Frommer's®

Sicily

4th Edition

by Darwin Porter & Danforth Prince

Here's what the critics say about Frommer's:

"Amazingly easy to use. Very portable, very complete."
—**BOOKLIST**

"Detailed, accurate, and easy-to-read information for all price ranges."
—**GLAMOUR MAGAZINE**

"Hotel information is close to encyclopedic."
—**DES MOINES SUNDAY REGISTER**

"Frommer's Guides have a way of giving you a real feel for a place."
—**KNIGHT RIDDER NEWSPAPERS**

WILEY

Wiley Publishing, Inc.

Published by:

WILEY PUBLISHING, INC.

111 River St.
Hoboken, NJ 07030-5774

ISBN 978-0-470-39899-9

Editor: Marc Nadeau
Production Editor: M. Faunette Johnston
Cartographer: Andrew Murphy
Photo Editor: Richard Fox
Production by Wiley Indianapolis Composition Services

Front cover photo: A girl attending a wedding waits by the West door at Monreale Cathedral, near Palermo, Sicily.
Back cover photo: A boat near a volcanic outcropping off Salina, in the Aeolian Islands.

For information on our other products and services or to obtain technical support, please contact our Customer Care Department within the U.S. at 877/762-2974, outside the U.S. at 317/572-3993 or fax 317/572-4002.

Wiley also publishes its books in a variety of electronic formats. Some content that appears in print may not be available in electronic formats.

Manufactured in the United States of America

5   4   3   2   1

CONTENTS

4 SUGGESTED SICILY ITINERARIES   61

5 SETTLING INTO PALERMO   72

6 EXPLORING PALERMO   98

7 SIDE TRIPS FROM PALERMO   130

8 MESSINA & THE TYRRHENIAN COAST   146

9 THE AEOLIAN ISLANDS   170

10 TAORMINA & MOUNT ETNA   187

11 CATANIA   214

12 SYRACUSE & THE SOUTHEAST   244

13 RAGUSA & PIAZZA ARMERINA   272

LIST OF MAPS

AN INVITATION TO THE READER

In researching this book, we discovered many wonderful places—hotels, restaurants, shops, and more. We're sure you'll find others. Please tell us about them, so we can share the information with your fellow travelers in upcoming editions. If you were disappointed with a recommendation, we'd love to know that, too. Please write to:

Frommer's Sicily, 4th Edition
Wiley Publishing, Inc. • 111 River St. • Hoboken, NJ 07030-5774

AN ADDITIONAL NOTE

Please be advised that travel information is subject to change at any time—and this is especially true of prices. We therefore suggest that you write or call ahead for confirmation when making your travel plans. The authors, editors, and publisher cannot be held responsible for the experiences of readers while traveling. Your safety is important to us, however, so we encourage you to stay alert and be aware of your surroundings. Keep a close eye on cameras, purses, and wallets, all favorite targets of thieves and pickpockets.

Other Great Guides for Your Trip:

Frommer's Amalfi Coast with Naples, Capri & Pompeii

Frommer's Florence, Tuscany & Umbria

Frommer's Italy

Frommer's Northern Italy

Frommer's Rome

Frommer's Rome Day by Day

Frommer's Venice Day by Day

Irreverent Guide to Rome

Italy For Dummies

Pauline Frommer's Italy

Rome For Dummies

FROMMER'S STAR RATINGS, ICONS & ABBREVIATIONS

Every hotel, restaurant, and attraction listing in this guide has been ranked for quality, value, service, amenities, and special features using a **star-rating system**. In country, state, and regional guides, we also rate towns and regions to help you narrow down your choices and budget your time accordingly. Hotels and restaurants are rated on a scale of zero (recommended) to three stars (exceptional). Attractions, shopping, nightlife, towns, and regions are rated according to the following scale: zero stars (recommended), one star (highly recommended), two stars (very highly recommended), and three stars (must-see).

In addition to the star-rating system, we also use **seven feature icons** that point you to the great deals, in-the-know advice, and unique experiences that separate travelers from tourists. Throughout the book, look for:

(**Finds**)	Special finds—those places only insiders know about
(**Fun Facts**)	Fun facts—details that make travelers more informed and their trips more fun
(**Kids**)	Best bets for kids and advice for the whole family
(**Moments**)	Special moments—those experiences that memories are made of
(**Overrated**)	Places or experiences not worth your time or money
(**Tips**)	Insider tips—great ways to save time and money
(**Value**)	Great values—where to get the best deals

The following **abbreviations** are used for credit cards:

AE	American Express	**DISC**	Discover	**V**	Visa
DC	Diners Club	**MC**	MasterCard		

FROMMERS.COM

Now that you have this guidebook to help you plan a great trip, visit our website at **www.frommers.com** for additional travel information on more than 4,000 destinations. We update features regularly to give you instant access to the most current trip-planning information available. At Frommers.com, you'll find scoops on the best airfares, lodging rates, and car rental bargains. You can even book your travel online through our reliable travel booking partners. Other popular features include:

- Online updates to our most popular guidebooks
- Vacation sweepstakes and contest giveaways
- Newsletter highlighting the hottest travel trends
- Podcasts, interactive maps, and up-to-the-minute events listings
- Opinionated blog entries by Arthur Frommer himself
- Online travel message boards with featured travel discussions

What's New in Sicily

Situated at the center of the Mediterranean, the island of Sicily was once one of the great centers of civilization in the Western world. Everything here is different from the Italian mainland, even the hybrid Sicilian dialect and the many place names tinged with Arabic, in memory of the island's long-ago conquerors. The Greeks, the Romans, the Muslims, the Normans, and the Spaniards all passed through here and left their marks. Much of that ancient past remains. But Sicily is also modern—and forever changing. Here are some of the latest developments.

PALERMO

HOTELS A once-dreary *pensione* has been turned into **Letizia,** a boutique hotel of charm in an 18th-century *palazzo* at Via Bottai 30 (℃ **091-589110**). The 13-unit hotel occupies two floors of an 18th-century building at the edge of the Kalsa district. Prices are among the most affordable in Palermo for a hotel of this style.

Even though it occupies a restored palace, **Plaza Opera Hotel**, Via Nicolò Gallo 2 (℃ **091-3819026**), is the epitome of cosmopolitan chic. Paintings and some antiques add grace notes, but it is a bastion of *moderno,* with beautifully designed bedrooms in a minimalist style.

The Count and Countess of Federico have opened their antiques-laden castle, dating from the 12th century, to paying guests. **Palazzo Conte Federico** stands at Via dei Biscottari 4 (℃ **091-6511881**). Its entrance torchlit at night, it rents out the most elegant apartments in town, with high ceilings and baroque frescoes. Apartments are not only elegant, but come with kitchenettes. For what you get, prices are most reasonable here.

With only 16 rooms, **Ucciardhome,** Via Enrico Albanese 34–35 (℃ **091-348426**), is one of the best boutique hotels of Palermo. The atmosphere in both the public and the private rooms is elegant and intimate, and special features range from a chic wine bar to soundproof bedrooms with terraces or balconies.

The former royal residence of Prince Alessandro Filangieri II has been converted into **Hotel Orientale** at Via Maqueda 26 (℃ **091-6165727**). In the center of the old city, the building retains many of its grand architectural features, including a marble staircase and hand-painted frescoes. The location is convenient to the Central Station.

RESTAURANTS Some of the most authentic of Sicilian recipes are now showcased at **Bellotero,** Via Giorgio Castriota 31 (℃ **091-582158**), lying in the city's new town. It has only 10 tables, so reservations are necessary. The chefs are known for their preparations of freshly caught fish and shellfish, and their zesty regional dishes, including mountain lamb with oven-roasted pistachios.

CATANIA

Opera lovers and devotees of native son, composer Vincenzo Bellini, have still been given no reopening date for the **Museo Civico Belliniano,** at Piazza San Francesco 3 (℃ **095-7150535**), which has been installed in this second-floor apartment once occupied by Catania's most famous resident. Check with the tourist office upon your arrival in Catania to see if this world-famous attraction is receiving visitors once again.

MARSALA

On the outskirts of this wine-producing town in Western Sicily, the German chain **Kempinski** has opened the most elegant and luxurious resort in this part of the island. **Kempinski Hotel Giardinodi Costanza,** Via Salemi, Km. 7, 1000 Mazara del Vallo (✆ **0923-675000**), is a 90-room resort with grand luxuries in a landscaped setting of sublime comfort and tranquillity. Its on-site spa is the best in Sicily, as are its children's programs.

MONREALE

Lying on the outskirts of Monreale, the most popular day trip from Palermo, **Casale del Principe,** Contrada Dammusi (✆ **091-8579910**), is an *agriturismo* (farm estate) that is only 23km (14 miles) south of Palermo in the Jato Valley. In the 18th century, the property, with its 16th-century watchtower, was a Jesuit monastery. Today it's been turned into an elegantly rustic country house where no two rooms are alike. The setting is among vineyards, orchards, and olive groves.

SYRACUSE

HOTELS   In the historic heart of Ortygia, **Agilà Ortygia Charme Hotel,** at Via Vittorio Veneto 93 (✆ **0931-465186**), has opened in a restored building with panoramic views over the Ortygia Sea. The antique architectural features have been preserved, even though modern amenities were added. Each of the rooms, opening onto a tranquil courtyard, contains antiques, and the restaurant serves both a Mediterranean and international cuisine.

A once-decaying palazzo has been restored and turned into the 17-room

Gran Bretagna, Via Savoia 21 (✆ **0931-68765**). The hotel was built on fortifications dating from the 16th century. Bedrooms are spacious and furnished with antique reproductions along with frescoed ceilings in some cases.

ATTRACTIONS   One of the city's major attractions, **Palazzo Bellomo,** an 18th-century palace that is home to one of the greatest art collections in Sicily, still remains closed at press time. Check its status with the tourist office when you arrive in Syracuse.

TAORMINA

This resort, the most chic in Sicily, has seen the opening of a government-rated, five-star hotel, **Gran Hotel San Pietro,** Via Pirandello 50 (✆ **0942-620711**), which is surrounded by the most elegant hotel gardens on the east coast of Sicily, featuring a large terrace and a deluxe swimming pool. The hotel is housed in a Mediterranean-style building, rising six floors on a hillside and overlooking the sea down below.

TRAPANI

On the outskirts of this city in Western Sicily, the **Duca di Castelmonte** has opened at Via Salvatore Motisi 3 in Xitta (✆ **0923-526139**). This is an *agriturismo* or farm estate renting little apartments that can house anywhere from two to six guests comfortably. In a setting of olive groves and orange trees, the hotel also offers an on-site restaurant serving traditional family recipes.

VULCANO

In the Aeolian Islands, **L'Approdo** at Via Porto di Levante (✆ **090-9852426**), has become the restaurant of choice, with its excellent regional food and shady garden. Under new management, the restaurant hires chefs expert at grilling the day's catch. Many of their dishes show flair, including carpaccio of swordfish or fresh tuna with wild fennel.

The Best of Sicily

The largest island in the Mediterranean Sea, Sicily is a land of beauty, mystery, and world-class monuments. It's an exotic mix of bloodlines and architecture from medieval Normandy, Aragonese Spain, Moorish North Africa, ancient Greece, Phoenicia, and Rome. Much of the island's raw, primitive nature has faded in modern times, as thousands of newfangled cars clog the narrow lanes of its biggest city, **Palermo.** Poverty remains widespread, yet the age-old stranglehold of the Mafia seems less certain thanks to the increasingly vocal protests of an outraged public. On the eastern edge of the island is **Mount Etna,** the highest active volcano in Europe. Many of Sicily's larger urban areas (**Trapani, Catania,** and **Messina**) are relatively unattractive, but areas of ravishing beauty and eerie historical interest are found in the cities of **Syracuse, Taormina, Agrigento,** and **Selinunte.** Sicily's ancient ruins are rivaled only by those of Rome itself. Agrigento's **Valley of the Temples,** for example, is worth the trip alone.

1 THE BEST TRAVEL EXPERIENCES

- **Walking among the Dead:** Outside Palermo, the Catacombe dei Cappuccini amazingly preserve the lifelike corpses of some 8,000 Palermitans entombed here from the late 16th century until 1920, when the last victim, a 2-year-old *bambina,* was laid to rest. In dimly lit, murky, subterranean corridors, you can wander among these mummies. It's a gory sight, but it's absolutely fascinating. See p. 104.

- **Wandering Palermo's La Kalsa:** The ancient quarter of La Kalsa, created during the city's Arab domination, is as close as Sicily comes to having a casbah typical of the North African cities to the south. This densely populated district of narrow streets and markets provides a view of local Sicilian life unlike anywhere else on the island. To make your experience more authentic, purchase some *babbaluci* from one of the many vendors. (These are marinated baby snails sold in paper cones for devouring on the spot.) Head for Piazza della

Kalsa, the heart of the quarter, and the day is yours. See p. 104.

- **Encountering the Sicilian Apennines:** The island isn't all coastline, even though most visitors rarely dip into the hinterlands. For a close-up view of life as lived in the "Sicilian Alps," head inland to explore Sicily's greatest national park, Parco Naturale Regionale delle Madonie, sprawling across 39,679 hectares (98,049 acres). Castles dotting the park's lofty villages evoke the Middle Ages; the town of Cefalù makes the best base. This area is the breadbasket of Sicily, so you'll pass through pretty farms and vineyards. Fields ideal for a summertime picnic give way to downhill skiers in winter. See p. 156.

- **Climbing the volcano:** Follow in the footsteps of the "disgraced" Ingrid Bergman, who came here in 1949 with her lover and director, Roberto Rossellini, to make the ill-fated film *Stromboli.* On the Aeolian island of Stromboli, the most spectacular of its archipelago, you can witness showers of flaring rock and sparks from its volcano. For the most dramatic viewings, visit at night, when you can witness up close the channels from which the lava flows toward the sea along *sciara del fuoco,* or "trails of fire." At the top, you'll be treated to fiery explosions, a great show that's gone on for centuries. Just wear something over your coiffure so that you, too, don't light up the night. See p. 184.

- **Cooling off in Gole dell'Alcantara:** Often visited from Taormina en route to Mount Etna, the Alcantara lava gorges are the best place to experience almost freezing waters when the temperatures in eastern Sicily soar from May to September. These gorges were carved by a river of the same name into rock-hard basalt, the creation of one of Mount Etna's ancient eruptions. You can rent thigh-length boots, but many

prefer to take along a bathing suit. This wonderland is the place to be a kid again: There's nothing quite like splashing around in these cooling waters. See p. 194.

- **Visiting medieval Erice:** This once heavily fortified and walled mountain town, left over from the Middle Ages, is suspended 755m (2,477 ft.) above sea level. Ancients called the city Eryx, and a glorious golden temple dedicated to Aphrodite at the pinnacle of the town was like a gleaming lighthouse for ancient mariners. You can wander its cobblestone streets and peer into flower-filled courtyards along twisting lanes. Nothing seems as foreboding as a walk down a *vanelle,* an alley so narrow that only one person can pass at a time. Many Sicilian men journey here looking for a wife, as the women of Erice have been considered the most beautiful in Sicily for centuries. See p. 301.

2 THE MOST ROMANTIC GETAWAYS

- **Atelier Sul Mare** (Castel di Tusa; ⓒ 0921-334295; www.ateliersulmare. com): Far off the beaten path is the most iconoclastic hotel on the island, created by an artist who has anointed himself the "Ambassador to Beauty." Some of the rooms are the creative statements of renowned artists who lived on the premises for months and made their rooms works of art. See p. 164.
- **Palazzo San Domenico** (Taormina; ⓒ 0942-613111; www.sandomenico. thi.it): No other hotel in Sicily offers the sweeping majesty of this time-tested icon whose rooms were installed in a 15th-century monastery. Grand comfort on a deluxe level goes hand in hand with such charming ecclesiastical touches as Madonnas in wall niches and centuries-old depictions of saints praying in ecstasy. See p. 196.

- **Hotel Villa Sonia** (Castelmola; ⓒ 0942-28082; www.hotelvillasonia.com): High above the resort of Taormina, this 1974 old-style villa is a true retreat for escapists. It's a cozy, tranquil nest, with beautiful public areas and rooms opening onto spectacular views. Its restaurant is so excellent, you won't want to leave the premises at night. See p. 201.
- **Villa del Bosco** (Catania; ⓒ 095-7335100; www.hotelvilladelbosco.it): Few island hotels evoke the stately aristocratic life of the 19th century as does this estate, 5km (3 miles) south of the center of Catania. Once a private home, it has been successfully converted into a first-class hotel that often attracts celebrities. Its on-site restaurant is another reason to stay here. See p. 220.
- **Eremo della Giubiliana** (Ragusa; ⓒ 0932-669119): A stone-built estate in sunny isolation, this is a baronial

compound of refinement and grace. A stay here is like a visit to the grand country estate of some Sicilian don of the non-Mafia type. All the luxuries of the 21st century are found here, as well as fine dining, but the aura is definitely Old World. See p. 275.

- **Foresteria Baglio della Luna** (Agrigento; ℂ **0922-511061;** www.baglio dellaluna.com): This is one of the grandest country inns of Sicily, meticulously restored by an antiques dealer and turned into a glamorous oasis of style, comfort, and elegance. Agrigento never had such a stylish place to stay. See p. 288.

3 THE BEST MUSEUMS

- **Galleria Regionale della Sicilia** (Palermo; ℂ **091-6230011**): This is the most magnificent collection of regional art in all of Sicily—in fact, the gallery is one of the finest in Italy. Housed in the Catalán-Gothic Palazzo Abatellis, its superb collections trace Sicilian painting and sculpture from the 13th to the 18th century. Some of its paintings, such as *Triumph of Death* from 1449, are among the most impressive masterpieces in the south of Italy. See p. 102.
- **Museo Archeologico Regionale** (Palermo; ℂ **091-6116805**): One of the greatest archaeological museums in Italy is filled with a virtual "British Museum" collection of rare finds that is particularly rich in artifacts from the Greek and Roman colonization of the island. The metopes dug up from the city of Selinunte alone are worth a visit. See p. 102.
- **Museo Mandralisca** (Cefalù; ℂ **0921-421547**): Come here for no other reason than to gaze in wonder at Antonello da Messina's *Portrait of an Unknown Man,* painted in 1465. It is the masterpiece of this great Sicilian artist. While here, check out the other art treasures of this regional museum, including everything from a Chinese puzzle in ivory to a vase from the 4th century B.C. See p. 159.
- **Museo Regionale** (Messina; ℂ **090-361292**): A former silk mill has been successfully converted into one of the island's most impressive regional museums, one that contains Sicily's greatest

collection of art from the 15th to the 17th century. See p. 102.
- **Museo Civico** (Termini Imerese; ℂ **091-8128279**): Housed in a 14th-century *palazzo* (palace) is one of the finest regional museums in Sicily, devoted to art and archaeology. The Hellenistic and Roman pottery are among its greatest treasures; the museum is also rich in medieval and Renaissance art. See p. 167.
- **Museo Archeologico Eoliano** (Lipari; ℂ **090-9880174**): One of the great archaeological museums of Italy lies hidden away on the volcanic Aeolian island of Lipari. Among its many celebrated exhibits are a stunning collection of ancient vases, many from the 4th century B.C., and a magnificent trove of theatrical masks unearthed from tombs of the same era. See p. 174.
- **Museo Civico Belliniano** (Catania; ℂ **095-7150535**): This museum pays homage to the composer Vincenzo Bellini, who was born here in 1801. The drab five-room apartment evokes old Catania and is filled with Bellini memorabilia, including original folios of his operas, his death mask, and even the coffin in which his body was transferred from Paris. See p. 227.
- **Museo Archeologico Regionale Paolo Orsi** (Syracuse; ℂ **0931-464022**): This is a showcase for some of the most important archaeological finds of southern Italy. Especially intriguing are the showrooms devoted to the Greek

colonization of Sicily, including the celebrated Landolina Venus. See p. 250.

- **Museo Regionale di Arte Mediovale e Moderna** (Syracuse; ✆ 0931-69511): One of Sicily's greatest art collections is housed in the 13th-century Palazzo Bellomo. The collections are finest in the painting and decorative arts of southeastern Sicily and include such masterpieces as *The Burial of St. Lucia,* by Caravaggio. See p. 255.

4 THE BEST CATHEDRALS & CHURCHES

- **Chiesa di Santa Cita/Oratorio del Rosario di Santa Cita (Palermo):** The church of Santa Cita, bombed in World War II, is visited mainly for its stunning oratory, representing the crowning architectural achievement of sculptor Giacomo Serpotta, who labored on it between 1686 and 1718. His cherubs and angels are a real romp. See p. 106.
- **Oratorio del Rosario di San Domenico (Palermo):** This 16th-century oratory is the stunning achievement of sculptor and baroque decorator extraordinaire Giacomo Serpotta. To many, it is the equal of the also glorious Santa Cita oratory (see above). Serpotta's stucco designs are among the greatest in southern Italy. See p. 106.
- **Oratorio di San Lorenzo (Palermo):** This is yet another great oratory that shows the magnificent decoration of master sculptor Giacomo Serpotta, who created this masterpiece between 1698 and 1710. See p. 106.
- **Monreale Duomo (Monreale):** This grand cathedral represents the pinnacle of the glory of Arabo-Norman art and architecture. Launched in 1174 by William II, the Duomo is the most stunning of the Norman churches of Sicily, the mosaics in its interior rivaling those of the celebrated Cappella Palatina in Palermo. See p. 134.
- **Duomo (Cefalù):** One of Sicily's most magnificent Norman cathedrals, built by Roger II, stands in this charming little north-coast town. The cathedral is known for its grand array of Byzantine-Norman mosaics, completed in 1148. They are a virtual tour de force of this type of painstaking art. See p. 151.
- **Duomo (Catania):** Dedicated to the martyred St. Agatha, this cathedral was built on the orders of Roger I, the Norman king, and was largely destroyed in the earthquake that devastated Catania in 1693. What was left was redesigned with parts that survived the catastrophe. The great opera composer Bellini is buried here, as are several Aragonese kings. See p. 226.

5 THE BEST & MOST EVOCATIVE RUINS

- **Tyndaris** (Capo Tindari): Tyndaris was a bustling place at its founding by Dionysius the Elder in 396 B.C. Later destroyed by pillaging conquerors, Tyndaris has now been unearthed, and the ruins of everything from a basilica to a Roman theater can be seen. The view of the sea is reason enough to visit. See p. 165.
- **Teatro Greco** (Taormina): Opening onto a view of Mount Etna in the background, this Greek amphitheater was hewn out of a rocky slope on Mount Tauro. What you see today is what's left after destruction by the Arabs in the 10th century. See p. 192.
- **Ortygia Island** (Syracuse): Famous in Greek mythology, this island is filled

with ancient ruins such as the Tempio di Apollo, the Greek temple dedicated to Apollo that dates from the 6th century B.C. and the oldest peripteral (having a single row of columns) Doric temple still left in the world. See p. 254.

- **Parco Archeologico della Neapolis** (Syracuse): Two of the greatest attractions of Sicily—both from the world of the ancients—lie in this city in southeastern Sicily. The Greek Theater is one of the great theaters of the classical period still remaining. The other attraction is the Latomia del Paradiso, or the "Ear of Dionysius," the most famous of the ancient quarries of Syracuse. See p. 248.

- **Villa Romana del Casale** (Piazza Armerina): This is one of the grandest of all Roman villas to have survived from the classical era. It contains a total of 40 rooms "carpeted" with the most magnificent mosaics in western Europe. Its most reproduced mosaics are those of 10 young women dressed in strapless two-piece bikinis that would not be out of style today. See p. 280.

- **Valle dei Templi** (Agrigento): Containing the largest and greatest collection of ancient Greek ruins in the world, the Valley of the Temples, outside the city of Agrigento, opens onto the southern coast of Sicily. The temples are especially stunning at night, when they're floodlit. The most impressive ones are those dedicated to Juno and to Concord. The latter is the most magnificent of all, with 13 wind-eroded columns still standing. See p. 283.

- **Selinunte's Archaeological Garden** (Selinunte, west of Agrigento): Guy de Maupassant called these ruins an "immense heap of fallen columns," and so they are, but they are also the remains of one of the greatest colonies of ancient Greece. The temples date from the 6th century to the 5th century B.C. See p. 296.

- **Tempio di Segesta** (Segesta): One of the world's most perfectly preserved monuments from antiquity, Tempio di Segesta was constructed in the 5th century B.C. Amazingly, 36 of its Doric columns still stand. A visit to this remote site in western Sicily also gives you a chance to see a large Greek theater in ruins. See p. 300.

6 THE BEST BEACHES

- **Mondello Lido** (Mondello): This is where the citizens of Palermo flock on summer days to escape the stifling heat of the capital city. In Sicily, Mondello Lido is outclassed in fashion only by the beaches at the foot of Taormina. Its wide, sandy beaches extend for 2km (1¼ miles) from Monte Pellegrino to Monte Gallo. See p. 136.

- **Mortelle:** The best sands in northeast Sicily are found at the resort of Mortelle, which is where the Messinese themselves go to escape the scalding heat in their capital. The resort lies 12km (7½ miles) north of Messina at the northeast tip of the island. The area is filled with good sandy beaches, so you can take your pick. The best-accessorized strip is Lido dei Tirreno. See p. 156.

- **Spiaggia Sabbie Nere** (Vulcano): Completely off the beaten trail, "Black Sands Beach" is the finest in the Aeolian archipelago—that is, once you get over the fact that its sands are black and not powdery white. Beaching it here is something to tell the folks back home about. See p. 181.

- **Lido Mazzarò** (Taormina): The best-equipped beach in Sicily, Lido Mazzarò is also one of the finest, a favorite sea-bordering strip of sand and gravel once frequented by the stars of Hollywood's golden age and still as interesting as ever. A 15-minute cable-car ride down from the medieval town of Taormina, the beach is a hot spot from April to October. Bars and restaurants border the sands. See p. 192.

- **Giardini-Naxos:** Situated on the waterfront near Taormina, Giardini-Naxos is one of the most sophisticated seaside resorts of Sicily. The sandy beach, one of the island's best, lies between Capo Taormina in the northwest and Capo Schisò in the south. It may lack Taormina's medieval charm, but it's filled with good hotels, fine swimming, and excellent restaurants. See p. 207.

- **Marina di Ragusa:** Southeastern Sicily has a number of beaches, some of them quite tacky, but Marina di Ragusa is the best of the lot. This is quite an appealing area, and if Ragusa is too hot in summer, you might drop anchor at a hotel here and visit the ancient city on a day trip. The resort also has the best ice-cream bars, pubs, and watersports in the area. See p. 275.

7 THE BEST WALKS

- **Old Palermo:** In the heart of this ancient city, you can take a walk into history that in 3 hours will bring you by some of the Sicilian capital's most fabled monuments and into some of its most charming squares, such as Piazza Pretoria. You'll marvel that so much of the antique still remains, yet at the same time enjoy watching the locals go about their daily lives past monuments that in some cases were left over by the Arabs or the Normans. See p. 117.

- **Ustica:** In just 3 to 4 hours, you can circumnavigate the small island of Ustica, which rises out of the waters of the Tyrrhenian Sea 57km (35 miles) northwest of Palermo (reached by boat). The best hike on this volcanic island is the coastal path north of the main settlement. The local tourist office will provide a map. You'll pass along steep cliffs, part of a marine reserve, and be rewarded with some of the most stunning sea views in this part of the world. At some point, you can strip down and cool off from your walk by going swimming. See p. 140.

- **Parco Naturale Regionale delle Madonie:** This park, which begins 6km (3²/₃ miles) south of the coastal town of Cefalù, is too vast to explore by foot unless you have days. It comprises 39,679 hectares (98,049 acres) in all. But you can take a full-day excursion to walk through what has been called a "botanic paradise," containing more than half the species known on the island. Our favorite part of the walk centers on the village of Santuario di Gibilmanna, from whose belvederes you'll have the most panoramic views of the island. From here, you can walk all the way to the idyllic town of Castelbuno, coming to a rest at its historic Piazza Margherita. See p. 163.

- **Vulcano:** This is the most visited of the offshore Aeolian Islands. In ancient times, it was known as Thermessa and was believed to be the home of the god Vulcan, but also the gateway to Hades. Its big attraction is the Gran Cratere, which hasn't erupted since 1890. The walk to reach the peak of this crater is one of the most heavily trod in the islands. Allow about 3 hours for the trek there and back. For your effort, you'll be rewarded with the greatest of all views, not only of Vulcano, but of the other Aeolian Islands as well. See p. 179.

- **Old Catania:** Overshadowed by Mount Etna, Catania is the second-largest and one of the most historic cities of Sicily. A walk through the heart of Catania is the best way to explore its monuments. But it's not all history: You'll also get to take in the sights of the bustling outdoor market in the historic core. It will take about $4^{1}/_{2}$ hours, however, to cover just the highlights of the monuments, including the "Fountain of 10 Rivers" and the ancient Duomo, which was built after the great earthquake of 1902. See p. 232.

- **Valley of the Temples:** Our favorite walk in all of Sicily is along the Valley of the Temples, in the city of Agrigento. This is one of the most memorable and evocative sights of the ancient world. You won't find such impressive Greek ruins even in Greece itself. We prefer to walk among these ruins either at dawn or sunset. Naturally, their mysterious aura is heightened even more in springtime, when all the wildflowers are bursting into bloom. The highlight of your walk will be the Tempio della Concordia (Concord), the best preserved Greek ruins in the world. See p. 283.

8 THE BEST LUXURY HOTELS

- **Villa Igiea Grand Hotel** (Palermo; ⓒ **091-6312111**): This old villa, built at the turn of the 20th century in the Art Nouveau style, is the grandest address in Palermo. Surrounded by a park overlooking the sea, it provides an old-world atmosphere but has all the modern comforts. See p. 82.

- **Grand Hotel Liberty** (Messina; ⓒ **090-6409436;** www.nh-hotels.it: This is one of the grandest hotels on the eastern coast of Sicily. It has been transformed into a bastion of comfort and tranquillity, with some of the island's best and plushest bedrooms. A stay here is a beautiful way to visit "messy" Messina. See p. 153.

- **Villa Meligunis** (Lipari; ⓒ **090-9812426;** www.villameligunis.it): This hotel is as good as it gets in the volcanic Aeolian Islands. A restored cluster of 17th-century fishermen's cottages forms the nucleus of the compound. All modern conveniences in this remote outpost have been added. See p. 176.

- **Grand Hotel Timeo** (Taormina; ⓒ **0942-23801;** www.framon-hotels.

com): Liz Taylor and Richard Burton have long vamoosed, but this deluxe hotel still attracts the rich and famous who want to enjoy the stately comfort of a 19th-century neoclassical villa near Taormina's Greek theater. It's lighthearted and baronial at the same time. See p. 196.

- **Excelsior Grand Hotel** (Catania; ⓒ **095-7476111;** www.thi.it): This is the leading hotel of Sicily's second city, a monument to the modernism of *la dolce vita* days of the 1950s. The city may be in decay, but the hotel is completely up-to-date, housing its guests in luxury and comfort. See p. 217.

- **Grand Hotel** (Syracuse; ⓒ **0931-464600;** www.grandhotelsr.it): This turn-of-the-20th-century hotel is so old, it's new again, following a major upgrade and renovation. Its stately, old-fashioned charm has been preserved, but its comforts are definitely 21st century. It's the best place to stay if you plan to visit the archaeological gardens of Syracuse. See p. 256.

9 THE BEST MODERATELY PRICED HOTELS

- **Palazzo Excelsior** (Palermo; © 091-7909001; www.excelsiorpalermo.it): With its faded 19th-century nostalgia, this is a very appealing choice lying on the most prestigious street of Palermo, but in an isolated spot. Much of the interior is appealingly dowdy. It's not for everyone, but it attracts those discerning guests who like staying in a living museum. See p. 86.
- **Hotel Grotta Azzurra** (Ustica; © 091-8449807; www.framon-hotels.com): This remote island off the northern coast of Sicily is home to a lush, resort-style Mediterranean retreat, set on a wide plateau above the ocean. The prices are most affordable. See p. 145.
- **Villa Carlotta** (Taormina; © 0942-626058; www.hotelvillacarlottataormina.com): Romantically positioned in a hilltop village, this affordable hotel is a little gem. You're in a beautiful setting amid good furnishings, but you'll pay only a fraction of the price charged by nearby competitors such as the deluxe Grand Hotel Timeo. See p. 198.
- **Villa Favorita** (Marsala; © 0923-989100): On the home turf of the most famous wine-producing town in Sicily, this elegant 19th-century retreat has been restored and turned into a government-rated four-star hotel, yet its tariffs remain moderate. It's part of the cultural heritage of Marsala. See p. 268.
- **Hotel Moderno** (Erice; © 0923-869300; www.hotelmodernoerice.it): In spite of its dull and misleading name, this is quite a good hotel in Sicily's most enchanting medieval town. Rooms are located in an attractively decorated main building or in a newer annex. All units have hints of 19th-century styling and open onto private balconies or terraces with views in all directions. See p. 303.

10 THE BEST RESTAURANTS

- **Il Ristorantino** (Palermo; © 091-512861): This restaurant is hailed by some Italian critics for its classic and authentic Sicilian and Mediterranean cuisine. Francesco Inzerillo presents a creative menu based on his imagination, yet also keeps alive his favorite old-time recipes. See p. 91.
- **La Scuderia** (Palermo; © 091-520323): Set at the foot of Monte Pellegrino, 5km (3 miles) north of the city, this is Palermo's grandest restaurant, with superb international and Italian cuisine. Talented chefs turn out a tempting array of dishes prepared with market-fresh ingredients and served on the town's prettiest terrace. See p. 91.
- **Charleston Le Terrazze** (Mondello; © 091-450171): Located in Palermo's fashionable beach resort, this restaurant serves a better cuisine than that found in the capital city itself. It's housed in a building from 1913. The chefs use the finest ingredients in preparing the Sicilian and international cuisine. See p. 140.
- **Osteria del Duomo** (Cefalù; © 0921-421838): Its location across from the town's most famous cathedral is touristy, but this first-rate restaurant is anything but. It's a bastion of some of the north coast's grandest cuisine, specializing in sophisticated Sicilian fare along with a discreet offering of international dishes that have attracted world celebrities. See p. 162.
- **Casa Grugno** (Taormina; © 0942-21208): Taormina has never had such a

temple of gastronomy. One of the most exciting restaurants in Sicily is the culinary showcase for Andrea Zangerl, an Austria-born chef. His modern takes on Sicilian cuisine and sublime international dishes draw the world to his doorstep. See p. 202.

- **Le Zagare** (Catania; © 095-7476111): There is no finer Grand Hotel–style dining on the eastern coast of Sicily than at this citadel of haute cuisine, serving the best of island dishes along with a well-chosen sampling of Continental recipes. The baroque city around it may be in decay, but the good life still holds forth here. See p. 223.
- **Osteria I Tre Bicchieri** (Catania; © 095-7153540; www.osteriaitre bicchieri.it): Upon opening in 2002, this quickly became Catania's finest restaurant. Naples-born wunderkind and chef Laquinangelo Carmine has won immediate acceptance with his

succulent Continental cuisine. He's known especially for his preparation of Mediterranean fish. See p. 224.

- **Il Duomo** (Ragusa Ibla © 0932-651265): One of the finest restaurants in southern Sicily, Il Duomo has been awarded Michelin stars. Its greatest devotees maintain that it is the best restaurant in Sicily, serving a deluxe island cuisine. In many cases, chefs perpetuate age-old cooking traditions in turning out their sublime culinary offerings. See p. 277.
- **Ristorante Il Dehor** (Agrigento; © 0922-511061): In a grand villa of a hotel, Foresteria Baglio della Luna, this is one of the best restaurants in all of Sicily, serving refined Sicilian and international cuisine. Winning rave reviews from the press in Europe, this place will tempt you with an array of fixed-price menus from its very talented chef. See p. 293.

11 THE BEST DOWN-HOME TRATTORIE

- **Lo Scudiero** (Palermo; © 091-581628): The capital's finest moderately priced *trattoria* is set across from the landmark Politeamo Theater. Honest, straightforward Sicilian food is served here at very affordable prices. See p. 92.
- **Bye Bye Blues** (Mondello; © 091-6841415): Though the name doesn't sound very Sicilian, this is one of the best places to go for true island cooking. A casual, relaxed place outside Palermo, this trattoria is run by a husband-and-wife team who are passionate about feeding you well from the island's bounty. See p. 140.
- **E Pulera** (Lipari; © 090-9811158): For some of the best Aeolian cooking, head here for time-tested recipes and some of the best fish specialties in the island chain, including a delectable

fishermen's soup. No one makes a better swordfish ragout than these folks. See p. 177.

- **Granduca** (Taormina; © 0942-24983): The most atmospheric choice in this chic resort looks like an antiques store with potted plants. It also contains an alluring terrace with panoramic views. But most people come here for the excellent food and repertoire of Sicilian and Italian specialties. See p. 204.
- **La Grotta di Carmelo** (Acireale; © 095-7648153): The setting looks touristy and gimmicky, as you dine in a cave carved into a rock-face wall. Forget that it's constructed of black-lava rock from Mount Etna; the restaurant serves really good food, both seafood and typical Sicilian fare. Much of the fish is brought in daily from the Ionian Sea. See p. 243.

- **Don Camillo** (Syracuse; © 0931-67133): One of the city's finest and most affordable dining rooms was constructed on the foundation of a 15th-century monastery. The cuisine of seafood and Sicilian recipes is among the most creative in town. It's a charmer. See p. 262.

- **Monte San Giuliano** (Erice; © 0923-869595): In the medieval hilltop village of Erice, the most spectacular in Sicily, you can dine at this undiscovered garden hideaway after making your way through narrow labyrinthine streets. Most of the foodstuffs are plucked from the sea. Some of the dishes, such as a seafood couscous, are inspired by North Africa. See p. 304.

2

Sicily in Depth

Sicily is a land unto itself, proudly different from the rest of Italy in its customs and traditions. On the map, in fact, the toe of the Italian boot appears poised to kick Sicily away from the mainland, as if it didn't belong to the rest of the country. The largest of the Mediterranean islands, it's separated from Italy by the 4km ($2^{1}/_{2}$-mile) Straits of Messina, a dangerously unstable earthquake zone, making the eventual construction of a bridge doubtful.

Although the island's economy is moving closer to those of Europe and the rest of Italy, its culture is still very much its own. Its vague Arab flavor reminds us that Sicily broke away from the mainland of Africa, *not* Italy, millions of years ago. Its Greek heritage lives on as well. Although there are far too many cars in Palermo, and parts of the island are heavily polluted by industrialization, Sicily is still a place where life is slower, tradition is respected, and the myths and legends of the past aren't yet forgotten.

Sicily has been inhabited since the Ice Age, and its history is full of natural and political disasters. It has been conquered and occupied over and over: by the Greeks in the 6th to 5th centuries B.C., then the Romans, the Vandals, the Arabs (who created a splendid civilization), the Normans, the Swabians, the fanatically religious House of Aragón, and the Bourbons. When Garibaldi landed at Marsala in 1860, he brought an illusion of freedom, soon dissipated by the patronage system of the Mafia. Besides the invaders, the centuries have brought a series of plagues, volcanic eruptions, earthquakes, and economic hardships to threaten the interwoven culture of Sicily.

The land has a deep archaeological heritage and is full of sensual sights and experiences: verdant vineyards and fragrant citrus groves, horses with plumes and bells pulling gaily painted carts, masses of blooming almond and cherry trees in February, Greek temples, ancient theaters, complex city architecture, and aromatic Marsala wine. In summer, the *sirocco* (hot wind) whirling out of the Libyan deserts dries the fertile fields, crisping the harvest into a sun-blasted palette of browns. Beaches are plentiful around the island, but most are rocky, crowded, or dirty. The best are at Mondello, outside Palermo, and around Taormina in the east.

1 SICILY TODAY

Sicilians sigh when asked about that long-delayed bridge that may finally link them to the mainland. There are those, especially in the Messina area, who predict that it will never be built.

There has been talk of a bridge to the mainland since 1865. The hope is to have a railway line over the Strait of Messina. Not all Sicilians want the bridge, particularly environmentalists. Leftists argue that the money should be spent on social programs to aid the poor, and naturally ferryboat operators are vigorously opposed to any bridge.

In the meantime, the sea still provides the chief way to reach the isolated island, though more and more people are flying in from such cities as Naples or Rome.

Sicily at times seems to function like an independent nation, and it still lives, at least in part, in the past. Because of its fertile soil and balmy Mediterranean climate, agriculture remains the chief economic activity, although in the past decade or so there has been a rapid rise in tourism.

Landownership reforms have led to an increase in the amount of soil available for crops. However, the still-influential Mafia has hampered government efforts to institute reforms, and large blocks of land remain in private hands. Stacked up against other members of the European Union, Sicilians still have a low per capita income and high unemployment. Many young people leave to seek jobs in such industrial cities in the north as Milan.

Through its chief ports of Catania, Messina, and Palermo, Sicily exports its agricultural products to the world, including cattle, citrus, olives, and wine grapes. Its refined petroleum, textiles, fertilizers, and leather goods, among other items, bring in much-needed revenue. Sicilian wines are appearing on more and more tables around the world. Tourism facilities since the millennium have been considerably upgraded.

More and more illegal immigrants are using Sicily as a stopover along the way as they try to make it to the Italian mainland where jobs are more plentiful for guest workers. Because Sicily is not as prosperous as the mainland, most of these migrants chose not to remain on the island. Immigrants come mainly from northern and central Africa.

Today the population of Sicily stands at five million people, more or less. That figure would be an additional 10 million if those of Sicilian descent had not emigrated to other parts of the world, including the United States, Argentina, and Australia, among other countries. Immigrants living on the island make up only about 75,000 of the population, and the majority of these are from Tunisia, followed by Moroccans, Sri Lankans, Albanians, and refugees from other Eastern European countries.

In recent years, the role of women has changed dramatically in Sicily. In the words of one small town mayor, who wisely did not want to be identified, "We Sicilian men no longer are able to keep our women in the kitchen—barefoot and pregnant."

Today thousands upon thousands of women are employed in jobs outside the home, and many have occupations that were once given out only to men, including those in the police department. These changes are occurring in the bigger cities such as Palermo or Catania. However, in the smaller villages and towns, a Sicilian woman is still primarily a housewife or *casalinga,* occupied with cooking, child-rearing, and other domestic chores such as growing vegetables in a private garden or tending to small domestic herds of cattle or sheep.

More and more women are concerned with their physical appearance, spending large sums of money on hair and beauty products, clothing, shoes, and jewelry. The entire island celebrated in 2008 when a Sicilian girl, Miriam Leone, from Acireale, was named Miss Italy.

2 LOOKING BACK AT SICILY

EARLY COLONIZERS

Of the Mediterranean, Plato wrote that conquerors flocked to its coastline like "frogs gathering at a pond"—an apt comparison for Sicily itself. Much of the history of this largest of Mediterranean islands is unknown. Perhaps many tales from the *Odyssey* were set in what is now

Sicily, adding to its allure as a land of myth and legend.

For 6,000 years, conquerors from both Europe and Africa have tried to turn Sicily into a colony. Sicilians are so used to foreign occupation that the most nationalistic of islanders even today believe they are living under "occupation" by mainland Italy and under the control of Rome.

Archaeology provides much of the evidence of early colonization. Of course, indigenous people already existed on Sicily when the Greeks arrived. The Siculi people, for whom Sicily was named, came from the Calabria peninsula on the mainland, settling in the eastern and southern central parts of the island. Tribes of Sicani from Iberia occupied the western frontiers, and the people of Elimi, claiming descent from the Trojans, inhabited the medieval hilltop town of Erice, on the west coast.

Arriving from Carthage, the Phoenicians—the last of the pre-Hellenistic invaders—settled into Solunto near present-day Palermo. The ruins of their settlement can be explored today (p. 132). The Phoenicians also founded Palermo, the capital of Sicily, calling it *Panormus.* The Chalcidians landed in the east to establish what is modern-day Messina, and the Megarians founded the colony of Megara

Hyblaea, the ruins of which can be explored north of Syracuse, once you pass through an industrial blight.

In time these tribes came in for Hellenization. Naxos, near today's Taormina, was launched around 735 B.C. by mariners, a group of Chalcidians from Greece. You can explore these ruins today (p. 187). Around the same time (734 B.C.), the Corinthians laid the first stones on the island of Ortygia, calling their city *Syracoussai,* which in time became today's Syracuse.

North of Syracuse, Megara Hyblaea was founded in 728 B.C., followed in 628 B.C. by the founding of Selinunte (p. 296), still among the great archaeological ruins of Sicily. The last of the great Greek cities, Agrigento, was founded in 581 B.C., its Valley of the Temples today remaining one of the great attractions of southern Italy (p. 283).

The growing power of Carthage in North Africa brought fear to Sicily. By the 7th century B.C., Carthage had allied itself with the Phoenicians against the Greek settlers. The colonies of Magna Graecia, or Greater Greece, thrived on trade. As the Greek colonies grew more powerful in Sicily, they fought each other out of greed and jealousy—all of which laid the groundwork for the "rule of the tyrants."

DATELINE

- **734 B.C.** Corinthians found Syracuse.
- **480 B.C.** Syracusans overrun the Carthaginian beachhead at the Battle of Himera.
- **415 B.C.** Athens sails a great armada against Syracuse but is defeated.
- **409 B.C.** Carthage attacks and destroys Selinunte and Himera.
- **211 B.C.** Syracuse is sacked as Romans declare victory.

- **535** Belisarius annexes Sicily to the Eastern Roman Empire.
- **827** Saracens' invasion of Sicily launched.
- **1032** Roger seizes Palermo, launching the Norman dynasty.
- **1190–97** Henry, a Hohenstaufen, rules Sicily after defeating the Normans.
- **1231** Frederick II issues the antifeudal Constitution of Melfi.

- **1282** A rebellion—the so-called Sicilian Vespers—breaks out in Palermo, spreading across the island.
- **1302** Peace treaty between the Angevins and the Aragonese gives Sicily to the Spaniards.
- **1513** Spanish Inquisition introduced.
- **1693** Earthquake destroys much of eastern Sicily, including Catania.

continues

THE RULE OF THE TYRANTS

In ancient times, the word "tyrant" described men who grabbed power instead of inheriting it, as in a royal lineage. Tyrants ruled over the Greek city-states of Sicily. The year 480 B.C. proved pivotal in the island's history. That was when the Carthaginians mounted a massive attack on the western possessions of Greece, including Sicily. Hamilcar, the African commander, sailed into Sicily's northern coast with an army of 300,000 mercenaries carried in 3,000 transport ships. The Carthaginian general besieged Himera outside Termini Imerese, and the tyrant of the area, Thereon, appealed to Syracuse for help. Syracuse sent 55,000 men marching across the heart of Sicily. Hamilcar asked for help from Selinunte on the south coast.

The Carthaginians fell for a variation of the old Trojan horse trick, mistaking the Syracuse forces for reinforcements from Selinunte. When their ranks opened, some 150,000 soldiers were slain and their ships torched. As a result, the winner of that battle, Gelon, the tyrant of Syracuse, became a towering figure in the Greek world. Seven decades would pass before Carthage would return to pillage Sicily.

The defeat of the Carthaginians led to a golden age for Sicily, as such classical figures as Archimedes, Theocritus, and Empedocles became household names. Plato and Aeschylus dropped in from Greece. The largest of the Greek temples were constructed in Agrigento, the biggest amphitheater in Syracuse. The period of growth and expansion was set back only by infighting among the city-states.

Syracuse was clearly the dominant power in Sicily, so much so that it dared challenge the supremacy of Athens itself. In response, in 415 B.C. Athens sent the largest armada ever assembled to subdue Syracuse. The Great Expedition from the east met with failure, and 7,000 soldiers from Athens were taken prisoner. The great city of Syracuse reached the apex of its power.

THE REVENGE OF CARTHAGE

Hannibal, son of Gisgo, arrived on the southern coast of Sicily with his mercenaries in 409 B.C., seeking revenge. He destroyed what had been a great city, Selinunte, its modern-day ruins a testament to his victory. Selinunte faded into history forever.

Hannibal then headed north to seek his revenge against Himera. He won a great victory here and tortured and murdered all the male survivors.

- **1713** Treaty of Utrecht assigns Sicily to House of Savoy.
- **1734** Spanish reclaim Sicily under Bourbon king, Charles I.
- **1812** A liberal constitution spells the doom of the feudal system.
- **1816** Ferdinand abrogates the constitution, creates Kingdom of the Two Sicilies.
- **1860** Garibaldi's forces chase out the Bourbons, as Sicilians vote for unification.
- **1908** Earthquake in Messina takes 80,000 lives.
- **1943** Allied armies under Patton and Montgomery capture Sicily from the Nazis.
- **1946** Sicily granted limited independence.
- **1951** A massive emigration from the island begins, eventually totaling one million Sicilians.
- **1980s–1990s** In spite of a campaign against it by the government, the Mafia
maintains a strong influence on the island.
- **2002** Mount Etna announces itself once again, belching smoke and fire and threatening tourist facilities near Catania.
- **2004** Sicilian Mafia rebuilds, but faces competition from Calabria.
- **2006** Mafia's number-one boss arrested near Corleone.

Hannibal came back in full force once again, and in 406 B.C. destroyed Agrigento (then called *Akragas*). At the time, Akragas was surpassed only by Syracuse in power and influence. During the siege a plague swept through his camp, and Hannibal succumbed to it. His successor, Himilkon, took over for the Carthaginians, offering his son, Moloch, as a sacrifice to the gods to show he meant business. After 8 months of siege, Akragas fell to the Carthaginians.

Blaming the generals in Syracuse for the defeat of Akragas, the demagogue Dionysius seized power in 405 B.C. and became one of the most famous of all the tyrants. The Carthaginians moved on Syracuse, but the plague swept over their forces and the remaining army returned to Africa.

THE ROMANS IN SICILY

The Greek hold over Sicily was coming to an end. With Carthage subdued, a new menace rose to threaten imperial Sicily: Rome. Sicily was largely spared during the First Punic War (264–241 B.C.), but the people of Syracuse sided with Carthage during the Second Punic War (218–202 B.C.). This war is memorable because of the exploits of Hannibal, the Carthaginian general, coming from Spain, scoring a series of victories and bringing terror and massive destruction. The Sicilian city of Syracuse sided with this famous general (not to be confused with the one mentioned previously).

For this, the newly emerged powers of Rome did not forgive Sicily, and in 211 B.C. the Romans conquered the island. In its defeat, Sicily became a "subcolony," and the formerly proud inhabitants of the island became slaves or servants, living in poverty. Slave revolts broke out periodically but were brutally suppressed by the Romans, who used the island as a breadbasket after felling its trees.

In the 3rd century A.D., when Sicilians were finally granted citizenship in the Roman Empire, it was a little late. The barbarians from the north were on the march.

BARBARIANS, BYZANTINES & THE SARACENS

As the Roman Empire collapsed to the invading Visigoths in A.D. 410, Sicily came under increasing attack from the Vandals, who launched warships from the coastline of Tunisia. The barbarian invasion of the island was short-lived, but for a while Sicily was temporarily reunited with Italy under the Ostrogoth Theodoric.

In A.D. 535, the Byzantine general Belisarius occupied Sicily. Amazingly, for a brief time in 663 Syracuse became the center of the eastern Byzantine Empire.

The Arabs, Berbers, and Spanish Muslims—known collectively as the Saracens—had become increasingly attracted to the prize of Sicily. By 700, the island of Pantelleria had fallen to them. By 827, a full-fledged Arab invasion of Sicily was successfully mounted. Their landing was at Mazara del Vallo, in the south. Four years later, Palermo fell to the Saracens, and by 965, the invading African forces had moved east to the Straits of Messina.

The Arabs made Palermo the capital of their new Sicilian empire, decorating it with gardens, mosques (some 300 in all), palaces, and domes. Unlike the Roman occupation, Sicily actually prospered under the Arab rulers, who made substantial breakthroughs in agriculture, introducing citrus trees, date palms, cotton, and other crops. Even religious tolerance was practiced, and many Christians abandoned their faith to Muslim beliefs.

But the Saracen rule, like so many others, would be short-lived. Because of internal Arab bickering, the Byzantine general George Maniakes decided that Sicily once again was ripe to be plucked. Although his forces never got much beyond Syracuse, a new menace loomed: The Normans were about to move in on Sicily, an island they regarded as a glittering prize.

THE MEN OF THE NORTH

If a visitor should wonder why there are so many blondes in Sicily today, it's because of the Norman conquest of the island. In 1061, an Arab emir in Messina called on Roger Hauteville for help in putting down a rebellion among fellow Saracens. Big mistake. The Normans came, they saw, and they conquered, although it took them another 3 decades to subdue the entire island.

Amazingly, the Normans sometimes enlisted the aid of the resident Arabs to fight other Arabs. At one of the series of bloody battles, the Normans ended up firmly entrenched in Palermo, making it their capital in 1072.

Although the Normans were to stay less than a century, ruling with a series of five kings, they left an architectural legacy that remains a distinctive feature on the Sicilian landscape, especially in Palermo. Sometimes they took over an already existing Arab mosque and turned it into an "Arabo-Norman" style of church. By 1200, the Arabic language was fading, giving way to French and Italian.

Count Roger, or Roger I (1031–1101), launched the Norman-Sicilian dynasty. He was followed by Roger II (1105–54), one of the great kings of Europe in the Middle Ages, who brought together some of the most creative forces in the Mediterranean and who was also a big patron of the arts. In addition, he extended his Sicilian kingdom to embrace parts of North Africa, southern Italy, and Malta. Weaker kings, such as William the Bad (1154–66), followed.

THE REIGN OF THE HOHENSTAUFENS

When the Norman king, William II (1166–89)—called William the Good—died in 1189 at the age of 36, the throne went to Tancred, his illegitimate son. The ascension to the throne was challenged by King Henry VI, a German Hohenstaufen, or Swabian. Tancred hung on until his death in 1194, surviving a sacking of Messina in 1190 by Richard the Lion-Hearted on his way to join the Third Crusade.

William III succeeded Tancred, but the Hohenstaufen fleet docked at Messina, and the short-term king was imprisoned and would eventually die in a castle. Henry (later to become the Holy Roman Emperor Henry VI) was declared king of Sicily in 1190.

Henry was to die of dysentery in 1197, the throne passing to Frederick I of Sicily, his son, who was only 3 years old. His mother, Constance, ruled for him. When he grew up, he proved to be a strong king, especially against such island rebels as the Arabs. As a promoter of science, medicine, and law, he was called *Stupor Mundi,* or "Wonder of the World." Under Frederick, Palermo became the most important city in Europe, a cultural center with no equal in the Western world. In 1231, he issued the antifeudal Constitution of Melfi, stripping the barons of much of their power. At his death in 1250, Sicily entered a period of decline.

A French pope eventually awarded the title of king of Sicily to Charles of Anjou, the brother of Louis IX, the French king. Under Charles, in 1266 Angevin forces fought and beat the armies of the Hohenstaufen rulers. Once in power, Charles of Anjou launched a punishing attack against those islanders who had supported the Hohenstaufens.

THE WAR OF THE VESPERS

The abject poverty and the stern rule of the Angevins sparked an uprising, known as the Sicilian Vespers, which began on Easter Sunday 1282. What sparked the uprising is not known for certain. One story has it that a gang of French troops raped a teenage girl; another that a French soldier insulted a local woman in Palermo.

At any rate, the tolling of a church bell for evening services, or Vespers, at the Chiesa di Santo Spirito set off a riot. Every French soldier in sight was slaughtered, the rebellion fanning out to eventually cover the island. Any Frenchman unable to pronounce the word *cicero* correctly was massacred.

There were many patriots, to be sure, but the general rioting and slaughter was also a time for many islanders to settle old scores with their enemies. A group of noblemen called upon Peter of Aragon for help. He landed in Tripani 5 months after that initial violent outbreak on Easter Sunday. In only a few days, he was proclaimed king.

The actual War of the Vespers was fought between the armies of Aragon and the forces of Angevin, who used Naples as their base. It was to last for 21 years. Slowly but effectively, Spain tightened its noose around Sicily. The rope would not be untied for 5 centuries.

RULE BY THE SPANIARDS

In 1302, the Peace of Caltabelotta concluded the war between the Vatican-leaning Angevins and the imperial Aragonese. Sicily was divided into two kingdoms, the Angevins retaining the territories in mainland Italy (such as Naples), but with Sicily itself going to the Spaniards. The Aragonese kings, based in Palermo, would rule the island directly until 1458.

Isolated in the Mediterranean, Sicily virtually "sat out" the great artistic and cultural movements sweeping mainland Europe in the 14th and 15th centuries. The Renaissance of Italy had virtually no impact in forgotten Sicily. Only one great artist arose from this depression: Antonello da Messina (1430–79), who had been inspired by Flemish art during his travels to the north.

If anything, feudal bonds were tightened as Sicily drifted back into the Middle Ages. The Spanish Inquisition, introduced

to Sicily in 1513, virtually silenced any inquiring minds.

THE 17TH & 18TH CENTURIES

As Spain drifted into its own long decline in the 17th and 18th centuries, so did its colony of Sicily, ruled by indifferent viceroys. Political corruption was rampant throughout the land.

In the hinterlands of Sicily, brigand bands, protesting against vast estates and their cruel owners, rose up to strike back. Calling themselves the *Mafiosi,* these outlaws butchered livestock, burned crops, and slaughtered local bailiffs to protest the outmoded feudal system.

As if the feudal system and its inherent evils weren't enough, in the 17th century Sicily was plagued by natural disasters. Mount Etna erupted in 1669, causing massive damage to the east coast and destroying Catania. The eruption was followed in 1693 by earthquakes along the same coastline, which killed about 5% of Sicily's population. Sicily was also struck by outbreaks of the plague.

Politically, the island became a pawn among the powers of Europe. After the death of Charles II of Spain in 1700, that country was plunged into the Wars of the Spanish Succession. In 1713, Sicily passed into the hands of the House of Savoy, according to the terms of the Treaty of Utrecht. In 1720, it was traded to the Austrians for Sardinia.

The Spanish came back in full force in 1734, reclaiming Sicily and placing it under the Bourbon king, Charles I (1734–59). Charles I was to visit Sicily only once. In time he gave up the kingdom to assume the title of King Charles III of Spain. He was followed by Ferdinand IV, who held power as Ferdinand IV of Naples in 1806. The island's so-called noblemen, living parasitically off the people of Sicily, tightened their feudal grips on the island, as new ideas unleashed by the French Revolution brought in winds of change.

THE COMING OF NAPOLEON

Napoleon Bonaparte, also known as the Little Corporal, never actually invaded Sicily, although his rearranging of the maps of Europe had an impact on the island. When Napoleon conquered Naples in 1799, Ferdinand IV was forced out when the crown went to Napoleon's brother, Joseph. Ferdinand fled to Sicily, where he was protected by British troops. Under pressure from the island commander of British forces, Lord William Bentinck, Ferdinand was compelled in 1812 to draw up a constitution for Sicily similar to that which governed Britain.

This document spelled the death of the feudal life, as a two-chamber Sicilian parliament was formed in Palermo. The court established in Palermo was to be free of the one presiding in Naples.

Once Napoleon was defeated in 1815, Ferdinand went back to Naples and abrogated the constitution. The British departed, and Ferdinand assumed control again, declaring himself Ferdinand I, king of the two Sicilies (that is, Naples and Sicily) in 1816. He repealed all reforms.

In protest, Sicily rebelled, but the rebellion was put down with the aid of mercenaries from Austria. Ferdinand died in 1825, and conditions only worsened under Ferdinand II (1830–59), who was named *Re Bomba* after his 5-day bombardment of Messina to quell insurrections there and in Palermo in 1848. In spite of the failures of the rebellions, the spirit of revolution remained. By 1860, the name Garibaldi was being whispered across the island.

REVOLT & THE ARRIVAL OF GARIBALDI

On April 4, 1860, an island-wide revolt against the Bourbon regime broke out. Seizing upon the news, the revolutionary leader Giuseppe Garibaldi decided the time to strike was at hand. Along with his famous *mille,* 1,000 red-shirted soldiers, he arrived at Marsala on the west coast of Sicily on May 11, 1860. He set about to conquer the island, aided by the peasants who joined his army.

A Bourbon army of 15,000 soldiers was defeated at Calatafimi on May 15, and within 2 weeks the capital at Palermo had fallen. By the time Garibaldi declared victory at the port of Milazzo on July 20, the Bourbons were in serious retreat. For the first time since 1282, Sicily was no longer under the yoke of the Bourbon regime.

On October 21 of that same year, an island-wide referendum was conducted. The results were staggering. Some 99% of the voters had opted to follow Garibaldi's plan and unify with mainland Italy. Many poor Sicilians not allowed to vote were cynical of the results, viewing the Piedmontese House of Savoy as the new "occupier" of the island.

FASCISM & WARS

Under the House of Savoy, Sicily indeed found itself in the same poor position it had endured over the centuries under many conquerors. The so-called aristocracy remained firmly in charge of the economy, and the peasants got nothing, not even the right to vote. In 1866, Turin crushed a rebellion in Palermo, just as previous rulers had done.

The *Mafiosi,* which later became the dreaded Mafia of the 20th century, acted as regent for the bailiffs, or landowners, extracting exorbitant rents from the peasant farmers. In desperation, some 500,000 Sicilians felt compelled to leave the island to settle in Australia, North America, and South America. Many of these people came from Messina, which was devastated in the earthquake of 1908, with some 80,000 lives lost.

The 20th century brought more grim realities, with the Italian conquest of Libya in 1912, followed by World War I, which devastated the economy of Sicily and took the lives of many of its young men.

In World War I, unlike World War II, Italy fought on the side of the Allies. It declared war on Austria in 1915 and later Germany. Because it was on the winning side this time around, it was awarded a vast hunk of the South Tyrol, which it took over from Austria and still controls to this day.

The aftermath of World War I was followed in 1922 by the emergence of Benito Mussolini, who had gained power in Rome. The island of Sicily was anything but his bastion of power, so the Italian dictator decided to crack down on Sicily's *Mafiosi,* a move that simply drove the criminals underground.

Mussolini sent his agent Cesare Mori to restore law and order to Sicily. To do so, Mori won the support of the landed gentry. To reward these large estate holders for their help, he reversed all agrarian reforms of the past decades. Amazingly, by the 1920s Sicily found itself plunged back into a feudal system.

By the 1930s, Mussolini took a page from the ancient Roman conquerors' playbook and came to regard Sicily as a breadbasket to feed his armies in his quest for empire. Wheat production on the island increased, but at great expense to the land, which suffered from erosion and soil depletion.

Suddenly, Sicily found itself caught up in a new war, World War II. Softening it for an invasion with aerial bombardments, the Allies attacked most of Sicily's major cities. Catania, Messina, and Palermo were heavily bombed.

In July 1943, General Patton and the American Seventh Army landed at Gela on the southern coast, as Montgomery's British forces put ashore at a point to the east. The Sicilians offered little resistance, but the Nazis fought back with venom, hoping to delay the Allied advance until

they could move their men and equipment across the Straits of Messina into Calabria.

Palermo fell to the Allied advance, followed by Messina. On September 3, as the Germans escaped to southern Italy, Sicilian authorities signed an armistice, becoming the first region of Italy to fall to the Allies, long before the invasion of Normandy in 1944. Amazingly, the Allies were greatly helped by the Mafiosi, who were eager to rid Sicily of the Fascists who had tried to wipe them out.

49TH STATE FOR THE U.S.?

With the devastation of World War II behind it, Sicilians reviewed their modern link with the Italian mainland, with thousands deciding the union had been a disaster. A Separatist movement gained hold, demanding complete independence for the island.

Sicilian Communists called for massive land redistribution. In an unlikely marriage, the landed gentry allied itself with the Mafia to keep a lid on "dangerous left-wing uprisings" throughout the land.

In 1946, bowing to pressure, the government in Rome agreed to give Sicily limited independence. Regional autonomy called for Sicily to have its own assembly and president. The role would be similar to what Scotland enjoys with England.

Many of the Separatists were even lobbying to be linked to the United States, becoming the 49th state. But with the coming of the elections of 1951, the Separatists faded into history.

For most of the latter part of the 20th century, Sicily was dominated by the Christian Democrats. This is the party more or less of the Catholic Church, with right-of-center leanings—a very conservative bunch. In an unspoken, almost hidden alliance, the Christian Democrats worked with the Mafia, as *clientilismo*—political patronage—became the rule of the land. Many a developmental fund ended up in the pocket of a Mafia don.

Even in the late 20th century and early 21st century, the Mafia has remained a strong influence on the island, in spite of a campaign against it by the governments presiding in the 1980s and 1990s. In 2004, the annual report of the Interior Ministry to the parliament in Rome claimed that the Mafia in Sicily was experiencing "a moment of renewal to overcome a structural crisis following the arrest of many top-ranking elements." The report also concluded that the so-called *Cosa Nostra* was trying to "regain credibility and competitiveness." The ministry report ominously concluded that the *Cosa Nostra* was pressing ahead with its traditional activities, such as gaining control of public-works contracts and practicing widespread extortion of Sicilian businesses for "protection" money.

Still, the more famous *Cosa Nostra* is facing competition from a rival syndicate: the *'ndrangheta* of Calabria, that section of the mainland forming the "toe" of the Italian peninsula. Moving in on traditional *Cosa Nostra* territory, the *'ndrangheta* has increased its hold on cocaine trafficking and has strong ties with Colombian drug cartels.

One novel approach to dealing with the *Cosa Nostra* is taking place in the town of Corleone, whose name was used for Marlon Brando's jowly don. Corleone has been confiscating the property of some of the more notorious Mafiosi and making this blood-soaked land bloom. Agronomists are planting melons, lentils, wheat, grapes, and chickpeas on estates once owned by the Mafia. And how is the mob striking back at this agricultural bounty? Retaliation has been relatively minor at this point; at one time, mob members let loose a herd of hungry sheep to devour wheat fields.

In 2006 the government of Sicily continued its pursuit of Mafia leaders, arresting Italy's reputed number-one Mafia boss, Bernardo Provenzano. The don was found 60km (37 miles) south of Palermo in Corleone, even though his former lawyer was telling newspapers that the elusive Mafia leader was dead. He was found very much alive and will go to court on an array of charges.

In 2008, work continued in Palermo at a fast pace in the restoration of the Kalso, that historic district that was bombed by Allied planes in 1943. For example, *Lo Spasimo,* a ruined 16th-century church and convent, was transformed into a site for temporary art exhibits, concerts, and theatrical presentations. Other buildings are being restored to their original glory as well, including a major restoration of the city library, originally built in 1760. Several of the city's *oratorios* are also being restored. These were simple structures—not churches—constructed over a period of 200 years, beginning in the 16th century as religious and social gathering places for Sicilian noblemen.

Looking forward, while it is estimated that some one million people left Sicily over a 20-year period beginning in 1951, today North Africans in hopes of a better life arrive by the boatload on such southern-tier islands as Lampedusa and Pantelleria.

3 ART & ARCHITECTURE 101

For decades, scholars have claimed that if you want to uncover the history of Western civilization, you need look no further than the island of Sicily. The original melting pot is a showcase of art and architecture of the Mediterranean, as each conqueror brought a different style and artistic statement to the island over 10,000 years of history. From the earliest graffiti found in caves to the glorious Doric temples at Agrigento to the pinnacle of Sicilian baroque in Catania, each wave of civilization has left its mark. Sometimes the styles of two different occupiers have been uniquely blended—witness the marriage of Arabic and Norman art and architecture into an "Arabo-Norman" style.

The bad news is that much of Sicily's artistic legacy has been damaged by volcanic explosions, earthquakes, and a range of man-made forces, from Hannibal's invading troops from North Africa to the Allied bombardments of 1943, which routed the Nazi occupiers. Much that remains is threatened by decay.

The Mafia hasn't helped either. The looting of the island's treasures for sale abroad to wealthy anonymous buyers has taken a vast toll on Sicily's artistic heritage.

PREHISTORIC ART

Artists have been at work in Sicily since prehistoric times, as rock paintings and graffiti discovered at Palermo and Messina reveal. Even in the Neolithic period, the first indigenous cultures, such as those who settled Lipari, were turning out artful **ceramics** and **terra cotta,** many of which remain to this day (see the Museo Archeologico Eoliano in Lipari, p. 174).

The most remarkable **cave paintings** were those found at Grotta del Genovese on Levanzo, one of the Egadi Islands off the western coast of Sicily. Discovered by accident in 1949, the Paleolithic wall paintings and Neolithic drawings are anywhere from 6,000 to 10,000 years old. Most of the drawings are of wild animals, such as deer and horses. Even the mighty tuna, traditionally found in these waters, show up here.

THE LEGACY OF THE GREEKS

From the 8th century on, the Greeks settled Sicily in waves, leaving great contributions to architecture before they were replaced by other conquerors. Much of

their heritage was destroyed by pillagers, but much still remains to delight us. The Greeks left a legacy of some of the best-preserved **temples** in the Western world, especially those at Agrigento in the Valley of the Temples, those in the ruined city of Selinunte, those in the archaeological gardens at Syracuse, and (best of all) the magnificent and still-standing Temple at Segesta. The temples constructed in Sicily were more innovative than even those of classical Greece.

The archaeological museums of Sicily are filled with artifacts from the Greek occupation: painted **ceramics** and **amphorae, sculptures** and **metopes,** and **bronzes** and **carved ornaments** for temple buildings.

The apogee, however, of Greek architectural contribution to Sicily is the **Doric temple,** which stood on a three-stepped base, its inner chamber housing a statue of the god to whom the temple was dedicated.

THE COMING OF THE ROMANS

Unlike the Greeks, the Romans did not leave a great artistic legacy in Sicily, except for the **Villa Romana (Roman villa)** at Casale, outside the town of Piazza Armerina (p. 280). The vast polychrome floor mosaics at this 40-room villa from the 3rd century A.D. are worth the trek across Sicily. Other traces of Roman architecture can be found in the amphitheaters of Taormina and Syracuse, as well as in Syracuse's Christian catacombs.

ARTISTIC FLOWERING UNDER THE NORMANS

Subsequent conquerors such as the Byzantines and the Arabs made little artistic impact on Sicily until invited back by later conquerors, the Normans. The Byzantines transformed Greek temples into Christian basilicas, while the Arabs built palaces, private residences, and religious buildings with such Asian characteristics as domes piercing the roofs. The Arab-Norman artistic expression—called the Arab or "Arabo-Norman" style—represented a flowering of art and architecture.

From the 11th century on, the Normans began to transform Sicily, and much of their achievement remains today. This trio of different cultures—Norman, Arabic, and Byzantine—created what came to be called the "Sicilian Romanesque" style.

The Normans erected **cathedrals**, or **duomos.** Their achievements—the cathedrals at Monreale and Cefalù and the Palazzo dei Normanini in Palermo—remain among the greatest sightseeing attractions on the island today.

Roger II (1131–54) launched the first major Sicilian cathedral at Cefalù, using a Latin cross plan with a chevron pattern. Pointed arches and angled columns particular to Sicily, as opposed to mainland cathedrals, still characterize this landmark church. The mosaic decorations in its interior alone would make this one of Sicily's greatest churches.

The mosaics in the cathedral at Monreale are even more stunning and beautiful. It was at Monreale that Sicily reached the apex of its contribution to medieval art in Europe. The Monreale Duomo also contains the most examples of Norman sculpture on the island, more than 200 slender columns with twin capitals. Each of these capitals is graced with a singular composition.

Palermo also has a splendid cathedral and important **churches** of the period, such as Martorana and San Giovanni degli Ermeti, along with the Arab-influenced **palaces** of La Cuba and La Zisa.

But the Normans lavished the most attention on the seat of their power, the mammoth Palazzo dei Normanni in Palermo. This sumptuous palace became the seat of the Hauteville dynasty. Using a palace originally constructed by the Arabs in the 9th century, the Normans greatly

extended it between 1132 and 1140. The crowning architectural glory of this palace is the **Cappella Palatina (Palatine Chapel),** with its Arab-inspired cupola and a stunning modern honeycomb ceiling based on Arab designs.

With the passing of the Normans and the arrival of the Hohenstaufen rulers in the 13th century, the great flowering of Sicilian art slowly died. The Hohenstaufens were more interested in fortifications and castles than in art. The dark ages of Sicilian art had descended on the island and would last for 4 centuries.

SICILY SLEEPS THROUGH THE RENAISSANCE

At the height of the Renaissance, Sicily remained under Spanish occupation. That may explain why Sicily virtually slept through the Renaissance, which began in Florence and swept across the rest of Italy. Although no great architectural heritage remains in Sicily from this era, painting and sculpture dominated the artistic firmament, revealing mainly Spanish but also Flemish influences.

Sicily's greatest artist, **Antonello da Messina** (1430–79), emerged during this period, initially inspired by the Flemish school and later showing the influence of his encounters with Piero della Francesca and Giovanni Bellini in Venice. One painting more than any other exemplifies his work: *Portrait of an Unknown Man,* in the Cefalù Museo Mandralisca. His other notable works, the greatest of Renaissance art in Sicily, are the *Polyptych of St. Gregory,* in the Museo Regionale in Messina, and the *Annunciation,* in the Palazzo Bellomo in Syracuse.

The **Gagini family** of sculptors and architects moved down from Lake Lugano and had an enormous impact on Sicily. The founding father of the Gagini school was Domenico Gagini (1420–92), who often worked in conjunction with his son, Antonello, born in Palermo in 1478. Their sculpture still adorns many of the churches of Palermo, and a Gagini school flourished in Sicily until the mid-1600s.

THE EXPLOSION OF THE BAROQUE

The baroque style swept Sicily, awakening the island from a long slumber since the Normans' departure centuries earlier. That observer of all things Italian, Luigi Barzini, saw the baroque as a metaphor for "a frenzied search for consolation and revenge against crude and overbearing foreign devils."

The baroque came into vogue as a result of a devastating earthquake in 1693 in eastern Sicily that leveled such cities as Catania. The style of their reconstruction was baroque, the founding father of which, in Sicily, was **Rosario Gagliardi** (1700–70). He designed the magnificent **Cattedrale San Giorgio** at Ragusa Ibla. Islanders combined the Spanish-inspired version of the baroque with Sicilian decorative and structural elements to create their own unique style.

The baroque city that emerged after the earthquake in Catania was created in part by **Giovanni Battista Vaccarini** (1702–69), who devoted 3 decades of his life to pulling a new Catania out of the ashes.

Noto, in southeastern Sicily, is another city that was rebuilt in the baroque style after the earthquake. The unity of the baroque style here remains unequaled anywhere else on the island.

In the west in Palermo, the baroque style came under the influence of Spanish dons who preferred *Spagnolismo,* or a love of ostentation. The **Quattro Canti** crossroads of the city remains today as the most lavish example of the dons' taste for overly adorned squares and streets. Private palaces, or *palazzi,* were also richly adorned, with sculptures ranging from angels to nymphs to gargoyles.

The master of the Palermitan oratories, **Giacomo Serpotta,** born in Palermo in 1656, specialized in adorning church oratories with molded plasterwork in ornamental frames. You can see one of his masterpieces today, Palermo's **Oratory of the Rosary,** in the church of Santa Zita—about which the author Paul Duncan once claimed: "You can almost hear the chortling, farting, and giggling of the *putti.*"

CONTEMPORARY ART

Now that the 20th century has ended, it can safely be said that few books will be written on modern art and artists in Sicily. The one exception is **Renato Guttuso** (1911–87). Painting in a style often called visceral, Guttuso became renowned around the world for his nudes, landscapes, and still lifes. Visitors to Palermo today need only drive just outside the city to the **Galleria Comunale d'Arte Moderna e Contemporanea,** at the town of Bagheria (p. 130), to see the best examples of Guttuso's work as well as his on-site tomb.

---

4 THE LAY OF THE LAND

Of all the islands of the Mediterranean, Sicily is the largest, spread across 40,965km (25,454 miles), and lying halfway between Gibraltar and the Suez Canal. It is surrounded by several archipelagos, the most important of which are the Aeolian Islands (see chapter 9), with such touristed spots as Stromboli, Lipari, and Vulcano. Other

island groups include Egadi, Pantelleria, and Pelagie, the latter centered at Lampedusa.

Bounded by the Tyrrhenian Sea to its north, the Sicilian Sea to its southwest, and the Ionian Sea on its eastern coast, Sicily is separated from southern Italy by the Straits of Messina. Though it's the country's largest region, Sicily is only the fourth highest in population.

Sicily enjoys a Mediterranean climate—it's the first part of Italy to heat up in the spring and the last to grow chilly in winter. It also suffers the longest, hottest summers, with July a scorcher.

An island of rivers, Sicily is also volcanic, the most threatening menace being Mount Etna, on the eastern coast. Some of the islands in the various archipelagos also have volcanoes, notably Stromboli, but most are long dormant.

The island is split by four mountain groups. First and foremost are the so-called Sicilian Alps, the Apennines, actually a continuation of the same mountain range that begins in Calabria on the mainland. These mountains stretch along the north coast, beginning at the Straits of Messina and going west to the Torto River. The Apennines are divided into a trio of ranges, including Peloritani, Nebrodi, and Madonie. Of the three, we recommend at least an exploration of Madonie, the most fascinating for touring.

Another mountain range is found in western Sicily to the west of the Platani and Torto rivers. The third member of the trio lies at the core of Sicily, looking out to the coast of North Africa 140km (87 miles) away, scene of so many embarkations of island conquerors. The southern and western half of Sicily, in terms of topography, is more similar to the Atlas Mountains of North Africa than the Sicilian mainland.

The ancient Greeks, among the first major settlers, called Sicily *Trinacria,* or triangle, because of its triangular shape. The island coastline covers much ground, a distance of 1,000km (621 miles). The smoothest and most uninterrupted flank stretches from the Straits of Messina to the Gulf of Palermo, overlooking the city of Palermo, Sicily's capital. The southern coast begins in the southeast at Capo Passero on the Golfo di Noto and heads west

along the Golfo di Gela, coming to an end at Capo Lilibeo south of Marsala of wine-making fame.

The eastern coast, opening onto Mare Ionio, or the Ionian Sea, begins at Capo Passero and heads north to Messina, bypassing the cities of Catania and Syracuse. Gólfo di Catania is the most important body of water in the east, providing the island's largest plain with a seafront.

As the coastline nears Messina, it becomes a series of towering cliffs broken up by a network of craggy inlets. For the visitor, the most stunning seascapes and landscapes are found around the resort of Taormina and the small city of Acireale, north of Catania.

FLORA & FAUNA The deforestation of the island has been a disaster since as far back as Roman times. Once rich in forests that provided it with abundant water, Sicily had vast tracts of woodland razed over the years to turn the island into the grain belt of the Roman Empire. This massive deforestation has left Sicily with a more foreboding climate—hot and dry.

The ancient Greek settlers brought with them the cultivation of the grape and the olive tree. The Arab conquerors brought date palms from Africa and encouraged the cultivation of citrus groves.

Typical Mediterranean flora, including the strawberry tree and myrtle, is found all over the island. Broom bushes set the countryside alive in spring, with miles of sunflower-yellow coloring. The spiny shrub, the so-called bastard olive, grows wild almost everywhere.

Island fauna have been horrendously affected by the gradual deforestation of Sicily. Other than sheep grazing in country fields, it is rare to see much wildlife as you travel the country roads of Sicily. Along the coast, of course, there is still plenty of birdlife, notably cormorants and seagulls. The viper is the only poisonous snake on the island, frightening tourists as it suns itself at various archaeological sites in summer.

The western coast dwellers of Sicily, who for centuries have depended on the mammoth schools of tuna for their livelihoods, are now facing diminishing returns. Huge Japanese trawlers in international waters are capturing more and more of these fish for shipment to the markets of Tokyo.

5 SICILY IN POPULAR CULTURE: BOOKS, FILMS & MUSIC

BOOKS

A great novel, and the masterpiece of Tomasi di Lampedusa, *The Leopard* traces the decline and fall of the House of Salina, a family of Sicilian aristocrats at the time of Italy's Risorgimento (ca. 1860). At the novel's 50th anniversary, the publisher has reissued the book with some previously unpublished material. Initially rejected by many publishers, the novel today is one of the best-selling Italian novels of the 20th century. Regrettably, Lampedusa died in 1957 before his world-famous book found a publisher. *The Leopard* was hailed around the world, and Lampedusa's style was compared to that of Flaubert and Stendhal. The book illustrates the changing face of Sicilian society.

The Day of Battle: The War in Sicily and Italy (1943–44), by Rick Atkinson, is a riveting story of the U.S. Army's campaign to capture Sicily in World War II. This is a "warts-and-all" detailed story of the Sicilian campaign, focusing on the major personalities (and sometimes the minor players) as well as the flaws and successes of the battle.

The Whorehouses of the World: Tales of Wartime Italy—Casablanca, Algiers, and Sicily, by Paul W. Brown, is not for the faint of heart. This story is a personal memoir of how a young man from Queens in New York survived deadly beaches, starvation-plagued towns and cities, and the stench of war. By describing his personal reactions to the war, the author provides a rare insight into the fact that war is not fought by generals but by ordinary men, who are often filled with terror at the horrific experiences they must undergo.

The Norman Conquest of Southern Italy and Sicily, by Gordon S. Brown, a retired ambassador and diplomat, is not dry, but a fascinating historical account of the Norman conquest of the south of Italy, including Sicily. At least the book answers the question of where did all those blue-eyed Sicilians come from. Well researched, it is eminently readable, telling the tale of how descendants of the Vikings replaced the Byzantine Empire.

In her fourth Italian memoir, *That Summer in Sicily: A Love Story,* the American writer Marlena De Blasi spins a romantic tale of love in the mountains of Sicily. This is a marvelous story about Sicily's bewildering culture. Much of the narrative spins around a woman named Tosca, the patron of the Villa Donnafugata, and her lifelong love story with the last prince of Sicily descended from the French nobles of Anjou.

Arabs and Normans in Sicily and the South of Italy, by Adele Cilento, is a coffee-table book of 275 full-color glossy pictures. It is the best illustrated account of the architecture, tapestries, manuscripts, paintings, and relics of the culture created in Sicily under both Arab and Norman rule. With the coming of the Normans, the artistic legacy of the Byzantine world was fused with Christian motifs.

The Kingdom of Sicily, 1100–1250: A Literary History, by Karla Mallette, is for serious readers who want an insight into medieval life on the island. The book deals with the complex nature of Sicily as a cultural crossroads between East and West, Islam and Christianity. The literary production of the island is surveyed in Arabic, Latin, Greek, and Romance dialects.

One of the great writers of Italian fiction, Giovanni Verga, was a son of Catania, born in 1840. He published his *Little Novels of Sicily* in 1883, and it has since become a classic. Verga's sketches of Sicilian life are some of the most evocative ever written. At the time of his childhood, Sicily was one of the poorest places in Europe. The *New York Times* claimed that the book has "that sense of the wholeness of life, the spare exuberance, the endless inflections and overtones, and the magnificent and thrilling vitality of major literature."

Sicily: Where Love Is, by Gerry Battista, captures a closely knit family and their friends. The lives and adventures of several generations of the Salerno family, strong on family ties and cultural values, are beautifully portrayed in vivid descriptions. You are "transported" to Sicily when reading this book, and you don't even have to have an Italian heritage to enjoy it.

A House in Sicily, by Daphne Phelps, with Denis Mack Smith, is a captivating memoir, recounting how Phelps inherited "the most beautiful house in Sicily." Arriving in Taormina with little money, she planned to sell the house but fell in love with Taormina, and began receiving guests, including illustrious ones such as Tennessee Williams and Bertrand Russell. The *Chicago Tribune* called the memoir "thoroughly alive."

Casa Nostra: A Home in Sicily, by Caroline Seller Manzo, does for Sicily what Frances Mayes did for Tuscany in another memoir. Food, family, and culture—even culture shock—are captured in this English woman's tale of her unpredictable adventures when she set out to renovate a villa. The unique beauty and history of western Sicily are also captured in this tale.

The Wine Dark Sea, by Leonardo Sciascia, explores "the Sicilian mind," as well as Mafia culture and other tantalizing details in this collection of short stories. The book presents a capsule history of the island as it travels over the centuries.

On Persephone's Island: A Sicilian Journey, by Mary Taylor Simeti, depicts the social life and customs of Sicily, using the changing seasons as a guide. Politics, geography, history, Sicilian life, and even horticulture, are touched upon.

FILMS

Cinema Paradiso brought a 1989 Oscar to Giuseppe Tornatore for this romantic tale of growing up in a remote Sicilian village. The filmmaker returns to his Sicilian hometown for the first time in 3 decades and takes a look back at his life. That life included time spent helping the projectionist at the local movie house.

Giuseppe Toratore followed *Cinema Paradiso* in 1995 with *L'Uomo Delle Stelle* (The Star Maker), which was the story of a Roman con man who arrives in Sicily posing as a talent scout. He journeys with his camera to poor villages in 1950s Sicily, promising stardom for a fee to the gullible islanders.

Seemingly much of the world saw *The Godfather* in 1972, director Francis Ford Coppola's masterpiece, which starred Marlon Brando as the aging patriarch, Don Corleone, of an organized crime dynasty. It was based on the Mario Puzo novel and won three Oscars. Trivia note: One of the most controversial scenes used a real horse's head placed in the bed of an intended victim. The head was acquired from a dog-food factory.

The film *Mafioso* (1962) was not appreciated upon its release. Alberto Sordi, one of Italy's finest actors, played Antonio, a worker in an auto factory in the north of Italy, who decides to take his wife and two daughters on a vacation to show them his native Sicily. Alberto Lattuada brilliantly directed this comedy/crime drama. When Antonio reunites with his past in Sicily, he finds out that there are more sides to being a Sicilian than he remembers.

Stromboli (1949), shot on one of the Aeolian islands, was a failure at the box office although it received worldwide publicity. Later generations have appreciated it more than those who first saw it. In disgrace, Ingrid Bergman was the star, Roberto Rossellini the director. The couple's "illicit" affair virtually destroyed the married Bergman's career (at least temporarily), and she was even denounced in the U.S. Senate. In our view, Rossellini and Bergman should have been denounced for this movie, not their love affair.

Politics and crime are bedfellows in Francesco Rosi's neorealist drama, *Salvatore Giuliano* (1962). The body of Giuliano, one of Italy's most "beloved" gangsters, was found on July 5, 1950, in Castelvetrano in Sicily. His body was punctured with bullet holes. Rosi paints a vivid portrait of this legendary bandit.

Il Gattopardo (The Leopard) was Luchino Visconti's 1968 film version of the celebrated Giuseppe di Lampedusa novel set in the revolutionary Sicily of the mid-1800s. A lush drama with a memorable ballroom scene, the film is a perfect evocation of a lost world. The masterpiece traces the decline and fall of the House of Salina, starring Burt Lancaster as a Sicilian prince trying to preserve his fading aristocratic way of life.

Visconti in 1948 also used Sicily as a backdrop for *La Terra Trema* (The Earth Trembles), an adaptation of Verga's *Malavoglia*. This story of a fisherman failed at the box office upon its release, but came to be viewed as a classic of the neorealistic movement.

Playing a Sicilian aristocrat, Marcelo Mastroianni starred in Pietor Germi's 1961 comedy, *Divorce, Italian Style*. Facing a midlife crisis, Mastroianni wants a divorce when it was not legal in Italy. He finds his wife, played by Daniela Rocca, annoying and he comes up with a scheme to make it appear that she is unfaithful and then kill her.

The first segment of Michelangelo Antonioni's masterpiece *L'Avventura* (1960) was filmed off the coast of Panarea and the satellite Sicilian island of Lisca Bianca. The movie paints a dim view of the aristocratic class in Italy. It tells of the disappearance of a rich woman. In the search for her, the woman's lover and best friend become "an item."

MUSIC

As the crossroads of the Mediterranean, Sicily has had a wide range of music, from *à capella* devotional songs to the vibrant jazz scene of today. Over the years the island has been a cultural melting pot of music, beginning with the Greeks and going on to the Normans, French, Spanish, and even Arabs from the Maghreb.

As the "granary of Italy," Sicily is also home to harvest songs and work songs. Sicily's flute music *(friscaletto)* has deep roots on island, with Carmelo Salemi the best-known performer of these traditional sounds.

Catania, with its splendid Teatro Massimo Bellini, built in 1890, is the hometown of the great Vincenzo Bellini (1801–35), who regrettably lived a very short life. The young composer still remains "the favorite son" of Catania.

A popular musician, Franco Battiato, fused rock 'n' roll with traditional and classical influences. His masterpiece, released in 1979, was called *L'era del cinghiale bianco*.

Messina's male choirs enjoy island renown, and Giancarlo Parisi is known for his traditional Sicilian music. In 1975 Luciano Maio founded the band, Taverna Mylaensis, and recovered much traditional Sicilian music before it died out—folk songs, folkloric dance music, provincial ballads, romantic poetry, and instrumental songs played on traditional instruments.

Alan Lomax, an American musicologist, made many recordings of traditional island music in the 20th century, including epic storytelling, religious music, dance music, and lullabies.

Recorded in 1954, the album *Sicily* (www.rounder.com) is a digitally remastered selection of mostly unreleased music from Lomax's sweeping Columbia World Library of Folk and Primitive Music project. Lomax was fortunate enough to record this music in preindustrial Italy, and he was able to capture on record every sound from the plaintive a cappella chorus of female almond sorters to a frenzied tarantella. He even managed to capture the sounds of a *ciaramedda a paru* (twin-chanter bagpipe). Yes, the bagpipe is not just confined to Scotland.

6 EATING & DRINKING IN SICILY

Good food is one of the main reasons to go to Sicily, especially now that the so-called Mediterranean diet—a cuisine comprised of fresh vegetables, fruit, fish, and olive oil—is being touted as healthy fare. But few heart-healthy diets are as enchanting as Sicilian fare, whether served in modest *trattorie* or in star kitchens.

A MELTING-POT CUISINE

Island fare is a blend of the cuisines of Sicily's many conquerors and cultures. The lush citrus groves around Catania were originally planted by the Arabs. Even those magnificently intricate pastries and rich desserts are a direct result of the Arab invasions, which brought a taste of North Africa to the shores of Catania.

In time, subsequent invaders, including Norman rulers and Spanish viceroys, left their own legacy of "aristocratic food," often as part of huge banquets prepared by enormous staffs and presented by a legion of servants. These extravagant excesses were in direct contrast to the diet of the fishermen, the land tillers, and other working people who set a simple table based mainly on fish and the bountiful harvest of vegetables from the Sicilian countryside.

THE TYPICAL SICILIAN DIET

Sicily is blessed with some of the finest raw culinary materials in Italy. Using this incredible array of fresh ingredients from the sea and field, the chefs of Sicily fashion a delectable display of enticing platters, many of them better and more original than those found anywhere on the mainland of Italy.

STARTERS Sicilian antipasti make a fine meal by themselves. Our favorite opening to a meal is the island specialty *caponata* (eggplant and caper salad). It's made with eggplant, sweet bell peppers, cauliflower, fresh tomatoes, olives, fat capers, onions, and celery in a sweet-and-sour sauce of vinegar and sugar.

Another savory starter is *arancini di riso,* little rice balls stuffed with peas, cheese, and meat, then coated with bread crumbs and deep-fried. These rice balls are strangely addictive, as is *bottarga,* the dried and salted roe of gray mullet or tuna, which is pressed into loaves, cut into paper-thin slices, and dressed with lemon-laced virgin olive oil.

We could begin any meal in Sicily with an *insalata di mare,* a deluxe seafood salad of boiled squid, tasty bits of octopus, fat shrimp, and chopped fresh vegetables with a dressing of olive oil flavored with lemon juice or vinegar.

PASTA ALLA SICILIANA For your *primi*, or first course, especially if you've skipped the antipasti, you'll be treated to delicious pasta and rice dishes or even couscous, the latter deriving from Sicily's centuries-old links with North Africa. Most pasta dishes are adorned with fresh fish or vegetables, such as **spaghetti alla Norma** (pasta with eggplant). Fishermen in particular love the classic **pasta con le sarde,** a simple but savory pasta with fresh sardines, served in a tomato sauce and wild fennel and given added zest with raisins, pine nuts, and capers. For us, there is nothing finer than **spaghetti alle vongole veraci.** This pasta is served with fresh clams steamed in wine with garlic, fresh parsley, and olive oil. Notice that instead of the relatively mild Parmesan, many islanders sprinkle **caciocavallo,** a particularly strong cheese, on their pasta dishes.

VEGETABLES & FRUITS Luscious local vegetables, used liberally in pastas and main courses, include vine-ripened tomatoes, spring-green zucchini, yellow onions, tangy capers, fat garlic cloves, many varieties of olives, multicolored peppers, and broccoli—each among the most flavorful in Italy.

On a visit to a citrus grove on the slopes of Mount Etna north of Catania, we were treated to some of the sweetest-tasting and most vividly colored blood-red oranges known to humankind (and we've lived in both Florida and California).

BOUNTY OF THE SEA Naturally, fresh fish and crustaceans—including sea urchins, mussels, cockles, and whitebait—are the dominant feature at most tables. The traditional *musseddu* (salted and fried tuna), is used to flavor many salads. The most popular fish dishes are tuna from the west and swordfish from the Straits of Messina. For

most gastronomes, fish is best served *alla griglia* (simply grilled) or else *arrosto* (roasted). After a sea harvest, you'll find what might be the world's best *zuppa di cozze* (mussel soup) resting in a bowl in front of you. Or try *cozze alla marinara,* fresh mussels steamed in wine with garlic and parsley. *Involtini di pesce spada,* grilled roulades of swordfish, are covered with bread crumbs and sautéed in olive oil. Sicilians are also fond of anchovies, using them in such dishes as *sfincione,* thick island pizza topped with anchovies, onions, and tomatoes. Many Sicilians don't consider *sfincione* pizza—it's sold in focaccerias, in bakeries, or perhaps from street vendors, but never in a pizzeria.

MEATS Traditionally, Sicilian cuisine is based largely on vegetables and the catch of the day harvested from coastal waters. But you can also fill your plate with marvelous meat specialties, including our favorite, a simple but tasty concoction called **costoletta alla Siciliana (thinly sliced veal with Parmesan and chopped garlic),** which is dipped in bread crumbs and sautéed. One of the better-known meat dishes is *falsomagro,* meaning "false lean." This rich, bountiful dish, a family favorite, is composed of a large slab of beef wrapped around Sicilian sausages, perhaps prosciutto, raisins, pine nuts, grated cheese, and even a boiled egg or two. The treat is tied with a string and stewed in a savory tomato sauce.

One Sicilian dish now served around the world is *pollo alla Marsala* (chicken in Marsala wine). A variation on this famous dish is veal Marsala, which originated among western Sicily's English families living here in the 19th century. Appearing on almost every menu is some form of *involtini,* a roulade made from grilled or roasted chicken or sliced beef, stuffed with a vegetable or meat filling. Sometimes a leafy vegetable such as radicchio is added to the filling.

SWEET STUFF One of the most succulent of the byproducts derived from the sweet blood-red oranges (and from Sicily's tangerines, lemons, and figs as well) is *frutta candita,* a sugared and preserved confection that explodes with flavor in your mouth and that is well worth the effort of taking home with you. Equally tempting are the fabulously lifelike replicas of pears, grapes, or apples concocted from almond paste and sugar (marzipan). The colors used in their fabrication and the realism with which they're crafted make them appear as if they had just been picked. In some cases, for added realism, the artisans add hints of a tiny bruise or blemish in each of the confections, partly for charm, partly for whimsy, and partly, we think, to show off their skills. Many of these techniques were originally developed by monks and nuns in monasteries and convents during the 17th and 18th centuries.

Sicilians are also known for their *gelato,* often produced in exotic flavors. (Have you ever had a velvety, creamy mulberry?) In summertime, you can order right from a street vendor a *granita di anguri,* a delectable, slushy watermelon ice. Sicily makes some of the best *granita* in the world, using purée of fresh fruit pulp— and not just watermelon, but *limone* (lemon), *fragola* (strawberry), and *pesca* (peach), among other flavors. Of course, they also do splendid chocolate, coffee, and vanilla versions.

Islanders point with justifiable pride to their desserts, one of the high points of dining in Sicily. Nothing is grander than a *cassata Siciliana,* Catania's most famous cake. It's a layered sponge cake sweetened with Marsala or orange liqueur and filled with ricotta cheese, chunks of chocolate, and candied island fruits. A different cake, *cassata al galleto,* is made with vanilla-flavored frozen custard and, perhaps, candied fruits, chocolate bits, hazelnuts, or pistachios.

Finally, never leave Sicily without sampling one of its classic *cannoli,* a crunchy tube of pastry filled with ricotta and studded with candied fruits, bits of chocolate, and the inevitable pistachios.

THE WINES OF SICILY

Sicily is celebrated for its wines. The most famous wine, **Marsala,** comes from the west coast from the city of the same name. Marsala is a fortified wine whose alcoholic content is about 20%; it's Sicily's version of port or sherry. A typical Marsala is amber yellow in color with wonderful depths of orange. With its special bouquet, it has a pleasing fragrance, both velvety and fruity, coming in both brut and sweet versions.

Moscata wines usually carry the designations *della Zucco, di Noto,* or *di Pantelleria* (an offshore western island). Moscata is made from the Muscat grape, which is sometimes fortified with Zibibbo or Corinto. Most often it is a golden or light amber dessert wine. It can also be sparkling—then it's called *spumante.*

Malvasia wine is associated with the volcanic island of Lipari. It is golden yellow, turning to amber, with a delightful aroma, both generous and strong. **Novello** is the island's nouveau wine, sold just months after the grapes are harvested and pressed. This is a red wine, both robust and fruity. **Faro,** which means "lighthouse," is a wine produced around Messina. It is a vivid ruby red, with a nutty flavor and fine bouquet; it's a good wine for roasts.

Planning Your Trip to Sicily

To see most of Sicily's highlights, plan on spending at least 5 to 7 days and moving a few times. Everything is very spread out—Sicily is the largest island in the Mediterranean, 177km (110 miles) north to south and 281km (175 miles) wide. Taormina, the most popular resort, is a great place to relax and play in the sun for a couple of days; from here you can also visit Mount Etna. The town is rather isolated in the east, however, so it may not be the best base for seeing the island's other highlights. The quickest and most efficient way to see the majority of Sicily is to fly into Palermo, rent a car, and travel east to Taormina; then return your car and fly back to the mainland from Catania. (Conversely, you can fly into Catania, perhaps from Rome, and end your itinerary in Palermo, returning the car there before flying back to Rome.)

This chapter is devoted to the where, when, and how of your trip—the advance planning required to get it together and take it on the road.

1 VISITOR INFORMATION

For information before you go, contact the Italian Government Tourist Board (www.italiantourism.com).

In the United States: 630 Fifth Ave., Ste. 1565, New York, NY 10111 (© 212/245-4822; fax 212/586-9249); 500 N. Michigan Ave., Ste. 2240, Chicago, IL 60611 (© 312/644-0996; fax 312/644-3019); and 12400 Wilshire Blvd., Ste. 550, Los Angeles, CA 90025 (© 310/820-0098; fax 310/820-6357).

In Canada: 175 Bloor St. E., South Tower, Ste. 907, Toronto, ON, M4W 3R8 (© 416/925-4882; fax 416/925-4799).

In the United Kingdom: 1 Princes St., London W1R 8AY (© 020/7408-1254; fax 020/7399-3567).

You can also write directly (in English or Italian) to the provincial or local tourist boards of the areas you plan to visit. Provincial tourist boards (**Ente Provinciale per il Turismo**) operate in the principal towns of the provinces. Local tourist boards (**Azienda Autonoma di Soggiorno e Turismo**) operate in all places of tourist interest; you can get a list from the Italian Government Tourist Office.

If you are in Sicily and need to get information, call toll-free © **800-117700** (only within Italy). If you are calling from another country, dial © **06-87419007.** This service is available daily from 8am to 11pm in five languages; it dispenses information concerning transportation, health assistance, events, museums, safety, hotels, and information points.

Online, check out the Italian Government Tourist Board's site, **www.italiantourism.com,** and the Italian State Tourism Board's site, **www.enit.it.**

MAPS Most local tourist offices will provide fairly detailed maps of their city or town plans. These are particularly helpful in that all of the major sightseeing attractions are usually marked. Since most of these attractions are in the historic core of a town or city, the highlights can usually be covered on foot, except in such spread-out cities as Palermo where you'll need to rely on public transportation to get around.

The **Automobile Club d'Italia** issues a free map, available at state tourist offices, if you're planning a motor tour of Italy.

For general touring, you can also check out the following websites: www.mapquest.com, www.maporama.com, and www.michelin.com.

2 ENTRY REQUIREMENTS

PASSPORTS

For information on how to get a passport, see "Passports" in the "Fast Facts: Sicily" section of appendix A—the websites listed provide downloadable passport applications as well as the current fees for processing passport applications. For an up-to-date, country-by-country listing of passport requirements around the world, go to the "Foreign Entry Requirement" Web page of the U.S. State Department at **http://travel.state.gov**.

VISAS

Visas are not needed by U.S., Canadian, Irish, Australian, or New Zealand citizens for visits of less than 3 months.

Under Italian law, all nonresidents are required to complete a *dichiarazione di presenza* (declaration of presence). Tourists arriving from Canada or the United States should obtain a stamp in their passport at the airport on the day of arrival. This stamp is considered the equivalent of the declaration of presence. It is important that applicants keep a copy of the receipt issued by the Italian authorities. Failure to complete a declaration of presence is punishable by expulsion from Italy. Additional information may be obtained (in Italian only) from the Portale Immigrazione at www.portaleimmigrazione.it and the Polizia di Stato at www.poliziadistato.it/pds/ps/immigrazione/soggiorno.htm. Americans staying in Italy for more than 3 months are considered residents and must obtain a *permesso di soggiorno* (permit of

stay). This includes Americans who will work or transact business and persons who want to simply live in Italy. An application "kit" for the *permesso di soggiorno* may be requested from one of 14,000 national post offices *(Poste Italiane)*. The kit must then be returned to one of 5,332 designated post office acceptance locations. It is important that applicants keep a copy of the receipt issued by the post office. Additional information may be obtained from an Italian immigration website via Internet at www.portaleimmigrazione.it, although the site is exclusively in Italian. Within 20 days of receiving the permit to stay in Italy, Americans must go to the local Vital Statistics Bureau *(Anagrafe of the Comune)* to apply for residency. It generally takes 1 to 2 months to receive the certificate of residence *(Certificato di Residenza)*.

Although European Union regulations require that non-E.U. visitors obtain a stamp in their passports upon initial entry, many borders are not staffed with officers carrying out this function. If an American citizen wishes to ensure that his or her entry is properly documented, it may be necessary to request a stamp at an official point of entry. Under local law, travelers without a stamp in their passports may be questioned and asked to document the length of their stay at the time of departure or at any other point during their visit, and could face possible fines or other repercussions if unable to do so.

April to June and late September to October are the best months for traveling in Sicily—temperatures are usually mild and crowds aren't quite so intense. Starting in mid-June, the summer rush really picks up, and from **July to mid-September,** the country teems with visitors. **August** is the worst month: Not only does it get uncomfortably hot, muggy, and crowded, but the entire island goes on vacation at least from August 15 to August 31—and many Sicilians take off the entire month. Numerous hotels, restaurants, and shops are closed (except at the spas, beaches, and islands, where you'll find 70% of the vacationing Sicilians). From **late October to Easter,** most attractions go on reduced winter hours or are closed for renovation. Many hotels and restaurants take a month or two off between **November and February,** when spa and beach destinations become padlocked ghost towns, and it can get much colder than you'd expect. The almond trees blossom in February, especially along the southern coast, and Taormina and Mount Etna are celebrated

for their riot of spring flowers. Easter is a time of major celebration on the island, with many traditional, religion-oriented festivals. **High season** on most airline routes to Rome/Palermo usually stretches from June to the beginning of September. This is the most expensive and most crowded time to travel. **Shoulder season** is from April to May, early September to October, and December 15 to December 24. **Low season** is from November 1 to December 14 and December 25 to March 31.

WEATHER

It can be very hot in summery Sicily, especially inland. The high temperatures begin in May, often lasting until sometime in October. Winters are mild.

For the most part, it's drier in Sicily than in North America, so high temperatures don't seem as bad because the humidity is lower. On the islands, temperatures can stay in the 90s Fahrenheit (30s Celsius) for days, but nights are most often comfortably cooler.

Average Temperatures & Rainfall in Palermo & Syracuse

		Jan	Feb	Mar	Apr	May	June	July	Aug	Sept	Oct	Nov	Dec
Palermo	Temp (°F)	54	55	56	60	66	72	78	79	75	69	62	56
	Temp (°C)	12	13	13	16	19	22	26	26	24	21	17	13
	Rainfall (in.)	2.80	2.60	2.30	1.70	1.00	.50	.20	.50	1.60	3.90	3.70	3.20
Syracuse	Temp (°F)	54	54	55	59	60	72	78	79	75	69	58	56
	Temp (°C)	12	12	13	15	16	22	26	26	24	21	14	13
	Rainfall (in.)	2.40	1.70	1.30	.70	.50	1.00	.10	.20	1.00	3.10	2.00	2.80

SICILY CALENDAR OF EVENTS

For major events for which tickets should be procured well before you arrive, check with **Keith Prowse** (© **800/223-6108;** www.keithprowse.com).

JANUARY

Epiphania (Epiphany), Piana degli Albanesi. Located 29km (18 miles) from Palermo in one of the Albanian colonies founded at the end of the 15th

century, the celebration of Epiphany is an ostentatious affair. A joyous procession of residents in traditional Albanian costumes parades through the streets.

Call © **091-8574144** or go to www. pianalbanesi.it. January 6.

Carnevale, Acireale. Carnevale is celebrated all over Sicily, but this is the most beautiful event. In a town north of Catania, it's marked by a colorful parade of masked participants and giant floats. Lemons and oranges from nearby citrus fields are used in abundance, creating an aromatic atmosphere. It's a weeklong party of fun and revelry. Contact the Catania tourist office at © **095-7306211.** Third week in January.

FEBRUARY

Almond Blossom Festival, Agrigento. Literally thousands of almond trees are in bloom around the Valley of the Temples at this festival heralding the arrival of the first fruits of spring. In Phrygian myths, the almond tree was viewed as the "father of the world." The event is marked with music, beauty pageants, parades, and puppet shows. All kinds of sweets made with almonds are sold. Contact the Agrigento tourist office at © **0922-20454** or 0922-20391. First half of February.

Feast of Saint Agata, Catania. Of pagan origin, this is a beautiful all-night religious celebration of the martyred patron saint of the city. A procession of candle-bearers, called *candelore,* parades through the city, accompanied by the mayor and his entourage in gilded horse-drawn carriages. High church officials add clouds of incense and all the requisite pomp and circumstance. There's also street theater and fireworks. Sweets based on centuries-old recipes from nunneries are sold. All-around mayhem prevails. Contact the Catania tourist office at © **095-7306211.** February 13 to February 15.

APRIL

Holy Week Observances, island-wide. Processions and age-old ceremonies— some from pagan days, some from the

Middle Ages—are staged in every city and town in Sicily. No matter where you are, you're likely to come across observances of this annual event. Particularly colorful and moving are the observances in Palermo and Catania along the coast. Trapani's procession of the *Misteri* is the island's most famous event staged during Holy Week. But the finest observance, in our view, is in the inland city of Caltagirone, a 2-hour drive southwest of Catania. Events are staged on such days as Holy Tuesday, Good Friday, and, of course, Easter Sunday itself. Local tourist offices can supply details. Week leading up to Easter.

The Dance of the Devils, Prizzi. Unique in Italy, a grotesque dance of the devils *(Il Ballo dei Diavoli)* takes place on Easter in this medieval town a 2-hour drive south of Palermo, deep in the Sicilian interior. The festival represents the age-old struggle between good and evil. Figures dressed as red devils, their faces covered with grotesque masks, parade through the streets, searching for souls to devour. Death is seen dressed in yellow and carrying a crossbow. All ends well when "angels" appear later to subdue the devils. Call © **095-7306255.** Easter.

MAY

Infiorata (Flower Festival), Noto. The residents of this little southeastern town prepare a magnificent carpet of flowers along Via Nicolaci, in the historic core. Themes are taken from religion and mythology. The festival features crafts shows, performances of sacred music, and tours of religious sites, followed by dances and parades of flower-bedecked antique carriages. Check with the tourist office at © **0931-573779** for exact dates. Beginning of May.

JUNE

Festa del Muzzini, Messina. *Muzzini* are ancient vases draped in silk that are carried in parades. This observance is actually a pagan rite to honor Demeter, the goddess of earth and fertility. It's rumored that many young women trying to have a child find themselves impregnated on the night of this celebration. Contact the Messina tourist office at ✆ **090-674236.** June 24.

JULY

The Feast of Santa Rosalia, Palermo. Holding a special place in the hearts of many residents, this festival is the most famous and popular in Sicily. During the week of the festival, Palermo becomes an open-air theater. The highlight is a 15m-high (49-ft.) float known as the *carro,* which is paraded through the streets along with a statue of Santa Rosalia on a huge cart drawn by horses. Torchlight processions are conducted to the saint's shrine on Monte Pellegrino, where the saint is said to have appeared in a vision to a hunter. Bands, dancers, African drums, religious choruses, fireworks, theatrical performances, and feasts (featuring everything from delectable tiny snails to fantastic gelato) characterize the event. Contact the Palermo tourist office at ✆ **091-583847.** July 10 to July 15.

AUGUST

Ferragosto (Assumption Day). This national holiday virtually shuts down the island of Sicily, marking the event where Mary was said to have been "taken up and assumed into heaven." This event always includes a feast of pagan origin, street parades, and fairs with young girls dressed in virginal white, sitting on oxen carts, their virtue menacingly protected by spikes. They toss fruit to the spectators. This observance is at its most colorful in Palermo; you can call its local tourist office at ✆ **091-968033;** www.palermotourism. com. Mid-August.

Palio dei Normanni, Piazza Armerina. Sicily's Norman past is observed during this historic celebration in which locals

dress in ancient costumes for parades. Even jousting takes place among knights in period costumes, looking like refugees from the pages of *Ivanhoe.* They fight against a puppet representing the dreaded Saracens. Contact the Piazza Armerina tourist office at ✆ **0935-682911;** www.italianvisits.com. Mid-August.

SEPTEMBER

International Couscous Festival, San Vito Lo Capo. This annual event outside Trapani means 3 days of dancing to live music and a bounty of local foods. The couscous competition draws some of the best cooks in the world, including those from North Africa where the dish originated. You'll gain 10 pounds if you participate in all of the feasting. Contact the Trapani tourist office at ✆ **0923-545511.** Mid-September.

OCTOBER

Maritime Festival, Porticello Santa Flavia. This festival takes place every year at a little fishing port to the east of Palermo. Sporting competitions include boat races among the fishermen. There's also a village festival dedicated to fish, a mainstay of the port's economy, especially the harvesting of anchovies and sardines. At night, there's a parade of boats illuminated with flaming torches, and an image of Maria is hauled to the water to be blessed. Naturally, stalls sell all the fish dishes you can consume. Contact the Palermo tourist office at ✆ **091-968033;** www.palermotourism. com. First Sunday in October.

NOVEMBER

Tutti Santi (All Saints' Day), islandwide. This ancient observance is celebrated all over Sicily as a national holiday including the "Day of the Dead." It's the Sicilian version of Halloween, in which the spirits of the dead are said to roam about. Originally more pagan in origin, it was tamed by the Catholic Church with the introduction of saints who are celebrated. Children are dressed in costumes for parades around the main squares of various towns. Pastry shops prepare a delectable confection, the ominously named "bones of the dead." Check with local tourist offices. November 1 and 2.

December

Christmas Fair, Syracuse. The major holiday fair of the south is conducted in this ancient city, which boasts the island's most colorful Christmas market. Many islanders drive for miles to purchase gifts here, including sweets, clothing, special embroidery, ornaments, and other items. It's conducted in the Epipoli section of Syracuse. Contact the Syracuse tourist office at ℂ **0931-481200.** From the second Saturday in December to December 21.

4 GETTING THERE & GETTING AROUND

GETTING TO SICILY
By Plane

High season for most airlines' routes to Sicily is usually from June to the beginning of September. This is the most expensive and most crowded time to travel. **Shoulder season** is from April to May, early September to October, and December 15 to December 24. **Low season** is from November 1 to December 14 and December 25 to March 31.

From July to October, **Eurofly** (www.euroflyusa.com) flies direct to Palermo from JFK in New York twice a week. If you're flying in August, reserve well in advance because seats are very limited because of heavy demand. Most visitors fly first to Milan or Rome, and then take a connecting flight to Sicily, most often using Palermo as their gateway to the island.

In the western part of the island, planes arrive at the **Aeroporto Punta Raisi,** 31km (19 miles) west of Palermo at Punta Raisi. In the east, planes land at Catania's **Aeroporto Fontanarossa,** 7km (4¹/₂ miles) south of the center of town. For Palermo airport information, call ℂ **091-7020111** (www.gesap.it) daily between 5:30am and 9:30pm; and for the Catania airport, call ℂ **095-7239111** (www.aeroporto.catania.it) daily between 8am and midnight.

Chances are you'll use **Alitalia** (ℂ **800/ 223-5730** in the U.S., or 8488-65643 for domestic flights within Italy; www.alitaliausa.com) for the Sicilian flights. For Alitalia flight information in Palermo, call ℂ **091-7020313** daily between 5am and 7:30pm; in Catania, call ℂ **095-252410** daily between 5am and 9pm.

Alitalia operates at least 17 flights a day from Rome to Palermo and about 13 from Milan. There is one direct flight a day from Turin to Palermo (far more if you stop over in Milan or Rome and make a connecting flight). For most visitors who are already in the south of Italy, the daily flight from Naples to Palermo is the most heavily booked. There are also six daily flights from Bologna to Palermo.

Alitalia also operates 12 daily flights from Rome to Catania. There are an additional eight flights a day that stop first in Naples. From Milan to Catania, there are 16 direct flights daily, or nine with stops in Rome. From Turin, Alitalia offers two direct flights to Catania (or 16 with stops in Rome). From Bologna, the airline flies three times daily to Catania, or 16 times with stops in Rome or Naples.

Meridiana (ℂ **0789-52682** or 06-65953880 in Rome, or 091-6512587 in Palermo; www.meridiana.it) is the second

Tips **Cutting Air Costs**

Regardless of how you fly, it's cheaper for transatlantic passengers to have a flight to Palermo written into their overall ticket when booking a flight to Italy from North America. If you book a flight to Palermo once you've arrived in Italy, it will cost much more.

major carrier serving Sicily. The airline shares some of its flights and reservations functions with Alitalia (see above). Most of Meridiana's flights to Sicily operate between Rome and Palermo (four direct flights daily) and can be booked separately or as part of a transatlantic itinerary through Alitalia.

In addition to its flights from Rome to Palermo, Meridiana offers two direct daily flights from Milan to Catania; one direct daily flight from Bologna to Palermo (three direct flights from Bologna to Catania); and one direct flight from Verona to Palermo (two direct flights from Verona to Catania). Surprisingly, Meridiana doesn't fly from Rome to Catania or from Naples to Catania.

From late March to late October, **Air Malta** (© 356-21-662-227; www.airmalta. com) offers two daily flights from Malta to Palermo, with a flying time of 50 minutes, and five daily flights from Malta to Catania, with a flying time of 45 minutes.

A final carrier serving Sicily is **Air One** (© **199-207080** or 06-48880069; www. flyairone.it in Rome). It flies from Rome to Palermo five times a day, and from Rome to Catania five times a day. There are three daily flights from Milan to Palermo, and four flights from Milan to Catania. There is also a daily flight from Turin to Catania, and four flights daily from Turin to Palermo. From Pisa there are 20 flights daily: 10 to Palermo and 10 to Catania.

By Car

If you're already on the Continent, particularly in a neighboring country such as

France or Austria, you may want to drive to Italy. However, you should make arrangements in advance with your car-rental company.

It's also possible to drive from London to Rome, a distance of 1,810km (1,125 miles), via Calais/Boulogne/Dunkirk, or 1,747km (1,086 miles) via Ostend/Zeebrugge, not counting channel crossings by hovercraft, ferry, or the Chunnel. Milan is some 644km (400 miles) closer to Britain than is Rome. If you cross over from England and arrive at one of the continental ports, you still face a 24-hour drive. Most drivers play it safe and budget 3 days for the journey.

Most of the roads from western Europe leading into Italy are toll-free, with some notable exceptions. If you use the Swiss superhighway network, you'll have to buy a special tax sticker at the frontier. You'll also pay to go through the St. Gotthard Tunnel into Italy. Crossings from France can be through the Mont Blanc Tunnel, for which you'll pay, or you can leave the French Riviera at Menton and drive directly into Italy along the Italian Riviera toward San Remo.

If you don't want to drive such distances, ask a travel agent to book you on a Motorail arrangement in which the train carries your car. This service, however, is good only to Milan, as no car and sleeper expresses run the 644km (400 miles) south to Rome.

Warning: You won't save a lot of money by driving to Sicily from another European country. Once you cross the frontier into Italy, you'll face a staggering number of tolls for riding the autostrade (express highways). Not only that, but gasoline costs are among the highest in Europe. Count on a lot of time, at least 17 hours of straight driving from the Swiss or French border to Villa San Giovanni, the point from which the car-carrying ferries sail to Messina in eastern Sicily.

By Train

For many visitors, this is the most convenient way to reach Sicily from the Italian mainland. Trains with connections from all over Europe, including Rome and Naples, arrive at the port of Villa San Giovanni, near Reggio di Calabria, in southern Italy.

Trains roll onto enormous barges for the 1-hour crossing into eastern Sicily. Passengers remain in their seats during the short voyage across the Straits of Messina, eventually rolling back onto the tracks once they reach Sicily. The trip from Rome to Palermo takes 11 to 13 hours, depending on the speed of the train. The trip from Naples to Palermo takes 10 hours.

For fares and information within Italy, call © **892021.** See individual town or city listings for more detailed train information and fares.

If you plan to travel a lot on the European or British railroads on your way to or from Sicily, you'd do well to secure the latest copy of the *Thomas Cook European Timetable of Railroads.* It's available online at **www.thomascooktimetables.com**.

New electric trains have made travel between France and Italy faster and more comfortable than ever. France's high-speed **TGV** trains have cut travel time between Paris and Turin from 7 to $5^1/_2$ hours and between Paris and Milan from $7^1/_2$ to $6^3/_4$ hours. Italy's **ETR** trains currently run between Milan and Lyon, a 5-hour ride, with a stop in Turin.

Rail Passes for North American Travelers

Many travelers to Europe take advantage of one of the greatest travel bargains, the Eurailpass which permits unlimited first-class rail travel in any country in western Europe except the British Isles (good in Ireland). Passes are available for purchase online (www.eurail.com) and at various offices/agents around the world. Travel agents and railway agents in such cities as New York, Montreal, and Los Angeles sell Eurailpasses. You can purchase them at the North American offices of CIT Travel Service, the French National Railroads, the German Federal Railroads, and the Swiss Federal Railways. It is strongly recommended that you purchase passes before you leave home as not all passes are available in Europe; also, passes purchased in Europe will cost about 20% more. Numerous options are available for travel in France.

The **Eurail Global Pass** allows you unlimited travel in 20 Eurail-affiliated countries. You can travel on any of the days within the validity period, which is available for 15 days, 21 days, 1 month, 2 months, 3 months, and some other possibilities as well. Prices for first-class adult travel are $745 for 15 days, $965 for 21 days, $1,199 for 1 month, $1,695 for 2 months, and $2,089 for 3 months. Children 4 to 11 pay half fare; those 3 and under travel for free.

A **Eurail Global Pass Saver,** also valid for first-class travel in 20 countries, offers a special deal for two or more people traveling together. This pass costs $629 for 15 days, $819 for 21 days, $1,019 for 1 month, $1,439 for 2 months, and $1,785 for 3 months.

A **Eurail Global Youth Pass** for those 12 to 25 allows second-class travel in 18 countries. This pass costs $485 for 15 days, $625 for 21 days, $779 for 1 month, $1,099 for 2 months, and $1,359 for 3 months.

The **Eurail Select Pass** offers unlimited travel on the national rail networks of any three, four, or five bordering countries out of the 22 Eurail nations linked by train or ship. Two or more passengers can travel together for big discounts, getting 5, 6, 8, 10, or 15 days of rail travel within any 2-month period on the national rail networks of any three, four, or five adjoining Eurail countries linked by train or ship. A sample fare: for 5 days in 2 months you pay $469 for three countries. **Eurail Select Pass Youth** for travelers 25 and under, allow second-class travel within the same guidelines as Eurail Selectpass, with fees starting at $305. **Eurail Select Pass Saver** offers discounts for two or more people traveling together, first-class travel within the same guidelines as Eurail Selectpass, with fees starting at $399.

WHERE TO BUY RAIL PASSES Travel agents in all towns and railway agents in major North American cities sell all these tickets, but the biggest supplier is **Rail Europe** (✆ 877/272-RAIL [7245]; www.raileurope.com), which can also give you informational brochures.

Many different rail passes are available in the United Kingdom for travel in Britain and continental Europe. Stop in at the **International Rail Centre,** Victoria Station, London SW1V 1JY (✆ **0870/5848-848** in the U.K.). Some of the most popular passes, including InterRail and Euro Youth, are offered only to travelers 25 and under; these allow unlimited second-class travel through most European countries.

Rail Passes for British & Other European Travelers

If you plan to do a lot of exploring by train, you might prefer one of the three passes designed for unlimited travel within a designated region during a predetermined number of days. These passes are sold in Britain and several other European countries.

The **InterRail Pass** (www.interrail.net) is available to passengers of any nationality, with some restrictions—passengers must be able to prove at least 6 months of

residency in a European or North African country (Morocco, Algeria, and Tunisia) before buying the pass. It allows unlimited travel through Europe, except Albania and the republics of the former Soviet Union. Prices are complicated and vary depending on the countries you want to include. For pricing purposes, Europe is divided into eight zones; the cost depends on the number of zones you include. For those 25 and younger, the most expensive option (399€/$519) allows 1 month of unlimited travel in all eight zones and is known as a "global." The least expensive option (159€/$207) allows 5 days of travel within 10 days.

Passengers 25 and older can buy an **InterRail Global Pass.** The cost varies from 359€ to 489€ ($467–$636) for 10 days to 599€ to 809€ ($779–$1,052) for 1 month. Passengers must meet the same residency requirements that apply to the InterRail Pass (described above).

For information on buying individual rail tickets or any of the aforementioned passes, contact **National Rail Inquiries,** Victoria Station, London (✆ 020/7278-5240 or 0845/748-4950; www.nationalrail.co.uk). tickets and passes are also available at any of the larger railway stations as well as select travel agencies throughout Britain and the rest of Europe.

By Boat & Ferry

As an island, Sicily is well linked via sea to mainland Italy. The major connection is from Villa San Giovanni in Calabria, the last mainland city approached before the ferry trip over to Messina, in eastern Sicily. Ferries *(traghetti)* depart frequently from Villa San Giovanni, making the trip of 12km (7¹⁄₂ miles) across the straits. If you don't have a car, the fastest way to go is by hydrofoil from Reggio di Calabria.

If you're already in Naples, it's easy to go by sea from there to Palermo. **SNAV** (✆ **081-4285555;** www.snav.it) operates hydrofoils that make 5-hour southern crossings to Sicily. There is also a car-carrying ferry service operated by **Traghetti Lines** (© 050-754492; www.traghetti. com), taking 11 hours to reach Palermo from Naples. Boat schedules are dependent on weather conditions. For details, see p. 35.

If you're in the north of Italy, you can also sail to Palermo from Genoa. **Grandi Navi Veloci,** Via Milano 51 (© 010-2094591; www.gnv.it), runs daily service to Palermo from July to September (Mon–Sat otherwise). The journey takes 20 hours and costs 200€ ($260) for foot passengers or 284€ ($369) per person for those bringing a vehicle; these fares are round-trip. Ferries in Genoa depart from Nuovo Terminale Traghetti.

Grandi Navi Veloci, Varco Galvali (© 0586-409804), operates ferries to Palermo from the port of Livorno. Daily ferry departures make the 12-hour run. Foot passengers are charged 178€ ($231) round-trip; a person in a vehicle pays 260€ ($338), also round-trip.

By Bus

There is no direct bus service to Sicily from outside Italy. Europe's major bus carrier, **Eurolines** (© 0870/514-3219 in London; www.eurolines.com), has its main office at Grosvenor Gardens, Victoria, London SW1. It runs buses to Rome in 33 hours. After that, you can take an Italian bus to Sicily unless you're completely exhausted. Buses leave England on Wednesday and Friday, heading for Milan and Rome. The cost, round-trip, ranges from 124€ to 143€ ($161–$186).

If you're in Rome and want to travel overland by bus into Sicily, you can book tickets at **Segesta,** Piazza della Repubblica (© 0935-565111; www.interbus.it). It has two departures daily from Rome's Piazza Tiburtina to Palermo; the trip takes 12 hours. The line also goes to Syracuse in 11 hours.

GETTING AROUND SICILY
By Plane

Unlike in mainland Italy, flying around Sicily is rarely an option. Once you've made a choice to fly into Palermo, as your western gateway, or Catania, as your eastern gateway, the chief means of getting about are train, bus, or rental car. There are domestic flights from Palermo to the Pélagie Islands, close to North Africa, and to the island of Pantelleria, also owned by Sicily.

By Train

Unless you're heading for remote towns and villages in Sicily, riding the rails is the best way to traverse the island without a private rental car. All of the major cities such as Palermo, Catania, Messina, Syracuse, Agrigento, Taormina, and Trapani have rail links. Trains on weekends and holidays tend to be crowded, so book in advance.

Train fares are generally very affordable in Sicily. See "By Train" listings under the individual town and city sections for trip times and point-to-point fares. Trains are operated by **Ferrovie dello Stato (FS),** the Italian State Railways. For general information on connections through Sicily, call © 892021 from anywhere on the island or within Italy itself; from outside Italy, call © 338/333-4844. For more information, search the website at **www.ferrovie.it**.

A **Trenitalia Pass** allows you to travel on the days you select so you can explore Sicily or Italy at your leisure. For 3 days in 2 months, the cost is $286 in first class or $228 in second class. Additional rail days cost $34 and $30, respectively. A budget version of this pass is the **Trenitalia Pass Saver,** requiring two people to travel together at all times. This pass costs $243 in first class or $194 in second class, with additional rail days costing $28 and $24, respectively. Again, the pass is valid for 3 days of rail travel in 2 months.

A supplement must be paid to ride on certain rapid trains, designated **ETR-450** or **Pendolino** trains.

You can buy all of these passes from any travel agent or by calling ⓒ **800/848-7245.** You can also call ⓒ **800/4-EURAIL (387245)** or 800/EUROSTAR (38767827); www.raileurope.com.

As a rule of thumb, second-class travel usually costs about two-thirds the price of an equivalent first-class trip. **InterCity trains** (designated **IC** on train schedules) are modern, air-conditioned trains that make limited stops; compared with the cost of the far slower direct or regional trains, the supplement can be steep, but a second-class IC ticket will provide a first-class experience.

An IC couchette (private fold-down bed in a communal cabin) requires a supplement above the price of first-class travel. Children ages 4 to 11 receive a discount of 50% off the adult fare, and children 3 and younger travel free with a parent. Seniors and travelers 25 and under can also purchase discount cards. Seat reservations are highly recommended during peak season, and on weekends or holidays they must be booked in advance.

Slower Sicilian trains—called **Diretto, Espresso,** and **Interegionale**—stop at only major towns or cities. Try to avoid a Regionale train (sometimes known as the Locale), as they stop in every hamlet and take forever.

Available at ticket offices is an FS booklet, *Treno Sicilia,* updated twice annually and usually distributed free.

By Bus

Where the train doesn't go, there is almost always a local bus to take you into the more remote villages and hinterlands, although you can generally go from city to city and town to town by bus as well. Bus fares are often more expensive than rail transportation. For individual city and town links, and for a general outline of fares, refer to the individual sections on cities and towns in later chapters.

The major bus company is **SAIS** (ⓒ **091-616028** in Palermo, or 095-536168 in Catania; www.saisautolinee.it), offering service from Palermo to Messina, Catania, and Syracuse. **Cuffaro** (ⓒ **091-6161510;** www.cuffaro.info) links Palermo in the north with Agrigento in the south. **Interbus** (ⓒ **094-2625301;** www.interbus.it) has service between the cities of Catania, Messina, Taormina, and Syracuse.

Sunday is a bad day to take the bus, as schedules are either curtailed or down completely. Keep in mind that large cities can have a number of bus depots. In smaller towns, buses generally pull into one central square, often the rail station.

Tickets are most often purchased right on the bus. In bigger cities such as Palermo, you can buy a ticket in advance at the office of one of the local companies. That way, you'll be more confident that you'll have a seat.

Only the cities and larger towns offer a bus system to get you from point to point. Tickets for city buses are bought before boarding and must be validated once you hop on, or else you'll be fined up to 60€ ($78) on the spot.

Tickets are generally purchased at ticket booths, *tabacchi* (tobacco shops), or newspaper kiosks. Most city buses charge 4.60€ ($6) for a ticket that is valid for only 60 to 90 minutes. Sometimes a city will offer a 24-hour transit ticket that can save you money if you plan to use the bus network extensively.

By Car

U.S. and Canadian drivers don't need an **International Driver's License** to drive a rented car in Italy or Sicily. However, if you're driving a private car, you will need such a license.

You can apply for an International Driver's License at any **AAA** branch. You must be at least 18 and have two 2×2-inch photos and a photocopy of your U.S.

driver's license with your AAA application form. The actual fee for the license can vary, depending on where it's issued. Remember that an International Driver's License is valid only if physically accompanied by your original driver's license and only if signed on the back.

To find the AAA office nearest you, call *C* **800/222-4357**, or go to www.aaa.com. In Canada, you can get the location of the **Canadian Automobile Association** office closest to you by calling *C* **800/267-8713** or going to www.caa.ca.

RENTALS Many of the loveliest parts of Sicily lie miles from the main cities, far away from the train stations. For sheer convenience and freedom, renting a car is usually the best way to explore the island. But you have to be a pretty aggressive and alert driver who won't be fazed by super-high speeds on the autostrada or by narrow streets in the cities and towns. Sicilian drivers have truly earned their reputation as bad and daring.

However, the legalities and contractual obligations of renting a car in Sicily (where accident and theft rates are very high) are a little complicated. To rent a car here, a driver must have nerves of steel, a sense of humor, a valid driver's license, and a valid passport, and must be (in most cases) more than 25 years old. Insurance is compulsory, though any reputable rental firm will arrange it in advance before you're even given the keys.

In some cases, slight discounts are offered to members of AAA or AARP. Be sure to ask.

It is generally cheaper to make arrangements for car rentals before you leave home. Of course, you can also rent a car once you arrive in Sicily. Although the price can vary greatly depending on the vehicle, the average rental on the island costs from 60€ to 120€ ($78–$156) per day.

The main rental agencies in Sicily include **Avis** (*C* **800/331-1212;** www.avis.com) and **Hertz** (*C* **800/654-3131;**

www.hertz.com). Avis has locations at Catania's Aeroporto Fontanarossa (*C* **095-340500**), in Catania itself at Via Guido Gozzano 53 (*C* **095-373909**), at Palermo's Aeroporto Punta Raisi (*C* **091-591684**), and in Palermo at Via Francesco Crispi 115 (*C* **095-586940**).

Hertz has locations at Catania's Aeroporto Fontanarossa (*C* **095-341595**), and at Palermo's Aeroporto Punta Raisi (*C* **091-213112**).

U.S.-based companies specializing in European car rentals are **Auto Europe** (*C* **800/223-5555;** www.autoeurope.com), **Europe by Car** (*C* **888/223-1516** or 212/581-3040; www.europebycar.com), and **Kemwel Holiday Auto** (*C* **800/678-0678;** www.kemwel.com).

GASOLINE *Benzina* (gasoline) is expensive in Sicily. Be prepared for sticker shock every time you fill up even a medium-size car with *super benzina,* which has the octane rating appropriate for most of the cars you'll be able to rent. In today's uncertain economy, prices can change from week to week, even day to day. Gas stations on the autostrade are open 24 hours, but stations on regular roads are rarely open on Sunday; also, many close from noon to 3pm for lunch, and most shut down after 7pm. Make sure the pump registers zero before an attendant starts refilling your tank. A popular scam in Sicily is to fill your tank before resetting the meter, so you pay not only your bill but also the charges run up by the previous motorist.

DRIVING RULES The Italian Highway Code follows the Geneva Convention, and Sicily, like the rest of Italy, uses international road signs. Driving is on the right; passing is on the left. Violators of the highway code are fined; serious violations might also be punished by imprisonment. In cities and towns, the speed limit is 50kmph (31 mph). For all cars and motor vehicles on main roads and local roads, the limit is 90kmph (56 mph). For the auto-strade, the limit is 130kmph (81 mph). Use the left lane only for passing. If a driver zooms up behind you on the auto-strada with his or her lights on, that's your sign to get out of the way. Use of seat belts is compulsory.

BREAKDOWNS & ASSISTANCE The **Automobile Club Italiano (ACI)** does not offer free roadside emergency help to stranded motorists in Sicily. If you call the ACI emergency number (✆ **803116**) in the event of a breakdown, you must pay a minimum of 110€ ($143), plus another 45€ ($59) to have your car towed to the nearest garage, plus tax and 1€ ($1.30) per kilometer. So getting stranded in Sicily has a serious cost. Not only that, but 20% is added to the bill between 10pm and 6am and on Saturday and Sunday. ACI offices are at Via delle Alpi 6, in Palermo (✆ **091-300468;** www.aci.it), and at Via Sabotino 1, in Catania (✆ **095-533380**).

SICILIAN ROADS The autostrada does not exist as extensively on Sicily as it does on the Italian mainland. The most traveled route is the A19 between Palermo and Catania, a convenient link between the island's two major cities. The other oft-traveled route is A20 going between Palermo and Messina. A18 links Messina and Catania on the eastern coast, whereas A29 goes from Palermo to the capital of the western coast, Trapani.

Sicily has nowhere near the burdensome tolls of mainland Italy, but there are some: For example, taking the autostrada from Messina to Catania costs 4.50€ ($5.85).

Unless you're traveling from main city to main city, you'll use the state roads, or *Strade statali,* single-lane, and toll-free routes. To reach remote villages, you'll sometimes find yourself going along a country lane and watching out for goats.

By Taxi

Taxi rates vary from town to town, but in general are pricey. In most cities, the meter begins at 3.50€ ($4.55), and then charges you 2.50€ ($3.25) for the first 154m (505 ft.), plus another .85€ ($1.10) per kilometer thereafter. There are supplements of 2€ ($2.60) from 10pm to 7am and on holidays. Depending on the size of the taxi, four or as many as five passengers are allowed. Taxis are found at all airport arrival terminals. In some cities, they can be called. When you reserve by phone, the taxi meter goes on when the cabbie pulls out of his station. In Sicily, taxis rarely stop if hailed on the street.

By Bicycle

Most Sicilian cities have bike-rental firms; otherwise, your hotel might help you make arrangements for one. Rentals in cities start at 10€ ($13) a day or 60€ ($78) a week. Even though helmets and lights are not legally required, they are prudent to have. It is forbidden to bike along the autostrade. Bikes are transported free on Sicilian ferries, but you must pay to carry them on most trains. Fast trains generally do not allow bikes, although conductors on IC trains let you put a bike in the baggage train for an extra 5€ ($6.50).

---

5 MONEY & COSTS

CURRENCY

The **euro,** the new single European currency, became the official currency of Italy and 11 other participating countries on January 1, 1999.

However, the euro didn't go into general circulation until early 2002. The old currency, the Italian lira, disappeared into history on March 1, 2002, replaced by the euro, whose official abbreviation is "EUR." The symbol of the euro is a stylized *E:* €.

Emergency Cash—The Fastest Way

If you need emergency cash over the weekend when all banks and American Express offices are closed, you can have money wired to you from **Western Union** (☎ **800/325-6000;** www.westernunion.com). You must present valid ID to pick up the cash at the Western Union office. However, in most countries you can pick up a money transfer even if you don't have valid identification, as long as you can answer a test question provided by the sender. Be sure to let the sender know in advance that you don't have ID. If you need to use a test question instead of ID, the sender must take cash to his or her local Western Union office rather than transfer the money over the phone or online.

Exchange rates of participating countries are locked into a common currency fluctuating against the dollar.

For more details on the euro, check out **www.europa.eu.int/euro**. At press time one 1€ was worth approximately $1.30 in U.S. currency.

ATMS

ATMs are prevalent in all Sicilian cities and even in smaller towns. ATMs are linked to a national network that most likely includes your bank at home.

The easiest and best way to get cash away from home is from an ATM (automated teller machine). Be sure you know your personal identification number (PIN) before you leave home and be sure to find out your daily withdrawal limit before you depart. Also keep in mind that many banks impose a fee every time a card is used at a different bank's ATM, and that fee can be higher for international transactions (up to $5 or more) than for domestic ones. On top of this, the bank from which you withdraw cash may charge its own fee. To compare banks' ATM fees within the U.S., use www.bankrate.com. For international withdrawal fees, ask your bank.

You can also get cash advances on your credit card at an ATM. Keep in mind that credit card companies try to protect themselves from theft by limiting the funds

someone can withdraw outside their home country, so call your credit card company before you leave home. And keep in mind that you'll pay interest from the moment of your withdrawal, even if you pay your monthly bills on time.

Important note: Make sure that the PINs on your bank cards and credit cards will work in Sicily. You'll need a **four-digit code** (six digits won't work); if you have a six-digit code, you'll have to go into your bank and get a new PIN for your trip. Be sure to check the daily withdrawal limit at the same time.

CREDIT CARDS

Credit cards are a safe way to carry money. They also provide a convenient record of all your expenses, and they generally offer relatively good exchange rates. You can also withdraw cash advances from your credit cards at banks or ATMs, provided you know your PIN. If you've forgotten yours, or didn't even know you had one, call the number on the back of your credit card and ask the bank to send it to you. It usually takes 5 to 7 business days, though some banks will provide the number over the phone if you tell them your mother's maiden name or some other personal information. Keep in mind that when you use your credit card abroad, most banks assess a 2% fee above the 1% fee charged

What Things Cost in Palermo

	US$	UK£
Taxi from the airport to city center	56.00	28.00
Bus from airport to city center	9.60	4.80
Ride on city bus	1.90	.95
Double at Central Palace (expensive)	301.00	151.00
Double at Hotel Sport Club Portorais (moderate)	200.00	100.00
Double at Albergo Hotel Joli (inexpensive)	157.00	79.00
Lunch for one, without wine at La Scuderia (expensive)	35.00	18.00
Lunch for one, without wine at Bar Alba (inexpensive)	13.00	6.50
Dinner for one, without wine, at Il Ristorantino (expensive)	72.00	36.00
Dinner for one, without wine, at Capricci di Sicilia (moderate)	48.00	24.00
Dinner for one, without wine, at Hirsch (inexpensive)	26.00	13.00
Slice of pizza	6.40	3.20
Glass of wine	4.80	2.40
Admission to Palazzo dei Normanni	9.60	4.80
Theater ticket	16.00	8.00

by Visa, MasterCard, or American Express for currency conversion on credit charges. But credit cards still may be the smart way to go when you factor in things like exorbitant ATM fees and higher traveler's check exchange rates (and service fees).

For tips and telephone numbers to call if your wallet is stolen or lost, see "Lost & Found" in the "Fast Facts: Sicily" section of appendix A.

In Sicily, the most commonly accepted credit cards are MasterCard and Visa. Of secondary importance are American Express and Diners Club.

6 HEALTH

STAYING HEALTHY

In general, Sicily is viewed as a "safe" destination, although problems, of course, can and do occur anywhere. You don't need to get shots; most foodstuffs are safe; and the water in cities and towns is potable. If you're concerned, drink bottled water. It's easy to get a prescription filled in towns and cities.

In case of **emergency,** dial © **113** for the police, or © **112** for the *Carabinieri* (army police corps): They can call an ambulance or help you in many ways. If your situation is life-threatening, go to the *pronto soccorso* (emergency department) at the local hospital.

Many, but hardly all, doctors in Sicily speak English. If you get sick, consider asking your hotel concierge to recommend a local doctor—even his or her own. You can also try the emergency room at a local hospital. Many hospitals also have walk-in clinics for emergency cases that are not life-threatening; you may not get immediate attention, but you won't pay the high price of an emergency-room visit. In the chapters that follow, we list hospitals and emergency numbers under "Fast Facts" in the sections on various cities.

Under the Italian national healthcare system, you're eligible only for free *emergency* care. If you're admitted to a hospital

Avoiding "Economy-Class Syndrome"

Deep-vein thrombosis, or as it's known in the world of flying, "economy-class syndrome," is a blood clot that develops in a deep vein. It's a potentially deadly condition that can be caused by sitting in cramped conditions—such as an airplane cabin—for too long. During a flight (especially a long-haul flight), get up, walk around, and stretch your legs every 60 to 90 minutes to keep your blood flowing. Other preventative measures include frequent flexing of the legs while sitting, drinking lots of water, and avoiding alcohol and sleeping pills. If you have a history of deep-vein thrombosis, heart disease, or another condition that puts you at high risk, some experts recommend wearing compression stockings or taking anticoagulants when you fly; always ask your physician about the best course for you. Symptoms of deep-vein thrombosis include leg pain or swelling, or even shortness of breath.

as an in-patient, even from an accident and an emergency, you're required to pay (unless you're a resident of the European Economic Area). You're also required to pay for follow-up care.

If you do end up paying for healthcare, especially if you're admitted to a hospital for any reason, some health-insurance plans and HMOs will cover at least part of the out-of-country hospital visits and procedures. Be prepared to pay the bills at the time of care, however. You'll get a refund after you've returned to your country and filed all the paperwork.

If you are traveling around Sicily over the summer, limit your exposure to the sun, especially during the first few days of your trip and, thereafter, from 11am to 2pm. use a sunscreen with a high protection factor and apply it liberally. Remember that children need more protection than adults do.

General Availability of Healthcare

Contact the **International Association for Medical Assistance to Travelers** (**IAMAT;** ℰ **716/754-4883** in the U.S., or 416/652-0137 in Canada; www.iamat. org) for tips on travel and health concerns in the countries you're visiting, and for lists of local, English-speaking doctors. The United States **Centers for Disease Control and Prevention** (ℰ **800/311-3435** or 404/498-1515; www.cdc.gov) provides up-to-date information on health hazards by region or country and offers tips on food safety. **Travel Health Online** (www.tripprep.com), sponsored by a consortium of travel medicine practitioners, may also offer helpful advice on traveling abroad. You can find listings of reliable medical clinics overseas at the **International Society of Travel Medicine** (www. istm.org).

WHAT TO DO IF YOU GET SICK AWAY FROM HOME

For travel abroad, you may have to pay all medical costs upfront and be reimbursed later. Medicare and Medicaid do not provide coverage for medical costs outside the U.S. Before leaving home, find out what medical services your health insurance covers. To protect yourself, consider buying medical travel insurance (see "Medical Insurance," under "Insurance," in appendix A).

Very few health insurance plans pay for medical evacuation back to the U.S. (which can cost $10,000 and up). A number of companies offer medical evacuation services anywhere in the world. If you're ever hospitalized more than 150 miles from home, **MedjetAssist** (© **800/527-7478**; www.medjetassistance.com) will pick you up and fly you to the hospital of your choice virtually anywhere in the world in a medically equipped and staffed aircraft 24 hours day, 7 days a week. Annual memberships are $225 individual, $350 family; you can also purchase short-term memberships.

U.K. nationals will need a **European Health Insurance Card (EHIC)** (© **0845/606-2030**; www.ehic.org.uk) to receive free or reduced-costs health benefits during a visit to an European Economic Area (EEA) country (European Union countries plus Iceland, Liechtenstein, and Norway) or Switzerland. The European Health Insurance Card replaces the E111 form, which is no longer valid. For advice, ask at your local post office or see www.dh.gov.uk/travellers.

If you suffer from a chronic illness, consult your doctor before your departure. Pack **prescription medications** in your carry-on luggage, and carry them in their original containers, with pharmacy labels—otherwise they won't make it through airport security. Carry the generic name of prescription medicines, in case a local pharmacist is unfamiliar with the brand name.

7 SAFETY

Don't think you'll be at the mercy of the Mafia the moment you step foot in Sicily, as popular belief around the world suggests. The Mafia is virtually invisible.

You'll face more danger from thieves, such as pickpockets, than you will from the *Cosa Nostra. Scippatori,* or purse snatchers and pickpockets, are the curse of such cities as Palermo, Messina, and Catania.

Country towns, of course, are far safer. Avoid walking on dark streets in the old towns of Sicily at night. Even during the day, relatively deserted inner-city streets can put you at risk of robbery. Although many tourists are robbed, violence against visitors is rare.

While there is little you can do to protect yourself from random terrorist attacks, petty crime is much more common. Although most tourists have trouble-free visits to Sicily each year, the principal tourist areas have been experiencing an increase in crime. Palermo and Catania, in particular, have reported growing incidents of muggings and attacks. Criminals frequent tourist areas and major attractions such as museums, monuments, restaurants, hotels, beach resorts, trains, train stations, airports, subways, and ATMs.

Travelers should exercise caution, carry limited cash and credit cards, and leave extra cash, credit cards, passports, and personal documents in a safe location. Crimes have occurred at all times of day and night.

Thieves often work in teams or pairs. In most cases, one person distracts a victim while the accomplice performs the robbery. For example, a stranger might wave a map in your face and ask for directions or "inadvertently" spill something on you. While your attention is diverted, an accomplice makes off with the valuables. Attacks can also be initiated from behind, with the victim being grabbed around the neck and choked by one assailant while others rifle through the belongings. A group of assailants may surround the victim, maybe in a crowded popular tourist area or on public transportation, and only after the group has departed does the person discover he/she has been robbed. Some attacks have been so violent that victims have needed to seek medical attention after the attack.

Theft from parked cars is also common. Small items like luggage, cameras, or briefcases are often stolen from parked cars.

Travelers are advised not to leave valuables in parked cars and to keep doors locked, windows rolled up, and valuables out of sight when driving. "Good Samaritan" scams are unfortunately common. A passing car will attempt to divert the driver's attention by indicating there is a mechanical problem. If the driver stops to check the vehicle, accomplices steal from the car while the driver is looking elsewhere. Drivers should be cautious about accepting help from anyone other than a uniformed Sicilian police officer or Civil Guard.

The loss or theft abroad of a U.S. passport should be reported immediately to the local police and the nearest U.S. embassy or consulate. U.S. citizens may refer to the Department of State's pamphlet *A Safe Trip Abroad* for ways to promote trouble-free journeys. The pamphlet is available by mail from the Superintendent of Documents, U.S. Government Printing Office, Washington, DC 20402, via the Internet at www.access.gpo.gov, or via the Bureau of Consular Affairs home page at http://travel.state.gov.

A U.S. Department of State travel advisory warns that every car (whether parked, stopped at a traffic light, or even moving) can be a potential target for armed robbery. In these uncertain times, it is always prudent to check the U.S. Department of State's travel advisories at http://travel.state.gov.

8 SPECIALIZED TRAVEL RESOURCES

TRAVELERS WITH DISABILITIES

Sicily is hardly in the vanguard of catering to travelers with disabilities. Only the most expensive first-class or deluxe hotels have facilities that accommodate persons with disabilities.

The narrow, cobblestone streets of Sicily's cities and villages, most of which date back to the Middle Ages, weren't built for people who get around in wheelchairs. Hysterical drivers and impossible parking don't help much either. Even if you're an Olympic athlete, getting across a street in the face of speeding traffic in Palermo is risky at any time.

We recommend that those with disabilities consider visiting Sicily on an organized tour specifically geared to provide assistance, which is vitally needed.

Organizations that offer a vast range of resources and assistance to travelers with disabilities include **MossRehab** (© 800/CALL-MOSS [225-56677]; www.mossresourcenet.org); the **American Foundation for the Blind** (AFB; © 800/232-5463;

www.afb.org); and **SATH** (Society for Accessible Travel & Hospitality; © 212/447-7284; www.sath.org). **AirAmbulanceCard.com** (© 877/424-7633) is now partnered with SATH and allows you to preselect top-notch hospitals in case of an emergency.

Access-Able Travel Source (© 303/232-2979; www.access-able.com) offers a comprehensive database on travel agents from around the world with experience in accessible travel; destination-specific access information; and links to such resources as service animals, equipment rentals, and access guides.

Many travel agencies offer customized tours and itineraries for travelers with disabilities. Among them are **Flying Wheels Travel** (© 507/451-5005; www.flyingwheelstravel.com) and **Accessible Journeys** (© 800/846-4537 or 610/521-0339; www.disabilitytravel.com).

Flying with Disability (www.flying-with-disability.org) is a comprehensive information source on airplane travel.

Also check out the quarterly magazine *Emerging Horizons* (www.emerginghorizons.com), available by subscription.

The "Accessible Travel" link at **Mobility-Advisor.com** (www.mobility-advisor. com) offers a variety of travel resources to persons with disabilities.

British travelers should contact **Holiday Care** (✆ 0845-124-9971 in the U.K. only; www.holidaycare.org.uk) to access a wide range of travel information and resources for disabled and elderly people.

For more on organizations that offer resources to travelers with disabilities, go to frommers.com.

GAY & LESBIAN TRAVELERS

Even though Italy since 1861 has had rather liberal legislation regarding homosexuality, Sicily remains one of the major bastions of homophobia in Europe. Some of the islanders express antigay attitudes that might belong more appropriately to the Middle Ages. Open displays of affection between same-sex couples meet with obvious disapproval by intolerant islanders.

Don't be misled: Sicilian men are often very affectionate, linking arms with one another and kissing on the cheeks to say hello or bid goodbye. This is how straight men behave, and such affection is not to be construed as overtly sexual.

There are few gay businesses in Sicily. If you're gay and still want to go, your best bet is the more sophisticated resort of Taormina, following in the footsteps of past visitors such as Tennessee Williams and his longtime companion, Frank Merlo.

If you really want a gay holiday in Italy, Sicily may not be for you. Consider *la dolce vita* as lived on the Isle of Capri (see *Frommer's Italy,* Wiley Publishing, Inc.).

If you have your heart set on Sicily, however, the following resources may be helpful.

The **International Gay and Lesbian Travel Association (IGLTA;** ✆ 954/630-1637; www.iglta.org) is the trade association for the gay and lesbian travel industry, and offers an online directory of gay- and lesbian-friendly travel businesses and tour operators.

Many agencies offer tours and travel itineraries specifically for gay and lesbian travelers. **Above and Beyond Tours** (✆ 800/397-2681; www.abovebeyondtours.com) are gay Australia tour specialists. San Francisco–based **Now, Voyager** (✆ 800/255-6951; www.nowvoyager.com) offers worldwide trips and cruises. And **Olivia** (✆ 800/631-6277; www.olivia.com) offers lesbian cruises and resort vacations.

Gay.com Travel (✆ 415/834-6500; www.gay.com/travel or www.outandabout. com) is an excellent online successor to the popular *Out & About* print magazine. It provides regularly updated information about gay-owned, gay-oriented, and gay-friendly lodging, dining, sightseeing, nightlife, and shopping establishments in every important destination worldwide.

The Canadian website **GayTraveler (www.gaytraveler.ca)** offers ideas and advice for gay travel all over the world.

The following travel guides are available at many bookstores, or you can order them from any online bookseller: *Spartacus International Gay Guide* (Bruno Gmünder Verlag; www.spartacusworld. com/gayguide) and *Odysseus: The International Gay Travel Planner, 17th Edition* (www.odyusa.com); and the *Damron* guides (www.damron.com), with separate, annual books for gay men and lesbians.

For more gay and lesbian travel resources, visit frommers.com.

SENIOR TRAVEL

Mention the fact that you're a senior when you make your travel reservations. Many hotels offer discounts for seniors. In most cities, people over the age of 60 qualify for reduced admission to theaters, museums, and other attractions, as well as discounted fares on public transportation.

Members of **AARP,** 601 E St. NW, Washington, DC 20049 (✆ 888/687-2277; www.aarp.org), get discounts on hotels, airfares, and car rentals. AARP offers members a wide range of benefits, including *AARP The Magazine* and a monthly newsletter. Anyone 50 and over can join.

Many reliable agencies and organizations target the 50-plus market. **Elderhostel** (© **800/454-5768;** www.elderhostel.org) arranges worldwide study programs for those aged 55 and over.

Recommended publications offering travel resources and discounts for seniors include the quarterly magazine *Travel 50 & Beyond* (www.travel50andbeyond.com) and the best-selling paperback *Unbelievably Good Deals and Great Adventures That You Absolutely Can't Get Unless You're Over 50 2007–2008, 16th Edition* (McGraw-Hill), by Joann Rattner Heilman.

Frommers.com offers more information and resources on travel for seniors.

FAMILY TRAVEL

Throughout this guide, look for our kid-friendly icons. Sicilians may love *bambini,* but they don't offer a lot of special amenities for them. For example, a kids' menu in a restaurant is a rarity. You can, however, request a half portion *(mezza porzione),* and most waiters will oblige. Most Sicilian hoteliers will let children 12 and younger stay for free in a room with a parent. Sometimes this requires a little negotiation at the reception desk.

At attractions, inquire if a kids' discount is available; Italians call it *sconto bambino.* European Community youths 17 and under get a big break: They're admitted free to all state-run museums.

Babysitting services are available through most hotel desks or by going to the local tourist office in the town where you're staying. Many hotels have children's game rooms and playgrounds.

Recommended family travel websites include **Family Travel Forum** (www.familytravelforum.com), a comprehensive site that offers customized trip planning; **Family Travel Network** (© **703/905-9858;** www.familytravelnetwork.com), an award-winning site that offers travel features, deals, and tips; **Traveling Internationally with Your Kids** (www.travelwithyourkids.com), a comprehensive site offering sound advice for international travel with children; and **Family Travel Files** (www.thefamilytravelfiles.com), which offers an online magazine and a directory of off-the-beaten-path tours and tour operators for families.

WOMEN TRAVELERS

Women traveling alone in macho Sicily will want to exercise caution and be wary of pickpockets and purse snatchers.

Women travelers may also want to check out the award-winning website **Journeywoman** (www.journeywoman.com), a "real life" women's travel information network where you can sign up for a free e-mail newsletter and get advice on everything from etiquette to dress to safety. The guide *Safety and Security for Women Who Travel,* by Sheila Swan and Peter Laufer (Travelers' Tales, Inc.), also offers common-sense tips on safe travel.

9 SUSTAINABLE TOURISM

Sustainable tourism is conscientious travel. It means being careful with the environments you explore, and respecting the communities you visit. Two overlapping components of sustainable travel are **eco-tourism** and **ethical tourism.** The

International Ecotourism Society (TIES) defines eco-tourism as responsible travel to natural areas that conserves the environment and improves the well-being of local people. TIES suggests that eco-tourists follow these principles:

- Minimize environmental impact.
- Build environmental and cultural awareness and respect.
- Provide positive experiences for both visitors and hosts.
- Provide direct financial benefits for conservation and for local people.
- Raise sensitivity to host countries' political, environmental, and social climates.
- Support international human rights and labor agreements.

You can find some eco-friendly travel tips and statistics, as well as touring companies and associations—listed by destination under "Travel Choice"—at the **TIES** website, www.ecotourism.org. Also check out **Ecotravel.com,** which lets you search for sustainable touring companies in several categories (water-based, land-based, spiritually oriented, and so on).

While much of the focus of eco-tourism is about reducing impact on the natural environment, ethical tourism concentrates on ways to preserve and enhance local economies and communities, regardless of location. You can embrace ethical tourism by staying at a locally owned hotel or shopping at a store that employs local workers and sells locally produced goods.

Responsible Travel (www.responsible travel.com) is a great source of sustainable travel ideas; the site is run by a spokesperson for ethical tourism in the travel industry. **Sustainable Travel International** (www.sustainabletravelinternational.org) promotes ethical tourism practices, and manages an extensive directory of sustainable properties and tour operators around the world.

In the U.K., **Tourism Concern** (www.tourismconcern.org.uk) works to reduce social and environmental problems connected to tourism. The **Association of Independent Tour Operators (AITO)** (www.aito.co.uk) is a group of specialist operators leading the field in making holidays sustainable.

Frommers.com: The Complete Travel Resource

It should go without saying, but we highly recommend **Frommers.com,** voted Best Travel Site by *PC Magazine*. We think you'll find our expert advice and tips; independent reviews of hotels, restaurants, attractions, and preferred shopping and nightlife venues; vacation giveaways; and an online booking tool indispensable before, during, and after your travels. We publish the complete contents of over 128 travel guides in our **Destinations** section covering nearly 3,600 places worldwide to help you plan your trip. Each weekday, we publish original articles reporting on **Deals and News** via our free **Frommers.com Newsletter** to help you save time and money and travel smarter. We're betting you'll find our new **Events** listings (http://events.frommers.com) an invaluable resource; it's an up-to-the-minute roster of what's happening in cities everywhere—including concerts, festivals, lectures, and more. We've also added weekly **podcasts, interactive maps,** and hundreds of new images across the site. Check out our **Travel Talk** area featuring **Message Boards** where you can join in conversations with thousands of fellow Frommer's travelers and post your trip report once you return.

Volunteer travel has become popular among those who want to venture beyond the standard group-tour experience to learn languages, interact with locals, and make a positive difference while on vacation. Volunteer travel usually doesn't require special skills—just a willingness to work hard—and programs vary in length from a few days to a number of weeks. Some programs provide free housing and food, but many require volunteers to pay for travel expenses, which can add up quickly.

For general info on volunteer travel, visit **www.volunteerabroad.org** and **www. idealist.org**.

Before you commit to a volunteer program, it's important to make sure any money you're giving is truly going back to the local community, and that the work you'll be doing will be a good fit for you. **Volunteer International** (www.volunteer international.org) has a helpful list of questions to ask to determine the intentions and the nature of a volunteer program.

10 PACKAGES FOR THE INDEPENDENT TRAVELER

Before you start your search for the lowest airfare, you may want to consider booking your flight as part of a travel package such as an escorted tour or a package tour. What you lose in adventure, you'll gain in time and money saved on accommodations, and maybe even food and entertainment, along with your flight.

Package tours are not the same thing as escorted tours. With a package tour, you travel independently but pay a group rate. Packages usually include airfare, a choice of hotels, and car rentals, and packagers often offer several options at different prices. In many cases, a package that includes airfare, hotel, and transportation to and from the airport will cost you less than just the hotel alone would have, had you booked it yourself. That's because packages are sold in bulk to tour operators—who resell them to the public at a cost that drastically undercuts standard rates.

One good source of package deals is the airlines themselves. Most major airlines offer air/land packages, including **American Airlines Vacations** (✆ 800/321-2121; www.aavacations.com), **Delta Vacations** (✆ 800/221-6666; www.delta vacations.com), **US Airways Vacations** (✆ 800/455-0123; www.usairwaysvacations. com), **Continental Airlines Vacations**

(✆ 800/301-3800; www.covacations.com), and **United Vacations** (✆ 888/854-3899; www.unitedvacations.com).

Vacation Together (✆ 800/839-9851 or 877/444-4547; www.vacationtogether. com) allows you to search for and book packages offered by a number of tour operators and airlines. The **United States Tour Operators Association** (✆ 212/599-6599; www.ustoa.com) has a search engine that allows you to look for operators that offer packages to a specific destination. Travel packages are also listed in the travel section of your local Sunday newspaper. **Liberty Travel** (✆ 888/271-1584; www.libertytravel.com), one of the biggest packagers in the Northeast, often runs full-page ads in Sunday papers. Or check ads in national travel magazines such as *Arthur Frommer's Budget Travel Magazine, Travel + Leisure, National Geographic Traveler,* and *Condé Nast Traveler.*

Package tours can vary by leaps and bounds. Some offer a better class of hotels than others. Some offer the same hotels for lower prices. Some offer flights on scheduled airlines, while others book charters. Some limit your choice of accommodations and travel days. You are often required to make a large payment upfront. On the plus side, packages can save you money, offering group prices but allowing for independent travel. Some even let you add on a few guided excursions or escorted day trips (also at prices lower than if you booked them yourself) without booking an entirely escorted tour.

Before you invest in a package tour, get some answers. Ask about the **accommodations choices** and prices for each. Then look up the hotels' reviews in a Frommer's guide and check their rates online for your specific dates of travel. You'll also want to find out what **type of room** you get. If you need a certain type of room, ask for it; don't take whatever is thrown your way. Request a nonsmoking room, a room with a view, or whatever you fancy.

Finally, look for **hidden expenses.** Ask whether airport departure fees and taxes, for example, are included in the total cost.

11 ESCORTED GENERAL-INTEREST TOURS

Escorted tours are structured group tours, with a group leader. The price usually includes everything from airfare to hotels, meals, tours, admission costs, and local transportation.

Many people derive a certain ease and security from escorted trips. Escorted tours—whether by bus, motorcoach, train, or boat—let travelers sit back and enjoy their trip without having to spend lots of time behind the wheel or worrying about details. You know your costs upfront, and there are few surprises. Escorted tours can take you to the maximum number of sights in the minimum amount of time with the least amount of hassle—you don't have to sweat over the plotting and planning of a vacation schedule. Escorted tours are particularly convenient for people with limited mobility. They can also be a great way to make new friends.

On the downside, an escorted tour often requires a big deposit upfront, and lodging and dining choices are predetermined. You'll get little opportunity for serendipitous interactions with locals. The tours can be jampacked with activities, leaving little room for individual sightseeing, whim, or adventure—plus they also often focus only on the heavily touristed sites, so you miss out on the lesser-known gems.

Before you invest in an escorted tour, ask about the **cancellation policy:** Is a deposit required? Can they cancel the trip if they don't get enough people? Do you get a refund if they cancel? If *you* cancel? How late can you cancel if you are unable to go? When do you pay in full? *Note:* If you choose an escorted tour, think strongly about purchasing trip-cancellation insurance, especially if the tour operator asks you to pay upfront (p. 318).

You'll want to get a complete **schedule** of the trip to find out how much sightseeing is planned each day and whether enough time has been allotted for relaxing or wandering solo.

The **size** of the group is also important to know upfront. Generally, the smaller the group, the more flexible the itinerary, and the less time you'll spend waiting for people to get on and off the bus. Find out the **demographics** of the group as well. What is the age range? What is the gender breakdown? Is this a trip mostly for couples or singles?

Discuss what is included in the **price.** You may have to pay for transportation to and from the airport. A box lunch may be included in an excursion, but drinks might cost extra. Tips may not be included. Find out if you will be charged if you decide to opt out of certain activities or meals.

Finally, if you plan to travel alone, you'll need to know if a **single supplement** will be charged and if the company can match you up with a roommate.

Visit Italy Tours, 9841 Airport Blvd., Ste. 1424, Los Angeles, CA 90045 (© **800/ 255-3537** or 310/649-9080; www.visit italytours.com), offers a popular 9-day, 7-night tour called "Sunny Sicily." It focuses on the grandest of the island's archaeological sites, including Segesta, Erice, Syracuse, Piazza Armerina, and Agrigento, and also visits volcanic Mount Etna, the fishing village of Trapani, and the beach resort of Taormina. Stops are also scheduled in Palermo and Monreale. Other tours are available, including a 15-day tour, "Archaeological Sicily," and a 9-day tour, "Sicilian Carousel," that focuses on such towns and villages as Syracuse, Ragusa, Cefalù, and Piazza Armerina.

One of the biggest escorted-tour operators is **Perillo Tours** (© **800/431-1515;** www.perillotours.com). Since it was founded in 1945, it has sent more than a million travelers to Italy. Perillo's tours cost much less than you'd spend if you arranged a comparable trip yourself. Accommodations are in first-class hotels, and guides tend to be well qualified. Tours in Sicily also include time in southern Italy, including 3 nights in Rome and 3 nights in Sorrento. The swing through Sicily itself, part of a larger tour, usually takes in 2 nights in Palermo, 1 night in Agrigento, and 3 nights in Taormina.

Globus and Cosmos Tours, working jointly, comprise one of Perillo's top competitors. **Globus** (© **800/338-7092;** www.globusandcosmos.com) also offers a 14-day grand tour of Italy and Sicily. **Cosmos** (© **800/276-1241**), the budget branch of Globus, sells the same itineraries. These tours must be booked through a travel agent and not directly.

Yet another option is **Insight Vacations** (© **800/582-8380;** www.insightvacations. com), which features art tours. Its 10-day tour of Italy and Sicily includes stopovers at the seaside resort of Taormina and visits to the temples at Agrigento and the art treasures of Palermo.

For a luxury tour, consider **Abercrombie & Kent** (© **800/554-7016** or 630/ 954-2944; www.abercrombiekent.com). Its 11-day tour of southern Italy includes Palermo, Agrigento, Piazza Armerina, Syracuse, and Taormina, with the option of adding a few nights in Rome to the itinerary.

12 SPECIAL-INTEREST TRIPS

For many visitors, a themed tour is the best way to explore the island.

For those who'd like to cycle along volcanic craters and rugged coastlines in sight of Greek ruins, an intriguing 8-day biking tour is offered by **VBT Bicycling Vacations** (© **800/BIKE-TOUR** [2453-8687]; www.vbt.com). It costs from $2,495 per person, including accommodations (airfare not included). Bike trips circle the craters of Mount Etna and go to Taormina and on to some of the Aeolian Islands, including Lipari and Salina.

Backroads (© **800/462-2848** or 510/ 527-1555; www.backroads.com), runs a 6-day biking and walking trip through Sicily that incorporates a boat ride to the Aeolian island of Panarea. It even offers a family version of this trip that's suitable for children as young as 9 years old. Both trips are around $4,250 per person (land costs only), double occupancy.

Butterfield & Robinson (© **866/551-9090** or 416/864-1354; www.butterfield. com) operates a ship-based tour that takes in Sicily and the Aeolian Islands by 32-passenger private yacht. Days bring opportunities for hiking, swimming, snorkeling, and diving. The 8-day tour starts at $9,995 per person (airfare not included).

Smithsonian Journeys (© **877/338-8687;** www.smithsonianjourneys.org)

features educational travel with guides who are experts in their fields. An 11-day "Legacy of Sicily" tour explores the island in great depth, visiting Palermo, Segesta, Selinunte, Agrigento, Piazza Armerina, Catania, and Taormina.

Academic Tours (© 800/875-9171 or 718/417-8782; www.academictours.com) is a real Sicilian specialist. It offers the best archaeological tours of Sicily, visiting such ancient cities and sites as Segesta, Erice, Selinunte, Piazza Armerina, Noto, and Syracuse. Typical prices for land arrangements are $1,325 to $1,399 in a double room for an 8-day tour.

To Grandmother's House We Go (© 718/768-4662; www.tograndmothers housewego.com) features cooking and cultural tours of Sicily. Cooking classes concentrate on simple, delicious food, and no more than 12 people participate at one time. The tour comprises not only food, but also historical sights as well as living history—that is, the shops of artisans, a winery, a tuna fishery, and more. The cost is $3,250 per person, excluding airfare.

13 STAYING CONNECTED

To call Sicily from the United States, dial the **international prefix, 011;** then Italy's **country code, 39;** and then the city code (for example, **091** for Palermo or **095** for Catania), which is now built into every number. Then dial the actual **phone number.**

A **local phone call** in Italy costs around .20€ (25¢). **Public phones** accept coins, precharged phone cards (*scheda* or *carta telefonica*), or both. You can buy a *carta telefonica* at any *tabacchi* (tobacco shop; most display a sign with a white T on a brown background) in increments of 2.50€ ($3.25), 5€ ($6.50), and 7.50€ ($9.75). To make a call, pick up the receiver and insert .50€ (65¢) or your card (break off the corner first). Most phones have a digital display that'll tell you how much money you've inserted (or how much is left on the card). Dial the number, and don't forget to take the card with you after you hang up.

To call from one city code to another, dial the city code, complete with initial 0, and then dial the number. (Note that numbers in Sicily range from four to eight digits in length. Even when you're calling within the same city, you must dial that city's area code—including the zero. A Catanian calling another Catanian number must dial 095 before the local number.)

To dial direct internationally, dial **00** and then the country code, the area code, and the number. **Country codes** are as follows: the United States and Canada, 1; the United Kingdom, 44; Ireland, 353; Australia, 61; New Zealand, 64. Make international calls from a public phone, if possible, as hotels almost invariably charge ridiculously inflated rates for direct-dial. Calls dialed directly are billed on the basis of the call's duration only. A reduced rate is applied Monday to Saturday 11pm to 8am and all day Sunday. Direct-dial calls from the United States to Sicily are much cheaper, so arrange to be called at your hotel if possible.

Italy has a series of **international phone cards** (*scheda telefonica internazionale*) for calling overseas. They come in increments of 50, 100, 200, and 400 *unita* (units), and they're usually available at *tabacchi* and bars. Rates for international calls using prepaid cards can vary, based on the country you call. Prepaid phone cards may offer rates that are much lower than a phone company's basic international charges. A toll-free access phone number and a personal identification number (PIN) are usually printed on each phone card. To make a phone call, you dial the access number and then enter the PIN. An automated voice will ask you to enter the phone number you are calling and will tell you how much time you have left on your card.

For **national telephone information** in Italy, dial **1254**; for **international information** call **892412**. Both services cost 3€ ($3.90) per minute.

To make collect or calling-card calls, drop in .20€ (25¢) or insert your card and dial one of the numbers here; an American operator will shortly come on to assist you. The following calling-card numbers work all over Italy: **AT&T,** ✆ 800/172-444; **MCI,** ✆ 800/905-825; and **Sprint,** ✆ 800/172-405. To make collect calls to a country besides the United States, dial ✆ **170** (free), and practice your Italian in order to relay the number to the Italian operator. Tell him or her that you want it *a carico del destinatario.* To make collect calls abroad is not free; it costs .20€ (25¢) per minute, plus a surcharge of .30€ (40¢).

Don't count on all Sicilian phones to have touch-tone service. You might not be able to access your voice mail or answering machine from Sicily.

CELLPHONES

The three letters that define much of the world's wireless capabilities are GSM (Global System for Mobiles), a big, seamless network that makes for easy cross-border cellphone use throughout dozens of countries worldwide. In general reception is good.

For many, **renting** a phone is a good idea. (Even world-phone owners will have to rent new phones if they're traveling to non-GSM regions.) While you can rent a phone from any number of overseas sites, including kiosks at airports and at car-rental agencies, we suggest renting the phone before you leave home. North Americans can rent one before leaving home from **InTouch USA** (✆ **800/872-7626** or 703/222-7161; www.intouch global.com) or **RoadPost** (✆ **888/290-1616** or 905/272-5665; www.roadpost. com). InTouch will also, for free, advise

you on whether your existing phone will work overseas.

Buying a phone can be economically attractive, as many nations have cheap prepaid phone systems. Once you arrive at your destination, stop by a local cellphone shop and get the cheapest package; you'll probably pay less than $100 for a phone and a starter calling card. Local calls may be as low as 10¢ per minute, and in many countries incoming calls are free.

INTERNET & E-MAIL
With Your Own Computer

More and more hotels, cafes, and retailers are signing on as Wi-Fi (wireless fidelity) "hot spots." Mac owners have their own networking technology: Apple AirPort. **T-Mobile Hotspot** (www.t-mobile.com/ hotspot or www.t-mobile.co.uk) serves up wireless connections at coffee shops nationwide. **Boingo** (www.boingo.com) and **Wayport** (www.wayport.com) have set up networks in airports and high-class hotel lobbies. IPass providers (see below) also give you access to a few hundred wireless hotel lobby setups. To locate other hot spots that provide **free wireless networks,** go to **www.jiwire.com**.

For dial-up access, most business-class hotels offer Wi-Fi for laptop modems. In addition, major Internet service providers (ISPs) have **local access numbers** around the world, allowing you to go online by placing a local call. The **iPass** network also has dial-up numbers around the world. You'll have to sign up with an iPass provider, who will then tell you how to set up your computer for your destination(s). For a list of iPass providers, go to www.ipass.com and click on "Individuals Buy Now." One solid provider is **i2roam** (✆ **866/811-6209** or 920/233-5863; www.i2roam.com).

Wherever you go, bring a **connection kit** of the right power and phone adapters, a spare phone cord, and a spare Ethernet network cable—or find out whether your hotel supplies them to guests.

Online Traveler's Toolbox

Veteran travelers usually carry some essential items to make their trips easier. Following is a selection of handy online tools to bookmark and use.

- **Airplane Food** (www.airlinemeals.net)
- **Airplane Seating** (www.seatguru.com and www.airlinequality.com)
- **Foreign Languages for Travelers** (www.travlang.com)
- **Maps** (www.mapquest.com)
- **Subway Navigator** (www.subwaynavigator.com)
- **Time and Date** (www.timeanddate.com)
- **Travel Warnings** (http://travel.state.gov, www.fco.gov.uk/travel, www. voyage.gc.ca, or www.dfat.gov.au/consular/advice)
- **Universal Currency Converter** (www.xe.com/ucc)
- **Visa ATM Locator** (www.visa.com), **MasterCard ATM Locator** (www. mastercard.com)
- **Weather** (www.intellicast.com and www.weather.com)

Without Your Own Computer

To find cybercafes check **www.cyber captive.com** and **www.cybercafe.com**. Cybercafes are found in large Sicilian cities, especially Catania and Palermo. But they do not tend to cluster in any particular neighborhoods because of competition.

Aside from formal cybercafes, most **youth hostels** and **public libraries** have Internet access. Avoid **hotel business centers** unless you're willing to pay exorbitant rates.

14 TIPS ON ACCOMMODATIONS

SURFING FOR HOTELS

In addition to the online travel booking sites **Travelocity, Expedia, Orbitz, Priceline,** and **Hotwire,** you can book hotels through **Hotels.com, Quikbook** (www. quikbook.com), and **Travelaxe** (www. travelaxe.net).

HotelChatter.com is a daily webzine offering smart coverage and critiques of hotels worldwide. Go to **TripAdvisor.com** or **HotelShark.com** for helpful independent consumer reviews of hotels and resort properties.

It's a good idea to **get a confirmation number** and **make a printout** of any online booking transaction.

SAVING ON YOUR HOTEL ROOM

The **rack rate** is the maximum rate that a hotel charges for a room. Hardly anybody pays this price, however, except in high season or on holidays. To lower the cost of your room:

- **Ask about special rates or other discounts.** You may qualify for corporate, student, military, senior, frequent flier, trade union, or other discounts.
- **Dial direct.** When booking a room in a chain hotel, you'll often get a better deal by calling the individual hotel's reservation desk rather than the chain's main number.

- **Book online.** Many hotels offer Internet-only discounts, or supply rooms to Priceline, Hotwire, or Expedia at rates much lower than the ones you can get through the hotel itself.

- **Remember the law of supply and demand.** You can save big on hotel rooms by traveling in a destination's off season or shoulder seasons, when rates typically drop, even at luxury properties.

- **Look into group or long-stay discounts.** If you come as part of a large group, you should be able to negotiate a bargain rate. Likewise, if you're planning a long stay (at least 5 days), you might qualify for a discount. As a general rule, expect 1 night free after a 7-night stay.

- **Sidestep excess surcharges and hidden costs.** Many hotels have adopted the unpleasant practice of nickel-and-diming their guests with opaque surcharges. When you book a room, ask what is included in the room rate, and what is extra. Avoid dialing direct from hotel phones, which can have exorbitant rates. And don't be tempted by the room's minibar offerings: Most hotels charge through the nose for water, soda,

and snacks. Finally, ask about local taxes and service charges, which can increase the cost of a room by 15% or more.

- **Book an efficiency.** A room with a kitchenette allows you to shop for groceries and cook your own meals. This is a big money saver, especially for families on long stays.

- **Consider enrolling in hotel chains' "frequent-stay" programs,** which are upping the ante lately to win the loyalty of repeat customers. Frequent guests can now accumulate points or credits to earn free hotel nights, airline miles, in-room amenities, merchandise, tickets to concerts and events, discounts on sporting facilities—and even credit toward stock in the participating hotel, in the case of the Jameson Inn hotel group. Perks are awarded not only by many chain hotels and motels (Hilton HHonors, Marriott Rewards, Wyndham ByRequest, to name a few), but individual inns and B&Bs. Many chain hotels partner with other hotel chains, car-rental firms, airlines, and credit card companies to give consumers additional incentive to do repeat business.

Suggested Sicily Itineraries

Vacations are getting shorter, and a "lean-and-mean" schedule is called for if you want to experience the best of Sicily in a limited amount of time. If you're a time-pressed traveler, as most of us are, with only 1 or 2 weeks for Sicily, you may find the first two itineraries helpful. Families should review the third option, "Sicily for Families," later in this chapter.

1 THE REGIONS IN BRIEF

A predominantly mountainous island, Sicily is separated from the mainland by the Straits of Messina. Culturally there is an even wider gap between Italy and its semi-autonomous island, Sicily, which feels a world apart.

This is a land of tempestuous elements, including active volcanoes and torrential rivers that can flood during the winter rainy season and dry up in the scorching summer months. While northern Sicily enjoys a milder clime, southern Sicily is often profoundly affected by the hot winds known as *sirocco* blowing in from the deserts of North Africa.

Sicily lies at the confluence of a trio of seas—in fact, the Greeks call it *Sikelia*, or "three points." The northern coast opens onto the Tyrrhenian Sea, the eastern coast (Catania and Taormina) onto the Ionian Sea, and the southern coast onto the Sicilian Sea.

Sicily also controls a string of offshore islands, including Ustica, off the coast of Palermo; the Aeolians (mainly Stromboli, Vulcano, and Lipari); and the Egadis, lying off the cities of Marsala and Trapani on the west coast. Lonely Pantelleria lies off the western coast, and the southernmost Pelagians are almost in North Africa.

Here's a rundown of the cities and regions covered in this guide.

AEOLIAN ISLANDS From the mud baths of Vulcano to the fiery explosions from the crater on Stromboli, the Aeolian Islands (Isole Eolie) are mysterious and exciting places to be, different from anything else in Italy. Awash in the Tyrrhenian Sea, these islands lie off the northern coast and are within easy reach of the port of Milazzo by hydrofoil or ferryboat. The three main islands to visit are **Vulcano** (closest to the Sicilian mainland), **Lipari** (where most of the tourist facilities are found), and **Stromboli** (still actively volcanic). Those travelers with unlimited time can also make day trips to such lesser islands as **Panarea, Filicudi, Salina,** and **Alicudi.**

AGRIGENTO Located on the southern coastline of Sicily, Agrigento was one of the most important centers of Magna Graecia, and its **Valle dei Templi (Valley of the Temples),** a mammoth array of temple ruins, is reason enough to go to Sicily. The home of the 5th-century philosopher Empedocles and of the playwright Luigi Pirandello, Agrigento was destroyed by Carthage in 406 B.C. But those invading armies left plenty of ruins for us to explore today. The town's Doric temples date from the 6th century to the 5th century B.C. and were erected to such deities as Hercules, Juno, and Jupiter.

CATANIA   The second city of Sicily opens onto the Gulf of Catania, lying at the foot of the southern slopes of Mount Etna, a volcano that has rained lava down on it for centuries. One of the oldest cities of Sicily, it dates from the 8th century B.C. Massively rebuilt after destruction by an earthquake in 1693, Catania today is called the "baroque city." You'll either love this massive sprawl or hate it. We love it, as did such hometown boys as the composer Vincenzo Bellini (1801–35).

MESSINA   Overlooking the Straits of Messina on the northeast coast of Sicily, the city of Messina is, for most visitors, the gateway into Sicily. Although it's possible to fly into Palermo, most people arrive by hydrofoil or ferryboat from the Italian mainland, disembarking at the port of Messina, where rail and bus connections can be made to other parts of Sicily. Shakespeare used the city as a setting for *Much Ado About Nothing,* although he never actually laid eyes on it. Messina today is a modern city, having been rebuilt after many disasters.

MOUNT ETNA   This is Sicily's greatest natural attraction and its highest mountain, and it's also the largest volcano in Europe and one of the most active in the world. The ancient Greeks viewed it as the home of Vulcan, god of fire, and home of the Cyclops, the one-eyed monster. Much of its surrounding landscape is covered with solidified lava, a surface for skiing in winter and hiking in summer. The crater is dangerously active, so you always feel a sense of adventure, or even danger, while touring or hiking in the area.

PALERMO   The island's largest city and its capital is also filled with the most sightseeing treasures. Palermo opens onto the Gulf of Palermo on the northwest coast of Sicily, the largest settlement in Conca d'Oro, a fertile land planted with citrus. Founded by the Phoenicians, it contains innumerable fine monuments, particularly in the baroque vein, along with an array of art that spans the centuries. It's difficult to navigate and crime-laden, but like its sister city of Naples, it's worth the effort for those who don't mind a certain inconvenience.

PIAZZA ARMERINA   This is not a piazza (square) but an actual town, and a spectacularly sited one as well, lying inland in central Sicily. It is visited mainly by those who want to see the famous Roman hunting lodge from the 4th century B.C. The mosaics found here are among the most spectacular in the world; they even include some bathing beauties in bikinis.

RAGUSA   Set on the southern slope of the Iblei mountain range, Ragusa lies inland from the sea and is one of the most intriguing cities in the southeastern sector of the island. It's actually two cities in one, Ragusa Ibla and Ragusa Superiore. Of medieval origin, with narrow twisting lanes, the old city, which suffered a major earthquake in 1693, retained much of its appearance when it was rebuilt.

SEGESTA & SELINUNTE   Your journey of discovery through Sicily should include these ancient ruins. Segesta lies in western Sicily in a setting of rolling hills. Its claim to fame is a Doric temple built around 430 B.C., with its 36 limestone columns still intact. On the southern coast, Selinunte was once a rival to Segesta until it was destroyed by Hannibal and the Carthaginians. Like Agrigento and Syracuse, Selinunte is visited for its impressive and scattered ruins of temple columns that speak of former glory.

SYRACUSE   Called *Siracusa* in Italian, this historic city, founded by the Greeks in the 8th century B.C., lies on the southeastern coast of the island. After Taormina and

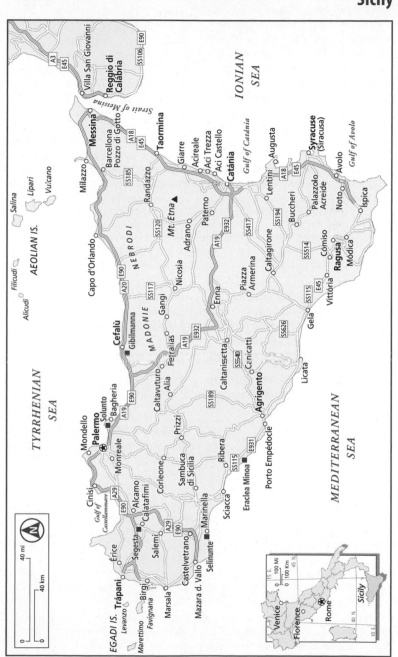

Palermo, it is the third-most-visited city in Sicily. Filled with medieval streets, but with an essentially baroque aura in architecture, its main draws are its classical ruins and works of art. These include a Greek theater and a Roman amphitheater, both from the 3rd century B.C.

TAORMINA   Sicily's grandest resort, first publicized by Goethe in 1787, has over time drawn a steady stream of celebrities, ranging from Oscar Wilde to Marlene Dietrich. Situated atop Monte Tauro, Taormina is not on the beach, but good sandy strips are easily reached along its eastern flanks. In spite of the hordes who descend on it every year from April to October, Taormina retains some of its medieval aura.

TRAPANI & ERICE   The major city on the western coast, Trapani lies in the northwest, opening onto the Egadi archipelago of three islands. It offers superior transportation links to the rest of Sicily and easy road links to Palermo. Trapani was founded by the Greeks, though eventually it fell to the Romans. The medieval hill town of Erice, to its immediate north, has far more antique charm, and if you have only a day to spend in the west, devote it to touring Erice. But if you have the time, Trapani and its monuments make for an intriguing day of sightseeing as well.

2 SICILY IN 1 WEEK

Use the following itinerary to make the most out of a week in Sicily, but feel free to drop a place or two to save a day to relax on the beach. In 1 week, you can visit **Palermo,** the historic capital, and make further trips to the medieval hilltop resort of **Taormina,** with a side trip to the volcanic slopes of **Mount Etna.** Not only that, you can explore the ancient archaeological gardens at **Syracuse** and even the Valley of the Temples at **Agrigento.**

Days ❶ & ❷: Arrival in Palermo ★★★

Take a flight that puts you as early as possible in Palermo, so you can spend most of **Day 1** sightseeing. Check into your hotel and enjoy your first Sicilian breakfast before setting out. Visit the **Palazzo dei Normanni** (p. 99) in 1½ hours, paying special attention to the **Cappella Palatina.** Either before or after lunch, head for the **Galleria Regionale della Sicilia** (p. 102) in the Palazzo Abatellis to see one of the greatest collections of art in all of Sicily. Cap the afternoon by taking our walking tour of Old Palermo (p. 117). Before the sun sets, drive 15km (9 miles) north to **Monte Pellegrino** (p. 128) for a panoramic view of the old city and its bay.

While still based in Palermo, begin **Day 2** with a visit to the magnificent **Monreale Duomo** (p. 134), or cathedral, 10km (6 miles) southwest of Palermo. Dating from 1174, the cathedral in this hilltop town of Monreale represents the zenith of art and architecture from the Arabo-Norman school. Return to Palermo in time for lunch and try to budget your time to see two final remaining attractions—**Museo Archeologico Regionale** (p. 102), one of the great archaeological museums of Italy, and the eerie **Catacombe dei Cappuccini** (p. 104), or the Catacombs of the Capuchins, where you'll encounter mummies so well preserved they look as if they're still alive. On your jaunts that evening, stop by Palermo's loveliest square, **Piazza Pretoria** (p. 120), to take in the beauty of its Pretoria Fountain, and visit **Quattro Canti** (p. 114), the "Four Corners" of Palermo.

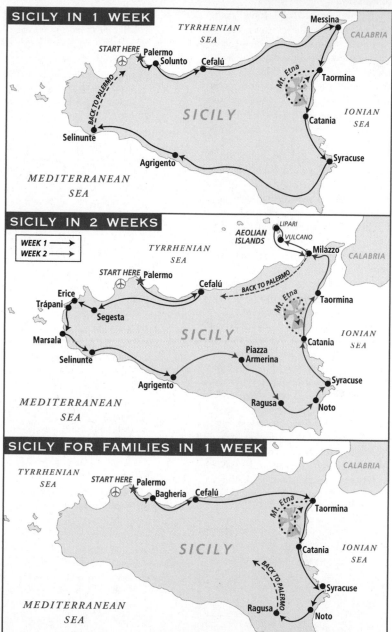

Day ❸: The Tyrrhenian Coast ★★★ to Messina

On the morning of **Day 3,** leave Palermo heading east for 18km (11 miles) to visit the ruins of **Solunto** set high on the slopes of Monte Catalfano. For the scenic route, take SS113 east from Palermo toward Porticello, where you follow the signposts into Solunto. Spend 1¹/₂ hours exploring what remains of the Carthaginian town of Solus, which was founded in the 8th century B.C. (p. 132).

Leave Solunto and cut south toward Bagheria, where you can follow the directions to the expressway (A19/A20) that takes you east toward **Cefalù** at a point 81km (50 miles) east of Palermo.

This former fishing village is our major stopover for the day along the Tyrrhenian coast. Explore its main street, **Corso Ruggero** (p. 158), and try to get in an hour at the beach. After lunch visit the **Duomo** (p. 158), or cathedral, to see a stunning array of mosaics.

Set out again along A20 east, which will take you for a scenic ride along the beautiful Tyrrhenian coast into Messina. In all, the trip from Palermo to Messina is 233km (145 miles). This is one of the grand motor trips in Sicily. Check into a hotel in Messina for the night.

The sights of Messina are minor, so you can treat it as a refueling stop to rest up for an early start the following day. Some of the greatest attractions of Sicily, mainly Greek and Roman ruins, lie south of Messina.

Day ❹: Taormina ★★★ & Mount Etna ★★

Leave Messina on the morning of **Day 4,** following A18 south to Taormina, a distance of 53km (33 miles), where you can check into a hotel for the night. The major sight here is the **Teatro Greco** (p. 192), or Greek Amphitheater, which you can see in the morning. After lunch, plan an excursion to **Mount Etna** (p. 210), the highest and largest active volcano in Europe, a

distance of 23km (14 miles) southwest of Taormina. This is still an active volcano, so check road conditions before setting out. After seeing this majestic but dangerous mountain, head back to Taormina for the night.

Day ❺: The Ruins of Syracuse ★★★

On the morning of **Day 5,** head south along expressway highway A18 to Catania, the second-largest city of Italy. On this driving tour, there will be no time to explore this massive sprawl. The distance between Taormina and Catania is 58km (36 miles). A18 feeds into E45 as it continues south into Syracuse, a distance between Catania and Syracuse of 62km (39 miles).

In **Syracuse** check into a hotel for the night and set out to explore this ancient city, beginning with the chief reason to visit, its **Parco Archeologico della Neapolis** (p. 248). In one of Italy's greatest archaeological gardens, you can see the highlights, including **Teatro Greco, Latomia del Paradiso,** and **Anfiteatro Romano.** After lunch, visit the **Museo Archeologico Regionale Paolo Orsi** (p. 250), one of the greatest of such museums in all of Italy, and head for **Ortygia Island** (p. 254) as the afternoon wanes. This island figures into Greek mythology. Syracuse is such an important sight, you could even schedule another full day here and not see everything. But to keep with our 1-week drive, plan to move on the next morning.

Day ❻: Agrigento ★★★ & the Valley of the Temples ★★★

On the morning of **Day 6,** leave Syracuse and drive to the ancient city of **Agrigento,** a distance of 217km (135 miles) west. To reach Agrigento, take SS115, bypassing the city of Gela, until you reach Agrigento in the west. Once in Agrigento, check into a hotel for the night.

Set out to spend 3 or 4 hours exploring the **Valle dei Templi,** one of the greatest sights left of the ancient world. The most majestic temples are the Temple of Juno, the Temple of Concord, and the Temple of Hercules. We suggest a return visit at night when these temples are lit, one of the most evocative sights of Sicily. If you have the time, two minor sights include the 13th-century church, **Abbazia di Santo Spirito,** and the **Museo Regionale Archeologico.**

Day ❼: Selinunte & Its Ruins ★★ En Route to Palermo

For your final look at Sicily on **Day 7,** head out in the morning from Agrigento and drive 113km (70 miles) to Selinunte. From Agrigento, take Route 115 southwest to Castelvetrano; then follow the signposted secondary road, Route 115,

and spend the rest of the morning exploring the archaeological garden here. This city was once one of the great colonies of Greece, but, alas, its ruins today are not as impressive as those of Agrigento.

After a visit and lunch, it's time to spend a good part of what remains of the afternoon driving back to Palermo where you can hook up with transportation to your next destination. It is a 122km (76-mile) drive northeast from Selinunte to Palermo. After Selinunte get on Route 115 going northwest to the town of Castelvetrano. From here an express highway (A29) carries you northeast into Palermo, where you can check into a hotel for the night.

67

---

3 SICILY IN 2 WEEKS

On this second tour we can hit all the highlights—not only the two major goals, **Palermo** and **Taormina,** but also the majestic Greek and Roman ruins at **Syracuse, Agrigento,** and **Selinunte.** This tour also allows us to see the Greek temple of **Segesta** (one of the best preserved in the world) and to take in such west-coast destinations as the medieval hill town of **Erice** and the wine-producing town of **Marsala.**

Days ❶ & ❷: Palermo ★★★: Gateway to Sicily

In two busy days you can see the highlights of the Sicilian capital. To do that, you can follow the agenda as outlined in Days 1 and 2 in "Sicily in 1 Week," above.

Day ❸: A Side Trip to Cefalù ★★

The ancient small city of **Cefalù** lies 81km (50 miles) east of Palermo and can be visited as a day trip, with a return to Palermo that night. If you don't want to make the drive back, you can overnight in one of the little hotels of Cefalù. Follow the same itinerary as outlined in Day 3 in "Sicily in 1 Week," earlier in this chapter, cutting out the final lap of that trip into Messina for the night.

Day ❹: Segesta ★★★ to Erice ★★★

From either Cefalù or Palermo, whichever you selected for your base for the third night, leave in the morning for the small village of **Segesta,** lying 75km (47 miles) southwest of Palermo. Take the autostrada (A29) running between Palermo and Trapani, turning off at the clearly marked exit to Segesta. When Segesta was the mysterious and ancient city of Elymi, the **Tempio of Segesta** (p. 300), one of the world's most perfectly preserved temples handed down from antiquity, could be seen. You can also enjoy one of the most panoramic views of Sicily from this vantage point.

After a visit, get back on the express highway (A29) and continue west to **Erice** for the night, a distance of only 96km (60 miles) southwest of Palermo. Check into a

SUGGESTED SICILY ITINERARIES

4

SICILY IN 2 WEEKS

hotel for the night and set about to wander through the medieval town (p. 301), the most perfectly preserved in Sicily, with panoramic views in all directions. Cover as many of the attractions as you can, but know that it is the town itself that is the main sightseeing target.

Day ❺: Trapani to Marsala

On the morning of **Day 5,** leave Erice, heading south to the west-coast city of **Trapani,** a distance of 14km (8³/₄ miles). There are two unmarked but signposted winding roads that take you southwest of Erice into Trapani. You can spend the rest of the morning exploring the *centro storico,* or medieval core, of Trapani, having lunch there. See p. 306.

In the afternoon, head south from Trapani along Route 115 into **Marsala,** a distance of 31km (19 miles). Overnight in Marsala. This is the home of the world-famous port wine, and you can take tours of the wineries such as **Cantine Florio** (p. 312). With the remaining time, you can visit some of the sights of the town.

Day ❻: The Ruins of Selinunte ★★

On the morning of **Day 6,** leave Marsala and drive east along the N115 to the little town of Castelvetrano where you can follow an offshoot road south to the sea and **Selinunte** (it's signposted). Here you can spend 2 hours wandering through the Selinunte ruins (p. 296). For a late lunch that day, you can find food in the neighboring village of Marinella. Since lodgings are few, we suggest you continue east to Agrigento for the night, a distance of 113km (70 miles). At night spend an hour or so driving through the floodlit ruins of the Valley of the Temples, one of the greatest and most evocative temple attractions of Sicily or southern Italy.

Day ❼: Agrigento ★★★ & the Valley of the Temples ★★★

To explore during the day, we suggest that you extend your hotel stay in **Agrigento** for **Day 7.** That way, you can follow the

itinerary outlined for Day 6 in "Sicily in 1 Week" (see earlier in this chapter).

Day ❽: Piazza Armerina & Ragusa ★

On the morning of **Day 8,** leave Agrigento and drive to **Piazza Armerina,** a distance of 124km (77 miles). To reach it, drive east from Agrigento (N115) to the city of Gela. At this point, head north on N1176 to Piazza Armerina. Once here you can visit one of the great attractions of Sicily, **Villa Romana del Casale** (p. 280), lying 6km (3³/₄ miles) from town. This is one of the greatest and best preserved of all the villas to have survived from the days of Imperial Rome. It is celebrated for its mosaics. After lunch, head south and backtrack along N1176 to the coastal city of Gela. Once in Gela continue east along N115/E45 to the city of **Ragusa,** where you can overnight. Except for the side trip to Piazza Armerina, the driving distance between your launch in Agrigento and your final stopover in Ragusa is 138km (86 miles). Chances are, you'll arrive in Ragusa in time to take the long stairway to its historic core, **Ragusa Ibla** (p. 274), which is the main reason to visit.

Days ❾ & ❿: Noto ★★ to Syracuse ★★★

On the morning of **Day 9,** leave Ragusa, driving for 55km (34 miles) east to the ancient city of **Noto** for a morning visit. Follow N115 east until you come to the city limits of Sicily's grandest baroque town. For guidance on how to tour it, see p. 265. After lunch in Noto, continue on N115 for another 31km (19 miles) to **Syracuse,** where you can check into a hotel for 2 nights, since there is so much to see. In the afternoon, head for the ancient and historic island of **Ortygia** (p. 254). For **Day 10** in Syracuse, follow the guidelines for Day 5 in "Sicily in 1 Week," above.

Day ⓫: Catania ★: Sicily's "Second City"

On the morning of **Day 11,** head north of Syracuse to **Catania,** a distance of 87km

(54 miles), following E45/N115/N114 all the way. Take our **walking tour of "Historic Catania"** (p. 232) and follow it up with lunch. In the afternoon, explore the southern slopes of **Mount Etna** (p. 210). The northern slopes of the active volcanic mountain can also be explored from a base in Taormina (see below). Overnight in Catania.

Day ⑫: Taormina ★★★: Sicily's Greatest Resort

On the morning of **Day 12,** drive north along the express highway, A18, arriving in the hilltop resort of **Taormina** after going 53km (33 miles). Plan to overnight here. If you haven't toured **Mount Etna** (see Catania, above), you can visit the northern rim of a base in Taormina. But we suggest that you tour Etna during your Catania stopover, leaving you free for the most fun along the trip—a day of R & R in Taormina with some time for its beaches that front the sea down below. You may have seen enough ruins already, but there is one more three-star attraction to explore: **Teatro Greco** (p. 192), the Greek amphitheater, one of the major attractions of Sicily. After that, we suggest you head for the best beach in the area, **Lido Mazzarò** (p. 192).

Days ⑬ & ⑭: Vulcano ★★★ & Lipari ★★

Decisions, decisions on **Day 13** in your driving tour. The average visitor, pressed for time, might want to end the tour in Taormina, perhaps heading for Messina north of Taormina, a distance of 53km (33 miles), reached along the express highway, A18. At Messina, transportation can be arranged back to the Italian mainland.

But with 2 days to spare, you can explore the best of the **Aeolian Islands:** Vulcano (our first choice) or **Lipari** (a runner-up). (**Stromboli,** more difficult to reach, would require almost an additional 2 days for those who can afford the time. Our coverage of this volcanic island begins on p. 184.)

Most visitors will settle for Vulcano, which is closer to the port city of **Milazzo,** where boat transportation to the Aeolians can be arranged. To reach the embarkation point at Milazzo, continue from Taormina to Messina (see above). Instead of stopping here, drive west on the autostrada (A20) until you arrive at Milazzo, a distance of 32km (20 miles) from Messina, in the east.

If you're traveling to the Aeolians in summer, make sure you've made reservations well in advance. The trip across the sea to Vulcano is 55km (34 miles). After checking in, set about exploring Vulcano, its chief attraction being the **Gran Cratere** (p. 181), a trip that will eat up 3 hours or more of your time. Better have lunch in town before setting out on this arduous journey with some of the greatest panoramic views in the Aeolians.

On the morning of **Day 14,** leave Vulcano sailing to Lipari, which is only 18km (11 miles) away. Once on Lipari, check into a hotel for the night and begin your exploration of the island. (Our detailed coverage of its attractions begins on p. 171.) The single most important sight is the **Museo Archeologico Eoliano** (p. 174), one of Southern Italy's greatest treasure-troves of the ancient world. The following morning, head back to the mainland. Depending on your transportation arrangements, you can return to Palermo in the west for flights or else take one of the seagoing vessels from the port at Messina.

4 SICILY FOR FAMILIES

The island of Sicily has many attractions that kids enjoy. Perhaps your main concern with having children along is pacing yourself with museum time. You can only hope that your kids get a kick from wandering among Greek and Roman ruins, because these are major reasons for first-timers to visit Sicily. Our suggestion is to explore **Palermo** for 2 days before heading east along the Tyrrhenian coast for an overnight at **Cefalù** before going east to the great resort of **Taormina,** which is for all the family. The trip concludes with major stopovers in such historic cities of the ancient world as **Syracuse** and **Agrigento.**

Days ❶ & ❷: Arrival in Palermo ★★★

On **Day 1,** your kids have probably been held captive on a long flight (maybe even with a change of planes) and will be eager for exercise. After a fortifying breakfast with some Sicilian pastries, set out for a long stroll by taking our **walking tour of Old Palermo** (p. 117). In the afternoon, promise your kids that they will find plenty to hold their interests in the **Palazzo dei Normanni** (p. 99) and the **Galleria Regionale della Sicilia** (p. 102), since you don't dare leave Palermo without seeing these world-class attractions. At the end of the afternoon, drive up to **Monte Pellegrino** (p. 128) for the grandest and most panoramic views in Palermo.

On the morning of **Day 2,** visit **Monreale** to see its spectacular Arabo-Norman **Duomo** (p. 158). Kids enjoy climbing up to the dramatic terraces with views in all directions. Fortify them with the famous cookies of the area, which are sold at **Bar Italia** (p. 136) near the Duomo. **Monreale** lies 10km (6 miles) southwest of Palermo. In the afternoon, if it's a summer day, head for the best beach in the area, **Mondello,** lying 12km (7 1/2 miles) west of Palermo.

Overnight for both nights in Palermo before heading east in the morning.

Day ❸: Bagheria to Cefalù ★★

On the morning of **Day 3,** leave Palermo, making the drive to the decaying villas at the old summer retreat of Sicilian nobles, **Bagheria,** lying 14km (8 3/4 miles) east of Palermo, reached along the coastal route (113), via Ficarazzi, which is more scenic and easier to access than the autostrada (A19). Once here, visit **Villa Palagonia** (p. 131), a bizarre monument known as the "Villa of Monsters," because of all the

grotesque statues. Your kids will think it's the setting for some scary movie. After a visit, follow Route 113 east into **Cefalù,** a distance of 81km (50 miles) from Palermo. Check into a hotel here for the night.

Before exploring the town itself, which can be done later in the afternoon, secure the makings of a picnic and set out to enjoy it and the scenery in one of Sicily's greatest national parks, **Parco Naturale Regionale delle Madonie** (p. 163), lying only 6km (3 3/4 miles) south of Cefalù.

When you return to Cefalù, take your kids on a stroll of the town, beginning at Piazza Garibaldi and heading along **Corso Ruggero,** the main street. Drop in at the **Duomo** (p. 158) to see the brilliant mosaics before heading up the rocky crag, **La Rocca** (p. 159), for one of the most panoramic views along the northern coast.

Days ❹ & ❺: Family Fun at Taormina ★★★

On the morning of **Day 4,** set out early to drive east in the direction of Messina, a distance of 170km (106 miles) following Route 113. At Messina, cut south along A18 (an autostrada), following it along the east coast into **Taormina,** a distance of 53km (33 miles) south of Messina. There is so much for all the family to see and do that we suggest you check into a hotel here for 2 nights.

After all that driving, your kids deserve some beach time, and **Lido Mazzarò** (p. 192), reached by cable car, is one of the best along the east coast. After 2 or 3 hours here, return to town in time to visit **Teatro Greco** (p. 192), one of the greatest of Greek amphitheater ruins in Italy. Spend the rest of the afternoon and early evening strolling the ancient streets of Taormina, enjoying an affordable dinner in a tavern.

On a very busy **Day 5,** get an early start, taking an excursion to the northern rim of the still active volcano, **Mount Etna** (p. 210 in chapter 10). This is the highest and largest volcano in Europe—and it's still active. Check on road conditions with the Taormina tourist center before setting out, as they are subject to change. The menace of Etna begins 23km (14 miles) southwest of Taormina.

Day ❻: The Ruins of Syracuse ★★★

On the morning of **Day 6,** leave Taormina, heading south on the A18 to Catania, second-largest city of Sicily, a distance of 53km (33 miles). Bypass the city, getting onto N114 for the final lap south into **Syracuse,** a distance of 87km (54 miles) from Catania. Check into a hotel for the night and set out—with kids in tow—to explore this ancient city of antiquity.

There will be much in the **Parco Archeologico della Neapolis** (p. 248) to fascinate children, including the **Latomia del Paradiso,** where the acoustics are so good the sound of a rip in paper evokes gunfire. Follow up with a visit to the eerie **Catacombe di San Giovanni** (p. 250), which is always a kid pleaser, with its honeycombed tunnels. If time remains, head for the **Museo Archeologico Regionale Paolo**

Orsi (p. 250), where we recently saw kids mesmerized by the skeletons of prehistoric animals, including dwarf elephants.

Day ❼: Noto ★★ & Ragusa ★ in the Southeast

On the morning of **Day 7,** leave Syracuse and drive 31km (19 miles) southwest to **Noto,** following Route 115. You can spend the morning here strolling through this baroque city (p. 265). As you wander about, pick up the makings of a picnic to be enjoyed later in the **Giardini Pubblici** (p. 266), a park shaded by palm trees. If the family is willing, take a break from driving and head for one of the sandy beaches at **Noto Marina** (p. 268), 6km (3³/₄ miles) from the center.

Packing up from the beach, continue on for the night at **Ragusa,** which lies 55km (34 miles) west of Noto. Plan to overnight here. Kids like to climb the long stairway to the old city, **Ragusa Ibla** (p. 274). Wander at leisure, taking in some of the most panoramic views in Sicily. A highlight here for the entire family is the beautiful public garden, **Giardino Obleo** (p. 275).

If time has run out at this point, and Palermo is your transportation hub for the island, you can cut back across Sicily the following morning to Palermo on the north coast, a drive of 267km (166 miles).

Settling into Palermo

Through all its vicissitudes, Palermo has continued to capture the imagination of world travelers. In 1768, the German romantic poet Johann Wolfgang Goethe had to see Palermo to add the city to his knowledge of classical culture.

In Goethe's travel diary, *Italian Journey*, he describes his arrival by sea and a magnificent setting at the foot of Monte Pellegrino, the "tops of trees swaying like vegetable glow-worms" and a haze tinting "all the shadows blue." So enraptured was Goethe with his first glimpse of Palermo that the captain had to urge him to disembark. Goethe had it right: The best way to appreciate Palermo for the first time is by an arrival by sea.

As a city, Palermo is both loathed and adored by visitors, praised and condemned. It's a mixture of panache and poverty, a place of beauty that is hideously ugly in places, and a great city in which to wear a money belt and keep an eye on your camera. There are a lot safer places to be in the world than Palermo after dark.

Palermo's Arabo-Norman buildings have no equal on the planet, and the entire city is a treasure-trove of museums (often dusty, forgotten ones) and baroque oratories. Its outdoor markets, such as raucous Vucciria, evoke North Africa and are still dominated by the influence of the Arabs who departed centuries ago.

To feel the pulse of Palermo, visit one of these markets. We are eternally fascinated by the sea creatures sold. We sigh at the beauty of mounds of purple artichokes, piles of blood-red oranges, and pyramids of oyster-white eggplant.

Get used to the roar of traffic and the wail of police sirens. Watch out for those cars racing down the street. Noise and pollution hang over the city as you ricochet your way among old monuments: Arab cupolas, Byzantine street markets, and Norman and baroque architectural gems.

Its summers are oppressive—"not fit for habitation," in the words of one visitor—and its street scenes frenetic. Think Tangier or Algiers.

Palermo still bears the imprint of its former conquerors. What it's not is a typically European city, nor even an Italian one for that matter. As one of its 700,000 residents was quick to point out, "We're Sicilian—*not* Italian."

Palermo is old, and in spite of certain "beauty marks," it looks it. The Phoenicians established a trading post here in the 8th century B.C. In time Palermo became the Carthaginian center of Sicily. When the Roman conquest came in 254 B.C., Palermo went into decline, as the new conquerors shifted their power and trading to Syracuse on the east coast.

As the centuries moved inexorably forward, Palermo played host to what seemed like never-ending armies of invaders. The Vandals came, then the Ostrogoths, and by 831 the city had fallen to the Arabs. Under the Arabs Palermo became one of the great emporiums of the Mediterranean, with splendid mosques and sumptuous palaces. It was the equal of Cairo in Egypt or Córdoba in Spain.

Even by the 11th century, with the Arabs in retreat, Palermo flourished. By 1072, it had fallen to Roger de Hauteville, marking the beginning of the Norman period. Under his son, King Roger, who ruled from 1130 to 1154, Palermo entered its golden age, with Muslims, Christians, and Jews living in harmony and prosperity.

Under King Frederick, who ascended to the throne of Sicily in 1208, Palermo became the capital of the Holy Roman Empire. The grand age of Hohenstaufen rule ended in 1266 when the French Angevins came to the throne, launching a despotic rule that ended in the Rebellion of the Sicilian Vespers in 1282.

In the aftermath, the Spanish Aragonese came into power and influence in Palermo. The Aragonese preferred Naples over Palermo as a capital, and in their departure the power vacuum was filled with feudal families and religious orders.

Palermo was never to regain the power and prestige it enjoyed in its long-ago heyday. The city's decay and decline stretched on for centuries. Then an even worse disaster descended on it in 1943, when the city was targeted for massive bombardments by Allied air forces stationed in North Africa.

In the aftermath of the war, Palermo was reconstructed haphazardly. In the postwar years, the city's very name became a synonym for corruption under the Mafia. And while the odious influence of this gang is on the wane, we suspect that there are still plenty of aging *Godfather* types hiding out behind all those closely guarded compounds.

A number of city officials will admit (off the record, of course) that many of the funds allocated in Rome or by the European Union to "rescue" Palermo have ended up in the pockets of the Mafia. But the unheard-of actually happened some 20 years ago: A series of informers, at risk for their lives, came forward to squeal on the Mafia.

Palermo headlines blared that "the tide was turning" against the *Cosa Nostra.* The fight continued under Leoluca Orlando, the city's mayor from 1993 to 2001. He refused to have the city do business with companies he suspected of having links with the Mafia. Even his own Christian Democrat Party disavowed him, but that didn't stop Orlando.

Along with the fight against crime, Palermo only belatedly came to realize the greatness of its architectural heritage. Interest in restoration has at long last arrived. The Teatro Massimo was restored and reopened in 1997, and old and historic quarters, such as Kalsa, are being restored and given a new lease on life with the opening of restaurants, galleries, and cafes. In Palermo, there is hope for the future.

An old-time resident, Giovanni Fatone, summed it up this way for us: "We have passion—sometimes—although it fades with age. We awake with energy but often lose strength in the scalding sun. We are warm and friendly but also rude and irksome when our mood changes quickly. We are a simple people but capable of great wisdom and sophistication when called upon. Palermo and its people are a controversial lot, and many bad things are said and written about us. But even our enemies agree on one point: We are the consumers of the pleasures of life."

1 ESSENTIALS

GETTING THERE   By Plane   Flights into Palermo from mainland Italy are obviously the fastest, most convenient links. Palermo's airport, **Punta Raisi,** is the island's largest, with the greatest number of flights; it's 31km (19 miles) west of Palermo on the A29 highway. For more detailed information on flights into Sicily, see p. 38. In Palermo, you can call ℂ **091-7020111** for information on domestic flights or international connections. Most likely you will be booked on a flight via Rome or Milan to your return destination.

From the airport, a local **bus** to Piazza Giulio Cesare (central train station) will cost 6€ ($7.80). A **taxi** is likely to charge at least 35€ ($46)—or more, if the driver thinks he can get away with it. It's also possible to rent a **car** at the airport (all the major firms are represented) and drive into Palermo. Allow 20 to 30 minutes—longer, if traffic is bad—to get to the center of town. See also "Getting Around," below.

By Train   Palermo has good rail links with the rest of Sicily and also to Italy. After a 3-hour ride from Messina, on the northeast coast, you'll arrive at Palermo's main terminal, **Stazione Centrale**, at Piazza Giulio Cesare (✆ 892021), which lies on the eastern side of town and is linked to the center by a network of buses and taxis. The ticket office here is open daily from 6:45am to 8:40pm, with luggage storage available.

The train ride from Catania, in the east, takes $3^1/_2$ hours, with frequent departures throughout the day. From Trapani, in the west, it's a $2^1/_2$-hour ride, with 11 trains arriving daily.

It's also possible to book trains from major Italian cities. From Rome, it's an 11-hour trip, with seven trains arriving per day. From Naples, visitors usually take the ferry, though the 9-hour train ride is also an option (there are about five trains daily).

Intraisland train tickets are cheap: 12€ ($16) from Catania; 11€ ($14) from Messina; 8€ ($10) from Agrigento; and 10€ ($13) from Trapani.

The big rail haul from Rome costs 44€ to 80 € ($57–$104) one-way, depending on the train. For rail information for Sicily, or for Italy in general, call ✆ **892021.**

By Bus   You can take a bus from Rome to Palermo, but we don't recommend it: The ride is long, dull, and boring. Palermo-bound buses leave Rome's Tiburtina station daily at 9:30pm; the trip takes 12 hours. For information, call **SAIS,** Via Balsamo 16 (✆ **091-6166028**).

If you prefer bus travel, we suggest it for shorter hauls on the island itself. There are convenient links to major cities by **SAIS,** Via Balsamo 16 (✆ **091-6166028**). From Messina, it takes $3^1/_4$ hours to reach Palermo; from Catania, $2^1/_2$ hours. Segesta also has bus links to Trapani in the west, a 2-hour trip. **Cuffaro,** Via Balsamo 13 (✆ **091-6161510**), runs between Palermo and the city of Agrigento in $2^1/_2$ hours.

The Palermo bus stations along Via Balsamo are adjacent to the rail station. The trip from Rome costs 45€ ($59), but most bus fares on the island are inexpensive. For example, the cost from Trapani is 7.50€ ($9.75); from Agrigento, 7.70€ ($10); from Catania, 14€ ($18); and from Messina, 15€ ($20).

By Car   Three autostrade (superhighways) link Palermo with the rest of Sicily. The most used routes are A19 from Catania and A20 from Messina. From the west, A29 comes in from Mazara del Vallo. In addition, two main highways link Palermo: SS113 from Trapani in the west or Messina in the east, and SS121 from Catania and Enna in the east. Palermo is cut off from mainland Italy. To reach it by car, you'll have to cross the Straits of Messina by ferries operated by FS, the state railway authority.

Once the ferry has landed at Messina, you'll still face a drive of 233km (145 miles) to Palermo. If you're planning to drive down from Naples or Rome, as many visitors do, prepare yourself for a long trip: 721km (448 miles) south from Naples, 934km (580 miles) south from Rome.

By Boat   This is our favorite way to get here from mainland Italy, since we always visit Palermo from Naples. From Naples, the most convenient service over to Palermo is provided by **SNAV** (✆ **081-4285555**). The ferry trip takes 11 hours and costs 50€ to 71€ ($65–$92) per person. A rival ferry is operated by **Tirrenia Lines** (✆ **892123**),

Tips   **The Next Pocket Picked May Be Yours**

Palermo is home to some of the most skilled pickpockets on the Continent, so be especially alert. Don't flaunt jewelry, cameras, or wads of bills; women who carry handbags are particularly vulnerable to purse snatchers on Vespas. Park your car in a garage rather than on the street, and don't keep valuables inside. Police squads operate mobile centers throughout the town to help combat street crime.

which takes 11 hours and costs 38€ to 90€ ($49–$117). Schedules vary depending on weather conditions, so always call on the day of departure even if you've already confirmed your reservation the day before. To call Tirrenia from abroad or from a cellphone, dial ℂ **081-0171998.**

VISITOR INFORMATION   Tourist offices are located at strategic points, including the Palermo airport (ℂ **091-591698**) and the main train stations (ℂ **091-6165914**). The principal office is the **Azienda Autonoma Turismo,** Piazza Castelnuovo 34 (ℂ **091-6058351**), open Monday to Friday 8:30am to 2pm and 3 to 6pm. In July and August this office is also open on Saturday 9am to 1pm. When you stop in, ask for a good city map.

CITY LAYOUT   The capital of Sicily has both an Old City and a so-called New City. The hardest part to navigate is the sector lying north of the rail depot. The street plan of the Middle Ages is still in effect here, so it's easy to get lost.

Two main roads cut across medieval Palermo, the **Old City,** virtually quartering it. The first main road is **Corso Vittorio Emanuele,** which begins at La Cala, the ancient harbor, and cuts southwest to the landmark Palazzo dei Normanni and the Duomo (the Palermo cathedral). Corso Vittorio Emanuele runs east-west through this ancient maze of streets known to the Arabs of long ago. The other street splitting the town into two sections is **Via Roma,** which runs north and south.

The Old City is split into quadrants at the **Quattro Canti,** the virtual heart of Palermo. This is the point where Vittorio Emanuele crosses **Via Maqueda,** an artery beginning to the west of the rail depot, heading northwest. Running roughly parallel to Via Maqueda to its east is **Via Roma,** which heads north from Piazza Giulio Cesare. Via Roma and the much older Via Maqueda, virtually parallel streets, shoulder the burden of most of the inner city's heavy traffic.

La Kalsa, the medieval core of Palermo, lies to the southeast of the busy hub of Quattro Canti. The residential neighborhood of **Albergheria** is to the southwest of Quattro Canti. This is the center of the sprawling Ballaro market. Like La Kalsa, Albergheria was heavily bombed in World War II.

Chances are, you'll have little reason to visit **Sincaldi,** the northwest quadrant, unless you want to go to the Capo market. The smallest of the districts of the quadrant is **Amalfitani,** the northeast sector. La Cala, the ancient harbor, eats up most of the space in the district.

Via Cavour divides the medieval core to the south and the **New City** to the north. In spite of its heavy traffic, the more modern section of Palermo is much easier to navigate. At the heart of this grid are the double squares of **Piazza Castelnuovo** and **Piazza Ruggero Séttimo.** Palermitans call this piazza maze **Piazza Politeama** (or just Politeama). At the double square, Via Ruggero Séttimo (a continuation of Via Maqueda; see above) crosses **Via Emerico Amari.**

Heading northwest from Politeama is Palermo's swankiest street, **Viale della Libertà,** home to smart stores and tony boutiques. It is also the street of many upmarket restaurants, bars, office blocks, and galleries. Libertà races its way to the southern tip of **Parco della Favorita.**

STREET MAPS   Even with a good map, you can get lost in the maze of central Palermo. The tourist office issues maps called "Carta Monumentale" that are sold all over Palermo. These are updated every year or so to take into account the many changes occurring in the city as it alters and restores itself. If you purchase a map, make sure it has a street index (some don't). Otherwise, you've wasted your money.

NEIGHBORHOODS IN BRIEF

Historically, the medieval quarters of Palermo were rigidly defined. You were born into one of the city quarters; you grew up there, married, had children, and died there. What you didn't do was intermarry with a man or woman from another quarter. When this was done, it met with social ostracism. Each quarter had its own dialect, palaces, markets, and shops. From an early age, children learned the boundaries of their quarter and stayed within it. Palermo today, of course, is hardly so rigidly confined, and its citizens move throughout the city. But Palermo still has its neighborhoods, beginning with **La Kalsa.**

La Kalsa   The Saracens created this quarter; in Arabic, *Khalisa* means pure, but little was ever pure about La Kalsa. Only now is it awakening to tourism. Always an interesting section, evocative of a city in North Africa, it was viewed as extremely dangerous after dark. The opening of bars and restaurants has changed that pattern, though it's still not a place to wander blithely about at night. The center of La Kalsa was destroyed in 1943 by Allied bombers, and for years in the postwar era, it remained a large bomb site. Today, that bombed area has been turned into a green park, but the neighborhood still has plenty of narrow alleys and streets to get lost in. Kalsa lies to the east of Albergheria, moving toward the harbor, and to the south of Corso Vittorio Emanuele.

La Vucciria   North of La Kalsa and north of Corso Vittorio Emanuele, La Vucciria moves east toward the harbor and the ancient port of La Cala. It is bordered to the west by the Palazzo dei Normanni and Porta Nuova and to the south by the bus terminal, Stazione Centrale. Its northern outpost is Piazza Verdi. Although famed mainly for its open-air market, Vucciria is also filled with monuments and is of major interest to art-loving visitors. This is the best known of all the quadrants that form the core of the medieval city. Like La Kalsa, it is still viewed as a dangerous place at night, especially along its dark maze of little alleyways. But few can resist a look at the market Leonardo Sciascia called a "hungry man's dream." In the book *Midnight in Sicily,* Peter Robb calls it "the belly of Palermo and its heart, too."

Il Ballaro   Most of this sector lies to the west of La Kalsa and to the south of Il Capo, which begins north of Corso Vittorio Emanuele, the northern fringe of Ballaro. Ballaro is known mainly for its market lying to the west of Piazza Ballaro. This district is also home to one of Palermo's most elegant baroque squares, Piazza Bologni. A statue of Emperor

Charles V stands in the heart of a rectangle of palaces decorated with coats of arms.

Il Capo One of the oldest quadrants of Palermo, Il Capo lies in the northwest, east of La Vucciria and directly north of Il Ballaro. You've entered it once you cross north from Corso Vittorio Emanuele. Il Capo, too, is filled with decaying streets, alleys, and lanes occasionally broken by little pockets of greenery. Our favorite square here is Piazza del Monte, which is planted with trees and has a friendly neighborhood bar or two. The palaces are decaying, and there's not a lot of tourist interest here, but we still like to wander about with no particular goal other than to appreciate the neighborhood and wonder what lives are led behind the rotting facades of all those once-noble *palazzi* (palaces). Eventually you'll come to Porta Carini, one of the major gates left over from the Middle Ages.

Albergheria South of Il Ballaro is this historic old district, bounded by Via Maqueda and Corso Vittorio Emanuele and lying to the northwest of the Stazione Centrale. Ripe in its decay, Albergheria is filled in part with palazzi, like all the other neighborhoods, particularly in the area that opens onto Via Maqueda. The most notable of these is the Palazzo Santa Croce, at the intersection of Via Maqueda and Via Bosco. Much of Albergheria's central area is absorbed by an open-air street market. The district is filled with a maze of narrow alleys and streets, and it also contains many fine churches (many in desperate need of funds). Several sections are very poor, and since poverty breeds crime, be sure to exercise caution both day and night. Much of the bomb damage from 1943 remains, simply because no one has ever had the money to fully restore the area.

New City As you head north of the medieval quarter, the streets grow broader but also more nondescript. The monumental and recently restored **Teatro Massimo,** at Piazza Verdi, marks the division between the Old City and the New City. Once Via Maqueda cuts through the medieval district, it becomes Via Ruggero Séttimo as it heads north through the modern town. This street explodes into the massive double squares at Piazza Politeama, site of Teatro Politeama Garibaldi. North of the square is Palermo's swankiest street, Viale della Libertà, running up toward Giardino Inglese.

GETTING AROUND   Parking is difficult in Palermo, and traffic is horrendous. There are treasures to be found here, but getting around to see them is more than difficult.

By Bus   The modernized bus system, once you learn to work it, is the best means of getting around the attractions on the periphery of Palermo, such as Monreale or Mondello. Most central lines cross Via Maqueda and its parallel street Via Roma, going through the quadrants of the old town. Other buses run east and west along the major dividing street, Corso Vittorio Emanuele.

In the New Town, Piazza Verdi, with its landmark Teatro Massimo, is a major hub, as is Piazza Politeama.

A ride on a municipal bus costs 1.20€ ($1.55). For information, call **AMAT,** Via Borrelli 16 (© **848-800817**). Most passengers buy their tickets at *tabacchi* (tobacco shops) before boarding.

A tourist bus called *City Sightseeing* begins and ends its circuit at the landmark Teatro Politeama (the Emerico Amari side). It stops at many major monuments, including the Duomo and the Royal Palace. From April to November 4 departures are daily at 9:30am; from November 5 to March 31, departures are at 10am. Tickets are sold on board; there are no advance reservations. The cost is 20€ ($26) per person. Children 11 and under are granted a 50% discount. For information, call ✆ 091-589429.

By Taxi   Getting around the inner core of Palermo by bus is very time-consuming and not easy, and driving a car around Palermo is a nightmare. In most cases, taxis are the best way to navigate the city center. Taxi stands are found at the main rail depot, at Piazza Verdi, at Piazza Indipendenza, and at Piazza Ruggero Séttimo, among other locations. The meter drops at 3.80€ ($4.95) and charges 2.55€ ($3.30) for the first 154m (505 ft.), plus .85€ ($1.10) per kilometer thereafter. If you can't find a taxi on the street, call ✆ 091-513311.

If you can afford it, consider renting a taxi for the day to explore Palermo attractions; it will cost 70€ to 100€ ($91–$130). Most drivers speak only a few words of English, but somehow they manage. You can request an English-speaking driver; perhaps one will be available. For further information on taxi sightseeing, call ✆ 091-512737.

On Foot   Palermo is a city designed for walking, especially to the museums, monuments, and palaces in the medieval core. But walking is exhausting and not at all practical if you want to take in attractions on the city's periphery. To go outside the center, rely on the network of buses (see above).

By Car   Driving around Palermo can be done, but it is guaranteed to take years off your life. You may want to rent a car for side trips to places such as Monreale, however. Rentals can be arranged at airport desks or at offices within central Palermo. The major firms include **Avis,** Punta Raisi Airport (✆ 091-591684), and Via Francesco Crispi 115 (✆ 091-586940). There are two leading Italian car-rental firms: **Maggiore** (✆ 091-591681) is at the airport, with a branch at the Notarbartolo Railway Station (✆ 091-6810801); **Sicily By Car** (✆ 091-591250) is also at the airport, as well as at Via Stabile Mariano 6A (✆ 091-581045). Rates average from 65€ to 80€ ($85–$104) per day.

Then there's parking. Parking spaces are like gold in central Palermo. One of the most convenient garages is **Garage Stazione Centrale** (✆ 091-6168297), at the rail station, which charges 15€ ($20) per night (closed Sun). Two other convenient garages—identified simply by the word GARAGE—are at Via Stabile 10 (✆ 091-321667), charging 15€ ($20) per night, and at Piazza Oliva (✆ 091-325444), charging 20€ ($26) per night.

By Organized Tour   The best tours are offered by **CST** (Compania Siciliana Turismo), 124 Via Emerico Amari. You can visit its office in person to discuss your interests and see what is available on any given day. CST arranges trips to such sights in Palermo as Monte Pellegrino or the Capuchin Catacombs, but they will also set up side trips to the Greek ruins at Segesta or day trips to western coastal towns such as Erice and Trapani. CST can be contacted by fax at **091-6197218** or by e-mail at cstmail@tin.it.

(*Fast Facts*)   **Palermo**

American Express   American Express services are available through a local agency, at **Giovanni Ruggieri e Figli,** Emerico Amari 40 (✆ **091-587144**), open Monday to Friday 9am to 1pm and 4 to 7:30pm, Saturday 9am to 1pm. Lose your card? Call ℂ **06-72282** at once.

Bookstore The best offering of English-language titles is found at **Feltrinelli,** Via Maqueda 395 (ℂ **091-587785**), open Monday to Saturday 9am to 7pm.

Consulates There's a **U.S. Consulate** at Via Vaccarini 1 (ℂ **091-305857**), open Monday to Friday 9am to 1:30pm. There's also a **U.K. Consulate** at Via Cavour 117 (ℂ **091-326412**), open Monday to Friday 9am to 1pm.

Emergencies For the police, dial ℂ **112;** for an ambulance, ℂ **118;** and to report a fire, ℂ **115.** For road assistance, dial ℂ **803116.** In a general crisis, call the *Carabinieri* (army police corps) at ℂ **113.**

Hospital The most convenient emergency center is at **Ospedale Civico,** Via Carmelo Lazzaro (ℂ **091-6661111**).

Internet Access The most central offering is **Aboriginal Internet Cafè,** Via Spinuzza 51 (ℂ **091-6622229**). It has 20 computers and charges 1.90€ ($2.50) per half-hour; open Monday to Saturday 9am to midnight.

Lost Property This service is handled by **Ufficio Oggetti Smarriti** at Via Macello 21 (ℂ **091-7405082**), open Monday, Tuesday, and Thursday 9am to noon. To reach it, take bus no. 211 from the Stazione Centrale.

Luggage Storage You can leave luggage at an office in the Stazione Centrale, open daily 6am to midnight. It charges 8€ ($10) per suitcase for 12 hours. For information, call ℂ **091-6033440.**

Pharmacies Convenient pharmacies in the city center are found at the following addresses: Via Roma 113 (ℂ **091-6164339**); Via Mariano Stabile 175 (ℂ **091-334482**); and Via Emerico Amari 2 (ℂ **091-585383**).

Police Dial ℂ **112.**

Post Office The main post office is at Via Roma 320 (ℂ **091-7535193**), open Monday to Friday 8am to 6:30pm, Saturday 8am to noon. Branches can be found at the train station (no phone), open Monday to Saturday 8:30am to 12:30pm; and at the airport (ℂ **091-212176**), open Monday to Friday 8:30am to 3:30pm.

Transit Information Call the local bus company, **AMAT,** at ℂ **848-800817.**

Travel Agencies See **"American Express,"** above. Budget-oriented travelers can try **Wasteels,** Via Francesco Paolo di Blasi 14 (ℂ **091-7308304**), open Monday to Saturday 7:30am to 2:30pm.

2 WHERE TO STAY

Hotels in Palermo come in all shapes, sizes, prices, and degrees of comfort, so you should not have trouble finding a room that suits both your desires and your pocketbook. You can live in first-class style or rather inexpensively; the city has more good and inexpensive accommodations than any other place in Sicily.

Because of the heat, July and August are the low season, whereas in such coastal resorts as Taormina those are the most expensive months to visit.

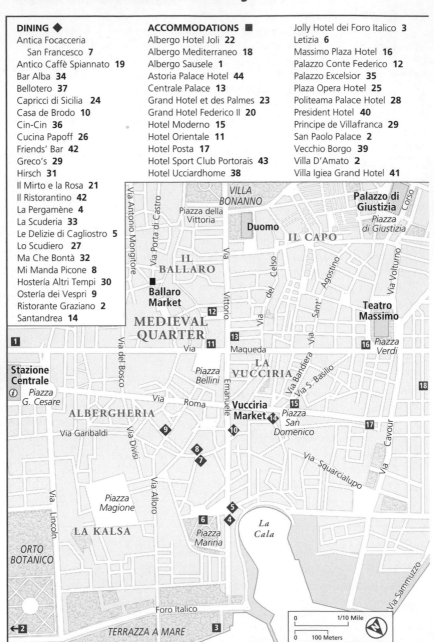

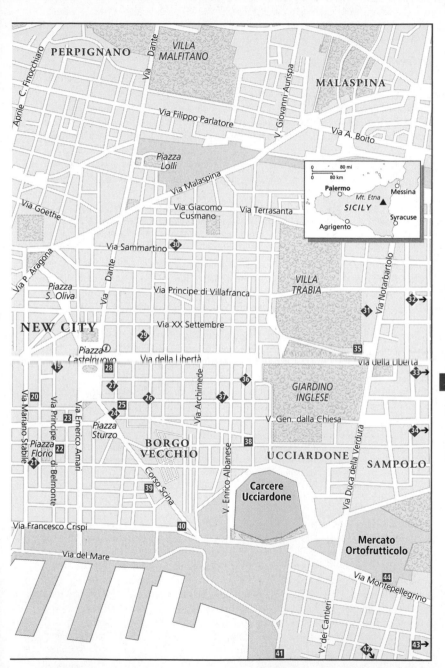

Budget hotels in Palermo are called *pensioni, locande,* or *alberghi,* and most of them lie at the southern frontiers of two parallel streets, Via Maqueda and Via Roma. Women traveling alone will feel safer checking into hotels on one of the main arteries and not down some narrow side street in the medieval quarters.

VERY EXPENSIVE

Grand Hotel Federico II ★★
One of Palermo's best hotels rises six floors in the center of town. It was created after a massive restoration of an old *palazzo* once owned by the aristocratic Granatelli family. The location is on a quiet residential street, although it lies close to Ruggero Settimo Avenue, a fashionable shopping and business district. The well-furnished and soundproof bedrooms for the most part are midsize, each decorated in an elegant way with marble and ceramics. The furnishings are refined with old paintings and period pieces. The first-class Caesar Restaurant was installed on the fifth floor in a former princely apartment, and on the terrace is a roof garden created for alfresco dining in summer.

Via Principe di Granatelli 60, 90139 Palermo. ℂ **091-7495052.** Fax 091-6092500. www.grandhotel federicoii.it. 60 units. 350€ ($455) double; 450€ ($585) suite. Rates include buffet breakfast. AE, DC, MC, V. Parking (nearby) 18€ ($23). Bus: 101 or 102. **Amenities:** Restaurant; bar; car-rental desk; room service; babysitting; laundry service; dry cleaning; nonsmoking rooms; roof garden; rooms for those w/limited mobility. *In room:* A/C, TV, minibar, hair dryer, safe.

Villa Igiea Grand Hotel ★★★
The best hotel in town, Villa Igiea, built at the turn of the 20th century, is a remarkable example of Sicilian Art Nouveau. Managed by Hilton, it is in better shape and more comfortable than the also highly rated Grand Hotel et Des Palmes, Palermo's other historic property. Once the private villa of the Fiorio family, whose claim to fame was coming up with the notion of putting tuna fish into a tin can, the villa hosts the moneyed elite of Sicily when they're in town for business or pleasure.

Located in the suburb of Acquasanta, 2.4km (1¹/₂ miles) north of the center and reached after you pass through a shabby district, the villa is surrounded by a park overlooking the sea. The old architecture has been preserved, including ceilings with stone vaults joining in an arch. Guest rooms contain valuable furnishings such as comfortable wrought-iron beds.

Salita Belmonte 43, Acquasanta, 90142 Palermo. ℂ **091-6312111.** Fax 091-547654. www.hilton.com. 124 units. 235€–424€ ($306–$551) double; 455€–600€ ($592–$780) suite. Rates include breakfast. AE, DC, MC, V. Free parking. Bus: 139. **Amenities:** Restaurant; bar; outdoor saltwater pool; tennis court; room service; massage; babysitting; laundry service; dry cleaning; nonsmoking rooms; rooms for those w/ limited mobility. *In room:* A/C, TV, minibar, hair dryer, safe, Wi-Fi.

EXPENSIVE

Astoria Palace Hotel ★★
Chances are good that if a CEO or even a president is bunking down in Palermo, he or she will be sheltered at this government-rated four-star selection. For sheer comfort and convenience, but not for those seeking accommodations dripping with atmosphere, we consider Astoria Palace the number-two hotel in town, ranked just after the charming but less efficient Villa Igiea. Don't let the word "palace" fool you, however. The name comes from the fact that it's a behemoth, not some classic antique. It is the biggest hotel in town and the setting for many large conventions. It is our sincere hope that you won't be here during one; you'll feel more welcomed and will get better service if you don't have to share the place with hundreds of conventioneers.

The rooms have modern but elegant furnishings. Not all accommodations are spacious; some are boxlike with just a small window. If you can afford it, go for a junior suite, which will be far bigger and more comfortable. Naturally, the best units are those on the top floor where the view is less obstructed.

Via Monte Pellegrino 62, 90142 Palermo. ℂ **091-6281111.** Fax 091-6372178. www.ghshotels.it. 326 units. 182€ ($237) double; 243€ ($316) triple; 282€ ($367) suite. Rates include American buffet breakfast. AE, DC, MC, V. Free parking. Bus: 139 or 721. **Amenities:** 2 restaurants; bar; business center; Wi-Fi in common areas; room service; babysitting; laundry service; dry cleaning; nonsmoking rooms; valet. *In room:* A/C, TV, minibar, hair dryer.

Centrale Palace ★★   For atmosphere and comfort, we'd still give the edge to Villa Igiea or the Astoria Palace—but Centrale Palace is a close runner-up. No other lodging lies as close to the Duomo, the Quattro Canti, and the monumental medieval heart of Palermo. The core of the hotel is a 17th-century private home, although guest rooms occupy adjacent buildings that are newer. The lobby is daringly painted in vivid colors associated with the Italian Renaissance, such as terra cotta and intense blues.

The original palazzo was converted into a hotel in 1892 during Palermo's Belle Epoque golden age. Some period or Empire antiques are placed about to take the curse off the *moderno.* But many furnishings, especially those in the guest rooms, have more function than flair. Doubles are generally medium-size to spacious; the quietest rooms are on the side streets, and double-glazing on the front windows blocks, but does not entirely keep out, Palermo's horrific street noise. Our favorite perch is the top-floor dining room, taking in views over the Palermo rooftops to Monte Pellegrino.

Corso Vittorio Emanuele 327 (at Via Maqueda), 99134 Palermo. ℂ **091-336666.** Fax 091-334881. www. angalahotels.it. 104 units. 188€–271€ ($244–$352) double; 221€–312€ ($287–$406) junior suite; 231€–850€ ($300–$1,105) suite. Rates include buffet breakfast. AE, DC, MC, V. Parking 18€ ($23). Bus: 103, 104, or 105. **Amenities:** 2 restaurants; bar; gym; sauna; room service; babysitting; laundry service; dry cleaning; nonsmoking rooms; solarium; rooms for those w/limited mobility. *In room:* A/C, TV, minibar, hair dryer, safe (in most).

Grand Hotel et Des Palmes ★   This is the most legendary hotel in Sicily, and it's still receiving guests even though its heyday is long past. For nostalgia buffs, however, there's nothing to top it. Since the 19th century, it has sheltered some of the island's most illustrious visitors, including Richard Wagner, who finished *Parsifal* here. The hotel has seen enough murders, suicides of poets, romantic but off-the-record liaisons, and aristocratic intrigue to fill a book the size of *War and Peace.* Classy furnishings, towering pillars, and antique chandeliers still evoke the greatness of a bygone era. The charm of this antique grande dame glows on its rooftop terrace as well.

Management is working to revive the place to its former glory, but it's an uphill battle, and a great deal depends on your room assignment. While the public rooms are still glamorous, some guest rooms can be disappointingly simple. The best ones feature antiques, heavy Italian fabrics, stucco ceilings, and parquet floors.

Via Roma 398, 90139 Palermo. ℂ **091-6028111.** Fax 091-331545. www.amthotels.it. 183 units. 221€–251€ ($287–$326) double; 371€–401€ ($482–$521) suite. AE, DC, MC, V. Parking 18€ ($23). Bus: 101, 102, 103, 104, or 225. **Amenities:** Restaurant; bar; room service; babysitting; laundry service; dry cleaning; all nonsmoking rooms; solarium; rooms for those w/limited mobility. *In room:* A/C, TV, minibar, hair dryer, safe.

Massimo Plaza Hotel ★ ⒱alue   Its major competitor, Principe di Villafranca, has better facilities, but we still applaud this little palazzo for its location in the historic center in front of the Teatro Massimo, reached after a steep climb up a flight of steps. It has a tasteful but subdued elegance that we like as well. The hotel oozes Sicilian style, from its welcoming atmosphere to its drawing-room-like bar; it also has a breakfast room and a reading room. Most small hotels in this category have cramped guest rooms, but the accommodations here are fairly spacious and comfortably furnished, each with a tub-and-shower bathroom and soundproofing against the curse of Palermo: traffic noise. The hotel has been refurbished as part of a general architectural restoration in the historic sector—but it still has no elevator.

Via Maqueda 437, 90133 Palermo. © **091-325657.** Fax 091-325711. www.massimoplazahotel.com. 15 units. 200€ ($260) double; 230€ ($299) triple. AE, DC, MC, V. Parking 15€ ($20). Bus: 101 or 102. **Amenities:** Bar; babysitting; laundry service; dry cleaning; nonsmoking rooms. *In room:* A/C, TV, fridge, hair dryer, safe.

Plaza Opera Hotel ★★   If you want a contemporary spin, check into this cosmopolitan hotel, one of the sleekest and most sophisticated in Palermo. It occupies a restored palace. In the heart of the city, it is convenient to theaters, to restaurants, art galleries, and wine bars, and you can visit most of the celebrated monuments on foot from the hotel's front door. Although the setting is completely modern, paintings and antiques add grace notes. From the moment you walk in the door to check in, you experience Sicilian hospitality, including a welcome cocktail. Bedrooms are beautifully designed and comfortably appointed with a sleek minimalist ambience. The helpful staff will book theater tickets or make restaurant reservations, performing any number of other tasks.

Via Nicolò Gallo 2, 90139 Palermo. © **091-3819026.** Fax 091-6127343. 47 units. 230€–290€ ($299–$377) double; 430€ ($559) suite. AE, DC, MC, V. Bus: 101 or 106. Parking 10€ ($13). **Amenities:** American bar; steam room nearby; babysitting; laundry service; car-rental kiosk. *In room:* A/C, TV, minibar, hair dryer, safe, Wi-Fi.

Principe di Villafranca ★★★ (Finds)   This charming 1998 property is the finest boutique-style hotel in Palermo. Stylish, intimate, and evocative of an elegant, unfussy private home, it occupies two floors of what was originally built as a low-rise apartment house. Its Sicilian theme includes enough antiques and architectural finesse to make you think the place is a lot older than it really is. Grace notes include Oriental rugs, marble floors, vaulted ceilings, and a baronial fireplace. The hotel and some of its neighbors were built within what was once one of Palermo's most beautiful gardens, the Ferriato, owned long ago by the princes of Villafranca.

Guest rooms are midsize to spacious, with tile, granite, and travertine bathrooms; Internet access; and a welcome variety of postmodern comfort and style. The excellent restaurant, Hippopotamus, specializes in a Sicilian and Argentine cuisine. In the bar, notice the valuable Liberty-era writing desk crafted by Basile, one of the luminaries of his era.

Via G. Turrisi Colonna 4, 90141 Palermo. © **091-6118523.** Fax 091-588705. www.principedivillafranca.it. 34 units. 230€ ($299) double; 280€ ($364) suite. Rates include buffet breakfast. AE, DC, MC, V. Free parking. Bus: 101 or 102. **Amenities:** Restaurant; bar; gym; room service; babysitting; laundry service; dry cleaning. *In room:* A/C, TV, minibar, hair dryer, safe.

Vecchio Borgo ★   Although not as grand as Hotel Federico II, this is another postmillennium hotel that was created by recycling an antique—in this case an eight-floor building constructed in 1937. The decor throughout is not cluttered but contains certain decorative flourishes. The midsize bedrooms are well furnished and beautifully maintained, each with a neatly kept and well-equipped bathroom with a hydromassage shower. There is no restaurant, although breakfast is served; many good *trattorie* are found in the neighborhood.

Via Quintino Sella 1–7, 90139 Palermo. © **091-6111446.** Fax 091-6093318. www.classicahotels.com. 38 units. 180€ ($234) double; 190€ ($247) junior suite. Rates include buffet breakfast. AE, DC, MC, V. Parking (nearby) 7€ ($9.10). Bus: 101 or 102. **Amenities:** Bar; room service; laundry service; dry cleaning; nonsmoking rooms; rooms for those w/limited mobility. *In room:* A/C, TV, minibar, hair dryer, safe.

MODERATE

Hotel Sport Club Portorais ★   This is the best and most appealing of the hotels near Palermo's airport, with very little of the aircraft noise you'd expect from such a location. Painted pink, and designed like a Mediterranean villa, it was built in the 1970s on a small bay lined with jagged boulders. Owned and operated by the Marchese family, it functions both as a resort and as an airport hotel.

Inside the hotel is a surprisingly interesting collection of art and antiques, including 18th- and 19th-century choir stalls, painted dowry chests, and an elaborately carved *portantina,* a cramped but gilded box with horizontal poles, wherein ladies used to be carried by hardworking members of their entourages. Many guests here spend their days beside the terraced, oval-shaped pool or at the private pebbly beach. The hotel's restaurant is excellent, and a dining pavilion opens directly onto a view of the sea. Rooms are high ceilinged and airy, with Asian art, tiled bathrooms, and, in many cases, private terraces or loggias.

Via Piraineto 125, 90044 Carini (Palermo). ⓒ **091-8693481.** Fax 091-8693458. www.hotelportorais.com. 44 units. 125€–210€ ($163–$273) double; 200€–250€ ($260–$325) suite. Rates include breakfast. AE, DC, MC, V. Free parking. **Amenities:** Restaurant; bar; outdoor saltwater pool; tennis court; gym; Turkish bath; laundry service; dry cleaning; small private beach. *In room:* A/C, TV, minibar.

Jolly Hotel Foro Italico ★   Many hotels of charm and grace now compete for the position of the top five or six "best in town." Given the added competition, this 1960s chain hotel, once one of the best, is now much lower on the food chain. That doesn't mean that it's fallen off in standards. It's still the same well-organized, well-run hotel it always was. Its major selling point is that it's the only hotel in the center with a swimming pool—and on an August day in Palermo, that's one heck of a selling point. Its location overlooking the sea and the Foro Italico adds to its allure.

A few steps from the Villa Giulia, the Jolly is also close to the harbor and the rail station. As was the style in Italy in the 1960s, rooms tend to be small. They are comfortable, however, and well organized, with lots of built-ins, frequently renewed bed linens, and tiled bathrooms. To escape the traffic noise, ask for one of the more tranquil units on the upper floors, which also have better views of the sea.

Via Foro Italico 22, 90133 Palermo. ⓒ **800/221-2626** in the U.S., 800/237-0319 in Canada, or 091-6165090. Fax 091-6161441. www.jollyhotels.it. 237 units. 165€–300€ ($215–$390) double; 250€–350€ ($325–$455) junior suite. Half board (breakfast and dinner) 35€ ($46) per person. Rates include breakfast. AE, DC, MC, V. Parking 15€ ($20). Bus: 139. **Amenities:** Restaurant; bar; outdoor pool (seasonal); room service; laundry service; dry cleaning; nonsmoking rooms. *In room:* A/C, TV, minibar, hair dryer.

Palazzo Conte Federico ★★★ (Finds)   Still inhabited by aristocracy, the Count and Countess of Federico, this is the most elegant and refined B&B in Palermo. Actually it is a torch-lit, antiques-laden castle that dates from the 12th century. In the heart of the old city, it is near the cathedral, and was constructed on the site of Roman city walls. Its tower on the south side is one of the few remaining parts of the former city wall. Restored and changed over the centuries, the castle still has high painted ceilings from the 1300s, baroque ceiling frescoes, and sculptures and fountains. Guest apartments are rented in the inner courtyard, complete with elegant beds, a kitchen area, a bathroom, and small living room.

Via dei Biscottari 4, 90134 Palermo. ⓒ **91-6511881.** www.contefederico.com. 6 units. 150€–400€ ($195–$520). No credit cards. Bus: 101, 104, or 105. **Amenities:** Dining room; cooking classes. *In room:* TV, Wi-Fi, no phone.

Palazzo Excelsior ★ Even though it was completely restored in 2005, this nostalgic favorite still exudes much of the aura of the 19th century. It was built for the National Exhibition of 1891 when it was called Hotel de la Paix. Many of the Art Nouveau stylings of that elegant era remain, at least in the public rooms with their atmosphere of Palermitan Belle Epoque. The location is in a quiet neighborhood at the northern end of Via Libertà. Bedrooms range from midsize to large and have been completely modernized, with well-equipped bathrooms. Many rooms open on a view of the hotel garden. The formal restaurant, where the staff is elegantly uniformed, serves first-rate Sicilian and international dishes.

Via Marchese Ugo 3, 90141 Palermo. ℂ **091-7909001.** Fax 091-342139. www.excelsiorpalermo.it. 117 units. 216€–302€ ($280–$293) double; 366€ ($476) junior suite. Rates include buffet breakfast. AE, DC, MC, V. Free parking. Bus: 101, 104, 107, 108, or 806. **Amenities:** Restaurant; bar; room service; babysitting; laundry service; dry cleaning; nonsmoking rooms; rooms for those w/limited mobility. In room: A/C, TV, minibar, safe.

Politeama Palace Hotel This is a very appealing hotel, with lots of regional charm and enough touches of international modernity to make tour groups from northern Europe feel at home. Built in 1977, and set behind an angular concrete facade, it rises nine stories above a point immediately adjacent to one of Palermo's most architecturally distinctive theaters, the Politeama, in the heart of the stylish Via Libertà district. Inside, expect a contemporary decor of polished granite, hardwood, leather, and Italian *moderno* styling. The best rooms overlook the heroic bronze chariots on the nearby theater and the square that contains it. All units contain elaborate woodwork, gilt touches, original art, dignified friezes that evoke baronial life in 19th-century Sicily, and small- to medium-size tile or stone bathrooms. Some rooms have Jacuzzis as well.

Piazza Ruggiero Settimo 15, 90139 Palermo. ℂ **091-322777.** Fax 091-6111589. www.hotelpoliteama.it. 94 units. 195€ ($254) double; 250€ ($325) suite. Rates include continental breakfast. AE, DC, MC, V. Bus: 101, 102, 103, or 104. **Amenities:** Restaurant; bar; babysitting; laundry service; nonsmoking rooms. In room: A/C, TV, minibar, hair dryer.

President Hotel This eight-story concrete-and-glass structure rising above the harbor remains a reliable choice in Palermo. After a much-needed renovation, the President emerged as one of the better and more moderately priced options in town. You'll pass beneath a soaring arcade before entering the informal stone-trimmed lobby. The amenities here are simple but comfortable. There's little stylish about the small rooms, but they are well kept, as are the adjoining tiled bathrooms. You needn't bother with the on-site restaurant and its clientele of tired businesspeople. All you have to do is walk out along the harbor to find a number of fine trattorie serving excellent fish.

Via Francesco Crispi 228, 90139 Palermo. ℂ **091-580733.** Fax 091-611588. www.shr.it. 129 units. 195€ ($254) double; 215€ ($280) triple. Rates include buffet breakfast. AE, DC, MC, V. Parking 10€ ($13). Bus: 139. **Amenities:** Restaurant; bar; room service; laundry service; dry cleaning. In room: A/C, TV, minibar, hair dryer, Wi-Fi.

San Paolo Palace ★ Built in 1990, this modern 14-story hotel offers serious competition to the Astoria Palace. Like the Astoria, San Paolo calls itself a "palace" hotel, which is hardly evocative of what it is: a large, sprawling though welcoming high-rise. In fact, if you're returning from a *trattoria* with too much *vino* under your belt, you might confuse the two properties.

Overlooking the sea, between Capo Zafferano and Mount Pellegrino, the hotel is not without its charms, among them a roof-garden restaurant with a spectacular view. The government gives San Paolo three stars instead of the four reserved for the Astoria, which means its rooms are slightly cheaper, yet you get basically the same deal. Guest rooms open onto the most famous gulf in Sicily and are extremely comfortable, though not particularly stylish. There's a wide choice of different bed arrangements, from king-size to cozy "matrimonial." Located a few minutes' ride from the town center, the hotel is a favorite of business clients and, like the Astoria, attracts conventions, which are hardly ideal times to stay here. As for maintenance, management rightly concedes that "so far we manage with a face-lift, a tuck here and there," not the major corrective surgery of a total renovation.

Via Messina Marine 91, 90123 Palermo. *C* **091-6211112.** Fax 091-6215300. www.sanpaolopalace.it. 290 units. 190€ ($247) double; 250€ ($325) suite. Rates include buffet breakfast. AE, DC, MC, V. Free parking. Bus: 221, 224, 225, 250, or 824. **Amenities:** 2 restaurants; bar; outdoor rooftop pool (seasonal); fitness center; room service; babysitting; laundry service; dry cleaning; nonsmoking rooms. *In room:* A/C, TV, minibar, hair dryer.

Ucciardhome ★ (**Finds**) One of the better boutique hotels of Palermo, this is an unexpected find. Rated four stars by the government, the hotel is known for its personal service by one of the city's most helpful hotel staffs. Ucciardhome has special features such as an exclusive wine bar that is both elegant and *intime.* The staff can make arrangements for you to visit a nearby gym, Turkish bath, or beauty salon. Room service will also provide special lunches and dinners. Honeymooners form a part of the clientele. Each of the spacious bedrooms is furnished with acute attention to detail, including minimalist designer furniture, precious materials, and dark wood, which is prominently featured in the hotel. Much use is made of ivory white marble floors, and each of the bedrooms comes with soundproofing, big windows, and terraces or balconies.

Via Enrico Albanese 34–35, 90139 Palermo. *C* **091-348426.** Fax 091-7303738. www.hotelucciardhome. com. 16 units. 102€–150€ ($133–$195) double; 162€–190€ ($211–$247) junior suite; 213€–250€ ($277–$325) suite. Rates include breakfast. AE, DC, MC, V. Bus: 101. **Amenities:** Wine bar; room service; laundry service. *In room:* A/C, TV, minibar, hair dryer, safe, Wi-Fi.

Villa D'Amato ★ (**Finds**) This little discovery, a completely renovated antique Sicilian villa opening onto the seafront, lies a 15-minute drive from the center. As a hotel, it is outclassed by Principe di Villafranca and Massimo Plaza Hotel, but it is not without its (considerable) charms. Set on its own parklike grounds, it is especially good for motorists who don't want to battle traffic in the heart of Palermo. We like it mainly for its gardens, a Mediterranean oasis. As you relax here, watching the plants grow, you'll be in Palermo but it won't feel like it. The guest rooms are completely comfortable, decorated in a sort of Italian Liberty style, yet they come off as rather plain. Small to midsize, each comes with a tiled bathroom. The good Sicilian/international cuisine is another reason to book here.

Via Messina Marine 178–180, 90123 Palermo. *C* **091-6212767.** Fax 091-6213057. www.hotelvilladamato. it. 37 units. 80€–150€ ($104–$195) double; 121€–180€ ($157–$234) junior suite. Rates include buffet breakfast. AE, DC, MC, V. Free parking. Bus: 221, 224, 225, 250, or 824. **Amenities:** Restaurant; bar; room service; babysitting. *In room:* A/C, TV, minibar, safe.

INEXPENSIVE

Albergo Hotel Joli Not to be confused with the Jolly chain, this is an inexpensive hotel on the third floor of a building on the beautiful old Piazza Florio. At the historic center of Palermo, it lies near the pricey Grand Hotel et des Palmes, a few blocks away from Piazza Castelnuovo. Of course, it's hardly comparable to des Palmes, which you might want to visit for a drink or a sumptuous meal. But if you're looking to save money and you don't demand elegance, this hotel offers small to midsize guest rooms; they're a bit boxy and furnished simply though comfortably, with compact tiled bathrooms. The best units come with small terraces overlooking the square. Convenient to both the port and the modern city, the hotel is also within walking distance of most points of historical interest. Considering its heartbeat location, the Albergo Joli provides a relatively tranquil setting.

Via Michele Amari 11, 90139 Palermo. ✆/fax **091-6111765**. www.hoteljoli.com. 30 units. 98€–108€ ($127–$140) double; 148€ ($192) junior suite. Rates include buffet breakfast. AE, DC, MC, V. Bus: 103, 106, or 108. **Amenities:** Breakfast room; bar; room service; babysitting; laundry service; dry cleaning. *In room:* A/C, TV, hair dryer, Wi-Fi.

Albergo Mediterraneo   One of our preferred government-rated three-star hotels, this angular 1956 building sits on a narrow commercial street in a blandly modern neighborhood. The granite-sheathed lobby leads to six upper floors with wide hallways and spacious dimensions, evoking a well-designed contemporary hospital. Rooms are bigger than you might imagine, with a sense of calm but absent of a lot of unnecessary furniture. Overall, this place is businesslike and highly recommendable.

Via Rosolino Pilo 43, 90139 Palermo. ✆ **091-581133**. Fax 091-586974. www.abmedpa.com. 106 units. 118€ ($153) double. Rate includes continental breakfast. AE, DC, MC, V. Parking 13€ ($17). Bus: 101, 104, or 107. **Amenities:** Restaurant; bar. *In room:* A/C, TV, minibar, safe.

Albergo Sausele (Value)   This family-run inn stands out amid the dreary rail station–area hotels. It boasts high ceilings, globe lamps, modern art, and new modular furnishings. The staff is hospitable, as is the resident Saint Bernard, Eva. Guest rooms with shower-only bathrooms are certainly small and modest, but are a pleasant choice. To avoid street noise, light sleepers should request a unit overlooking the peaceful courtyard. What makes this place special are the handcrafted and antique artifacts from around the world, collected by Giacomo Sausele on his travels.

Via Vincenzo Errante 12, 90127 Palermo. ✆ **091-6161308**. Fax 091-6167525. www.hotelsausele.it. 36 units. 92€ ($120) double; 123€ ($160) triple. Rates include continental breakfast. AE, DC, MC, V. Parking 10€ ($13). Bus: Any to Centrale Stazione. **Amenities:** Bar; 2 lounges. *In room:* A/C, TV, hair dryer.

Hotel Moderno ★ (Value)   One of the city's best cost-conscious options lies on the third and fourth floors of a stately looking building that's among the grandest in its busy and highly congested neighborhood. Don't expect the same kind of grandeur inside that you see on the building's neoclassical exterior: You'll take a cramped elevator to the third-floor reception area, and then proceed to a clean but very simple guest room. Each comes with a tiled bathroom; lots of artwork; and not a great deal of direct sunlight. In view of the oppressive heat outside, and in light of the reasonable prices, few of this hotel's repeat visitors seem to mind.

Via Roma 276 (at Via Napoli), 90133 Palermo. ✆ **091-588683**. Fax 091-588260. www.hotelmodernopa. com. 38 units. 75€ ($98) double. AE, DC, MC, V. Bus: 101, 102, 103, or 107. **Amenities:** Bar. *In room:* A/C, TV.

Hotel Orientale ★ (Value)   The former royal residence of Prince Alessandro Filangieri II, this 18th-century palace has been converted into a boutique hotel. Many of the original features were left intact, including a grand marble staircase, original hand-painted frescoes, and a courtyard. The location is in the historic center of the old city, near many famous landmarks, including the Teatro Massimo (p. 127). You can walk here from the central train station. We prefer room no. 7, because it is large and grandly comfortable, more like a ballroom than a bedroom. It was constructed over an archway through which traffic can reach the market streets behind the hotel. Antiques are mixed with 1950s-era furnishings.

Via Maqueda 26, 90134 Palermo. (C) **091-6165727.** Fax 091-6161193. www.albergoorientale.191.it. 24 units. 60€–70€ ($78–$91) double. AE, MC, V. Bus: 101, 102, 103, 104, 107, 122, or 225. **Amenities:** Cafeteria next door for breakfast; nonsmoking rooms; luggage storage. *In room:* A/C, TV.

Hotel Posta   The street housing the Hotel Posta is narrow, claustrophobic, and flanked with buildings with exteriors that could use a good cleaning. But the location is within a short walk of the Mussolini-era post office, several massive and very important churches, and the hubbub of a nearby street market. Despite the unprepossessing approach to the Posta, it is a celebrated address among writers, singers, artists, and actors appearing in productions at the local landmark theaters of Palermo. The controversial playwright, actor, director, and political activist Dario Fo (winner of the 1997 Nobel Prize in literature) is a frequent guest at the hotel, which has been run by the same family since the early 1920s. The Posta is small, functional, and unfrilly, with a tiny lobby; it's an intriguing blend of hypermodern design and antique stonework. The simple, fairly spacious guest rooms are accessible via a tiny elevator and come with small bathrooms.

Via A. Gagini 77, 90133 Palermo. (C) **091-587338.** Fax 091-587347. www.hotelpostapalermo.it. 27 units. 120€ ($156) double; 160€ ($208) triple. Rates include continental breakfast. AE, DC, MC, V. Bus: 101 or 104. **Amenities:** Nonsmoking rooms. *In room:* A/C, TV, minibar.

Letizia ★ (Finds   A once dreary *pensione* has been reincarnated as a boutique hotel of charm, grace, and elegance. Surrounded by decaying 18th-century palazzo from the golden age of Palermo, the hotel rises only two floors on the edge of Kalsa district, a half-block from the main drag, Corso vittorio Emanuele. The public rooms are gracefully decorated with antiques and Persian carpets. The small-to-midsize bedrooms contain much of the same type furnishings and are immaculately kept.

Via Bottai 30, 90133 Palermo. (C)/fax **091-589110.** www.hotelletizia.com. 13 units. 115€–125€ ($150–$163) double; 134€–150€ ($174–$195) suite. Rates include buffet breakfast. AE, MC, V. Parking 12€ ($16). Bus: 107 **Amenities:** Bar; room service; laundry service; babysitting. *In room:* A/C, TV, minibar, hair dryer, safe, Wi-Fi.

---

3 WHERE TO DINE

Many restaurants in Palermo are close to the sea, from which emerges much of the bounty on the trattoria table. *Pasta con le sarde* (pasta mixed with fresh sardines), spaghetti with clams or mussels, and grilled fish and seafood are the items to order on most menus.

Most of the cuisine is Sicilian, although there's more diversity in Palermo than anywhere else in Sicily. Tunisian and Chinese food are the most popular foreign offerings, although you can also find Spanish, Greek, French, Italian, and even Brazilian fare if you search hard enough. Many local dishes still show the influence of Palermo's long-departed conquerors, the Arabs.

If you're a street-food fanatic, Palermo is your kind of town. As you walk along any section of the city, you'll encounter peddlers touting the local specialties—such delights as *panelle* (fritters made with chickpea flour) and *calzoni* (deep-fried meat- or cheese-filled pockets of dough).

If you're with Mrs. Petrillo from *The Golden Girls,* and you want something authentically Sicilian, head for a food stall with a large cast-iron pot turning out fresh buns stuffed with thin strips of calves' spleen and ricotta cheese. The hot sauce that goes with it will have your tongue begging for mercy.

Desserts are also sold on the street. Some of the best concoctions are holdovers from the days of Arab occupation, including sweetened ricotta with cinnamon, pistachios, candied fruit, and cloves.

Budget eateries crowd the Stazione Centrale, but we generally avoid these tourist traps. Some of the best restaurants are hidden in the medieval Kalsa sector, to which you may want to take a taxi at night to avoid walking along streets where muggings occur.

Since Palermitans tend to be late diners (though not as late as the Spanish), most restaurants don't open until 8pm.

BREAKFAST & PASTRIES   If your hotel doesn't serve breakfast (most do), or even if it does but the menu is a la carte, you might want to begin your experience in Palermo by going to almost any bar or *pasticceria* for morning coffee and pastries. Our favorites are **Bar Alba** (p. 94) and **Caffè Mazzara** (p. 127).

In the Medaglie d'Oro area, a great cake shop/bar is **La Dolceria Pasticceria Coga,** Via Gustavo Roccella 56 (✆ **091-596944**). One of the city's oldest and most famous cake shops, **Antico Caffè Spinnato,** Via Principe di Belmonte 115 (✆ **091-583231**), in the Politeama area, turns out brioches, meringues, and croissants until midnight.

PIZZA PARLORS   The people of Palermo eat almost as much pizza as the Neapolitans. You should definitely sample the local pie, *pizza Palermitana,* made with bread crumbs, anchovies, pine nuts, olive oil, and cheese (and sometimes sausage, capers, olives, and grilled eggplant). **Antica Focacceria San Francesco** (p. 93) has been turning out pies fresh from the oven since 1834. A word to the frugal: A pizzeria is your cheapest option for a sit-down meal in Palermo; as such, they're packed on weekends, mostly with an under-25 crowd.

JUICE BARS   Not as plentiful as they once were, juice bars or kiosks used to line many of the city streets. They were—and some still are—an obligatory place to stop for a fruit ice. On a hot August day in Palermo, no one (in our view) has ever improved on lemon ice. For a change of pace, try a refreshing glass of sparkling water flavored with aniseed.

GELATERIE   These ice-cream shops are found all over Palermo, especially in the northern reaches of the city. Our favorite remains pistachio, although the flavors are more varied than the rainbow. Some gelato lovers even order ice cream for breakfast. The concoction is called *brioche con gelato,* or ice cream in a bun.

Al Gelato 2, Via de Gasperi 215 (✆ **091-528299**), in the Libertà neighborhood, serves Palermo's best ice cream. It also has the largest array of flavors of any gelateria. If you're a true ice-cream devotee and feel you've had your favorite food in all known flavors, scan the list of selections here: You're in for a surprise or two.

EXPENSIVE

Bellotero ★ SICILIAN   Lying in the Palermo new town, this is one of the most traditional of all Sicilian restaurants. The 10-table restaurant draws mainly Palermo foodies, who feast on such dishes as fresh fish and shellfish, beginning with a seafood appetizer of calamari, mussels, and shrimp. Many diners begin their meal with a lobster-studded pasta, and you can order such fare as spaghetti with sea bass or sea urchins with lemon zest, perhaps lamb with oven-roasted pistachios. The menu also features Sicilian rabbit and even serves filet of horse, which sounds revolting to many diners, although it is a traditional Sicilian dish with a long-standing reputation among gourmets. For dessert, we recommend the pistachio ice cream.

Via Giorgio Castriota 31. ✆ **091-582158.** Reservations required. Main courses 10€–20€ ($13–$26). AE, MC, V. Tues–Sun 1–3pm and 8–10:30pm. Closed Aug 1–20. Bus: 101 or 107.

Il Ristorantino ★★★ SICILIAN/MEDITERRANEAN   This restaurant is justifiably celebrated for its finely honed cuisine. Francesco Inzerillo, hailed as the city's top chef by gourmet Italian guides, presides over an establishment that's not only elegant but also one of the most stunningly modern in the city. The menu is creative, although old-time favorites are also included. He won our hearts with mackerel with caper sauce and a winning soup of zucchini and fresh seafood. Try the lobster tortellini with cherry tomatoes or the well-crafted swordfish au gratin. Desserts are luscious, so save some room. The restaurant lies in the suburbs north of the center and is best reached by taxi.

Piazzale Alcide De Gasperi 19. ✆ **091-512861.** Reservations required. Main courses 12€–20€ ($16–$26). AE, DC, MC, V. Tues–Sat 12:30–3:30pm and 8:30pm–midnight. Closed 2 weeks in Aug and Jan 1–7.

La Scuderia ★★ INTERNATIONAL/ITALIAN   On our latest tour of Palermo dining rooms, La Scuderia surfaced at the top of our list. Dedicated professionals run this restaurant surrounded by trees at the foot of Monte Pellegrino, 5km (3 miles) north of the city center near the stadium at La Davorita. The talented chefs change the menu according to what looks good at the market; the ingredients, as always, are of top quality. The imaginative cuisine includes a mixed grill of fresh vegetables with a healthy dose of a Sicilian cheese called *caciocavallo involtini* (roulade) of eggplant or veal; risotto with seafood; and *strettini* (homemade pasta) sautéed with mussels, tuna roe, fresh thyme, and lemon. A curiosity and a worthy dish as well is the filet of tuna with melon (yes, melon), mint, and toasted pine nuts. Everything is beautifully presented and served with typical Sicilian courtesy. In summer, the restaurant has one of the prettiest terraces in town, with tables sought after by lovers, families, and vacationing glamour queens alike.

Viale del Fante 9. ✆ **091-520323.** Reservations recommended. Main courses 11€–21€ ($14–$27). AE, DC, MC, V. Mon–Sat 12:30–3pm and 8:30pm–midnight. Closed 2 weeks in Aug. Bus: 107 or 603.

Ristorante Graziano ★★★ SICILIAN   The restaurant of Adriano and Franscesco Graziano is one of the best in Sicily. It's well worth the 45-minute drive from the center of Palermo to reach this elegant country house, where you'll dine in ultimate comfort and be attended to by the region's best-trained waitstaff.

The cuisine is meticulously crafted and backed up by a well-chosen wine *carte* of regional, national, and international selections. The chef takes superb ingredients to the limits of their innate possibilities, with a minimum of artifice and frills. The dishes of the day might include a sausage of fresh tuna flavored with mint, or perhaps a spicy *taglioni* (long pasta) with pesto. Freshly caught fish is a delight, cooked in a salt crust to seal in its juices and served on a platter of grilled vegetables. *Macco* (fava-bean purée) might be a staple dish of the poor, but in the hands of Nino, it becomes something of wonder, especially when it's paired with scampi, ricotta, peppercorns, and fried basil.

SS121, Località Bolognetta, Villafrati. ✆ **091-8724870.** Reservations required. Main courses 10€–15€ ($13–$20). AE, DC, MC, V. Tues–Sun 1–2:30pm and 8–10:30pm. Closed Jan 10–24 and July 6–26. From Palermo, take the autostrada east toward Catania, exiting where it's marked AGRIGENTO-VILLABATE SS121. Continue 17km (11 miles). The restaurant is on the right side of SS121.

MODERATE

Capricci di Sicilia Ⓥalue SICILIAN   Great care goes into the traditional Palermo cuisine here; to go really local, order *polpette* (fish balls of fresh sardines). The spaghetti with sea urchins is succulent; and the swordfish roulade is always dependable. Another good pasta dish is *caserecce Mediterranée* (homemade pasta sautéed with swordfish, tomatoes, almonds, and fresh mint). This is one of the best places to sample *cassata Siciliana*, Sicily's fabled dessert. In warm weather, meals are served in a small garden. The central location is close to Piazza Politeama.

Via Instituto Pignatelli 6 (off Piazza Sturzo). (C) **091-327777.** Reservations recommended. Main courses 9€–15€ ($12–$31). AE, DC, MC, V. Sept–July Tues–Sun 12:30–3pm and 8pm–midnight. Bus: 806 or 833.

Friends' Bar ★ SICILIAN   About 10km (6 miles) north of Palermo, this is one of the better restaurants in the region. Named after the four *amici* (friends) who opened it in the 1970s, it features an air-conditioned dining room and a gazebo-like structure that rises from a lush garden. A meal here is an event for many Sicilians, and a reservation (especially for the garden) might be hard to get. The antipasti, rich in marinated vegetables and grilled fish, are loaded onto a buffet table. The pastas tend to be strong, aromatic, and laced with such flavors as anchovies, fresh basil, and sardines. Grilled swordfish, calamari, and octopus are also a savory kettle of goodies. The house wine is redolent with the flavors and sunshine of southern Italy.

Via Filippo Brunelleschi 138, Michelangelo. (C) **091-201401.** Reservations required. Main courses 10€– 15€ ($13–$20). AE, DC, MC, V. Tues–Sun 10am–3pm and 7:30–11pm. Closed 3 weeks in Aug. Bus: 513, 540, or 675.

Le Delizie di Cagliostro ★ (Finds) SICILIAN/INTERNATIONAL   The restaurant that bears his name celebrates the dubious achievements of Sicily's most successful (and, ultimately, tragic) swindler, Giuseppe Balsamo (alias Count Cagliostro; 1743–95). His mystical mumbo jumbo and sleight of hand looted the purses and pride of commoners and aristocrats (including Marie Antoinette) alike, earning him a respected place in the pantheon of noteworthy Sicilian rogues.

Set on a busy boulevard in a commercial neighborhood, the restaurant boasts vaulted 18th-century ceilings covered with *trompe l'oeil* frescoes. Once you get past the overweening presence of the ghost of the count, you can sit back and enjoy the cuisine. Market-fresh ingredients go into dishes such as risotto with shrimp, cream, and curry; mushroom-stuffed crepes; and that Palermo favorite, pasta with fresh sardines. The platter of grilled vegetables, their flavors enhanced with olive oil and balsamic vinegar, is succulent.

Corso Vittorio Emanuele 150. (C) **091-332818.** Reservations recommended. Main courses 10€–15€ ($13–$20). AE, DC, MC, V. Daily noon–2pm and 7pm–midnight. Bus: 101, 102, or 105.

Lo Scudiero ★★ SICILIAN   Set directly across the busy street from the Teatro Politeama Garibaldi (site of the Galleria d'Arte Moderno), this cozy restaurant and brasserie (its name translates as "The Shield Bearer") is not to be confused with the grander and more expensive restaurant with a roughly similar name out in the suburbs near the soccer stadium. Honest, straightforward, and unpretentious, it's favored by locals, many of whom work or live in the nearby Via Libertà neighborhood. Fine raw materials and skilled hands in the kitchen produce such tempting dishes as grilled swordfish flavored with garlic and a touch of mint. The fish served here is really fresh, as the owner buys it every day at the market. This place gets our vote for some of Palermo's best roulades, grilled veal rolls with a stuffing of ground salami and herbs. Vegetarians can opt for the medley of grilled vegetables with balsamic vinegar and olive oil.

Via Turati 7. (C) **091-581628.** Reservations recommended. Main courses 8€–18€ ($10–$23). AE, DC, MC, V. Mon–Sat 12:30–3pm and 7:30–11:30pm. Closed Aug 10–20. Bus: 101 or 107.

Ma Che Bontà ★ (Finds) SICILIAN   Surely pasta dishes in Palermo don't get much better than this. The fettuccine arrives flavored with fresh mint, sautéed baby eggplant in virgin olive oil, and freshly caught swordfish. One platter contains two versions of ravioli: one stuffed with crabs, the other with sage-flavored mushrooms and rich cream. The tagliatelle is a taste sensation with tuna roe, almonds, pistachios, and fresh tomatoes. If you have room for a main course, stick to the fresh fish, such as tuna in a bittersweet sauce or swordfish roulades with an herb-flavored stuffing. "No! No! No!" everyone shouts at the suggestion of dessert—and then proceeds to devour the homemade cannoli and almond parfait with warm chocolate.

Viale Emilia 69. (✆) **091-511156.** Reservations recommended. Main courses 7€–10€ ($9.10–$13). AE, DC, MC, V. Mon–Sat 1–3:30pm and 8–11:30pm.

Mi Manda Picone ★ (Finds) SICILIAN   We like to come here for three reasons: to sample the excellent and well-chosen Sicilian wines, to enjoy the tasty food at affordable prices, and to admire the facade of that Romanesque gem, Chiesa di San Francesco, rising a few steps from the restaurant's entrance.

The specialty here is wine, mostly from Sicily (450 kinds), accompanied by platters of hearty, robust food. Sit on the terrace in front of the church or retreat to the woodsy, medieval-style interior, which once functioned as a stable. Light snacks include stuffed and deep-fried vegetables; a marvelous flan of fava beans and Pecorino cheese; fresh salads; and antipasti platters. More substantial fare includes grilled tuna or swordfish steaks with capers and black pepper.

Via Alessandro Paternostro 59 (Piazza San Francesco d'Assisi). (✆) **091-6160660.** Reservations not necessary. Main courses 10€–14€ ($13–$18). AE, MC, V. Wine 3.50€–7.50€ ($4.55–$9.75) per glass. Mon–Sat 7–11pm. Bus: 103, 108, or 164.

Osteria dei Vespri ★★ SICILIAN/ITALIAN   A few steps from Via Roma, this restaurant lies on the ground floor of Palazzo Ganci, a restored palace from the 18th century. A wine tavern and restaurant, it is filled with handcrafted wooden furniture resting on parquet floors. The wine list, with hundreds of vintages, is the best in town. Locals take out-of-towners here to this tucked-away little square deep in the heart of old town, knowing they will be served a well-prepared and savory regional cuisine.

The chefs, using a razor-sharp technique, impress with such starters as a soup of mussels, lentils, potatoes, saffron, and wild fennel. We are also impressed with their imaginative and finely crafted dishes, especially the roulade of fish and dried prunes, pine nuts, tuna roe, and cauliflower mousse. The pasta dish that merits the most raves is ravioli with ricotta and fresh basil, homemade tomato sauce, eggplant, and crispy onion. An imaginative use of ingredients continues with such delights as swordfish *cordon bleu*, with almonds, oregano, and ginger, or the braised beef with Nero d'Avola red wine and wild fennel on a potato purée with glazed onions. We want to go back to have our favorite dessert here, a mousse of black-and-white chocolate with glazed orange peel.

Piazza Croce dei Vespri 6. (✆) **091-6171631.** Reservations recommended. Main courses 14€–16€ ($18–$21); fixed-price menu 45€ ($59). AE, DC, MC, V. Mon–Sat 1–3pm and 8:30pm–midnight. Closed 2 weeks in Aug.

INEXPENSIVE

Antica Focacceria San Francesco ★★ (Kids) SICILIAN   All visitors need to make at least one stop at this local favorite, a tradition since 1834, in the Palazzo Reale/Monte di Pietà district. Nearly every kid in Palermo has feasted on its stuffed focaccia sandwiches and other inexpensive eats. High ceilings and marble floors evoke the era in which the eatery was born; the food has changed little since. You can still get *panino con la milza* (real hair-on-your-chest fare: a bread roll stuffed with slices of boiled beef spleen and melted cheese). The *panelle* (deep-fried chickpea fritters) are marvelous, as are the *arancini di riso* (rice balls stuffed with tomatoes and peas or mozzarella). Try the specialty, *focaccia farcita* (flat pizza baked with various fillings).

Via A. Paternostro 58. ℂ **091-320264.** Reservations not needed. Sandwiches 5€–8€ ($6.50–$10); pastas 7€–10€ ($9.10–$13). AE, DC, MC, V. Daily 10am–midnight. Bus: 103, 105, or 225.

Antico Caffè Spiannato ★★ PASTRIES/SNACKS   Established in 1860, this is the most opulent cafe in its neighborhood. Set on a quiet, pedestrian-only street, it's the focal point for residents of the surrounding Via Libertà district, thanks to its lavish displays of sandwiches, pastries, and ice creams. Buy coffee at the bar and be tempted by the elaborate cannoli and almond cakes. If you're hungry, sit at a tiny table—either indoors or out—for one of the succulent *piatti del giorno*. (These include fresh salads, grills, and succulent pastas such as spaghetti with sea urchins.) In the evenings, the focus shifts from coffee to cocktails and from pastries to platters. Live music entertains the nighttime crowd.

Via Principe di Belmonte 115. ℂ **091-583231.** Pastries 1€–3€ ($1.30–$3.90); platters 3€–12€ ($3.90–$16). AE, DC, MC, V. Daily 7am–1am. Bus: 101, 104, 107, or 806.

Bar Alba ★ SICILIAN   This bar has been a Palermo institution since 1955. We were still in college when we were first taken here to sample *cassata Siciliana* on native soil. This is the famous regional dessert of candied fruit, marzipan, and sponge cake—it's a delight if you're not afraid of a diabetic coma. The homemade ice creams deserve an award, especially the creations made with pistachio, and the *frutta di Martorana* (fruits made of almond paste) will dazzle you. You can also go whole hog on savory dishes—their *arancine* (rice ball with ham and cheese), a typical Sicilian specialty, is the best in town. The location is at the top of Via della Libertà, near the entrance to La Favorita Park.

Piazza Don Bosco 7C. ℂ **091-309016.** Reservations not needed. Pastries 1.50€–2€ ($1.95–$2.60); main dishes 4€–7€ ($5.20–$9.10). AE, DC, MC, V. Tues–Sun 7:30am–11pm. Bus: 603 or 833.

Casa del Brodo ★ SICILIAN   For more than a century, this Palermitan institution in the Palazzo Reale/Monte di Pietà neighborhood has handsomely fed some of the island's most discerning palates, such as the late Count Giuseppe Tasca of Almerita, once Sicily's premier vintner. In its two intimate, plainly decorated rooms, it attracts an equal number of locals and visitors, its atmosphere unchanged over the years.

With a name like "House of Broth," you could well imagine that broth is its specialty. And in truth, there is no kettle of broth finer in all of Sicily than that served here. But Casa del Brodo has many other dishes, too, including *macco di fave* (meatballs and tripe), a recipe that seems long forgotten in the kitchens of most Sicilians today. The one specialty we always order is *carni bollite* (boiled meats). Trust us: It may not sound enticing, but it is a tantalizing assortment of tender, herb-flavored meats, especially good when preceded by a savory risotto with fresh asparagus.

Corso Vittorio Emanuele 175. ℂ **091-321655.** Reservations recommended. Main courses 5€–15€ ($6.50–$20). DC, MC, V. Wed–Mon 12:30–3pm and 7:30–11pm. Bus: 103, 104, 105, 118, or 225. Closed Sun June–Sept.

Cin-Cin ★★ (Finds) SICILIAN   One of the culinary treasures of Palermo, this is a favorite spot with locals. Pronounced *chin-chin,* the restaurant's name is the Italian version of the toast "Cheers!" and suggests the camaraderie found here behind an unpretentious facade. It's reached by going down a flight of steps off Via Libertà, in the section between the Giardino Inglese and the Teatro Politeama. The fare is typically Sicilian, including such appetizers as eggplant *caponata* with octopus. Some of the best main courses feature spaccatelle (pasta) with pesto Ericino (a pesto typical of Erice made with basil, almonds, pistachio, pine nuts, and cherry tomatoes); risotto with red pumpkin and mascarpone cheese; swordfish rolls stuffed with basil, almonds, honey, and orange rind; and beef filet with mushrooms and mozzarella.

Via Manin 22, off Via Libertà. (✆ **091-6124095.** Reservations recommended. Main courses 7€–16€ ($9.10–$21). AE, DC, MC, V. Sept–June Mon–Fri noon–3pm and 8pm–midnight, Sat 8pm–midnight; July–Aug Mon–Fri noon–3:30pm. Bus: 101 or 107.

Cucina Papoff ★ (Finds) SICILIAN

With a name like "Papoff's Kitchen," you'll think you've landed in Bulgaria. The restaurant is named for its Bulgarian founder, but this friendly little trattoria actually serves some of the most traditional of all Sicilian dishes. The setting is an atmospheric 18th-century building with stone vaulting in the heart of Palermo, near Via Libertà and Politeama Piazza, just a few steps from the newly restored Teatro Massimo.

The basic recipes remain pretty much the same as they were 200 years ago. It was here that we became addicted to *maccu,* a creamy fava-bean soup flavored with wild fennel. We also recommend the batter-fried cardoon florets with the nutty taste of artichoke bottoms (only better). The stuffed radicchio is Palermo's best, as is the exquisite rabbit in red-wine sauce. You'll also see all those soul-food specialties that warm a Sicilian's heart, including *arancini di riso* (stuffed rice balls), potato croquettes, and *caponata* (eggplant salad). Although the wine *carte* has a number of European and even American selections, opt for one of the rare Sicilian vintages that are almost never found beyond the island's shores.

Via Isidoro La Lumia 32. (✆ **091-586460.** Reservations recommended. Main courses 8€–12€ ($10–$16). AE, MC, V. Mon–Fri 1–3:30pm and 8pm–midnight; Sat 8pm–midnight. Closed Aug. Bus: 101, 102, 104, or 106.

Hirsch ★ (Finds) GERMAN

A meal within Hirsch's rustic, wood-paneled interior provides a welcome change from a constant diet of Sicilian food. Except for the dusty sun-baked pavement outside and the palms and oleanders that line the street, you might imagine you're in Salzburg, thanks to the dark paneling, wrought iron, and *gemütlich* sense of kitsch that permeates the place. You'll find many of the time-tested Teutonic specialties here, including sauerbraten and Wiener schnitzel, as well as more exotic fare such as ostrich steaks and barbecued beef. And where else in Palermo can you order a fat roast goose? All of it tastes wonderful when accompanied by foaming steins of beer from the tap. Expect a table full of homesick Germans to be seated next to you.

Via Damiani Almejda 32A. (✆ **091-347825.** Main courses 8€–15€ ($10–$20). DC, MC, V. Tues–Sun 6pm–2am. Bus: 102, 103, 118, or 702.

Il Mirto e la Rosa ★ (Value) SICILIAN/VEGETARIAN

"The Myrtle and the Rose" is no longer a strict vegetarian restaurant. True, it still serves some of the most flavorful vegetarian dishes in Palermo, made with only the freshest harvests from the fields; but these days, its customers are also treated to an array of well-prepared meat and fish dishes. It's set in a Liberty-style building from the turn-of-the-20th-century Belle Epoque days; a dining terrace is open in summer. The North African–inspired vegetable couscous is the best in town, as are any number of rice and pasta dishes with tantalizing sauces, such as ravioli stuffed with eggplant with tomato mousse and basil jelly. We'd also rank the chef's veal Marsala as the best in Palermo. If you want generous portions and good flavor, order the delectable grilled steak Florentine. Seasonal produce is always emphasized on the menu.

Via Principe di Granatelli 30, off Piazza Florio. ② 091–324353. Reservations recommended. Main courses 8€–15€ ($10–$20); fixed-price menus 13€–21€ ($17–$27). AE, DC, MC, V. Mon–Sat noon–3pm and 7–11pm. Closed Aug 25–31. Bus: 101, 102, or 103.

Le Pergamène (Value) ITALIAN/SICILIAN   This is one of two alfresco restaurants that sit adjacent to one another at the edge of a pleasant but not very well-known public garden known as the Giardino Garibaldi, right at the point where the narrow streets of medieval Palermo open onto a network of 19th-century avenues and piazzas. The plastic armchairs of this restaurant are green, as opposed to the yellow chairs of the restaurant next door, with which there's a friendly rivalry. The menu lists two dozen pizzas; pastas that include the ubiquitous *pasta alla Norma* made with eggplant, as well as a version with either smoked salmon or smoked swordfish; and main courses that focus on grilled steaks (beef, pork, and veal), roulades, and fresh fish.

Piazza Marina 48–49. ② 091-6166142. Reservations not necessary. Pizzas 4€–8€ ($5.20–$10); main courses 7€–18€ ($9.10–$23). MC, V. Daily 5pm–2am. Bus: 103, 105, or 225.

Osteria Altri Tempi ★ (Value) SICILIAN   It's not that we don't like fancy restaurants—we do—it's just that we like to spend many a night in an unpretentious trattoria with wooden furniture and a decor of regional artifacts.

Before grandmother's cooking became a distant memory of childhood, Sebastiano Salanitro brought it back. Those foodies seeking authentic flavors—the very same dishes their ancestors tasted—can enjoy the old recipes here. When he opened the trattoria, Salanitro admitted that the culinary heritage of his tavern also embraces some of the best dishes that belonged to the various invaders who conquered Sicily. Where can you find a good sardine meatball these days? Osteria Altri Tempi serves them and does so exceedingly well. A tasty version of Sicilian lamb stew is offered, as is *vampaciucia c'anciova*. This homemade pasta dish is like lasagna but is studded with fresh anchovies and seedless white grapes and laced with the most savory tomato sauce we've enjoyed in Palermo. Finish off with a cannoli as Italians do in New York's Little Italy.

Via Sammartino 65. ② 091-323480. Reservations not needed. Fixed-price menu 25€ ($33). AE, DC, MC, V. Daily 12:30–3pm and 8–11:30pm. Closed Sun July–Aug and Aug 12–Sept 10. Bus: 101.

Santandrea ★ (Finds) SEAFOOD/SICILIAN   All of the bounty gathered at the Vucciria morning market is prepared with skill at this chic local favorite in the heart of La Kalsa. In fair weather, you can sit out on this old square to the south of Piazza San Domenico, looking at crumbling buildings from the 19th century. The waiter will recite the day's specials with obvious pleasure; go with the mixed antipasti, which always features fresh seafood. The pasta dishes are excellent, notably spaghetti prepared with sea urchins, a local delicacy, or spaghetti with fresh sardines. One of the habitués at an adjoining table once confided to us, "For a Sicilian, a day without fresh sardines is like a life without sex." The homemade desserts, especially the black chocolate mousse, are some of Palermo's most luscious.

Piazza Sant'Andrea 4. ② 091-334999. Reservations required. Main courses 7€–15€ ($9.10–$20). AE, MC, V. Mon–Sat 8–11:30pm. Closed Aug 13–17. Bus: 101, 103, 104, or 107.

Strascinu ★ (Finds) SICILIAN   It's a bit inconvenient to reach, as it's on the outskirts of town, but serious foodies head here knowing that it's worth the effort to reach it. This eatery has been a local favorite since it was opened in 1974 by Don Peppino, an expert on Sicilian gastronomy and a great devotee of island tradition. He wanted his restaurant to be typically Sicilian, not just in its cuisine but in its atmosphere. Inside the decor is adorned with Sicilian handicrafts. Made only with market-fresh ingredients, the local dishes are based on time-tested recipes—nothing experimental here. One dish, in fact—pasta with fresh sardines—dates from the Arab invasion. We like another pasta dish even better—spaghetti *alla pescatora* with mussels, clams, shrimp, squid, fresh tomato, and garlic. An appetizing array of meat dishes is highlighted by *arrosto misto di carne* (stuffed meat rolls, lamb cutlets, various slices of roasts, and sausages). You might also opt for the fresh prawns with chicory-flavored rice. The pizza oven is piping hot at night, turning out such pies as the amusingly named "Mafiosa." It's topped with tomato sauce, mozzarella, ham, mushrooms, artichokes, sausage, olives, and salami.

Viale Regione Siciliana 2286. ℂ **091-401292.** Main courses 8€–18€ ($10–$23). MC, V. Daily noon–4pm and 7:30pm–midnight. Closed Aug 14–30. There's no bus, so hop in a taxi to reach the place.

Exploring Palermo

Although relatively neglected by the casual visitor to Italy, Palermo is one of the great art cities of Italy. It may not be the equal of Venice or Florence, but it is a treasure nonetheless.

Down through the ages, writers have tried to capture Palermo's singular allure. Vincenzo Consolo, in his *Strolling through Sicily,* was overcome with the city's rich red earth "with springs of water where the palm grove rises tall and slender."

The oasis he wrote of is largely swept away today. In its place is one of the more difficult cities in southern Italy to explore. There's just too much traffic and pollution, and getting around in summer is an often dusty, humid affair, and even a risky one as you try to avoid cars, buses, and motor scooters.

Yet in spite of its difficulties, those willing to go to the trouble to uncover Palermo's hidden treasures will find much to appreciate here. In exploring Palermo, expect both sensuous sunshine and somewhat sinister shadows.

The Phoenicians were taken with the setting of Palermo way back in the 7th century B.C. They called it Ziz, which meant "flower." Palermo hasn't experienced a golden age since the 9th century, when, under Arab conquerors, the city became one of the great centers of Islamic culture in the Western world.

In 1072, the Normans arrived, bringing a style that merged with the local residents' into a kind of "Arabo-Norman" period.

All subsequent conquerors added their own particular style and alterations to the city's skyline, contributing new layers to Palermo's rich cultural heritage. Frederick II of Swabia arrived in 1212, ushering in a time of intellectual development and prosperity. Following the Swabians, the Angevins came—until the Spaniards drove them out. In the 18th century, the Bourbons of Naples arrived, embellishing everything with their baroque touch—not necessarily a good thing, as their architects and artisans destroyed much of the classical beauty.

Palermo spent most of the 20th century in decline, becoming a center for the notorious Mafia dons. It suffered severe damage in Allied air raids in 1943 and an earthquake in 1968. Much of its priceless medieval quarter has either been torn down or continues to decay.

Fortunately, matters are looking up these days, as more and more citizens are realizing what an artistic treasure Palermo is. Although not moving as fast as some preservationists would like, restoration is definitely in the air.

1 THE MAJOR ATTRACTIONS

You should give Palermo at least 3 days, and even then you will have grasped only some of its highlights. If your time here is severely limited, you can attempt to visit the city's top-10 attractions in a very rushed 2 days. If you can't spare even that much time and have only a day for the artistic monuments of Sicily's capital, here's how the top-five sights rank on a very short A-list:

Palazzo dei Normanni (Palace of the Normans) ★★   This is Palermo's greatest attraction and Sicily's finest treasure-trove. Allow 1¹/₂ hours and visit just this site if your time is really limited.

The history of the palace can be traced from the 9th century and the days of the Arab emirs and their harems, but probably goes back even further: The Arabs built the palace on an older Roman and Punic fortress. Over time it was abandoned by the Arabs, and the conquering Normans restored it into a sumptuous residence. The Normans came and went, and by the mid–16th century the palace was in serious decay until discovered anew by Spanish viceroys, who in 1555 began its rescue and once again turned it into a royal residence. Today it is the seat of Sicily's semiautonomous regional government.

If you enter from Piazza Indipendenza, you'll be directed to the splendid **Cappella Palatina (Palatine Chapel)** ★★★, representing the apex of the Arabo-Norman collective genius and built by Roger II from 1130 to 1140, when it was adorned with extraordinary Byzantine mosaics. You'd have to travel to Istanbul or Ravenna to encounter mosaics as awe-inspiring as these. The whole cycle constitutes the largest array of Islamic paintings to survive to the present day. Your appreciation of them, however, may be dimmed by the guardians trying to move people on their way, especially on days when too many tour-bus hordes arrive at the same time.

The chapel features a nave and two aisles divided by oval arches. The central area is surmounted by a hemispheric dome set on corner niches over a mosaic floor with walls of marble wainscoting. At the entrance to the nave is a mammoth **royal throne** encrusted in mosaics. Note the towering **Paschal candelabrum** ★ carved with figures, wild animals, and acanthus leaves, a masterpiece that has come down from the 12th century.

Covering the central nave is a honeycomb stalactite wooden **muqarnas ceiling** ★★, a true masterpiece and the creation of Arab artisans brought from North Africa. They depict scenes from daily life, including animal hunts and dances. Our favorite? The depiction of a "picnic" in a harem.

The mosaics were installed to teach the story of the Bible to an illiterate people. We're especially fond of Adam and Eve, each with the "forbidden fruit" in their mouths and greedily reaching for a second luscious piece. Ah, the symbolism.

There is no one set of mosaics to seek out: It is the sum total that adds to a miraculous artistic statement. Biblical scenes decorate the walls, with the image of Christ Pantocrator, surrounded by angels, on the cupola. The colors of the mosaics are vivid, the style realistic, the effect sometimes achieved by gold-backed tesserae and silver mosaic tiles. This mixed inlay makes the surfaces gleam in the soft light.

The mosaics in the nave are evocative of those at Monreale's Duomo (p. 107). If you don't have time to visit Monreale, you'll have seen the essence of this brilliant art here. Almond-eyed biblical characters from the Byzantine world create a panorama of epic pageantry, illustrating such Gospel scenes as the Nativity. The effect is enhanced by inlaid marble as well as by pillars made of granite shipped from the East.

Expect tight security as you wander around the **Royal Apartments** ★★ above, as this is still a seat of government. (On some days, visitors may not gain entrance at all.) You'll

Catacombe dei Cappuccini **1**
Chiesa del Gesù **7**
Chiesa della Martorana/
  San Cataldo **9**
Chiesa di San Domenico **22**
Chiesa di San Francesco d'Assis **19**
Chiesa di Santa Cita / Oratorio del
  Rosario di Santa Cita **21**
Chiesa di Sant 'Agostino **25**
Duomo **6**
Fontana Pretoria **10**
Galleria Regionale della Sicilia **15**

Giardino Garibaldi **11**
Giardino Inglese **28**
La Cuba **2**
La Gancia **16**
La Kalsa **12**
La Zisa **26**
Museo Archeologic Regionale **24**
Museo della Fandazione
  Mormino **29**
Museo Ethnografico Pitrè **30**
Museo Internazionale delle
  Marionette **17**

Oratorio del Rosario
  di San Domenico **23**
Oratorio di San Lorenzo **20**
Orto Botanico **13**
Palazzo dei Normanni/
  Cappella Palatina **3**
Palazzo Mirto **18**
Quattro Canti **8**
San Giovanni degli Eremiti **4**
Villa Bonanno **5**
Villa Giulia **14**
Villa Malfitano **27**

first enter **Salone d'Ercole,** from 1560, the chamber of the Sicilian parliament. The salon is named for the mammoth frescoes, created by Giuseppe Velasquez in the 19th century, depicting the *Twelve Labours of Hercules.* Only six panels are visible (the others are concealed behind the gallery). The most dramatic scene is the slaying of the multiheaded Hydra of Lerna. You definitely won't want to adopt the three-headed dog, Cerberus, as your pet.

The most intriguing room of the apartments is the **Sala di Ruggero II,** where King Roger himself slumbered. It's decorated with 12th-century mosaics. Look for depictions of the peacock; it was said, symbolically, that the flesh of the peacock would never rot. A charmer is the **Hall of Mirrors,** sometimes called the "Yellow Hall" because of all its stunning candelabras.

One of the most splendid courts of Europe once held forth in other rooms of the Royal Apartments. Here the Western world met the mysteries of the East, as Latin scholars conversed and exchanged ideas with Arab astronomers. Regrettably, little is left of those golden days, when this was the most magnificent of European medieval courts.

Piazza del Parlamento. 🕐 **091-6262833.** Admission 6€ ($7.80). Mon–Sat 8:30am–noon and 2–5pm; Sun 8:30am–12:30pm. Bus: 104, 105, 108, 109, 110, 118, 304, or 309.

Galleria Regionale della Sicilia (Regional Gallery) ★★★

This is the greatest gallery of regional art in Sicily and one the finest art galleries in all of Italy. It's housed in the **Palazzo Abatellis ★**, itself an architectural treasure, a Catalán-Gothic structure with a Renaissance overlay designed by Matteo Carnelivari in 1490. Carnelivari constructed the building for Francesco Abatellis, the praetor of Palermo. After World War II bombings, the architect Carlo Scarpa restored the *palazzo* in 1954.

The superb collection shows the evolution of the arts in Sicily from the 13th to the 18th centuries. Sculpture predominates on the main floor. Beyond room 2, the former chapel contains the gallery's most celebrated work, the *Triumph of Death* ★★★, dating from 1449 and of uncertain attribution (though it's sometimes credited to Pisanello). In all its gory magnificence, it portrays a horseback-riding skeleton (representing Death, of course) trampling his victims. The painter depicted himself in the fresco, seen with a pupil praying in vain for release from the horrors of Death. The modernity of this extraordinary work, including the details of the nose of the horse and the men and women in the full flush of their youth, is truly amazing, especially for its time.

The second masterpiece of the gallery lies at the end of the corridor exhibiting Arabic ceramics in room 4: the white-marble, slanted-eyed bust of *Eleanara di Aragona* ★★, by Francesco Laurana, who created it in the 15th century. This is Laurana's masterpiece.

The second-floor galleries are filled mainly with paintings from the Sicilian school, including a spectacular *Annunciation* ★★, the creation of Antonello da Messina, in room 11.

In the salon of Flemish paintings rests the celebrated *Triptych of Malvagna* ★★, the creation of Mabuse, whose real name was Jean Gossaert. His 1510 work depicts a Madonna and *bambino* surrounded by singing angels with musical instruments.

Via Alloro 4, Palazzo Abatellis. 🕐 **091-6230011.** Admission 6€ ($7.80) adults, 3€ ($3.90) children. Sat–Mon 9am–1pm; Tues–Fri 9am–1pm and 2:30–7pm. Bus: 103, 105, or 139.

Museo Archeologico Regionale (Regional Archaeological Museum) ★★★

This is one of the grandest archaeological museums in Italy, stuffed with artifacts from prehistoric times to the Roman era. Spread over several buildings, the oldest from the 13th century, the museum's collection includes major Sicilian finds from the Phoenician,

Punic, Greek, Roman, and Saracen periods, with several noteworthy treasures from Egypt. Even though some of the exhibitions appear shabby and the museum is definitely not state-of-the-art, its treasures are worth wading through the dust to see.

You'll pass through small **cloisters** ★ on the ground floor, centered on a lovely hexagonal 16th-century fountain bearing a statue of Triton. In room 3 is some rare Phoenician art, including a pair of **sarcophagi** that date from the 5th century B.C.

In room 4 is the *Pietra di Palermo,* a black diorite slab known as the Rosetta stone of Sicily. Dating from 2700 B.C., and discovered in Egypt in the 19th century, it was intended for the British Museum. Somehow, because of red tape, it got left behind in Palermo. It contains carved hieroglyphics detailing information about the pharaohs, including the delivery of 40 shiploads of cedarwood to Snefru.

The most important treasures of the museum, in room 13, are the **metopes of Selinunte** ★★. These finds were unearthed at the temples of Selinunte, once one of the major cities of Magna Graecia (Greek colonies along the coast of southern Italy). The Selinunte sculptures are remarkable for their beauty, casting a light on the brilliance of Siceliot sculpture in general. Displayed are three magnificent metopes from Temple C, a quartet of splendid metopes from Temple E, and, in the center, a 5th-century bronze statue, **Ephebe of Selinunte** ★. These decorative friezes cover the period from the 6th century B.C. to the 5th century B.C., depicting such scenes as Perseus slaying Medusa, the Rape of Europa by Zeus, and Actaeon being transformed into a stag.

Etruscan antiquities grace rooms 14 to 17. Discoveries at the Tuscan town of Chisu, such as the unearthing of funereal *cippi* (stones), shed more light on these mysterious people. The **Oinochoe Vase,** from the 6th century B.C., is one of the most detailed artifacts of Etruscan blackened earthenware (called *bucchero*).

Other exhibit halls on the ground floor display underwater archaeology, with the most complete collection of **ancient anchors,** mostly Punic and Roman, in the world.

Finds from Greek and Roman sites in western Sicily are to be seen on the second floor in rooms 2 and 12. Here are more artifacts from Selinunte and other ancient Sicilian sites such as Marsala, Segesta, Imera, and Randazzo. These include **funereal aedicules** (openings framed by two columns, an entablature, and usually a pediment), **oil lamps,** and **votive terra cottas.**

In room 7 is a remarkable and rare series of large Roman bronzes, including the most impressive, a supremely realistic **bronze Ram** ★★, a Hellenistic work from Syracuse. It's certainly worth the climb up the steps. Another notable work here is *Hercules Killing the Stag* ★, discovered at Pompeii, a Roman copy of a Greek original from the 3rd

EXPLORING PALERMO

6

THE MAJOR ATTRACTIONS

 Tips ## Where Mafia Wannabes Get Street Smarts

More and more foreigners are visiting at night, mainly to patronize some of the newly emerging restaurants—but still keep your wits about you. It's relatively safe to visit during the day, but even then, try not to walk around alone. Leave your valuables back in the hotel safe, hang on to your wallet, and take a taxi to your destination. Finally, never wander down dark, deserted labyrinthine streets.

century B.C. In room 8, the most remarkable sculpture is *Satyr Filling a Drinking Cup* ★, a Roman copy of a Praxitelean original.

On the third floor is a prehistoric collection along with Greek ceramics, plus Roman mosaics and frescoes. The highlight of the collection is panels illustrating **Orpheus with Wild Animals** ★, from the 3rd century A.D.

Piazza Olivella 24. ℂ **091-6116805.** Admission 6€ ($7.80) adults, 3€ ($3.90) children. Tues–Fri 8:30am–2pm and 2:30–6:30pm; Sat–Mon 8:30am–1:30pm. Bus: 101, 102, 103, 104, or 107.

Catacombe dei Cappuccini (Catacombs of the Capuchins) ★★   If you've got a secret yearning to join mummified cadavers, and your tastes lean to the bizarre, you should spend at least an hour at these catacombs under the Capuchins Monastery.

Some 350 years ago, it was discovered that the catacombs contained a mysterious preservative that helped mummify the dead. As a result, Sicilians from nobles to maids—at least 8,000 in all—demanded to be buried here. The oldest corpses date from the late 16th century. The last corpse to be buried here was that of 2-year-old Rosalia Lombaro, who died in 1920. She still appears so lifelike that locals have dubbed her "Sleeping Beauty." Giuseppe Tommasi, prince of Lampedusa and author of one of the best-known works of Sicilian literature, *The Leopard*, was buried here in 1957. His body was not embalmed, but buried in the cemetery next to the catacombs instead.

Visitors can wander through the catacombs' dank corridors among the mummified bodies. Some faces are contorted as if posing for Edvard Munch's *The Scream*. Although many corpses are still remarkably preserved, time and gravity have been cruel to others. Some are downright creepy, with body parts such as jaws or hands missing.

Capuchins Monastery, Piazza Cappuccini 1. ℂ **091-212117.** Admission 1.50€ ($1.95). Daily 9am–noon and 3–5pm (until 7pm in summer). Closed holidays.

La Kalsa ★★   In Arabic, the name *Khalisa* means "pure," although that is about the last word we'd use to describe this colorful district. Left over from the Middle Ages, the crumbling Quartiere della Kalsa is the medieval core of Old Palermo and its most intriguing neighborhood in spite of all the decay, wartime destruction, and poverty. It is rapidly being restored.

Located in the southwestern section of the old city, La Kalsa was designed and constructed by Arab rulers as a walled city for the emir and his ministers. Already in serious decline before World War II, La Kalsa was heavily bombed in 1943 by Allied bombers seeking to conquer Sicily from Fascist control (the neighborhood was on the bombers' radar for its strategic location near the city's port). In the postwar era, La Kalsa sank into deeper misery and squalor.

When the Albanian nun Mother Teresa visited La Kalsa, she lectured the well-heeled Palermitani, telling them that since Palermo was as poor as a third-world country,

---

(Tips)   Street Eats: What, You Haven't Tasted Babbaluci?

Around the heart of La Kalsa, at Piazza della Kalsa, you can do as the locals do and indulge in a savory treat. Several vendors can be seen cooking and peddling *babbaluci*, a gourmet delicacy to the people of the district. These baby snails are marinated in virgin olive oil, chopped fresh parsley, and garlic; sprinkled with red pepper; and sold to passersby in paper containers called cornets.

(Moments) The Church That Never Was

One of the most evocative moments you can experience in Palermo is to stand in the church ruins of Santa Maria dello Spasimo on a dying summer day, watching the remains of this late Gothic building catch fire with the rays of the setting sun. This sight evokes the spirit of Raphael, who came here to paint his famous portrait of the anguish of the Madonna before the cross. You'll have to go to the Prado in Madrid to see the actual masterpiece, but the inspiration for it is right here in La Kalsa.

"charity should begin at home." Today, after endless delays, Mother Teresa's words are finally being heard, and La Kalsa is slowly getting the restorative attention it deserves.

La Kalsa is bounded by the port of La Cala on one side and Via Garibaldi and Via Paternostro to the east and west, and by Corso Vittorio Emanuele and Via Lincoln to the north and south. One of its main thoroughfares is Via Butero.

A good place in the heart of the quarter to begin your rambling is the fancifully baroque church of **Santa Teresa alla Kalsa** (© 091-6171658), which opens onto the center square, **Piazza della Kalsa.** The church was constructed between 1686 and 1706. Two orders of Corinthian columns grace its stately facade. If it's open, visit the luminous interior to see the impressive stuccoes of Giuseppe and Procopio Serpotta. To reach Piazza della Kalsa, enter near La Cala, the harbor, through Porta dei Greci, right off the busy thoroughfare, Foro Italico. Arm yourself with a good, detailed map before venturing into the quarter.

From Piazza della Kalsa, walk north along Via Torremuzza until you come to **Via Alloro,** La Kalsa's main street in the Middle Ages. Head west along this street for a close encounter with the decaying district. The elegant palaces of yesteryear have been destroyed, torn down, or burned down; some are still standing, albeit most likely in a serious state of decay. One of the grandest extant palaces along Via Alloro is the **Palazzo Abatellis,** home today to the **Galleria Regionale della Sicilia** (p. 102).

After passing Palazzo Abatellis, you will shortly come to Via della Vetriera. At this point, head south for another close encounter with La Kalsa. This street will lead you to **Chiesa di Santa Maria dello Spasimo,** Via dello Spasimo (© 091-6161486). A melancholy aura hangs over this church, originally constructed in the late Gothic style in 1506. This is the only example of the Northern Gothic style on the island. The walls went up, as did a soaring apse; but the builders abandoned the project and it was never roofed. Naturally, its interior was never finished either. Two towering ailanthus trees adopted it and now grow tall and proud. The church ruins make a marvelous venue for performances in summer.

For a final look at La Kalsa, bid adieu to Santa Maria dello Spasimo and head west across Piazza della Spasimo. This will lead into the Piazza Magione. From here, you can enjoy the facade of **La Magione** or the **Chiesa della Santa Trinità** (© 091-6170596), an excellent example of a Norman church constructed in 1191 by the Cistercians. In 1197, Holy Roman Emperor Henry VI awarded it to the Teutonic Knights, who remained in control until 1492, when Pope Innocent VIII kicked them out of Italy. The knights are gone, but their marble funereal slabs can still be seen on the floor of the church's austere interior. The beautiful cloisters date from the founding of the original

Cistercian monastery; they were severely damaged when the 1943 Allied air raids bombed the church.

Chiesa di Santa Cita/Oratorio del Rosario di Santa Cita ★★★   The Oratory of the Rosary of St. Cita is a far greater artistic treasure than the church of St. Cita, on which Allied bombs rained in 1943. Only a glimmer of its former self, the church still contains a lovely **marble chancel arch ★** by Antonello Gagini. Look for it in the presbytery. From 1517 to 1527, Gagini created other sculptures in the church, but they were damaged in the bombing. In the second chapel left of the choir is a **sarcophagus of Antonio Scirotta,** also the creation of Gagini. To the right of the presbytery is the lovely **Capella del Rosario ★**, with its polychrome marquetry and intricate lacelike stucco-work. The sculpted reliefs here are by Gioacchino Vitaliano.

On the left side of the church, and entered through the church, is the **oratory,** the real reason to visit. This was the crowning achievement of the leading baroque decorator of his day, Giacomo Serpotta, who worked on it between 1686 and 1718. His cherubs and angels romp with abandon, delightfully climbing onto the window frames or spreading garlands of flowers in their path. They can also be seen sleeping, eating, and simply hugging their knees deep in thought.

The oratory is a virtual gallery of art containing everything from scenes of the flagellation to Jesus in the Garden at Gethsemane. The *Battle of Lepanto* bas-relief is meant to symbolize the horrors of war, while other panels depict such scenes as *The Mystery of the Rosary.* At the high altar is Carlo Maratta's *Virgin of the Rosary* (1690). Allegorical figures protect eight windows along the side walls.

Via Valverde 3. ℂ **091-332779.** Free admission (donation appreciated). Entrance to oratory 2€ ($2.60). Mon–Sat 9am–1pm. Bus: 107.

Oratorio del Rosario di San Domenico ★★★   Located in the area of the colorful open-air market, Mercato della Vucciria, the Oratory of the Rosary of St. Dominic was founded in the closing years of the 16th century by the Society of the Holy Rosary. Two of its most outstanding members were the sculptor Giacomo Serpotta and the painter Pietro Novelli, both of whom left a legacy of their artistic genius in this oratory.

In allure, this oratory is the equal of the Oratorio di San Lorenzo, which also displays Serpotta's artistic flavor. The sculptor excelled in the use of marble and polychrome, but it was in stucco that he earned his greatest fame. From 1714 to 1717, he decorated this second oratory with his delightfully expressive *putti* (cherubs), who are locked forever in a playground of happy antics.

Themes throughout the oratory are wide ranging, depicting everything from Allegories of the Virtues to the Apocalypse of St. John. Particularly graphic is a depiction of a writhing "Devil Falling from Heaven." At the high altar is a masterpiece by Anthony Van Dyck, *Madonna of the Rosary* (1628). Pietro Novelli frescoed the ceiling with the *Coronation of the Virgin.*

Via dei Bambinai. ℂ **091-332779.** Free admission. Mon 3–6pm; Tues–Fri 9am–1pm and 3–5:30pm; Sat 9am–1pm. Bus: 107.

Oratorio di San Lorenzo ★★★   No longer as rich in treasures as it once was, the Oratory of San Lorenzo lies to the left of and faces the church of San Francesco d'Assisi. A local Franciscan order, Compagnia di San Francesco, commanded this oratory constructed back in 1569. Its stunning mahogany pews, laced with mother-of-pearl, were created during the 18th century and rest on carved supports.

(Fun Facts) The Mystery of the Stolen Painting

In 1969, the art world learned in newspaper headlines that "the divine" Caravaggio's last large painting, *The Nativity*, had been stolen from the Oratory of San Lorenzo, where it once hung over the altar. Caravaggio created the work in 1609, a year before his death. No motive for the theft has ever been declared, and it is believed that the painting has been needlessly destroyed. The curator told us, "We keep hoping that one day it will come back to us, but as each day goes by, that hope grows dimmer and dimmer."

Of extraordinary elegance, the interior's **stucco decoration ★★** is the masterpiece of Giacomo Serpotta, who worked on it between 1698 and 1710. It features a series of 10 symbolic statues, plus panels relating the details of the lives of St. Francis and St. Lawrence. Art historians have written of these wall paintings as "a cave of white coral." Some of the most expressive of the stuccoes depict the martyrdom of St. Lawrence. Paintings alternate with statues of the Virtues. In total contrast to the serene Virtues and the solemn nudes is the cavalcade of *putti,* who romp gaily, making soap bubbles or kissing one another.

Near the old port of La Cala, just south of Corso Vittorio Emanuele. Via dell'Immacolatella. (C) **091-582370.** Free admission. Mon–Sat 9am–1pm. Bus: 101 or 102.

Duomo ★★   If too many cooks in the kitchen can spoil the broth, then too many architects turned Palermo's cathedral into a hodgepodge of styles. It is still a striking building, however, and well worth an hour or more of your time. Regrettably, the various styles—Greek, Roman, Norman, Arabic, Islamic—were not blended successfully with the overriding baroque overlay.

In 1184, during the Norman reign, the archbishop of Palermo, Gualtiero Offamiglio, launched the cathedral on the site of a Muslim mosque, which had been built over an early Christian basilica. Offamiglio was green with envy at the supremacy of the cathedral of Monreale. As the Palermo Duomo took shape, it became an architectural battleground for what was known as "The Battle of the Two Cathedrals."

Today, the facade is closed between two soaring towers with double lancet windows. The middle portal, dating from the 15th century, is enhanced by a double lancet with the Aragonese coat of arms. The four impressive campaniles (bell towers), date from the 14th century, the south and north porches from the 15th and 16th centuries.

But if anyone could be called the culprit for the cathedral's playground of styles, it is the Neapolitan architect Ferdinando Fuga, who went with the mood of his day and in 1771 and 1809 gave both the exterior and the interior of the Duomo a sweeping neoclassical style. In retrospect, he should have left well enough alone. The only section that the restorers didn't touch was the **apses ★**, which still retain their impressive geometric decoration.

The Duomo is also a pantheon of royalty. As you enter, the first chapel on the right contains six of the edifice's most impressive tombs, including that of Roger II, the first king of Sicily, who died in 1154. He was crowned in the Duomo in 1130. His daughter Constance, who died in 1198, is buried here along with her husband, Henry VI, who died the year before. Henry VI was emperor of Germany and the son of Frederick Barbarossa. Their son, another emperor of Germany and king of Sicily, Frederick II, was also buried here in 1250, as was his wife, Constance of Aragón, who died in 1222. The last royal burial here, Peter II, king of Sicily, was in 1342.

Accessed from the south transept, the **Tesoro,** or treasury, is a repository of rich vestments, silverware, chalices, holy vessels, altar cloths, and ivory engravings of Sicilian art of the 17th century. An oddity here is the bejeweled caplike **crown of Constance of Aragón** ★, designed by local craftsmen in the 12th century, and removed from her head when the tomb was opened in the 18th century. Other precious objects removed from the royal tombs are also on display here.

Piazza di Cattedrale, Corso Vittorio Emanuele. ℂ **091-334373.** www.cattedrale.palermo.it. Duomo: free (donation appreciated); crypt: 2€ ($2.60); treasury: 2€ ($2.60). Mon–Sat 9:30am–1:30pm and 2:30–5:30pm. Bus: 101, 104, 105, 107, or 139.

2 OTHER GREAT CHURCHES

Chiesa del Gesù   Constructed in 1564, but extended and modified by several later architects, this was the first church in Sicily built by the Jesuits. Regrettably, it was another victim of the 1943 Allied air raids and had to be considerably restored at the end of World War II. Don't judge this church by its somber facade. Its **interior** ★★ is a triumph of baroque indulgence. Everywhere you look is an outstanding example of exuberant Sicilian baroque, with marble adornments, stucco reliefs, polychrome intarsia, and an array of paintings and sculpted works. All of this overlay took centuries to complete.

The **frescoes** in the first bay of the vault of the nave are among the oldest pictorial decorations, created by Filippo Randazzo in 1743. The presbytery and apse also contain some of the original decorations, including sculptures by Gioacchino Vitaliano. Our favorite work of art here is the brilliant **chancel decor** ★, the work of the Serpotta brothers. It's a romp of cherubs harvesting grapes, playing musical instruments, and holding torches and bouquets. Seek out the second chapel on the right as you enter to view paintings of **St. Philip of Agira** and the even more expressive **St. Paul the Hermit** ★, both excellent examples of Pietro Novelli's work. The last figure depicted on the left in the St. Paul painting is actually a self-portrait of Novelli.

The magnificent porticoed courtyard gives access to the **Biblioteca Comunale,** the public library known as "Casa Professa." Filled with ancient manuscripts and incunabula, it also displays 300 portraits of illustrious men.

Piazza Casa Professa 21. ℂ **091-581880.** Free admission. Daily 7am–noon and 5–6:30pm. Bus: 101, 102, 103, 104, or 107.

Chiesa della Martorana/San Cataldo ★★   These two Norman churches stand side by side. If you have time for only one, make it La Martorana, as it is the most celebrated church in Palermo remaining from the Middle Ages. Visit it if only to see its series of spectacular **mosaics** ★★.

Named for Eloisa Martorana, who founded a nearby Benedictine convent in 1194, this church is dedicated not to her, but to Santa Maria dell'Ammiraglio (St. Mary of the Admiral). History was made here as well: It was in this church that Sicily's noblemen convened to offer the crown to Peter of Aragon.

Today's baroque facade regrettably conceals a Norman front. You enter through a beautiful combined portico and bell tower with a trio of ancient columns and double

| **Fun Facts** | **A Medieval Delicacy Lives On** |

In the Middle Ages, every convent in Palermo specialized in creating a different kind of confectionery. Many of those old recipes are gone forever, but one of the most enduring is still sold at *pasticceria* all over the city: *frutta martorana,* named after the old Benedictine convent of La Martorana. Originally this marzipan was molded into various fruit and vegetable shapes. Today, these almond-paste sweet-meats resemble anything from cats to sailboats. The *frutta martorana* are most abundant in the bakeries before the feast day of All Saints, in early November.

arch openings. The bell tower is original, dating from the 12th century. Once you go inside, you'll know that your time spent seeking out this church was worthwhile. The stunning mosaics were ordered in 1143 by George of Antioch, the admiral of King Roger and a man of Greek descent who loved mosaics, especially when they conformed, as these did, to the Byzantine iconography of his homeland. It's believed that the craftsmen who designed these mosaics also did the same for the Cappella Palatina. The mosaics are laid out on and around the columns that hold up the principal cupola. They're at their most beautiful in the morning light when the church opens.

Dominating the dome is a rendition of Christ, surrounded by a bevy of angels with the Madonna and the apostles pictured off to the sides. Even with the passage of centuries the colors remain vibrantly golden, with streaks of spring green, ivory, azure blue, and what one art critic called "grape-red."

On a visit to La Martorana, you can obtain a key from the custodian sitting at a tiny table to your right as you enter the chapel. This key allows entry into the tiny **Chiesa di San Cataldo** next door. Also of Norman origin, it was founded by Maio of Bari, chancellor to William I. But because he died in 1160, the interior was never completed. The church is famous for its Saracenic red golf-ball domes. Sicilians liken these bulbous domes to a eunuch's hat.

Piazza Bellini 2, adjacent to Piazza Pretoria. ⓒ **091-6161692.** Free admission. La Martorana: Mon–Sat 9:30am–1pm and 3:30–6:30pm; Sun 8:30am–1pm. San Cataldo: Tues–Fri 9am–5pm; Sat–Sun 9am–1pm. Bus: 101 or 102.

Chiesa di San Domenico   Although its oratory (p. 106) is a more intriguing artistic expression because of the delightful *putti* by Giacomo Serpotta, the Church of St. Dominic is one of the city's most remarkable baroque structures, its elegant baroque facade often depicted on postcards. It was constructed in 1640 to the design of the architect Andrea Cirrincione. The facade, however, wasn't added until 1726. Many antique buildings on the square were demolished to give this church more breathing room.

The facade rises in a trio of carefully ordered tiers, graced with both Corinthian and Doric pillars along with square pilasters that form a sort of picture frame for a statue of St. Dominic. Unlike the lavishly decorated oratory, the church has a severe interior that only emphasizes the beauty of the architecture. Its chapels, on the other hand, are richly decorated, forming a pantheon of tombs and cenotaphs of some of the more noble Sicilians, including Francesco Crispi, the former prime minister of Italy. The tomb of the painter Pietro Novelli (1608–47) is in the north aisle.

Adjacent is the headquarters of the Sicilian Historical Society, with its own tiny **Museo del Risorgimento,** containing mementos of Garibaldi. The fragmented 14th-century cloister was part of the first church erected on this site.

Piazza San Domenico. ℂ **091-584872.** Free admission to church, 2€ ($2.60) to cloisters. Mon–Fri 9–11:30am; Sat–Sun 5–7pm. Bus: 101.

Chiesa di San Francesco d'Assisi   Set in the medieval Kalsa district, north of Via Alloro, this church remains a gem in spite of earthquakes and the devastating bombardment by Allied planes in 1943. It was built between 1255 and 1277 as a shrine to St. Francis of Assisi. The church is known for its facade with a shallow porch and zigzag ornamentation. Its **rose window** ★ is one of the finest in Sicily, and its flamboyant **Gothic portal** ★ is from the original 13th-century structure.

After the 1943 bombardments, restorers set about to return the interior to its original medieval appearance, removing the overlay added by decorators who found the neoclassical style more alluring. The interior today is rather austere, with a trio of cylindrical piers and wide Gothic arches. But it still has the light, airy sense of space evocative of Franciscan churches erected in medieval times.

A few notable works of art survive. In the north aisle, fourth chapel on the left, note the magnificent **arch** ★★, superbly sculpted by Pietro de Bonitate and Francesco Laurana in 1468. This arch was the earliest major Renaissance work in Sicily. The sanctuary has beautiful **choir stalls** carved by Paolo and Giovanni Gili in 1520.

It's best to tie in a visit to this church with a look at the **Oratorio di San Lorenzo,** which is virtually next door.

Piazza di San Francesco d'Assisi, off Via Paternostro. ℂ **091-6162819.** Free admission. Mon–Fri 7am–noon and 4:30–6pm; Sat 9am–noon. Bus: 101 or 102.

Chiesa di Sant'Agostino   Even if you don't go inside, you won't miss much. The **facade** ★ is the most beautiful part of this church, which was financed in the 13th century by two prominent Palermo dynasties, the Chiaramonte and Sciafani families. Both the lava-mosaic-enclosed main portal and the distinctive rose window are in the Norman architectural style.

In contrast to the classic medieval front is the interior, which was reconstructed with baroque adornment centuries later. Here you'll see the last stuccoes of followers of the Serpotta School, completed between 1711 and 1729. You can still see Serpotta's mark, a *serpe* (Sicilian for "lizard"). The medieval cloister was originally built in the Catalán Gothic style, surrounding a central fountain. Lying at a corner of the cloister, the chapter house preserves many of its original 13th-century architectural features. Embedded into the wall of the stairs leading from the church's side entrance is an ancient Roman tomb.

Sant'Agostino lies adjacent to **Mercato di Capo,** a busy street market and one of Palermo's more intriguing sights.

Via S. Agostino. ℂ **091-584632.** Free admission. Mon–Sat 7am–noon and 4–5:30pm; Sun 7am–noon. Bus: 225.

La Gancia   Constructed in 1485 and dedicated to Santa Maria degli Angeli, this church stands next door to the Regional Gallery and can be easily visited at the same time. In the late Middle Ages, this was an enclave of the Franciscans. Much changed and altered over the centuries, the exterior of La Gancia contains a Gothic portal with a bas-relief on the arch. Inside, the nave is without aisles but contains a total of 16 side chapels and a marble floor in different hues.

The sculptor Giacomo Serpotta added baroque stucco decorations. The patterned **wooden ceiling** ★ is romantically painted with stars on a blue background. The chief treasure of La Gancia is a splendid **organ ★★** by Raffaele della Valle that dates from the late 1500s, making it the oldest in Palermo. At the marble pulpit, look for the **relief tondi of the *Annunciation,*** the work of Antonello Gagini in the 16th century. As a curiosity, note the **novice monk** ★ peering over the top of a cornice in the chapel to the left of the main altar.

Via Alloro 27. ℭ **091-6165221.** Free admission. Mon–Sat 9:30am–noon and 3–6pm; Sun 10am–12:30pm. Bus: Linea Gialla (Yellow Line).

San Giovanni degli Eremiti ★★   This is one of the most famous of all the Arabo-Norman monuments still standing in Palermo. It is certainly the most romantic building remaining from the heyday of Norman Palermo. Since 1132, this church, with its series of five red domes, has remained one of the most characteristic landmarks on the Palermo skyline. It is located on the western edge of the Albergheria district.

With an atmosphere appropriate for the recluse it honors, St. John of the Hermits (now deconsecrated), this is one of the most idyllic spots in Palermo. A medieval veil hangs heavily in the gardens, with their citrus blossoms and flowers, especially on a hot summer day as you wander around the cloister.

A single nave divides the simple interior into two bays, surmounted by a dome. A small cupola tops the presbytery. The right-hand apse is covered by one of the red domes. Surrounding the left-hand apse is a bell tower with pointed windows; it, too, is crowned by one of the church's red domes.

The small, late Norman **cloister ★**, with a Moorish cistern in the center, was part of the original Benedictine monastery that once stood here. It has little round arches supported by fine paired columns.

Via dei Benedettini 3. ℭ **091-6515019.** Admission 6€ ($7.80) adults, 3€ ($3.90) students, seniors, and children. Mon–Sat 9am–1pm and 3–7pm; Sun 9am–1pm. Bus: 109 or 318.

3 THE BEST OF THE PALACES

La Cuba ★   A less elaborate version of La Zisa (see below), and not as well-preserved, "Cuba" is a Sicilian derivation of the Arabic *Ka'aba,* meaning "cube" or "square-shaped structure." It has nothing to do with the Caribbean island of the same name. Built in 1180 by King William II, it was a kind of summer palace with royal gardens where the court came to escape the heat. A tall building with a rectangular plan, it is another magnificent piece of Fatimid architecture. The interior of the original structure had a hall that rose the full height of the building and was covered by a dome.

Giovanni Boccaccio made La Cuba a setting in his tales of *The Decameron.* After it fell from royal use, it was privately owned, becoming a leper colony. When the Bourbons came to power, they turned it into a cavalry barracks. Today, La Cuba is part of a military barracks. Visitors can enter, but not photograph, the military grounds.

Corso Calatafimi 100 (in the Tukory Barracks opposite Via Quarto dei Mille). ℭ **091-590299.** Admission 2€ ($2.60). Mon–Sat 9am–7pm; Sun 9am–1pm. Bus: 105, 304, 309, 339, 364, 365, or 389.

La Zisa ★   Only the shell of the former Moorish palace remains, and its claims to resemble the Alhambra in Granada are so far-fetched as to be ridiculous. But an aura of

Arabian Nights still lingers about the place. With a little imagination you can conjure up dancers who entertained the various sultans centuries ago.

Moorish craftsmen started the palace in 1166 under William I; it was finished in 1175 for his son, William II. La Zisa was the major building in a royal park that also embraced La Cuba. This beautifully landscaped park was called Genoard, meaning "terrestrial paradise," and was celebrated throughout Europe in the Middle Ages. The park was fenced in so that wild animals could roam about. Unfortunately, by the 16th century, the palace's heyday was all but a memory, and it was used as a depository for objects contaminated by the plague.

The structure you see today is high and compact. Two square towers flank the short sides of the castle. With its richness long stripped away, the interior is no longer remarkable, but you can still get some impression of the former sultan's palace. On the ground floor as you enter is the **Fountain Hall,** built on a cross plan. On the second floor is a good collection of Arabic art and artifacts.

Piazza Gugliemo il Buono (near Piazza Camporeale at the end of Via Dante). (**C**) 091-6520269. Admission 4.50€ ($5.85). Mon–Sat 9am–noon and 3–7pm; Sun 9am–1pm. Bus: 124.

Palazzo Mirto ★★   A visit to the nobleman's residence of the princes of Lanzi Filangeri is like a journey back in time. Though many of the other *palazzi* constructed at the same time lie rotting in the sun, this one is still relatively held together. Its history as a lavish abode dates back to the early 17th century; in 1982, the last surviving family member donated the palazzo to Sicily to preserve as a memorial to a vanished era.

Pause to take in the grace of the principal facade, with its double row of balconies, open to view on Via Lungarini. No other residence in Palermo can give you a better idea of a princely residence from the 18th and 19th centuries. As you enter the palazzo, look to the left, where magnificent **19th-century stables** ★ feature stalls and ornamental bronze horse heads. Take the fabulous red marble staircase up to the first floor, which is still decorated as it was when the last of the princes departed.

The first of the elegant drawing rooms is the **Sala degli Arazzi,** or tapestry hall, with mythological scenes that were painted by Giuseppe Velasco in 1804. Some of the salons open onto a patio garden with a flamboyant rococo fountain flanked by a pair of aviaries. Our favorite spot is the exquisite **Chinese sitting room** ★, with its *trompe l'oeil* ceiling, leather floor, and painted silk walls showing scenes from daily life. After dinner, the princes gathered here to smoke, talk, and play cards. As a note of curiosity, the next room has a series of remarkable Neapolitan plates from the 19th century, decorated with party costumes. At masked balls, each guest was assigned a plate that featured his or her costume. From the vestibule, you can visit another **smoking room** ★, this one painted and paneled with embossed leather. For a final bit of frippery, seek out the **Pompadour sitting room** ★, with a mosaic floor and silk walls embroidered with flowers, elegance so divine as to be decadent.

Via Merlo 2, off Piazza Marina. (**C**) 091-6167541. Admission 3€ ($3.90). Mon–Sat 9am–7pm; Sun 9am–1pm. Bus: 103, 105, or 139.

Villa Malfitano ★★   One of Palermo's great villa palaces, built in the Liberty style, sits within a spectacular **garden** ★★. The villa was constructed in 1886 by Joseph Whitaker—grandson of the famous English gentleman and wine merchant, Ingham, who moved to Sicily in 1806 and made a fortune producing Marsala wine. Whitaker had trees shipped to Palermo from all over the world to plant around his villa. These included such rare species as Dragon's Blood, an enormous banyan tree that happens to be the only one found in Europe. Local high society flocked here for lavish parties, and even British royalty visited. In World War II, Gen. George Patton temporarily stayed here as he planned the invasion of southern Italy. The villa today is lavishly furnished with antiques and artifacts from all over the world. The **Sala d'Estate (Summer Room)** is particularly stunning, with *trompe l'oeil* frescoes covering the walls and ceiling.

Via Dante 167. ℭ **091-6816133.** Admission 6€ ($7.80). Mon–Sat 9am–1pm. Bus: 103, 106, 108, 122, 134, 164, or 824.

4 OTHER GREAT MUSEUMS

Museo della Fondazione Mormino   This unusual, offbeat gallery is on the second floor of the Banco di Sicilia in the historic Villa Mormino. It displays the treasure-trove accumulated by banking interests over the years, ranging from artwork to Greek artifacts to rare coins. The collection of Italian majolica from the 16th century to the 18th century is among the finest in Italy; there is also a vast array of Greek vases. Look for the magnificent but tiny Etruscan mirror with a relief of Silenus. Of equal interest is the terra-cotta statue of a young boy, dating from the 3rd century B.C. The final section displays coins and medals, many from the 1200s.

Viale Libertà 52. ℭ **091-6085974.** Admission 4€ ($5.20) adults, 2€ ($2.60) children, students, and seniors. Mon–Fri 9am–1pm and 3–5pm; Sat 9am–1pm. Closed Aug. Bus: 101, 102, 702, or 704.

Museo Etnografico Pitré   This is the attic of old Sicily, a virtual time capsule of the way life used to be lived on the island. Nearly everything that it documents has been virtually swept away in the past half-century. Back in 1909, a great collector, Giuseppe Pitré, understood that the old ways were quickly vanishing, so he began to collect the tools of ordinary Sicilian life, accumulating some 4,000 objects that are today on exhibit at this museum.

Nothing is more evocative of old Sicily than the brightly painted, flamboyantly decorated **carts** ★, which Sicilians call *carretti*. A family's social standing was judged by its carts: The more elaborate and intricate the decoration, the more important the family. The museum also displays an intriguing collection of puppets and a vast array of handicrafts, ranging from ceramic holy water fonts to painted masks to 19th-century lace dresses.

Via Duca degli Abruzzi 1. ℭ **091-7404890.** Admission 5€ ($6.50) adults, free for children 17 and younger and seniors 61 and older. Tues–Sat 9am–7:30pm; Sun 9am–12:30pm. Bus: 101 to Stadio Partanna, then change to 614 or 645.

Museo Internazionale delle Marionette (International Puppet Museum) ★★ (Kids)   For those who are into puppets (or *pupi*, as the Sicilians say), this is the greatest museum of its kind in the world. In their shiny armor and with their stern expressions, these marionettes remain as an evocation of Norman Sicily, an era of legendary chivalry and troubadours. In the world of the puppet, the exploits of William the Bad (1120–66) and others live on, as do the legends of Charlemagne and the swashbuckling Saracen pirates. All of the puppets on display are handmade antiques, some of them centuries old, from Sicily as well as other parts of Italy. Most were used at one time in the *opera de pupi*, a local tradition fast dying out. The collection also includes puppets crafted in other parts of the world, notably Indonesia, India, and other countries from the Far East, as well

6

as the English "Punch and Judy." The most outstanding artisan represented here is Gaspara Canino, who achieved fame with his theater puppets in the 1800s.

Piazzetta Niscemi 1. (*) **091-328060**. Admission 5€ ($6.50) adults, 3€ ($3.90) children 11 and younger. Daily 9am–1pm; Wed–Fri 3:30–6:30pm. Bus: 103, 105, 139, or 225.

5 CITY LANDMARKS & TREASURES

Fontana Pretoria ★★   In the heart of Palermo's loveliest square, **Piazza Pretoria** ★★, stands this magnificent fountain, the work of the Florentine sculptor Francesco Camilliani in 1554 and 1555. It overlooks the facades of the two churches on the square, S. Caterina and S. Giuseppe dei Teatini. This fountain is hardly subtle: It's adorned with depictions of allegories, animal heads, nymphs, monsters, ornamental staircases and balustrades, and, of course, gods and goddesses comprising an encyclopedia of Mount Olympus. One of the statuettes guarding the ramps is Ceres, the classical patroness of Sicily, depicted with a horn of plenty. The fountain is floodlit at night, making it a 24-hour sight.

Quattro Canti ★   At the intersection of Via Vittorio Emanuele and Via Maqueda, the "Four Corners" of Palermo converge at a quartet of baroque palaces left over from the heyday of Spanish rule. The actual name of the square is Piazza Vigliena, although locals refer to it as Quattro Canti. Via Maqueda dates from the 1580s, when it converged with the ancient Via Càssaro, now called Vittorio Emanuele. The viceroy Vigliene ordered the construction of the four palaces at this crossroads, the buildings inspired by Rome's Quattro Fontane.

Each of the corners is decorated with a niche in three tiers. The first tier of each niche contains a fountain and a statue representing one of the four seasons. The second tier of each niche displays a statue of one of the Spanish viceroys. The third tier of each niche is dedicated to a statue of one of the patron saints of the city: Christina, Ninfa, Olivia, and Agata.

Unfortunately, Quattro Canti is no longer the meeting place of Palermitani as it was in the old days. Instead of creamy white buildings, think soot-blackened gray. And be careful when admiring the former beauty of the place, or you might be run down by a king of the road on a speeding Vespa.

6 PALERMO'S PARKS & GARDENS

The Arabs, a people who knew the joy of a green oasis, were the ones who introduced gardens into Palermo. The Normans extended the idea by creating parklands and

---

(Fun Facts   Shocking, Outrageous, Disgraceful!

When the **Fontana Pretoria** was first unveiled in 1575 at Piazza Pretoria, the outcry was so loud it could practically be heard across the city. Originally intended for a private Florentine villa and not a public square, the fountain is adorned with nude figures galore. In time, Palermitans learned to live with this "outrage," although they forever afterward referred to it as *Fontana della Vergogna,* or "Fountain of Shame."

summer palaces to escape the heat. Today, you can wander among gardens and greenery and encounter incredible banyan trees and other exotic plantings. If you have limited time to visit Palermo's parks, the most rewarding are Orto Botanico and Giardino Inglese, both described below.

GIARDINO GARIBALDI ★   In the very heart of Palermo, at Piazza Marina, lies this beautiful garden. Stunning **banyan trees ★★**, with their exposed, trunklike "aerial" roots, grace this park along with fig trees and towering palms.

In the 16th century, Aragonese weddings and military victories were celebrated at **Piazza Marina.** Sadly, it was also the site of public executions. After a long period of neglect, Piazza Marina has been spruced up and is once again a gathering place for residents. At night, it's an animated square with outdoor tables spilling from several pizzerie.

The largest palace on the square is **Palazzo Chiaramonte ★**, constructed in 1307 for one of Sicily's noblest and richest dynasties during the Aragonese era. Its most attractive feature can be seen on its facade—two tiers of delightful **windows ★★** with magnificent stone inlays. The palace is sometimes open for concerts.

GIARDINO INGLESE ★   The **English Gardens** lie to the north of the center, bordering Via della Libertà past Piazza Crispi. They were designed at the end of the 19th century. Always known as Palermo's prettiest little park, the gardens in the 1990s degenerated into a hangout for Palermo's drug-addicted population. Recently, however, the police have cracked down; unless conditions change, the park has been returned to its former self.

ORTO BOTANICO ★★   This is our favorite Palermo park, located at Via Abramo Lincoln 2B (✆ **091-6238241;** www.ortobotanico.palermo.it). These botanical gardens were laid out in 1795; the circular water lily pond from 1796 is still here. If for no other reason, make a visit just to see the amazing **banyan tree ★★**, the tallest and most impressive specimen in the garden. This fig tree with its "aerial" roots is more than 150 years old.

The garden is known to botanists the world over thanks to the richness and variety of its plant species, which range from gigantic tropical plants to spiny kapok trees with their bottle-shaped trunks. Among the curiosities are the *Bombacaceae* and *Chorisias* plants shipped here in the late 19th century from South America. These have swollen, prickly trunks and, in spring, bloom with beautiful pink flowers that turn into a strange fruit. Upon ripening, the fruit bursts open and drops its seed on the ground along with a thick hair "padding." Locals once harvested this padding and used it like horsehair.

Admission to Orto Botanico is 4€ ($5.20). It's open April to October daily 9am to 7pm; November to March Monday to Saturday 9am to 5pm, Sunday 9am to 2pm. Take bus no. 139, 211, 221, 224, 226, or 227. See below for a description of **Villa Giulia,** the park next door to the Orto Botanico.

PARCO DELLA FAVORITA   Reached by going 2.8km (1³/₄ miles) north of Palermo along Viale Diana is this large park at the foot of Monte Pellegrino. Parco della Favorita was part of an estate acquired in 1799 by Ferdinand of Bourbon, who came here after he was driven out of Naples by Napoleonic troops. He ordered that the land be laid out according to his rather Victorian taste. In time, it became the ruler's private hunting estate.

The fantastic **Palazzina Cinese (Chinese Palace)** built for Ferdinand is still standing. It was in this exotically decorated palace that the king, along with his wife, Maria Carolina, entertained Horatio Nelson and Lady Hamilton.

Note the marble fountain with a statue of Hercules. This is a copy of the celebrated *Farnese Hercules* that the king tried to abduct from Naples. Instead of the real thing, he got a copy.

In the 18th century, many noble families built summer villas around the park to escape the intense heat of the city. The most famous of these is **Villa Niscemi,** Piazza Niscemi (ⓒ **091-7494801**), which is also a venue for occasional cultural events. The villa is sometimes open on Sundays 9am to 1pm; call ahead to confirm.

VILLA BONANNO ★ Behind the Palazzo dei Normanni lies Villa Bonanno, among the most beautiful public gardens of Palermo. Enter from Piazza della Vittoria. The city added palm trees in 1905, making the park look like an oasis in North Africa. Note the roof covering the ruins of a trio of ancient Roman houses, the only such artifacts of their kind left in Palermo. Villa Bonanno adjoins Piazza del Parlamento, with its mammoth statue of Philip V of the House of Bourbon.

VILLA GIULIA Next door to the Orto Botanico, also opening onto Via Abramo Lincoln, is this Italianate oasis, created in 1778 and enlarged in 1866. This was the city's first public park and was named for its patron, Giulia Avalos Guevara, the wife of the ruling viceroy. Goethe came this way in 1787 and had much praise for the garden, which is also called "La Flora." Its beautiful trees and flowers are in better shape than the monuments. The best-known statue is called *Genius of Palermo,* by Marabitti.

7 ESPECIALLY FOR KIDS

Palermo is not the world's most child-friendly city. Because of roaring, dangerous traffic, it is difficult to walk the city's streets, especially the narrow ones, without constantly keeping an eye out for your *bambini.*

There is one attraction that kids adore in Palermo, however, and that's the **Museo Internazionale delle Marionette** (**International Puppet Museum,** p. 113). Sicilians call their famous puppets *pupi,* and they are truly works of folkloric art. Delightful puppet shows are staged here on Fridays between 5 and 6pm. These shows, costing from 5€ to 6€ ($6.50–$7.80) per ticket, are staged daily at 5:30pm, September through June only.

Each family who visits Palermo has to decide whether to take children to the **Catacombe dei Cappuccini** (p. 104), where mummified bodies and skeletons of some 8,000 Palermitans are on view. Young children in particular may be frightened by these ghoulish sights, which include a baby girl who died in 1920, her corpse amazingly lifelike even today.

Away from the traffic, noise, and pollution of Palermo, the city's public parks offer refreshing interludes for families. Especially inviting is the landscaped oasis of the **Orto Botanico,** or botanical gardens (p. 115).

Another delight for families is a trip up to **Monte Pellegrino** (p. 128), a mountain that looms over north Palermo. With its greenery and parkland, the 600m (1,969-ft.) mountain evokes Yosemite. Keep in mind that the park is likely to be crowded on Sundays with Sicilian families in search of a respite from Palermo's smog.

Finally, if you're in Palermo on a summer day, you might want to escape the city altogether and head for **Mondello Lido,** with its long, sandy beaches. Even on a summer night, this is the place to be; many families can be seen walking along the water and ducking into one of the pizzerie when the kids get hungry. For more on Mondello Lido, see p. 136.

START: San Giovanni degli Eremiti.
FINISH: Piazza Marina.
TIME: 3 to 3¹/₃ hours. (Interior visits, of course, will consume far more time.)
BEST TIME: Daily from 8am to noon and 3 to 6pm, when many of the museums and churches are open.
WORST TIME: During the lunch doldrums, from noon to 3pm, and after dark.

Begin your tour by the iron gates that protect the palm-shaded garden surrounding:

❶ San Giovanni degli Eremiti

The best known of all the Arabo-Norman monuments of Palermo, San Giovanni, at Via dei Benedettini, is a short block from roaring traffic arteries difficult to navigate. (*Tip:* To avoid walking through such heavy traffic, many visitors opt to take a taxi directly to the beginning of this walking tour.) Five typically Arab domes reveal the origins of the Moorish craftsmen who constructed this monastery for Roger II in 1132. It honors St. John of the Hermits. The church's tranquil, beautiful gardens are devoted to such species as the pomegranate and the rose. The gardens lead to the ruins of the original Benedictine monastery that once stood here, a structure built in 581 for Pope Gregory the Great.

After a visit, walk north toward the sound of roaring traffic coming from the nearby Piazza del Pinta. En route to the piazza, you'll pass a wall niche dedicated to Maria Addolorata, which is usually embellished with plants and fresh flowers.

Cross to the opposite side of Piazza del Pinta. From here, you'll see the severely dignified stone archway pierced with formidable doors, leading to:

❷ Palazzo dei Normanni

The chief attraction of Palermo, this mammoth palace and artistic treasure was constructed by the Arabs in the 11th century over the ruins of a Roman fort. Over time it was expanded and turned into the royal residence of Roger II, the Norman king. Much of the look of the present palace is from alterations it received from the 16th to the 17th century. The chief attraction

inside is **Cappella Palatina,** a magnificent example of the Arabo-Norman artistic genius.

Exit from the compound's stately entrance gate (the same one you entered), walk about 50 paces downhill, and then turn left onto Via del Castione. You'll have trouble seeing a street sign at first.

From here, you'll skirt the Norman Palace's massive and sharply angled foundations. After two narrow and claustrophobic blocks, climb the first set of granite steps rising upward from Via del Castione's left side. This will lead you into a verdant garden, called:

❸ Villa Bonanno

Imbued with the scent of jasmine and oleander, this public park separates the rear entrance of the Palazzo dei Normanni from the Duomo compound you'll be visiting soon. Dotting the garden are monuments and effigies erected in honor of such Sicilian patriots as Caetano Bucceri and Pietro Gullo. If it's a hot day, this is an idyllic place to cool off.

Walk through the garden, exiting at its opposite end, which will lead you to:

❹ Palazzo Arcivescovile

Lying across the busy Via Bonello, a street of heavy traffic, only a portal survives from the palace constructed here in 1460. The present structure is from the 18th century. Originally the Museo Diocesano was founded here, housing artifacts from the cathedral and other works of art from churches about to be demolished. Since it's been closed for many years, the palace can be appreciated only from its outside.

As a slight detour from this walking tour, stroll down a narrow lane behind Palazzo Arcivescovile to the **Oratorio dei**

SS. Pietro e Paolo. The interior contains stuccoes by Giacomo Serpotta and Domenico Castelli, plus a ceiling fresco by Filippo Tancredi. We've been able to see the interior of this oratory only one time over many years' worth of visits; it's been closed otherwise.

On the other side of Palazzo Arcivescovile on Via Bonello is the 16th-century **Loggia dell'Incoronazione,** with ancient columns and capitals that were incorporated into the present structure. The kings of Sicily used to "display" themselves to their subjects here following a coronation.

After viewing the palace, head east along the major artery, Corso Vittorio Emanuele. The sidewalk at this point becomes very narrow, barely passable, as cars roar by. The pavement will open within a short time onto a sweeping view of the:

⑤ Duomo

At Piazza di Cattedrale, right off Corso Vittorio Emanuele, the cathedral of Palermo, dedicated to Our Lady of the Assumption, was built on the site of an early Christian basilica, which was later turned into a mosque by Arab rulers. Although launched in the 12th century, the cathedral has seen many architects and much rebuilding over the centuries. The cathedral today is a hodgepodge of styles, its baroque cupola added in the late 18th century.

After a look or a visit, continue east along Corso Vittorio Emanuele on narrow sidewalks until you come to:

⑥ Biblioteca Centrale della Regione Siciliana

Once a Jesuit college called Collegio Massimo dei Gesuiti, this building is today the home of Palermo's main public library, providing shelter for more than half a million volumes and many ancient manuscripts, including several from the 15th and 16th centuries. A double arcaded courtyard is its architectural centerpiece. It is entered by the portal of the adjacent Chiesa di S. Maria della Grotta.

Continue to head east along Corso Vittorio Emanuele until you come to the intersection of Via SS. Salvatore. If it's open, you can duck into the dark, shadowy recesses of:

⑦ Chiesa SS. Salvatore

Palermo has far greater churches than this, so feel free to settle for just a look at its facade. Built in 1682 by Paolo Amato, the church was severely damaged during the 1943 Allied air raids, but it has since been restored—enough so that its oval interior is frequently a venue for weddings.

Our eastward trek continues along Corso Vittorio Emanuele to a point where the street widens into a square, the Piazza Bologni. It's time to:

TAKE A BREAK
The tables of **Liberty Bar,** Corso Vittorio Emanuele 350 (☏ **091-328929**), spread out onto the square. Here you can have your fill of excellent espresso or cappuccino, delicious ice cream as only the Italians know how to make it, and even sandwiches or a pizza.

After a refueling stop, continue east for a short distance until you come to:

⑧ Chiesa San Giuseppe dei Teatini

Near Quattro Canti (see below), this lavishly decorated church was built by the Theatine congregation. The interior has a dancing baroque spirit, although the facade, not completed until 1844, is along more severe neoclassical lines. The cupola of the church is adorned with majolica tiles. If you go inside (hours are Mon–Sat 8:45–11:15am and 5–7pm; Sun 8:30am–1pm), you'll find a two-aisle nave. Flanking it are towering columns resting under a frescoed ceiling, holding up walls covered with a marble polychrome decoration. The main altar is constructed of semiprecious gems, and the chapels are lavishly frescoed with stucco decoration. The church was designed by Giacomo Besio of Genoa (1612–45).

At this point of the walking tour, you are in the very heart of Old Palermo at the famous:

EXPLORING PALERMO

6

WALKING TOUR: OLD PALERMO

1 San Giovanni degli Eremiti
2 Palazzo dei Normanni
3 Villa Bonanno
4 Palazzo Arcivescovile
5 Duomo
6 Biblioteca Centrale
  della Regione Siciliana
7 Chiesa SS. Salvatore
  Liberty Bar

8 Chiesa San Giuseppe dei Teatini
9 Quatro Canti (Four Corners)
10 Piazza Pretoria
11 Chiesa San Cataldo
12 Chiesa della Martorana
  Pizzeria Bellini
13 Chiesa San Francesco di Assisi
14 Palazzo Mirto
15 Piazza Marina

Let the Horse Lead the Way

Consider hiring one of the horse-drawn carriages that line up on the Via Maqueda at Piazza Pretoria. A 60-minute ride for up to four passengers costs 60€ ($78). In a style that's romantic, nostalgic, or corny, depending on your point of view, it will haul you around for a view of the city's street life and a fast overview, from the outside, of monumental Palermo. For more information on carriage tours from a driver we find cooperative, call ℂ **380-5097646.**

❾ Quattro Canti (Four Corners)

Corso Vittorio Emanuele intersects with Via Maqueda, the latter street a famous piece of Palermitano civic planning, carved out of the surrounding neighborhood in the 16th century by the Spanish viceroy.

Architecturally, Four Corners is a melting pot of Arabo-Norman magnificence, Palermitan baroque, and the work of craftsmen of the Middle Ages. Each sculpted angle of the Four Corners celebrates seasons, a patron saint, or a Spanish viceroy.

Directly east of this "crossroads" of Palermo lies:

❿ Piazza Pretoria

This lovely square is Palermo's most famous. Its beautiful but controversial fountain, originally intended for a Tuscan villa, is bedecked with nude statues and mythological monsters—thus, it was called **Fontana della Vergogna,** or "Fountain of Shame," by outraged churchgoers. **San Giuseppe dei Teatini** is the church directly to the west; the eastern end of the square is flanked by **Chiesa Santa Catarina.** On the south axis stands **Palazzo Pretorio,** the city hall. Note the plaque on the front of the building commemorating Garibaldi's 1860 triumph, ending the Bourbon reign in Sicily.

Now walk to the southern edge of the Piazza Pretoria and go through the narrow gap between City Hall and the Church of Santa Catarina. A vista over the Piazza Bellini will open up before you. At its far end rise two of the most distinctive churches in Palermo, the first called:

⓫ Chiesa San Cataldo

Standing side by side with Chiesa della Martorana (see below), this is one of two Norman churches in Palermo. The church, with its rose-colored cupolas, was founded in 1154 by Maio da Bari, the despised emir of William I. After a checkered history—the church was turned into a post office in the 19th century—San Cataldo today is the seat of the Knights of the Holy Sepulchre.

Next door to San Cataldo is:

⓬ Chiesa della Martorana

With its handsome Norman bell tower, this is the more intriguing of the two churches. It is the loveliest Greek Church remaining in Sicily. It was founded in 1143 by George of Antioch, called Roger II's "Emir of Emirs." Regrettably, the linear symmetry of the original Norman church is today covered by a baroque facade.

After this intense spate of churchgoing, you'll probably think it's time to:

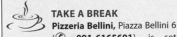

TAKE A BREAK
Pizzeria Bellini, Piazza Bellini 6 (ℂ **091-6165691**), is set directly at the base of the Church of San Cataldo, with a pleasant terrace that's shielded from the dust and congestion of the surrounding neighborhood by an evergreen hedge and latticework barrier. This is the kind of cafe where you almost fall into the chairs, then slug back a half liter of liquid refreshment. It doubles as a restaurant, in case you want a full meal, but most participants on this walking tour opt for gelato, a coffee, or a drink. Closed Mondays.

To resume the tour, retrace your steps along Via Maqueda north to Quattro Canti. Once at the Four Corners, continue east along Corso Vittorio Emanuele on the street's right-hand side. Here the neighborhood grows increasingly battered, commercial, and decrepit. In about 4 minutes, turn right onto Via Alessandro Paternostro, a narrow street 1 short block after Vicolo Madonna del Cassaro. Walk uphill along Via Alessandro Paternostro through a commercial section of shops. In less than 4 minutes, note the intricately carved Romanesque facade of the:

⑬ Chiesa San Francesco d'Assisi

This is one of our favorite churches in Palermo, thanks to its dignified simplicity and unusual combination of Romanesque and baroque detailing, plus the sense you get that it's still very much involved in the day-to-day life of this ancient parish. First constructed in the 13th century, it was destroyed by Frederick II after he was excommunicated by the pope. A new church was constructed and completed in 1277, although it's seen much alteration over the years. A 1943 Allied bombing didn't help matters, either.

From the square directly in front of the church (Piazza di San Francesco d'Assisi), head east on the narrow, unmarked street on the right-hand side of the church as you face it. Walk 1½ short blocks until you reach:

⑭ Palazzo Mirto

This is your greatest opportunity in Old Palermo to visit a palace from yesterday and to see how a Sicilian noble family lived. Of the many other palaces in the neighborhood, most are closed to the public and still not restored. Palazzo Mirto miraculously remains as it was, with its original furnishings. It dates from the 18th century, having been built over earlier structures that went back to the 15th century.

After a visit, walk a few steps to the west into the broad 19th-century vistas of:

⑮ Piazza Marina

This is the largest square in Palermo. Its most significant architectural monument is **Palazzo Steri-Chiaramonte,** constructed in 1307 by one of Sicily's most influential noble families. The palace was built in a Gothic style with Arabo-Norman influences. In the middle of Piazza Marina is the **Giardino Garibaldi,** a beautiful park where you may want to wind down and enjoy the splashing waters of its central fountain.

---

8 CITY MARKETS & SHOPPING

Palermo is like a grand shopping bazaar. You'll find a little bit of everything here, including boutiques of high fashion. Many shoppers seek out the expert craftspeople known for their skill in producing any number of goods, especially beautiful coral jewelry. Embroidered fabrics are another specialty item. Some visitors come to Palermo just to purchase ceramics.

Palermo markets (see below) are the most colorful in southern Italy. At these markets, all the bounty of Sicily—fruits, vegetables, fish—is elegantly displayed. Since it is unlikely you will be staying in accommodations with kitchen facilities, the markets are mainly for sightseeing, although they do offer an array of clothing and crafts as well.

For the best shopping, head for **Via della Libertà,** north of the city's medieval core within a 19th-century residential neighborhood of town houses and mid-20th-century apartment buildings that evoke some of the more upscale residential sections of Barcelona.

Within this same neighborhood, **Via Principe di Belmonte** is an all-pedestrian thoroughfare with many hip and elegant shops, as well as fashionable cafes such as Spinnato.

(Moments) Sugar Shock

You'll find traditional fruit-filled tarts as well as *cassata Siciliana* (tarts with a ricotta-based filling) at **Fratelli Magrì,** Via Isidoro Carini 42 (© **091-584788**). The shop also makes other types of sweets, as well as gelato in the summer, but come here for the authentic high-calorie pastries. **I Peccatucci di Mamma Andrea,** Via Principe di Scordia 67 (© **091-334835**), a celebration of local confections, will tempt you with the bounty of Sicily's traditional desserts. The best examples are pralines, *torrone, panetoni,* segments of fruit dripping with Sicilian honey, marzipan, and an age-old specialty known as *ghirlande di croccantini* (hazelnut torte). Get ready for sugar shock and lots of local color. Bus: 122 or 124.

The two other principal shopping streets in the old town are **Via Roma** and **Via Maqueda.**

Monday morning is the worst time to shop, as nearly all stores are closed. Otherwise, general shopping hours are Monday to Friday 9am to 1pm and 4 to 7 or 7:30pm, Saturday 4 to 8pm.

ART

Galleria Caravello   One of Palermo's largest and busiest galleries occupies the ground floor of a modern apartment building near the northern terminus of the Via di Libertà. It sells empty picture frames (the massively ornate and gilded kind) as well as contemporary-looking landscapes that will evoke Sicily and its vistas long after your return home. Via Marchese Ugo 64–70. © **091-6251736.** Bus: 101, 102, 104, 106, 107, or 306.

BOOKS

Libreria Altro Quando   This is Palermo's most visible counterculture bookstore, with a definite allegiance to things revolutionary, socialist, feminist, gay-liberated, and ecologically and politically conscious. Gay books tend to be shunted off to a mezzanine in back, which is accessible via a flight of hard-to-navigate stairs. Via Vittorio Emanuele 145. © **091-6114732.** Bus: 103, 104, 105, 108, 110, 139, 224, 225, 389, or 824.

Libreria Kalós   From a cool, contemplative hideaway within a walled compound in the heart of Palermo's well-heeled Via Libertà district, this shop sells books, holds poetry readings, sponsors chamber-music recitals, and publishes some of the finest books in the world on Sicily's artistic and architectural heritage. Come here for books (mostly in Italian, less frequently in English or French) and insight into the arts and letters of this distinct southern Italian city. Via XX Settembre 56B. © **091-322380.** Bus: 101 or 107.

CERAMICS

De Simone   For majolica-style stoneware, this old favorite, a family-run business, has been producing quality ware since the 1920s. It also offers some of the most tasteful ceramics and finest tiles in Palermo. Most tiles are painted with scenes of Sicilian country life, including seascapes and bird-filled landscapes. Also for sale are porcelain dinner and tea services, along with ceramic chandeliers. While visiting the shop, you can inquire about visits to the factory at Via Lanza di Scalea 960 (© **091-6711005**), open Monday through Friday from 8am to 5pm. Via Gaetano Daita 13B. © **091-584876.** Bus: 103, 106, 108, or 122.

Laboratorio Italiano ★ This is the sales outlet for the most dynamic and creative ceramic artists in Palermo. Set in the fashionable Via Libertà neighborhood, it sells inventories based on 19th-century Sicilian models, but always with a sophisticated, modern twist. The result is a shop that's often visited by owners of nearby beach houses and condos who stock up on jardinieres, planters, lace-edged bowls and platters, and holders for votive candles. We love the wall-mounted receptacles for holy water, priced at 40€ ($52); they show Madonnas, some of them black, "in conversation." Prices are lower than you'd expect. Via Principe di Villafranca 42. ✆ **091-320282.** Bus: 103.

DEPARTMENT STORES

Barone Confezioni-Abbigliamento-Corredi In business for some 6 decades, this is the best department store in Palermo. Its focus is mainly on high-end merchandise, with lots of popular labels in evidence. The store carries sportswear and casual wear as well as more formal suits and dresses. Women's fashions are found on the main floor, with departments for kids and men one floor down. Via Abramo Lincoln 146. ✆ **091-6165626.** Bus: 139, 211, 221, 224, 226, 227, 231, 234, 250, or 971.

ECCLESIASTICAL OBJECTS

Postolato Liturgico For devout Catholics visiting from around the world, this store represents a treasure-trove of church-related finery (or iconography, depending on your point of view). It's staffed by an international bevy of nuns, all in white habits, all of them members of the *Paoline Piedice* (Pious Disciples of the Divine Master) order. Inventories—some of them incredibly valuable—are usually displayed behind glass in a style that may remind you of a museum. You'll see chalices, monstrances, and medallions—some made of gold, others encrusted with gemstones—as well as some of the most gorgeous liturgical robes in Italy. Corso Vittorio Emanuele 454. ✆ **091-6512467.** Bus: 103, 104, 105, 108, 110, or 118.

FABRICS

Giuseppe Gramuglia Traditional Sicilian decor—at least that inspired by the late 19th century—usually involves lots of fabric, in the form of rich-looking upholsteries and heavy curtains that block out the intense sunlight. If you want to duplicate this look in your own home, consider a visit to this store. Set at the corner of Palermo's most fashionable shopping street (Via Principe di Belmonte), it contains hundreds of bolts of fabric, in every conceivable pattern. It also sells decorative ropes, fringes, and tassels. Via Roma 412–414 (at Via Principe di Belmonte). ✆ **091-583262.** Bus: 104, 107, 122, 124, 224, or 225.

FASHIONS FOR MEN

Carieri & Carieri This is a store for serious menswear shoppers—and if you express the slightest interest, a member of its staff is likely to "adopt" you, leading you to selections in your size and along a wide spectrum of fashion-related statements. The only thing wrong with this store is its intimidatingly large size, which might confuse you (or delight you) when you first walk in. The staff is about as upscale and attentive as any you're likely to find in Palermo, and if there aren't a lot of other customers, they're likely to descend upon you, en masse, to attend to your needs. The selection of suits and office wear is very extensive—the best and classiest displays in town. Via Enrico Parisi 4. ✆ **091-321846.** Bus: 101, 102, 104, 106, 107, 306, or 309.

(Moments) **Sampling the Local Vino**

Sicily's hot climate and volcanic soil nurture a wealth of vineyards, many of which produce simple table wines. Of the better vintages, the best known is **Marsala,** a sweet dessert wine produced in both amber and ruby tones. One name that evokes years of winemaking traditions, thanks to the winery's skill at producing Cerasucio di Vittoria and Moscato di Pantelleria, is **Corvo Duca di Salaparuta,** a 19th-century winery in the hills above Palermo. For information, contact the **Casa Vinicola Duca di Salaparuta,** Via Nazionale, SS113, Casteldaccia, 90014 Palermo (© **091-953988**). If you'd like to visit, call ahead to make an appointment and get directions. *Note:* This winery produces the Moscato di Pantelleria wine but not Marsala, which is produced only in Marsala.

FASHIONS FOR WOMEN

Le Gi di Valentino   Don't be fooled into thinking that the evening gown you buy here will be genuine (actually created by Valentino). What you'll get instead is a sense of fun, obscene amounts of silk taffeta arranged into tarty-looking flounces, and a genuine whimsy that might look fetchingly fabulous at a cocktail party back home. Clothes here manage to look "wenchy" and elegant at the same time, a real accomplishment if you're brave enough to wear them. Via Ruggiero Settimo 99–101. © **091-324197.** Bus: 101, 102, 103, or 124.

Motivi   The minimalist and often highly revealing clothing sold here might not be appropriate for any woman of a certain age, unless she's terribly pulled together, sexy, and well preserved. But if you're adventurous or merely curious about what's going on design-wise with Sicilian 20-somethings, take a look. The clothing is appropriate for the beach, for the disco, or for merely riding around in cars with boys. The venue is trendy—perhaps too much so—and, at its best, fun. Piazza Ruggiero VII 1–4. © **091-322158.** Bus: 101, 102, 103, or 124.

FOOD

I Peccatucci di Mamma Andrea ★   This small-scale boutique contains one of the most diverse collections of gastronomic abundance in Palermo, each item artfully wrapped into the kind of gift that will delight recipients back home. Elegant bottles contain liqueurs distilled from herbs or fruits you might never have thought suitable, such as almonds, basil, myrtle, fennel, figs, and rose petals. Jams and honeys showcase the agrarian bounty and aromas of Sicily. There is also an array of *peccatucci* ("small sins")—utterly delightful candies made from almond paste, sugar, and liqueur—that resemble fruit or sleeping cherubs. Via Principe di Scordia 67. © **091-334835.** Bus: 101, 102, 103, 104, 107, 122, 124, 224, or 225.

FRAMES

Meli   These family owners have worked for more than a century turning out hand-crafted tortoiseshell frames. They also specialize in reproductions of antique picture frames made of coral, along with jewel cases, stylish prints, etchings, and engravings from the 16th to the 19th centuries. Via Dante 294. © **091-6824213.** Bus: 103, 106, 108, or 122.

JEWELRY

Di Bella This is one of the better jewelry stores of Palermo, operating in a location near the old Capo marketplace. Top names in watches are featured along with tastefully styled rings, necklaces, and bracelets. Via Carini 22. © **091-320818.** Bus: 104 or 107.

Fiorentino A Palermo tradition since 1890, this jeweler is still going strong, offering both traditional and contemporary designs. The pieces are exquisite; there's also a vast array of gift items, silverware, and watches. The fashionable set along Via Libertà shop here. Via Roma 315. © **091-6047111.** Bus: 101, 102, 104, 106, 107, 303, 603, 702, 704, 721, 731, or 806.

LINENS

Frette This company's wares are highly prized by those who favor high-thread-count sheets and butter-soft linens. Frette has been the royal purveyors of linens to everyone from the pope to the former royal families of Italy. It offers sheets, tablecloths, towels, bedspreads, nightgowns, curtains, and tapestries, among other items. Via Ruggero Settimo 12. © **091-585166.** Bus: 101, 102, 103, or 124.

MARKETS

The Muslims were active traders, and Palermo's markets, which spill over into narrow alleys shaded by colorful awnings, still have an Arabic feel. Nothing else connects you with local life more than a visit to a bustling Palermo market.

The best, most famous market in Palermo is **La Vucciria ★★**. In Sicilian dialect, *vucciria* means "hubbub" or "voices," and that's what you'll hear here. The market spills onto the narrow side streets of Piazza San Domenico, off Via Roma between Corso Vittorio Emanuele and the San Domenico church. This is one of Europe's great casbahlike markets, with mountains of food ranging from fresh swordfish steaks to all sorts of meat and recently harvested produce, reflecting the bounty of the Sicilian countryside. The array of such items as wild fennel, long-stemmed artichokes, blood oranges, and giant octopus will astound you. This market trades Monday through Saturday until 2pm. Try to go before 10am, when it's at its most frenetic and colorful. The markets described below keep roughly the same hours.

(Moments) Feasting at the Markets

We like to visit the markets not only to look at the fabulous produce, but also to enjoy some of the tastiest snacks in Sicily. It's a great way to have lunch as you graze from stall to stall.

Some visitors stroll along while munching chopped **boiled octopus** (*purpu* in Sicilian) and delectable, freshly cooked **artichokes.** Naturally, there's plenty of **fresh bread** and luscious **vine-ripened fruit** as well.

You can also purchase absolutely delicious **panelle** (chickpea fritters) or **calzoni** (deep-fried meat- or cheese-filled pockets of dough). If you have an adventurous palate, dig in to a roll filled with beef spleen or tripe, called **pani cu' la meuza.** These pani are often topped with fresh ricotta or a velvety cheese known as *caciocavallo.* Hot sauce is sprinkled on at the last moment.

If you're seized with market fever, you can also visit **Mercato di Capo,** a large street market that captures some of the spirit of the city's Saracen past. This market sprawls around the area of Chiesa di Sant'Agostino. Clothing stalls flank the streets of Via S. Agostino and Via Bandiera; the items here tend to be cheap and poorly made. More interesting is the food section off Via Volturno, which spreads along Via Beati Paoli and Via Porta Carini. The most colorful part of this market converges around Piazza Beati Paoli. The stalls wind toward the old gate, Porta Carini, which used to be a part of the city wall surrounding Palermo.

The third great market of Palermo is **Ballarò,** in the Albergheria district, roughly between Piazza Carmine leading to Piazza Casa Professa and Piazza S. Chiara. This is mainly a food market, with mountains of fruits and vegetables along with fishmongers and hawkers of discount clothing.

MILITARY UNIFORMS

Romano Luigi, Sartoria Civile e Militare   This shop, along with three or four shops on either side, specializes in the uniforms and paraphernalia used by members of the Italian police and *Guardia Civile.* Get Michael Jackson on the phone. Ironically set directly across the street from shops that specialize in church vestments for the Catholic liturgy, it's a military fetishist's dream. Not everything can be (officially) sold to a layperson (such as some aspects of an official police officer's uniform), but the selection is intriguing for anyone who has ever completed a stint in the armed forces. Corso Vittorio Emanuele 453–455. ✆ **091-324457.** Bus: 104, 105, 108, 110, 118, 139, 224, 225, or 389.

PERFUMES & COSMETICS

Limoni   When it comes to toiletries and cosmetics for both women and men, Palermo shops don't get much better than this. Affiliated with one of Italy's most popular chains, this store features a wide array of scents. Many items are suitable as gifts. Corso Tukory 222. ✆ **091-6514324.** Bus: 103, 234, 246, or 318.

9 PALERMO AFTER DARK

For such a large city, Palermo has a dearth of nightlife. In the hot summer months, the townspeople parade along the waterfront of **Mondello Lido** to cool off (p. 136). Although they are improving somewhat, many Palermo areas with bars and taverns (such as La Kalsa or Albergheria) are not safe for walking around at night. And some of the bars and taverns in the medieval core of Palermo have the life span of sickly butterflies. The safest places for drinking, making conversation, and meeting like-minded companions are the many bars in the deluxe and first-class hotels. They are also the most sanitary.

The liveliest squares at night—and the relatively safest because lots of people are here—are **Piazza Castelnuovo** and **Piazza Verdi.** Another "safe zone" is a pedestrian strip flanked by bars and cafes, many with sidewalk tables, along **Via Principe di Belmonte,** between Via Roma and Via Ruggero Settimo. Some of these bars have live pianists in summer. If you like the sound of things, drop in for a glass of wine or a beer.

If you're interested in the arts and cultural venues, stop by the tourist office (p. 33) and pick up a copy of *Agenda,* which documents cafes and other venues offering live music in summer.

THE ARTS   Palermo is a cultural center of some note, with an opera and ballet season running from November to July. The principal venue for cultural presentations is the

(Finds) The Local Nerve Center

While in Palermo, you might want to make **Kursaal Kalhesa,** Foro Umberto I 21 (© **091-6167630**), your official headquarters. It's a beehive of activity and a great way to meet locals, most of whom are young and fluent in English. Situated in a restored palace near Piazza Marina, this is where Sicily meets New York's SoHo. An attractive crowd congregates at the bar, which is flanked by discreetly lit stone walls and a bookstore-cum-lounge. You can read English-language newspapers, listen to live music, get online at the Internet cafe, or pick up tourist info at the travel agency.

For serious eating, head upstairs for Sicilian and Tunisian fare. The chef's delectable dishes are served in a cavernous room decorated with blue and white tiles; in warm weather, there's terrace dining. The best dishes include artichoke pasta with a radicchio cream sauce, lemon-flavored swordfish with shrimp, and the famous lentils grown on the island of Ustica and flavored with squid ink, a local delicacy. Main courses cost from 8€ to 20€ ($10–$26).

The Kursaal building is open Tuesday through Sunday from 11:30am to 2pm and 4pm to 1am. As one local told us, "It's where I always go to hang my hat, even if people don't wear hats anymore."

restored **Teatro Massimo** ★★, Via Maqueda (© **800-907080**), across from the Museo Archeologico. It boasts the largest indoor stage in Europe after the Paris Opera House. Francis Ford Coppola shot the climactic opera scene here for *The Godfather: Part III*. The theater was built between 1875 and 1897 in a neoclassical style, and reopened after a restoration in 1997 to celebrate its 100th birthday. During the **Festival di Verdura,** from late June to mid-August, many special presentations, most often with international performers, are presented here. Ticket prices range from 10€ to 102€ ($13–$133). The box office is open Tuesday to Sunday 10am to 3pm. *Note:* The Teatro Massimo can be visited Tuesday to Sunday 10am to 3pm. Visits cost 5€ ($6.50). Bus: 101, 102, 103, 104, 107, 122, or 225.

If you have only 1 night for theater in Palermo, make it the Teatro Massimo. However, **Politeama Garibaldi,** Piazza Ruggero Settimo (© **091-6053315**), is also grandiose, and it, too, presents a wide season of operatic and orchestral performances. Again, the tourist office will have full details on what is being performed at the time of your visit. Bus: 101, 102, 103, or 124.

CAFES We like to start off an evening by heading to the century-old **Caffè Mazzara,** Via Generale Magliocco 15 (© **091-321443**), to sample wonderful ice cream, sip rich coffee, or try heady Sicilian wine. You'll run into us hanging out at the espresso bar and pastry shop on the street level. The cafe is open daily 7:30am to 11pm. Bus: 101, 102, or 103.

DANCE CLUBS Palermo's most popular dance clubs lie in the city's commercial center, although one good one is in north Palermo. The city's main club is **Candelai,** Via Candelai 65 (© **091-327151**). Mainstream rock blasts throughout the night in this crowded complex of gyrating 20-year-olds. The club is open Friday to Sunday 8pm, with no set closing time. There is no cover, but it is necessary to buy a membership card (valid for a month) for 15€ ($20).

PUBS One of our favorite pubs, **Nashville,** Via Belgio 4A (*©* **091-522980**), is a good place to spend an evening in fun company. You can order snacks or dessert here along with your drinks. A backdrop of rock, pop, or disco livens up the atmosphere. The pub attracts a mainly young crowd nightly 8pm to 1:30am. Bus: 100, 164, 529, 544, or 616.

Villa Niscemi, Piazza Niscemi 55 (*©* **091-6880820**), has a rustic bar, plus overflowing sidewalk tables in summer. The pub also has musical instruments; if you're the master of one (or even if you're not), you can play an instrument and hopefully entertain the patrons. Live music is featured on Fridays. A crowd of mostly 25- to 45-year-olds patronizes the joint, open daily 7pm to 3am. Closed Mondays in July and August. Bus: 614, 615, 645, or 837.

GAY & LESBIAN Gay and lesbian bars in Palermo are as scarce as a virgin at the Playboy mansion; most gay encounters occur on the streets, in cafes, and around squares. That said, gays and lesbians from 18 to 70 converge at **Exit,** Piazza San Francesco di Paola 39–40 (*©* **348-7814698**), daily 10pm to 3am. Live rock or pop is often presented. In summer, tables are placed outside, fronting the beautiful square. Bus: 108, 118, 122, or 124.

10 EASY EXCURSIONS

Palermo is graced with a number of satellite attractions that can be explored easily as side trips. Monreale, with its cathedral, is such an important sight that it is considered among greater Palermo's major attractions. In summer, there are the beaches of Mondello Lido. For a preview of what to see and do on the periphery of Palermo, see chapter 7, "Side Trips from Palermo."

If you don't have time to range far in your explorations, however, you can take an excursion to 600m (1,969-ft.) Monte Pellegrino, towering over the city.

MONTE PELLEGRINO ★

The parkland and nature preserve of the crown-shaped Monte Pellegrino looms over north Palermo. This green oasis and haven from the heat is where the Palermitani retreat on a summer day. During his visit, Goethe pronounced it "the most beautiful headland on earth." Avoid heading up this promontory on a Sunday, however, when half of the world's cars seem to have the same goal.

The mountain rises sharply on all sides except to the south. The headland here, known for its autumnal gold color, was occupied by the Carthaginian general Hamilcar Barca in the First Punic War and defended between 247 and 244 b.c. before it fell to the Romans.

You can reach the mountain from Piazza Generale Casino in Palermo, close to Fiera del Mediterraneo, the fair and exhibition grounds. From here, take Via Pietro Bonanno, following the signs toward the Santuario di Santa Rosalia (see below).

After a 15km (9-mile) drive to the north, you will reach the peak of Monte Pellegrino. Along the way to the top, you'll be rewarded with some of Sicily's most **panoramic views ★★★**, taking in the old city of Palermo and a sweeping vista of Conca d'Oro, the coastline. The paved road you see today dates from the 1600s, when it was a footpath for people climbing the mountain.

The chief attraction of Monte Pellegrino is **Santuario di Santa Rosalia** (*©* **091-540326**), a cave where the patron saint of Palermo lived. As you near the top (past endless souvenir shops hawking kitsch), you'll approach a belvedere, dominated by a statue of Santa Rosalia. If you stop here, you're treated to a **magnificent view ★** of the sea.

(Fun Facts)   The Legend of Santa Rosalia

No one knows for sure who Santa Rosalia was. She's more legend than real woman. She was born in 1130, supposedly to a patrician Norman family said to be descended from Charlemagne. Never a swinger, she was a very pious young lady. Unable to stand the pressures of hedonistic Palermo and its wicked ways, she fled to a cave in Monte Pellegrino in 1159 and died there in 1166.

When the Black Death swept over Palermo in 1624, the story goes, the figure of Rosalia appeared to a hunter. She directed him to her remains in the cave and ordered him to bring her bones to Palermo. She was then carried in a procession through the streets and properly buried.

After that, the plague disappeared. Ever since, Rosalia—now Santa Rosalia—has been revered as the patron saint of the city.

A festival held in her honor, every year on July 15, is a major social and religious event in Palermo. You can join the faithful on September 4, when the true believers walk barefoot from Palermo to the saint's sanctuary.

Santa Rosalia holds a special place in the hearts of the Palermitani, who have affectionately nicknamed her *La Santuzza,* or little saint. You enter the sanctuary through a little chapel constructed over a cave in the hillside, where the bones (read: alleged bones) of Rosalia were found in 1624.

Goethe has already given us his approval, finding the setting "so natural and pleasing one can hardly help expecting to see the saint breathe and move about." Supposedly a niece of William II, Santa Rosalia lived and died as a hermit on this mountain, retreating here in 1159.

Inside, a 17th-century statue of the saint, the work of Gregorio Tedeschi, is covered by a gilded silver mantle. Before the statue you'll find a massive pile of euros, a gift to her from the faithful. We suspect that someone else hauls in the loot at night—not the saint herself.

As a curiosity, note the thin spikes of flattened "steel cobweb" hanging from the ceiling. This isn't contemporary art; it's done to direct the water seeping from the ceiling into a container. The liquid is supposedly miraculous, and is highly prized by devout followers of the saint.

Admission is free, and the sanctuary (in theory, at least) is open daily from 7am to 8pm (closed at 6:30pm in winter). Frequent Masses may disrupt your visit.

Note the little pathway leading to the left of the chapel. If you take it, after about 30 minutes, you'll be at a cliff-top promontory with a view and a statue of the saint. The pathway to the right of the sanctuary leads to the top of Pellegrino, a leisurely hike of about 40 minutes. Families use the grounds and trails on Pellegrino as a picnic site.

If you're not driving, you can take bus no. 812 from Piazza Sturzo (Politeama) in Palermo (trip time: 30 min.). You can take the bus back or else descend from the mountain along the **Scala Vecchia,** a stepped path that winds down the mountain by the sanctuary going all the way to the Fiera del Mediterraneo fairgrounds.

7

Side Trips from Palermo

In spite of the fact that Palermo holds Sicily's greatest artistic monuments and treasures, it is also a city of noise and pollution. One of the pleasures of a visit to the island's capital is to escape it. A side trip makes a welcome respite.

At your doorstep are any number of treasures, ranging from the golden sands of **Mondello Lido** to **Ustica,** an offshore volcanic island of mysterious origins. The cathedral town of **Monreale** contains an ecclesiastical compound greater than anything in Palermo. But that's not all: You can also wander at leisure through the decaying aristocratic villas of **Bagheria** and later stroll among the ruins of the Greco-Roman town of **Solunto.**

1 BAGHERIA: DECAYING VILLAS

14km (8³/₄ miles) E of Palermo

In the 18th and 19th centuries, Bagheria became the summer retreat of the noble class, who built magnificent villas here to escape the scorching heat of Palermo. The agriculturally rich setting, on the southern slopes of Mount Catalfano at the eastern extension of the Gulf of Palermo, was home to citrus plantations and vineyards. The novelist Dacia Maraini, in her memoir, *Bagheria,* recalled "the atmosphere of a summer garden enriched by lemon groves and olive trees, poised between the hills, cooled by the salt winds."

As family fortunes disappeared and dynasties faded, however, Bagheria fell into a splendid decay. Many of its villas still exist, but ugly modern buildings and factories have encroached upon this once bucolic locale.

In the latter part of the 20th century, Bagheria earned the dubious distinction of being a center of Mafia activities. You can just imagine the international deals plotted behind the decaying walls of Bagheria's heavily guarded villas.

GETTING THERE   Several trains on the Palermo-Messina line stop at Bagheria, which also lies on the Santa Flavia–Solunto-Porticello line. Buses operated by AST also run here from Palermo, leaving from both the Stazione Centrale and Piazza Lolli. By car from Palermo, taking the coastal route (113) via Ficarazzi is easier than going to the trouble of getting on the autostrada (A19).

VILLA VIEWING

Villa Cattolica ★   Visit this baroque villa for a combination of antique architecture and modern art. It was originally constructed by Giuseppe Bonanni Filangeri, prince of Cattolica, and completed in 1736, during the Ottocento vogue for ostentatious country villas. An art gallery, **Galleria Comunale d'Arte Moderna e Contemporanea,** was established here in 1973. Most of the works in the gallery were donated by Renato Guttuso, a neorealist painter born in 1912 and the island's best-known modern artist. A staunch anti-Fascist during the Mussolini era, and later anti-Mafia, Guttuso evokes Picasso in some of his works. Beginning in 1958, the artist fell heavily under the influence of expressionism, abandoning realism for strong colors and daringly decisive lines. His Jazz

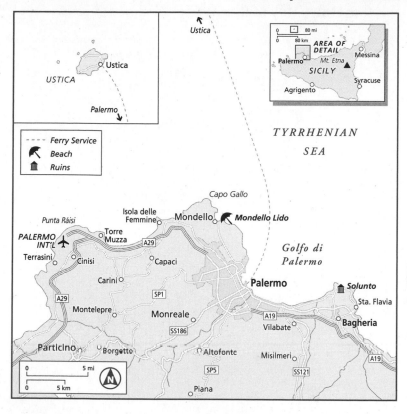

Age portraits and still lifes evoke the 1930s, while his works from the 1970s are startlingly sensuous. Note Gattuso's portrait of French Impressionist Paul Cézanne. Gattuso died in 1987, and his sculptor friend Giacomo Manzù designed a surreal "blue capsule" tomb for him. Set among scrubby cacti and citrus trees in the shadow of the villa, the tomb evokes the blue of the Sicilian sky.

After visiting the museum, you can walk through the gardens and see Gattuso's tomb as well as a *Camera dello Scirocco,* an artificial cave built under a seigniorial mansion that provided refuge on days when the scorching winds from Africa swept across the land.

Villa Consolare 9. © **091-943902.** Admission 5€ ($6.50) adults, 4€ ($5.20) students and children 17 and under. Tues–Sun 9am–6pm.

Villa Palagonia ★★ This is one of the most bizarre monuments of baroque decadence in Europe, known around the world as the "Villa of Monsters." When Goethe came this way, he was appalled by its "bad taste and folly." It was designed in 1705 by Tommaso Maria Napoli for Francesco Gravina, prince of Palagonia. But it was hideously decorated by the prince's eccentric grandson, the hunchbacked Ferdinando Gravina Alliata.

Hometown Boy Makes Good: *Cinema Paradiso*

The filmmaker Giuseppe Tornatore was born in Bagheria on May 27, 1956. Before making films, he was an award-winning still photographer and later a director of TV documentaries. In 1985, he made his feature movie debut with the film *Il Camorristal (The Professor)*. But it wasn't until 1989 that he received world acclaim for *Cinema Paradiso* (aka *Nuovo Cinema Paradiso*), a nostalgic and unabashedly sentimental tribute to the influence of movies on a young boy's life, shot on location in Tornatore's hometown of Bagheria.

The film won a Grand Jury Prize at the Cannes Film Festival and an Oscar as Best Foreign Film of the Year. In 2002, Tornatore restored 52 minutes to his 1989 film and rereleased it, entitled *Cinema Paradiso—The New Version*. Among other changes, the film has an entirely different, mood-altering last act. New ending or old, the director's films are said to "touch the soul of Sicily."

Francesco ordered that a series of tufa statues be inserted along the top of the wall in front of the facade. Of the original 200 statues, some 60 remain. Goethe described this parade of hideous figures as "beggars of both sexes, men and women of Spain, Moors, Turks, hunchbacks, deformed persons of every kind, dwarfs, musicians, Pulcinellas." He also commented on the depictions of animals: "deformed monkeys, many dragons and snakes, every kind of paw attached to every kind of body, double heads and exchanged heads."

In addition to his hunched back, Ferdinando was said to have a deformed mind. His wife was known to have had many lovers, so he ordered artisans to make frightening caricatures of these men to embarrass his wife and her male harem. He also created an eccentric interior, with spikes hidden under inviting velvet seats and sets of lovely Chinese porcelain glued together in a sticky mess. Mirrors were often built into the walls to distort the figures of visitors—thus, the hunchback got his revenge on those who stood tall and straight. A Hall of Mirrors remains, although in disrepair.

Unfortunately, most of the decorations that so infuriated Goethe are gone today, and the entire villa, while richly evoking the glories of its baroque past, is in sad need of a major restoration.

Piazza Garibaldi (at the end of Corso Umberto I). (C) **091-932088.** www.villapalagonia.it. Admission 4€ ($5.20) adults, 2€ ($2.60) students and children 17 and under. Apr–Oct daily 9am–1pm and 4–7pm; Nov–Mar daily 9am–1pm and 3:30–5:30pm.

2 SOLUNTO: EVOCATIVE RUINS

3km (1³/₄ miles) NE of Bagheria, 18km (11 miles) E of Palermo

Set high on the slopes of Monte Catalfano, the ruins of the city of Solunto may not be the most impressive in Sicily, but they are evocative, and the panoramic view of the sea and the beautiful setting amid aromatic wildflowers make the trip appealing. At a location 374m (1,227 ft.) above the bay, Solunto was the Carthaginian town of Solus and was actually founded as early as the 8th century B.C. Along with Palermo and Mozia, it was one of three Phoenician colonies in Sicily.

In 397 B.C., Dionysius of Syracuse destroyed the city. The present ruins are from the small city that existed here in the mid–4th century B.C. In time, Solunto was captured by the Romans, its dwellers fleeing their homes sometime during the 2nd century A.D.

The conquerors would not leave poor Solunto alone, even when it was nearly empty of life. The Saracens, for reasons known only to them, practically destroyed what remained after the Roman destruction.

GETTING THERE   Bagheria (p. 130) is generally the gateway for visitors continuing on to Solunto. By train, Solunto is one stop beyond Bagheria on the Santa Flavia–Solunto-Porticello line. Once you get off the train, go over the tracks and head toward the sea. In 300m (984 ft.), you'll see a signpost pointing to the ruins. From here, it's a 15- to 20-minute hike to the site.

Motorists generally arrive first in Bagheria. Solunto is signposted from Piazza Garibaldi at the entrance to Villa Palagonia in Bagheria. You can also reach Solunto by taking SS113 east from Palermo toward Porticello.

EXPLORING THE RUINS ★

On the way to the **Parco Archeologico di Solunto (Solunto Archaeological Garden),** you'll pass an **Antiquarium** just inside the gate. Everything of any real value was hauled off to Palermo a long time ago, but you might stop in for a look at some artifacts removed during excavations, including bas-reliefs, statuettes, ancient coins, and architectural fragments.

Immediately to the north lie the ruins of the **Terme,** the old thermal baths, with a mosaic floor remaining. Brick supports from below held up the rooms, allowing hot air to circulate.

The Terme fronts Via della Terme. If you head north and then right, you'll be walking along the main street of Solunto, **Via Dell'Agorà ★★.** The first ruin of any interest is the so-called **Gymnasium,** actually a patrician house with a peristyle and atrium more or less intact. Partially restored in 1866, the building has a trio of Doric columns and a partial roof. Directly east of it is an even more impressive patrician house, **Casa di Leda ★,** with a wall frescoed with a scene of Leda and her amorous swan. This house was built around a peristyle with an elaborate cistern system for collecting rainwater. In one room you can see the remains of a fresco similar to those discovered in the ruins of Pompeii.

The **Agorà,** the center of public life in old Solunto, lies east of Casa di Leda. Directly north of the square are the ruins of the **Odeon,** a small theater, and to its immediate east the larger ruins of what must have been an impressive theater in Hellenistic times, although not much remains today.

Admission is 2€ ($2.60). The park is open Monday to Saturday 9am to 7pm (closes at 3:30pm in winter), Sunday 9am to 2pm. Call ℂ **091-904557** for more information.

WHERE TO DINE

Antica Pizzeria Solunto/La Grotta   SICILIAN/PIZZA   Set on the uppermost promontory of Bagheria, with views over the ruins of Solunto and the nearby hamlet of Porticello, this is the most panoramic restaurant in the district. It has an outdoor terrace and two floors of seating, tended by a jaded staff. Frankly, the food and the service could both be better, but the view and the ambience here go a long way toward the creation of a magical Sicilian evening.

Parco Archeologico di Solunto. © **091-903213.** Reservations not necessary. Pizzas 6€–10€ ($7.80–$13); main courses 8€–18€ ($10–$23). AE, DC, MC, V. Fri–Wed 7:30pm–1am; Sun 1–3pm.

3 MONREALE: A MAGNIFICENT CATHEDRAL ★★★

10km (6 miles) SW of Palermo

This hilltop town has one of the greatest cathedrals in all of Italy and a panoramic view over the bay, Conca d'Oro. In the distance you can see the rise of Palermo.

During Norman rule, the kings chose Monreale as their royal hunting ground. When William II launched the celebrated cathedral and attached a royal residence and a monastery to it, Monreale was put on the maps of the world.

Since that time, pilgrims from virtually everywhere have flocked here to see this wonder. Even if you have to miss all the other sights in the Palermo environs, try to schedule 2 or 3 hours to make the trek to Monreale. It dwarfs other sights in this chapter and is, in fact, one of the major attractions of southern Italy.

GETTING THERE   From Palermo, take bus no. 389, departing from Piazza Indipendenza, which, 40 minutes later, will drop you off at Monreale's Piazza Vittorio Emanuele. During the day, three buses per hour leave for Monreale, costing 1.20€ ($1.55) one-way. Motorists can approach Monreale by Corso Calatafimi from Porta Nuova in Palermo.

MONREALE DUOMO ★★★

Arabo-Norman art and architecture reached the pinnacle of its beauty in this cathedral, launched in 1174 by William II. Like the grand Alhambra in Granada, Spain, the Duomo hides behind a relatively drab facade, giving little indication of the riches inside. William issued orders "to spare no expense" as he set about to out razzle-dazzle the glory of Palermo's Cappella Palatina (p. 99), which was the crowning architectural achievement of his grandfather Roger II. Today, the Monreale Duomo is the last and most stunning of the Norman churches of Sicily and is viewed as one of the architectural wonders of the Middle Ages.

The facade lies between two towers, one of which was never finished. Interlacing Arabic arches crown an 18th-century classical portico. If you stand on the Via dell'Arcivescovado, you can see where the original royal palace was absorbed by the Archbishop's Palace.

Bonanno Pisano, the sculptor and architect who created the Leaning Tower of Pisa, designed the cathedral's splendid **bronze doors** ★★ in 1185. He created 46 bas-reliefs of biblical scenes from both the Old and New Testaments. Beneath a portico from the 1500s, the lateral entrance is also graced with bronze doors, the 1179 work of Barisano da Trani, depicting saints, battles, animals, and scenes from the life of Christ. It is through this door that you enter the Duomo.

Once you step foot inside the golden interior, your eye won't know where to look first. The **mosaics** ★★★ here evoke the Cappella Palatina in Palermo, but on a much grander scale. This splendiferous cycle of 12th- and 13th-century art occupies the aisles, the choir, the transepts, and the entire nave, vividly bringing to life scenes from the Old and New Testaments. Craftsmen from Venice were brought in to create some of these mosaics, which show an amazing attention to detail. *Christ Pantocrator* ★ dominates the middle apse with majestic splendor; this is the most imposing of all such figures in any church on the island. Overall, there are more than 2,000 mosaics here—even more than in St. Mark's in Venice. The mosaic cycle is the second largest on earth, topped only by Istanbul's Hagia Sofia.

In the north apse, **Cappella del Crocifisso** ★ is gloriously baroqued to its teeth. The **treasury** shelters various precious objects and reliquaries, along with other ecclesiastical artifacts such as vestments, silverware, and goldsmithery dating from the Middle Ages or the Renaissance.

The plan to make this a Norman royal pantheon was never carried out, although you can see the porphyry sarcophagus of William I (d. 1166) and William II (d. 1190) before the entryway into the Cappella di San Benedetto, with decorations dating from the 16th century.

Well worth the steep climb uphill from the cathedral is an ascent to the **terraces** ★★★. Once you reach the top, you're rewarded with a sweeping vista over the cloisters and another stunning **view of the apses** ★★. From the more elevated terrace is a **dramatic panorama** ★★ to the sea and the bay of Conca d'Oro.

Descending from the terraces, you can visit the **cloisters** ★★★, which represent the flowering of Islamic architecture in Sicily. Devout Sicilians often refer to these cloisters as a "preview of Paradise." Pointed arches link 228 twin columns, each with a different design, many decorated with mosaics or reliefs. Each of the splendid **Romanesque capitals** ★★ is imaginatively conceived and carved. The artisan who depicted Adam and Eve hiding their genitalia in shame definitely had a sense of humor.

In the southwest corner is a **minicloister,** with one of the most delightful fountains in town. A dozen lionlike mouths gush water into the basin below.

Piazza Guglielmo il Buono. © **091-6404413.** Free admission to cathedral. Cloisters 4.50€ ($5.85); treasury 2.05€ ($2.70); ascent to terraces 1.55€ ($2). May–Sept daily 8am–6pm; Oct–Apr daily 8am–12:30pm and 3.30–6pm.

WHERE TO STAY
Baglio Conca d'Oro ★ (Finds) This 18th-century paper mill at Borgo Molara was completely restored and turned into a retreat of old-fashioned charm with 21st-century comforts. Guest rooms are modernized and come with small bathrooms with shower stalls. Most units open onto panoramas of the beautiful bay of Conca d'Oro, Monreale itself, or the Gulf of Palermo. In the antique redbrick building, the use of dark wood and Oriental rugs adds to the allure. You'll find this a convenient base for exploring both Palermo and Monreale.

Via Aquino 19, Borgo Molara 90126. © **091-6406286.** Fax 091-6408742. www.hotelbaglioconcadoro. com. 27 units. 170€–195€ ($221–$254) double; 230€–263€ ($299–$342) suite. AE, DC, MC, V. Located 3km (1¾ miles) from Monreale. From Palermo, take Viale Regione Siciliana and follow signs to Sciacca and N624. **Amenities:** Restaurant; bar; room service. *In room:* A/C, TV, minibar, hair dryer, safe.

ON THE OUTSKIRTS
Casale del Principe ★★ (Finds) This is an *agriturismo* (farm estate) lying 23km (14 miles) south of Palermo in the Jato Valley. The historic residence, turned into a delightful country hotel, grew from a 16th-century watchtower and was converted into a Jesuit monastery in the 18th century. Most guests arrive to enjoy the regional cuisine at its 150-seat restaurant, but you can also spend the night in a setting of vineyards, fruit orchards, and olive groves. The interior is rustic but elegant with a fireplace, paintings,

and country furniture. No two rooms are alike, and most of the accommodations open onto a private terrace with a panoramic view.

Contrada Dammusi, 90046 Monreale. © **091-8579910.** Fax 091-8579168. www.casaledelprincipe.it. 7 units. 50€ ($65) double; 80€ ($104) suite. Rates include buffet breakfast. AE, DC, MC, V. Follow the SS624 Palermo-Sciacca truck road to the San Giuseppe Jato exit (signposted from this point). **Amenities:** Restaurant; bar. *In room:* A/C, TV.

WHERE TO DINE

Drop in at **Bar Italia,** Piazza Vittorio Emanuele (© **091-6402421**), near the Duomo. The plain cookies are wonderfully flavorful; in the morning, order a croissant and a cappuccino, Monreale's best. Open Wednesday to Monday 5am to 1am.

Peppino SICILIAN For a modest meal, consider this simple *trattoria* that's positioned within a maze of narrow streets, about 4 blocks uphill (and west) from the cathedral. During clement weather, the preferred seating is on the cobble-covered terrace. Inside, you'll find a pizza oven and a TV that's likely to be blaring the latest football (soccer) match. The straightforward cuisine is typical of what you might find in the home of a local family: roulades (thin slices of veal that are stuffed, rolled, and fried), lamb or veal cutlets, and Spaghetti alla Norma (somehow eggplant always tastes better in Sicilian pastas). Your best bet might be the catch of the day, which is usually grilled along with roasted vegetables. Two specialties include *caserecce* (a homemade pasta) with fresh sardines and fennel, very Sicilian, or roasted Sicilian sausages.

Via B. Civiletti 12. © **091-6407770.** Reservations not necessary. Main courses 7€–10€ ($9.10–$13). AE, DC, MC, V. Fri–Wed 12:30–2pm and 7:30pm–midnight.

Taverna del Pavone ★ SICILIAN/ITALIAN The most highly recommended restaurant in Monreale faces a small cobblestone square, about a block uphill from the cathedral. Inside, you're likely to find a friendly greeting, an artfully rustic environment that's akin to an upscale tavern, and tasty Sicilian food. You might take delight in the zucchini flowers braised in a sweet-and-sour sauce; a delightful *pennette* with fava-bean sauce; and the house-made *maccheroni,* which was loaded with country cheese and absolutely delicious. For dessert, the most soothing choice is *semifreddo*—whipped cream folded into ice cream, given extra flavor with baked almonds.

Vicolo Pensato 18. © **091-6406209.** Reservations recommended. Main courses 9€–16€ ($12–$21). AE, DC, MC, V. Tues–Sun noon–3:30pm and 7:30–11:30pm.

4 MONDELLO: FUN AT THE BEACH

12km (7 1/2 miles) W of Palermo

When the summer sun burns hot, when the old men on the square seek a place in the shade, and when *bambini* tire of their toys, it's beach weather. For Palermo residents, that means Mondello Lido. Before this beachfront town started attracting the wealthy class of Palermo, it was a fishing village, and you can still see rainbow-colored fishing boats bobbing in the harbor. A good sandy beach stretches for about 2km (1 1/4 miles), filled to capacity on July and August days. *Tip:* Some women traveling alone find Mondello more inviting and less intimidating than Palermo.

GETTING THERE To reach all of the locations below by bus, take no. 806 to Mondello, leaving from Piazza Sturzo in the center of Palermo, close to Teatro Politeama. By car, take Viale Regina Margherita from the northern end of Parco della Favorita, going through the dreary suburb of Pallavicino beneath the western slope of Monte Pellegrino. On your way back, you can drive from Valdesi, at the southern tip of Mondello, along the Lungomare Cristoforo Colombo toward the heart of Palermo, going via the rock-strewn coastline at the foot of Monte Pellegrino.

HITTING THE BEACH As a seaside resort in Sicily, Mondello is outclassed only by Taormina. But if you find yourself in Palermo in July or August, **Mondello Lido** ★★ is the place to be. The wide, sandy beach extends for 2km (1¼ miles) from Monte Pellegrino to Monte Gallo.

Opening onto a half-moon-shaped bay between Monte Pellegrino and Capo Gallo, Mondello is the place for showing off your most daring swimwear and for living the good life, including lots of late-night staggering along with the young Palermitani from bar to bar (largely in the center, around **Piazza Mondello**).

Otherwise, Mondello Lido holds little of historical interest. What remains of the original fishing village lies at the far north of the bay—but it's hardly worth the trek. Between the wars, Mondello was a snobbish retreat for the upper crust, evoking the most fashionable parts of the French Riviera. After World War II, it more democratically became a "beach for everyone."

In the center of the beach, rising from concrete piers above the surface of the water, and connected to the Sicilian "mainland" with a bridge, you can still see the *kursaal*, a whimsical bathhouse (now a restaurant, **Charleston Le Terrazze;** p. 140) designed in the Art Nouveau style and adorned with sea dragons and other mythological creatures.

WHERE TO STAY

Albergo Conchiglia d'Oro (Value) Situated a 6-minute walk inland from the Lido (beach) in a residential neighborhood loaded with bougainvillea and private homes, this well-maintained hotel has a setting that's calmer and more sedate than those of other hotels close to the oceanfront frenzy. It's sometimes favored by Palermo-based business travelers who appreciate the easy parking after a day in the big sweaty city. Guest rooms are contemporary and somewhat generic-looking, though very comfortable. The hotel's garden—in the midst of which is a swimming pool—is one of the most appealing in Mondello. The beach is private. The in-house restaurant is large, airy, and welcoming, serving a good regional cuisine.

Via Cloe 9, 90151 Mondello, Palermo. ✆ **091-450032.** Fax 091-450359. www.hotelconchigliadoro.com. 50 units. 65€–93€ ($85–$121) double. AE, DC, MC, V. Free parking. **Amenities:** Restaurant; bar; outdoor pool. *In room:* A/C, TV.

Mondello Palace Hotel ★★ This is the most prestigious hotel in Mondello, set on its own private beach. It's favored by resortgoers and business travelers who prefer the relative peace of Mondello to the crush of Palermo. Modern and minimalist, it has an appealing kind of simplicity—a hint of the 1950s-derived glamour of *la dolce vita*. Originally built in 1953, it sits on prime real estate that's separated from the sands of the Lido only by a garden, an iron fence, and a busy oceanfront boulevard. The mix of privacy and seclusion on one side of the hedge and the crush of holiday-making flesh on the Lido is very appealing. Guest rooms are conservative, contemporary, and comfortable. Most contain private balconies; the luxurious bathrooms have tub/shower combinations.

Viale Principe di Scalea, 90151 Mondello, Palermo. ✆ **091-450001.** Fax 091-450657. www.mondello palacehotel.it. 93 units. 175€–215€ ($228–$280) double. Extra bed 70€ ($91). AE, DC, MC, V. **Amenities:**

"This Thing We Have": Men of Dishonor

In Sicily, they don't call it the *Mafia* (from the Arabic *mu'afah,* or "protection"). They call it *Cosa Nostra,* literally "our thing," but more accurately "this thing we have." Its origins are debated, but the world's most famed criminal organization seemed to grow out of the convergence of local agricultural overseers working for absentee Bourbon landowners—hired thugs, from the peasant workers' point of view.

Members of the Sicilian Mafia (or "Men of Honor," as they like to be called) traditionally operated as a network of regional bosses who controlled individual towns by setting up puppet regimes of thoroughly corrupt officials. It was a sort of devil's bargain between the regional bosses and the national Christian Democrat Party, which controlled Italy's government from World War II until 1993 and, despite its law-and-order rhetoric, tacitly left *Cosa Nostra* alone as long as its bosses got out the party vote.

The *Cosa Nostra* trafficked in illegal goods, of course, but until the 1960s and 1970s, its income was derived mainly from funneling state money into its own pockets, low-level protection rackets, and ensuring that public contracts were granted to fellow *mafiosi* (all reasons that Sicily has experienced grotesque unchecked industrialization and modern growth at the expense of its heritage and the good of its communities). But the younger generation of Mafia underbosses got into the highly lucrative heroin and cocaine trades in the 1970s, transforming the Sicilian Mafia into a major player on the international drug-trafficking circuit. This ignited a clandestine Mafia war that throughout the late 1970s and 1980s generated lurid headlines of bloody Mafia hits. The new generation was wiping out the old and turning the balance of power in their favor.

This situation gave rise to the first of the Mafia turncoats, disgruntled ex-bosses and rank-and-file stoolies who opened up and told their stories, first to police prefect Generale Alberto Dalla Chiesa (assassinated in 1982) and later to crusading magistrates Giovanni Falcone (murdered in May 1992) and Paolo Borsellino (murdered in July 1992), who staged the "maxi-trials" of mafiosi that

Restaurant; bar; outdoor pool; watersports equipment/rentals; gym; room service; babysitting; laundry service; dry cleaning. *In room:* A/C, TV, minibar, hair dryer.

Splendid Hotel La Torre ★ (Value   Tucked away at the distant edge of Mondello's fishing port, this postmodern building rises in stark contrast to the low cement structures that line the harbor. Inside the hotel, you'll find clean lines, oak floors, skylights, sweeping views of the sea, and mobs of European tourists, many of them on group tours. Originally built in 1959, the hotel has a hip but busy staff and midsize guest rooms filled with comfortable, bland-looking furnishings and tub/shower combinations. One highlight is this hotel's location, on a rocky peninsula jutting into the sea at the edge of the harbor. Terraces descend several steps to sweeping views over the water and the sands of the Lido, about 1km (¹/₂ mile) away. Also on-site are a park, garden, and solarium.

sent hundreds to jail. It was the magistrates' 1992 murders especially that attracted public attention to the dishonorable methods that defined the new Mafia and, perhaps for the first time, began to stir true shame.

On a broad and culturally important scale, it is these young mafiosi, without a moral center or check on their powers, who have driven many Sicilians to at least secretly break the unwritten code of *omertà*, which translates as "homage" but means "silence," when faced with harboring or even tolerating a "man of honor." The Mafia still exists in Palermo, the small towns south of it, and the provincial capitals of Catania, Trapani, and Agrigento. Throughout the rest of Sicily, however, its power has been slipping. The heroin trade is a far cry from construction schemes and protection money, and the Mafia is swiftly outliving its usefulness.

Even in Palermo, the grip of *Cosa Nostra* seems to be loosening. In the closing days of 2000, the city hosted a United Nations conference on combating organized crime. Palermo's mayor, Leoluca Orlando, proclaimed that his fragile city was "battling a great evil" and paid homage at the conference to those who died fighting the Mafia. As local officials have worked to fight the mafiosi's corruption and stifling of Sicilian society, their efforts have been hailed as a Palermo Renaissance.

As late as June 2006, Italian police arrested 45 people in an anti-Mafia crackdown, including top mobsters allegedly ruled by Bernardo Provenzano, the reputed number-one "godfather" apprehended earlier that year. Investigators claimed that the arrests in Palermo struck at the heart of the Sicilian Mafia, dealing it a serious blow. But the police also warned that the arrests didn't "mean that the Palermo Mafia has been dismantled."

In 2008 crackdowns continued to weaken the Mafia's grip on Sicily. Businesses are resisting age-old extortion techniques where they feared a destruction of their business—and possibly death. They are openly signing onto a website called "Addiopizzo" (Goodbye Pizzo), which unites them in a single purpose of banding together to defeat the Mafia.

Via Piano Gallo 11, 90151 Mondello, Palermo. ✆ **091-450222.** Fax 091-450033. www.latorre.com. 169 units. 136€–172€ ($177–$224) double; 161€–217€ ($109–$282) triple. AE, DC, MC, V. **Amenities:** Restaurant; piano bar; saltwater outdoor pool; tennis court; room service; babysitting; laundry service; dry cleaning; solarium; rooms for those w/limited mobility. *In room:* A/C, TV, minibar.

Villa Esperia ★ Finds Set on a busy commercial boulevard in the center of Mondello, this charming hotel occupies a majestic villa built around 1890. Touches of stateliness remain, thanks to high ceilings, a walled-in garden, and a Liberty-era decor that's more or less authentic to the late 19th century. Rooms are small to medium in size, with vague references to the 19th century, plus lots of cozy comfort. Those facing the street can be noisy, although air-conditioning and double layers of glass both help. Four of the rooms are in a comfortable annex that was originally conceived as a stable. The pleasant on-site restaurant has a glassed-in terrace.

Viale Margherita di Savoia 53, 90146 Mondello, Palermo. *C* **091-6840717.** Fax 091-6841508. www. hotelvillaesperia.it. 22 units. 99€–150€ ($129–$195) double. Rates include continental breakfast. AE, DC, MC, V. **Amenities:** Restaurant; bar; outdoor pool; tennis court. *In room:* A/C, TV, hair dryer.

WHERE TO DINE

Bye Bye Blues ★★ (**Finds**) SICILIAN Savvy locals all know of this place, an innocuous-looking private house that's set alarmingly close to a busy street in the neighborhood of Valdesi. The cuisine is among the finest in the greater Palermo area, though it falls just short of the viands concocted at Charleston (see below). The casual, relaxing dining room is run by Antonio, who used to work on American cruise ships, and his wife, Patrizia, who inherited time-tested Sicilian recipes from her mother and grandmother. The kitchen shapes raw materials from the surrounding countryside into dishes filled with flavor and passion. We were won over by the mussel soup with potatoes and pumpkin flowers; the extraordinary pasta with prawns; and the grilled calamari, a fragrant delight. If the watermelon gelatin tart is too experimental for you, finish with the hot chocolate cake.

Via del Garofalo 23. *C* **091-6841415.** Reservations required. Main courses 8€–20€ ($10–$26). AE, DC, MC, V. Wed–Mon 8pm–midnight. Closed Nov 1–15.

Charleston Le Terrazze ★★★ SICILIAN/INTERNATIONAL No restaurant in Mondello—or Palermo, for that matter—achieves the culinary perfection of this long-established citadel of fine cuisine. It's housed in the most charming building in town, built in 1913 on concrete pilings above the sea, just offshore from the Lido and connected to the "mainland" by bridge. Conceived as an Art Nouveau fantasy and crowned with artful depictions of sea monsters, it's the setting for this most memorable of Mondello restaurants. If weather permits, sit on the terrace that's open to the stars; otherwise, you'll dine in a high-ceilinged room that evokes the Gilded Age. Meals feature classy fare that artfully combines fish or meat with exceedingly fresh vegetables, excellent wines, and attentive service. The marinated swordfish is done to elegant perfection, the prosciutto with seasonal fruit is hard to resist, and the risotto with shellfish is a savory delight. Dessert might be an almond parfait or crêpes suzette.

Stabilimento Balneare, Viale Regina Elena, Mondello. *C* **091-450171.** Reservations required. Main courses 12€–20€ ($16–$26). AE, DC, MC, V. Daily 1–3:30pm and 8:30–11:30pm. Closed Wed Nov–Mar and Jan 7–31.

5 USTICA: A VOLCANIC ISLAND

57km (35 miles) NW of Palermo

Rising from the waters of the Tyrrhenian Sea and linked to the capital by hydrofoil and ferry, this holiday resort goes by the touristic name of the "Black Pearl of the Mediterranean." In this case, the name fits, as the volcanic island is composed of dark, petrified, rather foreboding-looking lava. The Romans, in fact, named it *ustum* ("burnt"), because it looked to them like a large black rock.

Both this turtle-shaped island and its main port are called Ustica. A visit here is a trip to unknown, offbeat Sicily. Even many Palermitans, who live a short ferry ride away, have never visited Ustica.

The village of Ustica is set on a tufa ledge between two inlets, lying in the shadow of Capo Falconara, whose summit is crowned with the remains of a fortress erected by the Bourbons.

The history of the island is ancient; it was once inhabited by the Phoenicians. In time they were followed by the Greeks, who named the island Osteodes ("ossuary"), in memory of the skeletons of 6,000 Carthaginians, mutineers who were brought here and abandoned without food or water.

Saracen pirates raided the island over the years, carrying off the prettiest women. Attempts to colonize it in the Middle Ages failed because of raids by Barbary pirates. The Bourbons repopulated it in 1762 with people from the Aeolian Islands and Naples. They constructed a trio of towers to defend the island against pirates.

As late as the 1950s, Ustica was a penal colony, a sort of Alcatraz of Sicily. Antonio Gramsci, the theorist of the Italian Communist Party, was once imprisoned here. And, in one of the most secret meetings of World War II, British and Italian officers met here in September 1943 to discuss a switch in sides from Mussolini to the Allies.

Ustica is tiny, only 8.6 sq. km ($3^1/_3$ sq. miles). The top of a submerged volcano, it is the oldest island in the Sicilian outer archipelago—even older than the Aeolian Islands, one of which is Lipari, which it resembles. Because its jagged coastline is riddled with creeks, bays, and caves, Ustica is best explored by a rented boat (see below) circling the island.

In 1987, Sicily designated part of the island a national marine park, and today its clear waters and beautiful sea, filled with aquatic flora and fauna, attract snorkelers and scuba divers from around the world. Divers are also drawn to its ancient wrecks and the now-submerged city of Osteodes, 1.6km (1 mile) west of the island, which sank into the sea in unrecorded times.

Ustica has a population of some 1,370 islanders. Visit them in such idyllic months as June or September; a trip here in July or August is so hot, it's like a journey to Hades.

ESSENTIALS

GETTING THERE   Hydrofoils and ferries operate daily from Palermo's Stazione Maríttima to Ustica. The ferry is the cheapest and slowest transport, costing 18€ ($23) each way and taking $2^1/_2$ hours. The hydrofoil, at a cost of 23€ ($30), does it in half the time. For tickets for either transport, go to **Siremar,** at Via Francesco Crispi 118 in Palermo (© **091-336632**), and on Piazza Bartolo in Ustica (© **091-8449002**). Hydrofoil service runs from April to December; ferries run year-round, but not on Sundays in winter.

GETTING AROUND   Arrival from Palermo is at Ustica village, the only port and home to 90% of the islanders. The heart of the village is reached by climbing a flight of steps from the harbor. You'll emerge onto the main square of town—actually a trio of interlocking squares that include the piazzas of Bartolo, Umberto I, and Vito Longo. We recommend that you take care of any shopping needs before you leave Palermo; otherwise, you'll have to buy it here, as whatever Ustica has to offer is found in this area.

Once you arrive, you can always do as the locals do and rely on your trusty feet. Otherwise, take one of the orange minibuses that circumnavigate the island, hugging the coastline. These leave from the center of Ustica village daily on the hour. Figure on $2^1/_2$ hours for the entire bus ride around the island; a ticket between any two points along the route costs 1€ ($1.30).

Summer boat excursions are run by local fishermen who not only know the most scenic beauty spots, but also will allow you time out for swimming during an island trip.

(Moments) Exploring a Watery Wonderland

J. Y. Cousteau claimed that the waters off the coast of Ustica were among the most beautiful he'd ever seen, ideal for both diving and underwater photography—and we agree. The best spot for diving is the **Grotta del Gamberi,** near Punta Gavazzi, at the southern tip of the island beyond Grotta del Tuono. Nearby is the famous **Sub-Aqua Archaeological Trail,** lying off the headland, Punta Gavazzi, with its lighthouse. Many anchors and even Roman amphorae can still be seen in these waters.

The best dive spot on the north coast is **Secca di Colombara,** to the west of Grotta dell'Oro. Here you can see a vast array of gorgonians and Ustica's most beautiful sponges. **Scoglio del Medico** ★★, or "doctor's rock," lies off the west coast of the island directly north of the bay called Baia Sidoti. This outcropping of basalt, riddled with grottoes and gorges, plunges to murky depths in the Atlantic, and offers a panoramic seascape unequaled anywhere else in Sicily.

Hotel Ariston, Via della Vittoria 5 (© 091-8449042), organizes sightseeing boat trips, rents boats to scuba divers, and hires out motorcycles. Its three-seater boats cost 50€ ($65) a day, gasoline not included. A boat trip around the island, which lets you see the caves and stop at secluded spots for swimming, lasts 2¹/₂ hours and costs 20€ ($26). If you'd like to tour on your own—expect rough roads—it costs 29€ to 40€ ($38–$52) a day to hire a motorcycle, with gas and two helmets included.

Scuba divers can go to **Ailara Rosalia,** Banchina Barresi (© 091-8449605), which rents boats for 70€ ($91) a day. You should bring your own diving gear, however.

VISITOR INFORMATION   The tourist office has closed due to financial reasons. However, you can visit the headquarters of **Parco Marino Regionale,** on the main square of town (© 091-8449456). The staff here can provide information about the marine park. Hours are daily 8am to 8pm.

FAST FACTS   For a medical emergency, call **Guardia Medica** (© 091-8449248). Serious cases are immediately transported to Palermo. The police or *Carabinieri* can be reached at © 091-8449049.

ATTRACTIONS NEAR THE PORT

It's fun just to stroll around the village, taking in views of the bay, Baia Santa Maria. The little town is made more festive by a series of murals that decorate the facades of the buildings.

Directly south of the village stands **Torre Santa Maria,** housing the **Museo Archeologico** (no phone). It's open daily from 9am to noon and 5 to 7pm; admission is 3€ ($3.90). Its most fascinating exhibits are fragments and artifacts recovered from the ancient city of Osteodes, now submerged beneath the sea. Many of the artifacts, such as crusty anchors, were recovered from ships wrecked off the coast. You'll see amphorae, Bronze Age objects from the prehistoric village of Faraglioni, and contents of tombs from the Hellenistic and Roman eras.

To the east of the tower are the ruins of a Bronze Age settlement, **Villaggio Preistorico,** at Faraglioni. Excavations began in 1989 on what was a large prehistoric village dating from the 14th century to the 13th century B.C. The foundations of some 300 stone-built houses were discovered, and the defensive walls of the settlement are among the strongest fortifications of any period known in Italy. It is believed that these early settlers came over from the Aeolian Islands. Admission is free; the site is always open.

If you walk north of Ustica village, you'll come to the remains of the **Rocca della Falconiera,** at 157m (515 ft.). Figure on a 20-minute walk. (Along the way you'll see many cisterns, as water remains a precious commodity on Ustica, even though a desalination plant has been installed.) The defensive tower was constructed by the Bourbons to protect the island from raids by pirates. This site was first settled back in the 3rd century B.C. by the Romans. If you look toward the sea you'll see the lighthouse, **Punta dell'Uomo Morto (Dead Man's Point)** on a cliff, where a cave contains vestiges of centuries-old tombs.

From the fort you can take in a view of **Guardia dei Turchi,** at 244m (801 ft.). This is the highest point on the island. That object you see in the distance, evoking a mammoth golf ball, is in fact a meteorological radar system installed by the Italian government.

The **view** ★ from the fortress ruins stretches from the harbor to the core of the island, with the mountains of **Monte Costa del Fallo** and **Monte Guardia dei Turchi** clearly outlined.

EXPLORING THE ISLAND

Since it is the top of an extinct volcano, Ustica doesn't have sandy beaches. But as you traverse the island, you'll find jumping-off points for swimming. The biggest attraction is the grotto-lined coastline, and because distances are short, hiking is a viable option.

Wildflowers cover the island except in late July and August, when the blistering sun burns them away. You'll also see produce grown by the islanders, such as lentils, figs, capers, grapes, prickly pears, wheat, and almonds.

Of all the caves or grottoes on the island, the most celebrated and fascinating is the **Grotta Azzurra** ★★, the first cave south of Ustica village as you head down the coast by boat. It's named for the more fabled cave in Capri, but both grottoes share an incredible iridescent glow from light reflections from the sea.

Almost as stunning is the next sea cave directly to the south, **Grotta Pastizza** ★. This is a stalactite cave behind a great pyramidal rock. Directly down the coast, another grotto, **Grotta della Barche,** is also intriguing. *Barche* means "boat," and Ustica fishermen anchor in this safe haven during storms.

PARCO MARINO REGIONALE ★★

The Marine National Park was created in 1986, the first marine reserve ever established in Italy. Since Ustica lies in the center of an inward current surging through the Straits of Gibraltar directly from the Atlantic Ocean, its waters are always clean and free of pollution.

Underwater photographers flock to the park to film the stunning **aquatic flora and fauna** ★★★. A splendid seaweed, *Poseidonia oceanica,* is called "the lungs of the sea" because it oxygenates the water. You may also see an array of magnificent red gorgonians, stunning black coral, plentiful turtles (now that they are protected), swordfish, lobster, and *cernia* (a kind of sea perch). Some divers claim to have had close encounters with grouper as big as a Fiat 500.

The park comprises three zones. **A area** extends along the western part of the isle from Cala Sidoti to Caletta and as far as 935m (3,068 ft.) offshore. Swimming is allowed here, but no boats and no fishing. **B area** extends from Punta Cavazzi to Punta Omo Morto, taking in the entire southwest-to-northeast coastline, and extending out into the sea a distance of 3 nautical miles. Swimming is permitted here. Finally, **C area** is a partial reserve made up of the rest of the coast. Swimming is allowed here, as is fishing.

HIKING AROUND USTICA

You can circumnavigate the island in 3 to 4 hours, depending on your pace. The best hike is along the coastal path heading north of town, where you'll see the Municipio, or island headquarters. Head left here, taking the trail along the north coast that leads past an old cemetery. This hike hugs the steep cliffs on the northern side of the island, part of the marine reserve, and the views are stunning.

Eventually you'll come to **Punta di Megna,** on the western coast, on the exact opposite side of the island from Ustica village. The offshore rock so appreciated by scuba divers, **Scoglio del Medico,** can be seen from here.

The road continues along the southwestern coast as far as the battered ruins of the old tower, **Punta Spalmatore,** where you can go swimming. (There is no beach here, however.)

Below this point, at **Punta Cavazzi,** along the southern rim of the island, is **Piscina Naturale** ★, a sheltered seawater pool and the best place on Ustica for swimming. If there are a lot of tourists on the island at the time of your visit, this "hole" is likely to be crowded with bathers in the briefest of swimwear.

At this point, the route no longer follows the coast and cuts inland all the way northeast to Ustica village once again.

WHERE TO STAY

Accommodations are scarce and fill up quickly from April to September. Many islanders rent rooms when the hotels are fully booked, but if you count on that, you're taking a chance. It's far preferable to arrive with a reservation. If you don't have one, go to the Piazza Umberto and start asking around for a *camera,* or room. In winter, many places close down.

Hotel Clelia (Value) This is the most typical of Ustica's little island inns, situated off Piazza Umberto I, the main square of Ustica village. It was the first little boardinghouse on the island to receive visitors, who began arriving in 1950 during the lean postwar years. It is also one of the island's best bargains. For most of its life, it was a *pensione,* or boardinghouse. But after so many improvements, it has been upgraded by the government to three-star status. Nonetheless, its prices have remained reasonable in spite of the installation of soundproof windows and modern furnishings. Guest rooms are small but comfortable, each with a little shower-only bathroom. Hotel extras include a lovely patio with scenic views, a shuttle bus that makes trips around the island, and scooter and boat rentals. This is one of the few places that remain open year-round.

Via Sindaco I 29, Ustica 90010. (C) **091-8449039.** Fax 091-8449459. www.hotelclelia.it. 26 units. 65€–150€ ($85–$195) double; 84€–195€ ($109–$254) triple. Rates include continental breakfast. AE, DC, MC, V. **Amenities:** Restaurant; bar; babysitting; laundry service; rooms for those w/limited mobility. *In room:* A/C, TV, minibar, hair dryer, safe.

Hotel Diana ★ (Finds) Located on the beach at Contrada San Paolo, this is one of the island's oldest hotels, but it's still in good shape following renovations. Opened in 1973 at the dawn of tourism on the island, the Diana's most attractive feature is its landscaping, which features fruit trees and wild island plants. The hotel's panoramic position allows some good views from the terraces of its guest rooms. Accommodations are a bit bare-bones but comfortable, with good beds, marble floors, and small bathrooms. The helpful owner/manager can offer advice on setting up island tours.

Contrada San Paolo, 90010 Ustica. ©/fax **091-8449109.** www.hoteldiana-ustica.com. 30 units. 55€–80€ ($72–$104) per person double. Rates include half board. AE, DC, MC, V. Closed Sept 25–Mar 31. **Amenities:** Restaurant; bar; outdoor pool. *In room:* A/C, TV.

Hotel Grotta Azzurra ★★

This is Ustica's best hotel bet, lying a 5-minute walk from the center. This modern and comfortable choice stands on a wide plateau above the ocean, with a steep drop to a spot for swimming. A natural grotto carved out of a cliff face below gives the hotel its name and its most alluring feature. All of the well-appointed guest rooms open onto sea views; each comes with a small but neat private bathroom with shower. Set among lush gardens, this hotel feels like a Mediterranean retreat, with such resort-style amenities as beach towels and umbrellas. Sports-oriented people can rent scooters and boats for island tours, sailing, and windsurfing. The hotel also attracts a lot of divers. Even if you're not a guest, consider a meal at **La Cala dei Fenici,** known on the island for its refined Sicilian cuisine.

Contrada San Ferliccio, Ustica 90010. © **091-8449807.** Fax 091-8449396. 51 units. 160€–285€ ($208–$371) double. Rates include breakfast. AE, DC, MC, V. Closed Oct–May. **Amenities:** Restaurant; bar; outdoor pool; hydromassage; babysitting. *In room:* A/C, TV, minibar, safe.

Villaggio Lirial Punta Spalmatore ★

Sicily's coastal towns are riddled with self-contained tourist villages, and this is the island's best such choice. Set 4km (2¹/₂ miles) from Ustica village on the western coast, it's entirely surrounded by native trees and plants. Most visitors spend their days in the terraced pool area with a panoramic view of the ocean; some guests from Palermo never even leave the grounds. The buildings rise only two floors, and accommodations are in bungalows with small but comfortable guest rooms and shower-only bathrooms. The cuisine is typical resort fare, but much use is made of fresh produce when available. Otherwise, foodstuffs have to be shipped over from Palermo. The wide range in rates depends on when you're here—the highest prices are charged in July and August.

Località Punta Spalmatore, Ustica 90010. © **091-8449388.** Fax 091-8449472. 110€–230€ ($143–$299) double. Rates include continental breakfast, lunch, and dinner. AE, MC, V. Closed Sept 20–May 31. **Amenities:** Restaurant; bar; outdoor pool; gym; wellness center; Jacuzzi; sauna; massage. *In room:* A/C, fridge.

WHERE TO DINE

There aren't many places to dine in Ustica. Most of the little *trattorie* are found in the village around the trio of central squares. The hotels also offer restaurants, with roof terraces opening onto views of the water.

Schiticchio SICILIAN/SEAFOOD

This modest establishment, near town hall in the center of Ustica village, offers a rustic decor, a staff that seems to try harder than average to please its patrons, and good homemade food prepared with the freshest ingredients on the island. Ask about the fresh fish of the day, which is often grilled to perfection. The pizza oven turns out succulent pies, and we delighted in a homemade pasta with a tangy pesto sauce.

Via dei Tre Mulini. © **091-8449662.** Reservations recommended. Main courses 8€–15€ ($10–$20). AE, DC, MC, V. Daily 1–3pm and 7:30pm–2am (until midnight in winter).

Messina & the Tyrrhenian Coast

The coastal road (A20) that runs from Messina westward to the capital at Palermo is one of the most frequented routes in Sicily. You can, of course, drive straight through to Palermo and not see a thing, but if you do, you'll miss some of the treasures of Sicily.

The coast is riddled with sandy beaches, small resorts, and villages. If you have time for only one stopover, make it Cefalù, the premier destination along the coast thanks in part to its famous Romanesque cathedral.

For those who want to cut inland to view a national park, we suggest you set aside a day to explore **Parco Naturale Regionale delle Madonie,** one of Sicily's most important nature reserves.

The best beaches lie to the east of Cefalù. They are sandy, clean, and unpolluted, though filled with visitors in July and August.

The coast also contains some of north Sicily's more impressive ruins, including those at **Himera** (near Termini Imerese) and at **Tyndaris,** west of Milazzo.

1 MESSINA

233km (145 miles) E of Palermo, 683km (424 miles) SE of Rome, 469km (291 miles) S of Naples

Overlooking the Straits of Messina, with the mainland city of Reggio di Calabria across the sea and to the east, Messina lies at the foot of the Peloritani Mountains. Only 5km (3 miles) separate the city of Messina from the Italian mainland. For most passengers arriving from the mainland, the tacky industrial and port city of Messina is their gateway to Sicily—a shame, really. But since you're here, what the hell? You might as well enjoy what Messina has to offer—and it does have some treasures if you're willing to seek them out.

Sicily's third-most populous city wasn't always this dismal. Mother Nature did a better job with Messina than mankind did. However, earthquakes and warplanes have done their damage. Because it has had to be rebuilt over and over, Messina is the most modern city on the island.

Messina was founded in the 8th century B.C. by the Siculans, who named it *Zancle* (sickle) because of its hooked promontory protecting the harbor. The Greeks from Cumae and Chalcis occupied the site in the 5th century. It fell to the dreaded Anaxilas, tyrant of Reggio, who changed the town's name to *Messána* to honor his native Messenia in the Peloponnesus.

By the 3rd century B.C., Messina had come under Roman influence. Messina's fame in the Middle Ages rested on its position as a launching pad for many of the Crusades. It was a flourishing city until the 17th century, when it lost trading privileges as punishment for protesting against the Spanish viceroys.

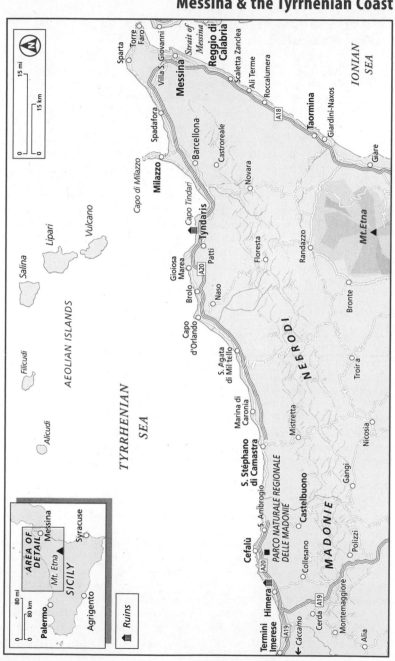

Not-So-Fun Facts: So You Think You've Got Bad Luck?

Aside from the fact that Shakespeare set his *Much Ado About Nothing* in Messina, it has rarely been blessed. Get a load of these disasters.

The Black Death, or bubonic plague, swept over Messina in 1743, killing more than 40,000 people. Forty years later, an earthquake leveled the city. Angered by Sicilian demands for independence, the Bourbon ruler Ferdinand II bombarded Messina to a pulp in 1848. Still reeling from the blows, the city was swept by a cholera epidemic in 1854. It staggered back to its feet by 1894, in time for another devastating earthquake. Messina had barely recovered when, on December 28, 1908, tremors shot through the city once again. Before the day was over, some 85,000 residents were dead. The earthquake was so violent that the coast sank 20 inches into the sea.

Under the dictatorship of Mussolini, the city was rebuilt and stood proudly once again. But in 1943, with Italy at war with Britain and the United States, Allied bombers were determined to knock out Messina and take Sicily as a prelude to the invasion of southern Italy. Bombs rained from the sky like raindrops falling on a roof; Messina was flattened once again.

Messina boasts one of the deepest and safest harbors in the Mediterranean. With a population of some 275,000, Messina also is one of southern Italy's most bustling cities. Rebuilt after devastation by the 1908 earthquake and the 1943 Allied bombings, it is a city of wide boulevards and low buildings. The structures hug the earth to prevent more danger in the event of another earthquake.

The long-delayed development in Messina was announced in 2002: the Straits of Messina bridge project, which will link the city with mainland Italy. Construction began in late 2005 but was discontinued for 3 years. It may start again sometime in 2009. The project has been a mess since its inception. Check out www.strettodimessina.it for updates, drawings, and even computer simulations of the new bridge.

ESSENTIALS

GETTING THERE By Boat Messina is linked to the Italian mainland by both ferries and hydrofoils crossing the Straits of Messina from either Villa San Giovanni or Reggio di Calabria.

Ferries leave from Villa San Giovanni, which is 12km (7¹/₂ miles) north of Reggio and closer to Messina. Ferry services are called *traghetti;* **FS** (© **892021** in Villa San Giovanni) is state run, while **Caronte** (© **090-37183214**) is independent. Offices for both companies can be found at the harbor where the ferries depart. Both ferries charge a fare of 8€ ($10) to Messina.

If you're leaving from Reggio di Calabria, you can take a ferry operated by **Meridiano** (© **0965-810414**), which charges 1.55€ ($2) for the 40-minute crossing to Messina.

Barnes & Noble Booksellers #1979
2289 Broadway
New York, NY 10024
212-362-8835

STR:1979 REG:005 TRN:9768 CSHR:STEPHANIE G

Frommer's Sicily
  9780470398999
  (1 @ 18.99)   18.99

Subtotal   18.99
Sales Tax (8.875%)   1.69
TOTAL   20.68
ELECTRONIC GIFT CARD   20.68
  Card#:   XXXXXXXXXXX8001
  Auth: 000536
  Entry Method: Swiped
  Card Balance: 5.36

A MEMBER WOULD HAVE SAVED   1.90

Thanks for shopping at
Barnes & Noble

101.21A   06/20/2010 05:55PM

CUSTOMER COPY

After 14 days of without a sales receipt, returns or exchanges will not be permitted.

Magazines, newspapers, and used books are not returnable. *Product not carried by Barnes & Noble or Barnes & Noble.com will not be accepted for return.*

Policy on receipt may appear in two sections.

Return Policy

<u>With a sales receipt</u>, a full refund in the original form of payment will be issued from any Barnes & Noble store for returns of new and unread books (except textbooks) and unopened music/DVDs/audio made within (i) 14 days of purchase from a Barnes & Noble retail store (except for purchases made by check less than 7 days prior to the date of return) or (ii) 14 days of delivery date for Barnes & Noble.com purchases (except for purchases made via PayPal). A store credit for the purchase price will be issued for (i) purchases made by check less than 7 days prior to the date of return, (ii) when a gift receipt is presented within 60 days of purchase, (iii) textbooks returned with a receipt within 14 days of purchase, or (iv) original purchase was made through Barnes & Noble.com via PayPal. Opened music/DVDs/audio may not be returned, but can be exchanged only for the same title if defective.

<u>After 14 days or without a sales receipt</u>, returns or exchanges will not be permitted.

Magazines, newspapers, and used books are not returnable. *Product not carried by Barnes & Noble or Barnes & Noble.com will not be accepted for return.*

Policy on receipt may appear in two sections.

Return Policy

<u>With a sales receipt</u>, a full refund in the original form of payment will be issued from any Barnes & Noble store for returns of new and unread books (except textbooks) and unopened

By Plane   The nearest airport to Messina is on the Italian mainland at Reggio di Calabria. **Aeroporto dello Stretto** (℃ 0965-640517) is 5km (3 miles) south of Reggio. Once you land at the airport, you can take one of the buses operated by **Autolinee Federico,** Via Lagani (℃ 090-644747), to Messina.

By Train   Eight trains arrive daily from Rome, the trip south taking 8 to 9 hours and costing 45€ ($59) one-way. A train link from Naples takes 5¹/₂ hours, costing 35€ ($46). There are also frequent rail links to Palermo, with a dozen or more trains going between Messina and the island's capital, taking approximately 3¹/₂ hours and costing 11€ ($14) one-way. The major attraction along the Tyrrhenian coast is Cefalù; trains from Messina go there throughout the day in 2¹/₂ to 3¹/₂ hours, costing 8.60€ ($11). There are also hourly trains between Messina and Taormina, Sicily's major resort to the south, taking 1 hour and costing 4.50€ ($5.85) each way. For rail information, call ℃ 892021.

By Bus   SAIS, Piazza delle Repubblica 6 (℃ 090-771914), operates buses to Catania nine times a week, taking 1¹/₂ hours and costing 7.50€ ($9.75) one-way. There are seven buses per day to Palermo, a 3¹/₄-hour trip that costs 15€ ($20). Many visitors use **Interbus** (℃ 090-661754), with offices to the left of the Stazione Centrale. It runs a dozen buses per day to Taormina, taking 1¹/₂ hours and costing 5.50€ ($7.15) one-way.

By Car   From the mainland of Italy, follow A3 south to Reggio di Calabria, getting off at Villa San Giovanni and taking a car ferry across the Straits of Messina to Messina itself. Along the northern coast, travel the A20/SS113 east from Palermo and Cefalù. The A18 from Taormina runs north to Messina.

VISITOR INFORMATION   For information and a map, head to the **Azienda Autonoma per L'Incremento Turistico,** Via Calabria 301 (℃ 090-674236), near Piazza della Repubblica and Stazione Centrale. It's open Monday to Thursday 9am to 1:30pm and 3 to 5pm and Friday 9am to 1:30pm.

ORIENTATION   Messina grew around its harbor, which is shaped like a sickle. You'll see this geographic configuration as you sail into the harbor. The tip of the sickle is marked by a towering statue, **Madonna della Lettera,** atop one of the tall towers of **Forte San Salvatore,** built in 1546 by the Spanish viceroys.

Via Garibaldi, running parallel to the sea, is the main street. It goes through **Piazza del Duomo,** the town's major square. South of this square is the second-most important square in Messina, **Piazza Carducci,** site of the university, founded in 1548 and reconstructed in 1927.

Ⓣⓘⓟⓢ   Rolling on, Rolling off Across the Sea

Train or bus travel across the Straits of Messina involves large-scale engineering on a most massive scale: Your train or bus will roll from the terra firma of the Italian mainland directly into the hold of a container ship for transport across the water. Passengers are allowed to remain in their seats on the train or bus, or they can stroll around the ship's upper decks for a breath of fresh air and a visit to the snack bar. A few minutes before landing, passengers head back to their seats on the train or bus, just before it rolls from its berth in the ship's hold onto the highway or railway tracks of Sicily.

To the east, the port is protected by the lighthouse known as the **Lanterna di Raineri,** on the peninsula of the same name. **Via 1 Settembre** leads from the sea to the heart of town. The transportation hub of Messina is **Piazza della Repubblica,** in front of Stazione Centrale. Most of the major bus lines converge on this square. To reach the heart of Messina from Piazza della Repubblica, head straight across the busy square and walk directly north along Via 1 Settembre to **Piazza del Duomo,** a square crowned by Messina's cathedral.

If you come by hydrofoil or ferry from Reggio di Calabria, you'll arrive 1km ($\frac{1}{2}$ mile) north of Stazione Centrale on Via Vittorio Emanuele II. Those taking a ferry from Villa San Giovanni reach land 3km ($1\frac{3}{4}$ miles) farther on or about 500m (1,640 ft.) north of Fiera, the site of Messina's trade fairs.

GETTING AROUND   Most hotels and attractions lie in the center and are best reached on foot. If you need to go farther afield, **ATM** buses depart from the transportation hub, Piazza della Repubblica. Bus tickets can be purchased at *tabacchi* (tobacco shops) or news kiosks throughout the city; they cost 1€ ($1.30) for a ticket valid for $1\frac{1}{2}$ hours or 2.60€ ($3.40) for an all-day ticket. The most useful route is no. 79, which stops at the Museo Regionale and the *duomo.*

Taxis are found mainly at the Stazione Centrale, at Piazza Cairoli, and along Via Calabria. For a 24-hour radio taxi, call ✆ **090-2934880.**

(Fast Facts   Messina

Currency Exchange The most convenient currency exchange is **Cambio/Ufficio Informazioni** (✆ **090-675234**), inside the Stazione Centrale. Open daily 7am to 9pm. There are also ATMs in the station.

Emergencies Call ✆ **113** for the police, ✆ **118** for first aid.

Hospitals Try **Ospedale Policlinico Universitario,** Via Valeria (✆ **090-2211**), or **Ospedale Piemonte,** Viale Europa (✆ **090-2221**).

Internet Access **Internet Caffè,** Via Garibaldi 72 (✆ **090-662758**), is open Monday to Saturday 9am to 8pm and charges 3€ ($3.90) per hour.

Luggage Storage A kiosk at the Stazione Centrale will store your bags for 4€ ($5.20) per day; open daily from 6am to 10pm.

Post Office The main post office is on Corso Cavour 138 (✆ **090-6015752**). Open Monday to Saturday 8am to 6:30pm.

EXPLORING THE CITY ON FOOT

As you wander around Messina, you'll come to the ruins of the church of **Santa Maria Alemanna,** built in 1220 by the crusading Teutonic Knights. The church—or what's left of it—stands at the corner of Via dei Mille, off Corso Garibaldi, directly north of Via del Vespiro and to the immediate west of Piazza Cavallotti. It's one of the few Gothic churches on the island, as the Gothic style of architecture never swept Sicily the way it did other parts of Europe. The Messinese seemed to dislike the style, and the unfinished church was left abandoned in the 15th century.

Chiesa SS. Annunziata dei Catalani When the Messinese saw their beloved church on this square after the 1908 earthquake, they called it a miracle. In an amazing feat, the earthquake stripped away much of the latter-day alterations and additions to the church, leaving its original 12th- and 13th-century architectural style intact. But because the quake leveled the earth on which the church sits, the structure seems to be sinking into the street today. Try to view the church from its western facade, where you'll see a trio of 13th-century doors.

The interior, now used as the chapel for the university, is in red, yellow, and white stone with tall Corinthian columns. The most outstanding feature is the **apse** ★, a stellar example of the Norman composite style. A nave and two aisles run to the apse, resting under a severe, brick-built cupola. This church is a kind of Arabic-Byzantine hodgepodge: Romanesque architecture blended with such Moorish features as geometrical motifs, with suggestions of the Byzantine.

In back of the church is a famous statue of **Don Juan of Austria,** the "natural" son of Emperor Charles V and a hero in the 1571 Battle of Lepanto. Amusingly, he's depicted with his foot resting proudly on the head of the Ottoman commander, Ali Bassa. The sculptor Andrea Calamech carved this monument in 1572. Incidentally, an even more famous sailor sailed from Messina to take part in that battle: Miguel de Cervantes, author of *Don Quixote.* Wounded, he was brought back to recover in a local hospital.

Piazza dei Catalani, Via Garibaldi. ✆ **090-6684111.** Free admission. Mon–Sat 9:30–11:30am; Sun 9–11:30am.

Duomo ★ This Romanesque and Norman cathedral has had a rough time of it since Roger II ordered it built in 1160. Henry VI, the Holy Roman Emperor, attended its consecration in 1197. Earth-shaking events like the 1908 quake and a 1943 Allied firebomb didn't help. The cathedral has more or less been reconstructed from scratch, although some original architectural features remain.

Its **central doorway** ★ was reconstructed using fragments originally from the 15th century. The lower part of the facade is decorated with 15th-century carvings depicting Sicilian agrarian life. The gray-and-pink interior has a trio of aisles divided by ogival arches and columns, resting under a trussed and painted ceiling. Many of the *duomo's* treasures were re-created, using fragments pulled from the ruins after the Allied bombings.

The statue of **John the Baptist** in the south aisle is attributed to Antonello Gagini in 1525. Dominating the main altar is a copy of the Byzantine **Madonna della Lettera,** the original having been destroyed by the 1943 firebombing. A pupil of Michelangelo, Jacopo del Duca, designed the **Cappella del Sacramento** in the north apse. It holds the cathedral's only original mosaic, a 14th-century work that depicts the Virgin seated with saints, queens, and archangels.

The church's treasure-trove is found in its **Tesoro,** which contains valuable candlesticks, chalices, and gold reliquaries. Much of the silverwork was created by artisans from Messina in the 17th and 18th centuries. Displayed for the first time in 3 centuries is the **Manta d'Oro,** or golden mantle, a special cover for the Virgin and Bambino on the *duomo's* altar.

Piazza del Duomo. ✆ **090-675175.** Free admission. Guided tours in English 5€ ($6.50) adults, 3.50€ ($4.55) for children 17 and under and seniors 65 and over. Oct 15–Apr 15 Mon–Sat 9am–1pm, Sun 10am–1pm and 4–6:30pm; Apr 16–Oct 14 daily 9am–1pm and 3:30–6:30pm.

Orologio Astronomico ★   The Duomo is upstaged by its 60m (197-ft.) campanile, or bell tower, with its astronomical clock standing to the left of the cathedral facade. Created in 1933 in Strasbourg, France, the clock puts on "the show of shows" at noon every day. With Schubert's *Ave Maria* scraping away on a loudspeaker in a note of high camp, the bronze automata goes into action. A lion waves his banner and roars, while a cock flaps its wing and crows. Dina and Clarenza, the heroines of Messina at the time of the Sicilian Vespers, take turns ringing the bell, and Jesus pops out of the tomb for instant resurrection. Be sure to gather in the square to check out this show.

Piazza del Duomo. Tower open to view 24 hr. Free show at noon.

Fontana di Orione ★   Standing in the center of the cathedral square, this elegant fountain was the prebaroque creation of Giovanni Angelo Montorsoli in 1547. It honors Orion, the city's mythical founder, who is seen surmounting a bevy of giants, nymphs, and crocodile-wrestling *putti* (cherubs). The fountain was built to honor the construction of the city's first aqueduct. The major figures represent the rivers Nile, Ebro, Camaro, and Tiber.

Piazza del Duomo. Open to view 24 hr.

Museo Regionale ★★   Situated in a former silk mill from 1914, the Museo Regionale, north of the Duomo, is one of Sicily's finest provincial museums and contains the island's greatest collection of art from the 15th to the 17th centuries. Its main collection consists of works rescued from the 1908 earthquake.

Its most precious relic to the devout is found in the atrium: a dozen **18th-century gilded bronze panels** that relate the tale of the Holy Letter. As legend has it, during a famine the Madonna sent the Messinese a boat filled with food but devoid of crew. The Virgin is also said to have sent along a letter containing a lock of her hair.

The museum displays many medieval and baroque treasures, including a mosaic of the Virgin and Child, known as *La Ciambretta* and dating from the 13th century. A marble low relief of **St. George** is attributed to Domenico Gagini. For us, there is nothing finer than Antonello da Messina's beautiful but damaged **polyptych ★★** of the Madonna with St. Gregory, St. Benedict, and the Annunciation, from 1473. Also on exhibit are two large **Caravaggio masterpieces ★★**, the work of "the divine" artist during his sojourn in Messina from 1608 to 1609. They represent the raising of Lazarus and the Nativity.

Greek and Roman antiquities are on view in the newly created garden pavilion. Look for the magnificent 1742 **Senator's Coach ★**, with its flamboyantly painted panels. The statues of **Neptune, Scylla,** and **Charybdis** removed from the Fontana di Nettuno (see below) are also on display.

Viale della Libertà. *(C)* **090-361292.** Admission 5€ ($6.50). June–Sept Tues–Sat 9am–1:30pm and 4–6:30pm, Sun 9am–12:30pm; Oct–May Tues–Sat 9am–1:30pm, Tues, Thurs, and Sat 3–5:30pm, Sun 9am–12:30pm.

Fontana di Nettuno   This landmark fountain stands on the seafront, at the intersection of Via della Libertà and Via Garibaldi. It's a reconstruction of the heavily damaged fountain created by Montorsoli in 1557. The original of the muscular marble god has been in the Museo Regionale ever since the statue was "castrated" by some roaming youths from Palermo. The sculpture of Neptune is depicted pacifying the sea, guarding the Straits of Messina from those wicked terrors, Scylla and Charybdis. Enjoy this fountain during the day, as the port area here isn't safe at night.

Antonello da Messina: Hometown Artist

Born around 1430 in Messina, Antonello went on to become one of the greatest masters of the Italian Renaissance and southern Italy's leading painter. Although much of his life remains a puzzle to biographers, it is known that he was very much influenced by the Flemish school, especially by the works of Jan van Eyck. Antonello was the first of the great Italian painters to master the art of working in oil. What is also known is that after many travels across Europe, this brilliant artist returned to his home city of Messina in 1476, remaining here until his death in 1478.

Antonello's works are characterized by their sense of light and attention to detail. Many of his portraits show a three-quarter view of the sitter. His paintings show intense psychological depth and are remarkable for their breakthroughs in texture, shadow, and brilliant light.

While in Sicily, you can see masterpieces of Antonello at Messina's Museo Regionale (p. 152) and Cefalù's Museo Mandralisca (p. 159).

WHERE TO STAY

For such a large city, Messina has a dearth of accommodations; its budget options are a disaster. At some, you might check in with luggage, with no guarantee that your suitcase will be there when you return to your claptrap chambers.

We've recommended only safe accommodations below, and though they offer comfort, they cater mainly to commercial travelers whose expense accounts might be greater than your vacation budget. Chances are you'll be in Messina for only a night and therefore won't feel the pinch too severely.

Expensive

Grand Hotel Liberty ★★★ This is the most elegant, appealing hotel in Messina. In fact, it's one of the finest hotels in Sicily. It originated as a battered rooming house, but the Framon chain transformed it from a sow's ear into one of the most beautiful hotels on the island. Throughout, you'll find rich paneling, marble-inlaid floors, ornate plasterwork, and lavish stained-glass windows. Guest rooms are as plush as anything you'll find in Sicily, with marble-trimmed bathrooms, fine hardwoods, high ceilings, and color schemes of champagne and gold. Thanks to this and to the welcome that's extended with genuine concern to single women traveling alone, the hotel enjoys one of the highest occupancy rates in town.

Via I Settembre 15, 98123 Messina. ⓒ **090-6409436.** Fax 090-6409340. www.nh-hotels.it. 51 units. 156€–187€ ($203–$243) double; 202€–225€ ($263–$293) suite. Rates include buffet breakfast. AE, DC, MC, V. **Amenities:** 2 bars; room service; babysitting; laundry service; dry cleaning; all nonsmoking rooms; rooms for those w/limited mobility. *In room:* A/C, TV, minibar, hair dryer, beverage maker, safe.

Moderate

Jolly Hotel Messina It isn't as architecturally dramatic, plush, or well located as its rival, Grand Hotel Liberty, but this boxy-looking *moderno* (ca. 1953) member of the nationwide hotel chain draws goodly numbers of loyal travelers, many of them in town on business. It was the first large-scale modern hotel in Messina, and was once the reigning choice in town. All rooms have double windows for insulation from the roar of traffic, and about half open onto views of the harbor. Units are well maintained, modern, and a bit banal looking but very comfortable, each with a tiled bathroom. The in-house restaurant is reviewed under "Where to Dine," below.

Via Garibaldi 126, 98100 Messina. ℂ **090-363860.** Fax 090-5902526. www.hotelclub.com. 96 units. 155€–255€ ($202–$332) double. AE, DC, MC, V. Free parking. **Amenities:** Restaurant; bar; room service; babysitting; laundry service; nonsmoking rooms; 1 room for those w/limited mobility. *In room:* A/C, TV, minibar.

Royal Palace Hotel   Built in the 1970s and recognized as a reputable hotel for business travelers, this large, boxy-looking staple of Messina's hotel scene lacks the high-blown style and elegance of its sister hotel, the Grand Hotel Liberty, but both are operated by the same chain. It's a suitable choice, thanks in part to its comfortable guest rooms, its allegiance to streamlined styling, and a genuinely charming lobby bar.

Via T. Cannizzaro 224, 98123 Messina. ℂ **090-6503.** Fax 090-2921075. www.nh-hotels.it. 107 units. 127€–150€ ($165–$195) double; 165€–240€ ($215–$312) suite. Rates include buffet breakfast. AE, DC, MC, V. **Amenities:** Restaurant; bar; room service; babysitting; laundry service; dry cleaning; nonsmoking rooms. *In room:* A/C, TV, minibar, beverage maker (in some), Wi-Fi.

WHERE TO DINE

Baked with herbs, sautéed with garlic, or even stewed into a *pesce stucco, pesce spada* (swordfish) has the people of Messina hooked. The fish is plentiful in the Straits of Messina, and as you walk along the harbor, you can see the tall-masted *felucche* (swordfish boats) patrolling the narrow channel. May and June are the best months for ordering swordfish.

Expensive

Jolly Restaurant dello Stretto ★ ITALIAN/SICILIAN   This contemporary hotel restaurant has the most panoramic view (in this case, of the wharves that service the ships coming in from Reggio Calabria) in town, along with a floor crafted from mollusk-encrusted russet marble and a sense of *la dolce vita* pizazz. To start, select an array of smoked local fish; there's nothing better on the menu. The chefs continue year after year to turn out such reliable dishes as breast of chicken with a Sicilian citrus sauce. The staff does very well with even a simple dish such as cream of fresh tomato soup with basil.

In the Jolly Hotel Messina, Via Garibaldi 126. ℂ **090-363860.** Reservations recommended Fri–Sat. Main courses 14€–18€ ($18–$23); fixed-price menus 30€–35€ ($39–$46). AE, DC, MC, V. Daily 1–3pm and 8–10pm.

Moderate

Piero ⓋValue SICILIAN   This is one of the town's most recommended restaurants, with a history dating from 1959 and an attractive interior that's outfitted with exposed paneling, terra-cotta floors, and a sense of bustling good cheer and workaday efficiency. Menu items may remind many Sicilians of their childhoods: spaghetti with mussels and crabmeat (our favorite), pennette sautéed with swordfish, clams, shrimp, tomatoes, and capers, and, finally, scampi prepared any way you ask for it. Don't overlook the luscious temptations of the antipasti table—it's a serve-yourself buffet that shouldn't be missed.

Via Ghibellina 119. ℂ **090-6409354.** Reservations recommended Fri–Sat nights. Main courses 8€–20€ ($10–$26). AE, DC, MC, V. Mon–Sat 12:30–3:15pm and 8–11:30pm. Closed Aug.

Tips   Night Wandering: Do So at Your Own Risk

Some young men in Messina earn a living picking the pockets of foreign men and snatching the purses of foreign women. A woman wandering the streets at night does so at her own risk. Although men aren't as likely to get abducted or raped, they may be at risk of being mugged. The area near the Stazione Centrale, the main rail depot, is the most dangerous part of town—that and the harbor are places to avoid after dark.

Inexpensive

Al Padrino MESSINESE/SICILIAN   Part of the charm of this place is its rough-edged, unpretentious nature. Virtually no effort has been spent on the glaringly white decor (which offers nary a hint of mystery or romance), and tables are hot and cramped, yet Al Padrino has flourished for a quarter of a century in a dreary neighborhood of heavy industry. The impossibly small kitchen churns out Messinese-style food that includes a creamy homemade *maccheroni;* spaghetti with shrimp and zucchini; swordfish meatballs with a fresh tomato and olive sauce; and many different preparations of beef. Flavors are robust and hearty, portions large. Get ready for loud voices, an in-your-face welcome, and an insight into working-class Messina at its most vivid.

Via Santa Cecilia 54–56. ✆ **090-2921000.** Main courses 8€–15€ ($10–$20). MC, V. Mon–Fri noon–3pm and 7–11pm; Sat noon–3pm. Closed Aug.

Le Due Sorelle Value SICILIAN   Set beside the square that flanks the front entrance to Messina's town hall, this restaurant occupies a long, narrow room that contains fewer than 10 tables, walls covered with wine bottles, and a carved screen that rises high above the terra-cotta floor. At lunchtime, the place is loaded with municipal office workers, one of whom happens to be the town's mayor. The unpretentious fare includes two different versions of couscous; veal with roasted vegetables; a *padellata di pesce* (panful of fish) with vegetables; and a full roster of house-made desserts.

Piazza Municipio 4. ✆ **090-44720.** Reservations recommended on Fri–Sat nights. Main courses 10€–16€ ($13–$21). MC, V. Mon–Fri 1–3pm and 8pm–midnight; Sat–Sun 8pm–midnight. Closed Aug.

Pasticceria Irrera PASTRIES   Set directly beside Messina's largest and most verdant square, this well-known cafe was established in 1910. The marble bar serves coffee and drinks; the *granita* tastes especially wonderful on warm days; and the pastry shop is widely renowned for its almond-based *Fiori di Mandorlo,* its succulent *Torta Letizia* (made with almonds and vanilla), and a chocolate-covered version of almond paste known as *Le Amarilde.*

Piazza Cairoli 12. ✆ **090-673823.** Pastries 2€–6€ ($2.60–$7.80). AE, DC, MC, V. Tues–Sat 8am–1:30pm and 4–8pm; Sun 4–8pm.

MESSINA AFTER DARK

If you're here in July or August, head for Piazza del Duomo, the central cathedral square where free concerts devoted to rock, jazz, or classical music are presented. Posters advertise cultural events, and the tourist office (see "Visitor Information," on p. 33) will have details.

If your hotel has a bar, that's often your best and safest bet for a drink. The noisiest (and most fun) *birreria* is **Gli Antenati Pub,** Corso Cavour 109 (② **090-672430**); its major drawback is that it's closed during the scorching months of June through August. Otherwise, it's a reliable place for a cold beer and pizza. The **Duck,** Via Pellegrino 107 (② **090-712772**), is a British-style pub where you'll encounter U.S. sailors stationed with NATO forces around Messina. It's closed on Mondays and from July 15 to September 15.

EASY EXCURSIONS TO THE BEACH

If the streets look a little deserted in July or August, that tells you that the Messinese are hanging out at **Mortelle,** the beach resort 12km (7¹/₂ miles) north of the city, at the northeastern tip of the island. The beachfront is a narrow strip of pebble-strewn sand known as the **Lido del Tirreno** (② **090-321001**). Thanks to large numbers of parasols and chaise longues, as well as easy access to beachfront restaurants, it's the best-accessorized beach in and around Messina. Entrance costs 4€ ($5.20) per person; parking is free. A day's rental of a *cabine* goes for 7€ to 8.50€ ($9.10–$11), while a chaise longue and parasol cost 7€ ($9.10).

From Messina, Mortelle is an easy ride on bus no. 79 or 81. Even when the sun goes down, Mortelle continues to stay busy until late at night; be careful not to get run down by cycles and scooters. The area is filled with pizzeria and bars, and in July and August, open-air films are screened at Arena Green Sky, opposite Duc Palme pizzeria.

If you find Mortelle too crowded, continue to the west, where you'll find more sandy beaches and little seaside resorts, the best of which is **Acqualadrone.**

Where to Stay

Grand Hotel Lido di Mortelle (Kids)   Set at the Messina end of the best beachfront in Mortelle, this government-rated three-star hotel was built in the late 1970s as the best lodging in town. The simple, airy guest rooms attract holiday-makers from the region, including families with young children. Nothing is particularly plush, but in this simple and unpretentious beach resort, no one really seems to mind. Access to the nearby beach is free.

SS113, Mortelle, 98164 Messina. ② **090-321017.** Fax 090-321666. www.giardinodellepalme.com. 24 units. 70€–110€ ($91–$143) double; 180€–260€ ($224–$338) triple. DC, MC, V. Free parking. **Amenities:** Restaurant; bar; outdoor pool; babysitting; laundry service; dry cleaning; nonsmoking rooms. *In room:* A/C, TV, minibar.

---

2 CEFALÙ ★★

81km (50 miles) E of Palermo, 38km (24 miles) NE of Termini Imerese, 170km (106 miles) W of Messina

The major destination along the Tyrrhenian coast, the former fishing village of Cefalù has grown into one of northern Sicily's premier stopovers. It hardly rivals Taormina in appeal, but it's trying. The town was captured in the Oscar-winning film *Cinema Paradiso.*

You can tour Cefalù in half a day and spend the rest of your time enjoying its beach. The town is not only in possession of a great patch of sand; it's also blessed with a Romanesque cathedral and a museum that houses Antonello da Messina's masterpiece *Portrait of an Unknown Man.*

Anchored between the sea and a craggy limestone promontory, Cefalù is a town of narrow medieval streets, small squares, and historic sights. Towering 278m (912 ft.) above the town is La Rocca, a massive and much-photographed crag. The Greeks thought it evoked a head, so they named the village *Kephalos,* which in time became Cefalù.

Known to be inhabited since the 9th century B.C., Cefalù was founded by the Sikels. By the 5th century B.C., it had become the fortified western outpost of Imera. The Byzantine era saw Cefalù thriving as the seat of a Greek bishop. But Saracen raids in the 8th century drove its residents away from the sea to seek refuge on top of La Rocca. Cowering in fear, the inhabitants didn't descend again until 1131, when Roger II ordered that the town be reconstructed along with his grand design for a cathedral.

ESSENTIALS

GETTING THERE   By Train   From Palermo, some three dozen trains head east to Cefalù (trip time: 1 hr.). The cost is 4.70€ ($6.10) one-way. From Messina, about a dozen trains run daily, costing 8.50€ ($11) and taking about 3 hours. Trains pull into the Stazione Termini, Piazza Stazione (© 892021).

By Bus   SAIS, Via Balsamo 20, in Palermo (© 091-6171141), runs buses between Palermo and Cefalù, charging 6€ ($7.80) one-way for the 1¹/₂-hour trip.

By Car   Follow Route 113 east from Palermo to Cefalù; count on at least 1¹/₂ hours of driving time (longer if traffic is bad). Once in Cefalù, park along either side of Via Roma for free, or pay 1€ ($1.30) per hour for a spot within one of the two lots signposted from the main street; both are within an easy walk of the town's medieval core.

VISITOR INFORMATION   The **Cefalù Tourist Office,** Corso Ruggero 77 (© 0921-421050), is open Monday to Saturday 8am to 7:30pm, Sunday 9am to 1pm. Closed on Sunday in winter.

GETTING AROUND   Taxis are the easiest way to get about and take advantage of the city's history-rich environs. **Cefalù Taxi** (© 0921-422554) operates the taxis, most of which can be found clustered at Piazza Stazione or Piazza Colombo.

Fast Facts   Cefalù

Currency Exchange   Go to **Banca Credito Siciliano,** at Via Roma and Via Giglio (© 0921-423922), near the rail depot. Open Monday to Friday 8:30am to 1:30pm and 2:45 to 3:45pm. The **Banco di Sicilia,** Piazza Garibaldi (© 0921-421103), has 24-hour ATM access.

Emergencies   For the police, call © 0921-420104; for first aid, © 0921-424544; and for Guardia Medica, © 0921-423623. The latter is open daily 8pm to 8am and located at Via Roma 15.

Hospital   The **Cefalù Hospital** is at Contrada Pietrapollastra (© 0921-920111).

Internet Access   The most central option is **Kefaonline,** Piazza San Francesco 1 (© 0921-923091), at Via Mazzini and Via Umberto; it is open Monday to Saturday 9:30am to 1:30pm and 3:30 to 7:30pm and charges 6€ ($7.80) per hour.

Pharmacies The two most central drugstores are **Cirincione,** Corso Ruggero 144 (*✆* **0921-421209**), open Monday to Friday 9am to 1pm and 4:30 to 8:30pm, Saturday and Sunday 4:30 to 11pm; and **Dr. Battaglia,** Via Roma 13 (*✆* **0921-421789**), open Monday to Saturday 9am to 1pm and 4 to 8pm.

Police The municipal police headquarters are along Via Roma (*✆* **0921-420104**).

Post Office The post office is at Via Vazzana 2 (*✆* **0921-923930**). Open Monday to Friday 8am to 6:30pm, Saturday 8am to 12:30pm.

SEEING THE SIGHTS

Getting around Cefalù on foot is easy—no cars are allowed in the historic core. The city's main street is **Corso Ruggero** ★, which starts at Piazza Garibaldi, site of one of a quartet of "gateways" to Cefalù. This is a pedestrian street that you can stroll at leisure, checking out the shops and viewing the facades of its *palazzi,* even though these are hardly comparable to those found in Palermo's medieval core.

The Romans designed a main street to bisect the village on a north-south axis. Basically that same plan is carried out today. The medieval sector is found to the west, where the poor folks once lived. Noblemen and their families and the rich clergy settled in the more posh eastern sector.

Across from the tourist office lies **Osteria Magno,** at the corner of Via Amendola and Corso Ruggero. Constructed in the 1300s but massively altered over the years, this was the legendary residence of Roger II. The palace remains closed but serves occasionally as a venue for temporary art exhibitions. For information on what's happening here, call the tourist office at *✆* **0921-421050.**

Duomo ★★   Set along Corso Ruggero, this magnificent Norman cathedral opens onto a wide square that is the center of town. Legend has it that Roger II ordered this mighty church to be constructed after his life was spared following a violent storm off the coast. Construction stretched on until 1240.

Your first impression may be that you've arrived at a fortress rather than a cathedral. Anchored at the foot of towering La Rocca, the twin-towered facade of the Duomo forms a landmark visible for miles around. Splitting the facade is a two-story portico that had to be rebuilt in the 1400s. We enjoy viewing this splendid facade in the late afternoon, when the building is bathed in golden light.

To the right of the facade on the south side, you'll find an entrance that may disappoint, if you've already been dazzled by the mosaics of Palermo's Cappella Palatina or Monreale's Duomo. But press on to the apse and vault, where you'll find a stunning array of **mosaics** ★★★ in all their shimmering glory. Completed in 1148, they are the oldest Byzantine-Norman mosaics in Sicily and among the world's most brilliant. The tour de force of the cycle is the Byzantine figure of the Pantocrator in the apse. Since this was a Norman church, Christ is depicted as a blond, not a brunette; but his nose and mouth look Greek, his brows and beard black like a Saracen's.

Regrettably, there's little else to see here. The Duomo seems to be in a perpetual state of restoration, hampered by lack of funds.

Piazza del Duomo. *✆* **0921-922021.** Free admission. Summer daily 8am–noon and 3:30–7pm; off season daily 8am–noon and 3:30–5pm.

Museo Mandralisca (Overrated) We come here just to gaze at the wonder of *Ritratto* *di un Uomo Ignoto (Portrait of an Unknown Man)* ★★, the 1465 work of Antonello da Messina. Unfortunately, the painting is badly framed and a velvet rope requires you to keep your distance. Still, this is clearly a masterpiece by the great Renaissance artist from Messina.

After being dazzled by Antonello, you may find the rest of the exhibitions disappointing. Baron Enrico Piraino di Mandralisca (1809–64) seemed to have randomly purchased anything that caught his fancy, including coins and medals, artifacts unearthed at digs at Lipari, and even such esoteric items as a Chinese puzzle in ivory. After searching for something intriguing, we did come upon a **4th-century-b.c. vase** ★, depicting a fish vendor and a customer in heated argument. After that, you must face a barrage of 20,000 shells.

Via Mandralisca 13. ⓒ **0921-421547.** Admission 5€ ($6.50). Daily 9am–1pm and 3–7pm.

La Rocca ★★ During the dog days of August, it's a long, hot, sweaty climb up to this rocky crag, but once you're here, the view is panoramic, one of the grandest in Sicily. If you're stout-hearted, count on 20 minutes to approach the ruins of the so-called Temple of Diana and another 45 huffing-and-puffing minutes to scale the pinnacle.

From Piazza Garibaldi, along Corso Ruggero, a sign—ACCESSO ALLA ROCCA—will launch you on your way. In summer, we recommend taking this jaunt either in the early morning or when evening breezes are blowing.

In Cefalù's heyday, this was the site of the acropolis of Cephaloedium, with a temple dedicated to Hercules on the top. Over the centuries, residents from below used this zone as a stone quarry.

You'll come first to the ruins of the **Tempio di Diana,** which popular tradition has attributed as a temple to the goddess Diana. Now consisting of mammoth trapezoidal blocks, the temple was constructed or reconstructed in various stages from the 9th century to the 4th century B.C.

As you continue to the top, you'll see the restored **ancient Arab** and **medieval fortifications.** From here, you can see all the way to the skyline of Palermo in the west or to Capo d'Orlando in the east. The lookout tower here, now in ruins, was called Torre Caldura and guarded an unfriendly coastline. On a clear day you can't see forever, but you will get a stunning view of the Aeolian Islands.

HITTING THE BEACH

Cefalù's crescent-shaped beach is one of the best along the northern coast. Regrettably, it's always packed in summer. In town, we prefer **Lido Poseidon.** At the best bar here, **Poseidon,** Via Lungomare Giuseppe Giardino (ⓒ **0921-424646**), you can rent an umbrella or a deck chair for 7€ ($9.10). It's open daily May to September. **Spiaggia Attrezzata,** in town just off the Lungomare, is another good beach, with brilliant white sand and turquoise shallows. You'll also find free showers here. Other recommended beaches are found west of town at **Spiaggia Settefrati** and **Spiaggia Mazzaforno.**

WHERE TO STAY

If you want to spend the night in Cefalù, and you have wheels, you'll find the hotels outside of town more comfortably satisfying.

Astro Hotel Originally built in 1969 and intelligently renovated several times since, this is the first hotel many visitors see when they approach Cefalù from its western outskirts. Small-scale and unpretentious, with a hardworking and sensitive staff, it offers well-equipped albeit simple rooms, each with terrazzo or tile floors and a shower-only bathroom. (*Note:* Hot water here means tepid.) About a third of the rooms have balconies. Parking is usually difficult in the traffic-clogged neighborhoods adjacent to the city's car-free inner core, but here it's free and readily available within a walled-in lot directly across the street. The hotel lies just uphill from the private beach, about a 12-minute walk from the medieval core.

Via Roma 105, 90015 Cefalù. (℃ **0921-421639.** Fax 0921-423103. www.astrohotel.it. 30 units. 80€–180€ ($104–$234) double; 110€–220€ ($143–$286) triple. Rates include buffet breakfast. AE, DC, MC, V. Free parking. **Amenities:** Restaurant; bar; babysitting; laundry service. *In room:* A/C, TV.

Hotel Tourist (Value)   Despite its lackluster name, this is a desirable hotel dating from 1970 but much renovated. It enjoys a tranquil position on the beach, about a 10-minute walk from the center, and is situated to offer scenic views of not only the water but also Cefalù itself. Bedrooms are midsize and simply adorned, each equipped with a shower-only bathroom. The most desirable units have balconies with views of the sea. A private beach lies across the highway from the hotel. The staff is one of the most helpful in the area, serving an excellent breakfast to fortify you for the day ahead.

Lungomare Giardina, 90015 Cefalù. (℃ **0921-421750.** Fax 0921-923916. www.touristhotel.it. 46 units. 90€–230€ ($117–$299). Rates include continental breakfast. AE, MC, V. Free parking. **Amenities:** Restaurant; bar; outdoor pool; laundry service. *In room:* A/C, TV, minibar, hair dryer, safe.

Kalura ★ (Kids)   Set amid palm trees, Kalura has something of a North African feel to it. This snug retreat is 3km (2 miles) east along the coast on a little promontory, a 20-minute walk from the center of Cefalù (follow the street signs from town to reach it). Run by the same family for nearly 3 decades, it's a friendly, inviting oasis. Guest rooms are well furnished; most open onto a sea view. Nothing is too elaborate here, including the simple shower-only bathrooms. A special park is reserved for children, one reason this is a very family-friendly place. The private beach offers good swimming in unpolluted waters. The hotel is also the most sports-conscious in the area, and can arrange excursions to nearby attractions as well.

Via Cavallaro 13, 90015 Contrada Caldura. (℃ **0921-421354.** Fax 0921-423122. www.hotel-kalura.com. 73 units. 190€ ($247) double. Rates include continental breakfast. AE, DC, MC, V. Closed Nov 1–Mar 7. **Amenities:** Restaurant; 2 bars; outdoor pool; tennis; watersports equipment/rentals; mountain bikes; children's park; room service; babysitting; laundry service; dry cleaning; rooms for those w/limited mobility. *In room:* A/C, TV, hair dryer.

Riva del Sole ★   The town's finest accommodations are in a three-story building rising along the seafront. Completely refurbished, it has its own discreet charm and harmonious styling in both its public and private rooms. Run by the Cimino family since it opened in 1966, it offers both attentive service and a welcoming atmosphere. Special features include a graceful garden, a solarium, a panoramic terrace, and an intimate bar. Bedrooms are midsize, tastefully furnished, and well equipped, each with a private balcony or veranda opening onto the water. The chefs do best with their take on Sicilian cuisine, but also turn out well-crafted Italian dishes and international specialties.

Lungomare G. Giardina, 90015 Cefalù. (℃ **0921-421230.** Fax 0921-421984. www.rivadelsole.com. 28 units. 140€–150€ ($182–$195) double; 190€–200€ ($247–$260) triple. Rates include buffet breakfast. AE, MC, V. Free parking. Closed Oct to mid-Dec. **Amenities:** Restaurant; bar; room service; babysitting; laundry service; dry cleaning; all nonsmoking rooms. *In room:* A/C, TV, minibar, safe.

If you're heading out on an excursion, perhaps to Parco delle Madonie (p. 163), you can pick up the makings for a delightful picnic at **Gatta Gaetano Alimentari e Salumeria,** Corso Ruggero 152 (© **0921-423156**). This well-stocked deli offers the best of Sicilian cheeses and sausages, along with cured meats, to-die-for olives, and luscious fruits—everything except bread, which you'll find sold in many places all over town.

For the best cakes and cookies, stop by **Pasticceria Serio Pietro,** V. G. Giglio 29 (© **0921-422293**), which also sells more than a dozen flavors of the most delicious gelato in town.

Moderate

Al Porticciolo ★ SICILIAN At the seafront end of the old town, nearly adjacent to the old port, this restaurant is set within a cavelike stone-sided room that used to be a storage point for fish (long before the days of refrigeration). During the day, dine indoors in air-conditioned comfort to avoid the heat, but at night (when all traffic is stopped along this street), opt for an outdoor table. The traditional pasta with sardines is well prepared here, but we're also fond of the tagliatelle of octopus, the addictive grilled radicchio, and the country-style kettle of mussel soup—just right for a seafaring town. The *cassata Siciliana* (layered sponge cake filled with ricotta, chocolate, and candied fruits) here is among the best we've ever tasted.

Via Carlo Ortolani di Bordonaro 66. © **0921-921981.** Main courses 8€–19€ ($10–$25); fixed-price menus 20€–35€ ($26–$46). AE, DC, MC, V. Thurs–Tues noon–3pm and 7pm–midnight. Closed Nov to mid-Dec.

Kentia ★★ ITALIAN This restaurant manages to evoke a bit more glamour, and a lot more style, than some of its nearby competitors. It's a cool hideaway from the oppressive sun, thanks in part to tiled floors, high masonry vaulting, and an understated elegance. A dozen homemade pasta dishes are prepared daily, and you'd have to walk to Messina to find swordfish as good as that grilled here. We generally stick to the *pesce del giorno* (catch of the day), which can be grilled to your specifications. The chefs also prepare a daily vegetarian fixed-price menu as well as one devoted entirely to fish.

Via N. Botta 15. © **0921-423801.** Reservations recommended. Main courses 7€–15€ ($9.10–$20); fixed-price vegetarian menu 18€ ($23); fixed-price fish menu 30€ ($39). AE, DC, MC, V. June–Sept daily noon–3pm and 7:30–11pm; Oct–May Wed–Mon noon–3pm and 7:30–11pm.

La Brace SICILIAN This has been a landmark restaurant in Cefalù since 1977. It's near the Duomo, on an impossibly narrow cobblestone street about a block downhill from the center of town. The Sicilian cuisine here has a number of imaginative Asian and other international touches—a surprise in this part of the world. We recommend the tagliatelle with porcini mushrooms and the mouthwatering *spiedini di pesce spada* (marinated swordfish roasted with sweet peppers and served in a lemony mustard sauce). As a bow to Tex-Mex cuisine, chili con carne appears on the menu, but serious foodies prefer the gratin of octopus. Other recommended main dishes include turkey filet with cherry sauce, swordfish kabob with a mustard lemon sauce, and spaghetti with prawns and swordfish. The house dessert, justifiably celebrated locally, is a banana doused with orange liqueur, baked, and then topped with whipped cream.

Via XXV Novembre 10 (off Corso Ruggero). © **0921-423570.** Reservations recommended. Main courses 7€–15€ ($9.10–$20); fixed-price lunch 19€–35€ ($25–$46); fixed-price dinner 29€–40€ ($38–$52). AE, DC, MC, V. Tues–Sun 1–2:30pm and 7–11:30pm. Closed Dec 15–Jan 15.

MESSINA & THE TYRRHENIAN COAST

8

CEFALÙ

Osteria del Duomo ★★ SICILIAN/INTERNATIONAL The hippest, most sophisticated restaurant in Cefalù is right in front of the town's famous cathedral, at the bottom of steps that have been trod upon by Norman knights and *La Dolce Vita* movie stars alike. Many tables sit in the open air on cobblestones, others under the vaulted ceiling of the air-conditioned interior. We think the chefs here top those at La Brace (Michelin's Cefalù favorite): They will enthrall you with their smoked fish, their seafood salads are the town's best (and the ideal food on a hot summer day), and their truly excellent carpaccio of beef will appeal to serious carnivores. Count on freshly made salads and desserts as well.

Via Seminario 3. ℂ 0921-421838. Reservations recommended Sat–Sun. Main courses 8€–16€ ($10–$21). AE, DC, MC, V. Tues–Sun noon–midnight. Closed mid-Nov to mid-Dec.

Inexpensive

Al Gabbiano SICILIAN/SEAFOOD Unlike most of the other restaurants in Cefalù, which are tucked into hideaway alleys within the medieval core, this one sits directly across from the town's most popular beach, allowing sun-kissed diners access throughout the day and evening. The atmosphere evokes a woodsy-looking tavern with breezy access to the outdoors and touches of heavy timbers and exposed stone. Fresh fish, a menu constant, tastes best grilled and served with spinach or fava beans. The mainstay of the north coast, swordfish, is served here with a tasty onion sauce. You can also order couscous with fresh fish. No pasta in town compares to this place's linguine with shrimp, clams, and mussels. And one of our favorite items is zucchini flowers, which the chefs are skilled at deep-frying or grilling.

Via Lungomare Giardina 17. ℂ 0921-421495. Reservations not necessary. Main courses 7€–12€ ($2.10–$16). AE, DC, MC, V. Thurs–Tues noon–3pm and 7:30–11pm.

L'Antica Corte SICILIAN The authentic Sicilian cuisine served here is market fresh and satisfying, despite the restaurant's slight touristic bent (the waiters, for example, appear with red bandannas and sashes like those worn by the Saracen pirates of yore). In good weather, try to get a table set under grapevines in the old courtyard. Otherwise, you'll find the air-conditioned seats inside a welcome relief from the heat. The pizzas are among the best in town—try the "Drago," with spicy sausage. Tempting pastas include one with hot peppers *(all'arrabbiata)* and another with shrimp, mushrooms, and a dousing of limoncello. The best bet is the catch of the day, which the chefs flavor with herbs and grill to your specifications.

Cortile Pepe 7, off Corso Ruggero. ℂ 0921-423228. Reservations recommended. Main courses 9€–13€ ($12–$17); pizza 5€–9€ ($6.50–$12); menu turístico 15€ ($20). AE, MC, V. Fri–Wed noon–3pm and 7–11:30pm; Sat–Sun only in Feb and Nov.

Lo Scoglio Ubriaco (The Drunken Rock) SICILIAN This restaurant is set high atop a rocky cliff at the edge of the old town. Walk in boldly and bypass the less desirable tables in the narrow dining room. Near the back, you'll find a staircase that meanders down onto a terrace perched atop jagged rocks, just above sea level and overlooking the fortifications on either side of the old port. If a table is available, this is where you should sit. Menu items are well prepared, albeit relatively predictable in light of the roughly equivalent food served in the town's other restaurants. A tangy mussel soup might tempt you before you proceed to the mixed grill of either fish or meat. The house-style tagliatelle is understandably a local favorite, served with a well-flavored mussel and cream sauce. You can also order another pasta dish, farfalle with tuna roe.

Via Carlo Ortolani di Bordonaro 2-4. © 0921-423370. Reservations recommended. Main courses
8€-18€ ($10-$23). AE, MC, V. July-Aug daily noon-2:30pm and 7pm-midnight; Sept-June Wed-Mon
noon-2:30pm and 7pm-midnight.

CEFALÙ AFTER DARK

Many townspeople like to go home, eat their catch of the day, and retire early after watching some TV. The liveliest spot in Cefalù is **Bip Bop Pub, Bar & Bistro,** Via Nicolà Botta 4 (© **0921-923972**). The rock-'n'-roll music and youthful (or at least young-at-heart) crowd in this English-style pub pull you very far away from the medieval setting of old Cefalù. Opt for a cocktail or beer on tap, crepes, sandwiches, salads, or a plate of pasta. Open daily from 11am to 4am; closed Mondays from October to March.

EASY EXCURSIONS

On Cefalù's doorstep lies an array of some of Sicily's greatest attractions, including a national park, **Parco Naturale Regionale delle Madonie;** the ruins of ancient **Tyndaris** (which date from 1500 B.C.); and the ceramic capital of **Santo Stefano di Camastra,** among many other sights.

You can easily schedule 3 nights for a visit to Cefalù, allowing 1 day to explore the town and another 2 days to see the highlights in the surrounding environs.

Parco Naturale Regionale Delle Madonie ★★

Since 1989, some 39,679 hectares (98,049 acres) of the most beautiful land in Sicily has been set aside as a national park. The park begins just 6km (3³/₄ miles) south of Cefalù. You can explore it on your own if you have plenty of time. There are no guided tours of the park.

The park has been called a botanic paradise, as it contains more than half of the 2,600 species known in Sicily. Some of the most ancient rocks and mountains on the island are found here, along with some of the most spectacular peaks. Among them, **Pizzo Carbonara,** at 1,979m (6,493 ft.), is the highest mountain in Sicily outside of Mount Etna.

The park is far from a wilderness—it is inhabited and contains any number of charming villages. To reach it from Cefalù, follow the road directions south for 14km (8³/₄ miles) to the **Santuario di Gibilmanna.** From the belvedere at this town, in front of the little 17th-century church, you can take in a **panoramic view** ★★ of the Madonie, including the peak of Pizzo Carbonara.

The Santuario di Gibilmanna is a shrine to the Virgin Mary. The Madonna is said to have shown signs of life in the 18th century when she was restoring sight to blind pilgrims and speech to a mute. Since the Vatican confirmed this claim, Gibilmanna has been one of the most important shrines in Sicily, drawing the devout.

After taking in the view, continue southeast, following the signs to **Castelbuono,** an idyllic town that grew around a *castello* (castle) constructed in the 1300s. You can stop over to visit its historic core, **Piazza Margherita.** The church here, **Madrice Vecchia,** dates from the 14th century, when it was built on the ruins of a pagan temple.

If you arrive during the lunch hour, your best bet for a bite to eat is **Romittaggio,** Località San Guglielmo Sud (© **0921-671323**), 5km (3 miles) south of Castelbuono. Specializing in simple mountain food, the restaurant is installed in a monastery from the Middle Ages. In summer, you can request a table in the arcades of the cloister. Meals range in price from 8€ to 18€ ($10-$23). The restaurant is closed from June 15 to July 15 and on Wednesdays year-round.

The road continues south to **Petralia Soprana** ★★, at 1,147m (3,763 ft.) the loftiest town in Madonie and one of the best-preserved medieval villages of Sicily, with narrow streets and houses of local stone. A grand belvedere is found at Piazza del Popolo, with a **stunning vista** ★★ toward Enna in the east.

At the end of Via Loreto, you can visit the church of **Santa Maria di Loreto,** built on the site of a Saracen fortress and framed by a set of campaniles. In back of the church is **Madonie's greatest panorama** ★★★, with glorious views of volcanic Mount Etna.

The next stopover is **Petralia Sottana,** overlooking the River Imera Valley. This little village, perched on a rocky spur 1,000m (3,281 ft.) above sea level, is the headquarters of the national park service, **Ente Parco,** Corso Paolo Agliata 16 (© **0921-684011**). The office is open Monday to Friday 9:30am to 1:30pm and 3:30 to 6:30pm.

At this point, head west along S120, stopping at **Polizzi Generosa,** another hilltop magnificently situated on a limestone spur. The **view** ★★★ at Piazza XXVII Maggio is one of the most spectacular in Madonie, taking in its loftiest peaks and the scenic valley of the River Himera.

Here you can begin your journey north back to Cefalù, passing through little **Scillato** until you reach **Collesano,** a vacation resort where the aura of the Middle Ages still lingers.

It is deceptively simple in its exterior, but the **Chiesa Madre,** reached by going up a flight of stairs, is filled with art treasures. This church contains masterpieces by the 16th-century painter Gaspare Vazzano, who signed his name "Zoppo di Gangi"; his cycle of **frescoes** ★ illustrates scenes from the lives of Jesus Christ, St. Paul, and St. Peter. He also painted another magnificent canvas, *Santa Maria degli Angeli* ★, found in the north aisle.

After viewing Collesano, you can continue north until you reach autostrada A20, which will take you back to Cefalù, your best base for the night.

Castel Di Tusa

This pleasant little town on the sea is only of minor interest. It opens onto one of the most beautiful "bayscapes" on the island, but not a lot happens here. Despite a ruined feudal fortress that rises from the highest hill, Castel di Tusa might pass for an uneventful fishing village surrounded by rocky, scrub-covered landscape. What makes it worthwhile is an overnight stay at one of Sicily's most remarkable hotels (see below). You can also use the hotel as a base for exploring Madonie Park (see above).

You'll really need a car for getting around the area. Take autostrada A20 from Cefalù, which becomes the SS113 for its final stretch to Castel di Tusa, a distance 25km (16 miles) east of Palermo.

Atelier Sul Mare ★★★ (Finds)   Sometimes defined as an "arts-oriented ashram," the most unusual hotel in Sicily occupies a boxy, concrete building that was erected in the 1960s as a conventional hotel with access to a nearby beach. Any vestiges of its original decor were ripped out long ago by the iconoclastic owner, Messina-born Antonio Presti. Today, the hotel artfully combines aspects of Bauhaus architecture, pop art, psychedelics, hints of flagrant and very permissive sexuality, and good doses of Italian-based socialist politics.

The black-and-white lobby's only adornments are hundreds of photocopies of articles about the place. About 25 of the guest rooms are comfortable, "conventional" units, each with original art and a sense of whimsy. The other 15 rooms were each decorated by an artist who lived on the premises for several months while completing the work. Examples include a sinuously curved all-black room by Chilean artist Raoul Ruiz, with a circular bed and a square-shaped skylight that blasts sunlight representing a spiritual liberty from oppressive governments and cultures. A room decorated in honor of filmmaker and gay activist Pasolini was conceived as a mud-built grotto that might remind you of a miniature mosque.

Via Cesare Battisti 4, 98070 Castel di Tusa. ℭ **0921-334295.** Fax 0921-334283. www.ateliersulmare.com. 40 units. 110€–180€ ($143–$234) conventional double; 160€–230€ ($208–$299) designer double. Rates include buffet breakfast. DC, MC, V. Free parking. **Amenities:** Restaurant; bar; occasional classes in pottery and ceramics. *In room:* A/C, no phone.

Santo Stefano Di Camastra

Heading east of Cefalù for 33km (21 miles), you'll approach one of the ceramic capitals of Sicily. A visit here can easily be tied in with a stopover at Castel di Tusa (see above). Santo Stefano lies 13km (8 miles) east of Castel di Tusa.

If you're driving, follow A20 east from Cefalù, which becomes the SS113 on its approach to Santo Stefano. The town is also on the main rail link from Palermo/Cefalù, heading east into Messina.

Santo Stefano lies at the western end of the **Parco dei Nebrodi,** one of the natural beauty spots to the east of Parco delle Madonie (p. 163). Following a disastrous landslide in 1682, the town was laid out in a geometric grid said to have been copied from the gardens of Versailles.

On the approach roads in and out of town, you'll see dozens of vendors hawking ceramics and pottery. The industry grew here because the area in the hinterlands is said to have some of the best clay in Sicily. Most of the pottery styles are traditional, but others are glaringly *moderno.* Would you believe a set of tableware devoted to the late Princess Di? In this vast array of merchandise, not all is of equal quality. Some items are shoddily made and filled with imperfections. Examine each piece before buying, and be prepared to haggle over prices.

If the many choices overwhelm you, head for the shop we've found the most reliable over the years: **Ceramiche Franco,** Via Nazionale 8 (ℭ **0921-337222**). Craftsmanship and skill go into the Franco family's ceramics, which are inspired by various artistic movements in Italy, especially the Renaissance and the baroque. Hours are Monday to Saturday 9am to 7:30pm.

Before actually buying anything, you might want to familiarize yourself with the area's wares by visiting the **Museum della Ceramica** ★, Via Palazzo (ℭ **0921-331110**), in the heart of town in the Palazzo Trabia. The restored palace itself is a thing of beauty, especially its **tiled floors** ★, **antique furnishings** (mainly from the 1700s), and beautifully **frescoed ceilings.** You'll learn how varied ceramics can be and the technique and skills that go into making them. It's open from May to September, Tuesday to Sunday 9am to 1pm and 4 to 8pm; and from October to April, Tuesday to Sunday 9am to 1pm and 3:30 to 7:30pm. Admission is free.

Tyndaris ★

At Capo Tindari, approximately 85km (53 miles) from Cefalù, stand the ruins of Tyndaris, on a lonely, rocky promontory overlooking Golfo di Patti. It was known to the ancients since it was founded by Dionysius the Elder in 396 B.C. after a victory over the Carthaginians. For a long time it formed a protective union with its ally, Syracuse, until that eastern Sicilian city fell to the Romans in 256 B.C. Tyndaris has had a rough time of it: It was partially destroyed by a landslide in the 1st century A.D., and then suffered an earthquake in A.D. 365. The Arabs in the 10th century were particularly vicious in destroying its buildings.

The **view** ★★ alone is almost reason enough to go; it stretches from Milazzo in the east to Capo Calavà in the west. On a clear day, there are stunning vistas of the Aeolian Islands, with Vulcano the nearest.

The most serious excavations of the site began after World War II, although digs were launched much less successfully in the 19th century. Most of the ruins you see today date from the days of the Roman Empire, including the **basilica,** the exact function of which remains unknown. Just beyond the basilica is a **Roman villa,** which is in rather good condition (you can still see the original mosaics on the floor). Cut into a hill at the end of town is a wide **theater,** built by the Greeks in the late 4th century B.C. The **Insula Romana** contains the ruins of baths, patrician villas with fragments of mosaics, and what may have been taverns or drinking halls. Beyond the entrance to the site on the left is a small display of artifacts dug up on the site. You can also see the ruins of defensive walls constructed during the dreadful reign of Dionysius.

The ruins are open daily from 9am until 1 hour before sunset. Admission is 2.10€ ($2.75) for adults, 1.05€ ($1.40) for students and children. For information on the archaeological area, call ☏ 0941-369023.

The site is also a place of pilgrimage for the devout who flock to the **Santuario di Tindari** (☏ 0941-369003), which contains a Byzantine Black Virgin, or the *Madonna Negra*. Legend has it that this Madonna washed up on the shores of Tyndaris centuries ago. The sanctuary is open Monday to Friday 6:45am to 12:30pm and 2:30 to 7pm, Saturday and Sunday 6:45am to 12:30pm and 2:30 to 8pm. Admission is free.

The site is best reached by private car. From Cefalù, motorists continue east approximately 85km (53 miles) along the main coastal route (A20/SS113). A small tourist office (☏ 0941-241136), at the site at Piazza Marconi, offers limited information. Open Monday to Friday 9am to 1pm and 3 to 7pm, Saturday 9am to 1pm.

3 TERMINI IMERESE

40km (25 miles) E of Palermo

Long known for its thermal waters, this town might merit a couple hours of your time. Although it is used mainly as a base for those wishing to take side trips from here, it does offer a few treasures.

Cáccamo, to the south, is one of the island's biggest and most magnificent bastions, and Himera, to the east, is the site of the ruins of a 7th-century-B.C. Greek settlement. For the dedicated sightseer, both Cáccamo and Himera are more rewarding than Termini Imerese itself, its name deriving from the Latin *Thermae Himerenses,* meaning "Hot Springs of Himera." Among those who came for the cure was the Greek poet Pindar. In a rather fanciful endorsement, Diodorus claimed that the springs were created by three nymphs and that Hercules was the first to enjoy the baths.

The town is split into two sectors—**Termini Bassa (Lower Termini)** and **Termini Alta (Upper Termini).** The upper town comprises most of the spa's historic center, whereas the transportation hub for the area is in the lower town. Once enclosed by fortified walls, the city lost most of its charms to the creeping industrialization that followed the end of World War II, including some hideously ugly petrochemical factories.

Moments **Palms, Pines, Ficus & Roman Remains**

In back of the cathedral, Via Belvedere leads up to a panoramic terrace offering one of the **grandest seascapes ★★** along the Tyrrhenian coast. The sea is set against the backdrop of Monte Calógero. From here, you'll also have a vista of the lower town and the port. Try not to let the industrialization spoil this otherwise idyllic vision for you. A short walk to your left leads to the "always locked" church dedicated to **Santa Caterina d'Alessandria** in the 14th century. Continue along at this point to the park, **Villa Palmieri,** laid out in 1845. Here you will see the ruins of an ancient Roman curia. Follow Via Anfiteatro from the park to the ruins of a **Roman amphitheater** from the 1st century A.D.

ESSENTIALS

GETTING THERE **By Train** Trains arrive from Palermo on the main Palermo-Messina line every hour (trip time: 20 min.). A one-way ticket from Palermo costs 3.10€ ($4.05). For rail information, call ✆ **892021.**

By Bus Buses run by **SAIS,** Via Balsamo 20, Palermo (✆ **091-6171141**), make frequent runs to Termini Imerese throughout the day. A one-way ticket costs 3.50€ ($4.55).

By Car From Palermo, head east along A19, the Palermo-Messina autostrada. The exit for Termini Imerese is clearly marked.

EXPLORING THE TOWN

Duomo Largely rebuilt in the 17th century, this cathedral has been much modified over the years. Its facade, which dates mainly from 1912, was designed to fit a quartet of early-16th-century statues (the present ones are copies). Inside are some treasures, most notably 19th-century sculptures including an 1842 marble relief, *Madonna del Ponte ★*, found in the fourth chapel on the right. In the Chapel of San Bartolomeo, look for an elaborate **Venetian rococo sedan chair,** and in the chapel dedicated to the Immaculate Conception, seek out the **wooden statue** by Quattrocchi from 1799. The *Crucifix* at the main altar was painted on both sides by Pietro Ruzzolone in 1484.

Piazza del Duomo. No phone. Free admission. Daily 9am–7pm.

Museo Civico ★ Founded in 1873 in an abandoned 14th-century *palazzo,* this is one of the finest regional museums along Sicily's northern coast. A visit here is like taking a class in the art, archaeology, and natural history of the area. Prehistory is even represented, with displays of artifacts recovered from nearby caves inhabited in Paleolithic and Neolithic times. The most precious relics are those removed from the ruins of Himera, including the **head of a lion ★** that came from the Temple of Victory between 480 and 460 B.C. A large stone slab with Arabic inscriptions may have been mounted over the gates of Termini Imerese during the days of its Saracen rule. You can also see mosaics, sarcophagi, and even the lead pipes used by the Romans for their plumbing (the lead eventually poisoned them). Look for a Byzantine triptych and paintings by Mattia Preti, pupil of Caravaggio. A most impressive triptych, *Madonna and Saints ★*, is by Gaspare da Pesaro from 1453.

Via del Museo Civico. ✆ **091-8128279.** Free admission. Tues–Sat 9am–1pm and 4–6:30pm; Sun 9am–1pm.

Grand Hotel delle Terme ★   This 19th-century hotel stands right over the spring whose famous waters won an endorsement from Plutarch. Even today you can enjoy the same curative waters as the Roman soldiers of yore: In the basement is a thermal spa that offers such treatments as mud therapy. The hotel offers modernized rooms with traditional furnishings, mostly in teak. Half of the guest rooms come with bathrooms with tubs, the other half bathrooms with showers; suites have Jacuzzis. The place is located in the commercial center of the lower town near the port.

Piazza delle Terme 2, 90018 Termini Imerese. ℂ **091-8113557.** Fax 091-8113107. www.grandhotel delleterme.it. 69 units. 80€–100€ ($104–$130) double; 45€ ($59) extra suite. AE, DC, MC, V. **Amenities:** Restaurant; bar; outdoor pool; Jacuzzi; gym; spa; sauna; salon; room service; massage; laundry service; dry cleaning. *In room:* A/C, TV, minibar, hair dryer.

WHERE TO DINE

Ristorante Pub Santi e Peccatori SICILIAN/SEAFOOD   The best restaurant in town serves tempting dishes for discriminating palates, often visitors from Palermo, who know of this place's charm and attractively priced cuisine. Sicilians claim that the waters of Termini Imerese make the best pasta in Sicily, and they may be right: We still recall a memorable spaghetti marinara with shrimp, mussels, and—as an added surprise—pistachios. For a main course, we recommend the fresh fish of the day grilled with aromatic herbs.

In the Hotel Il Gabbiano, Via Libertà 221. ℂ **091-8113262.** Reservations not needed. Main courses 8€–15€ ($10–$20). AE, DC, MC, V. Wed–Mon noon–3pm and 8pm–midnight.

EASY EXCURSIONS

You may opt to spend less time in Termini Imerese and more time in its environs, exploring two of the north coast's most impressive attractions: Himera and Cáccamo.

HIMERA   This was the site of a 7th-century-B.C. Greek settlement, 15km (9 miles) east along the coast. It's famous for the remains of the **Tempio della Vittoria (Temple of Victory)** ★, situated on a coastal plain at the mouth of the Imera River off Route SS113. Frankly, these ruins are not as impressive as those of Solunto outside Palermo (p. 132), but they're worth an hour or so of your time.

In 480 B.C., Himera was the site of one of the major battles of Sicily. The Greeks had settled in the east, the Carthaginians in the west. The Greeks from Agrigento and Syracuse defeated a massive army led by Hamilcar, who was killed in battle. The Tempio della Vittoria was constructed to honor this Greek victory; the labor was supplied by the Carthaginians taken prisoner. The triumph was short-lived, however. In 409 B.C., Hamilcar's nephew, Hannibal, attacked Himera in revenge for his uncle's death. He razed the city, killing most of its inhabitants.

Himera's temple contains little more than its foundation, with no standing columns. Yet the setting and the view make it worth a visit, especially if you have the imagination to bring it alive. If your imagination fails you, you can visit a modern antiquarium that shows diagrams of how the temple looked in its heyday. The remains of two other temples are also found in this archaeological park.

To get to the temple site from Termini Imerese, you can take one of four daily buses run by **Nancini** (ℂ **091-8144497**); the round-trip costs 4.50€ ($5.85). Buses depart from the train station at Termini Imerese. The site charges admission of 2€ ($2.60). It's open Monday to Saturday 9am until 1 hour before sunset, Sunday 9am to 2pm.

CÁCCAMO The Middle Ages live on at **Castello Cáccamo** ★, a huge 12th-century fortress overlooking the San Leonardo River Valley. This is the greatest fortress in Sicily and one of the most majestic in all of southern Italy. Dominating the tranquil village of Cáccamo, the feudal castle was built by the Normans on the site of an older Saracen fortress. The entrance is from Via Termitana on a rocky spur.

With its massive towers and battlements, the gray stone castle looks like something Disney might have created, but it's the real thing. It has some 130 rooms, its most impressive being **Sala della Congiura.** You can visit the theater hall, the court chapel, the 17th-century residence of various lords, the gatehouse, the knight's house, the keep, and the guard tower as well as the ramp wall. The castle is rather bare-bones inside, but worth seeing is the **panoramic view** ★ from the tower, **Torre Mastra.**

Castello Cáccamo, on Corso Umberto (© **091-8103248**), is 12km (7¹/₂ miles) south of Termini Imerese and 52km (32 miles) southeast of Palermo. If you're taking the Palermo-Catania autostrada, the exit for Cáccamo is signposted, 10km (6 miles) to the south. Buses bound for Cáccamo leave throughout the day from Termini Imerese's main train station. The castle is open daily 9am to 1pm and 3 to 7pm. Admission is 2€ ($2.60) for adults, free for children 17 and younger.

Don't get your hopes up if you're hungry: Restaurants at Cáccamo are very limited. The finest dining choice in town is **A Castellana,** Piazza Caduti 4 (© **091-8148667**), located in the stables of the castle and serving hearty, affordable Sicilian fare. The pastas are the best, with more than a dozen varieties prepared fresh every day. The chefs also make 55 different pizzas.

After you visit the castle, take an hour to walk around the medieval village. The highlight is the main square, **Piazza Duomo** ★, built on two different levels. The higher part contains a spectacular complex of structures, including the 17th-century **Palazzo del Monte di Pietà,** flanked on the right by **Chiesa delle Anime Sante del Purgatorio** and on the left by **Oratorio del Santissimo Sacramento.** The whole square looks like a stage set.

On the western side of the square is the town's most interesting church, **Chiesa Madre,** open Monday to Saturday 8am to 1pm. Dating from 1090, it was largely rebuilt in the 1400s and given a heavily baroque overlay centuries later. The church contains some treasures, including a painting from 1641 by Mattia Stomer, called the *Miracle of Sant'Isidoro Agricola.*

For information, contact the **Ufficio Turismo del Commune di Cáccamo,** Piazza Duomo (© **091-8122032**). It's open in July and August, Monday and Friday 7:30am to 2pm, Tuesday to Thursday 7:30am to 2pm and 3 to 6pm; and September to June, Wednesday and Friday 8am to 2pm, Tuesday and Thursday 8am to 2pm and 3 to 6pm.

9

The Aeolian Islands

The Aeolian Islands (Isole Eolie o Lipari) have been inhabited for more than 3,000 years, in spite of volcanic activity that even now causes the earth to issue forth sulfuric belches, streams of molten lava, and hissing clouds of steam. **Lipari** (36 sq. km/14 sq. miles) is the largest and most developed island, **Stromboli** (13 sq. km/5 sq. miles) is the most distant and volcanically active, and **Vulcano** (21 sq. km/8 sq. miles), with its brooding, potentially volatile cone and therapeutic mud baths, is the island closest to the Sicilian "mainland." The remaining islands (**Salina, Filicudi, Alicudi,** and **Panarea**) offer only bare-bones facilities and are visited mainly by day-trippers, if at all.

Despite the potential for volcanic activity, the area attracts visitors (mainly Germans and Italians) thanks to its crystalline waters that offer prime snorkeling, diving, and spearfishing and its photogenic beaches composed of hot black sand and rocky outcroppings jutting into the Tyrrhenian Sea. The volcanoes themselves offer hikers the thrill of peering into a bubbling crater.

Ancient Greek sailors believed that these seven windswept islands were the home of Aeolus, god of the winds. He supposedly lived in a cave on Vulcano, keeping the winds of the world in a bag to be opened only with great caution. "All the winds of the world" do seem to converge here at times. Until tourists began to arrive, the Aeolian Islands were one tough place to make a living. Many of its inhabitants long ago emigrated to a better life in the United States or Australia; even today, the islands remain sparsely populated.

Because of frequent ferry and hydrofoil service, the Aeolian Islands are easy to reach from the Sicilian mainland. The conquering hordes descend here in summer, with much overcrowding because of limited accommodations (hence, reservations are important). We prefer the less crowded times of late May, early June, and September. We've also made several winter visits, when most tourist businesses are closed and the island is sometimes bathed in brilliant sunshine. At other times the winds blow furiously, and the islands can be lashed by storms, especially between October and March. The sea can be so turbulent that ferry and hydrofoil service to mainland Sicily is suspended, and you may find yourself stranded.

GETTING THERE Ferries and hydrofoils service all of the Aeolian Islands from the port of Milazzo, on the northeastern coast of Sicily 32km (20 miles) west of Messina. Both **Società Siremar,** Via Dei Mille (© **090-9283242;** www.siremar.it), and **Ustica Lines,** Via Rizzo (© **090-9287821;** www.usticalines.it), operate ferry and hydrofoil routes.

The Milazzo-Vulcano-Lipari-Salina ferry lines leave Milazzo twice daily at 7am and 9am. It takes 1½ hours to reach Vulcano; a one-way ticket costs 10€ ($13). Lipari is 2 hours from Milazzo; a one-way ticket costs 11€ ($14). To reach Stromboli, take the Milazzo-Panarea-Stromboli ferry line, departing Milazzo at 7am and 2:30pm Tuesday through Saturday, and at 2:30pm Monday, and Sunday. The Stromboli trip takes 5 hours and costs 15€ ($20) one-way.

For a faster option, take the Milazzo-Vulcano-Lipari-Salina hydrofoil line, which reaches Vulcano in 30 minutes; a one-way ticket costs 15€ ($20). It takes 1 hour to reach Lipari and costs 16€ ($21)

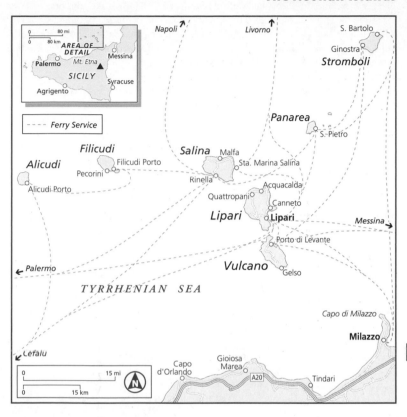

one-way. Siremar makes the trip 6 to 12 times daily from 7:05am to 6:10pm, while Ustica Lines makes six runs daily from 6:20am to 7:10pm. To reach Stromboli, use the Milazzo-Panarea-Stromboli hydrofoil line, which takes 2¹/₂ hours and costs 21€ ($27) one-way.

For more information on ferry and hydrofoil connections, call 🕻 **0923-873813** or 892123 (within Italy only).

If you're driving from Messina in the east, take S113 west to Palermo until you come to the turnoff for the port at Milazzo.

---

1 LIPARI ★★

37km (23 miles) N of Milazzo, 41km (25 miles) W of Messina

Homer called it "a floating island, a wall of bronze and splendid smooth sheer cliffs." The offspring of seven volcanic eruptions, Lipari is the largest of the Aeolians and is also the name of the island's only real town. It's the administrative headquarters of the Aeolians (except autonomous Salina). The town sits on a plateau of red volcanic rock on the southeastern shore, framed by two beaches: **Marina Lunga,** which functions as the harbor, and **Marina Corta.**

Nearly all activity is centered in Lipari town, which contains the largest concentration of tourist facilities in all of the Aeolian Islands, and as such makes the best base for exploring the entire archipelago. There are also four other villages, including **Canneto,** which is only 2km (1¼ miles) north of Lipari town. **Acquacalda** is found on the northern tip of the island. Inland and to its southwest is **Quattropani.** If you're heading southeast from Quattropani back to Lipari town, you'll pass through the small town of **Pianoconte.**

Marina Lunga and Marina Corta lie on either side of the *castello,* or cliff-top citadel, still surrounded by walls built in the 1500s for defensive purposes. Inside these walls are the Duomo, the archaeological museum (the major sight on the island), and two decaying baroque churches.

The major artery of Lipari town, **Corso Vittorio Emanuele,** goes north-south and is the site of most of the businesses catering to visitors, including bars, banks, and *trattorie.*

ESSENTIALS

GETTING AROUND Ferries from Milazzo dock at the deepwater port of Marina Lunga, while hydrofoils pull in at Marina Corta. Much of what there is to see, aside from the island's scenic wonders, lies between these two small ports. Lipari is serviced by a limited bus network.

Buses leave from Marina Lunga about every hour (more frequently in summer), taking you across the island. No point on the island is less than a half-hour ride away. A bus schedule is available at **Urso Guglielmo,** Via Cappucini 9 (© 090-9811262), above Marina Lunga. Tickets cost 2€ ($2.60) and can be purchased on board from the driver. Urso buses also operate tours of the island from July to September. Three buses at a time leave at 9:30am, 11:30am, and 5pm, costing 4€ ($5.20) for the circuit. Along the way you'll pass the highlights of Lipari's scenery. It's also possible to summon one of the independently operated taxis, most of which are found at Marina Corta.

A final transportation option is to rent a bike (10€/$13 daily) or motor scooter (15€/$20 daily, not including fuel). A security deposit is required: a large sum, a credit card, or a passport. Two rental outlets are **Da Marcello,** Via Sottomonastero, Marina Lunga (© 090-9811234); and **Da Tullio,** Via Amendola 22, Marina Lunga (© 090-9880540).

VISITOR INFORMATION The **tourist office** in Lipari is at Via Vittorio Emanuele 202 (© 090-9880095). In July and August, it is open Monday to Friday 8:30am to 2pm and 4:30 to 7:30pm, Saturday 8am to 2pm. From September to June, hours are Monday to Friday 8:30am to 2pm and 4:30 to 7:30pm.

FAST FACTS **Ferry** and **hydrofoil** tickets are available at Siremar offices at Via Mariano Amendola, Marina Lunga (© 090-9811312), and at the Terminal Aliscafi, Marina Corta (© 090-9812200). Hours are Monday to Friday 9am to 1pm and 4:30 to 7:30pm. The two major **pharmacies** are Farmacia Morsillo, Via Marina Garibaldi 72 (© 090-9811428), and Farmacia Internazionale, Via Vittorio Emanuele 128 (© 090-9431011). For a **hospital** emergency, call © **090-983040;** for **first aid,** © 090-9811010. For the local *Carabinieri* (army police corps), call © **090-9811333.** The **post office** is at Corso Vittorio Emanuele 207 (© **090/9810051**); open Monday to Friday 8am to 6:30pm and Saturday 8am to 12:30pm. For Internet access, go to **Net Cafe,** Via Garibaldi 61 (© 090-9813527), which charges 3.50€ ($4.55) per half-hour.

LIPARI
Acquacalda **6**
Canneto **2**
Cave di Pomice **3**
Lipari **1**
M. Chirica **8**
M. Pilato **9**
Pianoconte **10**
Porticello **4**
Quattropani **7**
Rocche Rossi **5**

VULCANO
Gelso **14**
Gran Cratere **13**
Porto di Levante **12**
Porto di Ponente **11**

The major bank is **Banca Monte dei Paschi di Siena,** Via Vittorio Emanuele 209 (✆ **090-9880432**), which has an on-site ATM available 24 hours.

EXPLORING THE ISLAND
Citadel/Upper Town

Most of the man-made sights of Lipari are centered in this citadel area surrounded by the walls of Lipari's castle. The *castello,* or what remains of it, dates from the 16th century, when it was constructed by the Spaniards. The citadel is approached by heading up Via Garibaldi.

You must traverse long steps cut through thick walls to reach the Upper Town. Part of the area here is an archaeological park (see below), where stratified clues about civilizations dating from 1700 B.C. have been unearthed. From these ruins, archaeologists have learned much about settlements in other Mediterranean cultures.

Take the steps at Via del Concordato to climb to the **Cattedrale di San Bartolomeo,** which replaced an earlier Norman cathedral destroyed by Barbarossa on his killing rampage in 1544. A Benedictine cloister from the 1100s is all that remains from Redbeard's assault on the cathedral. Today, the cathedral lies behind an impressive baroque facade and is dedicated to St. Bartolomew. A silver statue of the saint, dating from 1728, can be found in the northern transept. The church is open daily from 9am to 1pm.

To the south of the Duomo is the **Parco Archeologico,** its stones going as far back as Neolithic times. You can view Greek and Roman burial grounds here, along with a contemporary Greek-style theater where concerts and ancient plays are performed in July and September (see the tourist office for details). Major finds dug up here are displayed in the archaeological museum (see below). Parco Archeologico is open from April to September, Monday to Saturday 9am to 7pm; off season, daily 9am to 4pm. Admission is free.

Museo Archeologico Eoliano ★★   This is one of southern Italy's greatest archaeological museums, housing one of the world's finest Neolithic collections. It's divided into two buildings: One lies just south of the cathedral in the 17th-century **Palazzo Vescovile,** or bishop's palace, and contains Neolithic and Bronze Age exhibits. The other, the **Sezione Classica,** is on the south side of the Duomo and focuses on the classical and Hellenic periods.

The collection is laid out chronologically, beginning with the Neolithic to Bronze Age discoveries unearthed nearby. You'll see lustrous red ceramics, known as the "Diana style," from 3000 to 2500 B.C.; a display of obsidian, the glasslike black volcanic rock that was crafted into blades used throughout the ancient world before it was eventually replaced by metal; and the only Late Bronze Age (8th-c.-B.C.) necropolis found in Sicily.

Over in the Sezione Classica section is a rich array of classical and Hellenic artifacts, many dug up in the nearby necropolis. Particularly noteworthy are **burial urns** from Milazzo; archaeologists discovered that in the 11th century B.C., Lipari islanders buried bodies in fetal positions in large jars. The upper level holds a stunning collection of **decorated vases ★★**, many from the ancient Roman site of Paestum, that depict gods and goddesses, satyrs and courtiers, and scenes of daily life in ancient times. The museum also contains the world's greatest collection of **theatrical masks ★★★**, unearthed in tombs from the 4th century to the 3rd century B.C. Those gruesome grins on the masks of Hercules and Hades will haunt your dreams.

The final and least interesting section of the museum is the **Sezione Epigrafica,** in a smaller adjoining building. It displays engraved stones and the remains of several Greek and Roman burial tombs.

Via del Castello. ✆ **090-9880174.** Admission 6€ ($7.80) adults, free for children 17 and under. Daily 9am–1:30pm and 3–7pm.

Lower Town

After visiting the enclosed citadel, you will have seen the best of Lipari town. The only sight of interest in the lower town is the **Parco Archeologico Contrada Diana,** west of Corso Vittorio Emanuele, the main street. Here you can see the remains of Greek walls dating from the 5th and 4th centuries B.C., as well as the ruins of several Roman villas. Ancient tombstones reveal an eerie necropolis from classical days. The burial grounds are visible off Via Marconi. The park is usually locked, so you can only stroll by and look in. Any major finds discovered here are housed in the archaeological museum in the Upper Town.

Around the Island

Twenty-nine kilometers (18 miles) of road circle the island, connecting all of its villages and attractions. Buses run by **Urso Guglielmo,** Via Cappuccini (✆ **090-9811262**), make 10 circuits of the island per day. The trip to the little towns of Quattropani and

Acquacalda, on the north coast, costs 2€ ($2.60). Closer destinations cost 1.50€ ($1.95). Buses leave Lipari town from Marina Lunga, opposite the service station.

The major destination is the little town of **Canneto,** 2km (1¹/₄ miles) away, where the best beaches are found. Canneto can be reached by bus or a 30-minute walk. It's on the eastern coast of the island, directly to the north of Lipari town. Just north of Canneto is **Spiaggia Bianca,** named for the white sand that was originally found here, although today it's rather grayish. White sand is an oddity here—the rest of the island's beaches are predominantly black volcanic sand. To reach the beach from Canneto, take the waterfront road, climbing the stairs along Via Marina Garibaldi, and then veer right down a narrow cobbled path for 297m (974 ft.). Other than its beaches, nothing in Canneto need detain you.

Buses run north of Canneto, passing the **Cave di Pomice** at Campobianco, located between Spiaggia Bianca and Porticello. Other than tourism, pumice is the principal industry of Lipari. Pumice is used for everything from a building material to an ingredient in toothpaste. Some daring visitors slide down a pumice chute directly into the waters along the north coast.

From Cave di Pomice, you can see **Mount Pilato,** at 476m (1,562 ft.). This is the ancient crater of a volcano that last erupted in A.D. 700. Fields around this crater are the source of the pumice. You can walk to the crater, passing through barren fields locals call *Rocce Rosse,* or the "red rocks," because of the hue of the stone. A path leading to the crater from the northern tip of Campobianco stretches for 1.2km (³/₄ mile).

The bus stops in the village of **Porticello,** which has a beach. We suggest you avoid it, however, as it's rocky and not very special. If you do stop here, the most rewarding feature is the **panoramic view** ★★ of the other Aeolian Islands such as Alicudi, Filicudi, and Salina.

The island's northernmost little town is **Acquacalda,** or "hot water," a settlement known for its obsidian and pumice quarries. But few people go to the black-sand beaches here because they're rocky and there's also no shade. Acquacalda itself is virtually a one-street town with some snack bars and waterfront dives.

The bus moves along the northern tier of Lipari and then heads southwest to the little town of **Quattropani,** which is to the west of Mount Chirica at 602m (1,975 ft.). In the town, you can make a steep climb to **Duomo de Chiesa Baraca,** where the point of interest is most definitely not the "cathedral," but the **panoramic view** ★ from the grounds of the church. The distance between Quattropani and Acquacalda is 5km (3 miles); some hikers prefer to traverse this route on foot, enjoying scenic vistas at every turn.

There is yet another grand view to be enjoyed before leaving Lipari. West of Lipari town, and reached by buses departing from Marina Lunga, is a lookout point at **Quattrocchi** ("four eyes"). It's 4km (2¹/₂ miles) from Lipari town. Once at Quattrocchi, you can make the steep climb to **Quattrocchi Belvedere,** which will reward you with one of the most **panoramic vistas** ★★ in the Aeolian Islands.

WHERE TO STAY
Expensive
Gattopardo Park Hotel ★★ Set in an 18th-century villa and enveloped by white bungalows, this is the island's most architecturally interesting hotel. In comfort, it also ranks among the top choices on the island. Spacious terraces opening onto scenic views are yet another allure. The hotel provides free minibus service to some of the best beaches on the island, although there's also free swimming from the rocks in a bay nearby. For

Aeolian style, this place is unbeatable, with beautifully planted grounds, tiled floors, and wood-beamed ceilings. The furnishings are a blend of antique and modern, the rooms come with small shower-only bathrooms, and the best units are some of the most comfortable in Lipari. The dining and drinking facilities are among the island's best.

Vico Diana, 98055 Lipari. © **090-9811035.** Fax 090-9880207. www.gattopardoparkhotel.it. 78 units. 120€–260€ ($156–$338) double. Rates include half board (breakfast and dinner). AE, DC, MC, V. Closed Nov–Feb. **Amenities:** Restaurant; bar; outdoor pool; room service; babysitting. *In room:* A/C, TV, hair dryer.

Giardino sul Mare ★   This first-class option is only minutes from Marina Corta, opening onto the sea. It's a real Mediterranean resort hotel, with covered terraces for dining and a smallish pool surrounded by chaise longues and umbrellas. Guest rooms are well tended and comfortably furnished, with small shower-only bathrooms. Many European guests spend all their vacation time here except for an occasional island trip. The drinking and dining facilities equal those found at Villa Meligunis.

Via Maddalena 65, 98055 Lipari. © **090-9811004.** Fax 090-9880150. www.giardinosulmare.it. 46 units. 170€–270€ ($221–$351) double. Rates include half board. AE, DC, MC, V. Closed Oct 30–Mar 21. **Amenities:** Restaurant; bar; outdoor pool; room service; babysitting; laundry service; dry cleaning; rooms for those w/limited mobility. *In room:* A/C, TV, hair dryer, safe.

Hotel Carasco   This hotel enjoys the most dramatic location in Lipari, with its own private stretch of rocks opening onto the water and panoramic views from a bougainvillea-draped pool. The Carasco consists of two buildings that sit on a lonely bluff by the sea. The cool interior, with its terra-cotta floors and dark-wood furniture, contrasts with the bright heat of the outdoors. Each comfortable, well-furnished guest room comes with a ceiling fan, rustic artifacts, and a bathroom with shower or tub; ask for a room with a private balcony. Grace notes include an afternoon tea service and piano music in the lounge after dinner. *Note:* Although citing the beauty of the location, some readers have complained about the food and the service.

Porto delle Genti, 98055 Lipari. © **090-9811605.** Fax 090-9811828. www.carasco.it. 89 units. 40€–175€ ($52–$228) per person. Rates include continental breakfast. MC, V. Closed Oct 13–Easter. **Amenities:** Restaurant; bar; outdoor pool; room service; babysitting; laundry service; dry cleaning; all nonsmoking rooms. *In room:* A/C, minibar, hair dryer.

Villa Meligunis ★★   This first-class hotel is as good as it gets in the Aeolian Islands. Less than 45m (148 ft.) from the ferry docks, the appealingly contemporary villa rose from a cluster of 17th-century fishermen's cottages at Marina Corta. It oozes stylish charm, from its lovely fountain to its dramatic rooftop terrace to its wrought-iron bedsteads used by fashion photographers as backdrops. Guest rooms are comfortably furnished with summery pieces and well-maintained bathrooms with either tubs or showers. The restaurant serves excellent regional specialties.

Via Marte 7, 98055 Lipari. © **090-9812426.** Fax 090-9880149. www.villameligunis.it. 32 units. 150€–300€ ($195–$390) double; 225€–380€ ($293–$494) suite. Rates include continental breakfast. AE, DC, MC, V. Free parking. **Amenities:** Restaurant; 2 bars; outdoor pool; room service; babysitting; laundry service; dry cleaning; nonsmoking rooms. *In room:* A/C, TV, minibar, hair dryer, safe, Wi-Fi.

Moderate
Hotel Oriente ★   Located in the historic center of Lipari town, this hotel is only steps from the archaeological park and 300m (984 ft.) from the port. On a hot day, its shady terrace is one of the best places to be on the island. The interior is like a museum—it's stuffed with knickknacks and artifacts made from wrought iron. The rooms are light and

airy, with small tiled bathrooms that have hydromassage showers. A generous breakfast is served in the garden amid bougainvillea and citrus blossoms.

Via Marconi 35, 98055 Lipari. ℂ 090-9811493. Fax 090-9880198. www.hotelorientelipari.com. 32 units. 60€–130€ ($78–$169) double; 85€–170€ ($111–$221) triple; 110€–210€ ($143–$273) quad. AE, DC, MC, V. Closed Oct 30–Mar 30. **Amenities:** Bar; room service; babysitting; laundry service; dry cleaning. *In room:* A/C, TV, minibar, hair dryer, safe.

Hotel Poseidon   A favorite with scuba divers as well as discerning travelers in general, this well-run hotel lies off the main street, just 100m (328 ft.) from the sea, with guest rooms opening onto an inviting courtyard. Diving instruction can be arranged, as can equipment rentals, cylinder refills, and guided underwater trips. There is a fresh, breezy Mediterranean feel to this place. The guest rooms are well maintained, with wicker decorations and small tiled bathrooms.

Vico Ausonia 7, 98055 Lipari. ℂ **090-9812876.** Fax 090-9880252. www.hotelposeidonlipari.com. 18 units. 75€–150€ ($98–$195) double; 90€–180€ ($117–$234) triple. Rates include continental breakfast. AE, DC, MC, V. Closed Nov 15–Feb 28. **Amenities:** Bar; room service; babysitting; laundry service; dry cleaning; nonsmoking rooms. *In room:* A/C, TV, minibar, hair dryer, safe.

Villa Augustus ★ ⟨Finds⟩   Set in the historic center, close to the port, this hotel is surrounded by luxuriant gardens and has a dramatic roof terrace overlooking the sea. It's just 100m (328 ft.) above the main harbor and 2km (1¼ miles) from the whitish beaches north near the pumice quarries. The hotel is reached along a narrow island road and relatively hidden from the street. Rooms are attractively furnished; preferred, of course, are those with balconies or terraces. Attractive features include a reading room, a piano bar, and a solarium.

Vico Ausonia 16, 98055 Lipari. ℂ **090-9811232.** Fax 090-9812233. www.villaaugustus.it. 35 units. 110€–200€ ($143–$260) double. Rates include buffet breakfast. AE, MC, V. Closed Nov 1–Feb 28. **Amenities:** Restaurant; 2 bars; room service; babysitting; fitness room; sauna; massage; laundry service, dry cleaning; solarium; roof garden. *In room:* A/C, TV, hair dryer.

At Canneto

Casajanca ★ ⟨Finds⟩   It looks like a private home, and for good reason: Before it was converted into this little inn, Casajanca was the home of Ruccio Carbone, a native son who was celebrated as "the poet" of the Aeolian Islands. Rooms are little more than basic, motel-like accommodations, with small, shower-only bathrooms, but there is reasonable comfort here. Furnishings mix contemporary pieces with the occasional antique. The little garden is studded with tropical plantings and tables and chairs. The friendly owners provide a grand welcome to what they call "the inn of everlasting love."

Marina Garibaldi 115, Canneto (Lipari). ℂ **090-9880222.** Fax 090-9813003. www.casajanca.it. 10 units. 80€–200€ ($104–$260) double; 110€–243€ ($143–$316) triple. Rates include continental breakfast. AE, DC, MC, V. **Amenities:** Bar; room service. *In room:* A/C, TV, minibar, safe.

WHERE TO DINE

E Pulera ★★ SICILIAN/AEOLIAN   Owned by the same family that runs the Filippino (see below), this restaurant emphasizes its Aeolian origins. Artifacts and maps of the islands fashioned from ceramic tiles are scattered about. Some tables occupy a terrace with a view of a flowering lawn. Specialties include a delightful version of fishermen's soup, swordfish ragout, and risotto with squid in its own ink. A delightful pasta dish is fettuccine with yellow pumpkin, shrimp, and wild fennel.

Via Diana. ℂ 090-9811158. Reservations recommended. Main courses 10€–13€ ($13–$17). DC, MC, V. Daily 8pm–midnight. Closed Oct–May 15.

Salina: A Dream Vacation

For the ultimate dream vacation, head to one of the lesser-known Aeolian islands, **Salina,** where unexpectedly you'll come across one of the chicest hotels in Sicily (see below).

Some of the best beaches in the Aeolians make Salina an undiscovered paradise. It may be close to Lipari in size and distance, lying 15km (9 miles) to the north, but it's not overrun by visitors. The landscape is untouched and not developed at all. For a unique beach experience, head for the dramatic **Spiaggia di Pollara** ★★, a beach lying 100m (328 ft.) straight down from a series of cliffs in the midst of a semicircular volcanic crater. Seeing is believing.

Salina is also the highest of the Aeolians, its **Mount Fossa delle Felci** rising to some 915m (3,002 ft.). Inland is riddled with vineyards producing the Malvasia dessert wine, and the coast is studded with fishing villages.

Lying in the village of Malfa, on the north coast, **Hotel Signum** ★★, Via Scalo (② **090-9844375;** fax 090-9844102; www.hotelsignum.it), is a 30-room gem, run by Clara Ramette and Michele Caruso, who had a dream of creating a luxury hotel in the village of their birth. The location is only a 10-minute walk from the sea, and the hotel consists of a cluster of traditional white-painted Aeolian buildings. The comfortable bedrooms, each spacious, are in rustic Sicilian style with wrought-iron beds resting on terra-cotta floors. Rooms are filled with antiques, some with balconies, others with terraces, each with a panoramic view. Each unit comes with air-conditioning, TV, minibar, and safe. The pool is the best on the island, and the grounds are studded with fragrant lemon trees. The hotel operates a spa that features a steam bath, massages, thermal baths, and various beauty treatments. Traditional Aeolian dishes are served, with freshly caught fish, homemade pasta, and seasonal vegetables. Depending on the room, prices range from 130€ to 340€ ($169–$442) with breakfast included.

The Milazzo-Vulcano-Lipari-Salina ferry runs here (see "Getting There," earlier in this chapter).

Filippino ★★ SICILIAN/AEOLIAN It's a pleasant surprise to find such a fine restaurant in such a remote location. Filippino has thrived in the heart of town, near the town hall, since 1910. You'll dine in one of two large rooms or on a terrace ringed with flowering shrubs and potted plants. Menu items are based on old-fashioned Sicilian recipes and prepared with flair. The chef's signature pasta dish is "Aeolian orchids," a curly pasta topped with tomatoes, pine nuts, capers, garlic, basil, mint, and pecorino cheese. A specialty is swordfish with basil and the eggplant *caponata.*

Piazza Mazzini. ② **090-9811002.** Reservations required July–Aug. Main courses 8€–15€ ($10–$20). AE, DC, MC, V. Daily noon–2:30pm and 7:30–10:30pm. Closed Nov 10–Dec 26.

La Nassa ★ (Finds) SICILIAN/AEOLIAN At this enchanting restaurant, the delectable cuisine of Donna Teresa matches the friendly enthusiasm of her son Bartolo, who has thousands of interesting stories to tell. The food is the most genuine on the island, prepared with respect for both old traditions and modern tastes. After the *sette perle* (seven pearl) appetizer, a combination of fresh fish, sweet shrimp, and spices, you can try your choice of fish, cooked to your specifications. Local favorites include *sarago, cernia,* and *dentice,* as delicate in texture as their names are untranslatable. For dessert, try cook- ies with Malvasia wine.

Via G. Franza 41. ℂ **090-9811319.** Reservations recommended. Main courses 8€–18€ ($10–$23). AE, MC, V. Apr–June Fri–Wed 8:30am–3pm and 6pm–midnight; July–Oct daily 8:30am–3pm and 6pm–midnight. Closed Nov–Easter.

Ristorante Pizzeria Pescecane Ⓥalue SICILIAN/AEOLIAN   The oldest restaurant on the island is a warm, rustic place located right on the main street of town. It offers tables both inside and out on a terrace. The pastas are savory, especially those made with freshly caught seafood. *Lipparata* is the most regional pasta dish, prepared with capers, olives, anchovies, and tomatoes. Pizzas are also good, especially the Desirée, made with mozzarella, fresh tomato, and ham.

Via Vittorio Emanuele 249. ℂ **090-9812706.** Reservations recommended. Main courses 5€–10€ ($6.50– $13); fixed-price menu 15€ ($20). AE, DC, MC, V. Daily 10:30am–3pm and 6pm–midnight. Closed Nov–Dec.

LIPARI AFTER DARK

On a summer night, most of the scantily clad visitors congregate around one of the bars with outdoor tables at Marina Corta. The early evening begins at the **Net Cafe,** Via Garibaldi 61 (ℂ **090-9813527**), where people come not only to surf the Web, but also to enjoy drinks and burgers, the big-screen TV, and a beautiful garden. **Turmalin** (ℂ **338-6418362**) is a summer dance club off Piazza Municipio near the castle. May through August, it's open nightly from 11pm to 6am, charging a cover of 15€ ($20).

Otherwise, nightlife consists of bars and more bars. Both live and recorded music are featured at **Chitarra Bar,** Salita San Giuseppe 5 (ℂ **090-9811554**), drawing a young to middle-aged crowd. In summer, it's open daily from 7pm to 4am (until midnight in winter). It shuts down completely in January and February. A hard-drinking place, **Bar Caffè La Vela,** Piazza San Onofrio 2 (ℂ **090-9880064**), is open 24 hours a day in summer, daily from 7am to midnight off season.

---

2 VULCANO ★★★

55km (34 miles) NW of Milazzo, 18km (11 miles) NW of Lipari

Vulcano, the ancient Thermessa, figured heavily in the mythologies of the region. The island was thought to be not only the home of Vulcan but also the gateway to Hades; Ulysses even stopped here in Homer's *Odyssey,* further delaying his return home to Ithaca. Thucydides, Siculus, and Aristotle each recorded eruptions. Other dormant volcanoes (including Vulcano Piano and Vulcanello) exist on the island, but a climb to the rim of the active **Gran Cratere (Big Crater),** or Vulcano della Fosse, draws the most attention. It hasn't erupted since 1890, but one look inside the sulfur-belching hole makes you understand how it inspired the hellish legends surrounding it. The 418m (1,371-ft.) peak is an easier climb than the one on Stromboli, taking just about an hour—though it's just as hot, and the same precautions prevail.

For centuries, the island was uninhabited because of fear of the volcano. Today, however, Vulcano is a stamping ground of the party crowd. Rich Italians from the mainland have erected fancy villas here as second homes. Vulcano's thermal baths, known for their curative powers and said to be especially helpful in relieving rheumatic suffering, also draw visitors.

The Romans had a small colony here, but the Bourbon rulers paid more attention to Vulcano. Under their reign, the whole island became a working farm, with labor provided by convicts shipped over from Lipari. A Welshman, James Stevenson, tried to bring agriculture and vineyards to the island in the 19th century, but most of his efforts failed because of a violent volcanic eruption. The last such explosive action occurred in the years 1888 and 1890, after which the volcano fell silent.

Vulcano is the island closest to the Sicilian mainland. Ferries and hydrofoils stop here before going on to the other islands. If the wind is blowing in the right direction, you can smell the island's prevalent sulfurous fumes. Vulcano also has the best beaches in the Aeolians, if you don't find black volcanic sands off-putting.

ESSENTIALS

VISITOR INFORMATION   The tourist office no longer operates here. Information on Vulcano is available by calling the tourist office in Lipari (© **090-9880095**).

GETTING AROUND   Most people walk, but a private company, **Scaffidi** (© **090-9853017**), runs buses from the port area to Piano, a village in the southwestern interior of the island, and to Gelso, at the southern tip. Seven buses operate Monday through Saturday; two operate on Sunday. If you'd rather rent a bike or scooter, go to **Da Paolo,** Via Porto Levante (© **090-9852112**), open May through November daily from 8am to 8:30pm. Mountain bikes cost from 6€ to 10€ ($7.80–$13) per day; scooters range from 15€ to 40€ ($20–$52).

FAST FACTS   The **Banco di Sicilia,** Via Marina Garibaldi 152 (© **090-9811140**), has an ATM and keeps regular banking hours Monday through Friday. Money can also be exchanged at the **Thermessa Agency,** Via Porto Levante (© **090-9852230**), open daily from 6:30am to 8:30pm. You can purchase hydrofoil tickets here as well, or try **Vulcano Viaggi,** Piazza Vulcano Levante 3 (© **090-9852149**), for both hydrofoil and ferry tickets. For **medical services** from June to September, a doctor is on call at © **090-9852220.** The island **pharmacy,** Bonarrigo, Via Favaloro 1 (© **090-9852244**), is open daily 9am to 1pm and 7 to 9pm. The *Carabinieri* (army police corps) can be called at © **090-9852110.** The **post office** is on Via Piano, off Porto di Levante (© **090-9853143**).

EXPLORING THE ISLAND

It might be, as the ancients believed, the entrance to hell. Nonetheless, Vulcano is the most visited of the Aeolian Islands, no doubt because of its proximity to the Sicilian mainland. Only the late, great Fellini could have done justice to a film about visitors flocking here to bathe in the mud.

To reach these fabled mud baths, **Laghetti di Fanghi,** go to the docks and enter along Via Provinciale. Walk over to a 56m-high (184-ft.) *faraglione,* or "stack": It's one massive pit of thick, sulfurous gunk that is said to greatly relieve certain skin diseases and rheumatic suffering. Be warned that the mud discolors everything from clothing to jewelry, which is one explanation for the prevalent nudity. In summer, expect to encounter muddy pools brimming with naked, package-tour Germans and other Europeans. Since the mud baths are also radioactive, you are warned not to stay in them for more than 10 to 15 minutes. The water from the sea bubbles up like a giant Jacuzzi nearby, and it's here that mud bathers wash off the gunk. Take care that you don't scald yourself while cleaning yourself off. The beach nearby isn't bad, but the aroma from the mud baths may have you holding your nose if you attempt to sunbathe here. The baths are open from Easter to October, daily from 6:30am to 8pm; admission is 1€ ($1.30).

You can, of course, skip this muddy cauldron altogether and head directly to the dramatic **Spiaggia Sabbie Nere (Black Sands Beach)** ★, the finest in the archipelago. Regrettably, its black sand gets so hot by midday that flip-flops are a virtual necessity if you plan to while away your day here. This beach is on the distant side of the peninsula from Porto di Levante to Porto di Ponente; get here by going along Via Ponente. Porto di Ponente is a 20-minute walk north from the mud baths.

If you tire of the black sands, leave the beach, and take the only road north to **Vulcanello** at the northern tip. Locals call this a "volcanic pimple." It erupted from the sea in 183 B.C., spiking its way up through the earth to become a permanent fixture on the island's landscape. As late as 1888, this toylike volcano erupted a final time, creating what the islanders call a *Valle dei Mostri* (Valley of Monsters) of bizarrely shaped lava fountains.

The Gran Cratere ★★★

To the south of Porto di Levante lies one of the greatest attractions in the Aeolians, the Gran Cratere. From Porto di Levante, follow Via Piano away from the sea for about 182m (597 ft.) until you see the first of the AL CRATERE signs. Once you do, follow the marked trail; allow 3 hours to make it there and back. *Tip:* This walk is unshaded, so go early in the morning or late in the day; load up on sunscreen and water; and wear sturdy hiking shoes.

For your trouble in making this steep, hot climb, you'll be rewarded with **dramatic views ★★** of some of the other Aeolian Islands. As you near the mouth of the crater, you see rivulets caused by previous eruptions. At the rim, peer down into the mammoth crater itself. Vapor emissions still spew from the crater, whose lips measure 450m (1,476 ft.) in diameter. The steam is tainted with numerous toxins, so you may not want to hang out here for long.

South to Gelso

Most of the tourist activity is concentrated in northern Vulcano, but an offbeat excursion can be made by taking a bus that cuts inland to the remote, almost forgotten villages of **Piano** and **Gelso.** For details on the island buses, see "Getting Around," above.

Islanders who live inland are likely to reside in the remote village of Piano, 7km (4¹/₃ miles) from the port. Piano lies between two peaks, **Mount Saraceno,** at 48m (157 ft.), and **La Sommata,** at 387m (1,270 ft.). There's not much here, and many of the homes are abandoned in the off season. If you continue on the bus to the southernmost village of Gelso, you can view the inland scenery of Vulcano along the way. At Gelso, the end of the line, you'll find some summer-only places to eat and good sea bathing. *Gelso* is Italian for "mulberry," one of the crops cultivated here along with capers.

The best beach is immediately east of Gelso. **Spiaggia dell'Asino** is a big cove reached by a steep path from the village of Gelso. Hydrocycles, deck chairs, and umbrellas can be rented from kiosks on the beach in summer.

Another little road goes to **Capo Grillo,** which has some of the best **panoramic views ★★** on the island, with a sweeping vista of the Aeolians.

BOAT EXCURSIONS ON VULCANO

You can rent your own boat at **Centro Nautico Baia Levante,** Porto di Levante (© **339-3372795**). With a boat, you can visit the hamlet of Gelso and explore the caves and bays that riddle Vulcano's western shores. Rentals range in price from 120€ to 500€ ($156–$650) per day, fuel not included.

If you'd like to use Vulcano as a base to visit other Aeolian Islands, excursions can be arranged through **Centro Nautico Baia Levante,** Porto di Levante (© **339-3372795**), open April through October daily from 8:30am to 8pm. Day excursions, which head for the islands of Lipari, Filicudi, Alicudi, and Salina, begin at 10am and last until 6pm. Because many options are available, the cost can range from 20€ to 90€ ($26–$117) per person. Night excursions begin at 6pm and end at midnight, with similar costs.

WHERE TO STAY

Hotel Conti ★ This is the second-best hotel on the island, surpassed only by Les Sables Noirs (see below). Just a few minutes' walk from the port where the hydrofoils and ferries pull in, the hotel opens onto the black sands of Ponente Bay. It's quite Aeolian in architecture, with luxuriant vegetation surrounding the main building and bungalows. Inside, you'll find cool tiled floors and dark-wood furnishings. Guest rooms are simply though comfortably furnished, each with a private entrance opening onto the gardens and a small tiled bathroom. The terraces, solarium, and restaurant (serving excellent Aeolian specialties) all boast sea views.

Via Porto Ponente, 98050 Vulcano. © **090-9852012.** Fax 090-9852064. www.contivulcano.it. 67 units. 54€–97€ ($70–$126) per person double. Rates include half board. AE, DC, MC, V. Closed Oct 21–Apr 30. **Amenities:** Restaurant; bar; laundry service; dry cleaning. *In room:* TV, hair dryer, safe.

Hotel Eolian ★ Ⓥⓐⓛⓤⓔ This hotel opens onto Ponente Bay. In typical Aeolian style, the main building is surrounded by stucco bungalows and set in a lush garden studded with palms. None of the bungalows has a view of the water—that's reserved for the restaurant and bar—but most guests spend their days beside the sea anyway. Guest rooms are midsize and furnished in a minimalist style; each has a tiled bathroom. Walk down from the terrace of the bar to reach the beach, where you can indulge in various watersports or rent a small boat to explore the more remote parts of the coastline. The thermal sulfurous pool is said to aid poor circulation.

Via Porto Levante, 98050 Vulcano. © **090-9852151.** Fax 090-9852153. www.eolianhotel.com. 88 units. 124€–176€ ($278–$229) double; 148€–214€ ($192–$278) per person with half board. Rates include continental breakfast. AE, DC, MC, V. Closed Oct to mid-May. **Amenities:** Restaurant; bar; 2 outdoor saltwater pools; tennis court; babysitting; laundry service; dry cleaning; nonsmoking rooms. *In room:* A/C, TV, minibar, hair dryer.

Les Sables Noirs ★★ Les Sables Noirs is the most elegant place to stay on Vulcano, offering a surprising level of luxury and excellent service in this remote outpost. Its rooms overlook a black-sand beach and front a panoramic sweep of the Bay of Ponente. The stucco and bamboo touches evoke a Caribbean resort. Accommodations are spacious, comfortably furnished, and decorated in typical Mediterranean style; many units open onto a wide balcony. There's a solarium as well. Another reason to stay here is the restaurant, which serves impressive regional specialties and opens onto a broad terrace in front of the beach.

Via Porto di Ponente, 98050 Vulcano. © **090-9850.** Fax 090-9852454. www.framonhotelgroup.com. 48 units. 230€–290€ ($299–$377) double; 270€–350€ ($351–$455) suite. AE, DC, MC, V. Closed Oct–Mar. **Amenities:** Restaurant; 2 bars; outdoor pool; babysitting; laundry service; dry cleaning; nonsmoking rooms; solarium. *In room:* A/C, TV, minibar, hair dryer, safe.

WHERE TO DINE

Il Palmento AEOLIAN/SEAFOOD The terrace opening onto the beach is a potent lure, but so is the cuisine. Although the food never rises to the sublime, it's still good, hearty fare. There is an accurate and thorough understanding of flavor here, especially in the house specialty: spaghetti with chunks of lobster in a zesty tomato sauce. The fish soup with homemade croutons was the best we sampled in Vulcano, and that Sicilian classic, pasta with fresh sardines, was prepared admirably here, with tomato sauce, olive oil, pine nuts, and wild fennel.

Via Porto Levante. ℂ **090-9852552.** Reservations not needed. Main courses 6€–16€ ($7.80–$21); fixed-price menu 22€ ($35). MC, V. Daily noon–4pm and 6pm–12:30am. Closed Nov 1–Mar 30.

L'Approdo ★ AEOLIAN/SICILIAN   Known for its shady oasis of a garden and its good food, this local dive is decorated in a typical Aeolian style, with white walls, tile floors, and dark wooden tables. Most of the ingredients are shipped over from mainland Sicily, although the fish is caught locally and some of the foodstuffs are grown on the island. Chefs are expert at grilling the fresh fish. They also reveal their skilled technique in their combinations of flavors, such as octopus salad with olive oil and lemon flavoring or the swordfish carpaccio. Linguini is paired with clams, thyme, and parsley. Another pasta dish, pennette, comes with fresh tuna and wild fennel.

Via Porto di Levante. ℂ **090-9852426.** Reservations recommended. Main courses 8€–16€ ($10–$21). AE, DC, MC, V. Daily noon–3pm and 7:30–11:30pm. Closed Nov 1 to the week before Easter.

Ristorante Belvedere AEOLIAN/SICILIAN   We like to come here for the food, of course, but we also enjoy sitting out on the beautiful terrace with a view of some of the other Aeolian Islands. The seafood dishes are typically superb; we favor the catch of the day grilled with fresh herbs and a squeeze of lemon. Grilled Sicilian lamb is another savory treat. Our all-time favorite pasta here is the homemade ravioli stuffed with ricotta and spinach.

Via Reale 42. ℂ **090-9853047.** Reservations recommended. Main courses 7€–13€ ($9.10–$17). AE, DC, MC, V. Daily 1–3pm and 8pm–midnight. Closed Oct 1–Mar 30.

Vincenzino (Value SICILIAN/AEOLIAN   This is the most appealing of the trattorie lurking near the ferry port. Known for its hefty portions and affordable prices, it serves clients in a rustic setting. You might begin your meal with spaghetti with crayfish, capers, and a tomato sauce. We're fond of the risotto *alla pescatora,* with crayfish, mussels, and other sea creatures. Another good choice is the house-style macaroni with ricotta, eggplant, tomatoes, and herbs. From October to March, the menu is limited to a simple array of platters from the bar.

Via Porto di Levante. ℂ **090-9852016.** Reservations recommended. Main courses 8€–10€ ($10–$13); fixed-price menu 20€ ($26). AE, DC, MC, V. Daily noon–3pm and 7–10pm.

VULCANO AFTER DARK

One of your best bets for a drink is **Ritrovo Remigio,** Porto di Levante, open daily from 6am to 2am. It offers terrace seating overlooking the port at Porto di Levante, where the ferries and hydrofoils from the mainland come in. In addition to its soothing cocktails, it serves excellent pastries and gelato.

The best nightlife—in fact, virtually the only nightlife—is found at **Cantine Stevenson** ★, Via Porto di Levante (ℂ **090-9853247**), the former wine cellars of James Stevenson, a virtual Renaissance man who did much to change the face of the island. Born in Wales, Stevenson's many interests led him to Vulcano, where he exported sulfur and pumice. In 1870, he purchased most of the island and planted the first vineyards. Here, in his former wine cellars, live music is featured nightly—whether folk, Sicilian, pop, rock, jazz, or blues—and more than 600 types of wine are sold. The old-style cantina, with seats outside in summer, is open April through September, daily from noon to 3am.

3 STROMBOLI ★★★

63km (40 miles) N of Milazzo, 40km (25 miles) N of Lipari

This is the most famous island of the Aeolians for the simple fact that its volcano is still active. The volcano, its single cone measuring 926m (3,038 ft.), has caused the island to be evacuated several times, although today Stromboli maintains a small population and attracts summer visitors.

The island has two settlements. **Ginostra,** on the southwestern shore, is little more than a cluster of summer homes with only 15 year-round residents. **Stromboli,** on the northeastern shore, is a conglomeration of the villages of Ficogrande, San Vincenzo, and Piscita, where the only in-town attraction is the black-sand beach. You won't see volcanic eruptions from any of these villages, as they occur on the northwest side of the volcano.

The entire surface of Stromboli is the cone of a sluggish but still-active volcano. Puffs of smoke can be seen during the day. At night along the **Sciara del Fuoco (Slope of Fire),** lava glows red-hot on its way down to meet the sea with a loud hiss. The main attraction is a steep, difficult climb to the lip of the 92m (302-ft.) **Gran Cratere.** The view of bubbling pools of ooze is accompanied by rising clouds of steam and a sulfuric stench.

The most distant island in the archipelago, Stromboli achieved notoriety and became a household word in the United States in 1950 with the release of the Roberto Rossellini *cinéma vérité* film *Stromboli,* starring Ingrid Bergman. The American public was far more interested in the love affair between Bergman and Rossellini than in the film. Although tame by today's standards, the affair temporarily ended Bergman's American film career, and she was even denounced on the Senate floor. Movie fans today are more likely to remember Stromboli from the film version of the Jules Verne novel *Journey to the Center of the Earth,* starring James Mason.

ESSENTIALS

GETTING AROUND Although several agencies at the port hawk deals ranging from cruises to boat trips, **Sabbia Nera,** Via Marina (© **090-986390**), is the most reliable. From Easter to September, it's open daily 9am to 1pm and 3 to 7pm. Boat rentals for tours around Stromboli begin at 140€ ($182) a day (fuel extra). You can also rent a scooter here for 20€ ($16) a day (fuel extra). The staff can arrange guided boat excursions to Vulcano, which leave at 6am and return at midnight; the cost is 30€ ($39) per person. Guided excursions to Panarea leave Stromboli at 10am and return at 6pm; the cost is 45€ ($59) per person. The excursion to Filicudi and Alicudi begins at 10am and ends at 6pm, costing 85€ ($111) per person. The agency can also book boat trips around Stromboli, calling at Ginostra and Strombolicchio. Trips last 3 hours and cost 20€ ($26) per person. Trips at night to see Sciara del Fuoco last 2¹/₃ hours and cost 25€ ($33). Most of these excursions leave from the beach at Ficogrande.

FAST FACTS To book hydrofoil or ferry rides, head for the office of **Siremar** (© **090-986016**) along the harbor road at the port and easy to spot. Boats arrive from Milazzo from April to September only. From July to September, it's possible to book hydrofoil tickets on Ustica Lines from Stromboli direct to Naples for 57€ to 62€ ($74–$81) per person one-way. Siremar offers year-round boat trips from Stromboli to Naples at 38€ to

48€ ($49–$62) per person. The local **pharmacy** is **Farmacia Bonarrigo Pietro**, Via Favaloro 1 (© **090-9852244**), open daily from 8:30am to 1pm and 4:30 to 9pm (8am–midnight Aug). The **post office** is at Via Roma (© **090-986261**), open Monday to Friday 8am to 1:30pm and Saturday 8am to 12:30pm.

EXPLORING THE ISLAND

By law, the cone of the volcano, **Gran Cratere** ★★★, can be visited only with a guide. **Guide Alpine Autorizzate** (© **090-986211**) charges 20€ ($26) per person and leads groups on the 3-hour one-way trip up the mountain, leaving at 5pm and returning at 11pm. (We don't recommend taking the trip during the day—it's far less dramatic then.) The trip down takes only 2 hours, but you're allowed an hour at the rim. About halfway up is a view of the **Sciara del Fuoco** ★, which is a strikingly fiery red at night.

Climbing the volcano is the big deal here; otherwise, there isn't much to see in town. Film buffs can follow Via Vittorio Emanuele to the **Chiesa di San Vincenzo,** a church so unremarkable it barely merits a visit. However, just two doors down on the right, near the Locanda del Barbablu, is the **little pink house** where Ingrid Bergman and Roberto Rossellini "lived in sin" during the filming of the 1950 flick *Stromboli.* The house can only be viewed from the outside.

On the northeast coast is a striking rock, **Strombolicchio,** a steep basalt block measuring 43m (141 ft.). It is reached by climbing steps hewn out of rock. Once at the top, you'll be rewarded with a **panoramic view of the Aeolians** ★★, and on a clear day you can see as far as Calabria on the Italian mainland.

WHERE TO STAY

B&B Ginostra ★ (Value) For the money, this guesthouse is the best deal on this volcanic island. It lies on a hill, a 5-minute walk from the sea, with its windows opening onto views of the port. The typical whitewashed Aeolian building has a certain charm and grace and offers much comfort in its simply furnished rooms with terra-cotta floors. The bedrooms are midsize and beautifully maintained, and each has a terrace overlooking the sea. The breakfast is homemade and generous.

Via S. Vincenzo (Ginostra), 98050 Stromboli. © **090-9811787.** 4 units. 45€–55€ ($59–$72) per person double. Rates include buffet breakfast. No credit cards. *In room:* Electric fan, no phone.

La Locanda del Barbablu ★ (Finds) This is a quirky choice, a charming little isolated Aeolian inn with only a few rooms, standing against turn-of-the-20th-century breakfronts. Rooms are small but comfortably furnished, often with four-poster beds encrusted with cherubs and mother-of-pearl inlay. A wide terrace opens onto dramatic views of the volcano and the sea. The restaurant is worth a visit even if you're not a guest.

Via Vittorio Emanuele 17–19, 98050 Stromboli. © **090-986118.** Fax 090-986323. www.barbablu.it. 6 units. 130€–210€ ($169–$273) double. AE, DC, MC, V. Closed Nov–Feb.

La Sirenetta Park Hotel ★★ This has the island's finest accommodations, a well-maintained, government-rated four-star hotel. It's the best equipped, with a scenic terrace, a nightclub, and a restaurant serving the best cuisine of any hotel here. It also has an idyllic location on the Ficograss Beach in front of Strombolicchio, the towering rock that rises out of the waters at San Vincenzo. Guest rooms are attractively furnished, with tiled floors and an airy feel. The hotel is justly proud of having the island's best pool as well, complete with hydromassage. Facilities include a fitness center and a dive center that also offers water-skiing, sailing, and windsurfing.

Via Marina 33, 98050 Ficogrande (Stromboli). ✆ **090-986025.** Fax 090-986124. www.lasirenetta.it. 60 units. 120€–300€ ($156–$390) double; 160€–370€ ($208–$481) double with half board. Rates include breakfast. AE, DC, MC, V. Closed Nov 1 to mid-Mar. **Amenities:** Restaurant; 2 bars; saltwater outdoor pool; tennis court; fitness center; watersports; room service; massage; laundry service; dry cleaning; nonsmoking rooms; rooms for those w/limited mobility. *In room:* A/C, TV, minibar, hair dryer, safe.

WHERE TO DINE

Il Canneto AEOLIAN   This typical island restaurant was constructed in the old style, with white walls and dark tables. Among the local trattorie, it's nothing fancy, but it's one of the more reliable joints in town. The specialty is always fish caught in local waters. A delectable pasta dish is the macaroni with minced swordfish or whitefish cooked in a light tomato sauce with fresh herbs. Swordfish roulades are also prepared with a certain flair here.

Via Roma 64. ✆ **090-986014.** Reservations recommended. Main courses 10€–18€ ($13–$23). AE, MC, V. Daily 7–11pm. Closed Oct–Mar.

La Locanda del Barbablu ★ SICILIAN/ITALIAN   This *locanda,* or inn, has enjoyed a certain renown since the early 1900s, when sailors used to stop here for some R & R en route to Naples. Today, the place is rather chic and has a lovely garden. The food is classically Italian, with no experimentation whatsoever. Excellent dishes include *ravioli di melanzane,* fried ravioli stuffed with eggplant and covered with a tomato sauce; *matarocco,* pasta flavored with tomato sauce, garlic, pine nuts, and fresh basil and parsley; and that old Sicilian reliable, pasta with fresh sardines.

Via Vittorio Emanuele 17–19. ✆ **090-986118.** Reservations recommended in summer. Main courses 8€–15€ ($10–$20). AE, DC, MC, V. Daily 7:30–11:30pm. Closed Nov 1–Feb 1.

Punta Lena ★★ AEOLIAN   The island's best cuisine is served at this old Aeolian house tastefully converted into a 17-seat restaurant, with a terrace opening onto the sea. The restaurant lies on the beach, a 10-minute walk from the center of town. There is a genuine effort here to cook with fresh products whenever possible. Stick to whatever the fishermen have brought in that day. The gnocchi *alla Saracena,* with whitefish, capers, olives, and tomatoes, is also excellent. The restaurant stocks the island's widest selection of wines.

Via Marina 8 (Località Ficogrande). ✆ **090-986204.** Reservations recommended. Main courses 8€–16€ ($10–$21). AE, DC, MC, V. Daily noon–2:30pm and 7–11pm. Closed Nov–Mar.

STROMBOLI AFTER DARK

As the sun sets and the volcano lights up the sky, it seems that everyone heads for **Bar Ingrid,** Via Michele Bianchi 1 (✆ **090-986385**). Naturally, it's named for Ingrid Bergman. Drinks, beer, and sandwiches are the casual offerings, but mainly people come here to see and be seen. It's open 6 days a week from 6pm to 2am. It closes Monday one week, Sunday the next.

Also popular is **Il Malandrino,** Via Marina (✆ **090-986376**), where you can hang out, drink, and even order a pizza. It's open 6 days a week from 5:30pm to 3am. It closes Monday one week, Sunday the next, a rotation it jointly maintains with Bar Ingrid.

For live music, head to **La Tartana,** Via Marina 33, Ficogrande (✆ **090-986025**), opening onto the beach. It's open June through September, daily from 9pm to 2am. Patrons come here to dance to disco or enjoy live pop. La Tartana is part of La Sirenetta Park Hotel, right near the port.

Taormina & Mount Etna

Sicily's greatest resort, Taormina, and its fiercest attraction, Mount Etna, can be combined in one powerful trip. Such writers as Goethe and D. H. Lawrence, besotted with the glories of Taormina's panoramic views of the bays beyond and Mount Etna looming in the background, spread word of the area's charm.

Taormina was built on a cliff, Monte Tauro, overlooking the sea. To the surprise of many first-time visitors, Taormina has no beach of its own. To reach the sands, you must take a steep cable-car descent down the hill. But the medieval charm of Taormina makes a stay high on the hill well worth your time.

The official high season lasts from April to October. If you're seeking a holiday by the beach and prefer to enjoy Taormina only on day trips, then **Giardini-Naxos** is your best choice. It has more style than many beach resorts in Sicily, which, frankly, tend toward the tacky. Seen from the terraces of Taormina, Giardini-Naxos opens onto a wide, curving bay with a beach that is justifiably one of the most popular on the island.

There are many possible excursions from Taormina, including a visit to the even loftier **Castelmola** and to the **Alcantara Gorges.** But nothing lures visitors quite like **Mount Etna,** the highest volcano in Europe. It's a potential menace, however: The entire coast of eastern Sicily is dominated by this volcanic peak, which continues to blow its top, sending deadly lava flows in all directions. The main crater is still dangerously active. At press time, Etna was at it again, opening up a new crater near Catania and spewing mile-high columns of smoke and ash into the air.

---

1 TAORMINA ★★★

53km (33 miles) N of Catania, 53km (33 miles) S of Messina, 250km (155 miles) E of Palermo

Taormina was just too good to remain unspoiled. Dating from the 4th century B.C., it hugs the edge of a cliff overlooking the Ionian Sea. The sea and even the railroad track lie below, connected by bus routes. Looming in the background is Mount Etna, an active volcano. Noted for its mild climate, the most beautiful town in all of Sicily seems to have no other reason to exist than for the thousands upon thousands of visitors who flock here for dining, barhopping, shopping, and enjoying the nearby beaches.

International visitors stroll back and forth along the one main street, Corso Umberto I, from April to October. After that, Taormina quiets down considerably. In spite of the hordes that descend in summer, Taormina has remained charming, with much of its medieval character intact. It's filled with intimate piazzas and *palazzi* dating from the 15th to the 19th centuries. You can dine in a different restaurant for every day of the week, linger at the many cafes, and browse the countless stores that sell everything from souvenir trinkets to antiques for well-heeled visitors. Hotels here tend to be pricey, but the good location can be worth it, as everyone gravitates to the top for dining and diversion—and those side roads from the bottom are quite steep to navigate.

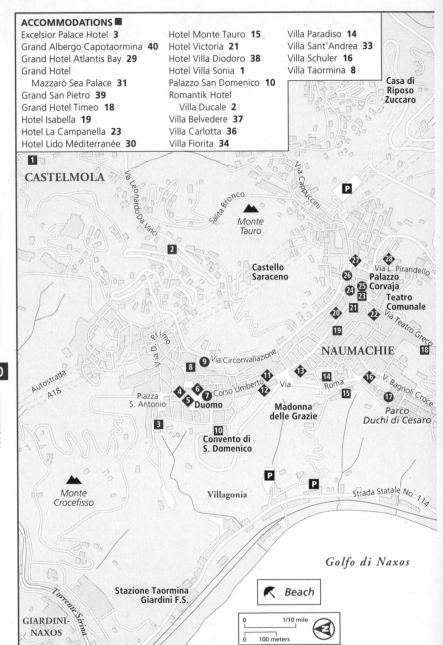

ACCOMMODATIONS ■

Excelsior Palace Hotel **3**
Grand Albergo Capotaormina **40**
Grand Hotel Atlantis Bay **29**
Grand Hotel
    Mazzarò Sea Palace **31**
Grand San Pietro **39**
Grand Hotel Timeo **18**
Hotel Isabella **19**
Hotel La Campanella **23**
Hotel Lido Méditerranée **30**

Hotel Monte Tauro **15**
Hotel Victoria **21**
Hotel Villa Diodoro **38**
Hotel Villa Sonia **1**
Palazzo San Domenico **10**
Romantik Hotel
    Villa Ducale **2**
Villa Belvedere **37**
Villa Carlotta **36**
Villa Fiorita **34**

Villa Paradiso **14**
Villa Sant'Andrea **33**
Villa Schuler **16**
Villa Taormina **8**

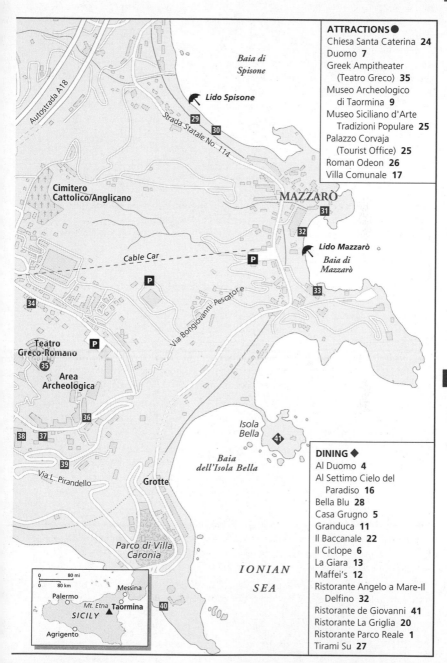

ATTRACTIONS ●
Chiesa Santa Caterina **24**
Duomo **7**
Greek Ampitheater
  (Teatro Greco) **35**
Museo Archeologico
  di Taormina **9**
Museo Siciliano d'Arte
  Tradizioni Populare **25**
Palazzo Corvaja
  (Tourist Office) **25**
Roman Odeon **26**
Villa Comunale **17**

DINING ◆
Al Duomo **4**
Al Settimo Cielo del
  Paradiso **16**
Bella Blu **28**
Casa Grugno **5**
Granduca **11**
Il Baccanale **22**
Il Ciclope **6**
La Giara **13**
Maffei's **12**
Ristorante Angelo a Mare-Il
  Delfino **32**
Ristorante de Giovanni **41**
Ristorante La Griglia **20**
Ristorante Parco Reale **1**
Tirami Su **27**

Baia di
Spisone

Lido Spisone

Autostrada A18

Strada Statale No. 114

Cimitero
Cattolico/Anglicano

MAZZARÒ

Lido Mazzarò
Baia di
Mazzarò

Cable Car

Via Bongiovanni Pescatore

Teatro
Greco-Romano

Area
Archeologica

Via L. Pirandello

Grotte

Isola
Bella

Baia
dell'Isola Bella

Parco di Villa
Caronia

IONIAN
SEA

Palermo
Messina
Mt. Etna Taormina
SICILY
Agrigento

80 mi
80 km

You can always escape the throngs during the day by seeking out adventures: perhaps climbing Mount Etna, walking to the Castelmola, or making a day trip to Syracuse (see chapter 12). In summer, you can hang out at the beaches below the town (although Taormina itself isn't right on a beach). At night, enjoy jazz and disco music or just spend time in a local tavern or restaurant.

Lots of people contributed to putting Taormina on the map. First inhabited by a tribe known as the Siculi, it has known many conquerors, such as the Greeks, Carthaginians, Romans, Saracens, French, and Spanish. Its first tourist is said to have been Goethe, who arrived in 1787 and recorded his impressions in his *Journey to Italy*. Other Germans followed, including Wilhelm von Gloeden, who photographed not only the town but also nude boys crowned with laurel wreaths. His pictures sent European high society flocking to Taormina. Von Gloeden's photos, some of which are printed in official tourist literature to this day, form one of the most enduring legends of Taormina. Souvenir shops still sell the pictures, which, considered scandalous in their day, seem tame—even innocent—by today's standards. In von Gloeden's footsteps came a host of celebs hoping to see what all the excitement was about: Truman Capote, Tennessee Williams, Marlene Dietrich, Joan Crawford, Rita Hayworth, and Greta Garbo. In time, another wave of stars arrived, including Elizabeth Taylor and Richard Burton, Cary Grant, and the woman who turned Grant down, Sophia Loren.

ESSENTIALS

GETTING THERE **By Train** You can make rail connections on the Messina line south. It's possible to board a train in Rome for the 8-hour trip to Messina, where you connect on to Taormina. Call ✆ **892021** for schedules. There are 19 trains a day from both Messina and Catania; trips from either town take 1 to 1¹⁄₂ hours and cost 3.60€ ($4.70) one-way. The Sicilian Gothic train station for Taormina/Giardini-Naxos is a mile from the heart of the resort, below the town. Buses run uphill from the station daily from 9am to 9pm, every 15 to 45 minutes (schedules vary throughout the year); a one-way ticket costs 1.50€ ($1.95). You can also take a taxi for 10€ ($13) and up.

By Bus You can also take the train as far as Messina and then hop a Taormina-bound bus. There are 15 a day, taking 1¹⁄₂ hours and costing 5€ ($6.50) one-way. For details, call **Interbus** (✆ **0942-625301**).

By Car From Messina, head south on A18. From Catania, continue north on A18. **Lumbi Parking,** Contrada Lumbi, is signposted off the Taormina Nord Autostrada junction; there's another garage at **Mazzarò Parking,** on Via Nazionale in Mazzarò, in the vicinity of the cable-car station off the coastal road. For 24-hour parking, count on paying 14€ to 16€ ($18–$21).

VISITOR INFORMATION The **tourist office** is in the Palazzo Corvaja, Piazza Santa Caterina (✆ **0942-23243**); open Monday to Saturday 8:30am to 2pm and 4 to 7pm. Here you can get a free map, hotel listings, bus and rail timetables, and a schedule of summer cultural events staged at the Greek Amphitheater.

SPECIAL EVENTS The Greek Amphitheater (p. 192) offers theatrical performances from July to September. Churches and other venues are the setting for a festival of classical music from May to September. Each summer, an international film festival is held in the amphitheater. Check with the tourist office for exact dates.

GETTING AROUND Within the heart of Taormina, use your trusty feet to get about. If you're venturing off on day excursions, a network of buses goes to such places as Giardini-Naxos and Mount Etna.

The more distant parts of Taormina are linked by minibus, which leaves from the terminal at Via Luigi Pirandello in town and costs .50€ (65¢) for a one-way ticket. Most visitors use the minibus that goes from the terminal to Madonna della Rocca, since it passes most of the major hotels. Service is daily 8am to 7:05pm.

Taxi ranks are found at Piazza Vittorio Emanuele and at Piazza San Pancrazio. These are used primarily if you're leaving the heart of Taormina and venturing into its hinterlands. A typical fare—say, from the center of Taormina to Madonna della Rocca—is 10€ ($13).

Many visitors prefer to rent a car in Taormina and explore at their leisure. A good local company is **Auto Europa** (© 800-334440); reservations should be made in advance in high season. The Taormina office is at Via Apollo Arcageta 4 (© 0942-21252). Vehicles rent for 34€ to 53€ ($44–$69) per day with unlimited mileage. Cars can be picked up in one Sicilian location and returned to another if you plan to explore beyond Taormina, perhaps taking a trip south to Syracuse and Agrigento.

Cable cars from Taormina run to the beaches below at Mazzarò, next to the Mazzarò car park. Service is daily 8am to 1am in summer, until 6pm in winter. A round-trip ticket costs 3.50€ ($4.55).

If you prefer to get around by moped, **Jet Car,** Via Nazionale 8 (© **0942-56190**), rents scooters for 35€ ($46) per day. It's open year-round daily 8am to noon and 4 to 8pm.

(Fast Facts Taormina

American Express The travel agency **La Duca Viaggi,** Via Don Bosco 39 (© **0942-625250**), handles AmEx clients Monday to Friday 9am to 1pm and 4 to 7:30pm. However, the most comprehensive travel agency in Taormina is **Dr. Silvestri Travel Bureau,** Corso Umberto I, 143–145 (© **0942-23052**). Established in 1905, it offers services ranging from car rentals and airline tickets to currency exchange and bus excursions. It's open Friday to Wednesday 9am to 1pm and 4 to 8pm.

Currency Exchange There are dozens of possibilities, especially at the banks along Corso Umberto I and Via Pirandello. **Cambio Valute,** Corso Umberto I, 224, near Piazza Sant'Antonio (© **0942-24806**), has ATMs and is the most convenient; open Monday to Saturday 9am to 1pm and 4 to 8pm. You can also get money exchanged at the post office at Piazza Sant'Antonio (© **0942-213011**), open Monday to Saturday 8am to 6:30pm.

Emergency Dial © **113** or 0942-23232.

Hospital Serving the entire Taormina area is **Ospedale San Vincenzo,** Piazza S. Francesco Di Paola (© **0942-628040**). In an emergency, call **Guardia Medica** (© **0942-625419**), open Monday to Friday 8am to 8pm, Saturday and Sunday 24 hours.

Internet Access The best place to go is the **Internet Café,** Calle Umberto I, 214 (© **0942-628839**), which charges 2€ ($2.60) per hour.

Left Luggage A kiosk inside the Taormina/Giardini-Naxos train station is open daily from 8am to 9pm; it charges 4€ ($5.20) per piece over a 24-hour period.

EXPLORING THE AREA

Many visitors to Taormina come for the beach, although the sands aren't exactly at the resort. To reach the best and most popular beach, **Lido Mazzarò** ★★, you have to go south of town via a cable car (*©* **0942-23605**) that leaves from Via Pirandello every 15 minutes. A one-way ticket costs 2€ ($2.60). This beach is one of the best equipped in Sicily, with bars, restaurants, and hotels. You can rent beach chairs, umbrellas, and watersports equipment at various kiosks from April to October. To the right of Lido Mazzarò, past the Capo Sant'Andrea headland, is the region's prettiest cove, where twin crescents of beach sweep from a sand spit out to the minuscule **Isola Bella** islet. You can walk here from the cable car in a minute, but it's more fun to paddle a boat from Mazzarò around Capo Sant'Andrea, which hides a few grottoes with excellent light effects on the seaward side.

North of Mazzarò are the long, wide beaches of **Spisone** and **Letojanni,** more developed but less crowded than **Giardini,** the large, built-up resort beach south of Isola Bella. A local bus leaves Taormina for Mazzarò, Spisone, and Letojanni, and another heads down the coast to Giardini.

The **Teatro Greco (Greek Amphitheater)** ★★★, Via del Teatro Greco (*©* **0942-23220**), is Taormina's most visited monument, offering a view of rare beauty of the seacoast and Mount Etna. In the Hellenistic period, the Greeks hewed the theater out of the rocky slope of Mount Tauro; the Romans remodeled and modified it greatly. What remains today dates from the 2nd century A.D. The conquering Arabs, who seemed intent on devastating the town, slashed away at it in the 10th century. That leaves us with a rather sparse and dusty ruin, less evocative than the Greek theater in Catania. On the premises is a display of artifacts from the classical and early Christian periods. Today, the Greek Amphitheater is the site of the annual Taormina film festival. It's open from April to September, daily from 9am to 7pm; and from October to March, daily from 9am to 4pm. Admission is 6€ ($7.80) for adults, 3€ ($3.90) for those ages 18 to 25, and free for seniors 65 and older and children 17 and younger. The ruins lie on the upper reaches of Taormina, near the Grand Hotel Timeo.

Behind the tourist office, on the other side of Piazza Vittorio Emanuele, is the **Roman Odeon,** a small theater partly covered by the church of Santa Caterina next door. The Romans constructed this theater around A.D. 21. Much smaller than the Greek theater and with similar architecture, it was discovered in 1892 by a blacksmith digging in the area. A peristyle (colonnade) was also discovered here, perhaps all that was left of a Greek temple dedicated to Aphrodite.

Chiesa Santa Caterina, Piazza Santa Caterina, off Corso Umberto I (*©* **0942-23123**), was consecrated to St. Catherine of Alexandria (exact consecration date unknown); it may have been built in the mid–17th century. It sits on a piazza that abuts

the highest point of the town's main street, Corso Umberto I. Within its severely dignified exterior are baroque detailing and a trussed wood-beamed ceiling. Chiesa Santa
Caterina is the temporary replacement for Taormina's cathedral, which will be closed for
some time. Open daily 9am to noon and 4 to 7pm.

Farther along the main drag, **Corso Umberto I** ★, you'll arrive at Piazza del Duomo
and the **Duomo,** or cathedral, of Taormina. Built around 1400 on the ruins of a church
from the Middle Ages, this fortress cathedral has a Latin cross plan and a trio of aisles.
The nave is held up by half a dozen monolithic columns in pink marble; a fish-scale
decoration graces their capitals in honor of the island's maritime tradition. For information, call ℂ **0942-23123.** The cathedral's role has been assumed by Chiesa Santa
Caterina (see above).

Museo Archeologico di Taormina, in the Palazzo Badia Vecchia, on Via Circonvallazione (ℂ **0942-620112**), is set on the site of the ancient Roman baths. It is a repository
for the hundreds of archaeological remnants discovered during excavations in and around
the city. Expect pottery shards and lingering artifacts of the ancient Roman world.
Admission is free; it's open Tuesday to Sunday 9am to 1pm, also on Tuesday and Thursday 4 to 8pm.

The Palazzo Corvaja, one of the most famous palaces in Taormina, contains the tourist office as well as the **Museo Siciliano di Arte e Tradizioni Popolari (Museum of Art
and Popular Traditions),** Piazza Santa Catarina at Corso Umberto I (ℂ **0942-23243**).
It's filled with 18th-century oil portraits, painted glass and donkey carts, and embroidery.
The most charming pieces in the collection are secular portraits of the mid-19th-century
Sicilian bourgeoisie. Entrance to the ground floor of the palace (also the town's tourist
office) is free. Admission to the museum is 2.60€ ($3.40). It's open Tuesday to Sunday
9am to 1pm and 4 to 8pm.

A local sightseeing oddity here is **Villa Comunale,** sometimes called **Parco Duca di
Cesarò** ★★, Via Bagnoli Croce, off Corso Umberto I. One of the most beautiful little
parks in all of Sicily, the gardens were the creation of Lady Florence Trevelyan in the late
19th century. This Scottish lady was "invited" to leave Britain after a well-publicized

Where Garbo's Big Feet Trod the Sands

The district's most appealing beach club, **Paradise Beach Club,** Via Lungomare, Letojanni (ℂ **0942-36944**), lies at the easterly end of the beachfront of
Letojanni, a hamlet that receives lots of traffic from hotel guests of Taormina
above. It was built on the site of a villa (ca. 1920s) that was the lair of Dr.
Gayelord Hauser, a dietitian and confidant of a long list of Hollywood stars that
included Greta Garbo. Come here for a half or full day, relax beside a freshwater
pool, enjoy a meal at the pleasant restaurant, or swim in the sea on a gravel
beach under supervision of a registered lifeguard. Platters of well-prepared
food in the open-air restaurant cost from 9€ to 18€ ($12–$23). At least some of
the clients here might be registered guests at Taormina's Villa Paradiso, which
maintains shuttle service between Taormina and this club. The club is open
June to October, daily 9am to 6pm. The entrance fee of 10€ ($13) includes all-
day use of a chaise longue and parasol.

(Finds) **For That Rainy Day**

Taormina has one of the most charming public libraries in Italy, **Biblioteca di Comune di Taormina,** Piazza XXV Aprile 3 (℃ **0942-610260**). It's weak in its range of books, but the setting is the severely dignified **Chiesa di Sant'Agostino,** originally built in 1448 and majestically transformed into a library around 1900. Open Monday to Friday 8:30am to 1:30pm, Tuesday and Thursday 3:30 to 6pm.

---

romance with the future king, Edward VII, son of Victoria. She built various amusements in the gardens, including a fanciful stone-and-brick pavilion that might have been conceived as a teahouse. The gardens are open daily 8:30am to 7pm (6pm in winter); admission is free.

Another flower-filled garden in Taormina is the **Giardino Púbblico (Public Garden),** Via Bagnoli Croce. It overlooks the sea, making it a choice spot for views. You can order drinks at a bar in the park. The garden is open from dawn until dusk.

It's worth a trip to the nearby village of **Castelmola** ★, 3km (2 miles) northwest of Taormina. This is one of the most beautiful places in eastern Sicily, with a panoramic view of Mount Etna on clear days. You might also visit the ruined *castello* (castle) on the summit of **Mount Tauro** (390m/1,280 ft.), about 3km (2 miles) northwest of Taormina along the Castelmola road. Hikers can follow a footpath here. Ruins of a former acropolis are visible, but most people come simply for the panoramas.

FARTHER AFIELD TO THE ALCANTARA GORGES

To see some beautiful rapids and waterfalls, head outside of town to the **Gole dell'Alcantara** ★ (℃ **0942-985010**), which is a series of gorges. The waters are extremely cold—uncharacteristic for Sicily, but quite refreshing in August. It's usually possible to walk up the river from May to September (when the water level is low), though you must inquire about current conditions before you do so. From the parking lot, take an elevator partway into the scenic abyss and then continue on foot. You're likely to get wet, so bring your bathing suit. If you don't have appropriate shoes, you can rent rubber boots at the entrance. Allow at least an hour for this trip. From October to April, only the entrance is accessible, but the view is always panoramic. It costs 4€ ($5.20) to enter the gorge, which is open daily 7am to 7:30pm. By car, head up SS185 some 17km (11 miles) from Taormina. Or take **Interbus** (℃ **0942-625301**) for the 1-hour trip departing from Taormina at 9:15am, 11:45am, 1:15pm, and 4:45pm. Buses from Gole dell'Alcantara return to Taormina at 9:25am, 12:35pm, 2:35pm, and 3:45pm. The round-trip fare is 5€ ($6.50). You can also go by taxi from Taormina, but you'll have to negotiate the fare with your driver; try calling Franco Nunzio at ℃ **0942-51094.**

WHERE TO STAY

The hotels in Taormina are the best in Sicily—in fact, they're the finest in Italy south of Amalfi. All price ranges are available, from army cots to sumptuous suites.

If you're coming primarily to hit the beach, at least in July and August, you may want to stay at **Mazzarò,** 5km (3 miles) from the center, and trek up the hill for shopping, nightlife, and dining. Mazzarò is the major beach and has some fine hotels (see the Grand

Hotel Mazzarò Sea Palace, later in this chapter). Buses connecting Mazzarò and Taormina leave every 30 minutes daily from 8am to 9pm; the fare is 1.50€ ($1.95). Otherwise, we recommend that you stay in Taormina—it has far more charm than anything down by the sea.

In summer, the curse of Taormina hotels is the noise, not only of traffic but also of visitors who turn the town into an all-night party. If you're a light sleeper and you've chosen a hotel along Corso Umberto, ask for a room in the rear—you'll be trading a view for a good night's sleep.

If you're driving to a hotel at the top of Taormina, call ahead to see what arrangements can be made for your car. Ask for exact driving directions as well as instructions on where to park—the narrow, winding, one-way streets can be bewildering once you get here.

Very Expensive

Gran Hotel San Pietro ★★★
The resort's latest government-rated five-star hotel is the only one to compete successfully with Palazzo San Domenico. Surrounded by the best hotel gardens on the eastern coast, it offers a huge terrace and pool, situated to evoke the bow of a ship. The interiors are bright and vast, everything graceful, including a wood-paneled library. Guest rooms are elegantly furnished, often in olive green, silver, gold, or apricot pink. They are rated classic and superior, or else junior and executive suites. The location of this Mediterranean-style building, rising six floors, is set on a hillside overlooking the sea, some 800m (2,625 ft.) from the center.

Via Pirandello 50, 98039 Taormina. © 0942-620711. Fax 0942-620770. www.gaishotels.com. Free parking. 63 units. 270€–462€ ($351–$601) double; 590€–792€ ($767–$1,030) suite. Rates include buffet breakfast. AE, DC, MC, V. **Amenities:** 2 restaurants; bar; outdoor pool; fitness center; room service; babysitting; laundry service; dry cleaning; nonsmoking rooms; private beach; 1 unit for those w/limited mobility. *In room:* A/C, TV, minibar, hair dryer, safe, Wi-Fi.

Grande Albergo Capotaormina ★★★
This barren cape was transformed in the 1960s with the addition of the most avant-garde architectural statement in or around Taormina—an oasis of posh comfort within a spectacularly inhospitable natural setting. Surrounded by the Ionian Sea on three sides, and with a layout that resembles an irregular pentagon, the hotel contains five floors with wide sun terraces. Elevators take you through 46m (151 ft.) of solid rock to the beach and to a large, free-form pool far below the level of the hotel, directly adjacent to the sea. Guest rooms are handsome and well proportioned, each with a private terrace and a spacious bathroom.

Via Nazionale 105, 98039 Taormina. © 0942-572111. Fax 0942-625467. www.capotaorminahotel.com. 202 units. 222€–500€ ($289–$650) double; 460€–1,100€ ($598–$1,430) suite. AE, DC, MC, V. Parking 15€ ($20). **Amenities:** 3 restaurants; 3 bars; outdoor seawater pool; golf; tennis; gym; seawater Jacuzzi; sauna; watersports program (supplemental charge) including deep-sea fishing and scuba; salon; room service; massage; laundry service; dry cleaning; nonsmoking rooms. *In room:* A/C, TV, minibar, hair dryer, safe, Wi-Fi.

Grand Hotel Atlantis Bay ★
This government-rated five-star hotel has its own private beach along the Taormina coast. Associated with the excellent Mazzarò Sea Palace, but with a less experienced management and a less gifted staff, it blends artfully into a landscape of pebbly beachfronts and cliffs. Great care was taken for an ecologically sensitive approach to the natural surroundings. The result is a jagged and earthy-looking combination of rough-hewed stones, terra-cotta tiles, and primal colors that don't stand out when viewed from afar. There's something stylish and postmodern about this youthful, sports-oriented hotel, with its bubbling aquariums and neo-Roman accessories in the lobby. Many guest rooms feature terraces.

Via Nazionale 161, 98030 Taormina Mare. ☎ **0942-618011.** Fax 0942-23194. www.atlantisbay.it. 86 units. 362€–555€ ($471–$722) double; from 570€ ($741) suite. Rates include continental breakfast. AE, DC, MC, V. Parking 35€ ($46). **Amenities:** 2 restaurants; 2 bars; outdoor pool; wellness center; fitness center; nonsmoking rooms; rooms for those w/limited mobility. *In room:* A/C, TV, minibar, hair dryer, Wi-Fi.

Grand Hotel Mazzarò Sea Palace ★★★ The leading hotel in Mazzarò opens onto the most beautiful bay in Sicily and has its own private beach. Completed in 1962, this government-rated five-star deluxe hotel has been renovated frequently since. From the coastal highway, you won't be able to see very much of this spectacular lodging—only a rooftop and masses of bougainvillea. You'll register on the top floor, and then ride an elevator down to sea level for access to a stylish, airy set of marble-sheathed public rooms. The hotel is very elegant, genuinely charming, and well staffed. Big windows let in cascades of light and offer views of the coast. Guest rooms are well furnished, filled with wicker and veneer pieces along with original art and wood or tile floors; most have panoramic views.

Via Nazionale 147, 98030 Mazzarò. ☎ **0942-612111.** Fax 0942-626237. www.mazzaroseapalace.it. 88 units. 332€–523€ ($432–$680) double; 556€–978€ ($723–$1,271) suite. Rates include breakfast. AE, DC, MC, V. Parking (nearby) 16€ ($21). **Amenities:** Restaurant; bar; outdoor pool; fitness center; room service; babysitting; laundry service; dry cleaning; nonsmoking rooms; rooms for those w/limited mobility. *In room:* A/C, TV, minibar, hair dryer, safe, Wi-Fi.

Grand Hotel Timeo ★★ Hidden in a tranquil private park just below the Greek Amphitheater, the Timeo opened in 1873 and has hosted everyone from King Umberto II to Liz Taylor. It's perched at the eastern edge of Taormina, on a precarious but panoramic terrace that's flooded with light and views upward to the amphitheater and down across town to the sea. A prestigious member of the Framon chain, it evokes a 19th-century neoclassical villa that manages to be lighthearted and baronial at the same time. It lacks the manorial dignity of the Palazzo San Domenico and has none of its ecclesiastical overlays; you get the feeling that the Timeo was built purely for pleasure, and it carries the aura of a sophisticated and very secular private villa. Guests are treated to a winning combination of old-world elegance and contemporary conveniences. The hotel has a private beach with lounge chairs and umbrellas; the staff will arrange tee times at nearby golf courses.

Via Teatro Greco 59, 98039 Taormina. ☎ **0942-23801.** Fax 0942-628501. www.framon-hotels.com. 87 units. 334€–565€ ($434–$735) double; 450€–1,735€ ($585–$2,255) suite. Rates include buffet breakfast. AE, DC, MC, V. Free parking. **Amenities:** Restaurant; piano bar; outdoor heated pool; fitness center; Turkish bath; car-rental desk; shuttle service to the beach; room service; massage; babysitting; laundry service; dry cleaning; nonsmoking rooms; rooms for those w/limited mobility. *In room:* A/C, TV, minibar, hair dryer, safe, Wi-Fi.

Palazzo San Domenico ★★★ This is one of the greatest hotels of Italy, with a pedigree so impressive that it evokes a national monument. Having housed such illustrious guests as François Mitterand and Winston Churchill, it's the envy of other hoteliers of Taormina. Set in the heart of the resort's oldest neighborhood, it originated in the 14th century as a semifortified Dominican monastery. Today, after generations of meticulous upgrades, it's surrounded by walled-in terraced gardens lit at night by flickering torches.

Don't expect the interior to look cutting edge and glossy, or as if a team of decorators has just finished moving in the furniture: What you'll find are massive and dignified areas (reception rooms, hideaway chapels, paneled salons) outfitted with museum-quality antiques that have been in place for at least 75 years, a genuinely impressive patina, and a physical setting that no one would ever dare modernize. The result is old-fashioned in the most appealing sense of the word.

(Moments) **When the Monks Come Out at Night**

If you stay at San Domenico, take a walk through the ecclesiastical-looking hallways, chapels, and courtyards late at night, when things are eerily empty and quiet, and when torches flicker exotically in the gardens. That's when the resident ghosts are said to make their appearances. It's the most mystical and otherworldly experience available at any hotel in Sicily.

Guest rooms are located in either the old monastery part of the hotel, where furnishings are severely dignified and very comfortable, or in the somewhat more opulent "newer" wings, those added in 1897, which evoke the Gilded Age and its aesthetics a bit more richly. Views extend out over the bougainvillea, palms, and citrus trees in the garden to the sea.

Piazza San Domenico 5, 98039 Taormina. (*C* **0942-613111.** Fax 0942-625506. www.sandomenico.thi.it. 108 units. 360€–567€ ($468–$737) double; from 790€ ($1,027) suite. Rates include buffet breakfast. AE, DC, MC, V. Free parking outside; 3 spaces inside (summer only) 20€ ($26). **Amenities:** 4 restaurants; piano bar; outdoor heated pool; gym; salon; room service; babysitting; laundry service; dry cleaning; nonsmoking rooms; rooms for those w/limited mobility. *In room:* A/C, TV, minibar, hair dryer.

Expensive

Excelsior Palace Hotel ★★   This government-rated four-star hotel in Taormina is used more aggressively by tour groups than virtually any other hotel in town. It's set on a rocky ridge in the lower reaches of Taormina, midway between a busy piazza and an isolated, somewhat dusty garden. Part of the allure of this place derives from its outrageous facade (ca. 1903), which artfully mimics the grand Moorish architecture you might expect in Marrakech. Most of the rather formal-looking guest rooms were recently upgraded and inspired by late-19th-century models. Older, not-yet-renovated rooms are a bit more bland but equally comfortable.

Via Toselli 8, 98039 Taormina. (*C* **0942-23975.** Fax 0942-23978. www.excelsiorpalacetaormina.it. 88 units. 250€ ($325) double. AE, DC, MC, V. **Amenities:** Restaurant; bar; outdoor pool; babysitting; laundry service; dry cleaning; solarium. *In room:* A/C, TV, minibar, hair dryer.

Hotel Isabella   Only one other hotel, the Victoria, enjoys a location directly on the main street of Taormina; the Isabella is the better rated of the two. Small-scale and chic in a way that only a boutique hotel can be, it welcomes visitors with a lobby that might remind you of a living room with a peaches-and-cream color scheme. Its pleasing decor was inspired by a sun-flooded English country house. Guest rooms are not particularly large, though cozy and plush. Some have views over the all-pedestrian hubbub of the town's main street. On the rooftop is a solarium.

Corso Umberto I 58, 98039 Taormina. (*C* **0942-23153.** Fax 0942-23155. www.gaishotels.com. 32 units. 112€–194€ ($146–$252) double. Rates include buffet breakfast. AE, DC, MC, V. **Amenities:** Restaurant; bar; free access to beach club w/watersports equipment/rentals, sunning, and swimming; babysitting; nonsmoking rooms; solarium. *In room:* A/C, TV, minibar, hair dryer, safe.

Hotel Monte Tauro   This hotel was built into the side of a hill rising high above the sea. Each room has a balcony with a sea view. Rooms are furnished to a high standard, with tiled bathrooms. Junior suites have Jacuzzis. The social center is the outdoor pool, whose cantilevered platform is ringed with dozens of plants.

Via Madonna delle Grazle 3, 98039 Taormina. ℂ **0942-24402.** Fax 0942-24403. www.hotelmontetauro. it. 100 units. 175€–295€ ($228–$384) double; 270€–380€ ($351–$494) junior suite. Rates include continental breakfast. AE, DC, MC, V. Closed Jan 15–Mar. **Amenities:** Restaurant; 2 bars; outdoor pool; room service; babysitting; laundry service; dry cleaning. *In room:* A/C, TV, minibar, hair dryer, safe.

Hotel Villa Diodoro ★ This is one of Taormina's better hotels, with tasteful design through and through. There are sunny spots where you can swim, sunbathe, and enjoy the view of mountains, trees, and flowers. The vistas of Mount Etna, the Ionian Sea, and the eastern coastline of Sicily are reason enough to stay here. Guest rooms are elegant and comfortable, with wrought-iron headboards, terra-cotta floors, balconies, and compact bathrooms. From June to October, a shuttle bus runs to the beach at nearby Lido Caparena.

Via Bagnoli Croce 75, 98039 Taormina. ℂ **0942-23312.** Fax 0942-23391. www.gaishotels.com. 99 units. 178€–326€ ($231–$424) double. Rates include buffet breakfast. AE, DC, MC, V. Free parking. **Amenities:** Dining room; lounge; outdoor pool; car rental; room service; babysitting; laundry service; dry cleaning; rooms for those w/limited mobility. *In room:* A/C, TV, minibar, hair dryer, safe.

Romantik Hotel Villa Ducale ★★ This restored old villa is a charming and romantic choice. Villa Ducale sits on a hillside, a 10-minute walk up from the center, in the quiet hamlet of Madonna della Rocca (midway btw. the heart of the resort and high-altitude Castelmola). It boasts magnificent views of the Mediterranean, the town, and Mount Etna. Each guest room has a veranda, terra-cotta floors, wrought-iron beds, and a compact bathroom. The service is warm and helpful. Breakfast is usually served on an outdoor terrace with a gorgeous view.

Via Leonardo da Vinci 60, 98039 Taormina. ℂ **0942-28153.** Fax 0942-28710. www.hotelvilladucale.it. 15 units. 100€–280€ ($130–$364) double; 200€–480€ ($260–$624) suite. Rates include buffet breakfast. AE, MC, V. Parking 10€ ($13). **Amenities:** Lounge; Jacuzzi; shuttle service to the beach; room service; laundry service. *In room:* A/C, TV, minibar, hair dryer, safe.

Villa Carlotta ★★ Finds Only Villa Ducale and Grand Hotel Timeo enjoy the same tranquillity and romantic position as this house, situated in a mock castle with an alluring roof garden—it's a charmer in every way. The staff, the service, the accommodations, and the price combine to make this a little gem. Furnishings are well chosen for comfort, tradition, and style, and each guest room is beautifully furnished and inviting. The cuisine at the restaurant is first-rate.

Via Pirandello 81, 98039 Taormina. ℂ **0942-626058.** Fax 0954-23732. www.hotelvillacarlottataormina. com. 23 units. 250€–320€ ($325–$416) double; 320€–480€ ($416–$624) suite. Rates include buffet breakfast. AE, DC, MC, V. Parking 15€ ($20). **Amenities:** Restaurant; outdoor pool; Jacuzzi; room service; babysitting; laundry service; dry cleaning; all nonsmoking rooms. *In room:* A/C, TV, minibar, hair dryer, safe, Wi-Fi.

Villa Sant'Andrea ★ Finds Staying here is like going to a house party at a pretty home. The atmosphere draws return visits by artists, painters, and other discerning guests. The Sant'Andrea lies at the base of the mountain, directly on the sea, and opens onto a private beach. Guest rooms are well maintained and comfortable, though size and decor vary. Many have balconies or terraces; the tiled shower-only bathrooms are small. A cable car, just outside the front gates, runs into the heart of Taormina.

Via Nazionale 137, 98030 Taormina Mare. ℂ **0942-23125.** Fax 0942-24838. www.framon-hotels.com. 80 units. 256€–388€ ($333–$504) double; from 420€ ($546) suite. Rates include buffet breakfast. AE, DC, MC, V. Parking 15€ ($20). Closed Nov 3–Apr 2. **Amenities:** 2 restaurants; 3 bars; fitness center; massage; boat rental; room service; babysitting; laundry service; dry cleaning; nonsmoking rooms. *In room:* A/C, TV, minibar, hair dryer, safe.

Villa Taormina ★★ (Finds) In the heart of Taormina, this antique residence is imbued with more Sicilian character than any other similar establishment in town. Not only that, but its terrace opens onto one of the resort's most panoramic views. The residence stands above the Piazza del Duomo, with the cathedral clearly visible from the balconies of the hotel. On a narrow, tranquil street, you get a combination of elegance, charm, and comfort in what might be called a glorified B&B. Filled with antiques and objets d'art, the villa is like lodging in the private home of some grand don of yesterday. Each spacious bedroom is individually decorated with hand-chosen fabrics, warm colors, Oriental rugs, and traditional Sicilian furniture. Baroque, neoclassical, and imperial styles are blended harmoniously. In other words, it's a class act. The superb bathrooms contain a hydromassage bathtub or shower, and even a courtesy beauty kit, and the bedrooms use hypoallergenic materials. Breakfast is served on a sun-filled terrace, opening onto views of the Mediterranean and Mount Etna in the distance. The location is just two flights up from the main street, Corso Umberto.

Via T. Fazzello 39, 98039 Taormina. ℂ **0942-620072.** Fax 0942-623003. www.hotelvillataormina.com. 8 units. 180€–280€ ($230–$364) double; 260€–350€ ($338–$455) suite. Rates include buffet breakfast. AE, DC, MC, V. Parking (nearby) 15€ ($20). Closed Jan–Feb. **Amenities:** Bar; Jacuzzi; room service; babysitting; laundry service; dry cleaning; all nonsmoking rooms. *In room:* A/C, TV, minibar, hair dryer, safe, Wi-Fi.

Moderate

Baia Taormina ★★ On a rocky hillside overlooking the sea, the building housing this government-rated four-star hotel is distinctly Mediterranean, with its local stone and Sicilian terra cotta. The resort lies only a 30-minute or a 13km (8-mile) drive north of Taormina. Those who seek it out can enjoy more sports facilities here than at resorts in the center. At Baia Taormina, you get not only two swimming pools (one saltwater, one freshwater), but can take part in such activities as hang gliding, tennis, rock climbing, water-skiing, and surfing. Others can relax in the health and beauty center, taking a Turkish bath, a hydromassage, a regular massage, or whatever. Il Picciolo Golf Club, on the slopes of Mount Etna, is a 30-minute drive from this luxury hotel. Admittedly, some of the bedrooms are small, but most are midsize, and each is furnished handsomely, comfortably, and attractively. All the rooms look out over the sea, and there is a sunbathing terrace. The Sicilian and international cuisine served here offers a mouthwatering roster of carefully prepared dishes.

Statale dello Ionio 39, 98030 Forza D'Agrò. ℂ **0942-756293.** Fax 0942-756603. www.baiataormina.com. 60 units. 88€–186€ ($114–$242) per person double; 150€–202€ ($195–$263) per person suite. Rates include buffet breakfast. AE, DC, MC, V. Free parking. **Amenities:** Restaurant; bar; 2 outdoor pools; wellness center; gym; room service; babysitting; all nonsmoking rooms; roof garden; rooms for those w/ limited mobility. *In room:* A/C, TV, minibar, hair dryer, safe, Wi-Fi.

Hotel Lido Méditerranée ★ (Value) Less stylish and a bit more dowdy than some of the five-star palace hotels that lie within a 3-minute drive along the coast, this solidly reliable four-star choice offers less expensive rates than those around it. Originally built in 1968 next to a gravel beach, and renovated a few times since, it resembles a private bougainvillea-draped villa. Guest rooms are unpretentious, reminiscent of a simple beachfront hotel in the Caribbean.

Via Nazionale, 98030 Taormina Mare (Spisone). ℂ **0942-24422.** Fax 0942-24774. www.taorminahotels. com. 72 units. 180€–280€ ($234–$364) double. Rates include continental breakfast. AE, DC, MC, V. Closed Nov–Easter. **Amenities:** Restaurant; piano bar; room service; massage; babysitting; laundry service; dry cleaning; nonsmoking rooms. *In room:* A/C, TV, minibar, hair dryer, Wi-Fi.

Moments   **An Evening Promenade**

We like to stroll at twilight along Corso Umberto I until we reach the resort's most charming small square. **Piazza IX Aprile** ★★ overlooks the sea with the grandest panoramas of Mount Etna looming in the background. One side of the square is open; its other three sides are enclosed by the 17th-century church of San Giuseppe, San Agostino (converted into a library), and Torre dell'Orologio, from the late 1600s. Choose any of the bars with outdoor seating and sit back to enjoy the show—Piazza IX Aprile is the favored rendezvous point for the young men of Taormina to meet ladies.

Villa Belvedere   With a friendly reception, professional maintenance, and old-fashioned style, this hotel near the Public Garden offers the same view enjoyed by guests at more expensive hotels nearby. Head to the cliff-side terrace in the rear to enjoy the vista of the Ionian Sea, the cypress-studded hillside, and smoldering Mount Etna. The small to midsize guest rooms feature functional furniture with a touch of class. Most units have slivers of balconies from which to enjoy views over the neighboring Public Garden to the sea; top-floor rooms have small terraces. The hotel is located near the cable car and the steps down to the beach.

Via Bagnoli Croce 79, 98039 Taormina. ℰ **0942-23791.** Fax 0942-625830. www.villabelvedere.it. 47 units. 120€–228€ ($156–$294) double; 190€–380€ ($247–$494) suite. Rates include breakfast. MC, V. Parking 10€ ($13). Closed late Nov to mid-Dec and mid-Jan to mid-Feb. **Amenities:** 2 bars; outdoor pool; room service; laundry service; dry cleaning; nonsmoking rooms. *In room:* A/C, TV, hair dryer.

Villa Paradiso ★ **Finds**   This charming boutique hotel originated in 1921 when the grandfather of the present owner bought a villa originally built in 1892. Today, it's the impeccably maintained domain of local patriarch Signore Salvatore Martorana. Set within a warren of narrow streets adjacent to the town's most beautiful public gardens, the Paradiso contains tastefully furnished public rooms outfitted with antiques and fine art. Each of the cozy, individually decorated guest rooms has a balcony, conservative furnishings, and a tiled bathroom. Between June and October, the hotel offers free shuttle service and free entrance to the also-recommended **Paradise Beach Club,** about 6km (4 miles) to the east, in the seaside resort of Letojanni. The hotel's restaurant, Al Settimo Cielo del Paradiso (p. 203), serves excellent cuisine on the panoramic rooftop.

Via Roma 2, 98039 Taormina. ℰ **0942-23921.** Fax 0942-625800. www.hotelvillaparadisotaormina.com. 35 units. 155€–222€ ($202–$289) double; 195€–245€ ($254–$319) junior suite. AE, DC, MC, V. Parking 15€ ($20). **Amenities:** Restaurant; bar; lounge; room service; massage; 1 room for those w/limited mobility. *In room:* A/C, TV, hair dryer, safe.

Inexpensive

Hotel La Campanella   This hotel is rich in plants, paintings, and hospitality. It sits at the top of a seemingly endless flight of stairs, which begin at a sharp curve of the main road leading into town. You'll climb past terra-cotta pots and the dangling tendrils of a terraced garden, eventually arriving at the house. The owners maintain clean, simple, homey guest rooms.

Via Circonvallazione 3, 98039 Taormina. ℰ **0942-23381.** Fax 0942-625248. lacampanella@tao.it. 12
units. 90€ ($117) double. Rates include continental breakfast. No credit cards. **Amenities:** Lounge. *In room:* Hair dryer.

Hotel Victoria It's unusual to find a good government-rated two-star hotel in Taormina, and this one is conveniently positioned smack in the middle of the nighttime action, on the town's all-pedestrian main street. It was established in 1885 within a 300-year-old, four-story building that has been frequently upgraded over the years. Rooms are accessible via a flight of stone steps; they're high-ceilinged, well maintained, and comfortable, with hints of manorial style. All but a few have air-conditioning; eight have minibars; and all contain shower-only bathrooms. Rooms overlooking the Corso Umberto I get more light but also more noise.

Corso Umberto I 81, 98039 Taormina. ℰ **0942-23372.** Fax 0942-623567. www.albergovictoria.it. 22 units. 93€–125€ ($121–$163) double. Rates include buffet breakfast. AE, MC, V. Closed Jan–Feb. *In room:* A/C, TV, hair dryer.

Villa Fiorita ★ ⓥⓐⓛⓤⓔ This small inn stretches toward the Teatro Greco from its position beside the road leading to the top of this cliff-hugging town. Its imaginative decor includes a handful of ceramic stoves, which the owner delights in collecting. A well-maintained garden lies alongside an ancient but empty Greek tomb whose stone walls have been classified a national treasure. The guest rooms are arranged in a steplike labyrinth of corridors and stairwells, some of which bend to correspond to the rocky slope on which the hotel was built. Each unit contains antique furniture and a shower-only bathroom; most have private terraces.

Via Luigi Pirandello 39, 98039 Taormina. ℰ **0942-24122.** Fax 0942-625967. www.villafioritahotel.com. 26 units. 125€ ($163) double; 165€ ($215) suite. Rates include breakfast. AE, MC, V. Parking 12€ ($16). **Amenities:** Lounge; outdoor pool; room service; nonsmoking rooms. *In room:* A/C, TV, hair dryer, safe.

Villa Schuler ★ ⓥⓐⓛⓤⓔ Filled with the fragrance of bougainvillea and jasmine, this hotel offers style and comfort at a good price. Family owned and run, it sits high above the Ionian Sea, with views of Mount Etna and the Bay of Naxos. It's only a 2-minute stroll from Corso Umberto I and about a 15-minute walk from the cable car to the beach below. Guest rooms are comfortably furnished, with bathrooms; many have a small balcony or terrace. Breakfast can be served in your room or taken on a lovely terrace with a panoramic sea view. Service is impeccable.

The most luxurious way to stay here is to book the garden villa suite with its own private access. It's spacious and beautifully furnished, with two bathrooms (one with a Jacuzzi). The villa comes with a kitchenette, patio, private garden, and veranda, and costs from 240€ ($312) per day for two, including breakfast.

Piazzetta Bastione, Via Roma, 98039 Taormina. ℰ **0942-23481.** Fax 0942-23522. www.villaschuler.com. 26 units, most with shower only. 128€–182€ ($166–$237) double; 182€–196€ ($237–$255) junior suite. Rates include continental breakfast. AE, DC, DISC, MC, V. Parking 15€ ($20) in garage; free outside. Closed Nov 23–Mar 6. **Amenities:** Bar; lounge; free bicycles; room service; laundry service; dry cleaning; library. *In room:* A/C, TV, hair dryer, safe, Wi-Fi.

In Castelmola
Hotel Villa Sonia ★ ⓕⓘⓝⓓⓢ Created in 1974 on the site of an old villa, this stylish brick-and-stone retreat is a short walk downhill from Castelmola's town square. The best-rated and most appealing hotel in Castelmola, it was built on a ridge beside the winding road that accesses the village, with spectacular views from both the front and back sides. Guest rooms feature modern lines and manorial Sicilian touches such as wrought-iron

headboards. The restaurant, Ristorante Parco Reale (p. 205), is especially noteworthy. Shuttle-bus transfers run twice a day from the hotel to central Taormina.

Via Porta Mola 9, 98030 Castelmola. © **0942-28082.** Fax 0942-28083. www.hotelvillasonia.com. 36 units. 215€ ($280) double; 340€ ($442) suite. Rates include buffet breakfast. AE, DC, MC, V. Free parking. **Amenities:** Restaurant; bar; outdoor pool; fitness room w/sauna; babysitting; laundry service; dry cleaning. *In room:* A/C, TV, minibar, hair dryer, safe.

WHERE TO DINE
Very Expensive
Casa Grugno ★★★ MODERN SICILIAN/INTERNATIONAL   The most exciting restaurant in Taormina is making a bold statement about modern Sicilian cuisine. Austrian-born chef Andreas Zangerl presides over this increasingly famous place, where the snows of the Austrian Tyrol seem to mingle with the torrid Sicilian scrublands. The setting is a stone-sided house that contains a bar, an ocher dining room outfitted like a *trompe l'oeil* rendition of Carnevale in Venice, and a walled-in terrace ringed with plants. The hip and alert young staff gets excellent supervision from the town's most successful *maître d'hôtel,* Stephano Lo Guidice.

The sublime food here is reinvented Sicilian cuisine at its finest, a haute cuisine that draws from a Pan-European sensibility. The fixed-price menus might include tuna steak with sweet-and-sour onion and mint sauce; pasta *alla Trapanese* (with almonds, tomatoes, and chili peppers); roasted pigeon with lentils from the island of Pantelleria; and an impeccable version of Parmesan eggplant that might be the most deliciously fragrant dish in this part of town.

Via Santa Maria de Greci. © **0942-21208.** Reservations recommended. Main courses 15€–25€ ($20–$33). AE, DC, MC, V. June–Sept daily 7:30pm–midnight; off season Thurs–Tues 7:30pm–midnight. Closed Nov 4–Dec 26 and Jan 4–Mar 4 (dates may vary).

Expensive
La Giara ★★ SICILIAN/ITALIAN   Glossy, airy, and reminiscent of Rome during the heyday of Gina Lollobrigida, La Giara evokes a warmed-over *la dolce vita.* The restaurant is almost excessively formal, and it has remained predictably stable since its founding in 1953. Views sweep from the veranda's outdoor tables over the bay of Taormina. The Art Deco ambience is also inviting, with marble floors and columns shaped from stone quarried in the fields outside Syracuse. The pastas are meals in themselves; we're especially fond of the ricotta-stuffed cannelloni and the ravioli stuffed with pesto-flavored eggplant (aubergine). The fresh fish of the day is grilled to perfection, and meats are cooked equally well. Other enticing menu items include filet of pork cooked with dried fruit and dressed with Marsala, or rolled sea bass stuffed with aromatic bread crumbs with cherry tomatoes and capers.

Vico la Floresta 1. © **0942-23360.** Reservations required. Main courses 19€–25€ ($25–$33). AE, DC, MC, V. Apr–July and Sept–Oct Tues–Sun 8:15–11pm; Nov–Mar Fri–Sat 8:15–11pm; Aug daily 8:15–11pm.

Maffei's ★ (Finds) SICILIAN/SEAFOOD   Maffei's is very small, with only 10 tables, but it serves the best fish in Taormina. Every day the chef selects the freshest fish at the market, and you simply tell him how you'd like it prepared. We often choose the house specialty, swordfish *alla Messinese,* braised with tomato sauce, black olives, and capers. The *fritto misto* (a mixed fry with calamari, shrimp, swordfish, and sea bream) is made superbly light by good-quality olive oil.

Via San Domenico de Guzman 1. © **0942-24055.** Reservations required. Main courses 10€–16€ ($13–$21). AE, DC, MC, V. Daily noon–3pm and 7pm–midnight. Closed early Jan to mid-Feb.

TAORMINA & MOUNT ETNA

10

TAORMINA

Al Duomo ★ SICILIAN/MESSINESE   Known for its romantic terrace dining (with a view of the square and cathedral), this restaurant prepares its dishes using the freshest local produce and regional ingredients. It's an attractive place, with brickwork tiles and inlaid marble tables. Try the stewed lamb with potatoes and red Sicilian wine; fried calamari sautéed in extra-virgin olive oil; or *rissolé* of fresh anchovies.

Via degli Ebrei 11. ℂ **0942-625656.** Reservations required. Main courses 9€–18€ ($12–$23). AE, DC, MC, V. Nov–Mar Mon–Sat noon–2:30pm and 7–11pm; Apr–Oct Thurs–Mon noon–2:30pm and 7–11pm.

Il Ciclope (Value) SICILIAN/ITALIAN   This is one of the best of Taormina's low-priced *trattorie*. Set back from the main street, it opens onto the pint-size Piazzetta Salvatore Leone. In summer, try to snag an outside table. The food is fairly simple, but the ingredients are fresh and the dishes well prepared. Try the fish soup, Sicilian squid, or grilled shrimp.

Corso Umberto I, 203. ℂ **0942-23263.** Main courses 7€–18€ ($9.10–$23). AE, DC, MC, V. Thurs–Tues noon–3pm and 6:30–10:30pm. Closed Jan 10–Feb 15 and Wed Oct–May.

Ristorante La Griglia ★ SICILIAN   This restaurant seems much older, thanks to its country-elegant location within the thick stone walls of what was a private *palazzo* in the 1600s. Our favorite seats are those against the most distant back wall, where windows overlook one of Taormina's oldest streets, a ravinelike alley known as Via Naumachia, whose walled edges were built by the ancient Romans. Start with one of the best selections of antipasti in town or with a classic island pasta dish—we enjoyed one prepared with swordfish and baby eggplant. The chef will be happy to prepare grilled fresh vegetables for vegetarians. The wine list is wonderful.

Corso Umberto I, 54. ℂ **0942-23980.** Reservations recommended for dinner during midsummer. Main courses 9€–18€ ($12–$23). AE, DC, MC, V. Wed–Mon noon–3:30pm and 7–11pm.

Inexpensive

Al Settimo Cielo del Paradiso ★ (Value) SICILIAN   It's far from being the most popular restaurant in Taormina, but in some ways it's our undisputed budget favorite, thanks to its superb view, sense of chic, and high-altitude view that seems to sweep over half of Sicily. To reach it, take an elevator from the lobby of the also-recommended hotel, and then dine on a rooftop where Orson Welles and John D. Rockefeller IV once ate. Dishes are likely to include well-crafted versions of pennette or risotto with salmon; succulent salads of grilled prawns with a limoncello sauce; and roulades of grilled swordfish layered with vegetables and herbs. *Note:* You must enter the restaurant between 7:30 and 9pm, as it has the shortest opening times of any place along the coast.

In the Hotel Villa Paradiso, Via Roma 2. ℂ **0942-23922.** Reservations recommended. Main courses 9€–20€ ($12–$26). AE, DC, MC, V. Daily 1–2pm and 7:30–9pm.

Bella Blu ★ SICILIAN/INTERNATIONAL   This chic international spot is a restaurant and pizzeria, as well as a piano bar and disco. In addition to offering fine cuisine, Bella Blu is one of the most entertaining places to be in Taormina after dark. Located a 150m (492-ft.) walk from the center, it has a rich, luxurious aura. Its menus and fine food are based on the freshest local ingredients. The chef specializes in barbecued and grilled meats flavored with fresh herbs, as well as fresh fish. Sicilian favorites include homemade pasta with fresh sardines in a savory tomato sauce with wild fennel and pine nuts.

Via Luigi Pirandello 28. ℂ **0942-24239.** Reservations required June–Aug. Main courses 7€–13€ ($9.10–$17); fixed-price menu 18€ ($23). AE, DC, MC, V. Daily 10am–3pm and 6–11pm.

(Fun Facts)   The Case of the Bouncing Check

The writer Truman Capote visited Taormina to finish his novel *Answered Prayers*. One drunken night at the San Domenico, he closed a deal to purchase the island Isola Bella. It's actually a gloriously conical peninsula—small, ringed with sand, and absolutely beautiful. The asking price from a local landowner was $10,000. Everyone was happy with this amazing deal until the check was returned from New York, marked "insufficient funds."

Granduca ★ (Finds) ITALIAN/SICILIAN   This is the most atmospheric choice in town, entered through an antiques store; it also serves an excellent, carefully executed cuisine. In fair weather, request a table in the beautiful gardens. Our favorite pasta here is spaghetti alla Norma (with tomato sauce, eggplant, and ricotta). If you want something truly Sicilian, ask for pasta with sardines. The best meat dish is the grilled roulades. At night, various pizzas are baked to perfection in a wood-fired oven.

Corso Umberto I, 172. *©* **0942-24983.** Reservations recommended. Main courses 8€–18€ ($10–$23). AE, DC, MC, V. Daily 12:30–3pm and 7:30pm–midnight.

Il Baccanale SICILIAN   This *trattoria*/grill serves what islanders call *Cucina Tipica Siciliana*. A slightly better dining venue than its many competitors that flank it, this eatery lies at the end of a pedestrian-only street. It's the Taormina equivalent of a French bistro, with checkered tablecloths and a bustling kitchen visible on an upper balcony. The 30 or so tables spill onto the piazza in front.

Piazzetta Filea 1 (Via Di Giovanni). *©* **0942-625390.** Reservations recommended. Main courses 9€–17€ ($12–$22). MC, V. Daily noon–3pm and 6–10pm. Closed Thurs Oct–Mar.

Tirami Su ★ (Value) SICILIAN   This is one of the most frequently praised inexpensive restaurants in Taormina, drawing appreciative comments from both residents and visitors. It's small and basic looking, set beside a busy, narrow commercial street. You'll enjoy dishes that may include beef with mushrooms and cream sauce; swordfish roulades; and spaghetti with seafood.

Via Costantino Patricio. *©* **0942-24803.** Reservations recommended. Main courses 8€–14€ ($10–$18); pizzas 5€–9€ ($6.50–$12). AE, DC, MC, V. Wed–Mon 12:30–3pm and 7:30pm–midnight.

In Mazzaro

Ristorante Angelo a Mare-Il Delfino MEDITERRANEAN/ITALIAN   This late-19th-century building is in Mazzarò, about 5km (3 miles) from Taormina and a 2-minute walk from the cable-car station. From the flower-filled terrace, you can enjoy views over the bay. Both decor and menu items were inspired by the sea. Specialties include mussels *Delfino* (with garlic, parsley, olive oil, and lemons), house-style steak (with fresh tomatoes, onions, garlic, capers, and parsley), and risotto *pescatoro* (fisherman's rice).

Via Nazionale. *©* **0942-23004.** Reservations recommended. Main courses 7.50€–18€ ($9.75–$23). AE, DC, MC, V. Daily noon–3pm and 6pm–midnight. Closed Nov–Mar.

In Isola Bella

Ristorante da Giovanni SICILIAN/ITALIAN   Perched precariously between the coastal road and the cliff that drops vertiginously down to the sea, this restaurant enjoys

a view that sweeps over the peninsula of Isola Bella. The glassed-in dining room is simple
and airy, accented with blue tile floors and very few adornments other than the view. The
flavorful menu items include a fish soup that might win the approval of Neptune, as well
as a mixed grill of fish caught that morning by fishermen working the Ionian Sea. For
our pasta fix, we gravitate to pennette with succulent crabmeat. Meat aficionados should
find the veal scaloppine with white-wine sauce heartwarming.

Via Nazionale, Isola Bella. © **0942-23531.** Reservations recommended. Main courses 8€–18€ ($10–$23).
AE, DC, MC, V. Tues–Sun 12:15–3pm and 8–11pm.

In Castelmola

Ristorante Parco Reale ★ (Finds) SICILIAN/INTERNATIONAL Artful and
romantic, the best restaurant in Castelmola offers lots of international pizazz. Some
members of the staff are Australian, with an offbeat sense of humor that might contribute
to your understanding of this very Sicilian venue. The airy and rambling dining room is
awash with displays of wine and rolling food carts. The menu is constantly changing, but
the grilled catch of the day is always done to perfection. We've also recommend the
risotto with fresh mushrooms; the macaroni with garlic, tomatoes, and ham; and the veal
escalope cooked in almond wine.

In the Hotel Villa Sonia, Via Porta Mola 9, Castelmola. © **0942-28082.** Reservations recommended for
dinner in midsummer. Main courses 8€–19€ ($10–$25). AE, DC, MC, V. Daily 12:30–2:30pm and
7–9:30pm.

SHOPPING

Shopping is easy—just find **Corso Umberto I,** the main street. The trendy shops here
sell everything from lacy linens to fashionable clothing to antique furniture. The more
adventurous can veer off the Corso and search out little shops on the side streets.

Bar Pasticerria A Chemi ★ Everything in this store comes from Sicily. The array of
candies is amazing: Expect at least four kinds of *torrone* (nougat); local honey fortified
with slices of dried fruit; and every conceivable kind of marzipan. Bottled Sicilian
liqueurs are also available, including a worthy collection of Marsalas and an almond-
flavored dessert wine. Corso Umberto I, 102. © **0942-24260.**

Carlo Panarello This shop offers a good selection of Sicilian ceramics, plus deluxe
umbrellas, tablecloths, and an eclectic mixture of antique furnishings, paintings, and
engravings. Corso Umberto I, 122. © **0942-23910.**

Gioielleria Giuseppe Stroscio ★ This is the best outlet for antique gold jewelry
from 1500 to the early 1900s. It also sells a good selection of modern jewelry. We've seen
more helpful staff, however. Corso Umberto I, 169. © **0942-24865.**

Giovanni di Blasi ★ Ceramics stores are found all over Sicily, but this is one of the
best in terms of quality and design. It specializes in the highly valued "white pottery" of
Caltagirone. Corso Umberto I, 103. © **0942-24671.**

Il Quadrifoglio Here you'll find a rich collection of amber jewelry from the Dominican Republic and the Baltic, antique jewelry from estate sales throughout Sicily, antique
porcelain from Dresden, and papier-mâché masks that might be suitable for Carnevale
in Venice. The venue is artsy, antiquey, and charming. Corso Umberto I, 153. © **0942-
23545.**

La Torinese Loaded to the rafters with the agrarian bounty of Sicily, this delicatessen
was established in 1936 by—you guessed it—a one-time resident of Torino. Pick up
cheeses, sliced meats, pâtés, bread, and pastries for a picnic on any of the city's panoramic

outcroppings. There's also an impressive collection of wines, liqueurs, and grappas. Corso Umberto I, 59. ✆ **0942-23321.**

TAORMINA AFTER DARK

Sicilian cities aren't known for their nightlife. The best—and certainly the most sophisticated—after-dark amusements can be found in Taormina. The resort is also the best spot in Sicily for gay and lesbian visitors. (Incidentally, drinks here are more expensive than elsewhere in Sicily.)

Many visitors are content to relax at cafe tables on outdoor terraces. The most popular form of evening entertainment is the *passeggiata,* or promenade, along the Corso Umberto I. Join in—it's fun.

You might also catch a bus to Giardini-Naxos (p. 207) for a waterfront stroll in the evening. Most bars and clubs there stay open until way past midnight, at least in the summer.

For a nightlife adventure, one of the most popular activities in Taormina is to take a CST bus tour, **Etna Tramonto,** for a sunset trip to the slopes of Mount Etna. The cost is 72€ ($94). Departures are Tuesday at 3pm (returning at midnight). For information and tickets, call **Legendary Sicily** at ✆ **0942-620061.**

Bar at the Palazzo San Domenico ★   For a (relatively) inexpensive way to see one of Italy's most legendary hotels, drop by here for a drink. Within a sprawling labyrinth of public areas—some of which evoke the Gilded Age, others the inner sanctums of medieval monasteries—you can order drinks and listen to live piano music. Bar service is technically available daily from 4 to 11:30pm, but the place is most romantic after 9pm, when flickering torches illuminate the gardens. Piazza San Domenico 5. ✆ **0942-613111.**

Bar San Giorgio   Perched on the main square of Castelmola, adjacent to a rocky drop-off guaranteed to induce vertigo, this might be the only building in the town's historic core that was able to beat the local building codes and alter its otherwise medieval-looking architecture. The result is a boxy, glass-sided upper story that looks like something from the German Bauhaus. Many visitors opt for coffee or gelato in the ground-floor cafe, but if you prefer to contemplate the Sicilian views that sweep over the surrounding hills, simply negotiate the steep steps that cling to the building's exterior to reach the upper story. The place serves only coffee, sandwiches, light snacks, and drinks. Open year-round, daily 7:30am to midnight. Piazza S. Antonio, Castelmola. ✆ **0942-28228.**

Bella Blu   On a crazy summer day, you can bet that the most fun is being generated by the high-energy 20- and 30-somethings who flock to this previously recommended restaurant/pizzeria (p. 203). It's also one of the most elegant and popular piano bars and dance clubs in town. The disco is open only on Saturday 11pm to 2:30am; the piano bar is also open only on Saturday, 9pm to 2am. Via Luigi Pirandello 28. ✆ **0942-24239.**

Caffè Wunderbar   We always begin our evening here, as Tennessee Williams did on his yearly visits to Taormina. This bar/cafe is on Taormina's main street, opening onto a panoramic view of the bay and Mount Etna beyond. Ice creams and *granite* (crushed-ice drinks) are served at outdoor tables or inside an elegant salon where you might hear the soft notes of a cafe concert. Open daily from 9am to 2:30am; closed Tuesdays from November to February. Piazza IX Aprile 7 (Corso Umberto I). ✆ **0942-625302.**

La Cisterna del Moro   The focal point of this restaurant/pub is a stone-sided cistern, built during the Middle Ages by the Arabs, that's set deep within a basement used for wine storage. A staff member will show it to you upon request, but you're more likely to be drinking and eating on the upper floors. Located in a narrow alley a few steps downhill from Corso Umberto, the club is most fun after 8pm. An attached restaurant, set on a terrace draped in bougainvillea, serves 25 kinds of pizza (including a version with grilled radicchio, smoked cheese, and bacon). Beer is the preferred drink. Open Tuesday to Sunday noon to 3pm and 6pm to midnight. Via Bonifacio 1. (℃ **0942-23001.**

Mocambo Bar ★   Our favorite outdoor bar in Taormina occupies an enviable location on the main square, smack in the center of the evening hubbub. It was established in 1952, during the peak of *la dolce vita,* when Truman Capote and Tennessee Williams held court at the sidewalk tables. You can opt for a seat on the piazza throughout the year, weather permitting, but during colder months many visitors migrate inside, where there's a satirical mural showing a busy night at the Mocambo. There's live piano music every evening between 9pm and midnight. Open in summer daily 8pm to at least 2am; in winter, Saturday and Sunday 9pm to 12:30am. Piazza IX Aprile 8. (℃ **0942-23350.**

Morgana Bar   This ultrahip bar is tucked into one of the narrow alleys that run downhill from Corso Umberto I. Centered around a semicircular bar, it spills onto a candlelit terrace with lighting guaranteed to make anyone look fabulous. Don't expect this place to even begin hopping until around midnight. The clientele is international and attractive, and mating games between regulars and incoming holiday-makers sometimes get serious. Open nightly 9pm to 5am. Scesa Morgana 4. (℃ **0942-620056.**

O-Seven Irish Pub   One of our favorite bars in Taormina is a woodsy, sudsy, high-ceilinged affair, staffed with attractive Europeans. It welcomes 20- and 30-somethings from around the world, many flirting and philosophizing with one another over foaming mugs of beer. Open from June to September, daily 4pm to 6am; October to May, Thursday to Tuesday 5pm to 2am. Larqo La Farina 6 (at Corso Umberto I). (℃ **0942-24980.**

Re di Bastoni   Favored by locals as a convivial and almost claustrophobically crowded hideaway, this bar gets impossibly loud after 10pm with its live or recorded music reverberating off sienna-colored walls, a beamed ceiling, and oversize paintings. Patrons usually come here late at night, sometimes with their pets, and always with their fetishes, to slurp down the house specialty of strawberry caipirinhas. Open Tuesday to Sunday 11am to 3am. Sandwiches are the only food served. Corso Umberto I 120. (℃ **0942-23037.**

2 GIARDINI-NAXOS

5km (3 miles) S of Taormina, 47km (29 miles) N of Catania, 54km (34 miles) S of Messina

Many first-time visitors to Taormina are disappointed when they find they have to commute from its hotels to the beach. At Giardini-Naxos, however, you can walk from your hotel room to the sands in short order. You can reach this resort by the sea in just 30 minutes by taking the Giardini-Naxos bus from the hilltop of Taormina.

The beach here opens onto the bay, lying between Capo (Cape) Taormina in the northwest and Capo Schisò in the south. Its point formed by an ancient lava flow from Mount Etna, Capo Schisò was the natural landfall for mariners rounding the toe of Italy on their way from eastern Mediterranean ports.

Thucydides tells us that Naxos was founded in 735 B.C. by Chalcidians under the leadership of the Athenian Thucles, who was the first Greek to land on Sicilian soil. From their base at Naxos, the Greeks branched out to take over more parts of Sicily. The colony at Naxos thrived until Dionysius of Syracuse destroyed it in 403 B.C. Even if you're staying in Taormina, you should set aside some time to visit the archaeological garden that remains here (see below).

Over the years, beach development at Giardini-Naxos has been so great that the resort now competes with Taormina for visitors, although it lacks the older resort's medieval charm. Since the 1960s, it's been catering mainly to package-tour operators from the north of Europe. (As a local said, "Taormina has the class, we have the sands.") Indeed, all the trappings of tourism are evident in this once-tranquil fishing village, with its many sports facilities and amusement parks, handicraft shops, antiques stores, hotels, trattorie, and beachside bars.

Much of the resort continues to function even during the short winter, when the winds can blow cold. Europeans from the frigid north will find Giardini-Naxos's weather balmy almost any time of year.

ESSENTIALS

Giardini-Naxos has a long main street, **Lungomare,** running parallel to the sea.

Interbus (© **0942-625301**) runs buses from the terminal in Taormina along Via Luigi Pirandello; a one-way ticket costs 1.50€ ($1.95). Service is daily, every half-hour from 8am to midnight.

Giardini-Naxos shares the same rail depot as Taormina (see "Getting There" earlier in this chapter). If you're driving from Taormina, take the SS114 south. From Messina, follow autostrada A18 south, exiting at the turnoff for Giardini-Naxos.

The **tourist office,** Via Lungomare 20 (© **0942-51010**), is open Monday to Friday 8:30am to 2pm and 4 to 7pm, Saturday 8:30am to 2pm.

EXPLORING ANCIENT RUINS

In a setting of citrus trees and prickly pears, on the headland of Capo Schisò, lie the ruins of the **Naxos excavations** ★, the site of the first Greek colony in Sicily. This site has been inhabited since 735 B.C., and has gone through the various tribulations of all such colonies, thriving and prospering until conquered and devastated—only to rise again out of the ashes.

If you're driving, head out on Via Naxos, which becomes Via Stracina. The ancient site lies in the dusty, barren scrubland above Giardini-Naxos. The actual excavations are behind a rusted iron fence facing the uphill (landward) side of the main road leading into Giardini-Naxos. Inside, you'll find the repository of artifacts that remained after Dionysius of Syracuse razed the city in 403 B.C.

This is not Pompeii, so don't be disappointed. What the tyrant didn't raze to the ground, centuries of builders carted off for other structures. Little remains today, with the exception of some structural foundations and the pavement stones of ancient streets.

The best of what was dug up is displayed in the **Archaeological Museum,** on two floors of an old Bourbon-built fort. The most evocative artifact is a statuette of Aphrodite Hippias from the 5th century B.C. As a curiosity, one exhibit displays objects removed from a surgeon's grave, including a strigil, a speculum used to examine injuries, and tiny ointment jars.

The site is open daily from 9am to 4:30pm. Admission is 2€ ($2.60) for adults, free for children 17 and younger. For information, call © **0942-51001.**

Arathena Rocks Hotel ★ (Value)   This government-rated three-star hotel contains one of the most appealing collections of decorative objects along the Taormina coastline. This includes bas-reliefs, sculptures, wrought-iron balustrades, gilded baroque door frames, and hand-painted tilework tastefully assembled into a complete whole. The overall effect is that of a whimsical private villa that happens to rent out rooms. Built in the 1970s atop a jagged strip of eroded lava rocks, it has compensated for its lack of sandy beach with a terraced pool and masses of potted flowers. Its rock-studded beach is private. Rooms are cozy and clean; many contain balconies or loggias. Half of the units have air-conditioning.

Via Calcide Eubea 55, 98035 Giardini-Naxos. ℭ **0942-51349.** Fax 0942-51690. www.hotelarathena.it. 50 units. 116€–130€ ($151–$169) double. Rates include continental breakfast. AE, DC, MC, V. Free parking. Closed Nov–Easter. **Amenities:** Restaurant; bar; outdoor pool; free shuttle transfers to Taormina. *In room:* TV.

Hellenia Yachting Club ★★   Set in the heart of Giardini-Naxos, closer to the town's bars than some of its competitors, this is a gracefully modern hotel whose public areas have some of the most lavish marble decoration anywhere, often with classical Greek touches. Built in 1978 and radically upgraded in 2004, it features a sun terrace (with a pleasant but not overly large pool) and black-lava steps that descend to a private gravel beach. The place has the aura of a private club—perhaps one in Greece that welcomes a nautically minded British clientele. Be warned that guest rooms are not as opulent as the lobby would imply. They have a sparsely furnished, somewhat cold decor, with hints of 18th-century French styling.

Via Jannuzzo 41, 98035 Giardini-Naxos. ℭ **0942-51737.** Fax 0942-54310. www.hotel-hellenia.it. 112 units. 230€ ($299) double; 360€ ($468) suite. Rates include buffet breakfast. AE, DC, MC, V. Free parking. **Amenities:** Restaurant; 2 bars; outdoor pool; tennis nearby; fitness room; room service; babysitting; laundry service; nonsmoking rooms; rooms for those w/limited mobility. *In room:* A/C, TV, minibar, hair dryer, Wi-Fi.

Hotel Sabbie d'Oro   The on-site restaurant (p. 210) is genuinely charming and more alluring than the hotel that administers it. Nonetheless, this simple lodging is acceptable in every way, though hardly grand. Built in 1990, and named after the public beach (Sabbie d'Oro/Golden Sands) that's just across the street, this government-rated three-star hotel is clean, only a bit battered, and completely unpretentious.

Via Schisò 12, 98035 Giardini-Naxos. ℭ **0942-51227.** Fax 0942-56913. www.hotelsabbiedoro.it. 39 units. 90€–120€ ($117–$156) double. Rates include buffet breakfast. AE, DC, MC, V. Parking 15€ ($20). **Amenities:** Restaurant; bar; wellness center; concierge; laundry service. *In room:* A/C, TV, minibar, hair dryer, safe.

Sant Alphio Garden Hotel ★   This is the biggest and most opulent hotel in Giardini-Naxos. Constructed in 1979 at the northern edge of the resort, its rich style evokes the scope and imagination of Las Vegas. Its centerpiece is a free-form outdoor pool with lavish landscaping and a swim-up bar, set directly adjacent to the best-looking cluster of swimming pools along the Taormina coastline. The hotel is outfitted in contemporary tones of navy and white, with touches of chrome and a jazzy combination of Sicilian and European styling. Bedrooms range from midsize to spacious, each with a well-maintained bathroom with shower or tub. Most visitors opt to spend at least a week here, decompressing from overburdened schedules in other parts of (usually northern) Europe. Come here for a retreat, with the understanding that the medieval attractions of Taormina are just an easy taxi ride away. A private beach lies within a 3-minute walk; tennis, horseback riding, and golf are available through outside concessions.

Marina di Recanati, 98030 Giardini-Naxos. ☎ **0942-51383.** Fax 0942-53934. www.santalphiohotel.com. 124 units. 130€–214€ ($169–$278) double; 230€–290€ ($299–$377) suite. Rates include buffet breakfast. AE, DC, MC, V. Free parking. **Amenities:** 2 restaurants; 2 bars; outdoor pool w/sunken bar; spa w/indoor heated pool; fitness center; Jacuzzi; sauna; steam room; room service; massage; babysitting; laundry service; dry cleaning. *In room:* A/C, TV, minibar, hair dryer, safe, Wi-Fi.

WHERE TO DINE

Ristorante Sabbie d'Oro SICILIAN   Amicable and laid-back, this restaurant sits in a covered open-air pavilion adjacent to both the beach and the hotel that manages it. You'll dine in a setting that evokes a woodsy tavern, with tables loaded with grappa and a ceiling draped with fishnets and nautical bric-a-brac. The cooks, though not world-class, are attentive. You'll enjoy such dishes as a curious marriage of beef and clams; pennette with swordfish and almonds; and macaroni with eggplant and fresh tomatoes.

Via Schisò 12. ☎ **0942-52380.** Reservations recommended Sat–Sun. Main courses 10€–20€ ($13–$26). AE, DC, MC, V. Daily noon–3pm and 7–11pm.

Ristorante Sea Sound ★★ SICILIAN/SEAFOOD   From a position beside a commercial street in the center of town, adjacent to the Hellenia Yacht Club Hotel, you'll walk for at least 4 minutes along a private footpath flanked by flowering vines. Just when you suspect you've made a wrong turn, you'll see a low-rise concrete bungalow adjacent to the sea. Its focal point is the terrace, surrounded by walls adorned with cheerful pottery. The antipasti selection, ranging from smoked tuna to swordfish, is the best in the area. More than a dozen pastas are made daily, including spaghetti *alla bottarga* (with tuna roe) and risotto with fresh seafood. Meat choices are limited, but dishes such as veal scaloppine in Marsala sauce are competently made. The chef specializes in freshly caught fish and grilled shrimp.

Via Jannuzzo 37A. ☎ **0942-54330.** Reservations recommended. Main courses 9€–22€ ($12–$29). AE, DC, MC, V. Daily 12:30–2:30pm and 7–11:30pm. Closed Nov–Easter.

3 MOUNT ETNA ★★

23km (14 miles) SW of Taormina, 31km (19 miles) N of Catania, 60km (37 miles) S of Messina

Looming menacingly over the coast of eastern Sicily, Mount Etna is the highest and largest active volcano in Europe—and we do mean active. The peak has changed in size over the years, but is currently in the neighborhood of 3,292m (10,801 ft.). Etna has been active in modern times (in 1928, the little village of Mascali was buried under its lava), and eruptions in 2001 and 2002 rekindled Sicilian fears. In October 2002, the air was thick and dirty over eastern Sicily as Mount Etna once again spewed out columns of ash that blackened skies as far away as Tripoli, on the coast of North Africa. Since then, there have been no major eruptions, but with Etna, danger can occur unexpectedly.

Etna has figured in history and in Greek mythology. Empedocles, the 5th-century-B.C. Greek philosopher, is said to have jumped into its crater as a sign that he was being delivered directly to Mount Olympus to take his seat among the gods. It was under Etna that Zeus crushed the multiheaded dragon Typhoeus, thereby securing domination over Olympus. Hephaestus, the god of fire and blacksmiths, made his headquarters in Etna, aided by the single-eyed Cyclops.

MONTE ETNA

PARCO DELL'ETNA

The Greeks warned that whenever Typhoeus tried to break out of his prison, lava erupted and earthquakes cracked the land. That must mean that the monster nearly escaped on March 11, 1669, the date of one of the most violent eruptions ever recorded—it destroyed Catania.

Visitors will have to decide whether to ascend Mount Etna from the northern or southern approach. We prefer the north-facing side, partly because it's cooler, more beautiful, and much richer in wildflowers that thrive in the volcanic soil. The north side is also more heavily forested. The south side, because of the eruptions during the last decade, is mostly covered with barren-looking lava flows. Its access routes are more crowded, and its views less appealing. Nonetheless, many visitors to Catania come up Etna's south side (for details, see chapter 11).

If you decide to come up the north side, simply take the highway to its end, Piano Provenzana, which stops at a complex of Alpine-inspired chalets selling souvenirs. During the heat of a Sicilian summer, they appear visibly out of place, but in winter, because of the high altitude (2,700m/8,858 ft.), they function as the centerpiece of a small-scale but thriving ski colony. The ski facilities include five downhill ski lifts and a network of cross-country ski trails.

It is from this artificial-looking alpine hamlet of Piano Provenzana that you buy tickets for bus excursions to the top of Mount Etna. The round-trip lasts 2 hours and costs 45€ ($59) for adults, 35€ ($46) for children 11 and younger. Departures are whenever business merits, but in summer, buses leave usually every hour.

The bus tours are loaded with bio-curious, bio-conscious folks from throughout Europe, especially France, who shoot away on their cameras as the specially equipped bus (more like an armored car) winds its way laboriously uphill, through gravel beds and rocky gullies, past barren, lichen-covered gray-green landscapes. Frankly, it's not all that exciting. At the top, the bus parks near a seismic exploration station, which is mostly abandoned, and visitors walk a bit farther to a point near the top, across gravel-covered landscapes of great brutality. There's no fire and brimstone to see—if there is, and if the crater is active, all bus trips are immediately discontinued. Note that visibility is poor on cloudy days; it's also generally clearer in the mornings.

A road around the foot of the volcano takes you through magnificent country where the rich soil has spawned many plantations and vineyards. Pistachio trees and prickly pears are commonplace. If you're driving around Etna in the morning, you can usually see the volcano, although it is often hidden in mist after lunch.

THE FOOTHILLS OF MOUNT ETNA

The village of Linguaglossa, 18km (11 miles) west of Taormina, is the best base for excursions to Mount Etna. From here, you can access Piano Provenzana at 1,800m (5,906 ft.), the main ski resort on Etna. It's at Piano Provenzana that four-wheel-drive vans are organized for those wanting to go on excursions to Etna's dangerous summit. Many hikers walk from Piano Provenzana to the cone of Etna in about 3 hours, following the track used by the shuttle vans.

Linguaglossa

Before climbing the mountain, you may want to linger in the village of Linguaglossa. Built from black lava, it is traversed by a main street called Via Roma. At the most distant end of this street is the 17th-century church **Chiesa Madre Madonna della Grazie,** capped with an iron cross and opening onto Piazza Matrice.

Via Roma is covered with large and very heavy black-lava cobblestones. It begins at the **Chiesa di San Francesco de Paola,** known for its lavish baroque frescoes and plasterwork. Via Roma continues to the 17th-century Duomo, which is also known as **Chiesa della SS. Annunziata.** The stately pink-stucco **Il Municipio (Town Hall)** opens on Piazza Municipio, overlooking a Liberty-style monument dedicated to the Italian dead of World War I.

The tourist office, **Associazione Turistica Proloco Linguaglossa,** Piazza Annunziata 7 (© **095-643094**), is open Monday to Saturday 9am to 1pm and 4 to 8pm (3–7pm in winter), Sunday 9:30am to noon. Pick up brochures for area attractions and check out the minidisplay that showcases the local geology, including insights on the abundant lava flows.

A bus from Giardini-Naxos (p. 207) leaves for Linguaglossa daily at 2:55pm. If you're driving from Taormina to Linguaglossa, take A18 south. After 12km (7¹/₂ miles), take the exit marked FIUMEFREDDO. After 815m (2,674 ft.), turn left and follow SS120 into Linguaglossa.

Where to Dine

Chalet delle Ginestre SICILIAN   As you navigate your way uphill through the scrubby pine forests and occasional snows of the north slope of Mount Etna, you'll find this

isolated, cement-sided chalet a welcome sight. Set 9km (5¹/₂ miles) from the uppermost
terminus of the highway, it was built in 2000 and offers a cozy, weatherproof venue for a
fortifying meal or drink. Menu items include a mixed grill of meat; asparagus with risotto,
butter, and sage; and roasted veal. The food is satisfying and filling—nothing more.

Strada Mareneve, Km 10.8. ✆ **0347-7629436.** Reservations not necessary. Main courses 7€–15€
($9.10–$20); fixed-price menu 25€ ($33). No credit cards. Oct–Feb Fri–Wed 12:30–4pm; Mar–Sept Fri–
Wed 12:30–4pm and 8–10pm. Closed 2 weeks in Nov.

Randazzo

After you explore Linguaglossa and Mount Etna, you may want to continue west to the
intriguing "black town" of Randazzo, 20km (12 miles) away on Route 120. Amazingly,
this town, built of lava and with a history going back to antiquity, has never been
destroyed by the volcano. Most of its destruction came from man, when the Germans
made Randazzo their last stand of resistance in August 1943. That dubious honor caused
Randazzo to be bombed by the Allies.

Chiesa di Santa Maria ★, Piazza della Basilica 5 (✆ 095-921003), is a study in
contrasts, its building materials of black lava contrasting with its white trim. Its black-
and-white tower is a prime example of brilliant Sicilian masonry. The church dates from
the 13th century and contains a 15th-century south portal built in the Catalán Gothic
style. The interior opens onto impressive black-lava columns. Open daily from 10am to
noon and 4 to 6pm.

The other notable church in town, **Chiesa di San Martino,** Corso Umberto I (✆ 095-
921003), is open daily 10am to noon and 4 to 6pm. Its impressive **campanile** ★, or bell
tower, is from the 13th century, although the church was reconstructed in the 17th
century. The black-and-white stone tower makes a dramatic contrast to the church,
whose facade is adorned with reliefs of martyrs and saints.

The **tourist office** is at Corso Umberto I, 197 (✆ 095-7991611). It's open daily 9am
to 1pm and 2 to 8pm.

Where to Stay

L'Antica Vigna ★ (Kids) Take the SS120 out of Randazzo to get to this stunningly
situated little hotel, located 4km (2¹/₂ miles) southeast of town at the foot of the volcano.
These charming accommodations are actually a converted farm surrounded by 3 hectares
(7¹/₂ acres) of olive trees. The farmyard menagerie includes horses along with the inevitable Sicilian goats. The place is ideal for families with children; there's even a small park
set aside for them. Guests are housed in small, comfortable villas, furnished with everything from kitchens to fireplaces.

Località Montelaguardia, 95036 Randazzo. ✆ **095-924003.** Fax 095-923324. 14 units. 50€ ($65) per
person (includes breakfast and dinner). No credit cards. **Amenities:** Restaurant; tennis court. *In room:* No
phone.

Where to Dine

Trattoria di Veneziano SICILIAN Randazzo's most elegant restaurant is separated
from the town's medieval zone by a deep valley, along the bottom of which runs a busy
boulevard. It's set on the ground floor of an airy, modern building decorated in tones of
Chinese red. Among the well-prepared menu items are grilled tenderloin steaks, grilled
and smoke-cured ham, salted codfish, grilled sausages, and rigatoni or pappardelle with
fresh mushrooms.

Via del Romano 8. ✆ **095-921418.** Reservations not necessary. Main courses 7€–13€ ($9.10–$17). AE,
DC, MC, V. Tues–Sat noon–3:30pm and 7–11:30pm; Sun noon–3:30pm.

Catania

Often neglected by visitors in their race toward Taormina, the baroque art city of Sicily deserves at least a day or two—and hopefully more—of your time. The capital of the eastern part of Sicily and its second-largest city after Palermo, **Catania ★★** has had a tormented history of conquest and devastation by nature. It's also one of the richest repositories of baroque architecture in Europe, with treasures well worth seeking out.

The city has suffered natural disasters throughout the centuries. Much of the history of Catania is linked to its volcanic neighbor, **Mount Etna.** It has also been a victim of earthquakes. In 1669, the worst eruption in Catania's history occurred when Etna buried much of the city under lava that literally ran through the streets. Catania had hardly recovered when a massive earthquake leveled much of the city in 1693, creating an economic crisis.

But the people of Catania bounced back, creating an even better city and rebuilding in the harmonious baroque style. Many of the buildings were fashioned from the black lava that had rained down upon it. An aura of the 18th century still lingers over much of the heart of Catania as a direct result of the city's rebuilding program.

Even though much of the city today is in decay, its art treasures, church museums, and Roman ruins make it a rewarding stopover—that and the chance to meet, argue with, converse with, and dine with the Catanian people.

Of course, looming in the background is that menace of a volcano, Mount Etna. If you didn't take our suggestion and visit Etna from a base in Taormina (p. 187), you can do so from the southern slopes, with a base in Catania.

This chapter concludes with our surprise destination: a side trip to **Acireale.** As Sicilian cities go, Acireale is a mere infant, having been founded in 1326. Built on streams of lava, the little city stands on cliffs above the sea and is filled with wonders, especially around its monumental inner core.

---

1 ESSENTIALS

52km (32 miles) S of Taormina, 60km (37 miles) N of Syracuse

Standing in the ominous shadow of Mount Etna, Catania is a city of lava. A bustling port opening onto the Ionian Sea, it's known as the "city of black and white." Black lava and white plaster and marble form major parts of its architectural look.

Catania is the second-largest city in Sicily, with a population of 380,000. It's a lively place, and the seat of a bishop and a great university. In deference to its hometown boy, **Vincenzo Bellini** (1801–35), Catania boasts one of Italy's grandest opera houses, where you can hear the operas and the eternal arias of this virtuoso composer.

Its second hometown boy who made good was **Giovanni Verga** (1840–1922), acclaimed as one of Italy's greatest writers. Known for his naturalistic fiction, he wrote such masterpieces as *Vita dei Campi* and *Mastro Don Gesualdo.*

If we can believe the historian Thucydides (he wasn't always right), Catania was founded in 729 B.C. It's had a rough go of it ever since. In 403 B.C., Dionysius of Syracuse sold off its citizens into slavery. Its patron saint, Agatha, in 253 B.C. had her breasts lopped off and has been carrying them around on a platter ever since—at least in artistic depictions of herself. That was the penalty she suffered for turning down the advances of the Roman praetor, Quintianus. Catania grew up on the Laestrygonian Fields known in Book 10 of the *Odyssey* as the home of the cannibalistic Laestrygones.

The Catania you see today, a city of wide boulevards, is a direct result of past disasters. The architect **Battista Vaccarini** (1702–68) was assigned the task of rebuilding. He decided to turn it into "the city of the baroque," since that was the fashionable architectural statement of the time. Many famous artists were commissioned, and fragments of solidified black lava were used extensively. This lava, and the way it was positioned into the masonry, gave added strength to the walls of various buildings. The result was so successful that in the 18th and 19th centuries Catania was a mandatory stopover for those rich dandies making the "Grand Tour" of Europe. Regrettably, the Allied bombing raids of 1943 did much to damage many monuments.

Grime and neglect have also taken their toll. Today Catania is often called the most degraded city of Europe, largely because of the decay of its once-beautiful historic core. Urban flight to the suburbs is common, with residents leaving behind an inferno of garbage, the despair of poverty, and crime. In fact, Catania vies with Palermo for the dubious distinction of crime capital of Sicily. Sicilians living elsewhere on the island generally express disdain for Catania.

Yet, in spite of its crime and poverty, the city's industry and burgeoning economy have earned it the appellation of "the Milano of the South." And the inner city has seen improvements in recent years, including a few brightly restored antique buildings.

Our verdict on Catania? You'll either love it or hate it. We're among its devotees because we don't judge a city by whether it's pretty or not or even by whether it's well kept. We gravitate to places that bustle with life, and Catania is blessed with plenty of that. In what some critics have called a "rotting urban carcass," we have found joy in its people, pleasure in its food, and spiritual fulfillment in its artistic treasures.

There is no greater symbol of Catania, a city wiped off the map at least seven times, than the hideously ugly but endearing puce-colored elephant in front of the Duomo. It's made entirely of lava spewed from Etna. Somehow this tough little elephant is an appropriate mascot for Catania itself: It symbolizes the city's ability to bounce back from one disaster after another, and even to create art from the lava that destroyed it.

Catania is a cauldron in summer, one of the hottest cities in Italy, with temperatures known to shoot up to 104°F (40°C). Winters are mild, but the best time to visit is spring or autumn.

GETTING THERE **By Plane** Flights from across Italy arrive at **Aeroporto Fontanarossa** (© **095-7239111**), 7km (4¹/₃ miles) to the south. Major links are via Palermo, Naples, and Rome.

Major carriers flying into Catania include the market leader, **Alitalia** (© **800/223-5730** in the U.S., or 062222 in Italy for information on domestic links). You can also fly in on **Meridiana** (© **892928 in Italy**) from Turin, Verona, Bologna, Florence, and Paris. To reach Meridiana from abroad, call © **0789-52682. Eurofly** (© **892928** in Italy, or 070-52650 from abroad) offers direct flights to Catania from Milan. A taxi into the city center costs around 18€ ($23). You can also take an Alibus to the Stazione Centrale, or rail depot, in the heart of Catania. Bus departures between the two points are every 20 minutes from 5pm to midnight. A ticket costs the same as a ride on a city bus (see "Getting Around," below).

Many people fly into Catania but choose to skip the city and go on to Taormina. If that suits you, you can catch a bus just outside the airport that will take you into Taormina in about an hour, for 8€ ($10) one-way.

By Train Arrivals are at the **Stazione Centrale,** Piazza Papa Giovanni XXIII (© **892021**). Catania is a 10-hour train ride from Rome, with five trains arriving daily and costing 50€ to 65€ ($65–$85), depending on the train. Catania also enjoys links with all the major cities of Sicily: Palermo (trip time: 3¹/₂ hr.), costing 12€ ($16); Agrigento (trip time: 4 hr.), costing 13€ ($17); Messina (trip time: 2 hr.), costing 6.45€ ($8.40); and Taormina (trip time: 1 hr.), costing 3.60€ ($4.70). For rail information, call © **892021.**

By Bus There is no central bus company; all operate independently and in total chaos. Companies are found on Via D'Amico across from the Stazione Centrale. The most useful for visitors include **SAIS Trasporti** (© **095-536201**), running eight buses per day to Agrigento (trip time: 3 hr.), costing 12€ ($16) one-way; and **SAIS Autolinee** (© **095-536168**), running 24 buses per day to Messina (trip time: 1¹/₂ hr.), costing 7.50€ ($9.75), and 14 buses per day to Palermo (trip time: 2³/₄ hr.), costing 14€ ($18).

By Car From Messina, which will probably be your gateway into Sicily, take A18 south, passing Taormina and continuing on to Catania.

VISITOR INFORMATION **Tourist offices** are found at the Stazione Centrale, Piazza Giovanni XXIII (© **095-7306255;** www.apt.catania.it), and at Via Cimarosa Domenico 10 (© **095-7306211**), both open daily 8am to 8pm. There is also a branch at the airport (© **095-7306266**), open daily 8am to 8pm.

CITY LAYOUT

Catania was rebuilt using antiseismic measures. Its major boulevards were made straight and wide, virtually eliminating anything that had existed from medieval Catania. Broad piazzas punctuate many streets. The aim was to make streets wide enough to allow Catanians to escape in case lava flows through the streets again.

In recent years, unchecked growth has sent Catania crawling up the southern slopes of the ferocious Etna and sprawling across the fertile lands of the Simeto River.

The old center of the city is the **Piazza Duomo,** with the aforementioned fountain of the ancient elephant. Splitting Catania in two parts is its main street, **Via Vittorio Emanuele II,** which begins east at **Piazza del Martini** running west past Piazza Duomo.

Running on a north-south axis, **Via Etnea** ★ is the grand boulevard of Catania that runs north from Piazza Duomo for 3km (1³/₄ miles). Along this avenue are the best restaurants and boutiques. Eventually Via Etnea reaches **Villa Bellini,** the beautiful public gardens.

In western Catania, **Via Crociferi** ★ is the city's gracious street of the baroque, flanked by churches and *palazzi*.

GETTING AROUND Traffic is not quite as horrendous as in Palermo, but it's still the second worst in Sicily. Don't even attempt to use a car. Go by bus or taxi. Most of the historic treasures in Catania can be covered on foot.

By Bus **AMT** (Azienda Municipale Trasporti), Via Plebiscito 747 (© **095-7519111**), operates a good network of buses, branching out across the city. Tickets cost 1€ ($1.30)

and are valid for 90 minutes. A ticket valid for a day goes for 2.50€ ($3.25). You can
purchase tickets at *tabacchi* (tobacco stands) and news kiosks. *Tip:* If you take circular
bus no. 410, you'll be treated to a round-trip of all the major sightseeing attractions for
the cost of a one-way fare. The service is run only by appointment; call ✆ 095-
7517111.

By Metro   The very limited subway system has trains running every 15 to 30 minutes
daily from 7am to 8:45pm, costing 1€ ($1.30) for a ticket valid for 90 minutes. Metro
tickets, like bus tickets, are available from news kiosks and tobacco shops. Service runs
from Stazione Centrale at Platform 11 south to Catania Porto and north and northwest all
the way to Catania Borgo, the terminus for the Stazione Circumetnea via Caronda 490.

By Taxi   CST (✆ 095-330966) operates 24-hour taxi service. Taxi ranks are found at
the Stazione Centrale and Piazza Duomo.

⟨*Fast Facts*⟩   **Catania**

American Express AmEx is represented by **La Duca Viaggi,** Viale Africa 14
(✆ **095-7222295**). Open Monday to Friday 9am to 1pm and 4 to 7:30pm, Saturday 9am to noon.

Currency Exchange Most banks lie in the center along Corso Sicilia; these include
Deutsche Bank, Piazza Buonarroti 14 (✆ **095-722931**), and **Banco di Sicilia,**
Corso Sicilia 8 (✆ **095-368215**), both open Monday to Friday 8:30am to 1:30pm
and 2:30 to 4pm. You can also exchange currency at the train station and at the
AmEx office (see above).

Emergencies Call ✆ **113.** For **first aid,** dial ✆ **118. Guardia Medica** is at Corso
Italia 234 (✆ **095-377122**).

Hospital The major hospital is **Garibaldi,** Piazza Santa Maria del Gesù (✆ **095-
7591111**).

Internet Access Your best bet is **WebCam,** Via Etnea 678 (✆ **095-434999**), open
Monday to Saturday 10am to 9pm. It charges 2.50€ ($3.25) per hour.

Pharmacies Ask at your hotel for the one nearest you. One night pharmacy is
Croceverde, Via Gabriele D'Annunzio 43 (✆ **095-441662**), open daily 4pm to
1am.

Police Dial ✆ **112.**

Post Office The main post office is at Via Etnea 215 (✆ **095-7155071**), next to
the Villa Bellini Gardens. It is open Monday to Friday 8am to 6:30pm, and Saturday 8am to 12:30pm.

CATANIA · 11 · WHERE TO STAY

---

2 WHERE TO STAY

EXPENSIVE
Excelsior Grand Hotel ★★★   No other hotel in Sicily so gracefully manifests the
flowing sense of *la dolce vita* modernism as Catania's leading establishment. It brought
postwar tourism to Catania with a stately and monumental facade, built in 1954, that's

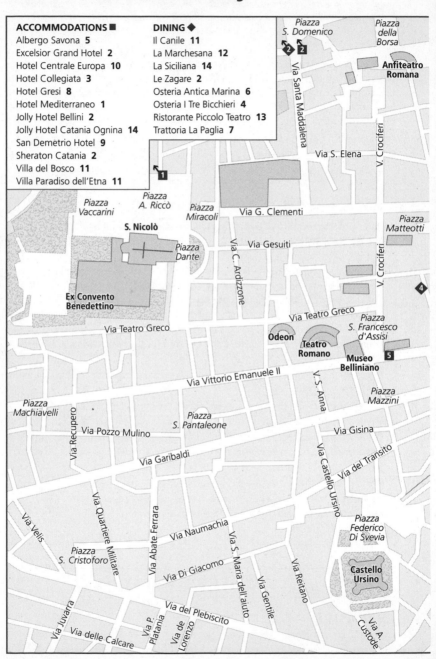

ACCOMMODATIONS ■

Albergo Savona **5**
Excelsior Grand Hotel **2**
Hotel Centrale Europa **10**
Hotel Collegiata **3**
Hotel Gresi **8**
Hotel Mediterraneo **1**
Jolly Hotel Bellini **2**
Jolly Hotel Catania Ognina **14**
San Demetrio Hotel **9**
Sheraton Catania **2**
Villa del Bosco **11**
Villa Paradiso dell'Etna **11**

DINING ◆

Il Canile **11**
La Marchesana **12**
La Siciliana **14**
Le Zagare **2**
Osteria Antica Marina **6**
Osteria I Tre Bicchieri **4**
Ristorante Piccolo Teatro **13**
Trattoria La Paglia **7**

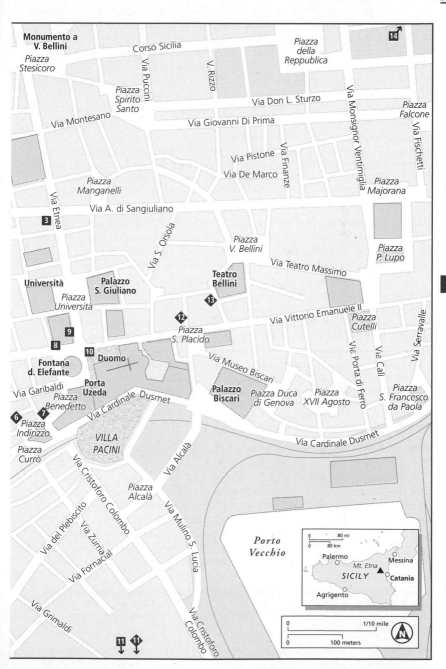

almost a mirror image of the Palazzo di Giustiza (Municipal Courthouse), which lies immediately across Piazza Verga, the most impressive square in Catania. A radical renovation retained the best aspects of this hotel's retro, Sputnik-era design and added zillions of new grace notes.

Expect a *moderno*-style lobby in perfect taste, with a resident pianist, deep and comfortable settees, and the kind of bar you'd expect in a posh hotel on Rome's Via Veneto. Half of the bedrooms overlook Piazza Verga and faraway Mount Etna, and all units are soundproof. These standard double rooms are called deluxe rooms, and each comes with a loggia-style balcony. The remainder ("superior rooms") are just as large, plush, and comfortable, but they face the back of the hotel and in most cases lack balconies. The in-house restaurant, **Le Zagare,** is reviewed on p. 223.

Piazza Verga, 95129 Catania. (C) **095-7476111.** Fax 095-537015. www.thi.it. 176 units. 215€–265€ ($280–$345) double; 275€–568€ ($358–$738) suite. Rates include breakfast. AE, DC, MC, V. Free parking. Bus: 443, 457, 721, or 722. **Amenities:** Restaurant; piano bar; fitness center; steam room; e-mail facilities in the lobby; room service; babysitting; laundry service; dry cleaning; nonsmoking rooms; rooms for those w/limited mobility. *In room:* A/C, TV, minibar, hair dryer, safe, Wi-Fi.

Sheraton Catania ★ This seaside resort lies in Cannizzaro, 5.6km (3¹/₂ miles) north of Catania's center. Set across the highway from the sea, and originally built in 1983, it offers a *moderno* lobby accented with fountains set into artificial grottoes, Lucite-trimmed balustrades, and a low-rise atrium that fills the interior with sunlight. This is not a "showcase" Sheraton (it's a member of the Sheraton franchise, but owned by a local investor), and its links to the international chain are relatively loose. It looks a bit dated when compared to more recently renovated places such as the Excelsior. But it's appealing and comfortable, graced with a surprising number of modern paintings. Guest rooms, accessible via a labyrinthine set of low-ceilinged hallways, have big windows, a sense of 1980s design, and generous space.

Via Antonello da Messina 45, 95020 Cannizzaro-Catania. (C) **095-7114111.** Fax 095-271380. www.sheraton.com. 170 units. 154€–257€ ($200–$334) double; 390€–460€ ($507–$598) suite. Rates include buffet breakfast. AE, DC, MC, V. Bus: 534 from Piazza Borsellino. **Amenities:** Restaurant; 2 bars; outdoor pool; tennis court; fitness center; health club; Jacuzzi; sauna; 24-hr. concierge; free shuttle bus to town center; business center; salon; room service; massage; nonsmoking rooms; solarium; rooms for those w/ limited mobility. *In room:* A/C, TV, minibar, iron, Wi-Fi.

Villa del Bosco ★★★ Guests at Villa del Bosco will enjoy a true taste of the aristocratic life of a landowning Sicilian family during the early 19th century. The stately looking Bosco is set behind a high wall that separates it from a suburban neighborhood, 5km (3 miles) south of Catania's historic core. It was originally built in 1826 as a private home and converted into a dignified boutique hotel, rich with antiques and a sense of another time. The hotel's social center is an elaborately detailed salon with a bar at one end. Guest rooms are elegant, with four-poster beds, plus tiled or stone-sheathed bathrooms. Suites come with either a Jacuzzi or else hydromassage showers. Its artfully frescoed breakfast room is the most beautiful in Catania. The in-house restaurant, **Il Canile,** is reviewed on p. 224.

Via del Bosco 62, 95125 Catania. (C) **095-7335100.** Fax 095-7335103. www.hotelvilladelbosco.it. 33 units. 240€ ($312) double; 300€–420€ ($390–$546) suite. AE, DC, MC, V. Bus: 129, 314, or 421. **Amenities:** Restaurant; bar; outdoor pool; laundry service; dry cleaning; nonsmoking rooms; rooms for those w/limited mobility. *In room:* A/C, TV, minibar, Wi-Fi.

Villa Paradiso dell'Etna ★★ (Finds) If you need to stay near the Fontanarossa airport, you might want to spend the night here, 11km (6³/₄ miles) from Catania. This elegant hotel lies on the slopes of Mount Etna, between the towns of San Giovanni La Punta and Viagrande. Surrounded by gardens, the hotel was opened in 1927 and has since been restored to its former glory. Its original furnishings are still here, and the atmosphere of the past lives on splendidly. Guest rooms are beautifully and comfortably furnished with antiques and old prints; all have views of Etna. The suites have hydromassage tubs. The villa also has a wine cellar, a panoramic roof garden, and a disco on summer Sundays.

Via per Viagrande 37, 95030 San Giovanni La Punta. © **095-7512409.** Fax 095-7413861. www.paradiso etna.it. 34 units. 270€ ($351) double; 420€ ($546) suite. Rates include buffet breakfast. AE, DC, MC, V. From Catania, follow the Catania-Messina motorway in the direction of Etna and San Gregorio. The hotel is signposted at the yellow signs leading to Le Zagare shopping center. **Amenities:** Restaurant; piano bar; lounge; outdoor pool; tennis court; fitness center; sauna; room service; massage; laundry service; dry cleaning; nonsmoking rooms; rooms for those w/limited mobility. *In room:* A/C, TV, minibar, hair dryer, safe.

MODERATE

Albergo Savona   A definite cut above the Hotel Centrale Europa, which sits across the street, this solid, well-located hotel lies a 2-minute walk from the Duomo. Converted into a hotel about a century ago, it has three floors of quiet, soundproof bedrooms with high ceilings, severely dignified yet comfortable furniture, and shower-only bathrooms. Guest rooms are accessed via a grandiose flight of marble-capped stairs flanked with elaborate wrought-iron railings. Although some have views of the cathedral, room nos. 102 and 104 are the best, with views over a medieval-looking courtyard. One of the best aspects of this place is the plush paneled bar, complete with soaring ceiling vaults, deep armchairs, and plenty of dignified style. It doubles as a breakfast room. As for some members of the staff, they need to go back and take Manners 101 again.

Via Vittorio Emanuele 210, 95124 Catania. ©/fax **095-326982.** www.hotelsavona.it. 30 units. 95€–150€ ($124–$195) double. AE, DC, MC, V. Bus: 401, 429, 432, or 457. **Amenities:** Bar; nonsmoking rooms; rooms for those w/limited mobility. *In room:* A/C, TV, minibar, safe.

Hotel Mediterraneo ★   Well designed and unpretentious, with three stars from the local tourist authorities, this is one of Catania's most modern hotels. In 2002, after a well-planned reconfiguration by celebrity architect Romeo Francesco, the place was reincarnated as a member of the Best Western hotel chain. The blue-floored lobby's best features include a tactful, hardworking staff and dramatic murals inspired by the great masterpieces of the Italian Renaissance. Guest rooms are predictably angular, simple, and uncomplicated, with big windows and bathrooms with tub/shower combinations.

Via Dottor Consoli 27, 95124 Catania. © **800/528-1234** in the U.S., or 095-325330. Fax 095-7151818. www.hotelmediterraneoct.com. 64 units. 160€ ($208) double. Rates include buffet breakfast. AE, DC, MC, V. Parking 10€–18€ ($13–$23) per day, depending on vehicle size. Bus: 431. **Amenities:** Lobby cafe and bar; laundry service; dry cleaning; nonsmoking rooms; rooms for those w/limited mobility. *In room:* A/C, TV, minibar, hair dryer, safe, Wi-Fi.

Jolly Hotel Bellini   This older (ca. 1959), more central of Catania's two Jolly Hotels has only three government stars, a low ranking for a chain more noted for its four- and five-star properties. Detractors find it a wee bit dated; we find it comfortable, well maintained, and, despite a few remaining touches of retro-dowdiness, an acceptable choice.

Piazza Trento 13, 95129 Catania. © **095-316933.** Fax 095-316832. www.jollyhotels.it. 130 units. 148€– 215€ ($192–$280) double. Rates include buffet breakfast. AE, DC, MC, V. Bus: 443, 721, or 722. **Amenities:** Restaurant; bar; room service; laundry service; dry cleaning; nonsmoking rooms; rooms for those w/ limited mobility. *In room:* A/C, TV, minibar, trouser press.

Jolly Hotel Catania Ognina ★   Set at the point in Catania where the city devolves into a seaside strip of beach resorts that eventually lead to such towns as Acireale, this boxy-looking, government-rated three-star hotel is favored by business travelers. A somewhat blasé staff will check you into a contemporary-looking guest room, outfitted with bland but comfortable furniture. About half of the units have harbor views. There's no on-site restaurant, but a respectable choice of dining options lies within a few minutes' drive or walk.

Via Messina 626–628, 95126 Località Ognina Catania. ℂ **095-7528111.** Fax 095-7121856. www.jolly hotels.it. 56 units. 170€ ($221) double. Rate includes breakfast. AE, DC, MC, V. Free parking. Bus: 334 or 448. **Amenities:** Bar. *In room:* A/C, TV, minibar.

INEXPENSIVE

Hotel Centrale Europa   This age-old government-rated two-star hotel occupies a site that's closer to the cathedral than any other lodging in town. It's been here since 1900, still evoking a battered but genteel *pensione* whose staff has seen thousands of art lovers and business travelers come and go. The small lobby is filled with sepia-toned photos of old Catania. Rooms are very simple and bland-looking, with few frills but acceptably comfortable furniture. More than half overlook the Duomo and the historic buildings around it. No meals of any kind, not even breakfast, are served, but the Caffè del Duomo (featured on p. 235 as part of our walking tour of Catania) lies a few steps away.

Via Vittorio Emanuele 167 (Piazza Duomo), 95124 Catania. ℂ **095-311309.** Fax 095-317531. www.hotel centraleuropa.it. 17 units. 85€ ($111) double; 105€ ($137) triple. AE, MC, V. Bus: 401, 429, 432, or 457. *In room:* A/C, TV.

Hotel Collegiata ★ Ⓕⁱⁿᵈˢ   All of the floors in this 17th-century building are devoted to private apartments except for two, which contain a series of high-ceilinged guest rooms that, however spartan-looking, are airy, comfortable, and bigger than you'd expect. The setting is close to one of Catania's most beautiful churches, La Collegiata, a short walk from the Duomo. The staff is hip and friendly.

Via Vasta 10 (at Via Etnea), 95100 Catania. ℂ **095-315256.** Fax 095-322848. www.lacollegiata.com. 14 units. 65€–85€ ($85–$111) double; 110€ ($143) triple. Rates include continental breakfast. AE, DC, MC, V. Bus: 448, 449, or 457. *In room:* A/C, TV, hair dryer.

Hotel Gresi   Small-scale and lacking any bona fide amenities, this would be nothing more than a tucked-away set of rooms fashioned from a once-private apartment except for the fact that the painted ceilings are as lavishly frescoed as those in any hotel in town. To reach the place, you'll pass through a stately looking courtyard, take a small elevator to the third floor, and register in a high-ceilinged anteroom whose painted ceiling is just one of many more to come. Most of the frescoes date from around 1850 in a style so lovely as to place them in almost surreal contrast with the hotel's simple furniture.

Via Pacini 28, 95124 Catania. ℂ **095-322709.** Fax 095-7153045. www.gresihotel.com. 23 units. 90€ ($117) double; 115€ ($150) triple. AE, DC, MC, V. Bus: 1–4. **Amenities:** Breakfast lounge. *In room:* A/C, TV.

San Demetrio Hotel ★ Ⓕⁱⁿᵈˢ   Small-scale, personal, and deeply idiosyncratic, this hotel occupies one of the upper floors of a grandiose building near the cathedral; it shares the floor with the branch of the local bureaucracy that fines motorists for parking and traffic violations. (To reach the entrance to the hotel, you pass somewhat scary-looking government offices, traverse a courtyard, and take a claustrophobic elevator to an upper floor.) The hotel was converted from a private apartment in 2000, and it still evokes a

> ### (Finds) A Farmhouse Retreat in the Shadow of Etna
>
> With Mount Etna rising ominously in the foreground, **Azienda Trinità,** Via Trinità 34 , 95030 Mascalucia (©/fax **095-7272156;** www.aziendatrinita.it), is a rural farm dating from 1609. It lies near the little Etnean town of Mascalucia, renowned for its 16th-century churches. The setting is a botanical park where Etna's lava breeds a collection of indigenous and exotic plants. Visitors can stay on the farm or in one of the modern apartments. Guest rooms are midsize and cozy, with wooden ceilings with traditional furniture. Each has air-conditioning, TV, and a small, shower-only bathroom. Meals are prepared with old Sicilian recipes using as much locally grown produce as possible, including the farm's own citrus fruit, olive oil, artichokes, zagara honey, mandarin liqueur, and baked olives. Half board (breakfast and dinner) costs 70€ to 85€ ($91–$111) per person. From the center of Catania, follow the signs to Tangenziale Ovest. Go along this road until you see the exit to Gravina. From here, follow the street signs to Mascalucia Etna.

private home. It is graced with some of the most beautiful ceiling frescoes of any hotel in Catania. The appealing paintings on the walls are done in a "post-Renaissance kind of modernism." Room no. 22 is particularly charming, but the others compete worthily with early-19th-century grace notes. In contrast, furnishings are spartan.

Via Etnea 55, 95124 Catania. (© **095-2500237.** Fax 095-311845. www.hotelsandemetrio.com. 6 units. 82€ ($107) double; 110€ ($143) triple; 135€ ($176) quad. Rates include continental breakfast. MC, V. Free parking. Bus: 448, 449, 457, 722, or 733. **Amenities:** Babysitting; laundry service; dry cleaning. *In room:* A/C, TV, hair dryer.

3 WHERE TO DINE

EXPENSIVE

Le Zagare ★★ CONTINENTAL/SICILIAN   When an army of designers renovated the dining room of the Excelsior Grand Hotel in 2001, they took pains to retain the original lines of its *dolce vita* decor (ca. 1954). The result is a genuinely elegant dining experience complemented by superb food and access to a terrace lined with flickering candles and flowering shrubbery. Menu items are a cut above the standard fare served in other hotel dining rooms. Delectable starters include Sicilian king prawn in a corn and cheese crust served on a bed of red onions and green tomatoes, or else purée of dried cod served on small pancakes of chickpeas, olives, and dried tomatoes. Natural flavors and the skill of the chefs combine to create such main dishes as grilled gilthead sea bream filets served with vegetables flavored with almond essence, or a casserole of Mediterranean fish and shellfish flavored with saffron. Desserts are especially yummy here, especially the crème brûlée flavored with pistachio or the crispy chocolate "pyramid" with iced nougat and orange sauce.

In the Excelsior Grand Hotel, Piazza Verga. ☎ **095-7476111.** Reservations recommended. Main courses 18€–27€ ($23–$35). AE, DC, MC, V. Daily 12:30–2:30pm and 7:30–10:30pm. Bus: 443, 457, 721, or 722.

Osteria I Tre Bicchieri ★★★ CONTINENTAL This is the finest and most appealing restaurant in Catania. Established in 2000 in partnership with one of the best-respected wine merchants (Benanti, Inc.) in Sicily, it welcomes visitors to a location on a narrow, quiet street 2 blocks northwest of the cathedral.

Note that this building contains two dining venues, the other a well-conceived wine tavern, called **Cantina,** in a woodsy-looking room near the front entrance. Food here includes the likes of fondue, steak tartare, carpaccio, pasta, and crepes, costing from 6€ to 15€ ($7.80–$20). But the real culinary vision of the place is found in the three high-ceilinged, vaulted rooms outfitted in a graceful 18th-century style, reached by walking through the Cantina and the kind of sliding, high-security door you might expect to see in a bank vault.

Part of the success of this place derives from the culinary vision of Naples-born chef Carmine Laquinangelo, whose creativity is fast becoming legend among local gastronomes. The best pasta we tasted in Catania was his tagliatelle with ragout of suckling pig. He does wonders with fish, especially *triglia,* a local saltwater fish served with onion-stuffed artichokes and a sauce of smoked foie gras. His signature gnocchi comes with a cheese from Ragusa. The wine list includes at least 1,000 Italian vintages, many from Sicily.

Note to wine experts: Make it a point to drop into the wine boutique, which sells both popular and very rare vintages. Best of all, it maintains a resident expert wine steward who really knows what he's talking about.

Via San Giuseppe al Duomo 31. ☎ **095-7153540.** www.osteriaitrebicchieri.it. Reservations required. Main courses 12€–20€ ($16–$26). AE, DC, MC, V. Mon–Sat 8pm–12:30am. Bus: 443, 457, 721, or 722.

MODERATE

Il Canile SICILIAN/CONTINENTAL Elegant and traditional, this restaurant in the Villa del Bosco hotel (p. 220) is very appealing. You can dine in a richly frescoed interior room or take a seat on a terrace without a hint of Sicilian traffic. Menu items include a *risottini* of porcini mushrooms from the slopes of Mount Etna. We sampled our finest seafood pasta in Catania here and went on to devour a succulent sea bream under an oven-crisp potato crust. The restaurant's name, which translates as "The Kennel," is taken from the pair of 18th-century stone dogs that stand near its entrance.

In the Villa del Bosco, Via del Bosco 62. ☎ **095-7335100.** Reservations recommended. Main courses 14€–21€ ($18–$27). AE, DC, MC, V. Daily 1–2:30pm and 8–11pm. Bus: 129, 314, or 421.

La Siciliana SICILIAN Decorated in a classic and rustic style, this restaurant was established in 1968 and is today managed by two sons of the original owner. Located in north Catania, it's set in a 19th-century villa that's furnished in provincial island style. In winter, diners sit in one of four cozy rooms; in summer, tables overflow onto a garden terrace. The cuisine is both innovative and respectful of tradition. We've enjoyed carpaccio of fresh swordfish, grilled stuffed calamari, and risotto with squid ink and fresh ricotta. For dessert, typical local favorites are always on the menu.

Viale Marco Polo 52A. ☎ **095-376400.** Reservations required. Main courses 6€–16€ ($7.80–$21). AE, DC, MC, V. Tues–Sat 12:30–3pm and 8–11pm; Sun 12:30–3pm. Closed July 1–15.

La Marchesana ★ (Value) SICILIAN/SEAFOOD   The charm of this place lies in its well-managed simplicity, the genuinely friendly welcome from the staff at the bar near the entrance, and the flavorful cuisine. Outdoor tables fill part of the quiet street during nice weather; otherwise, you can dine in a high-ceilinged, vaulted dining room that manages to stay cool even on hot days. The Di Dio family, well versed in welcoming diners from the English-speaking world, prepares dishes that include delectable risotto, salads, and succulent spaghetti with squid, cuttlefish, shrimp, and tomatoes.

Via Mazza 4–8 (at the Piazza San Placido). ℂ **095-315171.** Reservations recommended on weekends. Main courses 7€–12€ ($9.10–$16). AE, DC, MC, V. Daily 11am–4pm and 7pm–1am. Bus: 1–4.

Osteria Antica Marina SICILIAN   Only a handful of other restaurants convey as effectively the earthy, grimy, teeming maze of humanity that hauls food in and out of central Catania. Established just after World War II and sheathed with wooden panels, this *osteria* is set amid the densest concentration of open-air food stalls in town, two labyrinthine blocks south of the cathedral, on a piazza that by day teems with food merchants, but by night is calmer and quieter. You'll be separated from most of the hysteria outside by plate-glass windows and air-conditioning, but at the same time you'll get a sense of the freshness and variety of raw material just a few steps away. Menu items include ultrafresh homemade pasta, garnished (you guessed it) with seafood and shellfish, including sea urchins and scampi; every imaginable kind of grilled gilled creature in the Mediterranean; and fresh cuts of beef, pork, veal, and lamb.

Alla Pescheria di Catania, Via Pardo 29. ℂ **095-348197.** Reservations recommended. Main courses 12€–15€ ($16–$20). AE, DC, MC, V. Thurs–Tues 1–3pm and 8pm–12:30am. Bus: 1–4, 2–5, or 3–6.

Ristorante Piccolo Teatro INTERNATIONAL   Set a few steps from the Teatro Massimo is this cozy pub whose battered wood panels and prominent bar might remind you of an Italian beer hall. It attracts after-work business and a pretheater crowd of young hipsters and hipster wannabes. Expect dishes that include fresh fish (especially swordfish), risotto, and hot-weather favorites such as octopus salad and sorbets. "A dish for the gods," as one habitué described it, is spaghetti with sea urchins, eggs, and extra-virgin olive oil given additional flavor by fresh parsley, garlic, and hot peppers. Pennette with swordfish is made enticing by the addition of eggplant, fresh mint, pine nuts, and hot peppers.

Via Michele Rapisardi 6–8. ℂ **095-315369.** Reservations not needed. Main courses 9€–18€ ($12–$23). AE, DC, MC, V. Wed–Mon 8pm–12:30am. Bus: 14.

Trattoria La Paglia ★ (Finds) SICILIAN   If you like your food ethnic and your atmosphere hale and hearty, you can enjoy the most authentic Catanian dining experience at the site of the lively fish market. If you don't like the day's offerings, one of the staff might step out to the market and buy a fish you like, cooking it to your specifications. Start with *la triaca pasta,* an excellent pasta in fresh bean sauce, or *sarda al beccafico* (sardines fried in bread crumbs with pecorino cheese). We're also fond of the spaghetti whipped with sea urchins in an extra-virgin olive oil with fresh garlic. One local dish that's highly favored is *tonno con cipollata* (broiled tuna with onions and a dash of vinegar). Most of the dishes are based on the sea, and the atmosphere is very rustic.

Via Pardo 23. ℂ **095-346838.** Reservations required Fri–Sat. Main courses 7€–15€ ($9.10–$20). MC, V. Mon–Sat 12:30–2:30pm and 8–11pm. Bus: 457.

4 SEEING THE SIGHTS

Duomo ★   The cathedral at the very heart of Catania is dedicated to the memory of the martyred St. Agatha. The Duomo was originally ordered built by Roger I, the Norman king, but it was destroyed in the earthquake of 1693 and had to be reconstructed. Its **facade** ★ is its most enduring architectural legacy, the work of Battista Vaccarini (1702–68), who redesigned the city after the earthquake. For the granite columns of the facade, the architect "removed" them from the city's Roman amphitheater. Only the lovingly crafted medieval apses, made from lava, survived the devastation of that earthquake.

Many opera fans come here to pay their respects at **Bellini's tomb,** guarded by a life-size angel in marble. It's to the right as you enter the Duomo through its right door. The words above the tomb are from *Sonnambula* and in translation read, "Ah, I didn't think I'd see you wilt so soon, flower."

In the **Norman Cappella della Madonna,** also on the right, precious metals envelop a magnificent Roman sarcophagus and a statue of the Virgin Mary carved in the 1400s. To the right of the choir is the **Cappella di Sant'Agata,** to whom the cathedral is dedicated. In the sacristy is a fresco, said to have been created in 1774, that depicts the horrendous eruption of Mount Etna in 1669.

Piazza Duomo, Via Vittorio Emanuele II 163. ℂ **095-320044.** Free admission. Daily 7am–noon and 4:30–7pm. Bus: 448, 449, 457, 722, or 733.

Piazza Duomo   The Duomo is not the only attraction on this landmark square. Lying in the very heart of Catania, the Piazza Duomo was also created by the city's planner, Vaccarini. The baroque elegance of Catania's heyday lingers on here.

The symbol of the city, the **Fontana dell'Elefante** ★★, was created in 1735. It was obviously inspired by Bellini's monument in Rome's Piazza Minerva. The elephant was hewn from black lava spewed forth by Mount Etna and stands on a Byzantine platform. The elephant is a beast of burden here, carrying on its back an Egyptian obelisk lettered with hieroglyphics celebrating the cult of Isis.

The less-imposing **Fontana dell'Amenano** lies on the south side of the piazza. Water cascades down from its top basin, evoking a sheer veil that caused the Catanians to dub it *acqua a lenzuolo*. On the north side of the square are the facades of **Palazzo degli Elefanti** (today the city hall) and **Palazzo Senatorio.** Unless security forbids it, Palazzo degli Elefanti is usually open Monday through Friday from 8am to 7pm.

Standing beside the Duomo is the **Badia di Sant'Agata,** again dedicated to the patron saint of Catania. This is another stellar example of Vaccarini's mastery of baroque elegance. This church is one of seven in Catania dedicated to its patroness.

Lying east of Piazza Duomo is **Teatro Massimo** (or Bellini), one of the grandest and richest in Europe (p. 239).

Directly uphill from Piazza Duomo lies the entrance to the **Greco-Roman Theater,** Via Vittorio Emanuele II 266, dating from 415 B.C. The Roman theater, where gladiators battled wild beasts shipped from nearby Africa, was constructed on the site of an even earlier Teatro Greco. At its apex, 7,000 spectators could view the grisly entertainment here. The marble was coated by Mount Etna's eruption in 1669. In back of the theater is a similar but smaller **Odeon,** dating from the 2nd and 3rd centuries A.D. Concerts are sometimes staged here. The site is open daily from 9am to 1:30pm and 3 to 7pm; admission is free.

(Moments) The Green Lung of Catania

Escape from the city heat and congestion to **Villa Bellini** ★, the "Central Park" of Catania, reached by heading north along Via Etnea. Planted with such exotics as Brazilian araucarias, the park sprawls over several hills. This is one of the most attractive public parks in Sicily, and for some reason maintenance is higher here than it is in most of Catania's public monuments or gardens. The Catanians claim that the fig tree planted here is the world's largest. Unique in Italy is the floral clock and calendar on the hillside. Stand on a hill here and be rewarded with a panoramic view of Mount Etna.

Museo Diocesano This is dedicated to the cult of St. Agatha, patron saint of Catania. Agatha is also the patroness of all wet nurses, bell-founders, and jewelers. She suffered martyrdom by having her breasts lopped off. The museum is joined architecturally to the Duomo, its windows opening onto Piazza Duomo. Most of the artworks consist of vestments, altar furnishings, and relics from the bishops' palace. This minor museum need occupy no more than an hour of your time. The best of the treasure-trove is found in Hall II: Look for a relic arm of St. George as well as St. Cataldo's relic bust attributable to Paolo Guarna, one of the most famous goldsmiths of Catania in the 16th century.

Via Etnea 8. © **095-281635.** www.museodiocesicatania.it. Admission 5€ ($6.50) adults, 3€ ($3.90) children 17 and under. Tues–Sun 9am–12:30pm and 4–7:30pm. Bus: 448, 449, 457, 722, or 733.

Museo Civico Belliniano ★★ One of the trio of nearly adjacent museums honoring local sons (Verga, Emilio Greco, and Bellini museums), this is the most compelling and the one that most easily evokes an emotional reaction from Catanians, many of whom view it as a national shrine. To reach it, you enter a quiet courtyard off the Piazza San Francesco, and then climb to the drab, second-floor apartment where composer Vincenzo Bellini was born in 1801. Bellini is known for such titanic works as *La Straniera, Sonnambula, Norma, I Puritani,* and *I Cavalieri.*

Here you'll see original folios of his operas, his death mask, harpsichords and spinet pianos he rehearsed on as a child, and the coffin in which his body was transferred in 1876 back to Catania from its original burial place in Puteaux, near Paris. Signatures in the guest book read like a who's who of international musicians, ranging from Carlo Muti to Pavarotti. Many of the mementos of his life were donated by Rossini, a devoted latter-day fan of Bellini's brilliant *bel cantos.* If you're an opera fan, you will likely find this museum thrilling.

Note: At press time, this museum was still closed for renovations, with no set reopening date. Before you visit, call to check on its current status.

Piazza San Francesco 3. © **095-7150535.** Free admission. Tues–Thurs 9am–1pm and 3–6pm; Fri–Mon 9am–1pm. Bus: 1–4, 2–5, or 3–6.

Museo Emilio Greco ★ Larger, plusher, and obviously better financed than either the Bellini or the Verga museums, this second-story museum showcases the oil paintings and engravings of Sicilian artist Emilio Greco (1913–95). Many locals are not that familiar with Greco and his abstract nude forms. His fame is mostly derived from accolades he received in New York and Tokyo, not from adulation heaped upon him by other

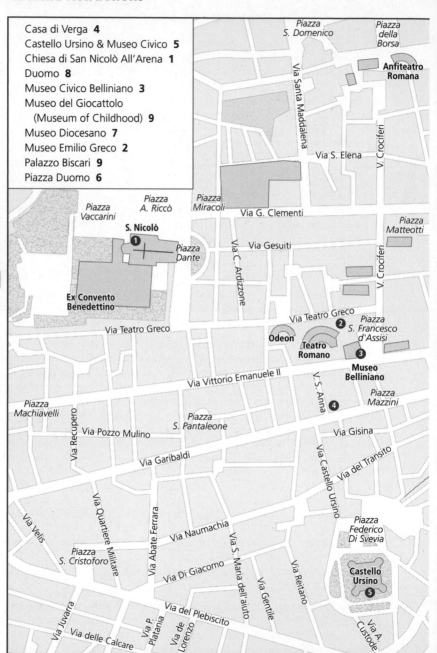

Casa di Verga **4**
Castello Ursino & Museo Civico **5**
Chiesa di San Nicolò All'Arena **1**
Duomo **8**
Museo Civico Belliniano **3**
Museo del Giocattolo
(Museum of Childhood) **9**
Museo Diocesano **7**
Museo Emilio Greco **2**
Palazzo Biscari **9**
Piazza Duomo **6**

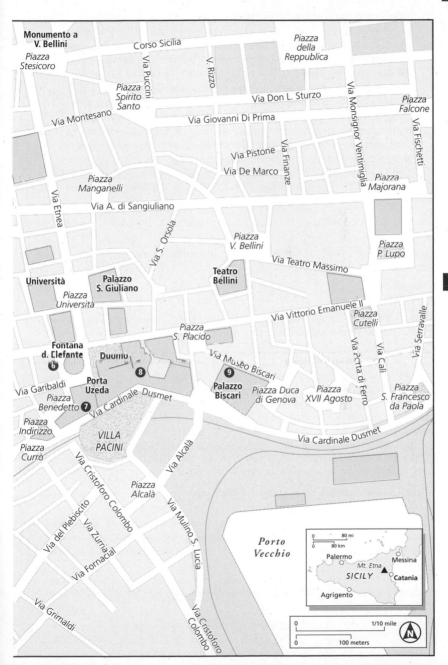

Where Gladiators Battled Lions

Lovers of antiquity should head to the Piazza Stesicoro, Via Vittorio Emanuele 260 (© **095-7150405**), for a very evocative site, the ruins of a **Roman amphitheater** dating from the 2nd century A.D. Although the ruins lie below street level, the gladiator tunnels are still visible. This is one of the largest of all Roman amphitheaters; it is believed that some 17,000 spectators were once entertained here by blood games. Only a tiny part of the theater survives, so you'll have to use your imagination to conjure up the ancient gore. The reason? The Ostrogoths, not devotees of Roman glory, used the amphitheater as a quarry. In fact, the Goths found the Roman gladiator contests too vicious and completely outlawed them. They converted the stones into churches and public monuments. The site is open daily 9am to 1pm and 3 to 7pm. Admission is free.

Sicilians. Sure, we admire Emilio Greco, but we couldn't help but wonder why works by other Sicilian artists weren't also on display in this magnificent space.

Piazza San Francesco 3. © **095-317654.** Free admission. Mon, Wed, and Fri–Sun 9am–1pm; Tues and Thurs 3–6pm. Bus: 31.

Casa di Verga   This is a memorial to Sicily's national poet, Giovanni Verga (1840–1922), who lived and wrote here for many years. Verga was a firebrand who wrote with poignancy about the plight of underpaid workers during the Industrial Revolution. Climb a flight of worn stairs for access to the battered, dusty, and not-particularly well-stocked museum that occupies the rooms where he completed some of his works. Despite the artist's powerful literature, you might leave with a sense of sadness that the local municipality has neglected this museum as obviously as it has. We recommend this place only for avid enthusiasts—the Bellini Museum, a few blocks away, is far more interesting.

Via Sant'Anna 8. © **095-7150598.** Admission 3€ ($3.90) adults, 2€ ($2.60) for ages 18–25, free for children 17 and younger. Tues and Thurs–Fri 9am–2pm and 3–7pm; Wed 9am–2pm and 3–5:30pm; Sat 9am–2pm. Apr–June also open Sun 9am–1pm. Bus: 1–4, 2–5, or 3–6.

Museo del Giocattolo (Museum of Childhood) (Kids)   Relatively unpublicized and almost chaotically disorganized, this museum offers exhibits designed to both entertain children and shape their creativity. The place is so confusing, the staff so unhelpful and inarticulate (even in Italian), that you may feel like Alice in Wonderland. Exhibits include dolls, electric train sets, and whimsical sculptures, many displayed beneath lavish frescoed ceilings from the late 18th or early 19th century.

In the Palazzo Bruca, Via Vittorio Emanuele 201. © **095-320111.** www.museodelgiocattolo.ct.it. Admission 3.50€ ($4.55) adults, 2€ ($2.60) for children 3–12. Tues–Fri 10am–1pm; Sat–Sun 10am–1pm and 4–7pm. Bus: 448, 449, 457, 722, or 733.

Palazzo Biscari ★   Today a private home, this is the most impressive *palazzo* in the city. To visit, you must call first and make an appointment. Constructed after the 1693 earthquake, the palace flowered in the mid–18th century as the home of Ignazio Paternò Castello, prince of Biscari, who held a passionate interest in art, archaeology, painting, music, and literature. When Goethe and others doing the Grand Tour of Europe passed **231** through Catania, they pronounced Palazzo Biscari the city's grandest attraction.

Partially constructed on the city's old fortress wall, the palace dances with a wealth of *putti* and caryatids. Balconies are the stunning work of Francesco Battaglia and his son, Antonino. In the courtyard is a grand stairwell, and on the second floor are the major reception rooms. The room at the far end has frescoes by Sebastiano Lo Monaco.

Prince Biscari installed an archaeological museum in his palace, but the collection has been moved to Castello Ursino (see below). Classical concerts are sometimes staged in the palace (check with the tourist office).

Via Museo Biscari 10–16. © **095-321818.** Free admission (donation appreciated). Call to arrange a visit. Bus: 1–4, 457, or 733.

Castello Ursino & Museo Civico ★

This castle, west of Piazza Duomo, was once the proud fortress of Frederick II in the 13th century. When it was originally built, the grim-looking fortress, surrounded by a moat, stood on a cliff overlooking the Ionian Sea. But Mount Etna's lava has shifted the land over the centuries. Now landlocked, Castello Ursino is reached by going through a rough neighborhood where caution is advised.

The castle was built on a square plan with a keep 30m high (98 ft.) on each corner and semicircular towers in the middle on each side. If you walk along the perimeter, you can still see the old moats and even some Renaissance windows imbedded in the south side.

The castle's *pinacoteca* (library) has an interesting (though hardly spectacular) series of paintings that date from the 1400s. Most of the work is from Sicily or southern Italy, including Antonello de Saliba's polyptych of the **Madonna Enthroned with Saints Francis and Anthony ★**; de Saliba was a pupil of the legendary Antonello da Messina. One of the best-known Catanian artists was Michele Rapisardi, who is represented by two lovely studies: the **Head of the Crazed Ophelia** and a **depiction of the Sicilian Vespers.** Surely the saddest **Grieving Widow** in all of Catania was that depicted by another homegrown artist, Giuseppe Sciuti. The art of Lorenzo Loiacono is also worth noting for his vivid, even theatrical efforts.

Housed inside are Prince Biscari's **archaeological collection** (see above), along with objects from San Nicolò Monastery, and some of the best Sicilian painted carts on the island.

Piazza Federico di Svevia. © **095-345830.** Free admission. Mon–Sat 9am–1pm and 3–7pm. Bus: 429.

CATANIA

11

SEEING THE SIGHTS

(Moments) **Something Fishy This Way Comes**

One of the largest, most bustling, and certainly most colorful *pescheria* (fish markets) in the Mediterranean is held Monday through Saturday mornings in a narrow warren of streets behind the Duomo. We doubt if even the late Jacques Cousteau could identify some of these creatures from the murky depths. "If it swims, we Catanians eat it," a local fishmonger told us.

Octopus, squid, eels, shellfish, and other writhing, twitching creatures are sold here. You can buy fresh mussels and sea urchins to eat on the spot. Vegetable and fruit stalls also spill into the offshoot lanes. The bloody butchers' tables surely inspired the paintings of Francis Bacon.

Chiesa di San Nicolò All'Arena   This is the largest and spookiest church in Sicily, stretching for 105m (344 ft.) with transepts measuring 42m (138 ft.). The cupola is 62m (203 ft.) high. Begun in 1687 by Giovanni Battista Contini, it was reconstructed in 1735 by Francesco Battaglia. Stefano Ittar designed the dome; the facade, with its mammoth columns, was left unfinished in 1796 but remains impressive. Catanians call it "mastodonic" because the pillars stick up like tusks. The interior is rather bare-bones. A beautiful 18th-century organ with 2,916 pipes is found behind the main altar. A meridian line was laid in the transept floor in 1841 to catch the sunlight precisely at noon. But because of the shifting volcanic land, today it catches the sun at 12:13pm. Sadly, the church will never be completed. Sporadic renovations try to keep it propped up, but the efforts seem doomed to failure.

The adjoining **Monastereo di San Nicolò All'Arena** is the second-largest monastery in Europe, rivaled only by Mafra, outside of Lisbon. This old Benedictine complex, dating from 1703, is part of Catania University, but frankly, it's in really bad shape. Depending on conditions at the time of your visit, you may or may not be able to enter.

Piazza Cavour. ⓒ **095-438077.** Free admission. Thurs 5–7:30pm; Sun 11am–1pm. Bus: 429 or 432.

WALKING TOUR   **HISTORIC CATANIA**

START:	Castello Ursino.
FINISH:	Piazza Università.
TIME:	4¹/₂ hours, including brief visits inside churches and monuments.
BEST TIMES:	Mornings before noon, when the food market is at its busiest.
WORST TIMES:	After dark, when the alleyways of the old town are unsafe.

Begin your tour amid the palms and palmettos of the piazza in front of the massive and forbidding-looking:

❶ Castello Ursino

Built on ancient Greek foundations, its soaring, severe-looking interior has some of the most impressive stone vaulting in Catania. The inside is devoted to a municipal museum that contains everything from archaeological remnants to 19th-century landscapes and portraits. When the *castello* (castle) was built in 1239, it directly fronted the sea, although since then, lava flows from Etna raised the ground level to the point where it now lies some distance inland. Look for patterns of both menorahs and crosses set into the medieval masonry, a hallmark left by the masons.

After your visit, with your back to the *castello,* walk diagonally to the right, across Piazza Federico de Svevia, heading to a point immediately to the left of the iron fence that fronts the railway tracks. Pass through an alley that funnels into an unnamed triangular piazza, and from there continue onto Via Auteri. At Via Auteri 26, note the 18th-century facade of the privately owned **Palazzo Auteri.** Said to be haunted, and long ago divided into private apartments (none of which can be visited), it's just one example of the many grand buildings dotting this historic neighborhood.

From Via Auteri, turn right onto Via Zappala Gemelli, site of the beginning of Catania's:

❷ Outdoor Fish, Meat & Produce Market

We can't even begin to describe the cornucopia of sights, sounds, and smells that rise from this warren of narrow streets. Pay attention to your footing: Don't slip on the slime from fish guts or rotting vegetables.

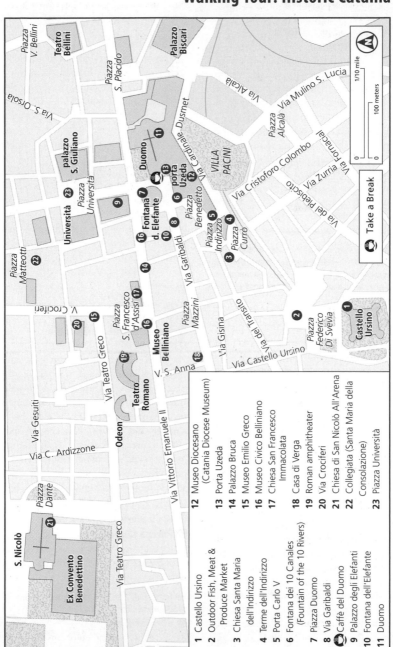

1 Castello Ursino
2 Outdoor Fish, Meat &
  Produce Market
3 Chiesa Santa Maria
  dell'Indirizzo
4 Terme dell'Indirizzo
5 Porta Carlo V
6 Fontana dei 10 Canales
  (Fountain of the 10 Rivers)
7 Piazza Duomo
8 Via Garibaldi
9 Caffè del Duomo
10 Fontana dell'Elefante
11 Duomo

12 Museo Diocesano
   (Catania Diocese Museum)
13 Porta Uzeda
14 Palazzo Bruca
15 Museo Emilio Greco
16 Museo Civico Belliniano
17 Chiesa San Francesco
   Immacolata
18 Casa di Verga
19 Roman amphitheater
20 Via Crociferi
21 Chiesa di San Nicolò All'Arena
22 Collegiata (Santa Maria della
   Consolazione)
23 Piazza Università

Continue downhill, through the souk, to the bulk that rises on the right-hand side of Via Zappala Gemelli, the:

❸ Chiesa Santa Maria dell'Indirizzo

Its elegant baroque facade—punctuated with a garish-looking neon sign declaring VIVA MARIA—stands above a square (Piazza dell'Indirizzo) that rises above that part of the food market specifically dedicated to meats. This is not a showcase church destined for the art books or tourist trade. It's the parish church of the meat- and fish-market district, with an evocatively battered interior, crumbling stucco, and scads of dusty baroque/rococo ornamentation. Opening hours are erratic, but are usually daily from 8am to noon and 3 to 6pm.

After your visit, walk to the church's southern side (the one on the left as you face it from the teeming meat market outside). Here, separated from the square by an iron fence, lies the ancient Roman ruins of the:

❹ Terme dell'Indirizzo

Constructed by the ancient Romans out of black volcanic rock and terra-cotta brick, with only a few of its original vaults and arches still intact, these baths are best admired from outside the fence. Look also for a tiny domed Greek-cross building, constructed of black lava. It's virtually never open except for qualified archaeologists. It's the ugliest monument on this tour—and the rocks have been cited as unsafe for climbing.

After your visit to the ruined baths, descend along basalt cobblestones in front of the Church of Santa Maria dell'Indirizzo. They lead downhill into the bowels of the rest of the food market. The largest open space in the market—a mass of parasols, blood, humanity, and grime—is the Piazza Pardo (also known as the Via Pardo), at the edge of which is the hard-to-see facade of a highly recommended restaurant, Osteria Antica Marina (p. 225).

With your back to the restaurant, turn left, noting the massive soaring archway, built of dark lava rock, on either side of which the food market teems wildly. It's the:

❺ Porta Carlo V

Punctuating the entranceway to the indoor section of the city's food markets, this is one of the rare structures of Catania that survived the earthquake of 1693. Pass beneath it and then turn left. After a few steps, you'll emerge into the open air again, into a neoclassical, traffic-free square filled with more food vendors selling, in this case, fish. Your map might identify it as the Piazza A. di Benedetto, but there is no sign. Most of the buildings date from the early 1600s. At the distant edge of this piazza, at the top of a short flight of stone steps, is a small stone obelisk marked FONTANA DELL'AMENANO. Built in 1867, it marks the location of a powerful underground river.

Visible at the bottom of a steep masonry-sided chasm from the obelisk's rear side is the:

❻ Fontana dei 10 Canales (Fountain of the 10 Rivers)

For years, this was the only water source in this neighborhood, and many local residents remember when a flood of water from this underground canal was diverted, thanks to conduits and channels, to an aboveground curtain of water used liberally by everyone in the food market. Today, because of urban renovations and difficulties with the plumbing, the waters remain mostly underground.

From here, walk to the top of the previously mentioned stone steps for a view over the:

❼ Piazza Duomo

At the edges of this piazza sit several of the monuments visited as part of this walking tour.

But before your visits, look left (westward) along the wide, upward-sloping vista of the:

❽ Via Garibaldi

At the most distant point on the street's faraway horizon, beyond the masses of people and cars, note the decorative triumphal arch that was built to celebrate the marriage, in 1768, of the Spanish king Ferdinand de Bourbon and Princess Carolina of Austria. About a century later, in 1862, it marked the processional route of Garibaldi for his triumphant entrance into Catania during the agonizing process of unifying Italy into a coherent political whole. The event marked Garibaldi's utterance, for the first time, of what eventually became a unifying political slogan, *"O Roma, o morte"* ("Give me Rome or give me death").

 TAKE A BREAK
Caffè del Duomo, Piazza Duomo 12 (© 095-7150556), is the most charming of the cafes flanking the square. Built in the late 1800s, it has a marble counter, hints of the Belle Epoque, and a lavish *tavola calda* (hot table) adjacent to the bar. You can choose from at least 15 different snack items, most priced between 1.50€ and 3€ ($1.60–$3.90). The cafe also sells some of the most artful almond candies in Catania, shaped like berries, pears, and apples. For a quick pick-me-up at the bar, do as the locals do and ask for seltzer water doctored with a tantalizing scoop of fruit-flavored *granita*. Open daily 5:30am to midnight.

After your refueling stop, walk across Piazza Duomo to the:

❾ Palazzo degli Elefanti

This palace is now the Municipio, or town hall, of Catania. From its central balcony, Mussolini once gave one of his rabble-rousing speeches. If it's open, walk into the building's central courtyard, where you'll see lava-rock foundations; bas-relief wall friezes dedicated to Catania's patron saint (St. Agatha); and a pair of 18th-century ceremonial coaches that are used every February to carry Catania's ecclesiastical and secular dignitaries (including the mayor) down the city thoroughfares for the Festival of St. Agatha. If the security

guard allows it, proceed into the second courtyard. Here, note the wall-mounted 19th-century copy of an ancient Greek sundial. Proud Sicilians claim that the ancient Romans learned the art and science of sundials from the Greek colonists of Sicily. Regrettably, unless you're on official civic business, the rest of city hall is usually closed to casual visitors.

After your visit, cross the Piazza Duomo and take time to admire:

❿ Fontana dell'Elefante

This fountain was created from black lava, and it is Catania's most famous monument. It stands on a Byzantine platform and carries on its back an ancient Egyptian obelisk covered with hieroglyphics. On top of that is an iron ornament that includes, among other symbols, a cross devoted to the patron saint, Agatha.

Piazza Duomo is dominated, naturally, by the:

⓫ Duomo

Begun by King Roger in 1070 and rebuilt by Caccarini after the earthquake, this cathedral used many ancient monuments of Catania in its construction, including stones from Roman theaters. Pause to admire its lugubrious baroque facade with granite columns. Norman apses can be viewed from Via Vittorio Emanuele. The church was built over the ruins of a vaulted Roman bath, and inside, a Romanesque basilica lies under the Duomo's nave. The cathedral is a pantheon of some Aragonese royalty.

After you exit from the cathedral, turn immediately left (with your back to the Duomo's entrance) and walk a few steps to a building that functioned for many generations as a seminary for theologians and is now the:

⓬ Museo Diocesano (Catania Diocese Museum)

Located at Via Etnea 8, this museum gives insight into the lavish traditions associated with one of Sicily's most powerful undercurrents of religious ecstasy, the Cult of St. Agatha. Inside, you'll see photos of modern-day religious processions as well as the massive silver sledge that holds the iconic effigy of St. Agatha, which is hauled through the streets every February as part of the mystical rites associated with this powerful cult.

After your visit, with your back to the entrance of the Diocese Museum, turn left and walk a few paces to the south, passing beneath the massive ceremonial stone portal known as:

⓭ Porta Uzeda

Originally built by Sicily's Spanish overlords during the early 18th century, this archway contains some interesting shops selling folkloric pottery. On its opposite side is a pleasant and verdant park, **Villa Pacini,** where you can rest for a few moments.

Now retrace your steps back into Piazza Duomo, walking diagonally across it toward Via Vittorio Emanuele, which flanks its northern edge. Continue westward. A point of minor interest en route is at Via Vittorio Emanuele 175, immediately adjacent to the Hotel de l'Europe. Here, note the **hidden doorway,** crafted from wood, whose panels were painstakingly designed to look like a continuation of the stone mullions of the building that contains it.

Continue west along the Via Vittorio Emanuele to one of Catania's quirkiest museums. Concealed behind a massive wall and an imposing doorway is the:

⓮ Palazzo Bruca

The palace, at Via Vittorio Emanuele 201, contains the **Museo del Giocattolo (Museum of Childhood),** reviewed on p. 230. This once private and still elegant palace is prefaced with an enormous, walled-in courtyard surrounding a heroic fountain of Hercules. If you're in the mood for another refueling stop, stop at the museum's cafe (hours are erratic) for pastries and cold drinks, which can be consumed on the panoramic rooftop or in the street-level entrance area.

After your visit, exit back onto Via Vittorio Emanuele and continue walking westward past some lesser churches and lots of baroque facades. Stop at the point where the street opens onto Piazza San Francesco, site of three important attractions, each noted below. You'll recognize the square thanks to the contemporary-looking statue devoted to Cardinal Dusmet, a 19th-century benefactor of Catania's poor. The inscription on its base translates as "Because we have bread, we give it to the poor."

The three attractions flanking the square include:

⓯ Museo Emilio Greco

Located at Piazza San Francesco 3, this archive-cum-museum displays the major artistic contributions of Catania citizen **Emilio Greco** (1913–95). He is most famous for his grand sculpture. For more information, see p. 227.

Accessible via the same entranceway on the western edge of the square is the more interesting:

⓰ Museo Civico Belliniano

The great **Vincenzo Bellini** (1801–35) was born in this house, which displays memorabilia and portraits. For details, see the review on p. 227.

Facing both of these museums at the eastern edge of Piazza San Francesco is:

⓱ Chiesa San Francesco Immacolata

The most interesting objects inside this church are the six massive, richly gilded candelabras—most at least 3.3m (11 ft.) high and incredibly heavy—that are proudly displayed in the nave. Carved at the beginning of the 20th century, they're carried on the shoulders of the faithful during the Feast Day of St. Agatha. The largest and heaviest of them was carved in 1913, gilded in 1935, and donated to the church and to St. Agatha by the city's bakers' guild.

After your visit, continue westward along Via Vittorio Emanuele, turning left in two short blocks onto Via Santa Anna. On that street, you'll find the small-scale baroque facade of the tiny Chiesa Santa Anna (it's almost always closed to casual visitors) and a few buildings later, on the left, the former home of one of Sicily's most famous writers:

⑱ Casa di Verga

Known for his naturalistic fiction, **Giovanni Verga** (1840–1922) became one of Sicily's greatest writers. He was celebrated in his day, making friends with such greats as Emile Zola. Much of Catania turned out for his 80th birthday, where Luigi Pirandello appeared as orator. For details of the building at Via Sant'Anna 8, see the review on p. 230.

Retrace your steps to Via Vittorio Emanuele and turn right, back toward the Piazza San Francesco. En route, along that street's northern edge, see the deceptively modern-looking stone entrance to one of Catania's most cherished archaeological treasures, the:

⑲ Roman amphitheater

Draped with ivy, and overlooked by a ring of 17th-century buildings and apartments, this charming theater at Via Vittorio Emanuele 260 is an ancient oasis concealed in the midst of an urban neighborhood. During classical times, it held as many as 17,000 spectators for plays and—to a lesser extent—water games, when boats would float on waters funneled in from then-nearby streams and aqueducts. It was also a site for gladiator contests. Ironically, part of the theater's graceful crescent-shaped seating structure is blocked by a black-lava bridge added during the early 17th century as the base for the since-demolished Via Grotte, once a densely populated street within this residential neighborhood.

Via Grotte, most of its bridgelike foundations, and all of its buildings were demolished in the 1950s by Catania's historic buildings committee as a means of returning the ancient theater to some semblance of its original purity. Vestiges of the street remain within the circumference of the Roman theater, however, cutting surreally across one edge of the theater's sweeping crescent-shaped bleachers.

Since Via Grotte was demolished, some former residents of the neighborhood have returned from prolonged sojourns in North America, Australia, or Argentina,

and have been shocked to find their childhood playgrounds (the Via Grotte and its offshoots) no longer in place.

Come with stamina, a good sense of balance, and sturdy walking shoes. Sandals are not recommended because of the steep, uneven steps, which lead visitors through ghostly tunnels that wind their way through and beneath the bleacher stands.

A smaller theater, the **Odeon,** is accessible near the back side of the Roman theater. To reach it, follow signs from the theater and walk uphill through some tunnels and steep vaulted stairs.

After your visit, return to Piazza San Francesco, stand in front of its mammoth church, and turn uphill to face the lowest end of one of the most richly embellished baroque streets in Catania:

⑳ Via Crociferi

Above its downhill entrance is a soaring stone bridge, **L'Arco San Benedetto,** which allowed nuns, many of whom were in seclusion, to access the buildings on either side of this street during the convent's heyday in the 17th to 19th centuries. Via Crociferi is so authentically baroque that it was filmed by Franco Zeffirelli for *Storie di une Copinere,* his cinematic tale of love gone awry during the baroque age.

In order of their appearance on this fabled but relatively short street, you'll see the following churches, convents, or monasteries: (1) **San Benedetto,** (2) **San Francesco Borgia,** (3) **San Giuliano,** and others whose facades aren't marked with name or number.

Three blocks from where you first entered Via Crociferi, turn left onto Via Gesuiti. Walk 4 blocks to reach Piazza Dante and the mammoth, never-completed:

㉑ Chiesa di San Nicolò All'Arena

The biggest church in Sicily was never completed, and it is almost ringed in scaffolding to keep it from falling down. Immediately adjacent is an abandoned monastery once intended as a library. Surrealistically large, this complex is Catania's symbol of the folly of large-scale projects gone awry. For more information, see p. 232.

Retrace your steps to Via Crucifero, turn left for about a block, and then turn right (downhill) onto Via San Giuliano. You'll be walking down the steep slope of a dormant volcanic crater that's associated with the geology of nearby Mount Etna. After 2 blocks, turn right onto Via Etnea and walk 2 blocks. On the right is a church with a baroque concave facade:

㉒ Collegiata (Santa Maria della Consolazione)

This royal chapel from 1768 is one of the masterpieces of the Catanese late baroque style, based on plans by Angelo Italia. The facade was completed by Stefano Ittar, and the vaults inside were frescoed by Giuseppe Sciti. It's dearly beloved to many Catanians who attended religious celebrations here during their childhoods.

After your visit, continue another block south along Via Etnea to the:

㉓ Piazza Università

This elegant urban piazza is often the site of political demonstrations. One side is devoted to the back of the previously visited Municipio (town hall), the other side to the symbolic headquarters of the University of Catania. The university was founded in 1434, but the bulk of it lies in a modern educational complex 3km (2 miles) to the east, in the suburbs. The square was constructed at the request of the duke of Camastra. It's dominated by the **Palazzo Sangiuliano,** built in 1745, and by the main university building, **Palazzo dell'Università,** which was finished at the end of the 1700s. One of the richest libraries in Sicily is housed in the **Università degli Studi di Catania,** founded by Alphonese of Aragon in 1434.

5 SHOPPING

Dolci di Nonna Vincenza Come here for marzipan and almond-based candies, made from recipes developed generations ago. You'll pay about 7€ ($9.10) per pound. The shop is on a quiet piazza, across from the main facade of the San Placido church. Piazza San Placido 7. (©) 095-7151844. Bus: 3–6, 259, or 334.

L'Artigianato Siciliano Chances are you'll eventually wander beneath the Porta Uzeda during your stay in Catania, either on our walking tour or as part of your logical exploration of the Piazza Duomo, which it fronts. Beneath it are vaulted spaces loaded with the fancifully hand-painted pottery skillfully made in Caltanissetta, a city in central Sicily that has churned out tons of the stuff during the past centuries. Look for gaily decorated serving dishes, candelabras painted like members of the 19th-century bourgeoisie, and all manner of art objects. Via Etnea 2 (beneath Porta Uzeda). (©) 095-345360. Bus: 448, 449, 457, 722, or 733.

Marella Ferrera ★★ Catania-born Marella Ferrera is the most successful women's clothing designer to emerge from Sicily. She's known for fashions that make women look like goddesses or lionesses, sometimes with outrageous flounces or appropriately inappropriate slits in indiscreet places. Prices begin at about 800€ ($1,040) for ready-to-wear, and from 3,100€ ($4,030) for couture. The shop evokes a cross between an Italian garden and a boudoir, with bolts of lace bursting from antique chests and paintings that evoke dream sequences in a style that could have been inspired by Dalí. Viale XX Settembre 25–27. (©) 095-446751. Bus: 443, 721, or 722.

Lapis is a monthly bulletin issued by the tourist office, and available at hotels and bars throughout Catania. It documents special concerts or festivals, movies, or nightclubs (such as they are).

Music lovers should head for the **Teatro Massimo** ★, sometimes called Teatro Bellini in honor of the hometown composer. It's at Piazza Teatro Massimo, Via Perotta Giuseppe 12 (*©* **095-7306111**). Some of Italy's best operas and concerts are presented here, with tickets costing from 13€ to 70€ ($17–$91). Nothing is grander than hearing Bellini's *Norma* or *La Sonnambula* on its home turf. The opera and ballet seasons extend from mid-January to right before Christmas, whereas the concert season runs from mid-October to late May. The box office is open Tuesday to Friday 9:30am to 12:30pm, Monday and Saturday 9:30am to 12:30pm and 5 to 7pm. Bus: 429.

Pubs and dance clubs rule the night. One such option is **Royal Pub Ceres,** Via San Giuseppe al Duomo 17–21 (*©* **095-7152294**), on a block northwest of the Duomo. This woodsy-looking English pub comes complete with a carved Victorian-style bar and a crowd of good-looking people under 35. Its reputation for beers on tap is unequaled in Catania. The venue sometimes spills onto the narrow street outside. The place rocks daily from 7am (for that early libation) to 2am. Take bus no. 448, 449, 457, 722, or 733.

7 SIDE TRIPS FROM CATANIA

The looming menace of **Mount Etna** attracts those who did not explore the volcano from its northern tier (p. 210). In addition to Etna, the town of **Acireale,** like Catania, is adorned with baroque treasures—but here you can enjoy the sights without the traffic and the people.

MOUNT ETNA ★★★

Few who visit Catania can resist the temptation to explore Europe's most active volcano, Mount Etna, northwest of the city. At 3,292m (10,801 ft.), it is the highest volcano in Europe and one of the largest in the world. Taormina (see chapter 10) is the base for exploring it from the north. From the south, Catania is ideal for flirting with this still-active volcano.

For a good view of this ferocious mountain, take one of the **trains** that circumnavigate the base of the volcano. Trains are boarded at Via Caronda 352/A (*©* **095-541250**), in Catania off Viale Leonardo da Vinci.

A **bus** leaves from the Stazione Centrale in Catania at 8:15am daily, bound for Rifugio Sapienza (see below). The bus returns to Catania in theory at 4pm—but always check schedules locally, as they vary. The round-trip costs 7€ ($9.10).

You can also **drive** one of the many southern approaches to Etna from Catania. The quickest and most convenient route is to head northwest of Catania by following the road signs to Tangenziale Ovest. Drive along this road until you see the exit to Gravina. At Gravina, continue northwest along the road directing you to Mascalucia. Once there, you will see signs pointing to Nicolosi. At Nicolosi, follow a small road to the north for the final lap to Rifugio Sapienza.

In either Rifugio Sapienza, a little village on the southern slope of Mount Etna, or the little town of Nicolosi, you can book guided jeep tours of Mount Etna for a cost of 45€ ($59). The trip lasts 2 to 3 hours and takes you as close as you can get to the top without walking. In Nicolosi, tickets can be purchased at **Funivia dell'Etna** (© **095-911158**), Monday to Friday 9am to 2pm and 5:30 to 8pm, Saturday 9am to 1pm. Nicolosi is connected with Rifugio Sapienza by frequent shuttle-bus service. You can also purchase tickets in Rifugio Sapienza at **Contrada Cantoniera** (© **095-915321**), open daily from 9am to 4pm.

More private tours can also be organized at Rifugio Sapienza. For information on these, call the **tourist office** in Nicolosi at Via Garibaldi 63 (© **095-911505**).

From Rifugio Sapienza, it's possible to hike up to the **Torre del Filosofo (Philosopher's Tower),** at 2,920m (9,580 ft.). The trip there and back takes about 5 hours. At the tower, you'll have a panoramic sweep of Etna, its peaks and craters hissing with steam. This is a difficult hike and not for the faint of heart. The climb is along ashy, pebbly terrain, and once you reach the tower, you have another risky 2-hour hike to the craters. The craters can erupt unexpectedly (as they did in the early 1990s, killing 11).

Tours should only be taken with a guide who knows current conditions. If Etna shows signs of erupting or even "belching," guided tours are suspended. On the return from Torre del Filosofo to Rifugio Sapienza, you'll pass Valle de Bove, the original crater of Etna.

11 ACIREALE

Located 16km (10 miles) north of Catania, this makes for one of the most satisfying day trips along the eastern coast of Sicily. Many people find Acireale more interesting than those rather dull lava fields of Mount Etna.

Overlooking the Ionian Sea, Acireale lies in a fertile valley of Mount Etna surrounded by citrus groves. The town stands on seven streams of lava and has long been known for its hot springs and spa facilities. Like Catania, it is a city of the baroque, with many of its greatest treasures from the 17th century. The same 1693 earthquake that destroyed Catania also did major damage in Acireale.

The "Aci" in the town's name comes from the mythical river said to have been created in the wake of the death of Acis, the handsome youth in love with the graceful Nereid Galatea. Acis was, according to the story, slain by the jealous Polyphemus, the savage of Cyclops.

To reach the town, most visitors arrive by car. Drive north of Catania until you see the cutoff to the right leading to the sea and Acireale. Buses also run throughout the day from Catania.

Before walking about the town, stop at the **tourist office,** Via Scionti 15 (© **095-891999**), for a town map. Hours are Monday to Friday 8am to 2pm, Tuesday and Thursday 4 to 7pm.

Seeing the Sights

Piazza del Duomo ★ is the monumental baroque heart of Acireale, containing its most impressive attractions. Filled with gelato parlors and cafes, the square is dominated by its cathedral, the **Duomo ★**. Originally built in the late 16th century, the church has suffered abuse from Etna, and the present building has been vastly altered and reconstructed. Note the lavish tiled and cusped bell towers and the fine baroque portal, which leads into an interior with frescoed vaults. At the east end are beautiful frescoes by **Pietro Paolo Vasta** (1697–1760), a homegrown artist. In the right transept is the Cappella di

The Images of Lost Dreams

Although the art of Sicilian puppetry is rarely seen today, Acireale still carries on this ancient tradition, and the town is known for its puppet shows and theater. Sicilian families journey here to give their kids a treat (most adults enjoy the shows, too). Shows are staged at **Teatro dell'Opera dei Pupi,** Via Galatea 89 (✆ **095-606272**), from July to September on Thursdays and Sundays at 9 and 10:30pm. Tickets, which cost 10€ ($13), must be purchased just before the show, as there is no box office open during the day.

Santa Venera, dedicated to the patron saint of Acireale. Hours are daily 8am to noon and 4 to 7pm; call ✆ **095-601797** for more information.

Another important church on the square is **Basilica dei Santi Pietro e Paolo,** identified by its landmark bell tower. Although it was constructed in the 17th century, its facade is from the 18th century. The church's greatest artworks are by Pietro Paolo Vasta. Open daily 8am to noon and 4 to 7pm. For more information, call ✆ **095-601834.**

The 17th-century **Palazzo Comunale** is a rather bizarre example of the Spanish/Sicilian baroque style. Its wrought-iron balconies are held up by monsters and gargoyles. The entrance to the palace is on Via Lancasteri, right off Piazza del Duomo. Admission is free; hours are Monday to Friday 8am to noon.

A final church worth visiting is **Basilica di San Sebastiano** ★, Piazza Vigo (✆ **095-601313**), one of the loveliest of all the baroque churches on the island. We prefer it to the treasures of the Duomo. It boasts a magnificent **balustrade facade** ★, adorned with statues representing scenes from the Old Testament. In the transept and chancel are frescoes by Pietro Paolo Vasta (there's that name again) that depict episodes from the sad life of St. Sebastian, the saint to whom this church is dedicated. Get to the church by way of Corso Vittorio Emanuele, just beyond Piazza del Duomo. Open daily 8am to noon and 4 to 8pm.

After Piazza del Duomo, the next most impressive baroque square of Acireale is **Piazza San Domenico,** at the end of Via Cavour. Dominating this small square is the splendid baroque facade of the **Church of San Domenico.** The most beautiful building here is the 17th-century **Palazzo Musmeci,** celebrated locally for its graceful balconies and rococo windows.

Since the days of the Greeks and most definitely the Romans, the sulfur-rich Etna "volcanic waters" have lured visitors to Acireale. The tradition continues at **Terme di Acireale,** Via della Terme 47 (✆ **095-7686111**). Every illustrious person passing through Sicily in the 18th and 19th centuries seems to have taken the waters here, which are said to have miraculous powers to treat rheumatism, gynecological disease, skin diseases, and periodontal diseases. You can also come for massages and mud treatments, each costing 15€ to 30€ ($20–$39). There is talk—so far, just that—of modernization. Open daily from 7am to 12:30pm.

Shopping

Most islanders who visit Acireale go home with marzipan, as the town is famous for this confection. The best are sold at **El Dorado,** Corso Umberto 5 (✆ **095-601464**), open Monday through Friday from 6am to midnight. It also makes the town's best chocolate

CATANIA

11

SIDE TRIPS FROM CATANIA

cakes. A good competitor is **Castorina,** Piazza del Duomo (© **095-601546**); try *cassata Siciliana,* the island's most celebrated cake, and some divine almond *granita.* Open Monday through Saturday from 7am to 1am.

Where to Stay

Aloha D'Oro ★ This hotel was constructed in 1968 using materials and techniques evocative of the old farmhouses surrounding Mount Etna. Architectural grace notes include wooden windows, arches, handmade tiles, and wrought-iron adornments. This offbeat and very comfortable choice is one of the better stopovers between Taormina and Catania. The complex includes a main building, called the *castello,* and another 33 accommodations in outlying units. Opt for a room with a view, which in this case means in the rear, looking out onto the Ionian Sea and a government-protected nature reserve. The hotel is within walking distance of a good sandy beach and the thermal baths.

Via dei Gasperi 10, 95024 Acireale. © **095-7687001.** Fax 095-606984. www.hotel-aloha.com. 113 units. 88€–168€ ($114–$218) double. Rates include buffet breakfast. AE, DC, MC, V. Free parking. **Amenities:** 3 restaurants; bar; 2 outdoor pools (1 heated, w/Jacuzzi); sauna; wellness center; room service; babysitting; laundry service; dry cleaning; all nonsmoking rooms. *In room:* A/C, TV, minibar, hair dryer.

Grande Albergo Maugeri ★ (Value) Located close to the Duomo, this is your best bet for an overnight stopover in the heart of town. Many guests here use Acireale instead of Catania or Taormina as a base for exploring Mount Etna. Rated four stars by the government, the hotel opened in 2001 across from Villa Garibaldi Park. The traditionally furnished bedrooms come with modern bathrooms. The restaurant serves the best hotel cuisine in Acireale.

Piazza Garibaldi, 95024 Acireale. ©/fax **095-608666.** www.hotel-maugeri.it. 59 units. 200€ ($260) double; 115€ ($150) per person half board (breakfast and dinner). AE, DC, MC, V. Free parking. **Amenities:** Restaurant; bar; room service; laundry service; dry cleaning; nonsmoking rooms; rooms for those w/ limited mobility. *In room:* A/C, TV, minibar, hair dryer.

Where to Dine

All'Antica Osteria (Value) SICILIAN/PIZZA This rustic restaurant-cum-pizzeria prepares an array of local delicacies and specializes in grills, especially grilled seafood from the Ionian Sea. The chefs turn out such dishes as *maccheroni All'Antica Osteria* (homemade pasta flavored with a creamy pesto, Parmesan cheese, and fresh tomatoes). *Stocco* is a white fish cooked *alla Messinese*—with carrots, potatoes, raisins, celery, and pine nuts. The small, well-priced wine list offers some local gems.

Via Carpinati 34. © **095-7634135.** Reservations recommended. Main courses 7€–12€ ($9.10–$16); fixed-price menu 13€–20€ ($17–$26). AE, DC, MC, V. Daily noon–3:30pm and 7pm–midnight.

Al Molino SEAFOOD/SICILIAN This local favorite is adjacent to an antique water mill on the Lungomare, the boardwalk along the sea, a short walk from the center of Acireale. Outside is a small garden with a wooden grape arbor. Inside, the decorations are appropriately nautical. Since the menu is based on fresh fish, it can vary from night to night. You might begin with Acireale's best bowl of fish soup or homemade pasta made with fish. Raw marinated shellfish is another specialty. The restaurant uses old-fashioned recipes and is better than ever.

Via Molino 106. © **095-7648116.** Reservations recommended. Main courses 8.50€–10€ ($11–$13). AE, DC, MC, V. Thurs–Tues 1–3pm and 8pm–midnight. Closed 2 weeks in Nov or Dec.

La Grotta di Carmelo ★★ SEAFOOD/SICILIAN   Here's a chance to dine in a cave with a rock-face wall—hence the name of the joint. Much of the structure was built from black-lava rock from Mount Etna. But this is no touristy gimmick. Its tables are in demand more than any other restaurant in town, in large part thanks to its excellent seafood, much of it plucked fresh from the Ionian Sea. Start with a savory bowl of fish soup; it doesn't get much better than this. Our pasta favorite is homemade and served with squid ink along with tomatoes, garlic, olive oil, and hot peppers. The cooks are experts at grilling fish to your specifications; locals tend to prefer it a bit rarer than the average American. The delicately steamed fish with lemon and olive oil is memorable. Desserts, wine, and service are all first-rate.

Via Scala Grande 36. ⓒ **095-7648153.** Reservations required. Main courses 8€–16€ ($10–$21). AE, MC, V. Wed–Mon 1–3pm and 7–11pm. Closed Oct 15–Nov 1.

12

Syracuse & the Southeast

One of the centers of ancient Western civilization, southeastern Sicily is a sightseeing mecca filled with glorious, evocative ruins. The area's chief town is **Syracuse,** one of the most important cities of the ancient world of Magna Graecia (Greater Greece).

We'll even go out on a limb and suggest that if you're forced to choose between Agrigento (see chapter 14) and Syracuse, opt for the latter, whose wealth and size were once unmatched by any other city in Europe.

Those with extra leisure time should also explore the baroque city of **Noto** and its surrounding sites, populated by Bronze Age people between 2000 and 1500 B.C.

Today, many of the sights of this sun-baked land are decaying. Noto, especially, is in peril. Earthquakes have caused massive damage to monumental, centuries-old buildings. But a trip through towns that knew great glory centuries ago is one of the most rewarding jaunts to take in Sicily, not to mention all of Italy.

1 SYRACUSE ★★★ & ORTYGIA ISLAND ★★★

182km (113 miles) S of Messina, 87km (54 miles) S of Catania, 330km (205 miles) SE of Palermo, 256km (159 miles) E of Agrigento

Of all the Greek cities of antiquity that flourished on the coast of Sicily, Syracuse (Siracusa) was the most important, a formidable competitor of Athens. In its heyday, it dared take on Carthage and even Rome.

Colonists from Corinth founded Syracuse on the Ionian Sea in about 735 B.C. Much of its history was linked to despots, beginning in 485 B.C. with Gelon, the tyrant of Gela, who subdued the Carthaginians at Himera. Syracuse came under attack from Athens in 415 B.C., but the main Athenian fleet was destroyed and the soldiers on the mainland were captured. They were herded into the **Latomia di Cappuccini** at Piazza Cappuccini, a stone quarry. The "jail," from which there was no escape, was particularly horrid—the defeated soldiers weren't given food and, packed together like cattle, they were left to die slowly.

Dionysius I was one of the greatest despots, reigning over the city during its greatest glory in the 4th century B.C., when it extended its influence as a sea power. But in A.D. 212, the city fell to the Romans under Marcellus, who sacked its riches. In that attack, Syracuse lost its most famous son, the Greek physicist/mathematician Archimedes, who was slain in his study by a Roman soldier.

Although the ruins of Syracuse will be one of the highlights of your trip to Sicily, the city itself has been in a millennia-long decline. Today, it's a blend of often unattractive modern development (with supermarkets and high-rises sprouting along speedways) and the ruins of its former glory.

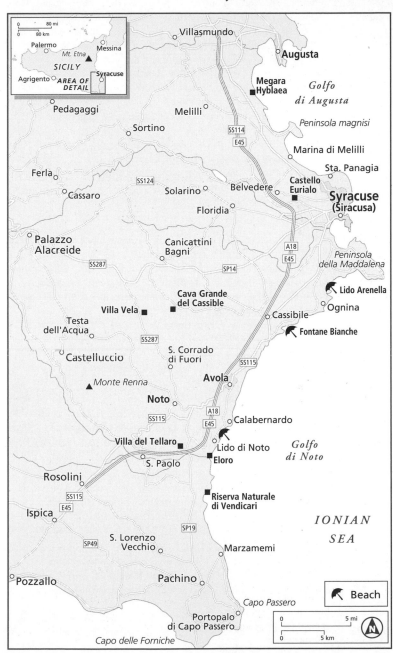

A lot of what you'll want to see is on the island of **Ortygia,** which is filled with not only ancient ruins but also crafts shops and boutiques. From the mainland, Corso Umberto goes to the Ponte Nuova, which leads to the island. Parking is a serious problem on Ortygia, so if you drive, leave your car in one of the garages near the bridge and then walk over and explore the island on foot. Allow yourself at least 2 hours to explore, plus another hour to shop along the narrow streets. You'll also want to sit on **Piazza del Duomo,** off Via Cavour—one of the most elegant squares in Sicily.

The ancient sites are a good half-hour's walk back inland from Ortygia, past a fairly forgettable shopping strip, so you might want to take a cab (they're easily found at all the sites). You'll find buses on Ortygia at Piazza Pancali/Largo XXV Luglio. The harbor is lined with 18th- and 19th-century town houses.

Syracuse is a cauldron in summer. Do as the locals do and head for the sea. The finest **beach** is about 19km (12 miles) away at **Fontane Bianche;** bus nos. 21 and 22 leave from the Syracuse post office, Piazza delle Poste 15. If you're driving, Fontane Bianche lies to the south of the city (it's signposted); take SS115 to reach it. The same buses will take you to **Lido Arenella,** only 8km (5 miles) away but not as good a beach.

ESSENTIALS

GETTING THERE   From other major cities in Sicily, Syracuse can be reached by **train,** although many visitors find the bus (see below) faster. By train, Syracuse is 1 1/2 hours from Catania, 2 hours from Taormina, and 5 hours from Palermo. Usually you must transfer in Catania. For information, call ☎ **892021.** Trains arrive in Syracuse at the station on Via Francesco Crispi, centrally located between the Archaeological Park and Ortygia. The nearest airport is at Catania.

From Catania, 18 Interbus **buses** per day make the 1 1/4-hour trip to Syracuse. The one-way fare is 6€ ($7.80). Call ☎ **0931-66710** in Syracuse, or 095-7461333 in Catania, for schedules.

By **car** from Taormina, continue south along A18 and then on E45, past Catania. Allow at least 1 1/2 hours.

VISITOR INFORMATION   The **tourist office** is at Via San Sebastiano 43 (☎ **0931-481232**), open Monday to Friday 8:30am to 1:30pm and 3:30 to 6pm, Saturday 9am to 1pm. There's another office in the historic center at Via della Maestranza 33 (☎ **0931-464255**), open Monday to Thursday 8:30am to 1:45pm and 2:45 to 5:30pm, Friday 8:30am to 1:45pm.

SPECIAL EVENTS   Some of the most memorable cultural events in Sicily are staged in May and June, when actors from the Instituto Nazionale del Dramma Antico present **classical plays** by Aeschylus, Euripides, and their contemporaries. The setting is the ancient Teatro Greco (Greek Theater) in the Archaeological Park. Tickets cost 30€ to 62€ ($39–$81). For information, contact **INDA,** Corso Matteotti 29, 96100 Siracusa (☎ **0931-487200**).

CITY LAYOUT   The chief attraction, **Isola di Ortygia,** is linked to mainland Syracuse by a bridge, **Ponte Umbertino.** The city's main street, **Corso Umberto,** runs from this bridge directly to the train station and crosses **Piazza Marconi,** a square from which most of the buses depart. Another main street is **Via Montedoro,** which runs parallel to and to the immediate north of Corso Umberto.

Other than Ortygia, Syracuse's grand attraction is the **Parco Archeologico della Neapolis.** To get to this garden of ruins from the heart of Syracuse, head north along **Corso Gelone.**

(Moments) Syracuse from the Sea

We like to see this ancient city the way the Greeks first came upon it—from the sea. Motor launches operated by **Compagnia del Selene** (© **0931-791033**) take you on a **panoramic trip** ★★ around Porto Grande and Ortygia. It lasts an hour, and the scenes of the ancient ruins are evocative and inspiring. The most memorable boat trips occur around twilight, when the monuments are floodlit.

If you'd like to drive along the boulevard fronting the Ionian Sea, head up the **Dionisio Grande** for panoramic scenery. This route will also take you to the **Latomia dei Cappuccini,** one of the most ancient of the limestone quarries that supplied blocks of limestone for the construction of the major buildings and monuments of Syracuse.

Off Via Cavour is **Piazza del Duomo,** one of the city's most elegant squares. A 5th-century temple that the Greeks dedicated to Athena became in time a Christian cathedral, or *duomo.*

From Piazza del Duomo, **Via Picherali** heads southwest to the sea and the **Fountain of Arethusa,** a freshwater spring beloved by the ancient Greeks, who claimed that this was where the nymph Arethusa was turned into a fountain.

The oldest street in town, **Via della Maestranza,** is a sightseeing attraction in its own right. It passes the island's most aristocratic residences, mostly baroque in style. The two most interesting palaces, which can be admired from the outside, are **Palazzo Interlandi Pizzuti,** at no. 10, and **Palazzo Impellizzeri,** at no. 17.

On the southernmost tip of Ortygia rises **Castello Maniace,** named in honor of George Maniakes, the Byzantine who, with aid from Norman soldiers, captured the city from the Muslims. Rebuilt by Frederick II in 1239, this castle is now a military barracks and is off-limits to the public. You can sail by the castle, however, if you take a boat tour (see "Syracuse from the Sea," below).

GETTING AROUND   Syracuse is served by a network of **buses** following circular routes, which means that many places will be quite a way from a bus stop. Buses leave from the center of Syracuse for Piazza della Posta, which lies across the bridge on Ortygia Island. The best place to catch a bus in Syracuse proper is Piazza Marconi (also called Foro Siracusano). The most frequented routes are nos. 21 to 23, which also stop at the rail depot.

Sometimes it's better to call a **taxi** (© **0931-69722**). The fare from the train station to Ortygia is about 10€ ($13).

(Fast Facts) Syracuse

Emergency Dial © **113.**

Internet Your best bet is **Internet Point,** Via Tunisi 36 (© **0931-411148**), lying on Ortygia Island. It offers 10 computers with fast connections, charging 3€ ($3.90) per hour. Open Monday to Saturday 10am to 9pm.

Luggage Storage A kiosk in the train station along Via Francesco Crispi is open daily 7am to 10pm, charging 4€ ($5.20) per piece.

Medical In case of medical emergency, **Guardia Medica,** Traversa Pizzuta 20 (*℡* **0931-484629**), is open Monday to Friday 8pm to 8am, Saturday and Sunday 2pm to 8am. The regular hospital is the **Ospedale Umberto I,** Via Testaferrata (*℡* **0931-724111**), near the end of Corso Gelone.

Pharmacy The **Farmacia Zecchino,** Viale Zecchino 199 (*℡* **0931-783384**), is open Monday to Saturday 8:30am to 1pm and 4:30 to 8pm. A list of pharmacies open at night is posted in the window.

Police Call *℡* **113.**

Post Office The post office is at Riva Posta 15 (*℡* **0931-796011**), open Monday to Friday 8am to 6:30pm, Saturday 8am to 12:30pm. There is also a currency exchange here.

SEEING THE ANCIENT SITES

Take bus no. 1 to reach these sites.

Parco Archeologico della Neapolis ★★★ Syracuse's Archaeological Park contains the town's most important attractions, all on the mainland at the western edge of town, to the immediate north of Stazione Centrale. The entrance to the park is down Via Augusto.

On Temenite Hill, the **Teatro Greco (Greek Theater)** ★★★, Viale Teocrito, was one of the great theaters of the classical period. Hewn from rock during the reign of Hieron I in the 5th century B.C., the ancient seats have been largely eaten away by time, but you can still stand on the remnants of the stone stage where plays by Euripedes were mounted. Today, the Italian Institute of Ancient Drama presents classical plays by Euripedes, Aeschylus, and Sophocles. In other words, the show hasn't changed much in 2,000 years.

Outside the entrance to the Greek Theater is the most famous of the ancient quarries, **Latomia del Paradiso (Paradise Quarry)** ★★, one of four or five from which stones were hauled to erect the great monuments of Syracuse in its glory days. Upon seeing the cave in the wall, Caravaggio is reputed to have dubbed it the "Ear of Dionysius" because of its unusual shape. But what an ear—it's nearly 60m (197 ft.) long. You can enter the inner chamber of the grotto, where the tearing of paper sounds like a gunshot. Although it's dismissed by some scholars as fanciful, the story goes that the despot Dionysius used to force prisoners into the "ear" at night, where he was able to hear every word they said. Nearby is the **Grotta dei Cordari,** where rope-makers plied their craft.

A rather evocative but gruesome site lies on the path down into the Roman amphitheater. The **Ara di Lerone,** or Altar of Heron, was once used by the Greeks for sacrifices involving hundreds of animals at once. A few pillars still stand, along with the mammoth stone base of this 3rd-century-B.C. monument. The longest altar ever built, it measured 196×23m (643×75 ft.).

The **Anfiteatro Romano (Roman Amphitheater)** ★ was created at the time of Augustus. It ranks among the top five amphitheaters left by the Romans in Italy. Like the Greek Theater, part of it was carved from rock. Unlike the Greek Theater with its classical plays, the Roman Amphitheater tended toward gutsier fare. Gladiators faced each

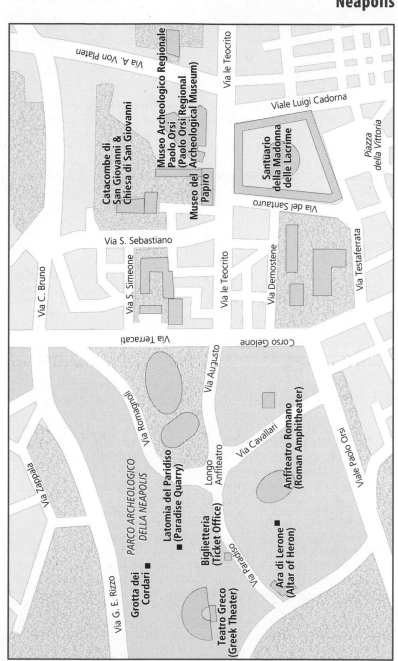

other with tridents and daggers, and slaves were whipped into the center of a battle to the death between wild beasts. If a man's opponent, man or beast, didn't do him in, the crowd would often scream for the ringmaster to slit his throat. The amphitheater is near the entrance to the park, but you can also view it in its entirety from a belvedere on the road.

Via Del Teatro (off the intersection of Corso Gelone and Viale Teocrito). ✆ **0931-66206.** Admission 6€ ($7.80). Apr–Oct daily 9am–5pm; Nov–Mar daily 9am–3pm.

Museo Archeologico Regionale Paolo Orsi (Paolo Orsi Regional Archaeological Museum) ★★★
One of the major archaeological museums in southern Italy surveys the Greek, Roman, and early Christian epochs. Crafted from glass, steel, and Plexiglas, and designed as an ultramodern showcase for the objects unearthed from digs throughout Sicily, this is the kind of museum that reinvigorates an appreciation for archaeology. Its stunning modernity is in direct contrast to the sometimes startling portrait busts and vases unearthed from around the island. Laid out like a hexagon, the museum is set in a garden dotted with ancient sarcophagi.

Section A takes us back before the dawn of recorded history. We're always fascinated by the skeletons of prehistoric animals found here, including dwarf elephants. Many artifacts illustrate life in Paleolithic and Neolithic times. Look for the stunning red-burnished **Vase of Pantalica ★**.

Section B is devoted to Greek colonization. The celebrated **Landolina Venus ★★** is here, without a head but alluring nonetheless. After all these centuries, the anatomy of this timeless Venus is still in perfect shape. A Roman copy of an original by Praxiteles, the statue was found in Syracuse in 1804. When he visited the town in 1885, Guy de Maupassant fell in love with this Venus and left a vivid description of her. Although it's not the equal of the Landolina Venus, the singular limestone block of a **Mother-Goddess ★** suckling twins dates from the 6th century B.C. and was recovered from a necropolis.

Section C brings the subcolonies and Hellenistic centers of eastern Sicily alive once more. It's a hodgepodge of artifacts and fragments, including votive terra cottas, sarcophagi, and vases from Gela. Interspersed among some rather dull artifacts are stunning creations such as an enthroned male figure from the 6th century B.C., a horse and rider from the same era, a terra-cotta goddess from the late 6th century B.C., and a miniature 6th-century-B.C. altar with a relief depicting a lion attacking a bull. You can also seek out three rare wooden statues from the 7th century B.C. (found near Agrigento).

In the gardens of the Villa Landolina in Akradina, Viale Teocrito 66. ✆ **0931-464022.** Admission 6€ ($7.80). Mon 3–5pm; Tues–Sat 9am–1pm and 3–5pm; Sun 9am–1pm.

Museo del Papiro
Located near the Paolo Orsi museum (see above), these galleries devoted to papyrus are unique in Italy. That's because Syracuse has the only climate outside the Nile Valley in which the papyrus plant can flourish. The word "paper," of course, comes from papyrus. But the plant has far more uses than making paper. Papyrus was used in the construction of lightweight boats, ropes, baskets, wigs, and fabric (papyrus sandals were all the rage in ancient Egypt). The most delicate part of the stalk might once have served as food. The most intriguing exhibit is of documents dating from the era of the pharaohs, featuring fragments from the Egyptian Book of the Dead.

Viale Teocrito 66. ✆ **0931-61616.** www.museodelpapiro.it. Free admission. Tues–Sun 9am–1:30pm.

Catacombe di San Giovanni (Catacombs of St. John) ★★
Evoking the more famous Christian burial grounds along Rome's Appian Way, the Catacombs of St. John

contain some 20,000 ancient tombs, honeycombed tunnels of empty coffins that were long ago looted of their "burial riches" by plundering grave robbers.

In Roman times, Christians were not allowed to bury their dead within the city limits, so they went outside the boundaries of Syracuse to create burial chambers in what had been used by the Greeks as underground aqueducts. The early Christians recycled these into chapels. Some faded frescoes and symbols etched into stone slabs can still be seen. Syracuse has other subterranean burial grounds, but the Catacombs of St. John are the only ones open to the public.

You enter the "world of the dead" from the **Chiesa di San Giovanni,** now a ruin. St. Paul is said to have preached on this spot, so the early Christians venerated it as holy ground. Now overgrown, the interior of the church was abandoned in the 17th century. In its heyday, it was the cathedral of Syracuse.

The church's roots date from the 6th century, when a basilica stood here, but it was eventually destroyed by the Saracens. The Normans reconstructed it in the 12th century, but in 1693 an earthquake destroyed it. A baroque church was then built, but was left in ruins by the earthquake of 1908. All that remain are roofless Norman walls and about half of the former apse. A beautiful rose window is still visible on the facade of the Norman church.

Underneath the church is the **Cripta di San Marciano (Crypt of St. Marcian),** constructed on the spot where the martyr is alleged to have been beaten to death. His Greek-cross chamber is found 5m (16 ft.) below the ground.

Warning: Make sure that you exit well before closing. Two readers who entered the catacombs after 5pm were accidentally locked in.

Piazza San Giovanni, at end of Viale San Giovanni. No phone. Admission 5€ ($6.50) adults, free for children 15 and younger. Tues–Sun 9:30am–12:30pm and 2:30–4pm. Closed Feb.

Santuario della Madonna delle Lacrime

The "Our Lady of Tears" sanctuary is one of the most bizarre monuments or churches in all of Sicily. Designed to evoke a gigantic teardrop, the structure was created by two Frenchmen, Michel Arnault and Pierre Parat, in 1994. It houses a statue of the Madonna that supposedly wept for 5 days in 1953. Alleged chemical tests showed that the liquid was similar to that of human tears. Pilgrims still flock here.

Although criticized by architectural purists, the contemporary conical structure dominates the skyline, rising 74m (243 ft.) with a diameter of 80m (262 ft.). The **interior ★** is amazing. You might get dizzy looking up at the vertical windows stretching skyward to the apex of the roof.

Lacrime is new, but just to the south of the sanctuary, on Piazza della Vittoria, you can stand and see the fenced-off excavations of an array of ancient Greek and Roman houses and streets.

Via Santuario 33. ✆ **0931-21446.** www.madonnadellelacrime.it. Free admission. Daily 8am–noon and 4–7pm.

Santa Lucia al Sepolcro

The original church here was constructed on the site where in A.D. 304 St. Lucy (Santa Lucia) was said to have been martyred. Dating from the Byzantine period, the church was vastly altered in the 12th century and completely reconstructed in the 17th century. Beneath this sanctuary is a vast labyrinth of dank catacombs dating from the 3rd century, most of which, even today, have not been explored and are closed to the public. You can, however, visit the sanctuary. The famous Caravaggio painting depicting the burial of Santa Lucia once hung here, but is now in the Palazzo Bellomo museum (p. 255).

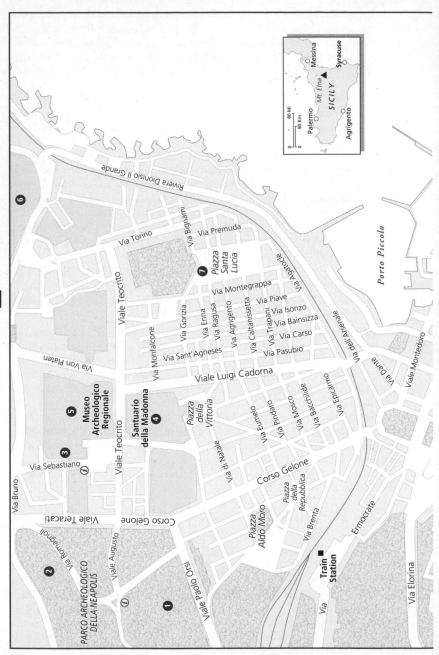

Riviera Dionisio Il Grande

Via Torino

Via Bignami

Via Premuda

Piazza
Santa
Lucia

Via Montegrappa

Viale Teocrito

Via Piave

Via Isonzo

Via Bainsizza

Via Montalcone

Via Gorizia

Via Enna

Via Ragusa

Via Caltanissetta

Via Agrigento

Via Trapani

Via Carso

Via Sant'Agnese

Via Pasubio

Via dell' Arsenale

Via Agatocle

Porto Piccolo

Via Dante

Viale Montedoro

Viale Luigi Cadorna

Via Von Platen

Museo
Archeologico
Regionale

Santuario
della Madonna

Piazza
della
Vittoria

Via Eumelo

Via Pindaro

Via Mosco

Via Bacchilide

Via Epicarmo

Viale Teocrito

Via Sebastiano

Via di Natale

Corso Gelone

Piazza
della
Repubblica

Via Bruno

Viale Teracati

Corso Gelone

Piazza
Aldo Moro

Via Brenta

Ermocrate

Via Romagnoli

Viale Augusto

PARCO ARCHEOLOGICO
DELLA NEAPOLIS

Viale Paolo Orsi

Via

Train
Station

Via Elorina

80 Mi
80 Km

Palermo

Messina

Mt. Etna

SICILY

Syracuse

Agrigento

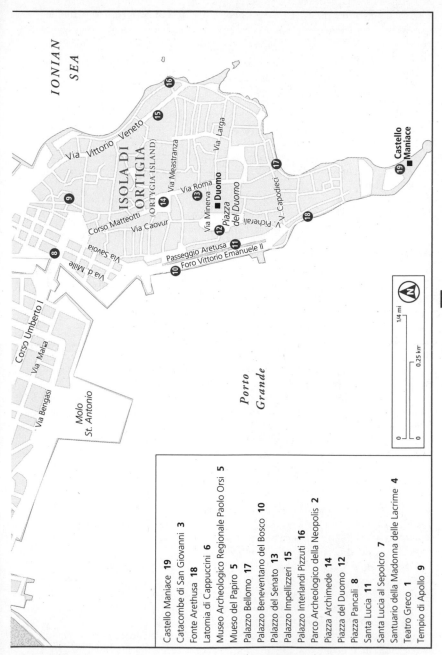

IONIAN SEA

Porto Grande

ISOLA DI ORTIGIA
(ORTYGIA ISLAND)

Via Vittorio Veneto
Via Meastranza
Via Larga
Via Roma
Via Minerva
Via Caovur
Via Savoia
Corso Matteotti
Passeggio Aretusa
Foro Vittorio Emanuele II
V. Picherali
V. Capodieci
Duomo
Piazza del Duomo
Corso Umberto I
Via Maia
Via Bengasi
Via d. Mille
Molo St. Antonio

■ **Castello Maniace**

1/4 mi
0.25 км

Castello Maniace **19**
Catacombe di San Giovanni **3**
Fonte Aretusa **18**
Latomia di Cappuccini **6**
Museo Archeologico Regionale Paolo Orsi **5**
Mueso del Papiro **5**
Palazzo Bellomo **17**
Palazzo Beneventano del Bosco **10**
Palazzo del Senato **13**
Palazzo Impellizzeri **15**
Palazzo Interlandi Pizzuti **16**
Parco Archeologico della Neopolis **2**
Piazza Archimede **14**
Piazza del Duomo **12**
Piazza Pancali **8**
Santa Lucia **11**
Santa Lucia al Sepolcro **7**
Santuario della Madonna delle Lacrime **4**
Teatro Greco **1**
Tempio di Apollo **9**

Indeed, there isn't much left to see of this church since all its former treasures have been hauled off. The doorway and apses are from Norman days, and a lovely rose window is from the 14th century. A granite column to the right of the presbytery marks the spot where Syracusans believe Santa Lucia suffered decapitation. Under the reign of Frederick III in the 16th century, the present ceiling was constructed with painted beams, reproducing a thick constellation of "stars" alternating with rose petals and small crosses.

Adjacent to the basilica and linked to it by a spooky 12th-century catacomb is a little baroque chapel containing the tomb of the martyred saint. She is long gone, however. In 1039, the Byzantine general Giorgio Maniace ordered that her corpse be sent to Constantinople. During the Crusades, the Venetians claimed the remains and shipped them back to Venice, where they remain today.

A marble statue placed under the sepulcher's altar is of particular, though morbid, fascination. From May 6 to May 8, 1735, eyewitnesses reported that this statue miraculously "sweated" profusely.

The sanctuary lies at the northern end of one of the loveliest squares in Syracuse, Piazza Santa Lucia, lined on three sides by rows of trees.

Via Gignami 1. (© 0931-67946. Free admission. Daily 9am–noon and 4–7pm.

Ortygia Island ★★★

Ortygia, inhabited for many thousands of years, is also called the Città Vecchia (Old City). It contains the town's Duomo, many rows of houses spanning 500 years of building styles, most of the city's medieval and baroque monuments, and some of the most charming vistas in Sicily. In Greek mythology, it's said that it was ruled by Calypso, daughter of Atlas, the sea nymph who detained Ulysses (Odysseus) for 7 years. The island, reached by crossing the Ponte Nuova, is about a mile long and half again as wide. Take bus no. 21 or 23 to get here.

Heading out the Foro Italico, you'll come to the **Fonte Arethusa ★**, also famous in mythology. The river god Alpheius, son of Oceanus, is said to have fallen in love with the sea nymph Arethusa. The nymph turned into this spring or fountain, but Alpheius became a river and "mingled" with his love. According to legend, the spring ran red when bulls were sacrificed at Olympus.

At Piazza del Duomo, the **Duomo ★** of Syracuse, reached by heading down Via Minerva from Piazza Archimede, illustrates more than any other structure in town the changing colonizations and architectural styles that have dominated the city over the centuries. The present cathedral incorporates architectural fragments from a 5th-century-B.C. temple honoring Athena. In its heyday, this Greek temple was spoken of in revered tones by the people of the Mediterranean. From miles away, sailors could see the golden statue of Athena shining like a beacon. Twenty-six of the temple's **Doric columns ★** are still in place. In 1693, an earthquake caused the cathedral's facade to collapse, and in the 18th century the structure was rebuilt in the baroque style.

Once inside, look in the first bay on the right for a beautiful **font ★** fashioned from a Greek marble krater. It is held up by seven stunning 13th-century wrought-iron lions. The Duomo is also rich in statues adorning its chapels, including one honoring patron saint Lucia. Entry to the Duomo is free; it's open daily from 8am to noon and 4 to 7pm.

The irregular **Piazza del Duomo ★** is especially majestic when the facade of the cathedral is dramatically caught by the setting sun or when floodlit at night. Acclaimed as one of the most beautiful squares in Italy, it's filled with fine baroque buildings. They include the striking **Palazzo Beneventano del Bosco,** with its lovely courtyard, and the Palazzo del Senato, with an inner courtyard displaying a senator's carriage from the 1700s. At the far end of the square stands another church, **Santa Lucia.**

The other important landmark square is **Piazza Archimede,** with its baroque fountain festooned with dancing jets and sea nymphs. This square is directly northeast of Piazza del Duomo, forming the monumental heart of Ortygia. It, not the cathedral square, is the main piazza of the old city. Original Gothic windows grace the 15th-century **Palazzo Lanza** here. As you move about Ortygia, you'll find that Piazza Archimede is a fine place from which to orient yourself. Wander the narrow streets wherever your feet will take you, and when you get lost, ask for directions back to Piazza Archimede.

Palazzo Bellomo ★★   This elegant 13th-century palace is today the home of the **Museo Regionale di Arte Medievale e Moderna,** which contains one of the great art collections of Sicily, dating from the high Middle Ages through the 20th century. It's located next to St. Benedict's church close to Fonte Aretusa.

The *palazzo* is from the Swabian era and was enlarged in the 15th century by the powerful Bellomo family. The art is arranged chronologically on two floors. Much of it was rescued from deconsecrated monasteries and churches.

We like to gaze upon two exquisite masterpieces: *The Burial of St. Lucia* (1608) ★, by the "divine" Caravaggio, and Antonello da Messina's exquisite *Annunciation* (1474) ★ . Caravaggio, the master of light, created a stunning canvas of grieving figures, graced with the serene expression of the martyr and the raw nudity of the gravediggers. The saint's death sleep was meant to signify her glorious rebirth in heaven. Though damaged, the *Annunciation* remains powerful in its imagery and majesty.

On the ground floor of the palazzo is an array of sculpture from the Middle Ages and the Renaissance, the most outstanding of which are from the Gagini school, including the tomb of Giovanni Cardinas, by Antonello Gagini, and a masterful *Madonna of the Bullfinch,* by Domenico Gagini. Look for the 17th- and 18th-century Sicilian carriages in the loggia.

The Tears of an Abandoned Mistress

One of the most evocative boat rides in and around Syracuse is along the **River Cyane,** 5km (3 miles) west of the city along Via Elorina. From May to September, a 2-hour boat trip can take you to the source of this river. Here you will see a pool that, according to legend, was formed by the tears shed by Cyane, a nymph attending her mistress, Persephone, who was abducted by Hades (Pluto in Roman mythology), leaving Cyane alone.

Along the way you'll see clusters of papyrus plants. The original plants were a gift from Ptolemy to Hieron II. The boat also goes by the meager ruins of **Olympeion,** a temple erected at the end of the 6th century.

Boat rentals cost between 8€ and 15€ ($10–$20) per person, depending on the number of passengers. For tickets and information on departure times, call ☎ **0931-69076.** To reach the departure site, take bus no. 21, 22, or 23 from Piazza della Posta and get off at Ponte delle Fiane.

The collection of Sicilian **decorative arts** ★ is full of charm and whimsy. It includes marble intarsia panels, ecclesiastical objects, 18th-century statuettes, church vestments, terra-cotta figurines, ceramics, and silver- and goldsmithery.

Note: At press time, this museum was closed for renovations. No reopening date has been announced. Before you visit, call to check on its current status.

Via Capodieci 16. (*C*) **0931-69511.** Admission 2.50€ ($3.25). Mon–Sat 9am–6:30pm; Sun 9am–1:30pm.

Tempio di Apollo   At the Piazza Pancali on the island of Ortygia, this Greek temple dating from the 6th century B.C. is the oldest peripteral (having a row of columns on each side) Doric temple in the world. The inscription says that the temple honors Apollo. However, after Cicero came to Syracuse, he wrote that the temple was dedicated to Artemis. Regardless, the temple faced a rocky future—it was first turned into a Byzantine Church before the Saracens took over and converted it into a mosque. Later, under Norman rule, it was turned back into a church. On a square across the bridge to Ortygia, the fenced-off ruins can be viewed at any time.

WHERE TO STAY

The best place to stay here is on Ortygia, at either the Grand Hotel or the Albergo Domus Mariae (see below). The island has far more character and charm than "mainland" Syracuse. On the downside, both of these hotels might be booked to capacity, especially in summer. In that case, we've included some backup choices.

Expensive

Algilà Ortygia Charme Hotel ★ (**Finds**)   In a restored building in the historic heart of Ortygia, this stately old building opens onto panoramic views of the ancient Ortygia Sea. The latest restoration saw the installation of the latest amenities, yet preserved its antique architecture. Each of the rooms is furnished differently with antiques, four-poster beds, and elegant decoration, and each contains a colorfully tiled bathroom. Rooms open onto a blissful inner courtyard. Both a Mediterranean and an international cuisine are served in the hotel restaurant, with a special menu offered to vegetarians.

Via Vittorio Veneto 93, 96100 Siracusa. (*C*) **0931-465186.** Fax 0931-463889. www.algila.it. 30 units. 112€–260€ ($146–$338) double; 217€–350€ ($282–$455) junior suite. AE, MC, V. **Amenities:** Restaurant; room service; laundry service. *In room:* A/C, TV, hair dryer.

Grand Hotel ★★★   Originally built in 1905, this is the best hotel in Syracuse, with a very appealing mix of modernity and old-world charm. It's set directly on the waterfront, near Ortygia's main access bridge to the Italian "mainland," in a stately four-story building that contains lots of inlaid marble and polished Belle Epoque hardwoods. The vaulted cellar has a bar with comfortable sofas and a collection of remnants—some museum quality—unearthed from this site during long-ago excavations. Guest rooms are contemporary and comfortable, with color schemes of beige and champagne. In some of the suites, duplex setups include interior staircases of polished steel. The in-house restaurant, **La Terrazza,** is reviewed on p. 262. The bus station is only 100m (328 ft.) away.

Viale Mazzini 12, 96100 Siracusa. (*C*) **0931-464600.** Fax 0931-464611. www.grandhotelsr.it. 58 units. 240€–250€ ($312–$325) double; from 300€ ($390) suite. Rates include buffet breakfast. AE, DC, MC, V. Free parking. **Amenities:** Restaurant; 2 bars; babysitting; laundry service; dry cleaning; 1 room for those w/limited mobility. *In room:* A/C, TV, minibar, hair dryer, safe, radio, Wi-Fi.

Grand Hotel Villa Politi ★   For decades after its inauguration in 1862, the Grand Hotel Villa Politi (not to be confused with Syracuse's Grand Hotel, described above) was one of the three most elegant and sought-after hotels in Sicily, rivaled only by Palermo's Villa Igiea and Taormina's Palazzo San Domenico. Today, it's a lot less prestigious, evoking, at least from the outside, either a hospital or a battered public school. But if you know what you're getting beforehand, *and* if you understand some of its history, you'll probably be content to stay on its unusual premises. The hotel is awkwardly located in a residential neighborhood that's connected by roaring boulevards, after a 10-minute drive, to the Archaeological Park. It's situated above what was used thousands of years ago as a rock quarry, the historic Latomie dei Cappuccini. The result is bizarre, even surreal, incorporating a dry, dusty garden with a deep chasm almost at the hotel's foundation, all of it surrounded by the urban encroachments of the 21st century. Most of the rooms reflect the somewhat dowdy tastes of someone's well-heeled but not widely traveled Sicilian aunt: lace curtains, high ceilings, comfy beds, and a definite sense of the south Italian bourgeoisie.

Via MP Laudien 2, 96100 Siracusa. ℂ **0931-412121.** Fax 0931-36061. www.villapoliti.com. 100 units. 190€–240€ ($247–$312) double; 360€ ($468) suite. Rates include buffet breakfast. AE, DC, MC, V. Free parking. Bus: 1 or 4. **Amenities:** 2 restaurants; bar; room service; outdoor pool; laundry service; nonsmoking rooms; solarium. *In room:* A/C, TV, minibar, hair dryer, safe, Wi-Fi.

Hotel Roma ★   A block from the city's magnificent cathedral, this government-rated four-star hotel opened in the much-renovated shell of a hotel that was originally built in the 1880s. The lobby's vaulted ceiling is crafted from chiseled stone blocks and ringed with Belle Epoque columns. Most of the well-appointed, very comfortable guest rooms have elaborate marquetry floors, original lithographs, and comfortable furniture vaguely inspired by Art Deco. About four of the rooms have computers. Overall, this is a fine hotel choice, with a location in the heart of monument-laden Ortygia Island.

Via Minerva 10, 96100 Siracusa. ℂ **0931-465626.** Fax 0931-465535. www.hotelroma.sr.it. 45 units. 110€–200€ ($143–$260) double; 254€ ($330) junior suite. AE, DC, MC, V. Parking 8€ ($10) per day. **Amenities:** Restaurant; bar; room service; gym; sauna; laundry service; dry cleaning; rooms for those w/limited mobility. *In room:* A/C, TV, minibar, safe, Wi-Fi.

Moderate

Albergo Domus Mariae ★ Finds   This small-scale hotel originated in 1995 when a Catholic elementary school was transformed into a decent, well-managed lodging. It's owned by an order of Ursuline nuns, and although the desk staff and porters are likely to be laypersons, its manager is a hardworking, habit-clothed member of the order. This is the only hotel in Syracuse with its own chapel and a genuinely contemplative reading room. There's also a rooftop terrace for sunbathing. Rooms are fairly priced, with modern furniture and a no-nonsense approach to decor. There are no attempts to foist religious education on guests—for most purposes, this is a conventional hotel, without any evangelistic mission. *Note:* The signs for this place are so small as to be almost invisible, especially if you're driving along the waterfront promenade that flanks it. Here's a tip: It's set directly across a tiny waterfront piazza from the baroque facade of San Filippo Neri Church.

Via Vittorio Veneto 76, 96100 Siracusa. ℂ/fax **0931-24854.** www.sistemia.it/domusmariae. 17 units. 140€–160€ ($180–$208) double. Rates include buffet breakfast. AE, DC, MC, V. Free parking. **Amenities:** Bar; room service; laundry service; dry cleaning; all nonsmoking rooms. *In room:* A/C, TV, minibar, hair dryer.

Gran Bretagna ★   No one knows the exact age of this once-decaying three-story palazzo, but it has been restored with sensitivity with the location between two restaurant-flanked side streets lying at the north end of the old city in the heart of Ortygia. During a wholesale renovation, workers uncovered parts of the city's 16th-century fortifications, which can be viewed through glass floor panels. In the courtyard you can also

Porto Piccolo

Riviera Dionisio II Grande

Via Bignami

Via Premuda

Via Torino

Piazza Santa Lucia

Viale Teocrito

Via Montegrappa

Via Gorizia

Via Enna

Via Ragusa

Via Agrigento

Via Caltanissetta

Via Piave

Via Trapani

Via Isonzo

Via Bainsizza

Via Carso

Via Pasubio

Via Montalcone

Via Sant'Agneses

Via Von Platen

Viale Luigi Cadorna

Via Agatocle

Via dell'Arsenale

Via Dante

Viale Montedoro

Museo Archeologico Regionale

Santuario della Madonna

Viale Teocrito

Piazza della Vittoria

Via di Natale

Via Eumelo

Via Pindaro

Via Mosco

Via Bacchilde

Via Epicarmo

Via Sebastiano

Via Bruno

Viale Teracati

Corso Gelone

Corso Gelone

Piazza della Repubblica

Piazza Aldo Moro

Via Brenta

Ermocrate

Via Romagnoli

PARCO ARCHEOLOGICO DELLA NEAPOLIS

Viale Augusto

Viale Paolo Orsi

Train Station

Via

Via Elorina

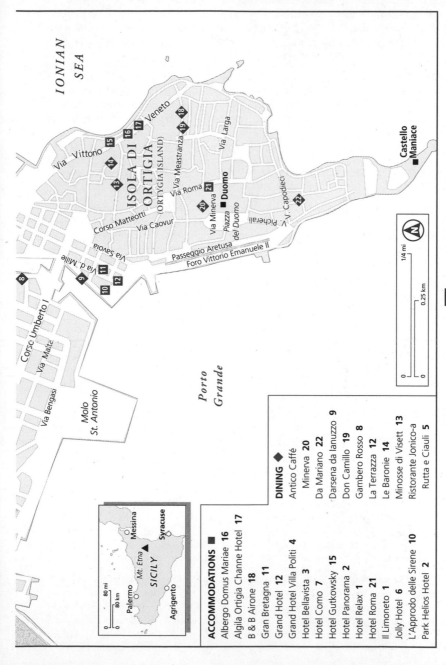

ACCOMMODATIONS ■

Albergo Domus Mariae **16**
Algila Ortigia Channe Hotel **17**
B & B Airone **18**
Gran Bretagna **11**
Grand Hotel **12**
Grand Hotel Villa Politi **4**
Hotel Bellavista **3**
Hotel Como **7**
Hotel Gutkowsky **15**
Hotel Panorama **2**
Hotel Relax **1**
Hotel Roma **21**
Il Limoneto **1**
Jolly Hotel **6**
L'Approdo delle Sirene **10**
Park Helios Hotel **2**

DINING ◆

Antico Caffé
  Minerva **20**
Da Mariano **22**
Darsena da Ianuzzo **9**
Don Camillo **19**
Gambero Rosso **8**
La Terrazza **12**
Le Baronie **14**
Minosse di Visett **13**
Ristorante Jonico-a
  Rutta e Ciauli **5**

view some of the ancient wall. Bedrooms are well furnished and exceedingly spacious, with antique reproductions and in some cases frescoed ceilings. Some accommodations are suitable for three or four guests.

Via Savoia 21, 96100 Siracusa. ⓒ/fax **0931-68765.** www.hotelgranbretagna.it. 17 units. 110€ ($143) double; 135€ ($176) triple. Rates include breakfast. AE, DC, MC, V. Free parking. **Amenities:** Bar; room service. *In room:* A/C, TV, minibar, hair dryer.

Jolly Hotel   A major stop for tour groups, the six-story Jolly is part of the chain that's Italy's answer to Holiday Inn. You get no surprises, just your basic motel room (albeit slightly worn) with a good bed and a small tiled bathroom. At least the view of the sea is panoramic. The location is on a dull but busy shopping street, about a 20-minute walk from Ortygia.

Corso Gelone 45, 96100 Siracusa. ⓒ **800/221-2626** in the U.S., 800/237-0319 in Canada, or 0931-4611111. Fax 0931-461126. www.medeahotels.com. 100 units. 136€–196€ ($177–$255) double. Rates include buffet breakfast. AE, DC, MC, V. Free parking. **Amenities:** Restaurant; bar; lounge; room service; laundry service; dry cleaning; nonsmoking rooms. *In room:* A/C, TV, minibar, hair dryer, safe.

Park Helios Hotel   The biggest hotel in Syracuse is architecturally uninspiring in its *moderno* statement, except for the private balconies, but it's still a solid, reliable choice. It offers airy, comfortably furnished guest rooms with tiled floors and mostly shower-only bathrooms. The service is good, though we found the restaurant rather mediocre. For the money, though, the place isn't a bad option.

Via Filisto 80, 96100 Siracusa. ⓒ **0931-412233.** Fax 0931-38096. 182 units. 100€–130€ ($130–$169) double. AE, DC, MC, V. Free parking. **Amenities:** Restaurant; bar; outdoor pool; room service; babysitting; laundry service; dry cleaning; nonsmoking rooms; solarium. *In room:* A/C, TV, minibar, hair dryer.

Inexpensive

B&B Airone   This converted old palazzo lies right in the historic center of Ortygia. It's the best bed-and-breakfast in the area, drawing young people, often backpackers, from all over the world. Furnishings are bare-bones yet comfortable, and the price is right. Only three of its units have private bathrooms, the others sharing a well-scrubbed hallway bathroom that's generally adequate for its purpose.

Via Maestranza 111, 96100 Siracusa. ⓒ **338-3739050.** www.bedandbreakfastsicily.com. 6 units. 50€–65€ ($65–$85) double with shared bathroom; 65€–80€ ($85–$104) double with private bathroom. Rates include buffet breakfast. No credit cards. **Amenities:** Lounge. *In room:* No phone.

Hotel Bellavista   This family-run hotel lies in the commercial center, close to the archaeological zone. It was built in 1956, but renovations have kept it up-to-date. The spacious lounge has leather chairs and semitropical plants. Guest rooms are informal and comfortable; most are furnished with traditional pieces and have sea-view balconies and tidy shower-only bathrooms. There's an annex in the garden for overflow.

Via Diodoro Siculo 4, 96100 Siracusa. ⓒ **0931-411355.** Fax 0931-37927. 47 units. 139€–150€ ($181–$195) double; 165€–185€ ($215–$241) triple. Rates include buffet breakfast. AE, DC, MC, V. Free parking. **Amenities:** Restaurant; bar; lounge; gym; sauna; room service; laundry service. *In room:* A/C, TV.

Hotel Como ★ Ⓥ**alue** Ⓚ**ids**   This small hotel, not far from the historic core, is one of the city's best bargains. It's located in the square at the train station and is convenient for those arriving on trains from Catania. It's little more than a utilitarian lodging, but many of the rooms are quite spacious and comfortably furnished. Since some of the units are triples, this is a favorite with families, often from other parts of Sicily. Plus, its low-slung design and sense of style set the place apart from a typically tacky train-station hotel.

20 units. 60€–100€ ($78–$130) double; 90€–120€ ($117–$156) triple; 150€ ($195) suite. Rates include buffet breakfast. AE, DC, MC, V. **Amenities:** Bar; laundry service; dry cleaning; nonsmoking rooms; 1 room for those w/limited mobility. *In room:* A/C, TV, minibar, hair dryer.

Hotel Gutkowski   Modern, unpretentious, and with a distinct sense of being alive to the creative arts scene of Syracuse, this small hotel opened in 1999 in a waterfront town house on Ortygia. Don't expect any particular luxury, as everything here is utilitarian and a bit less comfortable than rooms at the nearby Domus Mariae. It nonetheless has a welcoming atmosphere. The only meal offered is breakfast, which is served in a spartan room next to the reception desk.

Lungomare Vittorini 26, 96100 Siracusa. ℂ **0931-465861.** Fax 0931-480505. www.guthotel.it. 25 units. 110€ ($143) double; 130€ ($169) triple. Discounts of 10% available Oct–Mar. Rates include buffet breakfast. AE, MC, V. Free parking. **Amenities:** Wine bar; laundry service; dry cleaning; massage. *In room:* A/C, TV, minibar.

Hotel Panorama   Near the entrance to the city, on a rise of Temenite Hill, this bandbox-modern hotel sits on a busy street about 5 minutes from the Archaeological Park. Rated four stars by the government, it is close to where Greek plays are presented every summer. It's not a motel, but it does provide free parking. The small guest rooms are pleasant and up-to-date following a renovation, with comfortable but utilitarian furniture and small, shower-only bathrooms.

Via Necropoli Grotticelle 33, 96100 Siracusa. ℂ **0931-412188.** Fax 0931-412527. www.hotelpanoramasr. it. 51 units. 110€–165€ ($143–$215) double. Rates include continental breakfast. AE, MC, V. Free parking. Bus: 13. **Amenities:** Restaurant; bar; room service; laundry service; dry cleaning; 1 room for those w/ limited mobility. *In room:* A/C, TV, minibar, hair dryer, safe.

Hotel Relax   This Mediterranean-style hotel lies 2km (1¼ miles) from the center in a rather tranquil residential area. On the grounds are a garden, pool, and solarium, making it a good choice for those who don't want to stay in the center of hot, dusty Syracuse. Guest rooms are light and airy, furnished in a minimalist yet comfortable fashion. Suites are a good buy, but there are only two and they must be reserved in advance. The restaurant serves typical but quite good Sicilian and international cuisine.

Viale Epipoli 159, 96100 Siracusa. ℂ **0931-740122.** Fax 0931-740933. www.hotelrelax.it. 59 units. 108€ ($141) double; 145€ ($189) suite. Rates include buffet breakfast. AE, DC, MC, V. Free parking. Take any bus marked BELVEDERE. **Amenities:** Restaurant; bar; outdoor pool; kiddie pool; room service; laundry service; dry cleaning; solarium; rooms for those w/limited mobility. *In room:* A/C, TV, hair dryer.

Il Limoneto ★ Kids   What a discovery! This place brings you close to the heart of Sicily. The tranquil retreat of orange groves and orchards lies 9km (5½ miles) from the center of Syracuse along SP14 Mare-Monti. You can stay at this estate and visit not only Syracuse but also Noto (p. 265) and Ragusa (p. 272). Much of the food served here is grown on the grounds, and guests are invited to pick their own fruit. We enjoyed the hotel's house-party atmosphere, with guests gathering in the evening for wine and conversation. If you like the outdoors, this is the best choice in the area—you can take an aerobics class, or even archery instruction. Guest rooms are comfortably furnished in a farmhouse-rustic style. Families can opt for a room with a mezzanine, stashing the kids upstairs.

Via del Platano 3, 96100 Siracusa (Contrada Magrentino). ℂ **0931-717352.** Fax 0931-717728. www. limoneto.it. 10 units. 90€–120€ ($117–$156) double. Rates include continental breakfast. Dinner 30€ ($39) per person extra. MC, V. Free parking. Closed Nov. Take the Palazzolo bus from Syracuse's central station. **Amenities:** Restaurant. *In room:* A/C (in some), no phone.

L'Approdo delle Sirene (Value)   One of the town's best B&Bs is in an old palazzo by a canal; it's been restored and handsomely converted to receive guests. It offers excellent Sicilian hospitality with a panoramic terrace in a setting of jasmine and bougainvillea overlooking the sea. Despite the simple decor, there's a kind of elegance to the comfortably furnished midsize bedrooms.

Riva Garibaldi 15, 96100 Siracusa. © **0931-24857.** Fax 0931-483765. www.apprododellesirene.com. 8 units. 90€ ($117) double; 90€–120€ ($117–$156) triple. Rates include buffet breakfast. AE, DC, MC, V. Parking 18€ ($23). **Amenities:** Room service. *In room:* A/C, TV, minibar, hair dryer, beverage maker, Wi-Fi.

WHERE TO DINE

For just a drink, snack, or coffee, head for the elegant **Antico Caffè Minerva,** Via Minerva 15 (© **0931-22606**), in the vicinity of the Duomo. It's open Thursday through Tuesday from 7am to 1am.

Note: Only a few of the restaurants below lie on a bus line.

Expensive

La Terrazza ★ ITALIAN/SICILIAN   Set on the top floor of Ortygia's highest-rated hotel, this restaurant features a *dolce vita* ambience, formal service, and big-windowed views that sweep from the outdoor terrace way, way across Syracuse's bay. There's something festive about this place, and the fine food includes starters like smoked salmon with mint sauce; jumbo shrimp with citrus sauce; and an antipasti platter containing smoked turkey. Equally alluring are the main courses, such as risotto with monkfish and saffron. The cuisine is admirably authentic and satisfying, prepared with the freshest of ingredients.

On the top floor of the Grand Hotel, Viale Mazzini 12. © **0931-464600.** Reservations recommended. Main courses 10€–18€ ($13–$23). AE, DC, MC, V. July–Aug and Jan–Feb Wed–Mon 7:30–10:30pm; Sept–Dec and Mar–June daily 12:30–2:30pm and 7:30–10:30pm.

Ristorante Jonico-a Rutta e Ciauli ★ SICILIAN   This is one of the best restaurants in the area for typical Sicilian cuisine and wines. It's right on the sea, not far from Piazzale dei Cappuccini. The decor is pure Liberty (Art Nouveau) style. The antipasti array is dazzling, and the homemade pastas are superb—try pasta *rusticana,* with eggplant, cheese, ham, and herbs. Swordfish appears here in roulades with raisins, pine nuts, and bread crumbs. The dessert specialty is *cassatine Siciliane* (mocha-chocolate ice cream capped with sprinkles of coffee-flavored chocolate, all floating in a lake of English custard). A roof garden has a pizzeria serving typical Sicilian pizza.

Riviera Dionisio il Grande 194. © **0931-65540.** Reservations recommended. Main courses 7€–12€ ($9.10–$16); pizzas 5€–8€ ($6.50–$10). AE, MC, V. June–Sept daily noon–3pm and 8–10:30pm.

Moderate

Don Camillo ★ SEAFOOD/SICILIAN   This is one of the city's finest dining rooms, built near the historic center on the foundation of a 15th-century monastery that collapsed during an earthquake in 1693. The rather classy joint is full of atmosphere, with vaulted ceilings and potted plants. The cuisine is among the most creative in town, featuring lighter versions of time-tested Sicilian recipes. If you're a devotee of sea urchins (and not everyone is), the delectable morsels are particularly fresh-tasting here, especially when served with shrimp-studded spaghetti. All kinds of fish are served, and the catch of the day can be prepared almost any way you like it. Another specialty is grilled tuna steak with pepper jam. More than 450 different wines are on offer.

Via Maestranza 96. © **0931-67133.** Reservations recommended. Main courses 9€–12€ ($12–$16). AE, DC, MC, V. Mon–Sat 12:30–2:30pm and 7:30–10:30pm. Closed Nov.

Gambero Rosso SICILIAN/MEDITERRANEAN/SEAFOOD This large restaurant is housed in an old tavern near the bridge to the Città Vecchia. The dining room extends onto a terrace facing the port. Two reliable choices are *zuppa di pesce* (fish soup) and *zuppa di cozze* (fresh mussels in a tasty marinade). The meat dishes feature a number of choices from the kitchens of Lazio, Tuscany, and Emilia-Romagna.

Via Eritrea 2. ℂ **0931-68546.** Reservations recommended. Main courses 6.50€–13€ ($8.45–$17). AE, MC, V. Fri–Wed 11am–3pm and 7:30pm–midnight.

Minosse di Visetti ★ Finds ITALIAN This well-run restaurant is more formal and a lot more sedate than many of its quasi-hysterical competitors on Ortygia Island. It's set on an obscure alley in the heart of town, occupying a trio of paneled dining rooms. The restaurant entered the annals of local history in 1993, when it was selected as the dinner venue for the pope on the occasion of his inauguration of the Our Lady of Tears sanctuary (p. 251). The chef wins praise for his fresh mussels with cherry tomatoes. The spaghetti with seafood is marked by intense, refined flavors, and the fish soup is one of the best in town. One final and most recommended specialty is baked swordfish and shrimp pie.

Via Mirabella 6. ℂ **0931-66366.** Main courses 9€–17€ ($12–$22). MC, V. Tues–Sun noon–3pm and 7–11pm. Take any minibus leaving Piazza delle Poste and get off at Via Mirabella.

Inexpensive

Da Mariano SICILIAN Set on a cobble-covered alley, much too narrow for a car, a short block downhill from the Museo Bellomo, this hideaway has simple plastic tables and chairs, red-checkered tablecloths, and a good reputation. It offers only 70 seats in a cavelike warren of vaulted rooms that you'll find either charmingly intimate or impossibly claustrophobic. The chef's use of fresh ingredients is a compelling reason to dine here. We sampled a delightful homemade cavatelli with wild boar sauce. Many dishes, such as baked rabbit, Sicilian tripe, and perfectly sautéed calves' liver, are full of good old country flavor. The grilled swordfish is immensely tasty, as is farfalle pasta with braised radicchio. Other menu items include spaghetti with pumpkin flowers, cavatelli (pasta) with pork sauce, and grilled shrimp and calamari.

Vicolo Zuccolà 9. ℂ **0931-67444.** Reservations recommended. Main courses 7€–12€ ($9.10–$16). MC, V. Wed–Mon 1–3pm and 8–11:30pm. Closed 3 weeks in July.

Darsena da Ianuzzo ITALIAN/SICILIAN Well located, almost immediately adjacent to the older of the two bridges leading from the Sicilian "mainland" to Ortygia Island, this stylish enclave overlooks the artfully ratty harborfront life that gives Ortygia such color. A veranda overlooks the Ionian Sea. We've enjoyed some good meals here, but be warned: This is not the friendliest oasis in town. Only time-tested local recipes are served: One specialty is a savory fish soup; another is spaghetti with a mass of little sea urchins. *Conchigliette al ragù di pesce* (minced fish in a rich tomato sauce) is another well-prepared dish.

Riva Garibaldi 8. ℂ **0931-66104.** Reservations recommended. Main courses 8€–15€ ($10–$20). AE, DC, MC, V. Thurs–Tues noon–3pm and 7:15–11pm.

Le Baronie ★ Finds SICILIAN Expatriate Americans and longtime friends of ours living in Syracuse turned us on to this delightful *trattoria* in an old Sicilian villa. Laid out like a hexagon, it's set in a garden dotted with ancient sarcophagi and offers both patio and interior dining. The restaurant serves traditional island cuisine, but adds many creative touches. The result is highly personal, inventive food. Try the homemade pasta with a savory tomato sauce and shrimp. One of our other favorite pastas—and it's a delight— is pasta alla Siracusana (with capers, anchovies, and olives). A standard favorite with the locals is grilled swordfish or else grilled steak with a fresh salad. The chefs take justifiable pride in their gnocchi sautéed with shrimp, fresh zucchini, and cherry tomatoes.

Via Gargallo 24. ℂ **0931-68884.** Reservations recommended. Main courses 8€–15€ ($10–$20). MC, V. Tues–Sun noon–3pm and 7:30pm–midnight.

SHOPPING

Galleria Bellomo ★   Located across the narrow medieval street from the Museo Bellomo, this is an art gallery with a twist: It sells colorful still lifes and landscapes painted on papyrus that's manufactured on the premises. Part of the charm of this place involves a free demonstration of how this waterlogged reed is soaked, pressed, and layered between linen sheets to painstakingly produce the substance upon which the day-to-day business of ancient Egypt was conducted. Via Capodieci 15. ℂ **0931-61340.** Bus: 21 or 22.

Old Times/Davies of London Antiquario   This shop's entrance is set on the innermost rim of an antique courtyard, immediately adjacent to the Ortygia Island branch of Syracuse's tourist office. Inside is a wide array of mostly English art objects and porcelain, hauled down to Syracuse from estate sales in Britain by an expatriate who fell in love with southern Sicily many years ago. Via Cavour 18–20. ℂ **0931-60977.** Bus: 21 or 22.

SYRACUSE AFTER DARK

Much of the nightlife in summer takes place in satellite villages, particularly along the coast. Unless specifically stated, hours can be irregular; check before heading to one of the hot spots, especially those out of town.

In Syracuse itself, you can visit **La Nottola,** Via Gargallo 61 (ℂ **0931-60009**), on a small street near Via Maestranza. This stylish jazz club/piano bar/disco attracts a well-dressed younger crowd.

Syracuse has a number of worthy bars and cafes, including **Bar Bonomo,** Corso Gelone 48 (ℂ **0931-67845**), which is more of a bar/bakery. Its gelato is some of the best in town. The spacious **Bar del Ponte,** Piazza Pancali (ℂ **0931-64312**), is near Syracuse's most famous fountain and serves all kinds of drinks, snacks, and excellent gelato. Tables overflow onto the square in fair weather. Also in the vicinity of the fountain is the fashionable bar **Lungo la Notte,** Lungomare Alfeo 22 (ℂ **0931-64200**), open only at night. The panoramic setting overlooking the harbor attracts a young clientele.

On the Outskirts

The region's best disco is **La Piscina,** Viale Scala Greca (ℂ **0931-753633**). It contains a walled garden, a pool that at night seems mostly ornamental, and a crowd that's older than you'll find at the student hangouts closer to the town center. Take bus no. 5, 6, 8, 25, or 26.

SIDE TRIPS FROM SYRACUSE

For specific locations, see the "Syracuse & the Southeast" map, on p. 245.

CASTELLO EURIALO ★   This boat-shaped structure is one of the most formidable Greek fortresses to have survived from ancient times, set 9km (5½ miles) northwest of Syracuse along Via Epipoli, in the Belvedere district. The castle was adapted and fortified by Archimedes, the famous mathematician who was born in Syracuse in 287 B.C.

The castle was believed impregnable, but such was not the case. The Romans conquered it without a struggle. The approach road crosses the **Wall of Dionysius,** which once stretched for 27km (17 miles) across the Epipolae high plateau, enclosing the northern tier of Syracuse. Two parallel walls were built of limestone blocks, the center filled with rubble. The walls, launched by Dionysius the Elder in 401 B.C. after the Athenian siege, were finished in 385 B.C.

As you survey the ruins, know that they are the most complete of any Greek military work extant. Three ditches precede the west front of the fortress. The main castle consisted of a keep, barracks, and cisterns. A warren of underground passages was cut through the fortress. From the castle precincts, you can enjoy a **panoramic view ★** back to Syracuse.

Take bus no. 11, 25, or 26 from the Archaeological Park to reach the site, which is open daily 9am to sunset. Free admission. For information, call © **0931-711773.**

MEGARA HYBLAEA If you don't suffocate passing through the industrial horror, *Zona industriale,* with its polluting oil refineries, you'll reach ancient Megara Hyblaea, near the major port of Prilo along the coast of southeastern Sicily. The Greeks built the city to open onto the Gulf of Augusta, whose shoreline now contains the largest concentration of chemical plants in Europe. Pollution has killed nearly all marine life in the bay, and the air in this area is contaminated.

Should you be a serious-enough archaeologist, and if you have persisted this far, you'll come upon the ruin of what was Megara Hyblaea, 16km (10 miles) to the north of Syracuse and reached along SS114. Yellow signposts direct you to the excavations, which are open Monday to Saturday 9am to 2pm and Sunday 9am to 1pm. Admission is free.

The Megarians arriving in ships from Greece founded Megara Hyblaea in the 8th century B.C., making it one of the oldest of all Greek settlements in Sicily. It was leveled by the tyrant Gelon in 483 B.C. By 340 B.C., Timoleon had founded a second city, but it, too, fell to conquerors, this time the Romans in 214 B.C. Serious excavations of the site began in 1949 and continue to this day.

Outside the old town walls are the remains of a necropolis. After a look, you can walk into the heart of the ruins, exploring foundations of buildings from both the Archaic period (indicated by red iron posts) and the Hellenistic era (green posts). Of particular interest is a Hellenistic house from the 4th century B.C. (the entry is marked by iron steps). Nearly two dozen chambers were arranged around two patios.

To the left of the old agora, or marketplace, are the ruins of Hellenistic baths, with a boiler still discernible in the rubble. Nearby is a small Doric temple in bad shape, which dates from the 4th century B.C. You can also view the Hellenistic west gate with its two square towers.

Although Megara Hyblaea is the finest and most complete model of an Archaic city still extant, all the valuable artifacts dug up here have been transferred to the museums of Syracuse.

---

2 NOTO ★★

31km (19 miles) SW of Syracuse, 55km (34 miles) E of Ragusa

Justifiably the most popular day trip from Syracuse is to the little town of Noto, which is set amid olive groves and almond trees on a plateau overlooking the Asinaro Valley. Noto dates from the 9th century and knew Greek, Roman, Byzantine, Arab, Norman, Aragonese, and even Spanish culture before 1692, when an earthquake destroyed it. The town was constructed somewhat like a stage set, with curvilinear accents and wrought-iron balconies. Many Sicilian artists and artisans have worked hard to rebuild Noto into a baroque gem, with uniform buildings of soft limestone. It's even more magical at night, with all the buildings lit up—you may want to stay for dinner and then stroll around, or even stay overnight.

Mercifully, traffic has been diverted away from the main street, **Corso Vittorio Emanuele,** to protect its fragile buildings, on which restoration began in 1987—and not a moment too soon. Your best approach is through the monumental **Porta Reale (Royal Gate),** crowned by three symbols—a dog, a swan, and a tower, representing the town's former allegiance to the Bourbon monarchy. From here, take **Corso Vittorio Emanuele,** going through the old patricians' quarter. The rich-looking, honey-colored buildings along this street are some of the most captivating on the island. This street takes you to the three most important piazzas (see below).

ESSENTIALS

GETTING THERE   By Train   Noto is reached by trains (usually nine per day) heading southwest from Syracuse, which has good rail connections with the rest of Italy. The ride takes 30 minutes and costs 3.10€ ($4.05) one-way. The train station is on Via Principe di Piemonte, a 20-minute walk west of the historic core. For schedules, call © **892021.**

By Bus   Interbus (© **0931-66710**) offers 13 buses per day from Syracuse; the trip takes 50 minutes and costs 4€ ($5.20) one-way. The bus station is on Piazzale Marconi, near Giardini Pubblici just east of the center, a 5-minute walk to Porta Reale and the main street, Corso Vittorio Emanuele.

By Car   Head southwest along Route 115.

VISITOR INFORMATION   To get your bearings, stop first at the **tourist office,** at Via Gioberti 13 (© **0931-836503**), to pick up a map. Open from May to September, daily 9am to 1pm and 3:30 to 6:30pm; October to March, Monday to Friday 8am to 2pm and 3:30 to 6:30pm.

STROLLING THROUGH A BAROQUE CITY

The main thoroughfare, **Corso Vittorio Emanuele,** cuts through a trio of squares, each with its own church. The main axis begins at **Porta Reale,** a giant gateway to Noto patterned on a Roman-style triumphal arch, except this one dates from the 19th century rather than ancient times. The three squares are Piazza Immacolata, Piazza Municipio, and Piazza XVI Maggio.

If it's a hot day, you can rest in the **Giardini Pubblici,** immediately to the right of Porta Reale opening onto Viale Marconi. These public gardens are filled with palm trees and flowering bougainvillea. Don't bother trying to figure out all those local figures honored by marble busts. Even most of the people of Noto today have forgotten those men of dubious achievement.

Heading west on Corso Vittorio Emanuele, you'll first approach **Piazza Immacolata.** The square is dominated by the handsome facade of **Chiesa di San Francesco all'Immacolata** (© **0931-573192**), which contains notable artworks rescued from a Franciscan church in the old town. The major work of art here is a painted wooden *Madonna and Child* from 1564, believed to be the work of Antonio Monachello. The most impressive aspect of this church is its grandiose flight of steps. Open daily from 8:30am to noon and 4 to 7:30pm.

Immediately to the right of the church as you face it is the **Monastereo del Santissimo Salvatore,** which can be admired from the outside. The building, today a seminary, is characterized by windows adorned with "potbellied" wrought-iron balconies. The elegant tower is the hallmark of the fine 18th-century facade.

Like Venice, a City in Peril

The collapse of the dome of the Duomo in 1996 sent a dangerous signal racing through this little baroque city. After centuries of decay and neglect, the monuments of Noto are in grave danger. Complicating matters, much of the regional material—white tufa stone—is soft, and it was not meant to last through the ages like marble; unless it is constantly maintained, it can rapidly deteriorate. The only reason many of the buildings of Noto are still standing is because of wooden supports, and for some buildings it looks as if scaffolding is here to stay. Noto is hampered by lack of money, even though restoration is proceeding—but at a snail's pace, in some critics' view. What's the hope? That Noto will be approved as an addition to UNESCO's World Heritage Site list. This would mean funds for ongoing restoration. Until enough money is found, Noto continues to decline, with many of its most precious monuments in peril.

The next square is **Piazza Municipio ★**, the most majestic of the trio. It's dominated by the **Palazzo Ducezio,** a graceful town hall with curvilinear elements enclosed by a classical portico. The upper section of this palace was added as late as the 1950s. Its most beautiful room is the Louis XI–style **Salone di Rappresentanza (Hall of Representation),** decorated with gold and stucco. On the vault is a Mazza fresco representing the mythological figure of Ducezio founding Neas (the ancient name of Noto). The custodian will usually allow you a look around on the ground level during regular business hours; admission is free.

On one side of the square, a broad flight of steps leads to the **Duomo,** flanked by two lovely horseshoe-shaped hedges. The cathedral was inspired by models of Borromini's churches in Rome and was completed in 1776. In 1996, the dome collapsed, destroying a large section of the nave, and it's still under repair.

On the far side of the cathedral is the **Palazzo Villadorata,** graced with a classic facade. Its six extravagant **balconies ★★** are supported by sculpted buttresses of galloping horses, griffins, and grotesque bald and bearded figures with chubby-cheeked cherubs at their bellies. The palazzo is divided into 90 rooms, the most beautiful being the **Salone Giallo (Yellow Hall),** the **Salone Verde (Green Hall),** and the **Salone Rosso (Red Hall),** with their precious frescoed domes from the 18th century. The charming **Salone delle Feste (Feasts Hall)** is dominated by a fresco representing mythological scenes. In one of its aisles, the palazzo contains a *pinacoteca* **(picture gallery)** with antique manuscripts, rare books, and portraits of noble families. The building is under renovation and its status can change suddenly; check with the visitor center before heading here, or call ✆ **0931-573779** for up-to-date information.

The final main square is **Piazza XVI Maggio,** dominated by the convex facade of **Chiesa di San Domenico ★,** with two tiers of columns separated by a high cornice. The interior is filled with polychrome marble altars, but the church appears to have been shut indefinitely as it's in really bad shape. At least you can admire its facade. Directly in front of the church is a public garden, the **Villetta d'Ercole,** named for its 18th-century fountain honoring Hercules.

Right off Corso Vittorio Emanuele is one of Noto's most fascinating streets, **Via Nicolaci** ★, lined with magnificent baroque buildings.

In summer, Noto is also known for some fine **beaches** nearby; the best are 6km (3³/₄ miles) away at **Noto Marina**. You can catch a bus at the Giardini Pubblici in Noto; the one-way fare is 3€ ($3.90). Call ✆ **0931-836123** for schedules.

WHERE TO STAY

Camere Belvedere   Set at the highest elevation of the historic district, this elegant stone structure opens onto the "balcony of the city," a short walk from the crumbling Duomo. From its terrace, you're treated to a panoramic view of the baroque city, and on a clear day, you can see all the way to the seashore at Noto Marina and up to Portopalo, the extreme southeastern tip of the island. Constructed of ancient stones from other buildings, the belvedere is traditional all the way. Its guest rooms are sparsely furnished yet comfortable, resting for the most part under wood-beamed ceilings. Even though it's in the middle of a town, there is a rustic aura to this place.

Piazza Perelli Cippo 1, 96017 Noto. ✆/fax **0931-573820.** www.camerebelvedere.com. 4 units. 55€–65€ ($72–$85) double. Rates include continental breakfast. No credit cards. Free street parking. **Amenities:** Bar; breakfast room; solarium. *In room:* A/C, minibar.

La Sumalia Residence Ⓕⁱⁿᵈˢ   This ancient mansion, a real discovery, lies in the hills less than 1km (¹/₂ mile) from the center of Noto. From its perch, a panoramic view of the Gulf of Noto and the town unfolds. The property, which dominates a valley planted with almond and olive trees, has been restored and renovated with a number of its original architectural features intact. The small guest rooms have wood-beamed ceilings; rustic, comfortable furnishings; and small, shower-only bathrooms. Guests can take breakfast on the terrace and use the communal kitchen.

Contrada San Giovanni, 96017 Noto. ✆/fax **0931-894292.** www.lasumasumalia.com. 5 units. 60€–80€ ($78–$104) double. Rates include continental breakfast. AE, DC, MC, V. Buses depart from Piazza Marconi in Noto for Contrada San Giovanni. Free parking. **Amenities:** Bar. *In room:* A/C, TV, no phone.

Villa Canisello ★ Ⓕⁱⁿᵈˢ   Surrounded by lush vegetation, this offbeat discovery offers the chance to stay in a restored 19th-century farmhouse just a 10-minute walk from the historic core of Noto. You'll enter a world of peace and tranquillity here. The property has been restored with sensitivity, with tasteful decor throughout. The lounge in the garden is used as a reading room as well, and the public rooms display local crafts. Guest rooms are small but beautifully kept, each with a private entrance and a small, shower-only bathroom.

Via Pavese 1, 96017 Noto. ✆ **0931-835793.** Fax 0931-837700. www.villacanisello.it. 7 units. 75€–80€ ($98–$104) double. Rates include buffet breakfast. No credit cards. Free parking. **Amenities:** Bar; breakfast room. *In room:* A/C in some, TV, fridge, no phone.

Villa Favorita/Villa Giulia ★ Ⓕⁱⁿᵈˢ   These two 18th-century residences have been beautifully restored and filled with modern comforts. Located between Noto and Noto Marina (the beach area), they provide the best-equipped lodgings in the area. Under the same management, and very similar in style, they actually lie 10km (6¹/₄ miles) apart, but on the same road. Palm trees grace the grounds, and the look is one of elegance and serenity. Guest rooms are comfortably though somewhat austerely furnished. The dining rooms are handsomely appointed, and the cuisine of regional and international dishes is some of the best in the area.

The Sweetest Tooth in all of Sicily

The denizens of Noto are said to love sugary concoctions and confections more so than people anywhere else in Sicily. To satisfy that need they are celebrated for their marzipan and often for their ice creams. The town's leading pastry shop is the amusingly named **Mandorio in Fiore** ★★, or "almond in bloom." It stands at Via Ducezio 2 (✆ **0931-836615**), close to the Church of Saint Carmine. Dozens of cakes are on sale, along with sweet cookies and a huge array of candied fruits. Locals flock here for the famous Sicilian *cassata,* among the best we've had on the island. Another delight is the **Pasticceria La Fontana Vecchia,** Corso Vittorio Emanuele 150 (✆ **0931-839412**), whose specialty is *panedi spagna* or sponge cake. It's filled with a sweet ricotta, and the ice cream here pleases the most demanding gelato aficionados.

Contrada Falconara, 96017 Noto. ✆ **0931-820219.** Fax 0931-820220. www.villafavoritanoto.it. 73 units. 110€–180€ ($143–$234) double. Rates include buffet breakfast. AE, DC, MC, V. Free parking. From May–Sept, a bus leaves Piazza Marconi in Noto and heads for Marina di Noto, stopping at both hotels. Free parking. **Amenities:** Restaurant; bar; outdoor pool; room service; rooms for those w/limited mobility. *In room:* A/C, TV.

Villa Mediterranea ★   This is your best bet if you'd prefer to visit historic Noto on a day trip but stay on the best beach while in the area. This cozy hotel is set right along the seafront, in its own gardens with a pool. The beach is accessible through a private gate. The public lounges are stylishly furnished. Guest rooms contain comfortable beds, tiled floors, and tidy shower-only bathrooms. In the tradition of beach hotels, there is no attempt to overdecorate here.

Viale Lido, 96017 Noto Marina. ✆/fax **0931-812330.** www.villamediterranea.it. 15 units. 80€–150€ ($104–$195) double. Rates include buffet breakfast. AE, DC, MC, V. Free parking. Closed Nov–Mar. **Amenities:** Bar; outdoor pool; laundry service; dry cleaning. *In room:* A/C, TV, safe.

WHERE TO DINE

Al Buco ★ (Finds) SICILIAN   This restaurant is easy to reach, positioned only a few steps downhill from the town's main thoroughfare, Corso Vittorio Emanuele. Descend a flight of modern marble steps into a simply furnished interior that's kept cool by thick masonry walls and a location that's partially below the street's grade. The deep-fried zucchini blossoms here are the best we've ever had in Sicily. Fresh grilled tuna is a delight in its simplicity. Japan meets Sicily in the raw swordfish marinated in citrus sauce. Meat eaters don't get the same loving care fish devotees do, although steaks are good and served in a pepper cream sauce.

Via Giuseppe Zanardelli 17. ✆ **0931-838142.** Reservations recommended. Main courses 8€–14€ ($10–$18). MC, V. Sun–Fri noon–3:30pm and 7pm–midnight.

NOTO AFTER DARK

Café Sicilia   Small-scale, cozy, and prefaced with outdoor chairs and tables, this is Noto's most enduring cafe/bar. Part of its allure comes from architectural adornments in place since 1892. Its clientele seems reluctant to take coffee or drinks anywhere else. The absolutely luscious pastries include a bomb-shaped *savarin al Marsala.* Jars of Sicilian honey and liqueurs are available for sale. Corso Vittorio Emanuele 125. ✆ **0931-835013.**

La Fontana Vecchia Set at the monumental end of Noto's main walkway, this popular and well-positioned bar has a huge terrace and a reputation for being mobbed most evenings after sunset. Established in 1996, but with a turn-of-the-20th-century design that might make you think it's much older, it has a helpful and good-looking staff, a wide selection of cocktails, and *granite* that taste fantastic when a scoop is dissolved in soda water. Open April to September, daily 7am to midnight, and October to March, daily 7am to 10pm. Corso Vittorio Emanuele 150. © **0931-839412.**

SIDE TRIPS FROM NOTO

CAVA GRANDE DEL CASSIBILE ★★ The "Grand Canyon of Sicily" is a bit of a misnomer, but this remote section of the Iblei mountain range attracts hikers and nature buffs alike. To reach the site, drive north of Noto for 19km (12 miles) on Route 287 in the direction of the town of Palazzolo Acreide. When you reach the village of Villa Vela, with its Art Nouveau villas, you will be near the gorge's site. A little secondary road is signposted to Cava Grande. Go to the end of the road, where there is a car park with a stunning **panoramic vista ★** over the Cava Grande gorge: a canyon 250m (820 ft.) deep and some 10km (6¼ miles) long between towering limestone cliffs.

The ancients used the gorge as a burial ground, and thousands of tombs have been discovered here, dating from the 11th to the 9th century B.C. The most important artifacts were removed and taken to Syracuse museums.

If you descend into the gorge, allow at least 45 careful minutes. Figure on doubling your time for the climb back. The most stunning aspect of Cava Grande is a series of **natural rock pools ★** that were created by the Cassibilie River. You can swim, if you like. On a hot day, it's possibly the most refreshing place to be in inland Sicily. The site is always open.

ELORO The countryside surrounding this ancient city is lonely and lovely today, but it was one of the first cities founded by Syracuse back in the 7th century B.C. The location, overlooking the sea, is even more idyllic because it's set on a hill near the mouth of the Tellaro River.

What remains today only vaguely suggests what the little city must have looked like in its heyday. The ruins are in the early stages of excavation. So far, a bit of the ancient city walls have been unearthed. You can also see the ruins of a temple dedicated to Demeter (Ceres in Roman mythology). In the direction of the river lie the ruins of a theater that have also been dug out. The foundation of a temple believed to have been dedicated to Asclepius can also be viewed.

The admission-free site is open Monday to Saturday 8am to 1 hour before sunset. To reach it by car, drive 11km (6¾ miles) southeast of Noto. Follow the signposts to the beach town of Noto Marina. Eloro lies immediately to the south.

VILLA DEL TELLARO In 1972, a Roman villa dating from the 4th century A.D. was discovered with some of its magnificent polychrome mosaics still intact. Its location is 7km (4⅓ miles) west of the principal Noto/Pachino highway beside the Tellaro River. It is believed that this villa was once as richly adorned as the celebrated Villa Romana del Casale in the vicinity of Piazza Armerina (p. 280).

Constructed around a square peristyle, the building was obviously occupied by someone who had a lot of money and a taste for the exotic. The mosaics depict everything from erotica to the slaying of animals during a hunt.

Only the most serious archaeologists may want to seek out this place, which is located near the village of Caddeddi, signposted 1km (¹/₂ mile) off the main road. The ruins of the villa lie beneath a farmhouse. The farmer will show you through; a tip is expected. If you drop in, arrive at a reasonable hour (9am–4pm).

RISERVA NATURALE DI VENDICARI ★★   Created as a government-protected nature reserve in 1984, this stretch of coast south of the Tellaro River is one of the most beautiful spots in southeastern Sicily. Open daily 9am to dusk, with free entry, it covers 574 hectares (1,418 acres) of lovely marshland that is an oasis for migratory birds and serious birders. Guides are available at the **office** (© **0931-67450**) at the park entrance.

What you see depends on the season. In winter, all sorts of ducks can be spotted, ranging from the mallard to the red-crested pochard. In fall, you'll see the white egret, black stork, and even European flamingo. Most birds only check in and then fly away to other climes, with the exception of the black-winged stilt, the Kentish plover, and the reed warbler, which all breed here.

The reserve is always open, but it's best to go in the early morning or closer to twilight; don't forget binoculars. To get here from Noto, drive southeast to the coast. Then take the road south—signposted PACHINO—until you come to the marked entrance to the reserve.

If you first visited Eloro (see above), continue driving south for 5km (3 miles), where you'll see the **Torre Vendicari,** an abandoned Norman tower. This artifact from Sicily's conquerors of yesterday overlooks a beautiful crescent of golden sand near old salt pans. It's a great place to log some time on the beach.

Motorists with the time can continue all the way to the extreme southeastern tip of Sicily, at **Capo Passero.** You'll pass first through the pleasant town of Pachino before reaching the cape, which lies 7km (4¹/₃ miles) south of Pachino. A major tuna fishing grounds, the cape rewards visitors with a **panoramic view ★★** out to sea.

Ragusa & Piazza Armerina

Few foreign visitors cut into the inland trails of central Sicily to discover the treasures they hold. Sicily's coastline, with its Greek ruins, ancient cities, and fabulous beaches, is just too alluring, especially on a hot summer day. But even a short visit will give you a taste of the mountainous interior of this fascinating island, a land that is more representative of traditional Sicily than its port towns and villages.

In this short jaunt, we penetrate the wilds of central Sicily to discover one of the grandest Roman villas ever unearthed. Celebrated for its stunning mosaics, **Villa Romana del Casale,** outside the town of **Piazza Armerina,** is definitely worth the trek inland. It's one of the highlights of antiquity and may be Sicily's greatest single man-made attraction.

For another look at inland Sicily, visit the two cities of **Ragusa Superiore** and **Ragusa Ibla.** After Noto, Ragusa Ibla is one of the most stellar examples of the Sicilian baroque.

1 RAGUSA ★

267km (166 miles) SE of Palermo, 138km (86 miles) E of Agrigento, 104km (65 miles) SW of Catania, 79km (49 miles) SW of Syracuse

Ragusa is really two towns in one: an upper town, **Ragusa Superiore,** mapped out after a devastating earthquake in 1693, and **Ragusa Ibla,** constructed on an isolated spur. Ibla, in glaring contrast to the modern city, is one of the best-preserved old towns in Sicily, and well worth a day of your valuable time. The two parts of town are linked by a steep winding road or else by steps. Even if Ragusa Ibla weren't fascinating, the site would make an interesting trip because of the craggy valley that separates the two towns. It is a vista of winding pathways and plant-filled cliffs.

From the twin towns, panoramas of the countryside unfold. The landscapes around Ragusa are among the most memorable (and eerie) in Sicily. Many are crisscrossed with low-lying stone walls, pieced laboriously together without mortar, and lying in impoverished solitude beneath the punishing sun. These are the landscapes most often evoked in Sicilian literature and cinema, an oft-filmed terrain that has positioned Ragusa and its outlying districts in the forefront of Italian filmmaking.

If all this weren't enough, you can take a 25km (16-mile) drive to **Marina di Ragusa,** a thriving beach resort. Many visitors prefer to anchor here, visiting Ragusa Ibla for the day. Unlike the historic core of Ragusa Ibla, Marina di Ragusa is relatively modern, with its long, narrow, and unusually sandy beach strip. A boardwalk is lined with shops, bars, and restaurants. A party atmosphere prevails here in summer, when, by 10pm, the action is just getting started.

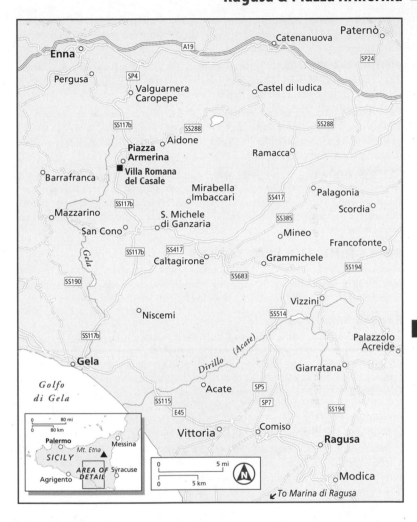

ESSENTIALS

GETTING THERE   From the east, Syracuse is often the rail gateway into Ragusa, with three trains per day making the 2-hour journey for a cost of 7.05€ ($9.15) one-way. It's also possible to take one of three trains per day from Palermo; the 6-hour trip costs 14€ ($18) one-way. There are no direct trains from Palermo—it is necessary to change trains in Caltanissetta or Gela.

Ragusa also has a bus link with Syracuse. **AST** (℗ **0932-681818**) runs seven buses per day on the 2-hour run; the fare is 5.80€ ($7.55) one-way.

The train and bus stations in Ragusa are at Piazza del Popolo and the adjoining Piazza Gramsci.

Motorists touring southeastern Sicily who visited Noto (p. 265) can continue southwest along Route 115 to the town of Ispica, at which point the highway swings northwest toward Ragusa.

VISITOR INFORMATION   The **tourist office,** Via Capitano Bocchieri 33 (© **0932-221511**), is open Monday, Wednesday, and Friday 9am to 1:30pm and Tuesday and Thursday 9am to 1:30pm and 4 to 6pm.

FAST FACTS   In case of **emergency,** dial © **113.** For a **medical emergency,** dial © **118.** The local hospital is **Ospedale Civile,** Via da Vinci (© **0932-600111**). Call the **police** at © **112.** The **post office,** at Piazza Matteotti (© **0932-232287**), is open Monday to Saturday 8am to 6:30pm.

GETTING AROUND   If you don't want to make the steep climb linking Ibla with Superiore, you can take city bus no. 3 departing from in front of the cathedral or from Piazza del Popolo; the fare is .80€ ($1.05) one-way. It's a hair-raising ride. The bus will let you off in Ibla at Piazza Pola or Giardini Iblei, most central for exploring the medieval and baroque town.

EXPLORING THE TWO TOWNS

If your time is limited, you can skip the upper town (Ragusa Superiore) and spend all your hours in Ragusa Ibla, as the older town holds far more intrigue. Those with more time can hike through the upper town, looking for the attractions that follow.

Ragusa Superiore

The long main street, **Corso Italia,** cuts through the upper town and makes for Ragusa's best promenade. The main attraction here is **Cattedrale di San Giovanni,** Via Roma 134 (© **0932-621658**), dating from the 18th century and dedicated to St. John the Baptist. Pause on the elegant square in front of the cathedral and look uphill to admire its decorative facade, which is made asymmetrical by a campanile on its western side. Its front elevation contains a wide terrace. The inside is ornate, especially the stucco decorations in the cupola. The Latin cross interior is notable for its two orders of pillars, each made of locally quarried asphaltite. Open daily 8:30am to noon and 4 to 7pm.

Museo Archeologico Regionale Ibleo, Palazzo Mediterraneo, Via Natalelli (© **0932-622963**), lies off Via Roma, within an easy walk of the Duomo, near the Ponte Nuovo bridge. The museum is rich in artifacts unearthed from ancient colonies in the province. The collection is at its best in remnants of the civilization that flourished in Greek days at Rovine di Camarina, 16km (10 miles) northwest of Marina di Ragusa. Assaulted by the Carthaginians, the colony was finally leveled by the Romans as early as 598 B.C. Some of the artifacts at the museum in Ragusa are from a temple here once dedicated to Athena. Various necropolis reconstructions hold great interest. Hours are daily 9am to 1:30pm and 4 to 7:30pm; admission is 2.10€ ($2.75).

Ragusa Ibla ★★

We prefer to reach the old town by taking a long stairway, **Santa Maria delle Scale ★,** heading down from Ragusa Superiore to the historic core of Ibla. Take this walk for the **panoramic vistas ★★** alone, some of the finest in southeastern Sicily.

Admittedly, the town is in deep decay, but it's a nostalgic remnant of yesteryear. Wander its narrow streets, checking out its crumbling baroque palaces.

Head east until you come to the **Duomo di San Giorgio ★**, Piazza del Duomo (✆ **0932-220085**), which is open daily 9am to noon and 4 to 7pm. Characterized by an impressive neoclassical dome, this is one of the best examples of Sicilian baroque in the south of Sicily, dating from the 18th century. The facade is a trio of tiers and looks like nothing so much as a glamorous wedding cake. In contrast, the interior may come as a disappointment, as it's quite plain.

Continuing east from the Duomo, you'll come to the **Chiesa di San Giuseppe ★**, Via Torre Nuova 19 (✆ **0932-621779**), open daily from 9am to noon and 4 to 6pm. It dates from 1590, and its oval-domed interior contains beautiful galleries and striking pavement crafted of black asphalt interspersed with majolica tiles. Among the notable artworks is the painting *Glory of St. Benedict,* by Sebastiano Lo Monaco (1793).

If you continue walking all the way east through Ragusa Ibla, you'll reach beautiful public gardens, **Giardino Obleo ★**, which are studded with religious buildings, notably **Chiesa di San Giacomo,** dating from the 14th century. It was struck by a 1693 earthquake, and much of the damage was never repaired. If it's open, you'll get to see a beautiful **triptych ★** by Pietro Novelli, depicting the Madonna flanked by St. Agatha and St. Lucy.

At the edge of the gardens, enjoy the **panoramic view ★** sweeping across the Valley of Irminio. The gardens are the perfect place for a picnic and can be visited daily from 8am to 8pm; there's no entry fee.

WHERE TO STAY

Ragusa Superiore

Mediterraneo Palace ★ A healthy hike from the center of medieval Ragusa, this government-rated four-star hotel is a boxy concrete structure, but it's the finest lodging for miles around. It offers a high level of comfort, with attractively and comfortably furnished guest rooms. The decor is so modernized and minimalist that you could be anywhere from Nigeria to Alaska. Those who like to eat in will find decent on-site dining and drinking facilities.

Via Roma 189, 97100 Ragusa. ✆ **0932-621944.** Fax 0932-623799. www.mediterraneopalace.it. 92 units. 139€ ($181) double; 278€ ($361) suite. AE, DC, MC, V. Parking 12€ ($16). **Amenities:** Restaurant; bar; room service; laundry service; dry cleaning; nonsmoking rooms; rooms for those w/limited mobility. *In room:* A/C, TV, minibar, hair dryer.

Montreal Set in the modern part of Ragusa, a hellish climb from the medieval quarter, this completely renovated hotel is short on style but big on creature comforts. The location is 10 minutes by car from the baroque-style Ragusa Ibla, the historic center. Guest rooms are without frills but contain sturdy furniture and small tiled bathrooms. The Montreal is a favorite with businesspeople visiting Ragusa to hawk their wares.

Via San Giuseppe 8 (at Corso Italia), 97100 Ragusa. ✆/fax **0932-621133.** www.chshotels.com. 50 units. 90€ ($117) double; 110€ ($143) triple. AE, DC, MC, V. Parking 8€ ($10). **Amenities:** Restaurant; bar; room service; laundry service; dry cleaning; nonsmoking rooms; rooms for those w/limited mobility. *In room:* A/C, TV, minibar.

Marina Di Ragusa

Eremo della Giubiliana ★★ (Finds About .6km (¹/₄ mile) inland from the barren highway, midway between Ragusa (7km/4¹/₂ miles to the north) and Marina di Ragusa, this stone estate is set in sun-blasted solitude against a landscape crisscrossed with low limestone walls. Maintained by local tenant farmers for at least a thousand years, the walls enclose grazing lands for cows and sheep. No other hotel we've seen in Sicily is as deceptive in the way it contrasts a baronial, severely dignified exterior with a walled-in compound of verdant greenery and lighthearted posh. Inside the compound, expect water fountains, lemon and almond trees, a kitchen garden burgeoning with life, and a truly unusual restaurant (p. 278).

To enter the compound, which functioned as a fortified monastery during the 1400s, you must navigate some signposted country roads that meander between the aforementioned stone walls, across a parched landscape that hasn't changed much in 300 years. After shouting your name into a microphone, you and your car will be "buzzed" in through massive iron gates that swing open soundlessly to reveal a walled-in world that might have been the home of a forbidding Sicilian don during the 19th century. Today, it's a warm, historically poignant hotel of discreet luxury and meticulous architectural detail. Guest rooms are cozy and as artfully authentic as rooms in a private home.

This is the only hotel in Sicily that maintains a private airstrip. One-day airborne excursions to offshore islands such as Lampedusa and Pantelleria cost 500€ ($650) for up to three passengers, with a chauffeured private car and lunch on the islands included.

Contrada Giubiliana, 97100 Ragusa. ✆ **0932-669119.** Fax 0932-669129. www.eremodellagiubiliana.it. 11 units and 5 self-contained cottages. 260€ ($338) double; 480€ ($624) suite; 220€ ($286) cottage. Half board (breakfast and dinner) 270€ ($351) for 2 persons in double or triple, 280€ ($364) in cottage. Rates include buffet breakfast. AE, DC, MC, V. From Ragusa, take SP25 southwest toward Marina di Ragusa. Eremo is signposted at Km 7. **Amenities:** Restaurant; bar; outdoor pool; laundry service; dry cleaning. *In room:* A/C, TV.

Hotel Terraqua ★   This is the most appealing hotel in the seaside resort of Marina di Ragusa. Configured as a cement-and-glass cube dotted with balconies, it was built in the 1980s, and identifies itself mainly as a beachfront hotel with clean rooms and frequent breezes. It usually shows its guests a good, albeit somewhat anonymous, time. Don't expect any personalized service from the staff—they're familiar with hordes of vacationers coming and going. But as a base for exploration of the neighborhood, including Ragusa Ibla, the hotel is a worthwhile choice. Guest rooms have tile floors and a beachgoing simplicity. The hotel is not directly on the sands of the beach—it's inside its own walled garden, a 5-minute walk from the water. It also has the best and biggest pool in town.

Via delle Sirene 35, 97010 Marina di Ragusa. ✆ **0932-615600.** Fax 0932-615580. www.hotelterraqua. com. 77 units. 120€–160€ ($156–$208) double; 160€–200€ ($208–$260) junior suite. Rates include buffet breakfast. AE, DC, MC, V. Free parking. **Amenities:** Restaurant; bar; outdoor pool; tennis court; outdoor Jacuzzi; babysitting; laundry service; dry cleaning; solarium. *In room:* A/C, TV, minibar, hair dryer.

WHERE TO DINE
Ragusa Superiore
Baglio La Pergola ★ SICILIAN   This elegant restaurant offers the finest dining in the modern town of Ragusa. It's decorated in a style evocative of the late 19th century, with a Belle Epoque aura, marble floors, and comfortable chairs. Dishes are full of flavor and prepared with a certain flair, as exemplified by the swordfish in lemon sauce with capers and toasted pine nuts. Succulent ravioli is filled with porcini mushrooms, chestnuts, ricotta cheese, and a whiff of marjoram. The best tortellini in town is served here, with fresh shrimp and a saffron sauce. Other tasty dishes include ricciola (a local fish) cooked with a pistachio crust and fennel, or else cannelloni with basil, ricotta, and mozzarella.

Contrada Selvaggio. ✆ **0932-686430.** Reservations recommended. Main courses 8€–15€ ($10–$20); fixed-price menus 25€–30€ ($33–$39). AE, MC, V. Wed–Mon noon–2:30pm and 8–11:30pm.

Il Barocco SICILIAN   The name comes from the elaborate baroque-style doorway, crafted in the 1600s, that dominates the restaurant's small, high-ceilinged dining room. (In fact, you might get the impression that the restaurant is rather uncomfortably crammed into the anteroom of a very grand *palazzo* or church.) Tiles and wrought iron decorate the interior, and plastic tables and chairs spill onto the pavement in front. Menu items are not as creative as what visitors will find at either of Ragusa's more prestigious eateries (Il Duomo and Locanda don Serafino), and the staff can be blasé, but food items are flavorful and filling. The best examples include lamb cutlets, crepes with ricotta and spinach, and a dessert specialty of orange mousse. The chef is also known for three of his pasta dishes—lasagna with pumpkin and ricotta; cavati with broccoli and anchovies; and tagliatelle with zucchini and sausage. *Note:* Don't confuse this restaurant with the gelateria, under the same name and management, about a block downhill.

Via Orfanotrofio 29. ℂ **0932-652397.** Reservations recommended. Main courses 8€–15€ ($10–$20). AE, DC, MC, V. Thurs–Tues 12:30–2:30pm and 7:30pm–midnight.

Il Duomo ★★★ SICILIAN   With its newly awarded Michelin stars, this restaurant is now one of the finest in Sicily—its devotees say *the* best. It lies on an impossibly narrow street, uphill and about a block behind the cathedral. Inside, the small rooms are outfitted like private parlors in a 19th-century country-Victorian style, some with views that sweep over the dry hillsides of southern Sicily. Come here for the intensely patriotic cuisine of Ciccio Sultano, a native *Ragusano* who commits himself passionately to the perpetuation of old-time traditions. Several varieties of bread are baked each day, using old-fashioned, increasingly hard-to-find strains of wheat. At least 20 types of olive oil are on display, and if you ask for help, a staff member will advise you on which variety is best with which particular bread or platter. Menus are based on the changing seasons, and many dishes make ample use of such local products as cherry tomatoes, pistachios, bitter almonds, wild fennel, and mint. Believe it or not, one of the most praised specialties is roasted baby pig with a chocolate sauce that has been caramelized with Marsala wine. One of the most succulent pastas is studded with freshly caught tuna and zucchini and served with a savory herb-laden pesto sauce.

Via Bocchieri 31. ℂ **0932-651265.** Reservations recommended. Main courses 9€–19€ ($12–$25); fixed-price menus 110€–120€ ($143–$156). AE, DC, MC, V. Aug Sun noon–2:30pm; July–Sept Mon 7–11pm, Tues–Sat noon–2:30pm and 7–11pm.

La Bettola SICILIAN   A short walk through narrow winding streets from the town's cathedral, this restaurant shows few hints of any changes that might have been made since the days of Mussolini. That, coupled with the 1940s-era decor, provides much of its charm. Tables and chairs are arranged on a large piazza in front, amid potted flowers and ample doses of old-fashioned Italy. The chef often tells diners to leave matters in his own hands, and he'll compose a meal for you—perhaps fresh ricotta followed by a tender, herb-infused chicken breast with delectable roulades stuffed with ham and onions.

Largo Camerina 7. ℂ **0932-653377.** Reservations recommended. Main courses 7€–10€ ($9.10–$13). MC, V. Mon–Sat 12:30–2:30pm and 7:30–11:30pm.

Locanda Don Serafino ★★ SICILIAN   This fine restaurant is set in a 17th-century palace in a labyrinth of intricately vaulted cellars, where the temperature remains cool in summer and comfortable even on the coldest days of winter. Any of the lavishly decorated tables presents a charming venue for lunch or dinner, but the most awe-inspiring are found in the deepest part of the labyrinth, a monastic-looking stone-sided room lined with wines selected personally by the owner. You'll enjoy dishes that may include *zuppa di pesce don Serafino;* spaghetti with sea urchins, ricotta, and squid; fresh fish cooked to perfection, and herb-and-garlic-infused lamb cutlets. In July and August, the restaurant does not serve lunch Monday to Wednesday.

Via Orfanotrofio 39. ② **0932-248778.** Reservations recommended. Main courses 18€–25€ ($23–$33); fixed-price menu 73€ ($95). DC, MC, V. Wed–Mon 12:30–2:30pm and 5:30–11:30pm.

Marina Di Ragusa

Eremo della Giubiliana SICILIAN   Even if an overnight stay at this hotel isn't practical, we heartily recommend it for its fine cuisine and its eerily antique location. The setting is inside a walled compound that originated in the 1400s as a fortified monastery and later evolved into a manorial home for some very tenacious landowners. Meticulously restored to its full limestone glory, and permeated with a discreet poshness, it serves well-prepared meals in a high-ceilinged room whose massive timbers are supported by soaring masonry arches. Lunches are relatively simple, consisting of a medley of omelets, salads, and focaccia (sandwiches stuffed with smoked fish, prosciutto, or local cheeses). Dinners are more elaborate, featuring *orecchiette* (one of their homemade pastas) with walnut sauce; roasted quail with spices; couscous; tuna carpaccio; and fresh salads usually culled from the hotel's walled-in garden. Come here as much for the sightseeing as for the food, and make an effort to see the surrounding landscape in the glare of daylight.

Contrada Giubiliana. ② **0932-669119.** Reservations recommended. Main courses 8€–16€ ($10–$21); lunch platters 6€–10€ ($7.80–$13); fixed-price Sun lunch 50€ ($65). AE, DC, MC, V. Daily 1–3pm and 7:30–10pm.

Ristorante/Pizzeria La Falena Value SICILIAN   Short on style but good in the kitchen, this rustic *trattoria* is known for its fresh fish, tasty pizzas, and welcoming reception. It attracts a beach-loving crowd for home-style dining, indoors or out. Quality ingredients go into the pasta with shrimp and arugula, the tortellini with ham and cream, and the savory rice dish with fresh shrimp, mussels, virgin olive oil, and garlic.

Via Porto Venere. ② **0932-239321.** Reservations required Sat–Sun. Main courses 8€–14€ ($10–$18). AE, DC, MC, V. Wed–Mon 12:30–2:30pm and 7:30pm–12:30am. Closed Jan.

RAGUSA AFTER DARK

Ragusa Ibla

Belle Epoque   Set in a tucked-away corner of the square directly in front of the cathedral, this place will welcome you for either daytime gelato or nighttime beer and cocktails. The homemade ice creams are likely to include *nocciola* (hazelnut), *pesca* (peach), and *arancia* (orange). From July to September, it's open daily 7am to 11pm or later. The rest of the year, it's closed on Monday. Via Convento, near Piazza Duomo. ② **0339-7528402.**

Marina Di Ragusa

Victoria Pub   Set directly across the street from the beach, this is the largest pub in Marina di Ragusa and one of the most whimsically decorated. The pseudo-Victorian decor includes pithy quotes from Shakespeare, expired New Jersey license plates, and banners advertising everything from Jack Daniel's to Newcastle Ale. The crowd tends to be young, on the make, and into rock 'n' roll. Open April to October, nightly 10pm to 4am; November to March, Saturday and Sunday 8pm to 4am. Lungomare Andrea Doria 20. ② **0339-2409247.**

2 PIAZZA ARMERINA

84km (52 miles) SW of Catania, 181km (112 miles) SW of Messina, 164km (102 miles) SE of Palermo, 103km (64 miles) NW of Ragusa, 134km (83 miles) NW of Syracuse

Art lovers journey from all over Europe and America to see the ruins of an extraordinary Roman villa at Casale, basing themselves in the little town of Piazza Armerina. Once known only as "Piazza," the town gets its name from Colle Armerino, one of a trio of hills on which it was constructed. The town is actually two-in-one: the original "Piazza," a village that dates from the heyday of the Saracens in the 10th century; and a 15th-century "overflow" town that extends to the southeast.

Graced with impressive but decaying *palazzi,* the town itself is worth a visit for at least an hour or two, although most tour buses rush through here delivering their passengers directly to Villa Romana del Casale.

ESSENTIALS

GETTING THERE One bus a day from Syracuse makes the 3-hour trip for 9€ ($12) one-way.

If you're driving from Ragusa, where we launched our inland tour of Sicily, continue north along Route 194, following the signs to the town of Caltagirone. At the town of Vizzini, continue northwest along Route 124 to Caltagirone. From here, the road will be signposted northwest all the way to Piazza Armerina.

VISITOR INFORMATION The **tourist office,** S. Rosalia 5 (℘ **0935-683049**), is open Monday to Friday 8am to 2pm, plus Wednesday 3 to 6:30pm.

GETTING AROUND If you've arrived in Piazza Armerina by bus, you can take yet another bus (no. B) to reach the Roman villa at Casale. From April to September, **Piccola Società Cooperativa** (℘ **0935-85605**) runs buses to the site daily 9 to 11am and 4 to 6pm (trip time: 15 min.). A one-way ticket costs 2€ ($2.60).

SEEING THE SIGHTS

Piazza Armerina is set on a plateau some 700m (2,297 ft.) above sea level. The city was founded during the Norman era, and today is filled with mansions showing both baroque and Renaissance architectural influences. Its historic **medieval quarter** ★ is graced with many beautiful churches, the most impressive of which is the Duomo, crowning the highest point in town at 720m (2,364 ft.).

Duomo, Via Cavour (℘ **0935-680214**), is open daily 8:30am to noon and 3:30 to 7pm. The old town's maze of narrow streets sprouted around this cathedral. The bell tower is from 1490, a surviving architectural feature of an even earlier church. The present building was inaugurated in 1627, the facade dating from 1719 and the dome from 1768. The facade is adorned with pilasters and columns, and the grand central door is surmounted by a large, square window topped by an eagle. The interior is spacious and filled with light. Among the best-known works of art here is the *Virgin delle Vittorie* ★, above the main altar at the far end of the nave in a 17th-century tabernacle. It is believed that it was given by Pope Nicholas II to Count Roger, ruler of Sicily. An impressive **wooden cross** ★ dating from 1455 is on view in the small chapel to the left of the chancel. Its back depicts a scene of the Resurrection that has been much reproduced in art books on Sicily.

Villa Romana del Casale ★★★   Located 6km (3¹/₂ miles) from Piazza Armerina, this magnificent villa is one of the largest dwellings of its kind to have survived from the days of the Romans. Its 40 rooms are "carpeted" with 11,340 sq. m (122,063 sq. ft.) of some of the greatest, most magnificent mosaics in western Europe.

It is obvious that a wealthy patrician built this mansion, and some scholars have even suggested that it was the hunting lodge of Maximanus, the "co-emperor" of Diocletian. The exact date of the villa's construction is hard to ascertain, however—perhaps the end of the 3rd century A.D. or the beginning of the 4th century. The complex was destroyed by fire in the 12th century and over the years was buried in mudslides. Parts of the villa were unearthed in 1881.

Many of the mansion's walls are still standing, but most visitors come to take in the mosaics on the floors and the surviving wall paintings. Many of the mosaic scenes are mythological. Since this was a hunting lodge, most of the tableaux involve the pursuit of wild animals.

Rooms branch out from a central courtyard, or peristyle. Among the discernible rooms still left are the **Terme,** or steam baths, which supplied water and also heated the villa with steam circulating through cavities in the floors and walls. In the **Sala delle Unizioni,** slaves are depicted massaging the bodies of their masters.

Caltagirone: A Ceramics Side Trip

A lovely drive 30km (19 miles) southeast of Piazza Amerina takes you to **Calta-girone,** an enchanting little town that earthenware potteries built. Glazed pottery is offered at shops throughout the town, whose most celebrated attraction is **Scala di Santa Maria del Monte ★★**, a stunning set of ceramic steps leading from old town to new town. There are 142 lava stair treads graced with majolica tiles—no two alike—that evoke everything from Moorish designs to baroque patterns.

As you go along, you'll encounter **Branciforti ★**, Scala di Santa Maria del Monte 3 (𝄚 **0933/24427**), which sells stunning ceramics in deep shades of blue with swirling arabesques. To learn more about ceramics, head for the little **Museo della Ceramica,** on Via Roma (𝄚 **0933-58418**), open daily from 9am to 6:30pm and charging an admission of 3€ ($3.90). Later you can relax in the shade of the **Giardino Pubblico,** a public garden nearby.

The **tourist office** is in Palazzo Libertini, Piazza Umberto (𝄚 **0933-53809**). Parking is available in a public lot near Chiesa San Francesco di Paola, approached before you reach Piazza Umberto. You can purchase parking tickets at various bars and tobacco shops throughout town.

If you'd like to spend the night, the **Grand Hotel Villa San Mauro,** Via Portosalvo 10 (𝄚 **0933-26500**), has 91 first-class rooms for 202€ ($262) per night. The best place to eat is **La Scala,** Scala Maria Santissima del Monte 8 (𝄚 **0933-57781**), where meals cost around 35€ ($46). It's near the base of the famous stairs, and may be unique for the mountain stream running through it.

The Peristylium, directly east of the peristyle, contains the splendid **Peristylium mosaic** ★★, which can be viewed on all sides of the portico. It's a romp of birds, plants, wild animals, and domesticated creatures such as horses. Adjoining it is the **Salone del Circo** ★★, the narthex (portico) of the Terme. Its name comes from the scenes of the Roman circus depicted in its mosaics. The chariot race at Rome's Circus Maximus can clearly be seen.

Directly south of the peristyle is the **Sala della Piccola Caccia (Room of the Small Hunt)** ★★★, with mosaics depicting everything from a sacrifice to the goddess of the hunt, Diana, to the netting of a wild boar.

To the immediate west of the peristyle is the **Ambulacro della Grande Caccia (Corridor of the Great Hunt)** ★★★, measuring 60m (197 ft.). The mosaics discovered here are among the most splendid from the ancient world. One of the most dramatic scenes depicts wild animals, ranging from rhino to elephant, being loaded onto a ship.

In a salon at the northwest corner of the peristyle is the most amusing room of all: **Sala delle Dieci Ragazze (Room of the 10 Girls).** Wearing strapless two-piece bikinis, the young women are dressed for gymnastic exercises. Their outfits would be appropriate for a beach in the 21st century.

Directly north of the peristyle is the **Triclinium** ★★★, a large central space that spills into a trio of wide apses. This was probably the dining area, and it's known for its magnificent rendition of the Labors of Hercules. In the central apse, the mosaics depict "The Battle of the Giants," five mammoth creatures in their death throes after being attacked by the poisoned arrows of Hercules.

Among the final salons is the **Vestibolo del Piccolo Circo (Vestibule of the Small Circus)** ★★, or depicting circus scenes such as chariot racing; and the **Atrio degli Amorini Pescatori** ★★, with mosaics illustrating fishing scenes.

Cubicolo della Scene Erotica ★ features a polygonal medallion depicting a panting young man locked in a tight embrace with a scantily clad seductress. Yes, there is a gratuitous bottom shot.

The site is open daily from 8am to 30 minutes before sunset. Admission is 6€ ($7.80).

WHERE TO STAY

Mosaici da Battiato (see "Where to Dine," below), also rents rooms.

Hotel Ostello del Borgo   This small hotel in the historic center occupies a wing of the ancient monastery of San Giovanni, once filled with Benedictine nuns and dating from the 14th century. It is the most atmospheric place to stay in the area. The small to midsize guest rooms are well maintained and equipped with small shower-only bathrooms. All the sights, including several restaurants, lie within easy reach of the front door.

Largo San Giovanni 6, 94015 Piazza Armerina. (**0935-687019.** Fax 0935-686943. www.ostellodel borgo.it. 20 units. 60€ ($78) double; 80€ ($104) triple. Rates include continental breakfast. MC, V. **Amenities:** Breakfast room. *In room:* TV, no phone.

Park Hotel Paradiso   This modern hostelry has the best location for those who want to be near the main attraction in the area, Villa Romana del Casale. Located right outside of town and surrounded by a forest, this is a well-kept building with comfortably furnished guest rooms. Each bathroom has either a shower or a hydromassage tub. The hotel has good on-site dining and drinking facilities, so you don't have to wander around Piazza Armerina at night.

RAGUSA & PIAZZA ARMERINA

13

PIAZZA ARMERINA

Contrada da Ramaldo, 94015 Piazza Armerina. ℂ **0935-680841.** Fax 0935-683391. www.parkhotel paradiso.it. 95 units. 95€–110€ ($124–$143) double; 150€–180€ ($195–$234) suite. Rates include buffet breakfast. AE, DC, MC, V. Free parking. Located 1km (¹/₂ mile) beyond Chiesa di Sant'Andrea. **Amenities:** Restaurant; 2 bars; outdoor pool; gym; fitness center; sauna; laundry service; dry cleaning; nonsmoking rooms; solarium; rooms for those w/limited mobility. *In room:* A/C, TV, minibar, hair dryer, safe, Jacuzzi (in superior rooms).

WHERE TO DINE

Al Fogher ★ (Finds) SICILIAN   This rustic restaurant, 3km (1³/₄ miles) north of Piazza Armerina, serves dishes based on local recipes. If you like to eat well but shun flashiness, you will instinctively warm to the cuisine here. The carpaccio of swordfish or tuna will get you started off beautifully. The chef's creativity is further expressed in such dishes as risotto with pumpkin, ricotta and gooseliver seasoned with fresh rosemary, and pork in a pepper sauce under a pistachio crust. The real specialty of the house is duck breast with a champagne vinegar sauce, dried tomatoes, and a green apple mousse. Equally good is the crispy red mullet filet with cream of yellow pepper, served with black rice studded with pistachio. The wine cellar is one of the best in the area, with 400 different local and international choices.

Contrada Bellia, Strada Statale 117. ℂ **0935-684123.** Reservations recommended. Main courses 10€–35€ ($13–$46). AE, DC, MC, V. Tues–Sat 12:30–2:30pm and 8–11pm; Sun 12:30–2:30pm. Closed July 20–Aug 5.

Mosaici da Battiato SICILIAN   This classic countryside restaurant lies 3km (1³/₄ miles) west of Piazza Armerina, en route to the famous mosaics. Unless a tour group has stopped off here (a frequent occurrence), this is a good place to order some of the best homemade Sicilian dishes in the area. Begin with a delectable pennette with rich cream, fresh tomatoes, and mushrooms. The rigatoni alla Norma is another succulent choice, made with eggplant (aubergine) and vine-ripened tomatoes. Most plates are reasonably priced, except the copious meat platter of grilled specialties—for trenchermen only.

The restaurant also rents 24 well-maintained, simply furnished guest rooms, each with a shower-only bathroom. A double costs 50€ ($65); a triple room goes for 65€ ($85).

Contrada Casale Ovest. ℂ **0935-685453.** Reservations recommended. Main courses 9€–15€ ($12–$20); fixed-price menu 20€ ($32). No credit cards. Daily 1–3pm and 7–11pm.

Trattoria La Ruota SICILIAN   Opt for a table on the terrace of this atmospheric restaurant, which was created from a defunct water mill. You'll be served a typical Sicilian lunch (the only meal offered) evocative of the plains of central Sicily. The good, homemade country cooking may include tagliatelle *alla Boscaiola* (with minced beef in a zesty tomato sauce laced with cream, fresh peas, and mushrooms); stewed rabbit with olives, capers, and tomatoes; and homemade grilled pork sausages.

Contrada Casale Ovest. ℂ **0935-680542.** Reservations recommended. Main courses 6€–8€ ($7.80–$10). AE, MC, V. Daily noon–3pm.

Agrigento & Selinunte

Two of the great cities of Magna Graecia—or what's left of them—can be explored along Sicily's southern coast. Both Agrigento and Selinunte knew greater glory than they experience today, but the remains of what they used to be are still relatively rich in spite of the looters and conquerors who have passed through. Of the two, Agrigento is the far greater attraction.

Once known as the Greek city of Akragas, **Agrigento** has seen many conquerors in its day, from the Romans to Byzantines and Arabs. The year 1087 saw the arrival of the Normans.

Agrigento's remarkable series of Doric temples from the 5th century B.C. are unrivaled except in Greece itself. All of the modern encroachments, especially the hastily built and often illegal new buildings, have seriously dimmed the glory of Agrigento, but much is left to fill us with wonder.

Selinunte, in contrast, was never built over as Agrigento was, and holds extensive remains of the acropolis, though none quite equal the charm of Agrigento's Valley of the Temples.

As you stand in the midst of a carpet of mandrake, acanthus, capers, and celery growing wild at Selinunte, you'll have to work hard to imagine what the city must have looked like at the apex of its power.

1 AGRIGENTO/VALLEY OF THE TEMPLES ★★★

129km (80 miles) S of Palermo, 175km (109 miles) SE of Trapani, 217km (135 miles) W of Syracuse

Agrigento's amazing **Valley of the Temples (Valle dei Templi)** is one of the most memorable sights of the ancient world. Greek colonists from Gela (Caltanissetta) called this area Akragas when they established a beachhead in the 6th century B.C. In time, the settlement grew to become one of the most prosperous cities in Magna Graecia. A great deal of that growth is attributed to the despot Phalaris, who ruled from 571 to 555 B.C. and is said to have roasted his victims inside a brass bull. He eventually met the same fate.

Empedocles (ca. 490–430 B.C.), the Greek philosopher and politician (also considered by some the founder of medicine in Italy), was the most famous son of Akragas. He formulated the theory that matter consists of four elements (earth, fire, water, and air), modified by the agents of love and strife. In modern times, the town produced playwright Luigi Pirandello (1867–1936), who won the Nobel Prize in literature in 1934.

Like nearby Selinunte, the city was attacked by war-waging Carthaginians, beginning in 406 B.C. In the 3rd century B.C., the city changed hands between the Carthaginians and the Romans until it finally succumbed to Roman domination by 210 B.C. It was then known as Agrigentium.

The modern part of Agrigento occupies a hill; the narrow casbahlike streets show the influence of the conquering Saracens. Heavy Allied bombing during World War II necessitated much rebuilding. The result is, for the most part, uninspired and not helped by all the cement factories in the area. But below the town stretch the long reaches of the Valley of the Temples, where you'll see some of the greatest Greek ruins in the world.

Visit Agrigento for its past, not for its modern incarnation. However, once you've been awed by the ruined temples, you can explore the *centro storico,* with its tourist boutiques hawking postcards and T-shirts, and enjoy people-watching at a cafe along Via Atenea. When it gets too hot (as it so often does), flee to a beach at nearby **San Leone.**

ESSENTIALS

GETTING THERE   The main rail station, **Stazione Centrale,** Piazza Marconi (✆ **892021**), is downhill from Piazzale Aldo Moro and Piazza Vittorio Emanuele. The train trip from Palermo takes 1¹/₂ hours and costs 7.60€ ($9.90) one-way; there are 11 trains daily. From Syracuse, you must first take one of four daily trains to Catania; the 6-hour trip costs 19€ ($25) one-way. Three trains a day make the trip from Ragusa to Agrigento, at a cost of 9.70€ ($13) one-way. This is an extremely awkward connection, as you have to change trains at Gela and then at Canicattì. Depending on the train, the trip can last from 5 to 9 hours.

   Cuffaro (✆ **0922-403150**) runs four buses per day from Palermo; the trip takes 2 hours and costs 9€ ($12) one-way. The company also has service from Syracuse, which takes 5 hours and costs 18€ ($23) one-way. By car from Syracuse, take SS115 through Gela. From Palermo, cut southeast along S121, which becomes S188 and S189 before it finally reaches Agrigento. Allow about 2¹/₂ hours.

VISITOR INFORMATION   The **tourist office,** Piazzale Aldo Moro 7 (✆ **0922-20454**), is open Sunday to Friday 8am to 1pm and 3 to 8pm, Saturday 8am to 1pm. Another tourist office is at Via Empedocle 73 (✆ **0922-20391**), open Monday to Friday 8am to 2:30pm and Wednesday 3:30 to 7pm.

SPECIAL EVENTS   The **Settimana Pirandelliana** is a festival of plays, operas, and ballets staged in Piazza Kaos during 1 week in July or August. The tourist office can supply details; tickets cost 7.50€ to 15€ ($9.75–$20).

GETTING AROUND   Agrigento is served by a network of orange **TUA buses** (✆ **0922-412024**). A ticket selling for 1€ ($1.30) is valid for 1¹/₂ hours. Bus no. 2 or 2/ runs to the beach at San Leone. Bus nos. 1 and 2 make frequent runs to the Valley of the Temples, and bus no. 11 goes to Casa di Pirandello. For **taxi** service in Agrigento, call ✆ **0922-21899** or 0922-26670.

FAST FACTS   In an **emergency,** call ✆ **113,** or the *Carabinieri* (army police corps) at ✆ **0922-596322.** The hospital for the greater area is **Ospedale Civile,** Via Rupe Atenea 1 (✆ **0922-492111**). The most central drugstore is **Farmacia Patti,** Via Atenea 129 (✆ **0922-20591**), open daily 9am to 1:30pm and 5 to 7:30pm. For Internet access, go to **A.M. Servizi Telematici,** Cortile Contarini 7 (✆ **0922-402345**), open Monday to Saturday 9am to 1pm and 3:30 to 9pm. It charges 3€ ($3.90) per hour. The **post office,** Piazza Vittorio Emanuele (✆ **0922-551605**), is open Monday to Friday 8am to 6:30pm and Saturday 8am to 6:30pm. Currency can be exchanged here.

WANDERING AMONG THE RUINS

Many writers are fond of suggesting that the Greek ruins in the **Valley of the Temples** (**Valle dei Templi**) be viewed at dawn or sunset, when their mysterious aura is indeed heightened. Regrettably, you can't get very close at those times. Instead, search them out under the cobalt-blue Sicilian sky. The backdrop is idyllic, especially in spring, when the striking almond trees blossom.

   Ticket booths are found at the west and east entrances (✆ **0922-26191**); they're 8€ ($10) for adults and free for those 17 and under. Hours are daily 8:30am to 7pm. Board

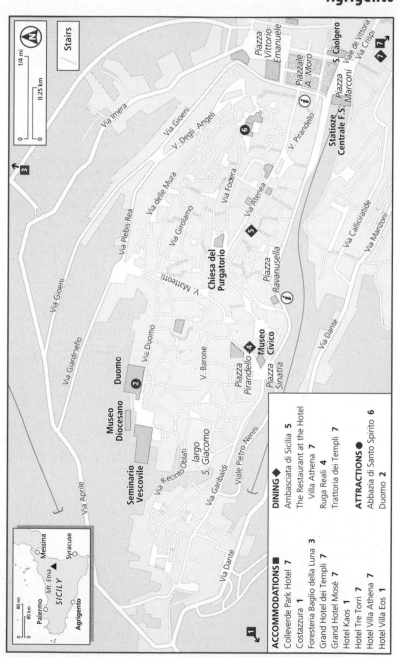

14

ACCOMMODATIONS ■
Colleverde Park Hotel 7
Costazzura 1
Foresteria Baglio della Luna 3
Grand Hotel dei Templi 7
Grand Hotel Mosé 7
Hotel Kaos 1
Hotel Tre Torri 7
Hotel Villa Athena 7
Hotel Villa Eos 1

DINING ◆
Ambasciata di Sicilia 5
The Restaurant at the Hotel
 Villa Athena 7
Ruga Reali 4
Trattoria dei Templi 7

ATTRACTIONS ●
Abbazia di Santo Spirito 6
Duomo 2

a bus or climb into your car to investigate. Riding out the Strada Panoramica, you'll first approach (on your left) the **Temple of Juno (Tempio di Giunone)** ★★, erected sometime in the mid–5th century B.C. Many of its Doric columns have been restored. As you climb the blocks, note the remains of a cistern as well as a sacrificial altar in front. The temple affords good views of the entire valley.

The **Temple of Concord (Tempio della Concordia)** ★★★, which you'll come to next, ranks with the Temple of Hephaestos in Athens as the best-preserved Greek temple in the world. With 13 columns on its side, 6 in front, and 6 in back, the temple was built in the peripheral hexastyle. You'll see the clearest example in Sicily of an inner temple. In the late 6th century A.D., the pagan structure was transformed into a Christian church, which might have saved it for posterity, although today it's been stripped down to its classical purity.

The **Temple of Hercules (Tempio di Ercole)** ★★ is the oldest, dating from the 6th century B.C. Badly ruined (only eight pillars are standing), it once ranked in size with the Temple of Zeus. At one time the temple sheltered a celebrated statue of Hercules. The infamous Gaius Verres, the Roman magistrate who became an especially bad governor of Sicily, attempted to steal the image as part of his temple-looting tear across the island. Astonishingly, you can still see black sears from fires set by long-ago Carthaginian invaders.

The **Temple of Jove/Zeus (Tempio di Giove)** ★ was the largest in the valley, similar in some respects to the Temple of Apollo at Selinunte, until it was ruined by an earthquake. It even impressed Goethe. In front of the structure was a large altar. The giant on the ground was one of several telamones (male caryatids) used to support the largest Greek temple in the world.

The so-called **Temple of Castor and Pollux (Tempio di Dioscuri),** with four Doric columns intact, is composed of fragments from different buildings. At various times it has been designated as a temple honoring Castor and Pollux, the twin sons of Leda and deities of seafarers; Demeter (Ceres), the goddess of marriage and of the fertile earth; or Persephone, the daughter of Zeus and the symbol of spring. *Note:* On some maps, this is called Tempio di Castore e Polluce. The temples can usually be visited daily from 8:30am until 1 hour before sunset. City bus nos. 1, 2, and 3 run to the valley from the train station in Agrigento.

MORE ATTRACTIONS

A combination ticket for admission to the Museo Regionale Archeologico and the Valley of the Temples costs 10€ ($13). The **Museo Regionale Archeologico (Regional Archaeological Museum)** ★, near San Nicola, on Contrada San Nicola at the outskirts of town on the way to the Valle dei Templi (📞 **0922-401565**), is open Tuesday to Saturday 9am to 7:30pm, Sunday and Monday 9am to 1:30pm. Admission is 6€ ($7.80), free for children 17 and younger. Its most important exhibit is a head of one of the telamones (male caryatids) from the Tempio di Giove. The collection of Greek vases is also impressive. Many of the artifacts on display were dug up when Agrigento was excavated. Take bus no. 1, 2, or 3.

Casa di Pirandello (Pirandello's House), Contrada Caos, Frazione Caos (📞 **0922-511826**), is the former home of the 1934 Nobel Prize winner, known for his plays *Six Characters in Search of an Author* and *Enrico IV.* Although Agrigentans back then might not have liked his portrayal of Italy, all is forgiven now, and Pirandello is the local boy who made good. In fact, the Teatro Luigi Pirandello at Piazza Municipio bears his name. His *casa natale* is now a museum devoted to memorabilia pertaining to the playwright's life. His tomb lies under his favorite pine tree, a few hundred yards from the house and grounds, which are open daily 9am to 1pm and 2 to 7pm. Admission is 2€ ($2.60). The

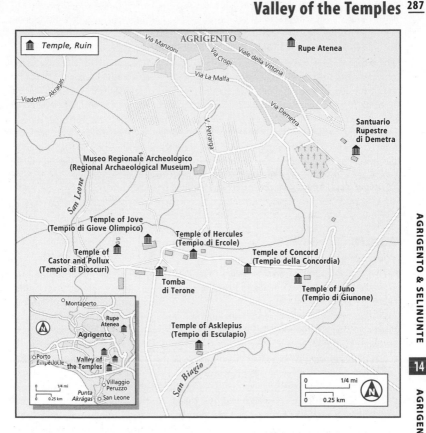

AGRIGENTO

Temple, Ruin

Via Manzoni

Viale della Vittoria

Via Crispi

Rupe Atenea

Via La Malfa

Viadotto Akragas

Via Demetra

V. Petrarga

Santuario
Rupestre
di Demetra

Museo Regionale Archeologico
(Regional Archaeological Museum)

San Leone

Temple of Jove
(Tempio di Giove Olimpico)

Temple of Hercules
(Tempio di Ercole)

Temple of
Castor and Pollux
(Tempio di Dioscuri)

Temple of Concord
(Tempio della Concordia)

Tomba
di Terone

Temple of Juno
(Tempio di Giunone)

Montaperto

Rupe
Atenea

Agrigento

Temple of Asklepius
(Tempio di Esculapio)

Porto
Empedocle

Valley of
the Temples

San Biagio

0   1/4 mi
0   0.25 km

Villaggio
Peruzzo

Punta
Akràgas

San Leone

0   1/4 mi
0   0.25 km

birthplace lies outside of town in the village of Caos (catch bus no. 1 from Piazza Marconi), just west of the temple zone.

THE CHURCHES OF AGRIGENTO

Abbazia di Santo Spirito ★ There is one good reason to venture into the tacky modern city itself. Although this 13th-century church is rotting away, it is still a worthy goal, as you'll realize when you stand at its impressive Gothic entrance surmounted by a rose window. The single nave is adorned with a baroque interior of fantastic stucco work with **four high reliefs ★** believed to have been created by Giacomo Serpotta. The scenes depict *The Adoration of the Magi, The Nativity, The Presentation of Christ at the Temple,* and *The Flight into Egypt.* Take the exit to the right of the facade to look at the cloisters. Here you'll note a **lovely entrance ★** into the chapter house, lined with Gothic arcades. A handsome doorway leads through a pointed arch. On each side are elaborate windows in the Arabo-Norman style. The nuns in the adjoining convent still sell a sweet confection called *kus-kus,* composed of chocolate and pistachio nuts.

Via Porcello at Via Santa Spirito. ℂ **0922-20664.** Free admission. Tues–Sat 9am–1pm and 4–7pm; Sun 9am–1pm.

Duomo ★   Founded in the 12th century, the cathedral of Agrigento has faced rough times. There are still remnants from the early Norman days, particularly the windows, but most of the church was reconstructed in the 13th and 14th centuries. It was vastly restored in the 17th century, and later rejuvenated from the effects of a landslide in 1966. The bell tower, or campanile, is graced with a series of Catalán Gothic single lancet windows. The tower is from 1470, but because it was never completed, it gives the cathedral a strange, disturbing look, as if it were the victim of a windstorm. The **beautiful interior** ★ rests under an **impressive wooden ceiling** ★, the tie beams adorned with scenes from the lives of various saints. This work was carried out in the 16th century. The Duomo itself is dedicated to a Norman, San Gerlando, the town's first archbishop. His tomb is set in the right wing of the transept. Guides are fond of positioning you under the apse, where you can clearly hear even the whispers of people at the other end of the nave 80m (262 ft.) away. Standing in odd contrast to the rather somber chapels is the choir, a baroque romp of angelic angels and golden garlands.

Piazza Don Minzoni, off Via del Duomo. (℃ **0922-490011.** Free admission. Tues–Sun 10am–1pm and 4–6pm. No bus.

WHERE TO STAY
Very Expensive
Foresteria Baglio della Luna ★★ (Finds)   In 1995, one of the most historic medieval sites in Agrigento was meticulously restored by a local antiques dealer. The resulting country inn has housed glamorous types who appreciate its stylish ways and its isolation from the crowds. The first impression you'll get is of a squarish medieval tower, ringed by a protective wall, in a well-landscaped compound that rises above a dusty, sun-blasted setting west of Agrigento. Originating in the 1200s as a watchtower, then rebuilt in the 1500s by Emperor Charles V, it eventually evolved into an aristocratic manor house that controlled hundreds of acres of the surrounding fields and orchards. You'll enter an immaculately maintained cobble-covered courtyard, off of which lie the stylishly decorated guest rooms. Each evokes a romantic lodging in an upscale home, and many have antique headboards, flowered upholsteries, and marble-clad bathrooms with showers and tubs. Some have faraway views of Agrigento's Greek temples. Hotel Villa Athena (see below) may have a closer view of the temples, but this place far surpasses it in charm and hospitality. To miss the experience of dining in the hotel's restaurant, **Ristorante Il Dehor**—the very best in this part of Sicily—would be unfortunate.

Note: This place can be hard to spot from the SS640. Look for the squarish medieval tower on the northern edge of the SS640, about 4.8km (3 miles) west of Agrigento, and turn at the exit marked SPIAGGIA DI MADDALUSA.

Contrada Maddalusa (SS640), Valle dei Templi, 92100 Agrigento. (℃ **0922-511061.** Fax 0922-598802. www.bagliodellaluna.com. 24 units. 245€–280€ ($319–$364) double; 350€–501€ ($455–$651) suite. Half board (breakfast and dinner) 45€ ($50) extra per person. AE, DC, MC, V. Bus: 1 or 3. **Amenities:** 2 restaurants; room service; babysitting; laundry service; Jacuzzi; dry cleaning; nonsmoking rooms. *In room:* A/C, TV, minibar, hair dryer, safe, Jacuzzi (in suites).

Expensive
Hotel Villa Athena ★ (Overrated)   This 18th-century villa rises from the landscape in the Valley of the Temples, less than 3km (1³/₄ miles) from town. It's worn and overpriced, but its location at the archaeological site is so dramatic that we like to stay here anyway, if only to see the ruins lit up at night from our room. Guest rooms are clean, with little

style, and the tiled bathrooms have tub/shower combinations and aging though still- **289**
functioning plumbing. Ask for a room with a view of the temple, preferably one with a
balcony. The perfect choice would be no. 205, which frames a panorama of the Temple
of Concord. During the day, guests sit in the paved courtyard, enjoying drinks and fresh
breezes. Even if you're not staying here, try to walk through the garden at night for an
amazing view of the lit temple. You can also park here during the day and take a 10-min-
ute walk along a trail to the temples.

Frankly, with a major overhaul this could be a great hotel. The staff is known for being
the most unfriendly in Agrigento, yet the setting is so compelling that there are those of
us who can overlook the drawbacks. At any rate, it remains the most popular and most
famous hotel in Agrigento—be sure to reserve at least a month in advance—although
celebrities now check in elsewhere. Because of its incomparable location and because of
its drawbacks, this is the only hotel in this guide that rates both a star and an overrated
icon.

Via Passeggiata Archeologica 33, 92100 Agrigento. ℂ **0922-596288.** Fax 0922-402180. www.athena
hotels.com. 40 units. 160€–260€ ($208–$338) double. Rates include continental breakfast. AE, DC, MC, V.
Free parking. Bus: 2. **Amenities:** Dining room; 2 bars; outdoor pool; room service; laundry service; dry
cleaning. *In room:* A/C, TV, minibar.

Moderate
Colleverde Park Hotel ★★   Sheathed in a layer of ocher-colored stucco, this is one
of our favorite hotels in Agrigento, partly for its verdant garden, partly for its helpful staff,
and partly for its location convenient to both the ancient and the medieval monuments of
Agrigento. It has the finest hotel garden in town, a labyrinth of vine-covered arbors, terra-
cotta terraces, and enormous sheets of white canvas stretched overhead as protection from
the glaring sun. The hotel's eminently tasteful glass-sided restaurant is the site of many local
wedding receptions. The decor throughout is discreetly elegant, providing refuge from the
hysteria that sometimes permeates Agrigento, particularly its roaring traffic. Guest rooms
have tiled bathrooms, lots of exposed wood, charming artwork, and big windows that in
some cases reveal views of the temples of Concordia and Juno.

Via Panoramica dei Templi, 92100 Agrigento. ℂ **0922-29555.** Fax 0922-29012. www.colleverdehotel.it. 48
units. 130€–190€ ($159–$247) double; 160€–210€ ($208–$273) junior suite. Rates include continental
breakfast. AE, DC, MC, V. Free parking. Bus: 1, 2, or 3. **Amenities:** Restaurant; bar; laundry service; dry cleaning; nonsmoking rooms; rooms for those w/limited mobility. *In room:* A/C, TV, minibar, hair dryer, safe.

Grand Hotel dei Templi ★   Don't confuse this relatively conservative government-
rated four-star hotel, which was originally built as a member of the upscale Jolly Hotel
chain, with the more radical-looking three-star Grand Hotel Mosé next door. Originally
built in an airy, high-ceilinged style in the mid-1970s, it's dignified and a lot more
restrained, with less of a "let's party with *or* without the kids" motif, than what you'll find
next door. It offers a pool surrounded by a wall, a tactful and reserved staff, and guest
rooms that are contemporary looking and comfortable—simple to the point of being a
touch banal. Each unit comes with a small private bathroom. The high-ceilinged,
extremely tasteful public areas reflect the best design standards of *la dolce vita* years.

Via Leonardo Sciascia, Villaggio Mosé, 92100 Agrigento. ℂ **0922-610175.** Fax 0922-606685. 146 units.
155€ ($202) double; 186€ ($242) triple. Rates include continental breakfast. AE, DC, MC, V. Free parking.
Bus: 3/. **Amenities:** 2 restaurants; bar; outdoor pool; room service; babysitting; nonsmoking rooms;
rooms for those w/limited mobility. *In room:* A/C, TV, minibar.

Hotel Kaos (**Kids**) Set 2km (1¹/₄ miles) southwest of the Valley of the Temples is this midsize hotel, which boasts a flowery garden, private beach, children's playground, and rooms opening onto the Mediterranean. The complex was formed by converting the residence of a former nobleman and two outbuildings once used to house servants. Many of the comfortable, well-furnished bedrooms have terraces; some units open onto the garden. Accommodations are well maintained and suitable for families, with tiled bathrooms. Unusual for a hotel of this size, Kaos contains three restaurants, each serving regional cuisine that features fresh produce.

Contrada Cumbo, Villaggio Pirandello, 92100 Agrigento. ✆ **0922-598622.** Fax 0922-598770. www.hotelkaos.it. 105 units. 199€–259€ ($259–$337) double; 229€–289€ ($298–$376) triple. AE, DC, MC, V. Free parking. **Amenities:** 3 restaurants; bar; outdoor pool; 2 tennis courts; babysitting; laundry service; dry cleaning. *In room:* A/C, TV, minibar, Wi-Fi.

Hotel Tre Torri Though it's near an unattractive commercial district 7km (4¹/₃ miles) south of Agrigento, this is among the area's busiest hotels. Behind a mock-medieval facade of white stucco, chiseled stone blocks, false crenellations, and crisscrossed iron balconies, Tre Torri is a favorite with Italian business travelers. The small guest rooms are comfortable, with modern furnishings and compact tiled bathrooms.

Strada Statale 115, Viale Canatello, Villaggio Mosè, 92100 Agrigento. ✆ **0922-606733.** Fax 0922-607839. www.hoteltretorri.eu. 118 units. 83€–130€ ($108–$169) double. Rates include continental breakfast. AE, DC, MC, V. Free parking. Bus: 3. **Amenities:** 4 restaurants; 3 bars; 2 pools (1 heated indoor); sauna; room service; laundry service; dry cleaning; nonsmoking rooms; solarium; rooms for those w/limited mobility. *In room:* A/C, TV, minibar (in some), hair dryer, safe (in some), Wi-Fi.

Inexpensive

Costazzura A government-rated three-star hotel, this is a sleek modern choice, with enough comfort but little charm. It's located in San Leone, the seaside resort of Agrigento, 3km (1³/₄ miles) from the Valley of the Temples. Guests here can combine the beach with a tour of ancient monuments on the side. Bedrooms are comfortably furnished though a bit stark; each has a private balcony and a tiled bathroom. On-site is a good family-run restaurant specializing in Mediterranean dishes.

Via delle Viole 2, San Leone, 92100 Agrigento. ✆ **0922-411222.** Fax 0922-414040. www.hotelcostazzurra.it. 32 units. 85€–130€ ($111–$169) double; 126€–168€ ($164–$218) triple. AE, DC, MC, V. Free parking. **Amenities:** Restaurant; bar; room service; Jacuzzi; laundry service; dry cleaning; nonsmoking rooms. *In room:* A/C, TV, safe, Wi-Fi.

Grand Hotel Mosé ★★ This government-rated three-star hotel (not to be confused with the more formal four-star Grand Hotel immediately next door) is a well-designed architectural oddity that evokes a touch of Las Vegas. It sits beside the main traffic artery of Mosé Villaggio, a modern suburb stretching to the north of medieval Agrigento. Sheathed in stucco with the same honey tones as the sandstone used to build the Valley of the Temples, it's theme-ish and imaginative, with a responsive staff and a bubbly kind of zest that can be a lot of fun. Guest rooms are simple, colorful, and slightly spartan, like something you might expect in a Club Med. Most of the units have tiled floors, shower-only bathrooms, wrought-iron headboards, and touches of manorial Sicilian flair. The most dramatic are the units on the hotel's rooftop, which are designed on the outside like mud-walled huts in a North African casbah, and which inside evoke a simple officer's barracks on the edge of the Sahara. The free-form pool is one of the most appealing in Agrigento.

Viale Leonardo Sciascia, Villaggio Mosé, 92100 Agrigento. ✆ **0922-608388.** Fax 0922-608377. www.iashotels.com. 102 rooms. 100€–140€ ($130–$182) double. Rates include continental breakfast. AE, DC,

MC, V. Free parking. Bus: 3. **Amenities:** Restaurant; bar; outdoor pool; shopping arcade; babysitting; laundry service; dry cleaning, solarium; nonsmoking rooms. *In room:* A/C, TV, minibar, hair dryer.

Hotel Villa Eos ★ (Value)   Small and personalized, but isolated in a barren stretch of land between the SS640 and the sea about 4.8km (3 miles) southwest of Agrigento, this ramshackle hotel evokes a rambling, contemporary private home, thanks in part to its well-meaning staff and small scale. It sits in an oasis of greenery with views over the sea. Guests here generally opt to swim in the hotel pool rather than head for the beaches, which require a taxi or bus ride. Rooms are simple, modest, and comfortably furnished. Some, but not all, have minibars. Frankly, the hotel is best for those with cars—you may be guaranteed peace and quiet here, but the location is something of an inconvenience if you want to avail yourself of the area's many nearby attractions and dining options.

Contrada Cumbo, Villaggio Pirandello, 92100 Agrigento. (C) **0922-597170.** Fax 0922-597188. www. hotelvillaeos.it. 25 units. 77€–150€ ($100–$195) double. Rates include continental breakfast. MC, V. Free parking. Bus: 1. **Amenities:** Restaurant; bar; outdoor pool; tennis court; babysitting; laundry service; dry cleaning. *In room:* A/C, TV, minibar.

At the Beach Resort of San Leone

Dioscuri Bay Palace ★★   The setting is more lavish than those of many nearby competitors, and this is a good choice if you want to be housed in comparative luxury close to Agrigento's beachfront. A member of the well-recommended NH chain, this modern hotel rises three floors above a small bay at the northwestern tip of the board-walks of Agrigento's waterfront resort of San Leone. Rooms are contemporary and comfortable, with tiled bathrooms.

Lungomare Falcone e Borsellino 1, 92100 San Leone (Agrigento). (C) **0922-406111.** Fax 0922-411297. 102 units. 121€–210€ ($157–$273) double; 290€ ($377) junior suite. Rates include buffet breakfast. AE, DC, MC, V. Bus: 2. **Amenities:** Restaurant; 2 bars; outdoor pool; Jacuzzi; car-rental desk; room service; babysitting; laundry service; dry cleaning; nonsmoking rooms; rooms for those w/limited mobility. *In room:* A/C, TV, hair dryer, safe, Wi-Fi.

Hotel Akragas   This is one of the most appealing budget-priced hotels of San Leone, located on the busy main road leading from Agrigento. It isn't particularly near the water, and other than its restaurant, it has very few amenities—but in light of its reasonable prices, no one seems to care. The boxy 1950s structure is a pleasant place that's completely unpretentious, family friendly, and conducive to low-key holidays near the beach. Rooms are spartan, clean, and comfortable, with small shower-only bathrooms.

Viale Emporium 16–18, 92100 San Leone (Agrigento). (C) **0922-414082.** Fax 0922-414262. www.hotel akragas.net. 12 units. 80€ ($104) double. Rates include continental breakfast. AE, DC, MC, V. Free parking. Bus: 2. **Amenities:** Restaurant. *In room:* A/C, TV.

WHERE TO DINE

Ambasciata di Sicilia ★ SICILIAN   This restaurant has been a city staple since the end of World War I, when a local family decided to celebrate the cuisine of their native Sicily in the form of this intensely vernacular *trattoria*. The cramped setting is accented with panels from antique donkey carts, frescoed ceiling beams, and marionettes salvaged from some long-ago street performance. In nice weather, the preferred seats are outside on four platforms built on the steeply sloping alley. (Some guests have commented that the flocks of birds that fly over the city rooftops far below are among the most soothing and mystical sights in Agrigento.) Menu items are based on 19th-century recipes. Stellar examples include beef roulades; an excellent *antipasti rustico* (sampling of antipasti); and linguine *al'Ambasciata* (prepared with meat sauce, bacon, calamari, and zucchini).

Via Gianbertoni 2, off Via Atenea. ℂ **0922-20526.** Reservations not required. Main courses 7€–12€ ($9.10–$16). AE, MC, V. Sept–July Tues–Sun 12:30–3:30pm and 7–11:30pm; Aug daily 12:30–3:30pm and 7–11:30pm. Closed 2 weeks in Nov.

La Trizzera ★ (Finds) SICILIAN   While visiting Pirandello's House (see above), you can also schedule a visit to this rustic trattoria. One reader called it "the best meal in Sicily." We're not that enthusiastic but found the food beautifully prepared, the ingredients fresh, and the flavors much to our liking. At first you may be turned off by the dusty stretch of road that runs in front, even the modesty of the place itself, but wait until you sample the food. Each item is prepared fresh that day. The chef shows his razor-sharp technique with *pasta alla Norma* (with chopped eggplant). You can also delight in a dish, *bucaneve*, a savory crepe stuffed with ham and local cheese. The most regional dish is *sarde a beccafico* (sardines stuffed with bread crumbs mixed with lemon juice and seasonings). A large variety of fish— either grilled or sautéed—is offered each day. The classic dessert, *cassata Siciliana* (made with ricotta cheese), is prepared with consummate skill here.

Via Fosse Ardeatine 57 (SS115), Contrada Caos, Villaseta. ℂ **0922-512415.** Reservations not required. Fixed-price menus 13€–23€ ($17–$30). AE, DC, MC, V. Tues–Sun noon–3pm and 7–11pm. Closed 2 weeks in Aug.

Restaurant at the Hotel Villa Athena ★ CONTINENTAL   The formally dressed staff here tends to be brusque, despite a long tradition of welcoming visitors from far away. But the site can be so magical, at least for first-timers to Agrigento, that a midsummer dinner on the terrace can be a memorable experience unaffected by food, staff, weather, or circumstances. If you opt for lunch here, it will be served in a crescent-shaped stone-and-stucco building whose curtains are usually closed against the noon glare. But it's at dinner that the true magic emerges: Views sweep from the torch-lit terrace to the nearby Temple of Concordia (which literally looms before you) in ways unmatched by any other establishment in Agrigento. In fact, whenever the city wants to impress representatives from parliament or the world of Italian fashion, the dinner that's held to celebrate their arrival is invariably conducted at this restaurant. Begin, perhaps, with a duet of smoked salmon and swordfish or else a fresh shellfish salad. We're fond of the sea bass flavored with saffron. The special risotto is made with pumpkin flowers, lobster, zucchini, and vodka. A "fantasy" of ice creams and sherbets is served to end the repast.

Via Passeggiata Archeologica 33. ℂ **0922-596288.** Reservations required. Main courses 10€–20€ ($13–$26). AE, DC, MC, V. Daily 12:30–2:30pm and 7:30–9:30pm (until 10pm June–Sept). Bus: 2.

Ruga Reali SICILIAN   Tables here spill onto one of Agrigento's most beautiful squares, high in the medieval center's upper zones. It's a short walk downhill from the cathedral, where there aren't a lot of other restaurants. We usually prefer the terrace, but if it's cold, rainy, or unbearably hot, descend into one of the nearby cellars, built in the 1400s as a stable, where other tables await. The chef shops at the nearby fish market, later concocting such delights as a savory fish couscous or else linguine with a shrimp sauce. Regularly featured is the filleted fish of the day served with fresh vegetables. The meat dishes are less inspired.

Piazza Pirandello (Piazza Municipio), Cortile Scribani 8. ℂ **0922-20370.** Reservations not necessary. Main courses 8€–17€ ($10–$22). AE, DC, MC, V. Daily noon–3pm and 7:30pm–midnight. Closed mid-Oct to mid-Nov.

Trattoria dei Templi ★ SICILIAN   This charming, discreet, and extremely well-managed restaurant sits at the bottom of the hill between medieval Agrigento and the

Valley of the Temples. Inside, you'll find brick-trimmed ceiling vaults, a polite crowd of diners from virtually everywhere in Europe, and excellent food that's served on hand-painted china. Menu items, served with efficiency by a staff of young, well-trained waiters, include *cavatelli valle dei Templi tipa Norma* (pasta with eggplant and cheese); *panzerotti della casa* (big ravioli stuffed with whitefish and served with a seafood sauce); and local fish with herbs, white wine, lemon juice, capers, olives, and orange zest.

Via Panoramica dei Templi 15. ✆ **0922-403110.** Reservations recommended. Main courses 7€–20€ ($9.10–$26). AE, DC, MC, V. Daily 12:30–3pm and 7:30–11pm. Closed Sun July–Aug and Fri Sept–June. Bus: 1, 2, or 3.

At the Beach Resort of San Leone

Il Pescatore ★ SICILIAN/SEAFOOD   Set right on the waterfront of Agrigento's beach resort of San Leone, this is the most famous of the 10 or so restaurants that flank it on either side. It's noted for its skillful preparations of fish, and also for a rough-and-tumble staff whose brusqueness is legendary—but which, almost perversely, has added to the restaurant's fame. The interior is more beautiful than you might expect, thanks to the four dining rooms' beamed ceilings and Romanesque-style columns and capitals salvaged from older buildings. Spaghetti with baby clams is always a smooth lead-in to a meal here, as is the *zuppa di cozze* (kettle of fresh mussels). Homemade bucatini comes with fresh sardines whipped into the pasta, and sole meunière is featured regularly. Also delectable is fresh fish with a pistachio cream sauce and a blending of fresh eggplant.

Lungomare Falcone e Borsellino, San Leone. ✆ **0922-414342.** Reservations recommended. Main courses 10€–15€ ($13–$20). AE, DC, MC, V. Sept–June Tues–Sun 12:30–3:30pm and 7:30–11:30pm; July–Aug daily 12:30–3:30pm and 7:30–11:30pm. Bus: 2.

Leon d'Oro SICILIAN/SEAFOOD   Set in an undistinguished, cement-sided modern building that originated as a garage and car-repair shop, this restaurant is uncomfortably close to the busy boulevard that funnels most of the traffic from Agrigento into San Leone. Its festive interior, however, reveals one of the most respected restaurants in town. Expect savory dishes based on time-tested recipes. Our favorite is *rotolini Emporium* (pasta with shrimp, tomatoes, fresh vegetables, and a pecorino cheese sauce).

Via Emporium 102, San Leone. ✆ **0922-414400.** Reservations recommended. Main courses 8€–16€ ($10–$21). AE, DC, MC, V. Tues–Sun 12:30–3:30pm and 7:45–11:30pm. Closed 2 weeks in Nov. Bus: 2.

Ristorante Il Dehor ★★★ SICILIAN/INTERNATIONAL   Set within the thick medieval walls of the Foresteria Baglio della Luna hotel (p. 288), 5km (3 miles) west of Agrigento, this is the finest restaurant in Agrigento, and one of the best in all of Sicily. Its excellence is the work of chef Damiano Ferraro, an Agrigento-born, London-educated culinary genius who has reinvented aspects of traditional Sicilian cuisine in ways that elicit rave reviews from discerning diners from throughout Europe. Guests dine on a terrace or in one of two rooms that are ringed with important 19th-century paintings and tapestries.

The 50€ ($65) fixed menu is traditional Sicilian and a bit cliché-ridden, but the 53€ ($69) tasting menu truly shows off the genius of this most talented chef. The appetizers are the best along the southern coast of Sicily—just wait until you sample the octopus and shrimp with new potatoes in a bisque flavored with escargot butter, or the sea scallops with king prawns on cannellini beans with candied lemon in a sea urchin sauce. We could return here every night for the pastas, such as tortellini of spiny lobster in a *jus* of summer truffles. Wild salmon is served in a consommé of cherry tomatoes with little ravioli of melted fennel and chopped garlic. Desserts don't get much better than the chocolate fondant with a pistachio parfait and two sauces.

In the Foresteria Baglio della Luna Hotel, Contrada Maddalusa (SS640), Valle dei Templi 92100. ℂ **0922-511061.** Reservations required. Main courses 10€–18€ ($13–$23); fixed-price menus 50€–53€ ($65–$69). AE, DC, MC, V. Tues–Sun 12:30–2pm and 7:30–10pm. Bus: 1 or 3.

2 LAMPEDUSA

240km (49 miles) S of Agrigento

After visiting the ancient glories of Agrigento, you can drive only 7km (4¹⁄₂ miles) southwest to the Porto Empédocle. Take the ferry to the African island of Lampedusa, which is owned by Sicily, for an offbeat adventure.

Little more than dry rocks, the remote and barren Isole Pelágie have at long last been discovered by visitors, mostly Italians from the mainland, who flock here in July and August. The main island is **Lampedusa,** which is the name of both the largest island and its chief town. It lies farther from the mainland of Sicily than Malta. Upon arrival, you'll think you've arrived in Tunisia or even Libya, which is not surprising. The islands belong to Sicily but are really islands of an archipelago of the African continent.

If you go by ferry (see below), you'll stop first at **Linosa,** the northernmost of the islands and the tip of a ancient submerged volcano. The ferry continues to Lampedusa, its final stop. Lampedusa lies 50km (31 miles) south of Linosa and is shaped like a giant raft inclined to one side.

In recent years, Lampedusa has become a major route for undocumented Africans immigrating to Europe. Lampedusa's flora and fauna are similar to those of North Africa nearby, and it's an arid island with a constant water shortage because of irregular rainfall.

ESSENTIALS

GETTING THERE   The quickest way is to fly from Palermo to Lampedusa year-round on **Air One** (ℂ **199-207080;** www.flyairone.it); the trip takes only 1 hour. The small airport lies on the southeastern side of town. Always book your hotel in advance, and chances are a courtesy bus will be arranged for you at the airport.

Most arrivals are from Porto Empédocle on a **Siremar** ferry, operating year-round and making the trip from Porto Empédocle to Lampedusa in 8 hours, 15 minutes. Ferries from Porto Empédocle leave daily at midnight, returning the following morning at 10:15am. The trip costs 31€ to 66€ ($40–$86) one-way, and cars are transported for 55€ to 104€ ($72–$72). The Sirremar office in Porto Empédocle is at Via Molo 13 (ℂ **0922-636683**); in Lampedusa, the office is on Longomare L. Rizzo (ℂ **0922-970003**). Ferries arrive at the harbor, Porto Vecchio, in Lampedusa, a 10-minute walk into town. Taxis await arrivals, or else you can take a minibus into town in summer.

VISITOR INFORMATION

The tourist office is on Via Vittorio Emanuele 80 (ℂ **0922-971379**). It is open April to October but keeps such erratic hours you'll never know when it's open.

If you wish, you can rent a bike at **Autonoleggio d'Agostino,** Via Bix 1 (ℂ **0922-970755**), and circle the island in a day. Bikes cost about 10€ ($13) a day, a motor scooter going for 25€ ($33) and up.

"We have the sun, we have the Mediterranean Sea," claims the island's director of tourism. "What more could you want?" That about says it.

The best beach on this 11km (6³/₄-mile) island is **Isola dei Conigli** or Rabbit Island, lying 7km (4¹/₃ miles) south of town. It's right off the shore, and you can swim over to it except when the tide is out and then you can walk over. In addition to good sandy beaches, there is a small nature reserve here where the endangered Caretta turtle lays her eggs between July and August. A small bus in town runs to the departure point for Rabbit Island every hour during the day. There are no facilities on Rabbit Island, so take what provisions you need.

In summer you can go down to the wharf in Lampedusa and negotiate a boat tour around the island with one of the local fishermen. Count on paying 15€ ($20) per person for the half-day trip. Double the price for a full-day jaunt, with lunch included. There is little in the interior of interest.

WHERE TO STAY

Cavalluccio Marino (Value)   This is one of the best bargains in town, although it's a simple place furnished very basically yet comfortably. Opened in 1980, it lies only 100m (328 ft.) from the sea and about 500m (1,640 ft.) from the center of town. Two of its units contain verandas and some of the others have balconies with a view. The food is good and hearty, with mainly fresh fish dishes.

Contrada Cala Croce 3, 92010 Lampedusa. ℂ **0922-970053.** Fax 0922-970672. www.hotel cavallucciomarino.com. 10 units. 82€–120€ ($107–$156) per person double. Rates include half board. AE, DC, MC, V. Free parking. Closed Nov–Mar. **Amenities:** Restaurant; bar; room service; laundry service. *In room:* A/C, TV, hair dryer, safe.

Cupola Bianca ★   At 1km (¹/₂ mile) from the center of town, this modern hotel—decorated in a Mediterranean Arabesque style—is the best in the archipelago. On a headland studded with olive and palm trees, it rises from the earth like an oasis in Morocco. Its garden setting is the most attractive on the island. Bedrooms are spacious for the most part, ranging from standard to superior. The most expensive are in a North African–like structure called Dammusi, with its extensive verandas. Furnishings are in rattan, and the place has great style for this remote part of the world.

Contrada Madonna, 92010 Lampedusa. ℂ **0922-971274.** Fax 0922-973885. www.hotelcupolabianca.it. 23 units. 100€–200€ ($130–$260) double; 250€–370€ ($325–$481) suite. Rates include half board. AE, MC, V. Free parking. Closed Nov–May. **Amenities:** Restaurant; bar; room service; laundry service; private boat for excursions; scooter rental and car rentals. *In room:* A/C, TV, hair dryer, safe.

Martello   This hotel could be placed in the center of Tangier and no one would know the difference. It lies on a spit of land dividing Cala Guitgia from Cala Salina, a small marina, at a point 80m (263 ft.) from the beach. Guests gather in the small garden to enjoy drinks and night breezes. Most of the rooms are spacious with a sea view from a private balcony. All are comfortably furnished in a standard motel style.

Contrada Guitgia, 92010 Lampedusa. ℂ **0922-970025.** Fax 0922-971696. www.hotelmartello.it. 25 units. 55€–110€ ($72–$143) per person. Rates include half board. AE, MC, V. Free parking. Closed Dec–Feb. **Amenities:** Restaurant; bar; solarium. *In room:* A/C, TV, hair dryer, safe.

WHERE TO DINE

In your search for a bar or restaurant, walk along **Via Roma** in the center of town at night. All the kitchens here serve fresh fish or else couscous from North Africa.

Gemelli MEDITERRANEAN/SICILIAN   This is the best restaurant in a town where the competition isn't very good. Nonetheless you get a cuisine that islanders have enjoyed for years. The local spaghetti appears with a fresh sardine sauce, and the chef even makes tasty Spanish paella. We are especially fond of the *seppie ripiene* or stuffed cuttlefish, and also couscous made with grouper. The Sicilian fish soup is also the best in town.

Via Cala Pisana 2. (**0922-970699.** Reservations recommended July–Aug. Main courses 10€–30€ ($13–$39). AE, DC, MC, V. Daily 7:30–11:30pm. Closed Nov–Mar.

---

3 SELINUNTE

122km (76 miles) SW of Palermo, 113km (70 miles) W of Agrigento, 89km (55 miles) SE of Trapani

Guy de Maupassant called the splendid jumble of ruins at Selinunte "an immense heap of fallen columns, now aligned and placed side by side on the ground like dead soldiers, now having fallen in a chaotic manner." Regardless of what shape they're in, the only reason to visit Selinunte is for its ruins, not for the unappealing modern towns (Mazara del Vallo and Castelvetrano) that have grown around it.

One of the superb colonies of ancient Greece, Selinunte traces its history from the 7th century B.C., when immigrants from Megara Hyblaea (Syracuse) set out to build a new colony. They succeeded, erecting a city of power and prestige adorned with temples. But that was calling attention to a good thing. Much of Selinunte's history involves seemingly endless conflicts with the Elymi people of Segesta (p. 299). Siding with Selinunte's rival, Hannibal virtually leveled the city in 409 B.C. The city never recovered its former glory and ultimately fell into decay.

ESSENTIALS

GETTING THERE   Selinunte is on the southern coast of Sicily and is best explored by **car,** as public transportation can be awkward. From Agrigento, take Route 115 northwest into Castelvetrano; then follow the signposted secondary road marked SELINUNTE, which leads south to the sea. Allow at least 2 hours from either Palermo or Agrigento.

If you prefer to take the **train** from Trapani or Marsala, you can make rail connections to Castelvetrano on the southern coast of Sicily, 23km (14 miles) from the ruins. The one-way rail fare from Marsala is 3.60€ ($4.70); from Trapani, 5.25€ ($6.85). The trip to Trapani to Castelvetrano takes 1 hour and 10 minutes; from Marsala, only 40 minutes. Once at Castelvetrano, board a bus for the final lap of the journey to Selinunte. **Lumia buses** ((**0922-20414**) run to Castelvetrano from Agrigento; call for schedule information. Buses arrive in Castelvetrano in front of the rail depot. From here, you must go the rest of the way by a bus operated by **Autoservizi Salemi** ((**0923-981120**); the one-way fare for the 20-minute trip is 1.50€ ($1.95).

VISITOR INFORMATION   The **tourist office,** Via Caboto Giovanni ((**0924-46251**), near the archaeological garden, is open Monday to Saturday 8am to 2pm and 3 to 8pm, Sunday 9am to noon and 3 to 6pm.

EXPLORING THE ARCHAEOLOGICAL GARDEN ★★

Selinunte's temples lie in scattered ruins, the honey-colored stone littering the ground as if an earthquake had struck (as one did in ancient times). Some sections and fragments of temples still stand, with great columns pointing to the sky. From 9am to 1 hour before

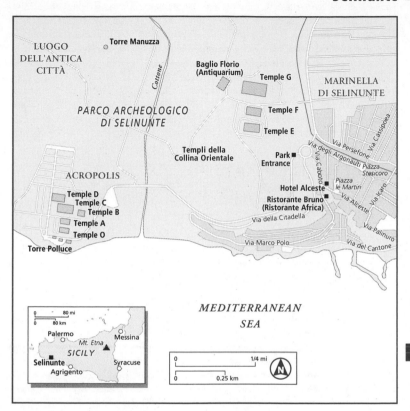

sunset daily, you can walk through the monument zone. Some of it has been partially excavated and reconstructed. Admission is 6€ ($7.80) for adults, free for children 17 and under.

The temples, in varying states of preservation, are designated by letters. They're dedicated to such mythological figures as Apollo and Hera (Juno); most date from the 6th and 5th centuries B.C. Near the entrance, the Doric **Temple E** contains fragments of an inner temple. Standing on its ruins before the sun goes down, you can look across the water that washes up on the shores of Africa, from which the Carthaginian fleet emerged to destroy the city. **Temple G,** in scattered ruins north of Temple E, was one of the largest erected in Sicily and was also built in the Doric style. The ruins of the less impressive **Temple F** lie between Temples E and G. Not much remains of Temple F, and little is known about it.

After viewing Temples E, F, and G, all near the parking lot at the entrance, you can get in your car and drive along the Strada dei Templi west to the Acropoli (or walk there in about 20 min.). The site of the western temples was the **Acropoli,** which was enclosed within defensive walls and built from the 6th century to the 5th century B.C.

The most impressive site here is **Temple C.** In 1925, 14 of the 17 columns of Temple C were re-erected. This is the earliest surviving temple of ancient Selinus, built in the 6th century B.C. and probably dedicated to Hercules or Apollo. The pediment, ornamented with a clay Gorgon's head, lies broken on the ground. Temple C towers over the other ruins and gives you a better impression of what all the temples might have looked like at one time.

Also here is **Temple A,** which, like the others, remains in scattered ruins. The streets of the Acropoli were laid out along classical lines, with a trio of principal arteries bisected at right angles by a grid of less important streets. The Acropoli was the site of the most important public and religious buildings, and it was also the residence of the town's aristocrats. If you look down below, you can see the site of the town's harbor, now overgrown. After all the earthquake damage, you can only imagine the full glory of this place in its golden era.

WHERE TO STAY NEARBY

The site of the ruins contains no hotels, restaurants, or watering holes of note. Most visitors come here on a day trip while based elsewhere. But there are a handful of accommodations in the seafront village of Marinella, less than 2km (1¼ miles) east of Selinunte. To reach Marinella, visitors must travel along a narrow country road.

Hotel Alceste This concrete structure is about a 15-minute walk from the ruins. Guest rooms have small tiled bathrooms with tub/shower combos. Most visitors, however, stop only for a visit to the plant-filled courtyard, where in summer there's musical entertainment, dancing, cabaret, and theater. In July and August, the hotel hosts what may be the highest percentage of academics of any accommodations in Sicily; they come from universities throughout the world. The somewhat shy and very kind owner, Orazio Torrente, is charming, as is his family. The airy, bustling restaurant is open daily for lunch and dinner, and is sometimes filled with busloads of visitors from as far away as Milan. Main courses cost from 7€ to 14€ ($9.10–$18).

Via Alceste 21, 91022 Marinella di Selinunte. ℂ **0924-46184.** Fax 0924-46143. www.hotelalceste.it. 30 units. 87€ ($113) double; 115€ ($150) triple. Rates include continental breakfast. AE, DC, MC, V. **Amenities:** Restaurant; lounge; room service; laundry service; dry cleaning; all nonsmoking rooms. *In room:* A/C, TV, hair dryer, safe.

WHERE TO DINE

Hotel Alceste, recommended above, is also a good choice for dining.

Ristorante Pierrot ★ Ⓥalue SICILIAN With a terrace opening onto the Mediterranean, this is the best place in the area for regional food. With a seafront table and a rustic decor, you can enjoy fresh produce from the market and fish caught that same day. Tired travelers visiting the ruins are quickly refreshed here with the invigorating cuisine prepared by skilled cooks. Since you're so close to North Africa, fish couscous regularly appears on the menu. *Orecchiette* (their homemade pasta) is served with succulent scampi. Another homemade pasta, and one we like even better is *spaccatelle con melenzane e pesca spada* (pasta sautéed with swordfish, eggplant, and tomato sauce). Nearly everyone orders one of the seafood pasta dishes, such as one with sea urchins, mussels, and shrimp. But you can also order your catch of the day grilled or sautéed to your specifications.

Via Marco Polo 108, Marinella. ℂ **0924-46205.** Reservations recommended. Main courses 8€–15€ ($10–$20); fixed-price menus 15€–30€ ($20–$39). AE, DC, MC, V. Daily 10am–3pm and 7pm–midnight.

15

Western Sicily

In the early days of 20th-century tourism to Sicily, the western part of the island was easily dismissed. On our first visit a long time ago, we were even discouraged from going there by a tourist official in Palermo. "What is there? A few Greek ruins and maybe some Mafia boys running about? Stay in Palermo, where we will wine and dine you."

Even today, most foreign visitors land in the east. But we have come to regard the western coast as one of our favorite areas for discovery. Much of Sicilian history was shaped along these shores, and much is left that is ancient, including the magnificent ruins at **Segesta,** whose temple has remained virtually intact for 2,500 years.

No hilltop medieval town, not even Taormina, equals **Erice.** And in spite of unfortunate modern building on its periphery, **Trapani** still has a historic core with a jumbled maze of narrow streets. Finally, **Marsala,** to the south, is known as the center for the making of world-famous dessert wines.

1 SEGESTA ★★★

30km (19 miles) E of Trapani, 75km (47 miles) SW of Palermo

There's only one reason to come to Segesta: to see a single amazing temple in a lonely field. For some visitors, that's reason enough because it's one of the best-preserved ancient temples in all of Italy. The trip here takes about an hour from Palermo, and makes a good brief stop en route to Trapani (p. 306).

Segesta was the ancient city of the Elymi, a people of mysterious origin who are linked by some to the Trojans. As the major city in western Sicily, it faced conflicts with the rival power nearby, Selinus (Selinunte). From the 6th to 5th century B.C., there were near-constant hostilities. The Athenians came from the east to aid the Segestans in 415 B.C., but the expedition ended in disaster, eventually forcing the city to turn for help to Hannibal of Carthage.

Twice in the 4th century B.C., Segesta was besieged and conquered, once by Dionysius and again by Agathocles. Segesta, in time, turned on its old but dubious ally, Carthage. Like all Greek cities of Sicily, it ultimately fell to the Romans.

ESSENTIALS

GETTING THERE   Nearly a dozen **trains** per day make the run from Trapani (p. 306) to the depot at Segesta, Segesta Tempio. A one-way ticket costs 3.10€ ($4). The station is only a 1km (1/2-mile) walk from the Doric temple. Segesta is also reached by **AST bus** (© **0923-23222**), leaving from Piazza Montalto in Trapani; the 25-minute ride costs 4€ ($5.20).

By **car,** take the autostrada (A29) running between Palermo and Trapani. The exit at Segesta is clearly marked.

A JOURNEY INTO ANTIQUITY

The **Tempio (Temple) of Segesta** ★★★ is one of the world's most perfectly preserved survivors from the days of antiquity. Unlike the sprinkling of columns in most Sicilian archaeological gardens, this is a full temple of scope and dimension, with its columns relatively intact. It stands on a 304m (997-ft.) hill, on the edge of a deep ravine carved by the Pispisa River.

The site is made all the more majestic by the deep valley that envelops it. In the fading gold and pink sunlight of a Sicilian afternoon, you can stand here and absorb the full view, the setting framed by the distant peaks of Monte Barbaro and Monte Bernardo. It is perhaps the most **magnificent view** ★★★ in all Sicily.

Constructed in the 5th century B.C., the well-preserved temple is supported by 36 Doric columns that in turn support its entablatures and pediments. Because the interior architectural elements are lacking, professors of antiquity believe that the temple was never finished due to a war with Segesta's archenemy, Selinunte.

The site is open daily 9am to 5pm; admission is 6€ ($7.80) for adults and 3€ ($3.90) for children 17 and under. The ticket office closes an hour before the temple park closes.

After visiting the temple, you can take a bus to the large **Teatro ★**, or theater, at the top of Mount Barbaro at 431m (1,414 ft.). The one-way fare costs 1.05€ ($1.40), and buses depart at the rate of two per hour during the day.

Dating from the 3rd century B.C., the theater was constructed during the Hellenistic period. A semicircle with a diameter of 63m (207 ft.), it was hewn right out of the side of the mountain. In ancient days, the theater could hold as many as 4,000 spectators, and the site is still used for the staging of both modern and classical plays presented from mid-July to August every even year (next in 2010 and 2012).

2 ERICE ★★★

96km (60 miles) SW of Palermo, 14km (8²/₃ miles) NE of Trapani, 45km (28 miles) NW of Marsala, 330km (205 miles) W of Messina

Originally established some 3,000 years ago, Erice is an enchanting medieval city. From its panoramic mountaintop setting, two sheer cliffs drop 743m (2,438 ft.) to vistas across the plains of Trapani and down the west coast of Sicily. On a clear day, you can even see Cape Bon in Tunisia, but the Sicilian aerie of Erice is often shrouded in mist that only adds to its mystique (or misery, especially in winter, when temperatures can plummet below Sicilian norms and snow is not uncommon).

Erice is a lovely place to spend an afternoon wandering the medieval streets, with their baroque balconies and flowering vines, and drinking in the vistas. The southwest corner of town contains the **Villa Balio** gardens, originally laid out in the 19th century. Beyond the gardens, a path winds along the cliff's edge up to Erice's highest point, the **Castello di Venere.** Today, little more than crumbling Norman walls surround the sacred site where a temple to Venus once stood.

ESSENTIALS

GETTING THERE If taking the **train** from Palermo, you'll pull into the station at Trapani (p. 306). **AST buses** (© 0923-23222) to Erice depart from Trapani's Piazza Montalto, at the rate of seven per day. Service is year-round, daily 6:40am to 7:30pm. The trip lasts 50 minutes and costs 2.20€ ($2.90) one-way.

By **car** from Trapani, head out on the Via Fardella to the end of the street. At some point near the end of the wide boulevard, you'll see signs pointing the way to Erice. Follow A29 all the way to Erice.

DISCOVERING A MEDIEVAL TOWN

Erice's chief attraction is the **medieval town ★★★**, although there are some individual points of interest worth seeking out as you make your way along its cobblestone streets. The historic core of Erice forms a triangle, with the southeastern corner framed by the **Castello di Venere** (see below). In the southwestern corner is the **Chiesa Matrice,** near Porta di Trapani, the best place to park your car before you explore the medieval center. The access road to Erice affords **panoramic vistas ★★** of the Trapani plains and the sea.

You can reach the medieval town by taking a **Funivia** (cable car), the ride costing 5€ ($6.50) round-trip and taking 12 minutes. The cable car station is on Via Capua on the eastern outskirts of Trapani (reached by bus no. 21 from the town center). The Funivia runs Tuesday to Friday 7:40am to 8:30pm, Saturday and Sunday 9:30am to midnight.

After leaving Porta di Trapani, your first discovery will be immediately to the northeast. **Chiesa Matrice di Erice,** Via Vito Carvini (℡ **0923-869123**), is the main church of Erice. Not quite a cathedral, it was constructed in 1314 using stones from the ancient Temple of Venus that once stood here. Its merlon-topped walls speak of the church's former role as a fortress and a place of worship. The rose window on the church facade is a thing of beauty, as is its Gothic porch.

If you climb the church's campanile, or bell tower, you'll be rewarded with a stunning view across the Gulf of Trapani to the Egadi Islands. Ordered built by Frederick of Aragon, the former watchtower has impressive Gothic mullioned windows. The church is open Monday to Friday 9:30am to 12:30pm and 3:30 to 5:30pm, Saturday and Sunday 9:30am to 1pm and 3:30 to 6pm.

If you walk north from the church, you can follow **Mura Elimo Puniche** ★, the Elimo Punic walls constructed by the Elimini (8th–6th c. B.C.) around the northeastern flank of Erice. Any attack on the town had to come from this direction, which was exposed. The best-preserved part of the walls lies along Via dell'Addolorata, stretching from Porta Carmine to Porta Spada, which is at the far northern end of the massive fortifications.

At Porta Spada, the end of your "wall walk," you'll find yourself at **Chiesa di Santa Orsola,** a 1413 church with its original Gothic rib-vaulting still on view in the nave. Directly to the east of this church is the **Quartiere Spagnola.** Launched in the 17th century but never finished, this "Spanish Quarter" building is no grand sight, but a **panoramic vista** ★ unfolds from here over the Bay of Cofano.

In the historic core of Erice stands the **Museo Civico Antonio Cordici,** Piazza Umberto I, at Corso Vittorio Emanuele (℡ **0923-869172**), open Monday and Thursday 9am to 1pm and 3 to 5pm; Tuesday, Wednesday, and Friday 9am to 1pm; admission is free. Named for a local historian, the building was originally a library dating from 1867. In its entrance hall is a magnificent 1525 relief of the *Annunciation* ★ by Antonello Gagini, one of his most impressive pieces of art. Upstairs are displays of the more intriguing artifacts from archaeological digs in the area, including a small Attic head of Venus dating from the 5th century B.C.

Heading east, you'll come first to **Giardino del Balio** ★, initially constructed by the Normans as a forward defense for their castle (see below). The gardens take their name from a former Norman governor and were mapped out in 1870 by Count Agostino Pepoli. Situated on the summit of a hill, the gardens open onto one of the most **spectacular views** ★★ in western Sicily, embracing the peaks of Monte Cofano with distant views of the Egadi Islands. On a clear day you can see all the way to Cap Bon in Tunisia, a distance of 170km (106 miles). The gardens are always open; entrance is free.

Saving the best for last, you'll come to **Castello di Venere,** or Castle of Venus, built atop Mount San Giuliano on the same spot where in ancient times a temple to the goddess stood. Dating from the 12th century, the present *castello* was constructed as a defensive fortification by the Normans. Massive and majestic, it became the seat of Norman authority in the west. It's still encircled by mammoth medieval towers. Above the entrance to the castle, note the coat of arms of Charles V and an original Gothic window. The castle provides an even more **memorable view** ★★★ than does the adjoining Giardino del Balio; you can see the plains of Trapani and the Egadi Islands to the southwest. In fair weather, you can even spot the offshore island of Ustica (p. 140).

After all the looting, burning, and destruction this castle has witnessed over the centuries, little is left of the ruins. But the view still makes it worthwhile. The castle is open daily 9am to 8pm year-round, with no admission fee.

SHOPPING

Altieri 1882   This small, charming shop lies a few steps uphill from the heart of Erice, Piazza Umberto I. It sells coral jewelry, silver frames, and Sicilian pottery, some of it produced locally. Via Cordici 14. ℂ **0923-869431.**

Bazar del Miele ★   This is one of the most impressive food shops in Sicily, with some items that are esoteric even by local standards. You'll see 15 different honeys; several preparations of anchovies; Marsala wines, arranged by vineyard, year, and degree of sweetness; and liqueurs, including a pale-green one made from fermented pistachios. The array of cheeses and almond-based candies is the most comprehensive in town. Via Cordici 16. ℂ **0923-869181.**

Ceramica Ericina ★   Erice craftspeople are as famous for their rugs as they are for their ceramics. This is basically a ceramics store, but we also found the best selection of Erice carpets here. These highly valued rugs are rigorously hand-woven, the most traditional colors being red, yellow, and blue. Sometimes the colors are broken up by even brighter hues, with both floral and geometric designs in zigzags and diamonds. There is also a good selection of Sicilian lace here. Via Vittorio Emanuele 7. ℂ **0923-869140.**

WHERE TO STAY
Expensive

Hotel Elimo ★   Set in the lower reaches of Erice's historic core, a few steps from the Hotel Moderno (see below), this arts-conscious hotel was built 400 years ago as a private *palazzo* and transformed into a hotel in 1986. Its public areas feature an appealing combination of old frescoed ceiling beams, antique masonry, Oriental rugs, and contemporary leather sofas, all nestled around a library-style TV den that adds considerable coziness to the space. The best views, seen through the enormous windows of the restaurant, sweep over the golden plains of western Sicily. We prefer this hotel's conventional guest rooms, which tend to be large and have well-styled modern furniture. Avoid the duplex suites, which some visitors find uncomfortably claustrophobic.

Via Vittorio Emanuele 75, 91016 Erice. ℂ **0923-869377.** Fax 0923-869252. www.hotelelimo.it. 22 units. 185€ ($241) double; 250€ ($325) suite. AE, DC, MC, V. **Amenities:** Restaurant; bar; laundry service; dry cleaning. *In room:* A/C, TV, minibar.

Moderate

Hotel Baglio Santa Croce ★ ⟨Finds⟩   This is a most delightful discovery and, for many, the most idyllic way to enjoy the pleasures of historic Erice without staying in the crowded center. Not far from town, this converted farmhouse dates from 1637 and lies on the slope of Mount Erice, opening onto the Gulf of Cornino. The original architectural materials, including wooden beams, have been retained. The delightful terraced gardens have panoramic vistas, and the atmosphere is one of charm and grace. Guest rooms are simply but comfortably furnished with tiled floors and wooden beams, along with olive-wood pieces and wrought-iron beds. The on-site restaurant serves good country cooking.

SS187, Km 300 (Contrada Ragosia), 91019 Erice. ℂ **0923-891111.** Fax 0923-891192. www.bagliosanta croce.it. 24 units. 108€–125€ ($140–$163) double. Rates include breakfast. AE, DC, MC. Free parking. Located 2km (1¼ miles) east of Valderice on N187. **Amenities:** Restaurant; bar; outdoor pool; laundry service; dry cleaning. *In room:* TV.

Hotel Moderno ★   It's cozy, it's warm, and it has a lot of charm, but don't let this hotel's name fool you: The kind of modernism it was named for dates from just after

World War II, when a 19th-century stone house and, later, the 14-room annex across the street were converted into one of central Erice's most appealing hotels. Rooms in the annex are bigger than those in the hotel's main core. Regardless of their location, all units have hints of 19th-century styling, the occasional antique, and bentwood, brass, and wicker furniture. About a dozen of the rooms open onto private balconies or terraces. If you arrive on a cold day, you're likely to be welcomed by a blazing fire. The on-site restaurant is highly regarded.

Via Vittorio Emanuele 67, 91016 Erice. ✆ **0923-869300.** Fax 0923-869139. www.hotelmodernoerice.it. 41 units. 95€–120€ ($124–$156) double. Rates include continental breakfast. AE, DC, MC, V. Free parking nearby. **Amenities:** Restaurant; bar; lounge; babysitting; laundry service; dry cleaning. *In room:* A/C, TV, minibar.

Inexpensive

Hotel Belvedere San Nicola ★ (Kids)   Positioned about 731m (2,398 ft.) downhill from the fortifications that surround medieval Erice, this inn stands in an isolated location that slopes down to views over the shoreline of Trapani. It markets itself as a family-friendly country inn that's less expensive than hotels in Erice's historic core. Built in 2000 adjacent to a community of Mediterranean-style town houses (mostly second homes and timeshares for holiday-making Europeans), it resembles a postmodern version of a thick-walled, big-windowed farmhouse. None of the compact, tile-floored guest rooms has air-conditioning, but thanks to Erice's high altitude and constant breezes, you won't need it. Some rooms have high, sloping ceilings, and all have an efficient, no-frills styling. The social center is the large outdoor pool.

Contrada San Nicola, 91016 Erice. ✆ **0923-860124.** Fax 0923-869139. www.pippocatalano.it. 10 units. 80€ ($104) double. Rates include continental breakfast. AE, DC, MC, V. Free parking. **Amenities:** Restaurant; bar; room service; outdoor pool; horseback riding grounds; bocce court; children's playground. *In room:* TV, hair dryer.

WHERE TO DINE

Monte San Giuliano ★ (Finds)   SEAFOOD/TRAPANESE   To reach this garden hideaway, negotiate your way through a labyrinth of narrow stone alleys that begin a few steps downhill from Erice's Piazza Umberto I, then pass through an iron gate and wander beyond stone walls and shrubbery to the restaurant's terraces and dining rooms. The setting is very rustic, typical of Erice. The freshest and finest seafood is served here. That the Arabs once ruled the land is evidenced in the seafood couscous. Our favorite pasta is something to savor: *busiate* (a homemade pasta) made with *pesto alla Trapanese,* which in this case means garlic, basil, fresh tomatoes, and—surprise—almonds. Other worthy pasta dishes include *caserecce* (a homemade pasta) with fresh shrimp and artichokes, or else fettuccine with sea urchins.

Vicolo San Rocco 7. ✆ **0923-869595.** Reservations recommended. Main courses 8€–15€ ($10–$20). AE, DC, MC, V. Tues–Sun 12:15–2:45pm and 7:30–10pm. Closed Jan 7–21.

Osteria di Venere   TRAPANESE/SICILIAN   This local dive has a staff not trained in the social graces, but it serves excellent regional cooking nonetheless. A mix of visitors and locals feasts nightly off the fat of the land. Start, perhaps, with the homemade pasta of the day. It's often made with a spicy sauce of garlic, tomatoes, fresh basil, and toasted almonds in the Trapanese style. The chef's namesake pasta, *alla Venere,* is made with tomatoes, eggplant, swordfish, and a surprising touch of mint. The menu is based mainly on meat in winter, with fish predominating in summer.

Impressions

In Italy, the pleasure of eating is central to the pleasure of living. When you sit down to dinner with Italians, when you share their food, you are sharing their lives.

— Fred Plotkin, *Italy for the Gourmet Traveler* (1996)

Via Roma 6 at Piazza San Giuliano. (C) **0923-869362.** Reservations required. Main courses 7€–16€ ($9.10–$21). DC, MC, V. Thurs–Tues 12:30–2:30pm and 8–10:30pm.

Ulisse SICILIAN   Enter this airy indoor/outdoor dining room by walking up a series of ramps and stairs that seem to go on forever, past hidden pockets of greenery loaded with hibiscus and palmettos. At the top of your climb is a family-managed restaurant lined with paintings by local artists. Pizzas are available here, but only at dinnertime, and they're less popular than the well-prepared fresh fish, meat, and pasta platters for which the place is best known. The house specialty is spaghetti with lobster. Another pasta favorite with locals is *pappardelle* (wide noodles) with fresh mushrooms.

Via Chiaramonte 45. (C) **0923-869333.** Reservations not required. Main courses 8€–16€ ($10–$21). AE, DC, MC, V. Sept–May Fri–Wed noon–3pm and 8pm–midnight; June–Aug daily noon–3pm and 8pm–midnight.

Pastries

Erice is renowned throughout Sicily for its pastries. These delectable goodies were carefully refined over the years by nuns based in Erice convents from the 14th to the 18th century. Even if you're dining in one of the restaurants in the central core, skip dessert and head to one of the best pastry shops in town.

Pasticceria Grammatico   Maria Grammatico is a former nun who became famous in Italy when she wrote *Bitter Almonds,* the story of her life. Coauthored with Mary Taylor Simeti, the book told of her recollections and recipes from a Sicilian girlhood spent in a convent. Her almond creations have made her celebrated in these parts, especially her crunchy almond cookies, rum-filled marzipan balls, and confections fashioned from chocolate-covered almond paste. The almond-paste creations are works of art, shaped into a variety of forms such as whimsical animals. The pastry shop also sells liqueurs such as a green, minty Marsala.

Via Vittorio Emanuele 14. (C) **0923-869390.** Pastries from 1.50€ ($1.95). No credit cards. Daily 7am–10pm.

Pasticceria Michele Il Tulipano ★   This is the most spectacular bakery in Erice, with a stand-up coffee-and-drinks bar where you can eat the goods on-site. Established on the town's main street in the early 1980s, it devotes itself to the intricately decorated pastries, many flavored with almonds or chocolate, that have made southern Italy famous. The most spectacular pastry we had in all of Sicily was a *cassatella*, a deep-fried fritter stuffed with sweetened ricotta, that's typical of the Trapani region. It tastes best with espresso and perhaps a glass of almond-flavored water.

Via Vittorio Emanuele 10–12. (C) **0923-869672.** Pastries from 1.50€ ($1.95). No credit cards. Daily 7:30am–9pm (until 2am July–Aug).

3 TRAPANI

100km (62 miles) SW of Palermo, 14km (8²/₃ miles) SW of Erice, 150km (93 miles) NW of Agrigento

The major city along the western coast of Sicily, Trapani may be your gateway to the west thanks to its superior transportation links to the rest of Sicily and its easy road links with Palermo.

Trapani lies below the headland of Mount Erice, with the Egadi Islands visible most days off its shore. Trapani is also the capital of its own province, which embraces the medieval hill town of Erice (see above). This most westerly of Sicilian provinces covers a land of great natural beauty, including a coastline that has many long beaches of white sand such as the one at San Vito lo Capo.

The city stands on a sickle-shaped promontory stretching into the sea. Its economy is based largely on fishing and winemaking along with salt mining, with tourism growing annually. A maze of narrow streets makes up its historic core, but it has none of the charm of Erice. If you have only a day for the west, your time is better spent in Erice to the north. But if you have an extra day, consider devoting it to historic Trapani, once a Phoenician outpost. Trapani's most dubious reputation is as a major Sicilian center of the Mafia.

Drepanon, as it was once called, was the key port in the Carthaginian defense of the island at the time of the Punic Wars. The Romans, led by Catulus, captured the city in 241 B.C., marking its decline. It regained some of its lost prestige during the 9th century when the Saracens landed to conquer it. Three centuries later they were followed by the Normans.

It was here in 1272 that Edward I of England pulled into port fresh from the Crusades to learn that he'd inherited the throne. More conquerors were to come, including Peter of Aragon, who landed here in 1282.

Architecturally, the worst blows to Trapani were the Allied bombardments in 1940 and 1943. The entire historic district of San Pietro was razed. Regrettably, the new Trapani bounced back with the building of several ugly modern blocks—think Soviet Union in the heyday of the Cold War. As a result of all this destruction, Trapani has fewer historic sites to visit than most Sicilian cities of its size—but there are some nuggets.

GETTING THERE   By Plane   The not very busy **Florio Airport** (② 0923-842502) is served by daily flights from Rome and the island of Pantelleria. It's located in Birgi on the road to Marsala, 15km (9 miles) from the center of Trapani. Buses, which leave from Piazza Malta, are timed for the arrivals and departures of the planes.

By Train   Most trains, at the rate of 6 per day, make the 2¹/₂-hour run from Palermo; a one-way ticket costs 9.70€ ($13). There are also 14 trains per day from Marsala, taking 30 minutes and costing 3.10€ ($4) one-way. Trains pull in at the **Piazza Stazione,** where luggage storage is available. For general rail information in Italy, call ② **892021.**

By Bus   AST (② **0923-23222**) runs seven buses per day to Erice, departing from Piazza Montalto in Trapani. The one-way ride takes 50 minutes and costs 2.20€ ($2.85).

By Ferry   Trapani is a major embarkation point for ferries and hydrofoils *(aliscafi).* Most departures are for the Egadi Islands of Marettimo, Levanzo, and Favignana. Service is also available to Ustica, Pantelleria, and even Tunisia in North Africa. Ferries depart from the docks near Piazza Garibaldi. Tickets are available from **Siremar** (② **892123**) and **Ustica** (② **0923-22200**).

By Car From Palermo, follow A29 all the way southwest into Trapani. From Marsala, head north along Route 115 to Trapani.

VISITOR INFORMATION The not very helpful **tourist office,** Via San Francesco d'Assisi (✆ **0923-545511**), is open Monday to Saturday 8am to 8pm, Sunday 9am to noon.

FAST FACTS Your hotel will point you to the nearest **pharmacy.** Pharmacies operate on a rotational system for night hours, with at least one open every night of the week. More serious medical needs are attended to at **Ospedale Sant'Antonio Abate,** Via Cosenza, in the northeast of the city (✆ **0923-809111**). For Internet access, head to **Phone Center GGE,** Stazione Marittima (✆ **0923-549840**), where the rate is 4€ ($5.20) per hour. The **post office,** Piazza Vittorio Veneto (✆ **0923-28914**), is open Monday to Saturday 8am to 6:30pm. The biggest and best travel agency is **Panfalone,** Via Ammiraglio Staiti 91 (✆ **0923-542470**), across the street from Trapani's harbor. The agency knows all the boat schedules and can sell tickets from Trapani to any of Sicily's offshore islands. It also sells boat tickets from, say, Palermo to Genoa, or from Palermo or Trapani to Corsica.

EXPLORING TRAPANI

Most visitors head first for the *centro storico* ★, the medieval core lying on the headland jutting into the sea. The most ancient part of this "casbah" was constructed in a typical North African style around a tightly knit maze of narrow streets. Originally these streets lay behind protective walls that guarded against sudden invasions from the sea.

The most intriguing street is **Via Garibaldi** (also known as Rua Nova, or "New Road"), which is flanked with churches and palaces. The Aragonese laid out this street in the 18th century. The best shops in the old town line **Via Torrearsa,** which leads down to a bustling *pescheria* (**fish market**) where tuna—caught in nearby waters—is king. The spacious central square, **Piazza Vittorio Emanuele,** laid out in 1869 and planted with palm trees, is a relaxing oasis.

The pedestrianized main street of Trapani is **Corso Vittorio Emanuele,** sometimes called Rua Grande by the Trapanese. Many elegant baroque buildings are found along this street, which makes for a grand promenade. At the eastern end of the street rises the **Palazzo Senatorio,** the 17th-century town hall, done up in pinkish marble.

Along the way, you can visit the **Cattedrale** (✆ **0923-432111**), open daily from 8am to 4pm. Built on the site of an earlier structure from the 14th century, the cathedral is dedicated to San Lorenzo (St. Lawrence) and has a 1743 facade. Artworks inside include a *Crucifixion* by Giacomo Lo Verde, a local artist, on the building's south side, fourth altar.

Another major church is **Chiesa Santa Maria del Gesù,** on Via San Pietro, with a facade that incorporates both Gothic and Renaissance features, dating from the first half of the 16th century. Its major work of art is a beautiful *Madonna degli Angeli* (Madonna with Angels), a glazed terra-cotta statue by Andrea della Robbia. Regrettably, the church is often closed.

Also worthy but perpetually closed is **Chiesa di Sant'Agostino,** Piazzetta Saturno, adjacent to the tourist office. This church is known for its lovely rose window from the 14th century, and even more so for occasional concerts staged here. Ask at the tourist office for details.

Another church in the heart of old town, **Chiesa del Purgatorio,** is in the 17th-century baroque style. In theory, it's open daily 8:30am to 12:30pm and 4 to 8pm. It's across from Stazione Marettima, 1 block up from Piazza Garibaldi. The entire atmosphere of this church remains medieval, with suffocating incense and otherworldly music. It houses the single greatest treasure in Trapani, however: the *Misteri* ★, 20 life-size wooden figures from the 18th century depicting Christ's Passion. Every bloody detail, including the Crucifixion, is shown.

A once major attraction, **Torre di Ligny,** built in 1671 as a defensive bastion on the tip of Trapani's "sickle," has closed its doors "for a very, very long time"—so we were told.

Villa Margherita lies between old and new Trapani. These public gardens offer a welcome respite from a day of tramping the cobblestone streets. Fountains, banyan trees, and palms rustling in the wind make for an inviting oasis. **Luglio Muscale Trapanese,** a festival of opera, ballet, and cabaret, is staged here in July, with nightly shows at 9pm. A kiosk inside the park gates sells tickets for 5€ ($6.50). For information, call *℃* **0923-21454.**

Modern Trapani has two sights worth a visit; otherwise, you can skip it without cultural deprivation. **Santuario dell'Annunziata** ★ is a 14th-century convent whose cloisters enclose the major museum of Trapani (see below). The 14th-century church was forever altered in the 18th century by new decorators, although its Gothic portal remains, surmounted by a lovely rose window. The **chapels** ★★ are a treasure and include two dedicated to the fishermen of Trapani who risk their lives daily to harvest the sea. The major chapel to seek out is the **Cappella della Madonna,** with its sacred Virgin and Bambino, attributed to Nino Pisano in the 14th century. The bronze gates to the chapel are from 1591. On its left flank is **Cappella dei Marinai,** a tufa structure crowned by a dome and built in the Renaissance style.

Adjacent to the church is Trapani's major museum: **Museo Regionale Pepoli** ★, Via Conte Agostino Pepoli 200 (*℃* **0923-553269**), open Monday to Saturday 9am to 1pm and Sunday 9am to 12:30pm. Admission is 4€ ($5.20). The former Carmelite convent has been converted into a showcase of regional art that emphasizes archaeological artifacts but also has a worthy collection of statues and coral carvings. The artistic Gagini family is better represented here than any other artist. Especially striking is *St. James the Greater,* by Antonello Gagini. The folk-art figurines are noteworthy, including a brutal depiction of the biblical legend of Herod's search for the Christ Child. Other works of art include a moving 14th-century *Pietà* ★ by Roberto di Oderisio and some impressive triptychs by anonymous artists.

SHOPPING

Cinzia Gucciardo   This is one of the few stores in Trapani that specializes in jewelry made from coral gathered in nearby waters. Inventories include necklaces, bracelets, and coral-crafted votive portraits of saints that are larger and more elaborate than anything else in Trapani. There's also a collection of 19th-century engravings and art objects, most of them focusing on 18th-century selections, usually in music rooms or salons. Corso Vittorio Emanuele 23–25. *℃* 0923-25542.

Gioielleria Enzo Catania   This might be the most elegant shop in town, the kind of place where a security system "buzzes" you inside after you're checked out by the staff through a plate-glass window. Inside, you'll find clocks, silver picture frames and chalices, religious icons, and impressive gold, silver, and platinum jewelry. Corso Vittorio Emanuele 39–41. *℃* 0923-21148.

Libreria del Corso   One of the town's best bookstores sells Italian-language (and to a lesser degree, English-language) books, many of them about Sicily and its art treasures. Corso Vittorio Emanuele 61. © **0923-26260.**

WHERE TO STAY

Crystal Hotel ★   A member of the NH chain, this is the most architecturally dramatic and urban-style hotel in Trapani. Constructed in the early 1990s, it's the most distinctive ultramodern building in town, characterized by an all-glass facade that curves above a piazza directly in front of the town's rail station. (Few trains come into Trapani every day, so the neighborhood is very quiet.) Guest rooms are comfortable and efficiently organized. Overall, this is a worthy choice and a modern refuge in the midst of an otherwise antique city.

Piazza Umberto I, 91100 Trapani. © **0923-20000.** Fax 0923-25555. www.nh-hotels.it. 70 units. 120€–190€ ($156–$247) double; 260€–290€ ($338–$377) suite. Rates include buffet breakfast. AE, DC, MC, V. Free parking. **Amenities:** Restaurant; bar; room service; babysitting; laundry service; dry cleaning; non-smoking rooms; rooms for those w/limited mobility. *In room:* A/C, TV, minibar, beverage maker (in some), safe, Wi-Fi.

Duca di Castelmonte ★ (Finds)   Motorists seeking lots of atmosphere and good food can drive outside of town to the best *agriturismo* or farmstead in the area. Here you are housed in rustic comfort in little flats which can accommodate two to six people, depending on how many beds you need to rent for the night. The dukes of Castelmonte still live at this castle. The original barns, stalls, and warehouses have been restored to turn into guest lodgings.

The setting is one of olive groves, citrus trees, and century-old pines. The owners grow their own vegetables, olives, and various fruits. The cooks prepare traditional recipes using time-tested family recipes that have been handed down from generation to generation. One of the best dinners in the area costs 23€ ($30).

Via Salvatore Motisi 3, 91020 Xitta (Trapani). ©/fax **0923-526139.** 30 beds. 48€ ($62) per person. Rates include breakfast. AE, MC, V. 5km (3 miles) west of Trapani along Via Florio. **Amenities:** Restaurant; outdoor pool; babysitting. *In room:* No phone.

Hotel Russo   Newer buildings have since taken over this hotel's role as the town's preeminent lodging, and by many standards the design (ca. 1950) and five-story ocher-fronted facade looks slightly outmoded. But a quick view of its art-filled lobby, and a quick understanding of its solid sense of respectability, will make you feel that you're about to stay at one of the most deeply entrenched hotels in western Sicily. There are marble and tile floors throughout, an amusing set of frescoes in the breakfast room, and a sense of old-fashioned Trapani everywhere. Rooms are well maintained, comfortable, and without any particular sense of drama or theatricality.

Via Tintori 4, 91100 Trapani. © **0923-22163.** Fax 0923-26623. www.sicily-hotels.net. 35 units. 77€–90€ ($100–$117) double. Rates include continental breakfast. AE, DC, MC, V. **Amenities:** Bar; room service; babysitting; laundry service; dry cleaning. *In room:* A/C, TV.

Hotel Vittoria   Set on the waterfront road, a short distance from the center of town, this hotel is less preferable to the Crystal but still acceptable in every way. The second-best hotel in town is a well-built, solid structure lacking any particular architectural charm or style. Nevertheless, it is exceedingly comfortable, and the staff is helpful. Guest rooms are furnished in a minimalist way, though the beds are inviting.

Via Francesco Crispi 4, 91100 Trapani. 📞 **0923-873044.** Fax 0923-29870. www.hotelvittoriatrapani.it. 65 units. 80€–100€ ($104–$130) double. Rates include breakfast. AE, DC, MC, V. Free parking. **Amenities:** Breakfast lounge; bar; room service. *In room:* A/C, TV, minibar, hair dryer, Wi-Fi.

WHERE TO DINE

Ai Lumi Tavernetta ★ SICILIAN   Many locals cite this artfully rustic tavern, established in 1993 on the ground floor of what used to be an important family-owned palazzo, as one of Trapani's best restaurants. It's located 2 blocks from the cathedral and features a long, narrow dining room capped with a series of medieval-looking brick arches. During the 17th century, it functioned as a stable, but today the venue is filled with wines from virtually everywhere, dark furniture, and a clientele that includes actors, politicians, and journalists. And, thanks to thick masonry walls and air-conditioning, it's a cool retreat from the blazing heat outside. The cuisine grows more proficient each time we visit. Flavorful dishes include roast lamb in a citrus sauce, local rabbit that's larded and then roasted, and seafood pasta with shrimp and calamari that tastes so fresh, they could have just leapt from the boat.

Corso Vittorio Emanuele 75. 📞 **0923-872418.** Reservations recommended Fri–Sat night. Main courses 8€–18€ ($10–$23). AE, DC, MC, V. Sept–July Mon–Sat 7:30–11pm; Aug daily 7:30–11pm.

P & G ⓥ**alue** SICILIAN/SEAFOOD   This restaurant, one of the best in town, is located near the train station across from the public gardens of Villa Margherita. It's also near the historic center, Via Fardella, and the shopping district. The decor is simple but classic, and service is among the finest in town. A highly recommended house specialty is *busiate,* the homemade pasta of the region, served with tomatoes, lots of garlic, anchovies, and almonds. Since North Africa is just across the sea, expect a wickedly delicious couscous prepared with fresh fish. Desserts are luscious, so save room.

Via Spalti 1. 📞 **0923-547701.** Reservations recommended. Main courses 7€–18€ ($9.10–$23). AE, DC, MC, V. Mon–Sat 10am–3:30pm and 7pm–midnight.

Ristorante da Peppe SICILIAN   Often convivial meals are served in this one-room restaurant, where large murals and a blue-green color scheme brighten up the varnished wood and white plaster. Menu items feature a well-rehearsed, oft-repeated medley of mostly Sicilian dishes, such as spaghetti with squid and squid ink; three kinds of couscous; risotto paella (a Sicilian adaptation of the famous dish of Valencia); and a time-honored favorite, *spaghetti rustica,* with swordfish, tuna, salmon, dried tomatoes, Abruzzi herbs, and bread crumbs.

Via Spalti 50. 📞 **0923-28246.** Reservations recommended Fri–Sat night. Main courses 8€–15€ ($10–$20); fixed-price menus 14€–22€ ($18–$29). AE, DC, MC, V. Daily 1–11pm.

Taverna Paradiso ★ SICILIAN   This tavern, established in 1996 in an old warehouse on the seafront, is the town's most prestigious restaurant. The warren of medieval-looking stone rooms is stylishly decorated with rustic artifacts that show off the antique masonry to its best advantage. The food is excellent, and prices not nearly as high as you might expect from a place of this quality. Care and precision go into every dish, especially the house specialties: a maritime version of couscous; spaghetti with tangy sea urchins; and a marvelous pasta dish with lobster, shrimp, and fresh artichokes. In winter, well-flavored meat and poultry dishes are likely to be featured when fish catches are slim due to rough waters.

Lungomare Dante Alighieri 22. 📞 **0923-22303.** Reservations recommended. Main courses 10€–18€ ($13–$23). AE, DC, MC, V. Mon–Sat 1–3:30pm and 8–11:30pm.

134km (83 miles) NW of Agrigento, 301km (187 miles) W of Catania, 124km (77 miles) SW of Palermo, 31km (19 miles) S of Trapani

Evoking a North African town with its tangle of narrow streets and alleys, Marsala is the home of the world-famous Marsala wine, a rival of port and Madeira. The wine was first popularized in 1770 when an Englishman, John Woodhouse, came ashore from a British ship that had been forced to anchor here during a violent storm. Woodhouse headed for a local tavern, and the rest is history.

The name Marsala dates from the port's occupation by the Saracens, who called it *Marsa el Allah,* or "Port of God." But it was the Carthaginians who founded the town on Cape Lilibeo (also called Cape Boeo) in 396 B.C. after fleeing nearby Mothia, which had been destroyed by armies from Syracuse. Marsala then fell to the Romans after a siege that lasted a decade (250–241 B.C.). The year 47 B.C. saw the arrival of Julius Caesar, who pitched camp here en route to North Africa.

One of the most famous events in Italian history occurred here on May 11, 1860, when Garibaldi and his brigade of 1,000 red-shirted men arrived to liberate Sicily from the Bourbons.

In 1943, Marsala sustained heavy damage from Allied bombers before their land invasion of Sicily.

Today, Marsala is a thriving little town on Cape Boeo, the westernmost tip of Sicily. Many of its hotels and restaurants are filled with businesspeople trading in Marsala wine. Although Erice (p. 311) is a more popular attraction, Marsala merits a day if you can spare it.

GETTING THERE   Multiple **trains** per day run south from Trapani (14 per day Mon–Sat, and 5 on Sun). The one-way trip costs 3.10€ ($4) and takes 30 minutes. For schedules, call ⓒ **892021**.

Buses for Marsala leave from Piazza Montalto in Trapani at the rate of three per day. The one-way trip costs 3€ ($3.90) and lasts 35 minutes. For schedules, call ⓒ **0923-21021**.

By **car,** head south from Trapani along Route 115.

VISITOR INFORMATION   The **tourist office,** Via 11 Maggio 100 (ⓒ **0923-714097**), is open Monday to Saturday 8am to 1:45pm and 2:10 to 8:10pm, Sunday 9am to noon.

GETTING AROUND   For a **taxi,** call ⓒ **339-5497849**.

FAST FACTS   In an **emergency,** call the *Carabinieri* (army police corps) at ⓒ **112.** The most convenient drugstore is the **Farmacia Calcagno,** Via 11 Maggio 126 (ⓒ **0923-953254**). When it's closed, a notice is posted listing what other pharmacies are open. For medical care, go to the **Hospital San Biagio,** Via Colocasio 10 (ⓒ **0923-782111**).

EXPLORING THE TOWN

The heart of this wine-producing town is the **Piazza della Repubblica,** site of the Chiesa Madre (see below) and the Palazzo Senatorio, dating from the 18th century and nicknamed "Loggia."

Branching off from this square is the main street, **Via 11 Maggio,** flanked by the town's most splendid *palazzi.* In the heyday of the Roman Empire, this street was called *Decumanus Maximus.* From Piazza della Repubblica, **Via Garibaldi** heads south to **Porta Garibaldi,** a magnificent gateway crowned by an eagle. Garibaldi is honored because it

Don't Even Mention Port in This Town

If you'd like to watch Marsala grapes crushed and turned into the town's "sweet nectar," Marsala wine, head for the **Cantine Florio,** Lungomare Via Florio (✆ **0923-781111**), which offers free guided tours of the winery. The 30-minute tours are offered Monday and Thursday at 11am and 3:30pm, Friday at 11am.

Devotees of Marsala also flock to **Cantina Sperimentale Istituto Regionale della Vite e del Vino,** Via Trapani 218 (✆ **0923-737511**), open Thursday to Monday 7:30am to 2pm and Tuesday and Wednesday 7:30am to 2pm and 3 to 7pm. You are allowed to sample a number of experimental wines here.

was at Marsala that he and 1,000 volunteers, dressed in red shirts, landed from Genoa. Their aim was to overthrow the Bourbon rulers, thus liberating the "Kingdom of the Two Sicilies."

The largest church in Marsala is **Chiesa Madre,** Piazza della Repubblica (✆ **0923-716295**), open daily 7:30am to 9pm. Originally constructed during the Norman occupation, it was massively rebuilt in the 1700s. The original church here was dedicated to St. Thomas à Becket. The dome collapsed in 1893 and was partially reconstructed in the 20th century. The facade is decorated with statues and flanked by two small campaniles (bell towers), completed as late as 1956. The three-nave interior is graced with slender pillars and contains many art treasures, including 15th- and 16th-century sculptures by the Gagini brothers. Seek out, in particular, the lovely *Madonna del Popolo* in the right transept, a 1490 creation of Domenico Gagini.

In back of the Chiesa Madre is the entrance to **Museo degli Arazzi,** Via Garraffa 57 (✆ **0923-711327**), open Monday to Saturday 9am to 1pm and 4 to 6pm, Sunday 9am to 1pm; admission is 2.50€ ($3.25). Its main attraction is a collection of eight **Flemish tapestries** ★, made in Brussels between 1530 and 1550. The skillfully created tapestries depict such scenes as the capture of Jerusalem and the war fought by Titus against the Jews in A.D. 66 to A.D. 67.

Marsala's other major museum, **Museo Archeologico di Baglio Anselmi,** at Lungomare Boéo (✆ **0923-952535**), is open Tuesday to Saturday 9am to 7pm, and Sunday 9am to 1pm. Admission is 3€ ($3.90). The museum is installed in a former warehouse for bottles of Marsala. Its chief attraction is the remains of a well-preserved **Punic ship** ★ discovered in 1971 off Isola Longa, north of Marsala. It measures 35m (115 ft.) long and was artfully reconstructed in 1980. The ship may have been originally constructed for the Battle of the Egadi Islands in 241 B.C.; it's amazing to think that a vessel dating from the First Punic War is still around in any form. Once manned by 68 oarsmen, this is the only known such war vessel ever uncovered.

Open for a look 24 hours a day is the **Insula di Capo Boeo,** at the end of Viale Vittorio Emanuele. Here are the ruins of a trio of Roman *insulae* (apartment complexes), including that of a spacious villa dating from the 3rd century B.C. Around the *impluvium* (basin built into the floor) you can see a quartet of mosaics depicting "The Battle of the Wild Beasts." Also here are the ruins of *terme* (baths) and salons containing mosaics. The head of Medusa is clearly visible.

Oviesse Set within about a block from the town's showcase church (Chiesa Madre), this is the department store that every local resident knows. Its enormous inventories include housewares, clothing, camping gear, and gift items. It's the kind of mass-market department store where you can acquire whatever objects you might have lost or forgotten on your way to Marsala, usually at prices a lot less expensive than in smaller, more stylish boutiques. Via Sebastiano Cammereri Scurti. ℂ **0923-951767.**

WHERE TO STAY

Delfino Beach Hotel This is the closest thing to a large-scale resort in Marsala. Set 5km (3 miles) south of town, behind a neobaroque facade across a busy highway from the beach, it was designed as a compound of cement-sided buildings within a walled garden, centered on a splashy-looking core that evokes a highly theatrical stage setting.

Accommodations include 16 apartments located near the main building. Most of the double bedrooms are midsize, with modern furnishings, often with a sitting area. Each is well supplied with modern gadgets, including individual controls for the air-conditioning. The well-furnished apartments are far more generous in size, with sitting and living areas separate from the bedrooms. Many of these are actually suites suitable for families of about four persons. The hotel restaurant and its beachfront lie a dusty 10-minute walk across the busy highway from the hotel's core. Frankly, despite the Vegas-inspired pool and nearby access to the beach, we prefer the Hotel President (see below), closer to the center of town.

Lungomare Mediterraneo 672, 91025 Marsala. ℂ **0923-751076.** Fax 0923-751647. www.delfinobeach. com. 50 units. 100€–180€ ($130–$234) double. Rates include half board. AE, DC, MC, V. Free parking. **Amenities:** Restaurant; bar; outdoor pool; tennis court; gym; room service; babysitting; laundry service. *In room:* A/C, TV, minibar, hair dryer, Jacuzzi (in some), safe.

Hotel Acos This boxy, government-rated three-star hotel was originally built in 1959 as a member of the now-defunct AGIP chain. It's set in back of a gas station on one of the town's busiest boulevards, on the south side of Marsala's commercial core. Favored by business travelers, it is a serviceable and reasonably priced choice. In spite of its setting, it is more stylish and elegant than it looks on its interior, and the restaurant San Carlo, immediately adjacent, serves a respectable Sicilian cuisine. The small to midsize guest rooms are well maintained and feature comfortably contemporary furnishings, along with tiled bathrooms.

Via Mazara 14, 91025 Marsala. ℂ **0923-999166.** Fax 0923-999132. www.acoshotel.com. 41 units. 85€– 100€ ($111–$130) double. Rates include buffet breakfast. AE, DC, MC, V. **Amenities:** Restaurant; bar; laundry service; rooms for those w/limited mobility. *In room:* A/C, TV, minibar.

Hotel President ★ Modern and pleasingly designed, this is Marsala's best and most prestigious hotel, with a whiff of jazzy insouciance that might have been inspired by Las Vegas. You may be surprised to learn that this favorite stopover of business travelers is rated only three stars by the local tourist authorities, since it looks very much like it deserves four. The entrance is prefaced with a row of palms; inside, a sheathing of travertine marble adds a touch of sober dignity. Guest rooms are located in two five-story towers, connected at the bases by a granite-floored lobby strewn with leather sofas and chairs. Guest rooms are comfortable, sunny, and relatively large, each with a bathroom that—with three separate kinds of marble sheathing and tub/shower combinations— looks like a testimonial to the stonemason's art.

Via Nino Bixio 1, 91025 Marsala. 🕿 **0923-999333.** Fax 0923-999115. www.presidentmarsala.it. 128 units. 105€ ($137) double. AE, DC, MC, V. Free parking. **Amenities:** Restaurant; 2 bars; outdoor pool; gym; room service. *In room:* A/C, TV, minibar.

New Hotel Palace ★ Kids This 19th-century estate was built by an English wine importer but it has been completely redone as a modern hotel with sleek Italian styling. Amazingly, the original architectural and historical appearance has been maintained as much as possible despite the addition of another 48 accommodations. The choice of rooms doesn't matter a lot because newer units duplicate the style of the original eight units in the main house. Bedrooms are spacious and furnished in the style of a grand hotel. Some of the units are adorned with frescoes by local artists. The bar is the spot for an elegant rendezvous, and the first-class restaurant serves market-fresh ingredients in delightful concoctions. A tree-lined park lies in front of the hotel, and stately old trees are a backdrop for the swimming pool. Children enjoy the playground.

Lungomare Mediterraneo 57, 91025 Marsala. 🕿 **0923-719492.** Fax 0923-719496. www.newhotelpalace. com. 56 units. 100€–297€ ($130–$386) double; from 300€ ($390) suite. Rates include buffet breakfast. AE, DC, MC, V. Free parking. **Amenities:** Restaurant; bar; outdoor pool; room service; massage; babysitting; laundry service; dry cleaning; all nonsmoking rooms; rooms for those w/limited mobility. *In room:* A/C, TV, minibar, hair dryer, safe.

Villa Favorita ★ Finds This elegant and offbeat choice was established in the early 19th century, when it became a rendezvous for Sicilian intellectuals and aristocrats. Today the elegant retreat is part of the cultural heritage of Marsala and has been given a new lease on life as a government-rated four-star hotel. Much of the original architecture of the main building has been preserved, with its wide oak floors and arched loggias opening onto a courtyard. You have a choice of a more traditional room in the main building or else, for greater privacy, a whitewashed igloo-shaped bungalow in the garden. The choice is yours. Bedrooms are spacious, and each of the accommodations comes with a well-maintained private bathroom. Both first-rate Sicilian and Italian dishes are a feature of the on-site restaurant.

Via Favorita 23, 91025 Marsala. 🕿 **0923-989100.** Fax 0923-980264. www.villafavorita.com. 29 bunga-lows, 13 units (in the main building). 80€–100€ ($104–$130) double in bungalow; 108€–130€ ($140–$169) triple in bungalow; 95€–120€ ($124–$156) double (in the main building); 120€–145€ ($156–$189) triple (in the main building). Rates include buffet breakfast. AE, DC, MC, V. Free parking. From the center of Marsala take the SS115 toward Trapani. The hotel is signposted. **Amenities:** Restaurant; bar; outdoor pool; tennis court; bowling green; playground; laundry service; dry cleaning; rooms for those w/limited mobility. *In room:* A/C, TV, minibar, safe.

ON THE OUTSKIRTS

Kempinski Hotel Giardinodi Costanza ★★★ Kids Set in a landscaped park of olive groves and vineyards, this German chain hotel operates the most elegant resort in western Sicily. You wander among fountains and gazebos before entering a refined world of understated elegance and sublime comfort. The spacious, beautifully furnished guest rooms are a harmonious blend of typical Sicilian decor and warm colors that open onto a private balcony or terrace. The wonderful, soft feather beds of goose feathers are per-haps the finest in the province.

The children's programs here are the best along the coast. The on-site spa is the best in Sicily, named for the noted Austrian aesthetician Daniela Steiner, whose clinics in St. Moritz and Monte Carlo are always packed. Steiner suggests preserving skin beauty by using natural methods, in this case Sicilian products such as sea salt. Patrons are also smeared with volcanic clay. The sublime Sicilian cuisine highlights regional produce. An hour's drive from Palermo, the location is ideal for exploring such ancient sights as Segesta and Selinunte, Erice, or Marsala itself.

Via Salemi Km. 7,1000 M 91026 Mazara del Vallo. (℃) **0923-675000.** Fax 0923-675876. www.kempinskisicily.com. 91 units. 200€–387€ ($260–$503) double; 640€ ($832) junior suite; 4,900€ ($6,370) penthouse suite. AE, DC, MC, V. **Amenities:** Restaurant; 2 bars; 2 pools (indoor and outdoor); spa; room service; laundry service/dry cleaning. *In room:* A/C, TV, minibar, hair dryer, safe, Wi-Fi.

WHERE TO DINE

Ristorante Delfino ★ SEAFOOD/SICILIAN This restaurant lies adjacent to the beachfront and across the highway from the hotel that bears the same name. It was established in the 1960s and has done rip-roaring business ever since. The setting is a very large, always bustling series of terrazzo-floored, slightly battered dining rooms, with a row of large windows and a terrace overlooking the sea. A huge array of antipasti, plus a steamy hardworking kitchen that's open to view, greet visitors as they enter. The fish soup is the best in town, but the homemade *bucatini* pasta in a tuna and mint sauce may be your starter of choice. Several kinds of carpaccio, often flavored with balsamic vinegar, are presented nightly. The chef is justifiably proudest of his wide variety of fresh fish, much of which is exhibited in a display case near the entrance.

Delfino Beach Hotel, Lungomare Mediterraneo 672, 91025 Marsala. (℃) **0923-998188.** Reservations not necessary. Main courses 8€–17€ ($10–$22); pizzas 5€–8€ ($6.50–$10); fixed-price menu 20€ ($26). AE, MC, V. Daily 8:30am–11pm. Closed Tues Oct–Mar.

Tenuta Volpara ★ **Finds** SICILIAN Follow a labyrinth of winding country roads, then pass between a stately pair of masonry columns, to reach Marsala's quintessential country inn—a jumble of light, noise, and energy in an otherwise isolated rural setting, 5.6km (3$^{1}/_{2}$ miles) south of the city center. Vast and echoing, with one of the largest dining rooms in western Sicily, it was rebuilt in 1993 on the site of a ruined tavern that had been here for centuries. Many of your fellow diners might be here as part of a wedding reception or baptism, which adds to this place's sense of fun. Beneath soaring stone arches, you'll dine on such items as steak braised in a Barolo wine sauce, homemade sausages roasted with an herb-flavored liqueur, fettuccine with fresh mushrooms, and the dessert specialty, *zabina,* a pastry laced with ricotta cheese.

Situated in an annex somewhat removed from the bustle of the restaurant are 18 motel-style guest rooms, each with a shower-only bathroom, air-conditioning, minibar, TV, and phone. With breakfast included, a double costs 80€ ($104).

Contrada Volpara. (℃) **0923-984588.** Fax 0923-984667. Reservations recommended Fri–Sat night. Main courses 7€–15€ ($9.10–$20); fixed-price menu 15€ ($20). AE, DC, MC, V. Daily 1:30–3pm and 8:30pm–midnight. Closed Mon Oct–Mar.

Trattoria Garibaldi **Value** SICILIAN/SEAFOOD Located in the historic center near the cathedral, this unpretentious restaurant has been feeding locals well since 1963. Patrons come here, some once or twice weekly, to enjoy the dishes, which despite their low prices are made with fresh, quality ingredients. The chef is justly proud of his array of antipasti, including succulent mussels and sea urchins, the latter dish an acquired taste for many. We especially like his *busiate* (their local homemade pasta) served with fresh fish. He also does a couscous with fish, inspired by Morocco. The signature dessert is *Cappidruzzi,* fried ravioli filled with ricotta. There's also an impressive list of Sicilian wines, all at affordable prices.

Piazza dell'Addolorata 35. (℃) **0923-953006.** Reservations recommended. Main courses 7€–13€ ($9.10–$17). MC, V. Mon–Fri noon–3pm and 7:30–10pm; Sat 7:30–10pm; Sun noon–3pm.

Trattoria delle Cozze Basirico ★ ⓕⓘⓝⓓⓢ SEAFOOD   Set on the southern outskirts of the town of Mazara del Vallo, about 5km (3 miles) from the center, this restaurant might remind you of an oversize railway car that just happens to serve vast amounts of seafood to hundreds of diners every night throughout the summer. Don't expect grandeur; this is a gutsy, two-fisted place whose walls are open to the sea breezes. The overworked staff is coyly clad in exaggerated sailor costumes. There are no printed menus here: A fast-talking waiter will tell you that the only options are selections from the buffet-style antipasti table, several different preparations of mussels, and steamed octopus in either lemon or tomato sauce. Drinks of choice include wine or beer, a suitable accompaniment for the restaurant's widely acknowledged specialty, mussels.

Litoranea Mazara-Granitola. ⓒ **0923-942323.** Reservations not accepted. Main courses 7€–10€ ($9.10–$13). AE, DC, MC, V. May–Sept daily 8pm–midnight. Closed Oct–Apr. Mazara del Vallo is reached by heading southeast of Marsala along Rte. 115 for 22km (14 miles).

MARSALA AFTER DARK

Many locals, especially young people, drop in at **E & N Café,** Via XI Maggio 130 (ⓒ **0923-951969**), if for no other reason than to enjoy the most delectable cannoli in town. Located on the most important commercial street of the historic center, the cafe is a bit small, but inviting. It's known for its *tavola calda* (panini, fresh rolls, and the like), as well as for its delicious ice creams. Note the showcase of marzipan fruit, which the friendly staff will convert into a "marzipan smoothie" for you. In fair weather, the cafe is open daily 7:30am to 2am, which is considered very, very late for sleepy Marsala. In winter, hours are Thursday to Tuesday 7:30am to 11pm.

Appendix A:
Fast Facts Sicily

AMERICAN EXPRESS Travel agencies representing AmEx are found in large cities, including **La Duca Viaggi,** Viale Africa 14, in Catania (ℂ **095-7222295**); **La Duca Viaggi,** Via Don Bosco 39, in Taormina (ℂ **0942-625255**); and **Giovanni Ruggieri e Figli,** Emerico Armari 40, in Palermo (ℂ **091-587144**).

AREA CODE Dial 011, then the country code for Italy (39), and then the city code (for example, 091 for Palermo or 095 for Catania). Then dial the specific phone number.

ATM NETWORKS See "Money & Costs," p. 45.

BUSINESS HOURS Regular business hours are generally Monday to Saturday 8 or 9am to 1pm and 4 to 7 or 8pm. The riposo (midafternoon closing) is observed in Sicily. If you're on the island in summer, when the heat is intense, you too may want to learn the custom of riposo, retreating back to your hotel for a long nap during the hottest part of the day. Banking hours vary from town to town, but in general are Monday to Friday 8:30am to 1:20pm and 3 to 4pm.

CASH POINTS See "Money & Costs" on p. 45.

CURRENCY See "Money & Costs" on p. 45.

DRINKING LAWS Wine with meals has been a normal part of family life for hundreds of years in Sicily. Children are exposed to wine at an early age, and consumption of alcohol isn't anything out of the ordinary. There's no legal drinking age for buying or ordering alcohol. Alcohol is sold day and night throughout the year because there's almost no restriction on the sale of wine or liquor in Sicily.

DRIVING RULES See "Getting There & Getting Around," p. 38.

DRUGSTORES Every farmacia (drugstore) posts a list of those that are open at night and on Sunday.

ELECTRICITY The electricity in Sicily varies considerably. It's usually alternating current (AC); the cycle is 50Hz 220V. Check the local current at the hotel where you're staying. We recommend obtaining a transformer if you're carrying any electrical appliances. Plugs have prongs that are round, not flat; therefore, an adapter plug is also needed.

EMBASSIES & CONSULATES There's a **U.S. Consulate** at Via Vaccarini 1, in Palermo (ℂ **091-305857**). The nearest **U.S. Embassy** is in Rome, at Via Vittorio Veneto 119A (ℂ **06-46-741**).

The **Canadian Embassy** is at Via Zara 30, in Rome (ℂ **06-854441**).

There's a **U.K. Consulate** at Via Cavour 117, in Palermo (ℂ **091-326412**), and a **U.K. Embassy** at Via XX Settembre 80A, in Rome (ℂ **06-422-00001**).

The **Irish Embassy** is at Piazza di Campitelli 3, in Rome (ℂ **06-697-9121**). For consular queries, call ℂ **06-697-9121**.

The **Australian Embassy** is at Via Antonio Bosio 15, in Rome (ℂ **06-852-721**). The **New Zealand Embassy** is at Via Zara 28, in Rome (ℂ **06-441-7171**).

EMERGENCIES For the police, dial ✆ **113;** for an ambulance, ✆ **118;** and to report a fire, ✆ **115.** For road assistance, dial ✆ **803116.** For a general crisis, call the *Carabinieri* (army police corps) at ✆ **112.**

GASOLINE (PETROL) See "Planning Your Trip to Sicily," p. 33.

HOLIDAYS Offices and shops in Sicily are closed on the following **national holidays:** January 1 (New Year's Day), Easter Monday, April 25 (Liberation Day), May 1 (Labor Day), July 15 (Santa Rosalia), August 15 (Assumption of the Virgin), November 1 (All Saints' Day), December 8 (Feast of the Immaculate Conception), December 25 (Christmas Day), and December 26 (Santo Stefano).

INSURANCE Medical Insurance For travel overseas, most U.S. health plans (including Medicare and Medicaid) do not provide coverage, and the ones that do often require you to pay for services upfront and reimburse you only after you return home.

As a safety net, you may want to buy travel medical insurance, particularly if you're traveling to a remote or high-risk area where emergency evacuation might be necessary. If you require additional medical insurance, try **MEDEX Assistance** (✆ **410/453-6300;** www.medex assist.com) or **Travel Assistance International** (✆ **800/821-2828;** www.travel assistance.com; for general information on services, call the company's **Worldwide Assistance Services, Inc.** at ✆ **800/777-8710**).

Canadians should check with their provincial health plan offices or call **Health Canada** (✆ **866/225-0709;** www.hc-sc. gc.ca) to find out the extent of their coverage and what documentation and receipts they must take home in case they are treated overseas.

Travelers from the U.K. should carry their European Health Insurance Card (EHIC), which replaced the E111 form as proof of entitlement to free/reduced cost medical treatment abroad (✆ **0845/606-2030;** www.ehic.org.uk). Note, however, that the EHIC only covers "necessary medical treatment," and for repatriation costs, lost money, baggage, or cancellation, travel insurance from a reputable company should always be sought (www.travel insuranceweb.com).

Travel Insurance The cost of travel insurance varies widely, depending on the destination, the cost and length of your trip, your age and health, and the type of trip you're taking, but expect to pay between 5% and 8% of the vacation itself. You can get estimates from various providers through **InsureMyTrip.com** (✆ **800/487-4722**). Enter your trip cost and dates, your age, and other information, for prices from more than a dozen companies.

U.K. citizens and their families who make more than one trip abroad per year may find an annual travel insurance policy works out cheaper. Check **www.money supermarket.com** (✆ **0845/345-5708**), which compares prices across a wide range of providers for single- and multitrip policies.

Most big travel agents offer their own insurance and will probably try to sell you their package when you book a holiday. Think before you sign. Britain's Consumers' Association recommends that you insist on seeing the policy and reading the fine print before buying travel insurance. The **Association of British Insurers** (✆ **020/7600-3333;** www.abi.org.uk) gives advice by phone and publishes *Holiday Insurance*, a free guide to policy provisions and prices. You might also shop around for better deals: Try **Columbus Direct** (✆ **0870/033-9988;** www.columbusdirect.net).

Trip-Cancellation Insurance Trip-cancellation insurance will help retrieve your money if you have to back out of a trip or depart early, or if your travel supplier goes bankrupt. Trip cancellation traditionally covers such events as sickness, natural disasters, and State Department advisories. The latest news in trip-cancellation insurance is the availability of **"any-reason"** cancellation coverage—which costs more but covers cancellations made for any reason. You won't get back 100% of your prepaid trip cost, but you'll be refunded a substantial portion. **TravelSafe** (𝒞 **888/ 885-7233;** www.travelsafe.com) offers both types of coverage. For details, contact one of the following recommended insurers: **Access America** (𝒞 866/807-3982; www.accessamerica.com); **Travel Guard International** (𝒞 800/826-4919; www. travelguard.com); **Travel Insured International** (𝒞 800/243-3174; www.travel insured.com); and **Travelex Insurance Services** (𝒞 888/457-4602; www.travelex-insurance.com).

LANGUAGE   Except in remote backwaters, Italian, of course, is the language of the land. (See p. 323 for a brief glossary of useful terms.) English is often understood at attractions such as museums and at most hotels and restaurants catering to foreigners. Even if not all of the staff speaks English at a particular establishment, such as a restaurant, sometimes at least one member of the staff does and can aid you. Most islanders also speak a Sicilian dialect. This is a patois comprised of words left over from various conquerors, including Arabic, Greek, French, and Spanish. It's a sort of linguistic amalgam, reflecting centuries of occupation (including American occupation).

LEGAL AID   The consulate of your country is the place to turn for legal aid, although offices can't interfere in the Italian legal process. They can, however, inform you of your rights and provide a list of attorneys. You'll have to pay for the attorney out of your pocket—there's no free legal assistance. If you're arrested for a drug offense, about all the consulate will do is notify a lawyer about your case and perhaps inform your family. If the problem is serious enough, most nationals will be referred to their embassies or consulates in Rome.

LOST & FOUND   Be sure to tell all of your credit card companies the minute you discover your wallet has been lost or stolen. Your credit card company or insurer also may require you file a police report and provide a report number or record of the loss. Most credit card companies have an emergency toll-free number to call if your card is lost or stolen; they may be able to wire you a cash advance immediately or deliver an emergency credit card in a day or two. Visa's emergency number in Italy is 𝒞 **800-819;** call collect. American Express cardholders should call collect 𝒞 **06/7220-348.** MasterCard holders should call collect 𝒞 **800-870-866.**

Identity theft and fraud are potential complications of losing your wallet, especially if you've lost your driver's license along with your cash and credit cards. Notify the major credit-reporting bureaus immediately; placing a fraud alert on your records may protect you against liability for criminal activity. The three major U.S. credit-reporting agencies are **Equifax** (𝒞 **800/766-0008;** www.equifax.com), **Experian** (𝒞 **888/397-3742;** www. experian.com), and **TransUnion** (𝒞 **800/ 680-7289;** www.transunion.com). Finally, if you've lost all forms of photo ID, call your airline and explain; they might allow you to board the plane if you have a copy of your passport or birth certificate and a copy of the police report you've filed. If you need emergency cash over the weekend when all banks and American Express offices are closed, you can have money wired to you via **Western Union** (𝒞 **800/ 325-6000;** www.westernunion.com).

MAIL   Mail delivery in Italy is notoriously bad. Your family and friends back home might receive your postcards in 1 week, or it could take 2 weeks (sometimes longer). Postcards, aerogrammes, and letters weighing up to 20 grams sent to the United States and Canada cost .85€

($1.10); to the United Kingdom, .60€ (.80¢); and to Australia and New Zealand, 1€ ($1.30). You can buy stamps at post offices and *tabacchi* (tobacco shops).

NEWSPAPERS & MAGAZINES In major cities, hotels and news kiosks often carry the *International Herald Tribune* and *USA Today*, as well as other English-language newspapers and magazines such as *Time* and *Newsweek*—but they're hard to find elsewhere. There are no English-language magazines or newspapers published in Sicily.

PASSPORTS The websites listed provide downloadable passport applications as well as the current fees for processing applications. For an up-to-date, country-by-country listing of passport requirements around the world, go to the "International Travel" tab of the U.S. State Department at **http://travel.state.gov**. International visitors to the U.S. can obtain a visa application at the same website. *Note:* Children are required to present a passport when entering the United States at airports. More information on obtaining a passport for a minor can be found at http://travel.state.gov. Allow plenty of time before your trip to apply for a passport; processing normally takes 4 to 6 weeks (3 weeks for expedited service) but can take longer during busy periods (especially spring). And keep in mind that if you need a passport in a hurry, you'll pay a higher processing fee.

For Residents of Australia You can pick up an application from your local post office or any branch of Passports Australia, but you must schedule an interview at the passport office to present your application materials. Call the **Australian Passport Information Service** at ℓ **131-232,** or visit the government website at www.passports.gov.au.

For Residents of Canada Passport applications are available at travel agencies throughout Canada or from the central **Passport Office,** Department of Foreign Affairs and International Trade, Ottawa, ON K1A 0G3 (ℓ **800/567-6868;** www. ppt.gc.ca). *Note:* Canadian children who travel must have their own passport. However, if you hold a valid Canadian passport issued before December 11, 2001, that bears the name of your child, the passport remains valid for you and your child until it expires.

For Residents of Ireland You can apply for a 10-year passport at the **Passport Office,** Setanta Centre, Molesworth Street, Dublin 2 (ℓ **01/671-1633;** www.irlgov. ie/iveagh). Those 17 and under and 66 and over must apply for a 3-year passport. You can also apply at 1A South Mall, Cork (ℓ **21/494-4700**) or at most main post offices.

For Residents of New Zealand You can pick up a passport application at any New Zealand Passports Office or download it from their website. Contact the **Passports Office** at ℓ **0800/225-050** in New Zealand, or 04/474-8100, or log on to www. passports.govt.nz.

For Residents of the United Kingdom To pick up an application for a standard 10-year passport (5-year passport for children 15 and under), visit your nearest passport office, major post office, or travel agency or contact the **United Kingdom Passport Service** at ℓ **0870/ 521-0410** or search its website at www. ukpa.gov.uk.

POLICE See "Emergencies," above.

SAFETY Don't think you'll be at the mercy of the Mafia the moment you step foot in Sicily, as popular belief around the world suggests. The Mafia is virtually invisible.

You'll face more danger from petty thieves, such as pickpockets, than you will from the *Cosa Nostra. Scippatori,* or purse snatchers and pickpockets, are the curse of such cities as Palermo, Messina, and Catania.

Country towns, of course, are far safer. Avoid walking on dark streets in the old towns of Sicily at night. Even during the day, relatively deserted inner-city streets can put you at risk of robbery. Although many tourists are robbed, violence against visitors is rare.

Never leave valuables in a car, and never travel with your car unlocked.

SMOKING In 2005 Italy launched one of Europe's toughest laws against smoking in public places, including bars and restaurants. All restaurants and bars come under the ruling except those with ventilated smoking rooms. Otherwise, smokers can retreat to the outdoors or private homes. Smokers face fines from 29€ to 290€ ($38–$377) if caught lighting up. Only 10% of italian restaurants currently have separate smoking areas.

TAXES As a member of the European Union (E.U.), Italy imposes a **value-added tax** (called **IVA** in Italy) on most goods and services. The tax that most affects visitors is the one imposed on hotel rates, which ranges from 9% in first- and second-class hotels to 19% in deluxe hotels.

Non-E.U. citizens are entitled to a **refund of the IVA** if they spend more than 155€ ($202) at any one store, before tax. To claim your refund, request an invoice from the cashier at the store and take it to the *dogana* (Customs office) at the airport to have it stamped before you leave. *Note:* If you're going to another E.U. country before flying home, have it stamped at the airport Customs office of the last E.U. country you'll be in (for example, if you're flying home via Britain, have your Italian invoices stamped in London). Once back home, mail the stamped invoice (keep a photocopy for your records) back to the original vendor within 90 days of the purchase. The vendor will, sooner or later, send you a refund of the tax that you paid at the time of your purchase. Reputable stores view this as a matter of ordinary

paperwork and are businesslike about it. Less-honorable stores might lose your dossier. It pays to deal with established vendors on large purchases. You can also request that the refund be credited to the credit card with which you made the purchase; this is usually faster.

Many shops are now part of the **"Tax Free for Tourists"** network (look for the sticker in the window). Stores participating in this network issue a check along with your invoice at the time of purchase. After you have the invoice stamped at Customs, you can redeem the check for cash directly at the Tax Free booth in the airport at Palermo or Catania, or mail it back in the envelope provided within 60 days.

TELEPHONES See "Staying Connected" on p. 57.

TIME ZONE Sicily is 6 hours ahead of Eastern Standard Time in the United States. Daylight saving time goes into effect in Italy each year from the end of March to the end of October.

TIPPING In **hotels,** the service charge of 15% to 19% is already added to your bill. In addition, it's customary to tip the chambermaid .50€ (65¢) per day, the doorman (for calling a cab) .50€ (65¢), and the bellhop or porter 1.50€ to 2.50€ ($1.95–$3.25) for carrying bags to your room. The concierge expects about 15% of his or her bill, as well as tips for extra services performed, which may include help with long-distance calls. In expensive hotels, these amounts are often doubled.

In **restaurants and cafes,** 15% is usually added to your bill to cover most charges. If you're not sure whether this has been done, ask, "E incluso il servizio?" (ay een-*cloo*-soh eel sair-*vee*-tsoh?). An additional tip isn't expected, but it's nice to leave the equivalent of an extra couple of dollars if you're pleased with the service. Restaurants are required by law to give customers official receipts. Checkroom

322 attendants expect .75€ ($1); washroom attendants, .35€ (45¢).

Taxi drivers expect at least 15% of the fare.

TOILETS All airport and rail stations have toilets, often with attendants who expect to be tipped. Bars, clubs, restaurants, cafes, gas stations, and hotels have facilities as well. Public toilets are also found near many of the major sights. Usually they're designated *WC* (water closet), or *donne* (women) or *uomini* (men). The most confusing designation is *signori* (gentlemen) and *signore* (ladies), so watch that final *i* and *e!* Many public toilets charge a small fee or employ an attendant who expects a tip. Carry tissues in your pocket or purse—they come in handy.

WATER Most Sicilians have mineral water with their meals; however, tap water is safe everywhere, as are public drinking fountains. Unsafe sources will be marked ACQUA NON POTABILE. If tap water comes out cloudy, it's only the calcium or other minerals inherent in a water supply that often comes untreated from fresh springs.

Appendix B: Glossary of Italian Terms & Phrases

1 BASIC VOCABULARY

English	Italian	Pronunciation
Thank you	Grazie	*graht*-tzee-yey
You're welcome	Prego	*prey*-go
Please	Per favore	*pehr* fah-*vohr*-eh
Yes	Si	see
No	No	noh
Good morning or Good day	Buongiorno	bwohn-*djor*-noh
Good evening	Buona sera	*bwohn*-ah *say*-rah
Good night	Buona notte	*bwohn*-ah *noht*-tay
How are you?	Come sta?	*koh*-may *stah*
Very well	Molto bene	*mohl*-toh *behn*-ney
Goodbye	Arrivederci	ahr-ree-vah-*dehr*-chee
Excuse me (to get attention)	Scusi	*skoo*-zee
Excuse me (to get past someone)	Permesso	pehr-*mehs*-soh
Where is . . . ?	Dovè . . . ?	doh-*vey*
the station	la stazione	lah stat-tzee-*oh*-neh
a hotel	un albergo	oon ahl-*behr*-goh
a restaurant	un ristorante	oon reest-ohr-*ahnt*-eh
the bathroom	il bagno	eel *bahn*-nyoh
To the right	A destra	ah *dehy*-stra
To the left	A sinistra	ah see-*nees*-tra
Straight ahead	Avanti (*or sempre* diritto)	ahv-*vahn*-tee (*sehm*-pray dee-*reet*-toh)
How much is it?	Quanto costa?	*kwan*-toh *coh*-sta
The check, please	Il conto, per favore	eel kon-toh *pehr* fah-*vohr*-eh
What time is it?	Che ore sono?	kay *or*-ay *soh*-noh
When?	Quando?	*kwan*-doh

English	Italian	Pronunciation
Yesterday	**Ieri**	ee-*yehr*-ree
Today	**Oggi**	*oh*-jee
Tomorrow	**Domani**	doh-*mah*-nee
Breakfast	**Prima colazione**	*pree*-mah coh-laht-tzee-*ohn*-ay
Lunch	**Pranzo**	*prahn*-zoh
Dinner	**Cena**	*chay*-nah
Monday	**Lunedì**	loo-nay-*dee*
Tuesday	**Martedì**	mart-ay-*dee*
Wednesday	**Mercoledì**	mehr-cohl-ay-*dee*
Thursday	**Giovedì**	joh-vay-*dee*
Friday	**Venerdì**	ven-nehr-*dee*
Saturday	**Sabato**	*sah*-bah-toh
Sunday	**Domenica**	doh-*mehn*-nee-kah

2 NUMBERS

1 **uno** (*oo*-noh)
2 **due** (*doo*-ay)
3 **tre** (tray)
4 **quattro** (*kwah*-troh)
5 **cinque** (*cheen*-kway)
6 **sei** (say)
7 **sette** (*set*-tay)
8 **otto** (*oh*-toh)
9 **nove** (*noh*-vay)
10 **dieci** (dee-*ay*-chee)
11 **undici** (*oon*-dee-chee)
20 **venti** (*vehn*-tee)
21 **ventuno** (vehn-*toon*-oh)

22 **venti due** (*vehn*-tee *doo*-ay)
30 **trenta** (*trayn*-tah)
40 **quaranta** (kwah-*rahn*-tah)
50 **cinquanta** (cheen-*kwan*-tah)
60 **sessanta** (sehs-*sahn*-tah)
70 **settanta** (seht-*tahn*-tah)
80 **ottanta** (oht-*tahn*-tah)
90 **novanta** (noh-*vahnt*-tah)
100 **cento** (*chen*-toh)
1,000 **mille** (*mee*-lay)
5,000 **cinque milla** (*cheen*-kway *mee*-lah)
10,000 **dieci milla** (dee-*ay*-chee *mee*-lah)

3 ARCHITECTURAL TERMS

Ambone   A pulpit, either serpentine or simple in form, erected in an Italian church.

Apse   The half-rounded extension behind the main altar of a church; Christian tradition dictates that it be placed at the eastern end of an Italian church, the side closest to Jerusalem.

Atrium   A courtyard, open to the sky, in an ancient Roman house; the term also applies to the courtyard nearest the entrance of an early Christian church.

Baldacchino (also ciborium)   A columned stone canopy, usually placed above the altar of a church; spelled in English *baldachin* or *baldaquin*.

Baptistery   A separate building or a separate area in a church where the rite of baptism is held.

Basilica   Any rectangular public building, usually divided into three aisles by rows of columns. In ancient Rome, this architectural form was frequently used for places of public assembly and law courts; later, Roman Christians adapted the form for many of their early churches.

Campanile   A bell tower, often detached, of a church.

Capital   The top of a column, often carved and usually categorized into one of three orders: Doric, Ionic, or Corinthian.

Cavea   The curved row of seats in a classical theater; the most prevalent shape was that of a semicircle.

Chancel   Section of a church containing the altar.

Cornice   The decorative flange defining the uppermost part of a classical or neoclassical facade.

Cortile   Courtyard or cloisters ringed with a gallery of arches or lintels set atop columns.

Crypt   A church's main burial place, usually below the choir.

Cupola   A dome.

Duomo   Cathedral.

Grotesques   Carved and painted faces, deliberately ugly, used by everyone from the Etruscans to the architects of the Renaissance; they're especially amusing when set into fountains.

Hypogeum   Subterranean burial chambers, usually of pre-Christian origins.

Loggia   Roofed balcony or gallery.

Narthex   The anteroom, or enclosed porch, of a Christian church.

Nave   The largest and longest section of a church, usually devoted to sheltering or seating worshipers and often divided by aisles.

Palazzo   A palace or other important building.

Piano Nobile   The main floor of a *palazzo* (sometimes the second floor).

Pieve   A parish church.

Portico   A porch, usually crafted from wood or stone.

Pulvin   A four-sided stone that serves as a substitute for the capital of a column, often decoratively carved, sometimes into biblical scenes.

Putti   Plaster cherubs whose chubby forms often decorate the interiors of baroque chapels and churches.

Stucco   Colored plaster composed of sand, powdered marble, water, and lime, either molded into statuary or applied in a thin concretelike layer to the exterior of a building.

Telamone   Structural column carved into a standing male form; female versions are called *caryatids*.

Thermae   Roman baths.

Transenna   Stone (usually marble) screen separating the altar area from the rest of an early Christian church.

Tympanum   The half-rounded space above the portal of a church, whose semicircular space usually showcases a sculpture.

Abbacchio   Roast haunch or shoulder of lamb baked and served in a casserole and sometimes flavored with anchovies.

Agnolotti   A crescent-shaped pasta shell stuffed with a mix of chopped meat, spices, vegetables, and cheese; when prepared in rectangular versions, the same combination of ingredients is identified as ravioli.

Amaretti   Crunchy, sweet almond-flavored macaroons.

Anguilla alla veneziana   Eel cooked in a sauce made from tuna and lemon.

Antipasti   Succulent tidbits served at the beginning of a meal (before the pasta), whose ingredients might include slices of cured meats, seafood (especially shellfish), and cooked and seasoned vegetables.

Aragosta   Lobster.

Arancini di riso   Rice balls stuffed with peas, cheese, and meat, then coated with bread crumbs and deep-fried.

Arrosto   Roasted meat.

Baccalà   Dried and salted codfish.

Bagna cauda   Hot and well-seasoned sauce, heavily flavored with anchovies, designed for dipping raw vegetables; literally translated as "hot bath."

Bocconcini   Veal layered with ham and cheese, then fried.

Bollito misto   Assorted boiled meats served on a single platter.

Bottarga   Dried and salted roe of gray mullet or tuna, which is pressed into loaves, cut into paper-thin slices, and dressed with lemon-laced virgin olive oil.

Braciola   Pork chop.

Bresaola   Air-dried spiced beef.

Bruschetta   Toasted bread, heavily slathered with olive oil and garlic and often topped with tomatoes.

Bucatini   Coarsely textured hollow spaghetti.

Cacciucco ali livornese   Seafood stew.

Caciocavallo   A semihard cow's-milk cheese with a particularly strong flavor, often used by Sicilians on pasta dishes instead of parmigiano.

Calzone   Pizza dough rolled with the chef's choice of sausage, tomatoes, cheese, and so on and then baked into a kind of savory turnover.

Cannelloni   Tubular dough stuffed with meat, cheese, or vegetables and then baked in a creamy white sauce.

Cannoli   Crunchy tubular pastry filled with ricotta and studded with candied fruits, bits of chocolate, and pistachios.

Caponata   Antipasti made with eggplants, capers, bell peppers, cauliflower, tomatoes, olives, onions, and celery in a sweet-and-sour sauce of vinegar and sugar.

Cappelletti   Small ravioli ("little hats") stuffed with meat or cheese.

Carciofi   Artichokes.

Carpaccio Thin slices of raw cured beef, sometimes in a piquant sauce.

Cassatta al galleto Cake made with vanilla-flavored frozen custard and, perhaps, candied fruits, bits of chocolate, hazelnuts, or pistachios.

Cassatta Siciliana A richly caloric dessert that combines layers of sponge cake, ricotta cheese sweetened with Marsala or orange liqueur, and candied fruit, bound together with chocolate butter-cream icing.

Costoletta alla siciliana Thinly sliced veal cutlet dredged in bread crumbs, fried, and flavored with Parmesan and chopped garlic.

Cozze Mussels.

Fagioli White beans.

Falsomagro Large slab of beef wrapped around Sicilian sausages, perhaps prosciutto, raisins, pine nuts, grated cheese, and even a boiled egg or two; then tied with string and stewed in a savory tomato sauce.

Fave Fava beans.

Foccacia Ideally, concocted from potato-based dough left to rise slowly for several hours and then garnished with tomato sauce, garlic, basil, salt, and pepper and drizzled with olive oil.

Fontina Rich cow's-milk cheese.

Frittata Italian omelet.

Fritto misto A deep-fried medley of whatever small fish, shellfish, and squid are available in the marketplace that day.

Frutta candita Sugared and preserved confection derived from fruits such as blood-red oranges, tangerines, lemons, and figs.

Fusilli Spiral-shaped pasta.

Gelato (produzione propria) Ice cream (homemade).

Gnocchi Dumplings usually made from potatoes *(gnocchi alla patate)* or from semolina *(gnocchi alla romana),* often stuffed with combinations of cheese, spinach, vegetables, or whatever combinations strike the chef's fancy.

Gorgonzola One of the most famous blue-veined cheeses of Europe—strong, creamy, and aromatic.

Granità Flavored ice, usually with lemon or coffee.

Insalata di frutti di mare Seafood salad (usually including shrimp and squid) garnished with pickles, lemon, olives, and spices.

Involtini Thinly sliced beef, veal, or pork, rolled, stuffed, and fried.

Involtini di pesce spada Grilled roulades of swordfish, covered with bread crumbs and sautéed in olive oil.

Minestrone A rich and savory vegetable soup usually sprinkled with grated parmigiano and studded with noodles.

Mortadella Mild pork sausage, fashioned into large cylinders and served sliced; the original lunchmeat bologna (because its most famous center of production is Bologna).

Mozzarella A nonfermented cheese, made from the fresh milk of a buffalo (or, if unavailable, from a cow), boiled, and then kneaded into a rounded ball, served fresh.

Mozzarella con pomodori (also caprese)   Fresh tomatoes with fresh mozzarella, basil, pepper, and olive oil.

Musseddu   Traditional Sicilian salted and fried tuna, used to flavor many salads.

Osso buco   Beef or veal knuckle slowly braised until the cartilage is tender and then served with a highly flavored sauce.

Pancetta   Herb-flavored pork belly, rolled into a cylinder and sliced—the Italian bacon.

Panettone   Sweet yellow-colored bread baked in the form of a brioche.

Panna   Heavy cream.

Pansotti   Pasta stuffed with greens, herbs, and cheeses, usually served with a walnut sauce.

Pappardelle alle lepre   Pasta with rabbit sauce.

Parmigiano   Parmesan, a hard and salty yellow cheese usually grated over pastas and soups but also eaten alone; also known as *granna*. The best is *Parmigiano-Reggiano*.

Peperoni   Green, yellow, or red sweet peppers (not to be confused with pepperoni).

Pesto   A flavorful green sauce made from basil leaves, cheese, garlic, marjoram, and (if available) pine nuts.

Piccata al Marsala   Thin escalope of veal braised in a pungent sauce flavored with Marsala wine.

Piselli al prosciutto   Peas with strips of ham.

Pizza   Specific varieties include *capricciosa* (its ingredients can vary widely, depending on the chef's culinary vision and the ingredients at hand); *margherita* (with tomato sauce, cheese, fresh basil, and memories of the first queen of Italy, Marguerite di Savoia, in whose honor it was first made by a Neapolitan chef); *napoletana* (with ham, capers, tomatoes, oregano, cheese, and the distinctive taste of anchovies); *quattro stagione* (translated as "four seasons" because of the array of fresh vegetables in it; it also contains ham and bacon); and *siciliana* (with black olives, capers, and cheese).

Pizzaiola   A process in which something (usually a beefsteak) is covered in a tomato-and-oregano sauce.

Polenta   Thick porridge or mush made from cornmeal flour.

Polenta de uccelli   Assorted small birds roasted on a spit and served with polenta.

Polenta e coniglio   Rabbit stew served with polenta.

Polla alla cacciatore   Chicken with tomatoes and mushrooms cooked in wine.

Pollo alla Marsala   Chicken cooked in Marsala wine.

Pollo all diavola   Highly spiced grilled chicken.

Ragù   Meat sauce.

Ricotta   A soft bland cheese made from cow's or sheep's milk.

Risotto   Italian rice.

Salsa verde   "Green sauce," made from capers, anchovies, lemon juice and/or vinegar, and parsley.

Saltimbocca   Veal scallop layered with prosciutto and sage; its name literally translates as "jump in your mouth," a reference to its tart and savory flavor.

Salvia   Sage.

Scaloppina alla Valdostana   Escalope of veal stuffed with cheese and ham.

Scaloppine   Thin slices of veal coated in flour and sautéed in butter.

Semifreddo   A frozen dessert; usually ice cream with sponge cake.

Seppia   Cuttlefish (a kind of squid); its black ink is used for flavoring in certain sauces for pasta and also in risotto dishes.

Sfincione   Sicilian pizzalike treat, topped with anchovies, onions, and tomatoes; sold in focaccerias and bakeries (but never in a pizzeria).

Sogliola   Sole.

Spaghetti   A long, round, thin pasta, variously served: *alla bolognese* (with ground meat, mushrooms, peppers, and so on); *alla carbonara* (with bacon, black pepper, and eggs); *alla Norma* (with eggplant); *al pomodoro* (with tomato sauce); *al sugo/ragù* (with meat sauce); and *alle vongole* (with clam sauce).

Spiedini   Pieces of meat grilled on a skewer over an open flame.

Strangolaprete   Small twisted nuggets of pasta, usually served with sauce; the name is literally translated as "priest-choker."

Stufato   Beef braised in white wine with vegetables.

Tagliatelle   Flat egg noodles.

Tonno   Tuna.

Tortelli   Pasta dumplings stuffed with ricotta and greens.

Tortellini   Rings of dough stuffed with minced and seasoned meat, and served either in soups or as a full-fledged pasta covered with sauce.

Trenette   Thin noodles served with pesto sauce and potatoes.

Vermicelli   Very thin spaghetti.

Vitello tonnato   Cold sliced veal covered with tuna sauce.

Zabaglione/zabaione   Egg yolks whipped into the consistency of a custard, flavored with Marsala, and served warm as a dessert.

Zuccotto   A liqueur-soaked sponge cake, molded into a dome and layered with chocolate, nuts, and whipped cream.

Zuppa di cozze   Mussel soup.

Zuppa inglese   Sponge cake soaked in custard.

INDEX

See also Accommodations and Restaurant indexes, below.

RESTAURANTS

FROMMER'S® COMPLETE TRAVEL GUIDES

Alaska
Amalfi Coast
American Southwest
Amsterdam
Argentina
Arizona
Atlanta
Australia
Austria
Bahamas
Barcelona
Beijing
Belgium, Holland & Luxembourg
Belize
Bermuda
Boston
Brazil
British Columbia & the Canadian
    Rockies
Brussels & Bruges
Budapest & the Best of Hungary
Buenos Aires
Calgary
California
Canada
Cancún, Cozumel & the Yucatán
Cape Cod, Nantucket & Martha's
    Vineyard
Caribbean
Caribbean Ports of Call
Carolinas & Georgia
Chicago
Chile & Easter Island
China
Colorado
Costa Rica
Croatia
Cuba
Denmark
Denver, Boulder & Colorado Springs
Eastern Europe
Ecuador & the Galapagos Islands
Edinburgh & Glasgow
England
Europe
Europe by Rail

Florence, Tuscany & Umbria
Florida
France
Germany
Greece
Greek Islands
Guatemala
Hawaii
Hong Kong
Honolulu, Waikiki & Oahu
India
Ireland
Israel
Italy
Jamaica
Japan
Kauai
Las Vegas
London
Los Angeles
Los Cabos & Baja
Madrid
Maine Coast
Maryland & Delaware
Maui
Mexico
Montana & Wyoming
Montréal & Québec City
Morocco
Moscow & St. Petersburg
Munich & the Bavarian Alps
Nashville & Memphis
New England
Newfoundland & Labrador
New Mexico
New Orleans
New York City
New York State
New Zealand
Northern Italy
Norway
Nova Scotia, New Brunswick &
    Prince Edward Island
Oregon
Paris
Peru

Philadelphia & the Amish Country
Portugal
Prague & the Best of the Czech
    Republic
Provence & the Riviera
Puerto Rico
Rome
San Antonio & Austin
San Diego
San Francisco
Santa Fe, Taos & Albuquerque
Scandinavia
Scotland
Seattle
Seville, Granada & the Best of
    Andalusia
Shanghai
Sicily
Singapore & Malaysia
South Africa
South America
South Florida
South Korea
South Pacific
Southeast Asia
Spain
Sweden
Switzerland
Tahiti & French Polynesia
Texas
Thailand
Tokyo
Toronto
Turkey
USA
Utah
Vancouver & Victoria
Vermont, New Hampshire & Maine
Vienna & the Danube Valley
Vietnam
Virgin Islands
Virginia
Walt Disney World® & Orlando
Washington, D.C.
Washington State

FROMMER'S® DAY BY DAY GUIDES

Amsterdam
Barcelona
Beijing
Boston
Cancun & the Yucatan
Chicago
Florence & Tuscany

Hong Kong
Honolulu & Oahu
London
Maui
Montréal
Napa & Sonoma
New York City

Paris
Provence & the Riviera
Rome
San Francisco
Venice
Washington D.C.

PAULINE FROMMER'S GUIDES: SEE MORE. SPEND LESS.

Alaska
Hawaii
Italy

Las Vegas
London
New York City

Paris
Walt Disney World®
Washington D.C.

FROMMER'S® PORTABLE GUIDES

Acapulco, Ixtapa & Zihuatanejo
Amsterdam
Aruba, Bonaire & Curacao
Australia's Great Barrier Reef
Bahamas
Big Island of Hawaii
Boston
California Wine Country
Cancún
Cayman Islands
Charleston
Chicago
Dominican Republic

Florence
Las Vegas
Las Vegas for Non-Gamblers
London
Maui
Nantucket & Martha's Vineyard
New Orleans
New York City
Paris
Portland
Puerto Rico
Puerto Vallarta, Manzanillo &
   Guadalajara

Rio de Janeiro
San Diego
San Francisco
Savannah
St. Martin, Sint Maarten, Anguila &
   St. Bart's
Turks & Caicos
Vancouver
Venice
Virgin Islands
Washington, D.C.
Whistler

FROMMER'S® CRUISE GUIDES

Alaska Cruises & Ports of Call

Cruises & Ports of Call

European Cruises & Ports of Call

FROMMER'S® NATIONAL PARK GUIDES

Algonquin Provincial Park
Banff & Jasper
Grand Canyon

National Parks of the American West
Rocky Mountain
Yellowstone & Grand Teton

Yosemite and Sequoia & Kings
   Canyon
Zion & Bryce Canyon

FROMMER'S® WITH KIDS GUIDES

Chicago
Hawaii
Las Vegas
London

National Parks
New York City
San Francisco

Toronto
Walt Disney World® & Orlando
Washington, D.C.

FROMMER'S® PHRASEFINDER DICTIONARY GUIDES

Chinese
French

German
Italian

Japanese
Spanish

SUZY GERSHMAN'S BORN TO SHOP GUIDES

France
Hong Kong, Shanghai & Beijing
Italy

London
New York
Paris

San Francisco
Where to Buy the Best of Everything.

FROMMER'S® BEST-LOVED DRIVING TOURS

Britain
California
France
Germany

Ireland
Italy
New England
Northern Italy

Scotland
Spain
Tuscany & Umbria

THE UNOFFICIAL GUIDES®

Adventure Travel in Alaska
Beyond Disney
California with Kids
Central Italy
Chicago
Cruises
Disneyland®
England
Hawaii

Ireland
Las Vegas
London
Maui
Mexico's Best Beach Resorts
Mini Mickey
New Orleans
New York City
Paris

San Francisco
South Florida including Miami &
   the Keys
Walt Disney World®
Walt Disney World® for
   Grown-ups
Walt Disney World® with Kids
Washington, D.C.

SPECIAL-INTEREST TITLES

Athens Past & Present
Best Places to Raise Your Family
Cities Ranked & Rated
500 Places to Take Your Kids Before They Grow Up
Frommer's Best Day Trips from London
Frommer's Best RV & Tent Campgrounds in the U.S.A.

Frommer's Exploring America by RV
Frommer's NYC Free & Dirt Cheap
Frommer's Road Atlas Europe
Frommer's Road Atlas Ireland
Retirement Places Rated